PROFESSIONAL PROBLEMS OF TEACHERS

T. M. STINNETT

Visiting Professor of Education in the Graduate College,
Texas A&M University

Professional
Problems
of Teachers

THIRD EDITION

The Macmillan Company, New York
Collier-Macmillan, Limited, London

First Printing

Earlier editions by T. M. Stinnett and Albert J. Huggett © 1956 and 1963 by The Macmillan Company

Library of Congress catalog card number: 68–16765

THE MACMILLAN COMPANY, NEW YORK
COLLIER-MACMILLAN CANADA, LTD., TORONTO, ONTARIO

PRINTED IN THE UNITED STATES OF AMERICA

To Mary Gantt Stinnett

Preface to the Third Edition

The several editions of this book have all had the same objective: to provide essential information for college students preparing for teaching and for experienced teachers regarding problems that they must face daily as practitioners and as members of the profession. The successive editions have been made necessary by the rapidly changing conditions in teaching. First there was the need to update data, which change significantly each year. Second, the nature of teaching and the role of teachers have both changed drastically in the decade since the first edition was issued. Third, teachers have, during that decade, rapidly increased their levels of preparation and competence and their assumption of aggressive attitudes toward their rights and responsibilities. Thus, the third edition bears little resemblance to the first.

This third edition has sought not only to include up-to-date statistics but also to reflect the arrival of a new breed of teachers in the elementary and secondary schools—more competent, more self-reliant, and determined to employ collective action to achieve a new status of creative participation in policy making in education. The nuances and implications of this new teachers' posture will be found in the revisions of already existing chapters. In addition, three new chapters have been added dealing directly with these new thrusts—"The Emerging Revolution in American Education" (Chapter 2); "The Competitive Struggle Among Teachers' Organizations" (Chapter 21); and "Collective Action by Teachers" (Chapter 22).

The prime intent of this edition, as of previous ones, is to seek to provide a basal document by which the members of the teaching profession may be oriented to their role as active participants in the inescapable tasks of improving education and their own status.

The author is indebted to the NEA Research Division and its staff and to former colleagues at NEA for helpful suggestions. Grateful acknowledgement is made of the contributions of Mrs. Edith Dodd and Mrs. Leatha Miloy, my graduate assistants at Texas A&M University, who participated in every phase of the preparation of the manuscript and the processing of the several steps in publication.

T. M. S.

College Station, Texas

Contents

PROFESSIONAL ORGANIZATIONS AND THEIR SYMBOLS

The following is a list of professional organizations for teachers to which frequent references are made in this book, together with the alphabetical symbols that identify them. Throughout this book, and quite commonly in educational literature, the symbols are used rather than the complete title, and the reader should familiarize himself with these abbreviations.

AAAS   *American Association for the Advancement of Science*
AAC   *Association of American Colleges*
AACTE   *American Association of Colleges for Teacher Education*
AAHE   *American Association for Higher Education*
AAHPER *American Association for Health, Physical Education, and Recreation*
AASA   *American Association of School Administrators*
AASL   *American Association of School Librarians*
AAU   *Association of American Universities*
AAUP   *American Association of University Professors*
ACE   *American Council on Education*
ACEI   *Association for Childhood Education International*
ACLS   *American Council of Learned Societies*
ACS   *American Chemical Society*
AERA   *American Educational Research Association*
AFT   *American Federation of Teachers*
AHA   *American Historical Association*

AIAA	*American Industrial Arts Association*
ASCD	*Association for Supervision and Curriculum Development*
AST	*Association for Student Teaching*
CCSSO	*Council of Chief State School Officers*
CEC	*Council for Exceptional Children*
DAVI	*Department of Audio-Visual Instruction*
DCT	*Department of Classroom Teachers (changed in 1967 to the Association of Classroom Teachers; ACT)*
DESP	*Department of Elementary School Principals*
DFL	*Department of Foreign Languages*
DHE	*Department of Home Economics*
DE-K-NE	*Department of Elementary-Kindergarten-Nursery Education*
DRE	*Department of Rural Education*
FTA	*Future Teachers of America*
MENC	*Music Educators National Conference*
NAEA	*National Art Education Association*
NASDTEC	*National Association of State Directors of Teacher Education and Certification*
NASSP	*National Association of Secondary-School Principals*
NBEA	*National Business Education Association*
NCA	*National Commission on Accrediting*
NCATE	*National Council for Accreditation of Teacher Education*
NCPT	*National Congress of Parents and Teachers*
NCSE	*National Commission on Safety Education*
NCSS	*National Council for the Social Studies*
NCTE	*National Council of Teachers of English*
NCTEPS	*National Commission on Teacher Education and Professional Standards*
NCTM	*National Council of Teachers of Mathematics*
NCTR	*National Council on Teacher Retirement*
NEA	*National Education Association*
NRTA	*National Retired Teachers Association*
NSBA	*National School Boards Association*
NSPRA	*National School Public Relations Association*
NSTA	*National Science Teachers Association*
PR&R	*National Commission on Professional Rights and Responsibilities*
SAA	*Speech Association of America*
SNEA	*Student National Education Association*

Part One
EDUCATION IN AMERICA

1: Development of the American System of Education

A ny real understanding of the problems that teachers in the United States face as members of a profession must be grounded in the knowledge of the American system of education. Where and how did the system begin? How has it grown? What are the historic landmarks in its development? What are the forces and influences that have shaped its evolution? Knight has written:

Few activities in American life are more conservative than education, and few are more afflicted by tradition and the dead hands of the past. Much of the work of the school is conventional or traditional. . . . A knowledge of the history of education is a necessary preliminary to educational reform and improvement. It leads educational workers to a willingness to re-evaluate and perhaps even to change their theories and practices in the light of the past. . . . It leads to a more exalted ideal of the teacher's work. By increasing his knowledge of the history of his occupation, it develops his desire for higher personal effectiveness and heightens his sense of the dignity and importance of teaching. . . .[1]

Only a superficial glance at the magnificent array of schools maintained by the American people is enough to convey the idea of the faith the people have had in education as a bulwark of freedom and as an instrument of progress. There are schools for everybody, of almost every conceivable type, from nursery schools to graduate schools in universities. There are public schools and private schools. There are schools maintained by local school districts, by municipalities, by counties, by states, and by the federal government. There are schools maintained by churches and by private corporations, and by individuals.

[1] Edgar W. Knight, *Education in the United States*, 3rd rev. ed. Boston: Ginn & Company, 1941, pp. 39–40.

3

In the school year 1964–65 there were 75,538 public elementary and 26,278 public high schools, or a total of 101,816 public schools. In the same year there were 14,800 nonpublic (or privately controlled and financed) elementary schools, and 4,451 nonpublic high schools, for a total of 19,251. Thus, there were in that year a grand total of 121,067 elementary and secondary schools available to American children.[2] Enrollments in these schools by 1966–67 were nearly 50,000,000, of which 44,000,000, or about 88 per cent, were attending public schools. There were in 1966–67 an estimated 23,335 school districts operated by 114,244 school board members.[3] Both the number of school districts and board members have declined significantly during the last three decades. For example, in 1931–32, there were more than 127,000 school districts and about 425,000 school board members.

But the foregoing is only a part of the vastness of the American school system. Almost 100 per cent of elementary school children (five to thirteen years of age) are enrolled; about 90 per cent of high school age (fourteen to seventeen) are enrolled; and almost 40 per cent of college-age youth (eighteen to twenty-one) are enrolled. At least 56,000,000 children and youth are enrolled in schools of some type; in addition, several million adults are enrolled in part-time or evening courses.

In 1965–66 there were 2,207 colleges and universities in the United States—787 public and 1,420 private. Included in the total were 664 junior colleges, 823 senior colleges (offering the bachelor's degree), 472 offering the master's degree, 227 offering the Ph.D. degree, and 21 offering other types of degrees. Every state supports from public funds one or more colleges or universities. The number of colleges of all types varies from one in Alaska and one in Nevada to 191 in New York. Enrollment in colleges in 1965–66 was estimated at about 6,000,000.

The 1966–67 high school enrollment of 16,409,860 represents an increase of about 5,500,000 since 1960, and an increase of almost 10,000,000 since 1950. At the beginning of this century, only a little more than one-half million were enrolled in high schools. Thus, the high school enrollment in the United States has multiplied more than 30 times since 1900. It will be noted that there was a very small increase in the decade 1940–50. This was due to the low birth rates of the depression years. By 1960, the postwar baby boom had begun to hit the high schools with great force.

The range of schools maintained by the American people is impressive. The federal government maintains special schools for Indian children living on reservations (these are now rapidly being merged with nearby

[2] U.S. Bureau of the Census, *Pocket Data Book, U.S.A. 1967*. Washington, D.C.: U.S. Government Printing Office, December, 1966, Tables 160 and 161, pp. 147–48.

[3] National Education Association, Research Division, *Estimates of School Statistics, 1966–67*, Research Report 1966-R20. Washington, D.C.: The Association, 1966, pp. 5–8.

TABLE 1   *Enrollment in American Public High Schools*

Year	Enrollment
1870	80,000
1880	110,000
1890	203,000
1900	519,000
1910	915,000
1920	2,200,000
1930	4,390,000
1940	6,601,000
1950	6,783,956
1960	11,374,707
1967	16,409,860

Source: For figures 1870–1940, U.S. Office of Education, Federal Security Agency, *Biennial Survey of Education in the United States, 1948–1950.* Washington, D.C.: U.S. Government Printing Office, 1952, Chap. 2. Figures for 1950, 1960 from National Education Association, Research Division, *Estimates of School Statistics, 1959–60,* Research Report 1959-R23. Washington, D.C.: The Association, 1959, p. 7. Data for 1967, *op. cit., Estimates of School Statistics,* Research Report 1966-R20. 1966, p. 5.

public school districts). The federal government also maintains an extensive school system, estimated to be the tenth largest in size of American public school systems, for the children of military personnel stationed in foreign countries. In 1966 there were about 300 such schools in 30 countries, with approximately 8,000 teachers and enrolling at least 175,000 children. These are called Overseas Dependent Schools. In fact, schools are provided for America for almost every range of human needs and operations.

HOW DID THE AMERICAN PEOPLE COME TO DEVELOP SUCH A SYSTEM?

The American System Is a Dual System

While the United States has come to symbolize the concept of the public free school, our system of education started with private schools; and we now have a dual system in which public and nonpublic schools function to supplement and complement each other. Although the number of public elementary and secondary schools presently far outnumber the nonpublic ones, and enrollment of the five-to-seventeen age group is predominantly in the public schools, these conditions do not obtain in higher education. There are about twice as many private colleges and universities as public; with the public institutions enrolling almost twice as many as the private institutions.

Background of American Schools

The background of the American system of education is largely English in heritage. Since the preponderance of our colonists were English, quite naturally English institutions were transplanted to the New World. The English theory of education reflected the class structure, which to a large degree was transplanted to the colonies. The English belief at that time was that the so-called common people were unfit to rule; that they were born to obey and not to govern; that their social and economic position, therefore, was fixed. The privileged were considered, even by the masses, as superior beings. The carry-over of this viewpoint is reflected in the fact that the thirteen colonies required the ownership of land, or other property of a specified value, as a qualification for voting. Learning among the masses, some believed, would lead to disobedience. Governor Berkeley of Virginia declared in 1671:

I thank God that there are no free schools and no printing presses in the Province; and I hope there will be none for a hundred years. Learning has brought disobedience and heresy, and sects into the world, and printing has divulged them, and libels against the best government. God keep us from both.[4]

With such a concept, which was widespread, it is not surprising that the notion persisted, during the seventeenth and much of the eighteenth centuries, that education was not a responsibility of the state. It is not surprising that the Sunday School (which also gave instruction in the three R's), the Dame Schools (taught by a housewife in her home for the masses of children), and the Lancastrian Schools (monitorial schools for poor children) flourished in England and were transplanted to early America. It was natural, also, for the class educational system to be transplanted to the colonies in the New World. The universities of Oxford and Cambridge were patterns for the founding of Harvard, William and Mary, Yale, Princeton, University of Pennsylvania (Academy and College of Pennsylvania), Columbia (King's College), Brown, Rutgers, and Dartmouth, all founded by 1769. The Latin Grammar Schools of England, established to prepare the sons of the privileged for college, became models for similar schools in all colonies except Georgia. Eton and Westminster, endowed preparatory academies, were copied in the New World with the founding of Symms and Eaton, Andover, Exeter, and many other private academies. The class distinctions were especially marked in the early colleges. At Harvard and Yale the names of students were not listed alphabetically but in the order of the social rank of their families. According to Knight, "At both institutions a name of renown was its own justifi-

[4] Edgar W. Knight, *op. cit.*, p. 64.

cation for an unrivalled place in the college lists; though at both an ample fortune seems also to have been taken into account in estimating family rank." [5]

In time, other European influences were introduced, and after the Revolution an independent nation began to make its own adaptations. Thus, a distinctly American system eventually emerged. For the first 175 years or so (from about 1600 to 1775) England was the home country of the vast majority of the colonists. The English governmental system was our system. And the English concept of education became our concept, to be modified in time, to be sure, but basically English in its origins.

Thus, our first schools were neither free schools nor universal ones. They were church schools, and restricted in attendance. In England the privileged classes sent their boys to private elementary schools and then to the "Grammar Schools" (the private secondary schools which, oddly enough, are still referred to as "public schools"), from which it was possible for them to enter the universities, such as Oxford and Cambridge. The education of girls in England was at this time restricted to private tutoring. There was little public concern for the education of the children of the poor. They had access only to the Dame Schools or church schools. Responsibility for education was not considered to be that of the government but of the parents and the church.

The colonists tended to transplant these concepts to the New World. The aristocratic influences in the southern colonies tended to place complete responsibility upon parents and the church for the schooling of children. The class system of England was transplanted here. Education was considered a privilege, not a right (as we have come to view it in modern America), except for orphans and pauper children, who were apprenticed and required to learn a trade.[6] The Middle Colonies, stretching along the Atlantic seaboard from New England to the South and settled by a number of religious groups, tended to reflect European backgrounds and to view education as a function of the church, for the purpose of instruction in the three R's and religion.

The Dutch in New Amsterdam (New York) copied the form of cooperation between church and state that had been worked out in the mother country. The Dutch West India Company was actually the governing power, appointing the school teacher and paying his salary. Schools were free only for the poor. The company demanded town rates or compulsory payments to support the schools for the poor. The schools were modeled after the parochial schools in Holland, and the church selected and certified the teachers, based on competence and religious orthodoxy.

The early development of schools in New England took a somewhat

[5] *Ibid.*, p. 79.
[6] H. G. Good, *A History of American Education.* New York: The Macmillan Company, 1956, p. 6.

different form. Here the state church dominated. The Puritans were firm believers in education as a means of salvation, in the necessity of all to be able to read in order to find from the Scriptures the means of salvation. They believed firmly, also, in an educated minister for every church. These beliefs made necessary the establishment of elementary schools for all children, both boys and girls, and Latin schools and colleges for the education of church leaders. It was inevitable that these beliefs would sooner or later find expression in law. It was inevitable, also, that these beliefs would become forerunners of the public school system, which eventually would be divorced from the church and sectarian religious instruction.

The First Public Schools

The first public elementary school to be established in the New World was founded in New Netherland in 1638. However, it was short lived because, in 1664, the English took over New York and resorted to the concept of limited governmental responsibility for schools. In Pennsylvania, William Penn attempted to establish a public school system but church controls of schools continued.

Massachusetts passed two laws in the 1640's that are often pointed to as the planting of the seeds of the American public school system. The schools established by these laws were not, in reality, public schools but arms of the established church; they were not secular, they were not compulsory, and the teachers were paid by the parents.

The first law, passed in 1642 by the Massachusetts Bay Colony, simply copied an act passed in 1641 by the Plymouth Colony, the latter adopting the principle of the English Poor Law of 1601, to the effect that the care of poor children was a public responsibility. The 1642 act required local officers to check on whether parents and masters were teaching their children to read and to understand the principles of religion and the capital laws of the country. These officers were also empowered to apprentice children whose parents were unable or unwilling to give such training.[7] Similar laws were subsequently enacted in Virginia, North Carolina, South Carolina, and Georgia. Obviously, these laws did not establish public schools in the sense that we understand the term today. They were efforts to mandate a degree of learning and vocational training, but not at public expense.

The 1647 law, commonly known as the "old deluder Satan" act, enacted by Massachusetts, was the first general school law in the colonies. This act of the General Court required every town of fifty householders to make provision for instruction in reading and writing. The language of the act, in modernized spelling, is as follows:

It being one chief object of that old deluder, Satan, to keep men from the knowledge of the Scriptures, as in former times by keeping them in an unknown

[7] Edgar W. Knight, *op. cit.,* p. 101.

tongue, so in these latter times by persuading them from the use of tongues, that so at least the true sense and meaning of the original might be clouded by false glosses of saint-seeming deceivers, that learning may not be buried in the grave of our fathers in the Church and Commonwealth, the Lord assisting our endeavors.

It is therefore ordered, that every township in this jurisdiction, after the Lord hath increased them to the number of fifty householders, shall then forthwith appoint one within their town to teach all such children as shall resort to him to write and read, whose wages shall be paid either by the parents or masters of such children, or by the inhabitants in general, by way of supply, as the major part of those that order the prudentials of the town shall appoint: *Provided,* Those that send their children be not oppressed by paying much more than they can have them taught for in other towns; and

It is further ordered, That where any town shall increase to the number of one hundred families or householders, they shall set up a grammar school, the master thereof being able to instruct youth so far as they may be fitted for the university: *Provided,* That if any town neglect the performance hereof above one year, that every such town shall pay five pounds to the next school till they shall perform this order.[8]

Despite the doubts that the intent of the act was to establish a public school system, it was the first of its type to be enacted, and it did contain some of the basic principles that were later incorporated into public school legislation. It did provide for public taxation, and the appointment of a teacher for all children who might come to him. Moreover, it was widely copied by other colonies. And by 1671, all of the New England colonies except Rhode Island had adopted some degree of compulsory education.

The 1647 law was unpopular from several standpoints. Parents resisted the compulsory attendance because they needed their children to help with the crops. The levying of a form of public taxation was resisted. Many features of the law were ignored or evaded. Not until much later were grammar schools, authorized by the law, established by the towns. And not until a century later did the schools begin to emerge as nonsectarian, secular schools, in which no particular religious doctrine was taught.

The establishment of schools in the colonies outside Massachusetts, New Hampshire, and Connecticut was haphazard, as settlers spread out from the towns following the westward migration of the Indians. This scattering of the children resulted, first, in the teacher serving several schools in one township, teaching a few months in one and then moving on to another. Finally, the townships were divided into several school districts, each with its own board and elementary school, operating three months out of the year. These districts, for the most part, came into being without legislation, being legalized later on. They were supported by public subscription rather than by taxes.

[8] *Ibid.,* p. 105.

FREE PUBLIC SCHOOLS IN A NEW NATION

By the time of the American Revolution (1776–1781), the groundwork had been laid for a system of free schools. As the colonists spread westward from the Atlantic seaboard, they took with them the traditions of the district schools, which had developed often without plan or legal authorization. The seed had been sown for a flowering of a universal, nonsectarian system of free schools supported by public taxation.

Great impetus in these directions was given by the Continental Congress (1785 and 1786) and by the Federal Constitution in 1789. The Continental Congress, provided for by the Articles of Confederation under which the independent colonies formed a loose organization between independence (1781) and the establishment of the Republic (1789), passed the Ordinance of 1785, which provided for a survey of the territory between the Ohio and Mississippi rivers (from which the states of Ohio, Indiana, Illinois, Michigan, and Wisconsin were later formed) and the setting aside of the sixteenth section of each township for the maintenance of schools, that is, one square mile, or 640 acres, of the 36 square miles (23,040 acres) in each congressional township. The Ordinance of 1787 (the Northwest Ordinance) provided a plan of administering the new territory. Article 3 contained the following provision:

Religion, morality and knowledge being necessary to good government and the happiness of mankind, schools and the means of education shall forever be encouraged.

This statement refers, of course, to the states to be formed from the new territory, but it and the land grant set a pattern for each new state added to the Union.

The Federal Constitution itself was silent on the matter of education, but Article X (Tenth Amendment) made education a state responsibility. There was a proposal made during the Constitutional Convention for insertion of a statement on responsibility for education, but no action was taken. State responsibility for education is an implied power under the Tenth Amendment, which reads as follows:

The powers not delegated to the United States by the Constitution, nor prohibited by it to the states, are reserved to the states respectively, or to the people.

Of the sixteen states forming the Union by 1800 (the thirteen original colonies and Vermont, Kentucky, and Tennessee), seven had inserted clauses in their constitutions establishing the state's responsibility for education. By the time the new states formed from the Northwest Territory were admitted to the Union, state responsibility had been firmly established. Thus, as new territory was acquired, Congress continued the principle of setting aside public lands for the maintenance of schools, except in Texas, which came into the Union by treaty and owned its own land, and Maine and West Virginia, which were carved from existing states. Since 1850 two sections of each township have been set aside by Congress for schools in each newly admitted state, except in Utah, Arizona, and New Mexico where four sections were allotted. And each new state made constitutional provision for a public school system.

MILESTONES IN THE DEVELOPMENT OF THE AMERICAN PUBLIC SCHOOLS

1638—First public elementary school established in New Netherland.

1642—Law adopted by Massachusetts Bay Colony incorporating the principles of the English Poor Law of 1601.

1647—Old Deluder Satan Act, enacted by Massachusetts, requiring establishment of elementary and grammar schools, to be in part supported by public funds.

1776–1800—Constitutional provision for public schools in Pennsylvania, North Carolina, Georgia, Masachusetts, New Hampshire, Vermont, and Delaware.

1785—Chartering of University of Georgia—first state university.

1785—Northwest Land Ordinance provided grant of each sixteenth section of land to be set aside for schools.

1791—Tenth Amendment to the Federal Constitution reserved to the states the responsibility for education.

1818—First grant of money by Congress to states for schools.

1821—First public high school established in Massachusetts.

1839—Opening of first normal school—Lexington, Massachusetts.

1850—All states in Union had constitutional provisions for public schools.

1862—Morrill Act of Congress—aid for land-grant colleges in states.

1867—Bureau of Education created by federal government.

1872—The Kalamazoo Case upheld right to tax for support of public high schools.

1917—Smith-Hughes Act—federal grants for vocational education.

1950—Impacted Area Aid.

1954—U.S. Supreme Court ruled segregation unconstitutional.

1958—National Defense Education Act.

1963—Higher Education Facilities Act.

1965—Elementary and Secondary Education Act.

Growth of the Idea of Public Schools

What were the factors that contributed to popular acceptance of the concept of state responsibility for the education of all the people, between the founding of the colonies and the founding of the new nation (1607 to 1789)? There were many factors, but two are dominant. First, there was the slowly expanding desire for political democracy. Property qualifications for voting, a concept transplanted from England, gradually were abolished. Then it became apparent that if a ruling, privileged class was to give way to rule of the people through the ballot, education of the masses was a necessity. The second factor, like the first a product largely of rugged pioneer conditions, was the deep feeling that a pauper or charity education was not in keeping with the spirit of an independent, proud people. The masses clearly saw that if their economic lot was to be improved for their children, the opportunity for education was basic. Another tradition transplanted from England was the jailing of people who were unable to pay their debts. Horror of the pauper status turned the thoughts of the people to the essentiality of education.

To be sure, there was opposition to the establishment of public schools. The taxing of all for their support met with great opposition. Compulsory school-attendance laws were unpopular. And many adhered to their European backgrounds in insisting that education was a family and a church responsibility. But the popular will for free schools, freely open to all, grew until it prevailed.

The First Public High Schools

Our first public schools were known as common schools, meaning available to all. These were elementary schools, and, in time, the term *common schools* came to connote elementary schools in the public mind. Massachusetts established the first public high school in 1821. Massachusetts passed laws in 1827 and 1835 requiring the establishment of high schools in communities of a specified size. In the meantime, private academies flourished, and their proponents opposed the establishment of competing schools supported by public funds. In 1850 there were 6,085 academies operating in the United States, with total enrollments of more than 260,000 pupils. The golden period of the private academies was the period from 1820 to 1860, when many states provided some public support for them.

The tide of this opposition was not turned until 1872, with the famous Kalamazoo Case. In that year a taxpayer filed suit to test whether he could be taxed to support a public high school, contending that it was not a common school authorized by constitutional and statutory provisions; that it was not an extension of the common school but a new kind of school not authorized by the state constitution. The Michigan Supreme Court in 1874 ruled that high schools were an extension of the common schools and that citizens could be legally taxed for their support. This decision led to a rapid expansion of the public high school (See Table 1, p. 5) and a consequent decline in the number of private academies.

Origin and Development of Public Colleges and Universities

As has been previously stated, our first colleges were all private institutions, for the most part esablished and maintained by churches. The first colleges were Harvard (1636), the College of William and Mary (1693), Yale (1701), Princeton (1746), University of Pennsylvania (1751), Columbia (1754), Brown (1764), Rutgers (1766), and Dartmouth (1769). By 1800, the number of colleges in existence was twenty-five. The University of Georgia was the first state university to be chartered, in 1785, but it did not begin operating until 1800. The University of North Carolina was chartered in 1789 and began operation in 1795. The first college for women was Mount Holyoke, established in 1838. Hampton Institute, founded in 1868, was the first college for Negroes. There were in 1860 a total of 264 colleges and universities in the United States, of which only 17 were public institutions. In 1965–66, about two of every three (of the 2,207) colleges and universities are private institutions. Total college enrollments had grown from about 150,000 in 1890 to about 6,000,000 in 1965.

The Latin Grammar Schools and Colleges were reserved for male students. Oberlin College was the first to admit women, in 1838. Some private schools taught girls penmanship, needlework, music, and languages. These were classical schools in the best tradition; such courses were considered the best possible preparation for the professions, and anything smacking of the "practical" was considered as diluting proper education. There were practical schools that developed in some of the cities. What they offered was sometimes called English education, as the basic language was English and the subject matter generally was an extension of the elementary schools. They were not college preparatory; the Latin Grammar Schools were. In the United States we have come to associate the term *grammar school* with elementary schools. In the English tradition they are secondary schools.

Of course, the Latin Grammar Schools in Colonial America were imitations of the English schools of the same name. The name derived from the fact that Latin was the basic language studied. The highly selective or aristocratic nature of these schools derives from the history of Latin as the language of the educated classes of Western Europe. Merchants, government officials, soldiers, and the Roman Catholic Church carried the language of Ancient Rome throughout Western Europe. While the natives continued their native tongues and dialects, Latin became the universal language, at least universal for Western Europe. Thus, it came to be associated with the cultivated people, as the prize possession of the well educated. It served to distinguish the cultured from the peasant.

The Latin schools were never very popular in the New World, as reflected by indifference to the 1647 law authorizing them. Some of the Latin schools in Massachusetts did not prepare a single student for college in ten or even twenty years.[9] And Harvard, in its first sixty years, graduated an average of eight students each year.

The private academy served to bridge the gap between the Latin Grammar School and the public high school, since its curriculum tended to reflect both, and since it was both college preparatory and terminal.

The three types of secondary schools that have abounded throughout the educational history of the United States are:

Type of School	Period in Which It Flourished
The Latin Grammar School	From settlement to the Revolution (1607–1775)
The Academy	From Revoluton to about 1875
The Public High School	From 1875–

These are not precise dates, of course; there was overlapping from one to the other, and all three types still exist.

SOME EARLY SCHOOLS AS FORERUNNERS OF THE PUBLIC SCHOOLS

Early Philanthropic Schools

The concept that the colonists brought with them from England, based upon the notion that education was not a public function but that private philanthropy or charity should support some kind of educational enterprise for the poor and the indigent, is reflected in some of the early schools established for this purpose.

The Lancastrian Schools

The basic idea of the Lancastrian School, because of the cost of teachers, was to use the older and more intelligent children to teach the younger and less gifted children in groups, through a monitorial system. The function of the teacher was to organize the total group of children into clusters of nine and assign a monitor (one of the pupils) to take charge of teaching them. The teacher did give special instruction to the monitors and encouraged and disciplined the pupils. But, thereafter, the monitors were in almost complete charge of their groups—checking attendance and truancy, handling instructional materials, examining and promoting pupils. By dispensing with qualified teachers and using the more advanced pupils as teachers, the inculcation of the rudiments of learning could be cheap indeed. Under this plan, one teacher could supervise the teaching of several hundred pupils. Organization was the key to the plan, to have each

[9] Good, *op. cit.*, p. 54.

group so organized as to keep things moving, every child kept continuously busy. But there were many weaknesses.

The Lancastrian School idea had its appeal in the United States largely because of its economy. The first American Lancastrian School was established in New York in the first decade of the 1800's, and the idea rapidly spread to other parts of the country. After wide use, the plan declined and disappeared before the Civil War period. The plan had some good by-products. It provided opportunity for some degree of learning for children who otherwise would have had little or no opportunity for schooling. And by reaching large numbers, it stimulated the desire for more learning and better school conditions. Moreover, it focused discussion on the need for special preparation of teachers. All in all, the Lancastrian system probably helped to hasten popular desire for a universal system of free schools. The system took its name from an English schoolmaster, Joseph Lancaster.

The Infant School

Another extension of the charity or philanthropy idea of education in the early part of the nineteenth century in the United States was the Infant School, borrowed from Scotland, which may have had some influence on the later establishment of kindergarten and primary schools as public institutions. At the time of their founding there was no ban on employing children in factories, even the very young. The idea was introduced into the United States in 1818, when Boston established Infant Schools as a supplement to the public schools. At that time the public schools of Boston did not admit children until they could read and write. Societies to provide the Infant Schools were founded in many Eastern cities. New York and Philadelphia founded such schools in 1827, and Providence in 1828.

Societies to Promote Schools

Voluntary organizations of citizens, known as "school societies," helped to hasten the establishment of free public schools. Their original purpose was to promote schools for our children. These societies have had many counterparts through the years since the public schools became well established. One of the notable examples has been the movement since 1930 to provide special schools or instruction in regular schools for handicapped children. The rather comprehensive program of "special education" now existing almost universally in good-size school districts is a direct result of the vigorous organizations in local communities of parents of handicapped children. The parents, rather than educators, promoted the idea until public support demanded that the public schools provide services for these children.

One of the early influential societies was the Society for Establishing a Free School in the City of New York, in 1805. Since New York did not have a public school system until 1842, the Society could be considered as a forerunner of a public school system. In fact, later, its name was changed to the Public School Society of New York. When a city school board was created in New York, the Society turned all of its property over to the new public school system.

Finally, a type of school now maintained by every church had great influence on promoting the establishment of public schools. This is the Sunday School, organized by churches to teach children to read and learn the Catechism. Originating in England for the purpose of serving children who worked in factories, it was transplanted to Virginia in 1786 and spread to other areas. It served two basic purposes: it brought together children of all classes in a "common" school of sorts, and it emphasized the need for a common school supported by all the people.

SOME EARLY LEADERS IN THE PUBLIC SCHOOL MOVEMENT

We have traced the economic and social forces prefacing the ultimate adoption of the public school concept: the aspirations of the working classes for education for their children, the recognition that a democracy must have enlightened voters, the revulsion of the rugged pioneers against the charity or philanthropy idea in education. We saw, also, the influence of certain early schools for the evolving concept of a free, common school for every man's child: the Lancastrian School, the Dame School, the Infant School, the secular Sunday School.

There was another powerful force that contributed significantly to the coalescing of public opinion behind the idea of a universal, publicly supported and controlled system of free schools. This force was a group of leaders whom history has evaluated as educational statesmen. The contribution of Franklin and Jefferson to the growing idea of the need of basic education for all had great influence in creating a climate of public opinion favorable to a mass system of education.

Benjamin Franklin

Benjamin Franklin's paper, "Proposals Relating to the Education of Youth in Pennsylvania" (1749), led to the founding of the Philadelphia Academy. The proposal was a "realist" (practical) education as contrasted with the classical. Subjects proposed for the curriculum were English, mathematics, history, handwriting, geography, oratory and debating, logic, morality, and natural history. Although Franklin's plans were not all incorporated into the Philadelphia Academy, he was clearly advocating what has evolved into the American comprehensive high school.

Thomas Jefferson

Thomas Jefferson prepared in 1779 the Virginia Bill for the More General Diffusion of Knowledge, which provided for a primary school for each township to be publicly controlled and supported in part by the public. Children were to attend three years free; beyond this period they were to pay tuition. The curriculum was to consist of reading, writing, arithmetic, and the history of Greece, Rome, England, and the United States. Twenty secondary schools were to be established in the state, and the brightest boys were to be enabled to attend these schools at public expense for two or more years. The full course was six years. The highest of this group were to be sent on to the College of William and Mary, and the rejects were to become the primary-school teachers. The sons of parents able to pay could be sent on through the full six years of secondary school and to the College of William and Mary. Jefferson, today, has often been vigorously attacked for presuming to limit free education of all to three years and for making education beyond that period highly selective. But it must be remembered that this was a radical proposal for his day. It has been assumed that Jefferson, being a practical statesman, meant his proposal to be only a first step in the implementation of a comprehensive program of public education. How far ahead of his time he was is indicated by the fact that his 1779 proposal was not acted upon by the Virginia Legislature until 1796, and then passed upon in an ineffective form. He was the founder and chief architect of the University of Virginia. He favored local control of the primary schools, holding that the people were the best judges of local issues. He believed that education should contribute to increased production, labor saving, preserving health, and improvement of agriculture (a forerunner of the Morrill Act and Land-Grant College Act of 1862).

There was another group which, building upon the past of the young nation—at that critical point in the 1830's and 1840's when the issue of whether we would continue to vacillate between public or philanthropic education seemed to hang in the balance—was able to persuade public opinion to embrace the public school concept. Some of the most influential of this group follow.

Horace Mann

The acknowledged giant of this era, sometimes referred to as the Father of the American Public School, was Horace Mann. Prepared as a lawyer at Brown University, Mann was a successful politician. But his abiding interest was in education, which he viewed as the means of the "infinite

Benjamin Franklin—Proposed in 1749 a practical educational program for youth which led to the founding of the Philadelphia Academy.

Thomas Jefferson—Author of a proposed public school system for Virginia (1779), providing a primary school in each township and twenty secondary schools. Three years of schooling to be free for all. Secondary schooling required tuition, except for a small select group.

Horace Mann—The "Father of the American Public School." First secretary of the Massachusetts State Board of Education. He led the fight to establish the first public normal school (1839) and to make the public school a secular institution.

Henry Barnard—Led in passage of law establishing the Connecticut State Board of Education and became the first secretary of the Board. Influenced establishment of the Rhode Island State Board of Education. Became the first United States Commissioner of Education (1867).

1640
1660
1680
1700
1720
1740
1760
1780
1800
1820
1840
1860
1880
1900
1920
1940

improvability of man." He served as the first secretary of the Massachusetts State Board of Education, serving twelve years in that position. With great forcefulness and utter dedication, he waged an uncompromising campaign for improvement of Massachusetts schools. The prevailing conditions in Massachusetts obtained generally: inadequate financial support of the schools, short terms (a few weeks), poor equipment, indifference to the attendance of children, and incompetent teachers. Boards violated the certification laws and hired teachers as they pleased. Mann used two weapons, skillfully and aggressively, to swing public opinion toward rectifying the deplorable conditions: his annual reports and his public addresses. In addition, he edited the *Common School Journal*. He was specific; he cited cases and prepared clear remedies. His eloquence, his command of language, and his utter devotion to his task had great effect upon the people.

Naturally, he had vigorous opposition. The conservatives considered him a radical and a "troublemaker." The churches were particularly vehement in their opposition. He was fighting for the secular schools, and in Massachusetts, it should be remembered, was the home base of the church-controlled school, supported in large part by public taxation. His advocacy of Bible reading without comment—in other words, the advocacy of the divorcement of public education from sectarian teaching—aroused bitter hostility on the part of the church leaders. He saw clearly that the teaching of religious creeds in the public schools would ultimately destroy these schools. So bitter was the opposition that an effort was made in the state legislature to abolish the State Board of Education and, therefore, his job. But Mann won. In 1855 the people of Massachusetts adopted a constitutional amendment establishing the public schools as secular, nonsectarain institutions. Mann's fight in Massachusetts had impact in other states, and gradually the states assumed control of the public schools, and church control was abolished. The establishment of this principle, the publicly supported and controlled nonsectarian public school, became a landmark in the American system of education.

Horace Mann's other accomplishments during the twelve years of his secretaryship of the State Board of Education were prodigious: school support was doubled, money was provided for school buildings, teachers' salaries were increased, the school year was lengthened, high schools were established, three normal schools were founded, school libraries were added, teaching methods were improved, and school supervision developed. The influence of Horace Mann upon the development of public schools, not only in the United States but also in other countries, was profound.

Henry Barnard

The parallelism in the career of Henry Barnard and Horace Mann is striking. A graduate of Yale and, like Horace Mann, prepared for the law, he turned to teaching. He studied for two years in Europe and became interested in the theories of Pestalozzi. In 1838, as a member of the Con-

TABLE 2   *Teachers' Monthly Wages (Exclusive of Board), About 1847*

State	Men	Women
Massachusetts	$24.51	$ 8.07
Pennsylvania	17.02	10.09
Connecticut	16.00	6.50
Ohio	15.42	8.73
Maine	15.40	4.80
New York	14.96	6.69
New Hampshire	13.50	5.65
Michigan	12.71	5.36
Indiana	12.00	6.00
Vermont	12.00	4.75

Source: H. G. Good, *A History of American Education.* New York: The Macmillan Company, 1956, p. 159, as adapted from Horace Mann's Eleventh Report.

necticut Legislature, he was instrumental in the passage of the law establishing a state board of education. Again, like Horace Mann, he became the first secretary of the board he had helped to create. Through much the same procedures Mann used in Massachusetts—annual reports, speaking, correspondence, and the founding of the *Connecticut Common School Journal*—he brought about a reawakening of public interest, which resulted in drastic reforms in the public schools of his state. Barnard aroused the same opposition as had Horace Mann, and the Connecticut Legislature abolished the State Board of Education in 1842, as well as Barnard's job as secretary (New York had taken a similar action in 1821). But Barnard, by a powerful speech before the Legislature of Rhode Island, influenced that body in establishing a state board of education, and Henry Barnard became the first commissioner of education in that state. His impact upon the schools of Rhode Island brought about similar advances to those of Horace Mann in Massachusetts. He later served as principal of the Connecticut Normal School, as president of the University of Wisconsin, as president of St. John's College, and became in 1867 the first United States commissioner of education. He helped to establish the American Association for the Advancement of Education, and edited the *American Journal of Education*. His book *Pestalozzi and Pestalozzianism* became a classic.

James G. Carter

Another spirit in the period of awakening of the American people to the need for an adequate public school system was James G. Carter. Known as the "Father of Normal Schools" because of his advocacy of professional preparation of teachers and his efforts to establish special institutions (normal schools) for this purpose, his crusade for school improvement predated those of Horace Mann and Henry Barnard. A graduate of Harvard in 1820, he became a teacher and a writer of great vigor. His "Letters on the Free Schools of New England" pointed up the great weakness of the schools and teachers, and concentrated public attention on corrective measures. He outlined a comprehensive plan for the education of teachers in his "Essays on Education." He was instrumental in the passage of the law creating the State Board of Education in Massachusetts, which Horace Mann was to serve with distinction.[10]

THE ORGANIZATION AND FINANCING OF AMERICAN SCHOOLS

Any review, however brief, of the development of the American system of education would be incomplete without some discussion of the types of organizational structures that have developed and the existing patterns of financial support. As for the nonpublic schools, the types of organizations vary according to the sponsoring agencies and the type of school. Private schools, or nonpublic schools, may be categorized as private nonprofit, preparatory, and church or parochial. In general, nonpublic schools must be chartered by the state and must meet certain prescribed minimal standards. As a general rule, nonpublic and public schools, at the respective levels, have many similarities. Financing of nonpublic schools comes from several sources, income from endowments, gifts, tuition, and foundation grants being the chief ones.

The public schools below the college level are organized around basic units of local school districts. These districts are authorized or created by the state legislature, and broad authority goes with their creation, such as the right of the voters to select the governing bodies (usually called school boards, committees, trustees, or boards of education), the right to establish schools and to levy taxes or propose tax levies, the right to issue bonds to erect school buildings, and the right to employ teachers and fix conditions of their work.

In 1966–67 there were 23,335 school districts (1,638 of which did not operate schools). These districts vary widely in size and number by states. In size, they vary from one square mile to about 18,000 square miles. Hawaii comprises one school district and Nebraska has 2,300. New York City is the largest in pupil population, with about 1,066,000 children and 50,000 teachers. Striking variations are also to be found in the ability of school districts within a given state to support their schools. Taxable wealth per child in some districts often is several times that of others in

[10] For a comprehensive treatment of the contributions of Horace Mann, Henry Barnard, James G. Carter, and other leaders of the awakening, see Edgar W. Knight, *op. cit.,* Chap. 7, "The Awakening," pp. 192–237.

the same state, or even of adjoining districts. There has been a drastic decline in the number of school districts in recent years. For example, since 1931 there has been a decline from 127,000 to 23,000, a decrease of 104,000 districts. This decline has resulted from better highways, good transportation, and the demand for better educational opportunities than could be furnished in the small school district. About 1,600 small school districts still exist as legal entities but operate no schools, either because there are too few children within their borders to foster the maintenance of a school or because it was found to be more economical to pay tuition and transport the children to a nearby school.

Types of School Districts

Local school districts are generally classified according to geographical size or areas served. Some serve a very small area: a town, a township, a county, or a state. Hawaii has a statewide school unit, and Alaska operates on a state basis all areas not a part of organized districts. A total of twelve states have county units (one school district serving an entire county). In eighteen states there are some county units, but for the most part the local or independent school district predominates. Thirty states have independent school districts, mixed with other types. In all, as has been stated, there are some 23,335 separate school districts each with its own governing board. In 1966–67, there were about 114,244 local school board members. The number of school board members, because of the reduction in the number of school districts, has declined from more than 400,000 in 1933 to the above number in 1966–67. Many of the school districts are too small and have insufficient resources to provide an adequate educational program for their children. Only about 13,000 are large enough to employ a superintendent of schools. Although some 8,000 one-room schools still exist, most of these are in school districts large enough to maintain well-rounded educational programs.

At the apex of the governing boards for public schools is the state board of education, the policy-making body for the state in school matters. All but two states (Illinois and Wisconsin) have such boards. These boards function through a state education agency, usually called a state department of education or state department of public instruction. The state agency consists of an executive officer, usually called state commissioner of education or state superintendent of public instruction, and a professional staff on which are experts in every area of concern to the schools. In some states, members of the state board of education are elected by a vote of the people and in some they are appointed by the governor or legislature. Likewise, the chief state school officer (commissioner or state superintendent) is elected in some states and appointed by the state board of education in others. State boards or departments of education are charged with the enforcement of minimum standards, as fixed by law or regulation, and with the responsibility for stimulating school districts to attain the best possible educational program for children.

How Public Schools Are Financed

The original source of support of the public schools, the local property tax, continues to be the major means of financing. For the school year 1966–67 local sources of taxation provided 52.1 per cent of the total support of the public schools, state sources provided 39.9 per cent, and federal sources provided 8.0 per cent. State legislatures authorize local school districts to levy and collect taxes to support their schools. Taxes on local property constitute the chief source of funds for schools, although in some states school districts may levy other forms, such as sales and income taxes. In some districts, local taxes are ample to operate the schools, but in others even the highest tax rates do not yield sufficient revenues. Thus, states have gradually developed programs to supplement local sources of support for the schools. These are statewide taxes—property, income, severance, and sales taxes are the major ones—which they apportion to the schools on formulas designed to assure reasonably equal educational opportunity. In general, states attempt to provide minimum foundation programs, which the local district may enrich according to its financial ability. This trend in states has grown rapidly since 1930. In 1929–30, for example, only 17 per cent of the total support of public schools came from state funds, in contrast to about 40 per cent in 1966–67. States vary widely in the extent of their support of public schools, ranging from about 5 per cent of the total in Nebraska to about 77 per cent in Delaware. Since 1961, the percentage of state support has remained constant, the percentage of local support has declined, and the percentage of federal support has more than doubled.

The total income of the public schools in 1966–67 was $30,195,908,000, of which $26,821,486,000 came from taxation and $3,373,422,000 from the sale of bonds (for capital outlay). The total estimated expenditure per pupil in average daily attendance in all public schools in 1966–67 was $564, ranging from $315 to a high of $912 among the states.

REFERENCES

BUTTS, R. FREEMAN, and CREMIN, LAWRENCE A., *History of Education in American Culture*. New York: Henry Holt and Company, 1953.

CHANDLER, B. J., *Education and the Teacher*. New York: Dodd, Mead and Company, 1961, Chap. 2, "How and Why American Public Schools Developed," pp. 23–52.

CUBBERLEY, ELLWOOD P., *Public Education in the United States*. Boston: Houghton Mifflin Company, 1919.

EDWARDS, NEWTON, and RICHEY, H. G., *The School in the American Social Order*. Boston: Houghton Mifflin Company, 1947.

ELSBREE, WILLARD S., *The American Teacher*. New York: American Book Company, 1939, Chap. 3, "Qualifications of Teachers During the Colonial Period," pp. 32–45; Chap. 11, "Educational Developments During the Early Days of the Republic," pp. 133–42; Chap. 12, "The Rise of the Public Normal School," pp. 143–54.

GOOD, H. G., *A History of American Education*. New York: Macmillan Company, 1956.

———, *A History of Western Education*, 2nd ed. New York: Macmillan Company, 1960.

HENDRICK, I. G., "History of Education and Teacher Preparation: A Cautious Analysis," *Journal of Teacher Education*, Spring, 1966, *17*:71–6.

HONEYWELL, ROY J., *Educational Work of Thomas Jefferson*. Cambridge, Mass.: Harvard University Press, 1931.

KNIGHT, EDGAR W., *Education in the United States*, 3rd rev. ed. Boston: Ginn & Company, 1951, Chap. 3, "The Background," pp. 50–69; Chap. 4, "The Colonial Climate," pp. 70–95; Chap. 5, "Early Practices," pp. 97–129; Chap. 8, "Horace Mann," pp. 201–2 and 210–18; Chap. 11, "The Training of Teachers," pp. 309–42.

MEYER, ADOLPHE E., *An Educational History of the American People*. New York: McGraw-Hill Book Company, 1957.

MESSERLI, J., "Horace Mann and Teacher Education," *Yearbook of Education* 1963: 70–84.

NATIONAL EDUCATION ASSOCIATION, Research Division. *Estimates of School Statistics, 1966–67* (Research Report 1966-R20). Washington, D.C.: The Association, 1966. (Issued annually.)

RICHEY, ROBERT W., *Planning for Teaching* (3rd ed.). New York: McGraw-Hill Book Company, 1963, Part IV, "Our Educational Heritage," pp. 305–58.

RUDY, S. WILLIS, "America's First Normal School: The Formative Years," *Journal of Teacher Education*, December, 1954, 5:263–70.

TYACK, D., "History of Education and the Preparation of Teachers: A Reappraisal," *Journal of Teacher Education*, December, 1965, *16*:427–31.

U.S. DEPARTMENT OF HEALTH, EDUCATION, AND WELFARE, Office of Education, *Fall 1965 Statistics of Public Schools*. Washington, D.C.: U.S. Government Printing Office, 1966.

WIMPEY, J. A., "After One Hundred Years: Horace Mann's Influence in Today's Schools," *Phi Delta Kappan*, February, 1959, *40*:206–8.

WOODY, THOMAS (ed.) *Educational Views of Benjamin Franklin*. New York: McGraw-Hill Book Company, 1931.

2: The Emerging Revolution in American Education

*T*here is an aphorism that controversy is the lifeblood of a free society. This is another way of saying that dissent is essential to the survival of democracy. At first glance these seem paradoxical principles, but carefully examined, they reveal not only the nature of a free society but the secret of its vigor.

Controversy is at the heart of progress in a democracy because it enables free men to make free decisions, to arrive at conclusions based upon evaluation of all sides of an issue. In an authoritarian society there is only one viewpoint: that of the prevailing authority. Free discussion is stifled, and dissent is a mark of disloyalty, even treason. Any debate on decisions of "higher authority" is considered seditious. Thus, popular thought, intellectual ferment, constant probing and questioning of the people about public policies and governmental laws and edicts are taboo. Obviously, such a system stifles intellectual activity, kills interest and participation of people in public affairs, and drives each citizen to silence and ultimately to sullenness and rebellion.

In the free society the key to intellectual vigor, pride in progress, is free discussion—freedom of speech and press. Every man is to have his say. Even when he enunciates "dangerous ideas," he still can say it. Why? Because if one man expresses an extreme, seemingly radical idea, another will counteract it with a moderate or even reactionary one. Somewhere in between, the people, after hearing or studying all expressions on a given issue, come to a conclusion as to the sound one. This principle of open and free discussion, of vehement dissent, differences of opinion, and often bitter controversy is difficult for many people to accept. A substantial proportion of people believe in free speech only if they agree with the speaker's viewpoint.

The public schools, belonging to all the people and subjected to popular will for support, will always be a subject of great controversy. Free schools were born in controversy. And evolution of the principle of free, public education in the United States moved forward on controversy. There is no reason to assume that the schools will ever be free of criticism, public discussion, and controversy. But this does not mean public antagonism, although some segments of the public may be violently opposed to the principle of public schools. It does not mean that a given critic is anti-public schools. He may be deeply committed to their maintenance but is skeptical of their procedures and wants them strengthened.

Causes of Present Criticism of Schools

While controversy has been present throughout the life of the public schools, the ferment of public criticism seems to be more heated during a national crisis, such as the threat of war, during war, or during a cold war such as that in which we are now involved. The present period of public school controversy began after Pearl Harbor, stilled somewhat during World War II, smoldered in the aftermath of the war, began to mount again with the Korean War, and flared in sizzling criticisms with the launching of the first Russian Sputnik in 1957. The decade 1950–60 has witnessed the most intense and perhaps the most bitter scrutiny of all education in the United States, with particular focus upon the public schools. There are, of course, many reasons why this decade brought forth such a development. Some of these are:

1. The frustration of the American people, after having fought two world wars and the Korean War, to find that peace was still an elusive search.

2. The concept that had been built up in the public mind, as an argument for establishment of free education for all and used repeatedly to secure increased financial support, that through education all our national problems would be solved—economic, moral, social, political, and military. In other words, the concept that education and more education of more and more people would automatically solve all the problems of human behavior, make all men good and wise, all voters enlightened and unselfish, all workers diligent and efficient, and all public servants invariably committed to the public welfare, claimed too much for the schools. No system of education can promise all these things as universal absolutes of attainment.

3. The public will always seek a scapegoat for its own failures. And schools, close at hand to every citizen, an instrumentality that he supports with his taxes, are always a prime object for scapegoating.

CURRENT ISSUES IN EDUCATION

What are the great issues in American education that are currently being debated with great heat and often with too little light? There are many, too many to enumerate here. The major ones (and each has numerous offspring that shoot the criticism into thousands of minor details) center on one or the other of the following: (1) Mass education is a failure; we should return to the European two-track system of one set of schools for the privileged (gifted) and one set for the poor and less gifted. (2) Our schools are soft and flabby, with curricula and teaching methods designed to encourage anti-intellectualism and sloth. (3) The intellectual subjects, especially mathematics, science, and foreign languages, are slighted. (4) The schools are too expensive. (5) Our teachers are incompetent, because their preparation has slighted the academic disciplines and glorified methods courses.

TEN CRITICISMS OF THE SCHOOLS

The NEA Research Division, in 1956, surveyed the issues as reflected in thirty lay magazines, made a frequency tabulation of criticisms discussed in articles in these publications, and grouped the criticisms under ten categories.[1] Then the study sought to evaluate these criticisms in the light of the facts as revelaed by research studies and their validity in light of research findings. The ten predominant criticisms examined in this study are:

1. Public school policy is in the control of professional educators.
2. Progressive education has taken over the public schools.
3. Life-adjustment education has replaced intellectual training in the public schools.
4. The policy of promoting all in the public school has robbed education of the stimulus of competition.
5. Lax discipline in the public schools has contributed to the increase in juvenile delinquency.
6. The teaching of classical and modern foreign languages is disappearing from the public secondary schools.
7. High school students are avoiding science and mathematics.
8. The public schools are neglecting the gifted child because they are geared to teach the average child.

[1] National Education Association, Research Division, "Ten Criticisms of Public Education," *Research Bulletin,* December, 1957, 35:131–75.

9. The public schools are neglecting the training of children in moral and spiritual values.

10. The standards of the schools of education are low, their programs of questionable value, and the intellectual qualities of preparing teachers are the poorest in the universities.[2]

Revolution in Education

It is interesting to review the charges and countercharges that reverberated in public forums and the public media between the close of World War II and the Sputnik frenzy. The issues of that period, already set forth, were to a large extent intramural arguments—some of them simply a restatement of old arguments—statements in a new context of long persisting differences of viewpoints about the purposes, the processes, and the philosophies of education in a free society.

During the decade 1950–60 the controversy rarely considered certain key factors lying obscured beneath the flowing surface of American life. In the meantime, the country was becoming highly industrialized and urbanized, changing the basic structure of its life and changing drastically the purposes and the aspirations of its society. At the same time, the school integration issue was for the most part a philosophical discussion. The extraordinary development of sophisticated technology by American industry, the civil rights movement, the development of mammoth slum ghettos in major cities, the slum child and his needs, the educational neglect of millions of American children of all races, the problems and impacts of chronic poverty—all these were yet to penetrate the national storm about education.

A glance at the issues just listed reveals how far the criticisms of our schools were missing the real, rising issues. Of course, all of these at the time were bitter issues, bitterly debated by critics and defenders of the lower schools. With the emergence of newer and vastly more complex conditions in our society, it turned out that these issues were geared to the older slower-paced social order where certain prestigious universities insisted upon the right to determine the nature and quality of education. Too, these issues were geared in large measure to the race with the Soviet Union for super-powerful defense systems.

Still obscured and mostly unnoticed were the growing problems of (1) automation, displacing thousands of workers and creating new jobs requiring new skills, (2) the educational neglect of millions of deprived children, crowded into cities by the unprecedented migration from rural

[2] For articles giving the pro's and con's regarding most of these issues and some additional ones, see C. Winfield Scott, Clyde M. Hill, and Hobert W. Burns (eds.) *The Great Debate,* Englewood Cliffs, New Jersey: Prentice-Hall, Inc., 1959, 184 pp.

areas to the cities, and (3) the continued ignoring of the real needs of the schools by our society.

The American people had been misled by the controversy about education in the "great debate" period. They had been deceived by the easy answer that the answer to curing the ills of the schools was to "get tough" in the lower schools. This was a vast oversimplification. There was need for a vast infusion of public funds to renovate school plants, which in many areas had deteriorated to an alarming degree; to check the outflow of qualified teachers to other fields; to utilize newly developed technological aids in the schools; and to develop new approaches to the effective teaching of the deprived children in the slum areas of large inner-cities.

These factors finally forced the federal government to embark on substantial school support, with the program of school legislation enacted beginning with the Kennedy administration in 1961 and accelerated by the Johnson administration. With the advent of this legislation, the educational revolution was propelled into full tide. The new legislation gave visible evidence that the American people were at long last fully conscious that education was indispensable not only to the survival but to the progress of their society.

The nature of the new and indispensable role of education in American life has been succinctly stated by Clark Kerr, former president of the University of California:

America's situation is unprecedented. Throughout most of history, education has been used for the advantage of one class or another, as the servant of the church or the aristocracy or some other institution. In the United States today, the educational complex is becoming both a servant of all the people and at the same time, with its capacity for new knowledge, an independent force in society. It is on the threshold of having a will of its own. Like the military-industrial complex that President Eisenhower once spoke of, the educational complex has the same capacity to perpetuate itself and to change the surrounding society. Perhaps even more significantly, it can change a country beyond the conscious will of its political leaders, as happens today in Russia wherever students and scholars demand more freedoms. In a free society, it seems to me, scholars must be the first to raise the painful question: Will education be as good a master as it has been a servant? [3]

Former U.S. Commissioner of Education Francis Keppel has written:

The first revolution in American education was a revolution in quantity. Everyone was to be provided an education of some sort. That revolution is almost won in the schools and is on its way in higher education. The second

[3] "Turmoil in Higher Education," *Look* Magazine, Vol. 31 (April 18, 1967), pp. 17–21. Interview with Clark Kerr, edited by G. B. Leonard and T. G. Harris.

revolution is equality of opportunity. That revolution is under way. The next turn of the wheel must be a revolution in quality.[4]

The first revolution to extend some form and degree of education to all American children was substantially achieved by the beginning of World War II. Although there were still vast pockets of educational neglect—of inadequate schools and schooling, the extent of the spread of popular education throughout the United States, from colonial days to the second great war, is probably unprecedented in the history of the world. This extension was accomplished at the grass roots of American society, largely by local communities. The states aided materially, but the federal government contributed relatively little to the movement. Some examples: The illiteracy rate was consistently reduced, in the total population 15 years of age and over, from 11.3 per cent in 1900, to about 2 per cent in 1965. The percentage of our population 17 years of age who graduated from high school increased from about 2 per cent in 1870 to over 76 per cent in 1964. Less than 1 per cent of American children between the ages of 6 and 13 are presently not attending school. About 94 per cent of children of high school age (14–17 years) are in school. Of the college age population (18–24) about 40 per cent attend college, and more than one half of the high school graduates go on to colleges and universities.

This is a record of popular, mass education unequaled elsewhere in the world. But beneath the surface data are educational failures and weaknesses that constitute one of the powerful causes for what Keppel terms the second revolution in education. Equality in educational opportunity still eludes American society to a striking and alarming degree. This faliure to achieve equal opportunity in education spreads across the entire school population, but with especial emphasis upon certain minority groups—Appalachian whites, Negroes, Puerto Ricans, Latin Americans (Mexicans), and American Indians.

Among the general school population about 30 per cent of children of high school age still drop out before graduation and one in 20 does not complete the eighth grade. As many as 15 per cent of the academically talented high school graduates—about one fourth of this group ranking in the upper quartile of high school graduates—do not go on to college. The chief reason for their failure to attend college is low family incomes.

The tragic extent of the failure of the nation to extend equality of educational opportunity to all children is reflected in the following tables. The data reveals that in 1960 in Iowa only 0.7 per cent of the 14-year-old and older residents were illiterate, and in Louisiana more than 6 per cent.

[4] Francis Keppel, *The Necessary Revolution in American Education.* New York: Harper & Row, 1966, p. 1.

The average for the country as a whole was 2.4 per cent. To state the data in another way, 99.3 per cent of the population of Iowa 14 years old or older was literate, while 93.7 per cent of Louisianans were literate. For the United States as a whole, 97.6 per cent were literate.

Per Cent of Population 14 Years Old and Older Illiterate in 1960

State	Per Cent	State	Per Cent
1. Iowa	0.7%	Delaware	1.9
		25. Maryland	1.9
2. Idaho	0.8	Oklahoma	1.9
Oregon	0.8		
		28. Pennsylvania	2.0%
Kansas	0.9		
Nebraska	0.9	Connecticut	2.2
South Dakota	0.9	29. Massachusetts	2.2
4. Utah	0.9	New Jersey	2.2
Washington	0.9		
Wyoming	0.9	32. Rhode Island	2.4
10. Minnesota	1.0	UNITED STATES	2.4
Montana	1.0	33. Florida	2.6
		34. West Virginia	2.7
12. Nevada	1.1	35. New York	2.9
Vermont	1.1	36. Alaska	3.0
		37. Kentucky	3.3
14. Indiana	1.2	38. Virginia	3.4
Wisconsin	1.2	39. Tennessee	3.5
		40. Arkansas	3.6
16. Colorado	1.3	41. Arizona	3.8
Maine	1.3		
		42. New Mexico	4.0
18. New Hampshire	1.4	North Carolina	4.0
North Dakota	1.4		
		44. Texas	4.1
20. Ohio	1.5	45. Alabama	4.2
21. Michigan	1.6	46. Georgia	4.5
22. Missouri	1.7	47. Mississippi	4.9
		48. Hawaii	5.0
23. California	1.8	49. South Carolina	5.5
Illinois	1.8	50. Louisiana	6.3

Source: U.S. Department of Commerce, Bureau of the Census. *Estimates of Illiteracy, by States: 1960.* Current Population Reports, Series P-23, No. 8. Washington, D.C.: Government Printing Office, Feb. 12, 1963, p. 2.

But the tragic picture of American educational failures is pinpointed in the following table. The average school years completed in 1960 ranges from 12.2 years in Utah to 8.7 years in Kentucky and South Carolina. The average for the nonwhite population ranges from 10.7 years in Maine to 5.9 years in South Carolina.

Median School Years Completed by Persons 25 Years Old and Older, 1960

State	All	White	Non-white	State	All	White	Non-white
1. Utah	12.2	12.2	10.1	28. New York	10.7	10.8	9.4
				29. New Jersey	10.6	10.8	8.8
2. Alaska	12.1	12.4	6.6				
California	12.1	12.1	10.5				
Colorado	12.1	12.1	11.2	UNITED			
Nevada	12.1	12.2	8.8	STATES	10.6	10.9	8.2
Washington	12.1	12.2	10.5	30. Illinois	10.5	10.7	9.0
Wyoming	12.1	12.1	9.3	Maryland	10.4	11.0	8.1
				Oklahoma	10.4	10.7	8.6
8. Idaho	11.8	11.8	9.6	31. South Dakota	10.4	10.5	8.6
Oregon	11.8	11.8	9.9	Texas	10.4	10.8	8.1
10. Kansas	11.7	11.8	9.6	Wisconsin	10.4	10.4	9.0
11. Massachusetts	11.6	11.6	10.3	36. Pennsylvania	10.2	10.3	8.9
Montana	11.6	11.7	8.7	37. Rhode Island	10.0	10.0	9.5
Nebraska	11.6	11.7	9.6	38. Virginia	9.9	10.8	7.2
14. Arizona	11.3	11.7	7.0	39. Missouri	9.6	9.8	8.7
Hawaii	11.3	12.4	9.9	40. North Dakota	9.3	9.3	8.4
Iowa	11.3	11.3	9.5	41. Alabama	9.1	10.2	6.5
17. New Mexico	11.2	11.5	7.1	42. Georgia	9.0	10.3	6.1
18. Delaware	11.1	11.6	8.4	43. Arkansas	8.9	9.5	6.5
19. Connecticut	11.0	11.1	9.1	Mississippi	8.9	11.0	6.0
Maine	11.0	11.0	10.7	North Carolina	8.9	9.8	7.0
21. Florida	10.9	11.6	7.0	46. Louisiana	8.8	10.5	6.0
New Hampshire	10.9	10.9	11.7	Tennessee	8.8	9.0	7.5
Ohio	10.9	11.0	9.1	West Virginia	8.8	8.8	8.4
Vermont	10.9	10.9	10.5	49. Kentucky	8.7	8.7	8.2
25. Indiana	10.8	10.9	9.0	South Carolina	8.7	10.3	5.9
Michigan	10.8	11.0	9.1				
Minnesota	10.8	10.8	9.9				

Source: NEA Research Division, *op. cit.*, Table 42, p. 31.

The harsh meaning of this data is found in examining statistics on the percentage of 18-year-old youth disqualified for military service for mental reasons as shown in the following table.

Per Cent of 18-Year-Old Youths Disqualified for Military Service for Mental Reasons July 1964 Through December 1965

	State	Per Cent		State	Per Cent
1.	Washington	5.8%	26.	Michigan	18.2%
2.	Minnesota	6.9	27.	California	19.5
3.	Oregon	7.4	28.	Delaware	20.8
4.	Wyoming	7.5	29.	Maine	20.9
5.	Iowa	7.7	30.	Colorado	21.2
6.	Utah	8.2	31.	Missouri	21.6
7.	Montana	8.3	32.	Oklahoma	23.3
8.	Wisconsin	9.4	33.	New York	24.9
9.	Idaho	11.4	34.	Arizona	25.9
10.	Nebraska	12.1	35.	Maryland	27.8
11.	Rhode Island	12.4		UNITED STATES	28.0
12.	South Dakota	12.6	36.	Hawaii	28.3
13.	Alaska	13.1	37.	New Mexico	29.4
14.	Kansas	13.5	38.	Florida	32.9
15.	Pennsylvania	13.7	39.	Arkansas	33.7
16.	Connecticut	13.8	40.	West Virginia	35.5
17.	Ohio	13.9	41.	Texas	38.6
18.	North Dakota	14.1	42.	Kentucky	39.1
19.	Indiana	14.2	43.	Georgia	43.2
20.	New Jersey	14.4	44.	Alabama	44.5
21.	Nevada	14.9	45.	Virginia	45.3
22.	Vermont	15.1	46.	Louisiana	46.0
23.	New Hampshire	16.1	47.	Tennessee	49.0
24.	Massachusetts	17.0	48.	North Carolina	53.0
25.	Illinois	17.8	49.	Mississippi	53.8
			50.	South Carolina	54.6

Source: U.S. Army, Office of the Surgeon General. "Results of the Examination of Youths for Military Service, 1965." *Supplement to Health of the Army*, 21: 1–47, July, 1966.

The percentage of rejections for military service for mental reasons ranged from 5.8 per cent in Washington, to 54.6 in South Carolina among the states. The percentage of rejections for the U.S. as a whole was 28.

FACTORS CONTRIBUTING TO THE EDUCATIONAL REVOLUTION

There is a complex of factors involved as causal influences in the current revolution in American education. It is impossible to compile a complete list. Only the major ones will be attempted. Also, it is impossible to list the major ones in any order of importance. All these factors overlap at points and duplicate at points.

The major causal factors appear to be:

1. The knowledge explosion.
2. The population explosion.
3. The technological revolution.
4. Advances in transportation and communication.
5. Urbanization of the American people.
6. The steady depletion of natural resources, forcing greater reliance upon the developed mind of man.
7. The school integration problem.
8. The need for new emphases upon the education of deprived children.
9. The need for continuing education.
10. The massive infusion of federal funds.

The Knowledge Explosion

The piling up of new knowledge at an unprecedented rate will inevitably require new approaches to teaching. This will require extensive use of educational technology, by which much of the rote factual drill will be done by machines, instead of direct communication of the teacher. Taped lectures, teaching machines and computers, programmed instruction, and the talking typewriter will take care of the objective testing of students. Much of this will happen before the student has any close contact with the teacher, who will serve to help students interpret and make adaptations of the learned material.

There was a time when society could boast of the encyclopedians— men who possessed all, or virtually all, of existing knowledge, such as Sir Francis Bacon and Richard Wundt. Under the impact of science, the rate of accretion of knowledge has increased so greatly in modern society that it is no longer possible for one individual to possess more than a fragment of total knowledge, even in a highly specialized field.

A popular expression, which typifies the vast accumulation of new knowledge, is that "Ninety per cent of all scientists who ever lived are still alive." Another widely-quoted statement is that knowledge in some fields is doubling every decade and this rate will increase. In other words, the increase of knowledge, which in earlier times was by a leisurely arithmetical progression, now is increasing by geometric progression.

More than a decade ago, David Sarnoff wrote:

The dominant physical fact in the next quarter-century will be technological progress unprecedented in kind and volume . . . . the last hundred years have been no more than a split second. Yet they have composed more technological achievement than the millennia that preceded. The harnessing of electricity to the purposes of light, power, and communication; demonstration of the germ theory of disease; discovery and application of the electron; invention of radio and television; development of anesthetics; the exploration of genes and mutations; invention of motor vehicles, evolution of the assembly line, and other mass production techniques; proliferation of organic chemistry; the splitting of the atom; development of antibiotics; the vast expansion of the known and measured universe of the stars and galaxies—these are only the highlights of recent progress.[5]

Other sources of energy will be discovered and harnessed—the sun, the tides, and the winds. Thousands of new materials—metals, plastics, fabrics, woods, glass—will be added, through man's capacity to rearrange the structure of matter. Transportation now with jet planes at 600 miles an hour will be replaced by the supersonic jet at 1,800 miles an hour, carrying about 600 passengers. These developments mean that no place on earth is far off anymore. In time will come the hypersonic jet flying at greatly multiplied speeds at heights probably approaching 100,000 feet. Instantaneous world-wide communication via Telstar and Comsat is already a reality, providing an informational fall-out that no human being can escape.

It is extremely doubtful that the accumulation of new knowledge can be assimilated by a "get tough" policy in our schools, or by drastic extension of the school day, week, and year. Although there probably will come extensions of educational time—in length of the school year and more years of education—the real answers to the dilemma of knowledge accretion appear to be (1) the "exclusion process"—dropping outdated materials and focusing on the essentials; (2) drastic revision of curricula; and (3) more realistic teaching methodology, with wide use of aids and technology.

The Population Explosion

There is a popular saying that assuming the continuation of current birth rates in the world and a continuing decrease in death rates, within a century or so, there will be "standing room only" in the world. Although this may prove to be an exaggerated estimate, there certainly are grounds for alarm. With all the progress of mankind in science and agriculture, a good portion of the world's peoples is faced with constant hunger, malnutrition, and famine.

It is estimated that there probably were 250 million people on earth at the time of the birth of Christ. It took about 16 centuries—roughly, to the time of the first colonial settlements in the United States—for this population to double to one half billion. During most of this period, the average life span was probably not in excess of 25 years (as contrasted with an average of about 70 years in the United States today).

By 1800, in an additional 200 years, the word's population is estimated

[5] David Sarnoff, "The Fabulous Future," *Fortune,* January 1955, pp. 85 ff.

to have been about 900 millions. In this period, the doubling rate was reduced to 250 years. By 1900, the world's population had reached 1.6 billions; by 1950, it had reached 2.5 billions; and in 1967, the total population of the world was 3.2 billions. During the nineteenth century, the doubling rate of the world's population was approximately 90 years; in the first half of the twentieth century this doubling rate was reduced to 75 years; and currently this doubling rate has declined to less than 40 years. Should the present doubling rate of population continue, the present 3.2 billions of people will grow to about 6 billions by 2014; to 13 billions by 2061; and to 25 billions by the beginning of the twenty-second century (a span of a little more than a century and a third).

The great problems—problems with which education must be concerned in the future as population continues to grow—are those of food, water, and minerals. With the rapid depletion of natural resources, the developed mind of man must be increasingly the source of new resources, new utilizations of nature's hidden treasures.

Man, through education, must find new ways of harnessing natural resources. The farming of the sea for food, chemicals, and minerals is only in the embryonic stage. The more efficient husbandry of rainwater is a necessity. Moreover, the conversion of the salt water of the sea to fresh water, through new and economical means of extraction by the use of nuclear energy, offers means of avoiding droughts and famine. Already, in many areas of the United States, the shortage of adequate water supplies is alarming. Vast land areas of the United States lie fallow for the want of water for irrigation.

New processes to tap the vast shale deposits of the Rocky Mountains and to provide the needed energy from oil yet remain untapped pools of vast proportions. The same is true of the oceans' hidden treasures. Doubtless in time man with new technologies will learn to harvest and import minerals from the asteroids. Pollution of our waters and air and smog in our great cities can be solved, but only as man through education learns the means of conquering them.

Education of the Deprived

The educational revolution has exposed to the American people the extent of the neglect of the deprived children of all races, but especially children of minority groups. Perhaps neglect is not the proper word, although in the past there certainly has been neglect on a wide scale. It is neglect in part, and in part it is failure to devise appropriate approaches to the education of the deprived. Again, the plight of the deprived children has been both a cause and a contributor to the revolution in education. The stark fact has been revealed to the American people that the very survival of the nation may depend upon finding quick and effective solutions to the education of our so-called slum children. This problem has its genesis, basically, in the system of segregation, both in education and in total life of the country. Through the Supreme Court decision on school integration in 1954, subsequent enactments of federal legislation (notably the Civil Rights Act of 1964), and certain appropriations acts for the schools, a massive assault on *de facto* and *de jure* segregation in various sections of the United States was begun.

The current proportion of Negroes in the population (about 11 per cent) will increase to about 13 per cent by 1980. Increasingly the Negro population is tending to cluster in the large inner-cities. And these inner-cities are tending to become vast ghettos.

An indication of the trend is reflected in the following figures: the Negro population of Washington, D.C., is now more than 60 per cent of the total in that city; and the school population is more than 90 per cent Negro. In certain large areas of the great cities, such as New York, Baltimore, Cleveland, Chicago, Los Angeles, New Orleans, and St. Louis, the Negro population ranges from 90 to 100 per cent. Since 1950, the white population in the large cities has generally decreased, the Negro population has generally increased. The whites tend to migrate to the suburbs, or a substantial proportion of white children living in the inner-cities are withdrawn from public schools and enrolled in the private or parochial schools. The result is *de facto* segregation in many respects with the ill effects of the *de jure* segregation existing before the Supreme Court decision. It is evident that American society must find a solution to this problem.

The federal government has poured in huge grants of money, set up Head Start programs and Job Opportunity programs, and made extra grants to school districts with large proportions of economically deprived families. Yet the progress in integrating the public schools since the Supreme Court decision in 1954 has been distressingly small, both in the South and in the North.

Extension of Education Upward and Downward

The opportunity for schooling at public expense will be extended downward to the kindergarten first, and this arrangement will be universal. Then, nursery schools will be made available generally, if not universally. There are several reasons why these extensions must take place. Among these are the changed nature of our society and economy and the changed pattern of family life.

Increasingly in American families both of the parents hold jobs. The lack of all-day association with one or both parents tends to rob the young child of the opportunity to learn, converse, develop a vocabulary, become articulate, and develop cognitive associations. Particularly are early preschool experiences indicated for the deprived child. Research has revealed that the child who begins the first grade (or at age six) behind his colleagues in intellectual achievement will fall further behind them as the school years progress. It is then too late to institute remedial work that will be wholly successful in curing the lag. Precious years have been lost and can never be completely recovered.

Free schooling will be extended upward to include the junior college years (and these years of schooling may eventually become compulsory). The junior college is the fastest growing area of higher education, both in school numbers and pupil enrollments. This extension is made necessary by two developments: (1) the need to relieve the pressures of enrollments on senior colleges and universities; (2) the higher levels of education and skills required by jobs in society with the advent of automation, the single job skills giving way to those requiring sophisticated, technological ones.

Both the junior colleges and high schools will provide for continuing adult education to enable adults to keep abreast of the need for new knowledge and new skills. It is estimated that presently more than 30,000,000 adults are continuing their education.

Time (in its issue of January 12, 1968) dramatically forecasted the expansion of education upward:

A tide of rising expectation in learning is sweeping the U.S. At the turn of the century, universal grade-school education was considered a high enough achievement, as was a high-school diploma by World War II. Now the day is fast approaching where some form of college-level learning will be the national norm.

THE SEARCH FOR QUALITY IN EDUCATION

The third phase of the American revolution in education, as indicated previously, is the quest for quality. This means that every American must be equipped with the highest possible level of education.

Any such quest must involve at least five factors: (1) the quality of teachers, (2) the curriculum provisions and procedures, (3) teaching methodology, (4) the use of technology, and (5) a reorganization of the learning situation.

A New Status for Teachers

With respect to the teachers, stepped-up levels of preparation are imminent. The teacher of the future, in the lower schools, will have an average preparation of five years and ultimately six years of college and university preparation. Presently Arizona, California, and the District of

Columbia have established the five-year standard for high school teachers, but they are not fully enforcing that standard. A total of 18 states are now mandating completion of the fifth year during teaching on the initial Bachelor's degree certificate.

Second, the teaching task must be made into a manageable one. Currently, teachers as a general rule are overloaded to the breaking point, with too many children, too many classes, and too many clerical, book-keeping, and custodial duties. The answer to this overloading appears to be the placing of the professionally competent teacher at the center of a cluster of helpers—technological and human. Thus, the teacher is made director of a team. There will be a media laboratory in each school, with a professionally prepared director with broad grounding in methodology, learning theory, and human growth and development, as well as expertness in the use of educational hardware. The director of the media lab will be the advisor on the use of technological aids in a given situation. There will be teacher aides—clerical, lay readers, teacher assistants—all classed as paraprofessionals. This cluster of helpers will free the teacher from much of the routine drill and other nonteaching duties for the essential task of working with individual children. This redeployment will lift the teacher to a new status level, to that of a director of a team.

The teacher of the future will be younger, the average age probably will be around 30. Presently, the median age of all teachers is 36 years; the median age for men is 33 and women, 40. The proportion of men in teaching will increase. Currently, the percentage of men in the total teaching force is 31, women 69. The teacher of the future will be bilingual or even trilingual, with a portion of his preservice preparation completed in foreign countries. The teacher of the future will be a self-propelling, self-determining, creative master of his own classroom. He will be an individualist, not a timid conformist. He will have tenure in his position and the right to participate in policy making for the school system through collective negotiation. Future salaries for teachers are bound to have a rapid escalation, with salaries starting at from $8,000 to $10,000 and reaching upper levels of $20,000 to $25,000. In all probability, we shall come to the year-round (11-month) school term in the lower schools, on a voluntary basis for both teachers and students, somewhat in the pattern of current practices in colleges and universities.

This projected scale of pay will permit the gifted, creative teacher to remain in the classroom, and preclude the necessity of seeking administrative positions because of economic pressures. The American public school teacher will become an individualist, thus teaching will be creative and inspiring. Conformism is usually the enemy of creativeness. No two teachers will perform in the classroom in precisely the same manner. With factual drill being performed largely by technology, this aspect of education which in the past has consumed most of the time and efforts of teachers, will become largely a self-teaching process.

This means that the need for common approaches will largely disappear. The teacher will be freed for guiding and motivating the individual student. Each teacher will develop his own methodology for challenging, questioning, stimulating education. The goal of teacher load should be not more than 15 periods a week before classes.

The individualistic teacher will have profound impacts upon the curriculum. The set curriculum patterns upon which, presently, professional committees, consultants, and teachers spend an inordinate amount of time, will give way to a flexible, cooperative, day-by-day search for meaningful knowledge.

It is equally obvious that the present rather rigid bureaucratic, vertical, unilateral structure of administering the public schools will become a horizontal, coequal, collegial structure in which the professional staff actually plans and executes the school program. In time, the school board will become somewhat like the board of regents of a university, in many instances becoming the legislative body for the will of the professional staff.

Of course, these changes in the status of teachers will not come about overnight. But changes toward these ends are already underway and discernible. The flow of the times and the growing complexity of educational needs and processes will speed up the rate of change.

The Dominant Purpose of Education in an Open-Ended Society

Of all the changes that the revolution in American education doubtless will bring about, perhaps the most radical will be that of the purpose of education.

In the past, too often the dominant purpose has been to fit children into the *status quo*, with a lock-step, rote drill kind of indoctrination, upon the assumption that factual information, rather arbitrarily selected and imposed, was the essential base of any education worthy of the name. Conforming to the *status quo* is, of course, essential to a frontier society in which protection against human enemies, wildlife, and the elements requires that each individual perform a given task and be in the proper place when danger to the group threatens. But America is no longer in that situation.

Thus, twin fears have tended to dominate the public schools. First, the fear of teachers of failure to measure up on the mythical standard, with which they have had little or nothing to do in establishing, of success in inculcating factual material. Second, the fear of children of failure as measured on this same norm. These routines have tended to foster the notion that schools are maintained to determine which children pass and which fail; drills, routines, and tests have been established to this end.

This concept tends to perpetuate schools dedicated to a competitive race between children with widely diverse talents, aspirations, and aptitudes. What is wrong with such procedures is the purpose of fitting children into their proper places by the use of somewhat arbitrary, predetermined yardsticks.

The inescapable obligation of the schools in a free society is to provide the opportunity for the fullest possible development of children, according to their needs and talents. The common set of knowledge, the common testing by which children are erroneously classified as superior and inferior will be replaced. The needs of the future probably will force the abandonment of marks or grades.

Curriculum and Methodology

Perhaps the most significant change of all in the revolution in education will be in the content and organization of the curriculum in the lower schools. The nature of teaching will change from that of the teacher being a rote master to that of the master guide and stimulator of children. The old order of the transmission of a common content to children to be given back in a common examination will give way largely to a day-by-day quest for meaningful knowledge and problem-solving by children.

Instead of expecting the mastery of a predetermined set of knowledges and values, children will be free to pursue interests and question where these may lead. Instead of seeking to indoctrinate children into a lock-step routine to find their places in the *status quo,* the search will be for the fullest possible development of children according to their individual needs and talents. Schools will shift from a competitive race to determine who fails and who succeeds among children of diverse talents and interests to the search for means of individual development. The system of grades by which in the past the schools have used to denote success or failure, to denote the superior and the inferior, will be abandoned. Instead of the fixed seat classroom children will work in large rooms, in groups, with a team consisting of the teacher and his helpers or several teachers and their helpers. Team teaching and non-graded schools will grow in use and effectiveness.

The above projections of the educational revolution are predicated upon the assumption of a massive infusion of federal funds. It is necessary, therefore, to review the history of federal support of schools and to project future trends in such support.

Federal Support of Schools

Since before the nation was founded under the present Constitution (in 1789), the issue of responsibility of the federal government for participating in the financial support of the public schools has been a highly controversial one. Beginning with the Northwest Ordinances of 1785 and 1787, when the Continental Congress allotted a section of land in each township for the maintenance of public schools, the Congress has nibbled at the problem. Many grants and laws having to do with some form of financial aid have been activated. Yet these have been indirect peripheral actions. Congress has yet to pass a general federal-support law applicable to all public schools and all programs in these schools.

FEDERAL GRANTS TO EDUCATION

Prior to 1960, the major grants by federal legislation for education, by categories of purposes, are set forth in the following compilation: [6]

Early Public Land Grants

1785—Land Ordinance.   Specified the manner in which the western lands should be surveyed and stipulated that "there shall be reserved the lot number 16 of every township for the maintenance of public schools within said township."

1787—Northwest Ordinance.   Stated that "religion, morality and knowledge, being necessary to good government and happiness of mankind, schools and the means of education shall forever be encouraged."

1802—Ohio Enabling Act.   Granted section 16 of each township, in the states carved from the public domain, to the township inhabitants for the support of schools. With the exception of Texas, Maine, and West Virginia, the same policy applied to all states admitted to the Union until 1848.

1803—Further Land Grants to New States. Granted a township to Ohio for a seminary of learning and stipulated that all educational land grants were to be "for schools and for no other use, intent or purposes whatever." Similar grants extended to other states carved from the public domain.

Land-Grant College Statutes

1862—Morrill Land-Grant Act.   Granted to each state an amount of 30,000 acres of public land (or its equivalent in scrip) per Congressman for the support of a college that would have as its primary purpose the teaching of "such branches of learning as are related to agriculture and the mechanic arts. . . ." Provision was also made for military training.

1890—Second Morrill Act.   Increased the support of the land-grant colleges and universities.

1908—Nelson Amendment to Morrill Act.   Increased the support of the land-grant colleges and universities.

[6] Source: National Education Association, Legislative Commission, *It's Older Than the Constitution—Federal Responsibility for Education.* Washington, D.C.: The Association, 1960 (pamphlet).

1935—Bankhead-Jones Act.   Increased annual appropriations for support of land-grant colleges and universities.

Vocational—Education Acts

1917—Smith-Hughes Act.   Provided grants for promoting vocational training in the public schools and for encouraging special education for teachers of vocational subjects. Contained exacting requirements and stipulations as to the use of the funds. Permanent annual appropriation amounts to $7,138,000.

1936—George-Deen Act.   . . . extended Smith-Hughes Act to include education in distributive occupations.

1946—George-Barden Act.   . . . Supplementary legislation to the Smith-Hughes and George-Deen vocational-education acts. Authorizes up to $29 million in federal grants. . . .

1956—Public Laws 911 and 1027, 84th Congress.   Amend the George-Barden Act to include federal aid for practical-nurse training of less than college level (up to $5 million a year for five years) and training in the fishery trades ($375,000 a year).

1958—National Defense Education Act.   Title VIII of Public Law 85-864 adds area vocational programs and emphasizes new technical skills. (For other details, see also "Defense Education.")

School Lunches

1946—National School Lunch Act (Public Law 396, 79th Congress).   Distributes funds and federally purchased foods to schools, public and nonpublic, to be used for school lunches.

1954—School Milk Program (Public Law 690, 83rd Congress).   An important adjunct to the school lunch program. In 1958, Public Law 85-478 extended this program until 1961 and authorized $75 million per year to make surplus milk available to nonprofit elementary and secondary schools, as well as child-care centers, settlement houses, and summer camps.

Veterans' Education

1944—Servicemen's Readjustment Act (Public Law 346, 78th Congress).   Provided for educational and training benefits for veterans on the basis of length of time spent in the service. The GI Bill of Rights.

1952—Veterans' Readjustment Assistance Act (Public Law 550, 82nd Congress).   The Korean GI Bill provided educational and training benefits for persons who served between June 27, 1950, and January 31, 1955.

1956—War Orphans' Educational Assistance Act (Public Law 634, 84th Congress).   Extends benefits of Korean GI Bill to orphans of servicemen killed in World War II or Korean conflict.

Federally Affected Areas

1941—Lanham Act.   Provided federal assistance, including school building aid, for communities adversely affected by federal activities.

1950—Public Laws 815 and 874, 81st Congress.   Provided assistance for school construction (PL 81-815) and maintenance and operation (PL 81-874) in federally affected areas. Authorized national school-facilities survey.

1958—Public Law 85-620. Continued federal assistance for construction and operation of schools in federally affected areas.

Rural Libraries

1956—Public Law 597, 84th Congress. Established a five-year program of federal grants to the states for extension of library services in rural areas. Federal appropriations up to $7.5 million a year are authorized.

1960—PL 86-679. Extends the act for five years.

Exceptional Children

1958—Public Law 85-926, the Fogarty-McGovern Act. Authorized federal grants to help train teachers for the mentally retarded.

1958—Public Law 85-905. Authorized federal funds to acquire and distribute films with printed captions for use with deaf persons.

Defense Education

1958—Public Law 85-864, the National Defense Education Act. Authorized $887 million in federal funds over a period of four years to strengthen critical areas in education.

Beginning in 1961, the federal government inaugurated a comprehensive program of financial support for schools that was to reach mammoth proportions during the Johnson Administration (see Table 3).

The federal appropriations of less than $1 billion in the fiscal year 1961 increased to about $4 billion in fiscal 1967. This mammoth increase indicates a drastic change in the policy of the federal government regarding education. The increase is both a consequence and a cause of the educational revolution. That is, (1) the revolution reaching such floodtide proportions under the impact of social forces impelled the federal government to become involved; and (2) the inflow of federal funds accelerated the revolution.

These appropriations do not indicate the total outflow of federal funds for education. Appropriations to other federal agencies, especially for the Head Start program, the Office of Economic Opportunity, the Job Corps and others, all related to education, were significant.

Halperin has stated:

Any speculation on this question (the extent of federal involvement) must take into account the great strides made by the 88th and 89th Congresses. . . . They enacted more than 30 education statutes. Federal funds for education were $3 billion a year when President Kennedy took office. They had increased to $5 billion when President Johnson succeeded him. Today (1967) the federal government is spending more than $10 billion for education.[7]

[7] Samuel Halperin, "Legislation in the 90th Congress," *Phi Delta Kappan*, February, 1967, 48:259–261.

TABLE 3   *Federal Appropriations for Major Programs for Fiscal Years 1966 and 1967* °

Program	Appropriation for the Year Ending June 30, 1966	Appropriation for the Year Ending June 30, 1967
Expansion and Improvement of Vocational Education	$ 253,441,000	$ 278,016,000
Elementary and Secondary Education Act	1,151,000,000	1,342,410,000
Higher Education	229,923,000	413,900,000
Teacher Corps	9,500,000	7,500,000
Student Loans	550,000	3,200,000
Higher Education Facilities	632,700,000	722,744,000
Grants for Libraries	55,000,000	76,000,000
Impacted Areas	438,078,000	439,137,000
National Defense Education Act	412,608,000	446,357,000
Educational Improvement for the Handicapped	25,500,000	32,600,000
Research and Training	70,000,000	70,000,000
USOE Salaries and Expenses	30,136,000	35,150,000
Other Programs	33,661,000	34,661,000
TOTAL	$3,342,097,000	$3,901,675,000

Source: Harold Howe II, "The U.S. Office of Education: Growth and Growing Pains," *Saturday Review*, December 17, 1966, pp. 68–69.

° This does not include programs such as Upward Bound and Head Start, which are not administered by the Office of Education.

REFERENCES

BREMBECK, COLE S., *Social Foundations of Education*. New York: John Wiley and Sons, 1966.

BODOH, R., "European vs. American Education," *Educational Leadership*, April, 1960, *17*:459, 461–63.

CAMPBELL, R. F., "Tomorrow's Teacher," *Saturday Review*, January 14, 1967, *50*:60+.

"Changing Directions in American Education: Symposium." *Saturday Review*, January 14, 1967, *50*:37–43+.

COREY, ARTHUR F., "The Real Attack is on Education for All," *Nation's Schools*, July, 1958, *62*:38–39.

FULL, HAROLD (ed.) *Controversy in American Education: An Anthology of Crucial Issues*. New York: Macmillan Company, 1967.

HALPERIN, SAMUEL, "Legislation in the 90th Congress," *Phi Delta Kappan*, February, 1967, *48*:259–261.

HOLLINSHEAD, BYRON S., "American and European Education: Why the Differences?" *NEA Journal,* February, 1959, *48*:56–59.

KEPPEL, FRANCIS, *The Necessary Revolution in American Education.* New York: Harper & Row, 1966.

KANDEL, I. L., "Revival of American Education," *Educational Forum,* March, 1960, *24*:271–78.

LEONARD, G. B., "What Your Child Can Teach His Teacher," *Look,* December 27, 1966, *30*:29–30.

LOUGHARTY, J. W., "Can Teachers Survive the Educational Revolution?" *Phi Delta Kappan,* January, 1967, *48*:204–7. Same condensed in *Education Digest,* April, 1967, *32*:16–19.

MILLER, RICHARD I., *Perspectives on Educational Change.* New York: Appleton-Century-Crofts, 1967.

NATIONAL EDUCATION ASSOCIATION, Legislative Commission, "It's Older Than the Constitution," Washington, D.C.: The Association, 1965, leaflet.

SCOTT, C. WINFIELD, HILL, CLYDE M., and BURNS, HOBERT W. (eds.) *The Great Debate: Our Schools in Crisis.* Spectrum Book. Englewood Cliffs, New Jersey: Prentice-Hall, Inc., 1959.

STINNETT, T. M., "Golden Years Upcoming—Maybe," National Commission on Teacher Education and Professional Standards, National Education Association, Washington, D.C.: The Association, 1967. Also, in *Journal of Teacher Education,* Fall, 1967, *XVIII*:1–16.

THAYER, V. T., "Life-Adjustment vs. Basic Education," *Phi Delta Kappan,* March, 1960, *41*:250–53.

———, *Public Education and Its Critics.* New York: Macmillan Company, 1954.

WAYSON, W. W., "Political Revolution in Education, 1965," *Phi Delta Kappan,* March, 1966, *47*:333–9.

Part Two
THE TEACHER
AS A MEMBER
OF A PROFESSION

3: The Profession of Teaching

*I*n the United States, teachers constitute the largest group of professional workers. The 1960 Census of the United States reported 5,288,457 workers in twenty-three selected professional groups, and 7,335,699 professional, technical, and kindred workers in a total experienced work force of 67,990,073. (See Table 4, p. 50.) The number of teachers reported was 1,862,346. But adding other teachers not clearly designated as such, the total would probably be at least 2,000,000. Thus, teachers in 1960 represented more than one third of the professional workers and more than one fourth of the professional, technical, and kindred workers. Table 4 also reflects that there are about two and one half times as many teachers as engineers, almost four times as many as nurses, nearly five times as many as accountants, and nine times as many as medical doctors.

In 1966–67, NEA estimated a total of 1,939,619 as the total professional staff in the public schools, of which 1,759,236 were classroom teachers. Adding to this an estimated 249,000 nonpublic school teachers, there were in that year more than 2,100,000 employed in the elementary and secondary schools. If the nearly 460,000 college teachers are added, then almost 2,700,000 teachers were employed in that year.

According to estimates of the NEA Research Division, about 68 per cent of public school teachers are women. In the elementary schools, the proportion is much higher: about 85 per cent women to 15 per cent men. In the high schools, men outnumber women, constituting 55 per cent of the total. The ratio of elementary to secondary school teachers is about nine to eight. Approximately 85 per cent of all the elementary and secondary school teachers are employed in the public schools and 15 per cent in nonpublic schools. Of the total professional personnel employed in the

TABLE 4 Selected Professional Groups in the United States, Census 1960

PROFESSION	NUMBER OF PERSONS		
	Male	Female	Total
Accountants and auditors	396,343	80,483	476,826
Architects	29,720	811	30,531
Authors	21,388	7,303	28,691
Chiropractors	12,957	1,403	14,360
Clergymen	197,109	4,727	201,836
College presidents and teachers	139,508	39,168	178,676
Dentists	81,249	1,949	83,198
Dietitians and nutritionists	1,945	24,757	26,702
Editors and reporters	64,552	38,305	102,857
Engineers, technical	864,178	7,404	871,582
Farm and home management advisers	7,136	6,385	13,521
Foresters and conservationists	32,874	892	33,766
Lawyers and judges	205,515	7,543	213,058
Librarians	12,249	72,431	84,680
Musicians and music teachers	86,294	111,235	197,529
Nurses, professional	14,791	577,038	591,829
Optometrists	15,399	682	16,081
Osteopaths	3,473	478	3,951
Pharmacists	85,482	7,228	92,710
Physicians and surgeons	213,918	15,672	229,590
Social and welfare workers	36,446	61,465	97,911
Teachers: elementary	143,936	866,746	1,010,682
secondary	275,592	244,975	520,567
not elsewhere classified	58,457	93,960	152,417
Veterinarians	14,600	306	14,906
TOTAL	3,015,111	2,273,346	5,288,457
Total professional, technical, and kindred workers	4,542,702	2,792,997	7,335,699
Total experienced civilian labor force	45,686,325	22,303,748	67,990,073

Source: Compiled from U.S. Department of Commerce, Bureau of the Census, "Occupation of the Experienced Civilian Labor Force and the Labor Reserve: 1960," *1960 Census of Population, Supplementary Reports, PC(S1)-40.* Washington, D.C.: The Bureau, December 31, 1962, Table 201, p. 3.

public schools (1,939,719) in 1966–67, about 90 per cent (1,759,236) were classroom teachers and about 10 per cent (180,483) were administrators, supervisors, and other professional staff. The number of professional personnel in the public schools ranged from 3,120 in Alaska to 181,200 in California. Seven states (California, Illinois, New York, Ohio, Michigan, Pennsylvania, and Texas) employed almost one-half of all public school teachers.

TABLE 5   *Where American Teachers Are Employed, 1966–67*

Where Employed	Number of Teachers
Public elementary schools	996,031
Public secondary schools	763,205
Public school administrative, supervisory, and special school services	180,383
Nonpublic elementary and secondary schools	249,000*
Colleges and universities	459,000*
TOTAL	2,647,619

Source: *Derived from NEA Research Division statistics.*
* Estimates of the U.S. Office of Education.

TABLE 6   *Distribution of Teachers According to Size of Staff*

	Elementary	Secondary	All Reporting
Number of teachers in the school			
Median	20.0	45.0	27.0
Per cent teaching in school of			
Mean	22.5	57.3	39.0
fewer than 10 teachers	15.9%	1.7%	9.1%
Per cent teaching in schools of			
50 or more teachers	3.9	45.9	23.8

Source: National Education Association, Research Division. *The American Public School Teacher, 1965–66,* Research Report 1967-4R. Washington, D.C.: The Association, 1967, pp. 16–17.

The median teacher in 1965–66 was in a school of 27 teachers; the median elementary school teacher was in a school of 20 teachers; the median secondary teacher was in a school of 45 teachers. About a fourth of all teachers were in a system enrolling 25,000 or more pupils; 44 per cent were in systems enrolling 3,000–24,999 pupils; 32 per cent in systems of 3,000 or less.

PROJECTION OF TEACHER DEMAND

Rapid increases in school enrollments and requirements of new federal programs indicate greatly increased teacher demands for the future. The U.S. Office of Education (See Table 7) projects a total need for the fall of 1974 of 3,014,000 teachers for all types of schools. This projection does not include noninstructional personnel which, in the public schools alone, would approximate 200,000. For the public schools alone, this projection indicates a demand to serve all needs of 1,385,160 of new certificated teachers from 1967 to 1974. This means on the average that about 200,000 new teacher graduates will be absorbed in the public schools each year of this seven year period. Because something like one third of the newly graduated teachers each year do not take teaching positions, about 300,000 teacher graduates will be required each year.

TABLE 7   *Projected Demand for Classroom Teachers in Public and Nonpublic Elementary and Secondary Schools and Colleges in 1974*

	Total Teacher Demand
Public Schools	2,097,000
Nonpublic Schools	291,000
Colleges, Public and Nonpublic	626,000
TOTAL	3,014,000

Source: U.S. Department of Health, Education and Welfare, "Projections of Educational Statistics to 1974–75" (1965 Edition). Washington, D.C.: U.S. Government Printing Office, 1965, 68 pp.

THE EMERGENCE OF TEACHING AS A PROFESSION IN THE UNITED STATES

While there is some evidence that teaching has not yet achieved full stature as a recognized profession, as will be discussed later in this chapter, it is clear that there has been in the last century a steady evolution toward this goal. When did teaching in the United States begin to take on the attributes of a profession? No one can say exactly. Probably the period that reflected a clear break with the past, in which teaching was considered an incidental or part-time occupation requiring no special preparation other than the possession of general knowledge, was when the nation began to establish normal schools—schools dedicated specifically to the preparation of elementary school teachers. The first of these was established at Lexington, Massachusetts, in 1839. Prior to this time, teachers for the academies (private high schools) and for the public high schools that were just beginning to develop were prepared by colleges as products of their general program of studies. Indeed, this was the general practice until the second decade of the twentieth century. Although a few universities and colleges began as early as 1850 to establish chairs of pedagogy or departments of education, the practice of providing professional preparation for high school teachers did not become general before about 1910.

Also, some private seminaries began offering preparation for elementary school teachers in the 1820's and 1830's. A few of these were given some public support. But the plan for subsidizing these private schools did not catch on, and the public normal schools were quick to take root and flourish as public teacher-education institutions.

The beginnings of these professional schools were modest, and not until about 1900 did they begin to gain status as collegiate institutions. Their founding, however, was significant in that they indicated the beginning of the effort to make teaching a profession.

By 1900, the foundations were laid for the rapid development of programs for the professional preparation of teachers. Although the movement for universal adoption and recognition of such preparation was at that time just beginning to get under way, it was clear that the movement would gain momentum and that there would be a steady evolution toward professional status for teaching. Of course, there are many other factors in the evolution of an occupation toward professional status, but perhaps the basic one is preparation based upon college and university curricula.

By the beginning of this century there were more than 300 normal schools in existence, either as parts of high schools or as separate institutions offering two years of college work. With the growth of public high schools and the increased demand for teachers for them, the normal schools began to be transformed into degree-granting state teachers colleges. This transformation developed rapidly between 1910 and 1930, when there were some 135 teachers colleges in existence. Since 1930, and especially in the last decade, teachers colleges have evolved into state colleges and many into state universities. By 1967, only 9 state and 11 private teachers colleges remained as single-purpose institutions. The trend is clearly toward the general or multiple-purpose institutions as the chief source of the preparation of teachers.

WHY DO WE CALL TEACHING A PROFESSION?

The term "teaching profession" has been widely used and, among educational workers especially, widely accepted as indicating an accomplished fact. Today, with virtually all teachers holding at least the bachelor's degree, and at least a fourth having the master's degree, teachers are approaching the preparation levels of other recognized professions. There is no question that, with the drastic accretion of new knowledge, this upgrading of preparation will continue.

The public attitude about such categorical classification is, perhaps, somewhat mixed. They understand that it requires competences that can only be developed by thorough professional preparation. At the same time, many others, perhaps remembering the meager preparation of their own teachers, regard teaching as a job that requires only a good general education. Probably most people do not, as yet, regard teaching in the same light as they do law or medicine. They ascribe somewhat less professional stature to teachers than they do to engineers or chemists or dentists or pharmacists or architects. And many in higher education hold these views.

There is good evidence, though, that the public classifies teaching as a profession. What evidence is there that teaching has become a profession? One of the purposes of this chapter is to analyze the marks that generally are associated with a profession and to indicate the factors that would seem to justify the classification of teaching as such.

At the outset, it should be pointed out that the term "profession" has been so loosely used that its meaning has become ambiguous.[1] The U.S. Census Bureau lists about fifty "professional, technical, and kindred occupations" in the United States. Many of the listed occupations doubtless would not meet the technical or generally accepted requirements of a profession. The Office of Education, U.S. Department of Health, Education, and Welfare, lists twenty-four professions, on the basis of recognized professional accrediting agencies filed with it, as follows: anaesthesia, architecture, Bible, business, chemistry, dentistry, engineering, forestry, journalism, law, library science, medicine, music, nursing, optometry, osteopathy, public health, pharmacy, podiatry, religious education, social work, teacher education, theology, and veterinary medicine.[2]

What, then, is a profession? And how does teaching measure up?

Characteristics of a Profession

There have been several listings of characteristics, or distinguishing marks, of a profession. One group has suggested the following criteria:[3]

1. A profession involves activities essentially intellectual.
2. A profession commands a body of specialized knowledge.
3. A profession requires extended professional (as contrasted with solely general) preparation.
4. A profession demands continuous in-service growth.

[1] For a full discussion of the meaning of profession, see Morris L. Cogan, "Toward a Definition of Profession," *Harvard Educational Review,* Winter, 1953, 23:33–50.

[2] Theresa Birch Wilkins, *Accredited Higher Institutions,* U.S. Department of Health, Education, and Welfare, Office of Education, Bulletin 1960, No. 24. Washington, D.C.: U.S. Government Printing Office, 1960, p. 3.

[3] National Education Association, Division of Field Service. "The Yardstick of a Profession," *Institutes on Professional and Public Relations.* Washington, D.C.: The Association, 1948, p. 8.

5. A profession affords a life career and permanent membership.
6. A profession sets up its own standards.
7. A profession exalts service above personal gain.
8. A profession has a strong, closely knit, professional organization.

Let us analyze the status of teaching in the light of these characteristics.

A Profession Involves Intellectual Activities

Certainly teaching meets this criterion. Because it involves activities that are predominantly intellectual in nature, and the work performed by its members is basic to the preparation for all other professional endeavors, teaching is sometimes referred to as the "mother of professions."

A Profession Commands a Body of Specialized Knowledge

There would immediately be differences of opinion as to whether teaching meets this requirement. Those in the field of education contend that teaching has developed a significant body of specialized content that is essential to the preparation of competent teachers. On the other hand, many people in higher education assert that teaching does not as yet possess a scientifically derived body of specialized knowledge. This viewpoint holds that general college education constitutes the major or exclusive preparation for teaching, and many people holding this viewpoint claim that teaching, therefore, cannot be classed as a profession. In other words, the first group claims that education is a science; the latter group contends that it is an art.

These differences of opinions and viewpoints invariably attend the development of any new science; and education, as its proponents would agree, is a relatively new science. Its beginning in the United States dates back to about 1823, with the publication of Samuel Hall's lectures, *Lectures on Schoolkeeping*.[4] Indeed, instruction in education began with one course called Principles of Teaching.[5] In the years since, however, hundreds of courses, extensive research, and a great body of literature have been developed. The arguments, which have accompanied these developments, as to whether teaching is a profession are understandable. The recognition of each new science has been vigorously resisted, and each new science has gained recognition as such only after achieving a significant and extensive body of unique knowledge that has been validated by careful research. While education unquestionably has developed a great body of specialized knowledge, its critics contend that too little of it has resulted from careful, thorough, scientific research. These critics

---

[4] Ellwood P. Cubberley, *Public Education in the United States.* Boston: Houghton Mifflin Company, 1919, p. 288.

[5] *Ibid.,* p. 289.

contend that too great a portion of the literature of education is based upon opinion, beliefs, and slogans. Educators point to the *Encyclopedia of Educational Research,*[6] a volume containing more than 1,500 pages of research findings, as evidence that the teaching profession has developed an extensive body of scientific knowledge. In addition, there are published each year thousands of pages reporting new research in education by graduate students and teachers in universities and by practitioners in the public schools.

That teaching has developed a body of significant, specialized knowledge there can be little doubt. But that this content has gained recognition as to quality and essentiality, to the extent that has been true of other professions, is not as clear.

A Profession Requires Extended Professional Preparation

Again, for teaching, the evidence concerning this criterion is mixed. A distinct characteristic of a profession, in contrast to a skilled occupation or trade, is that preparation for the former is secured by completing prescribed college or university curricula. Preparation for nonprofessional occupations is usually secured through practical experience or apprenticeship, or a combination of a study and apprenticeship.

Data in Table 8 indicate how slowly teaching has shifted from the

TABLE 8   *Numbers of States Enforcing the Degree Requirement for Beginning Elementary and Secondary School Teachers, by Decade 1900–1960*

YEARS	NUMBER OF STATES ENFORCING	
	For Elementary School Teachers	For Secondary School Teachers
1900	0	2
1910	0	3
1920	0	10
1930	2	23
1940	11	40
1950	21	42
1960	40	51
1967	47	52

Source: T. M. Stinnett, *A Manual on Certification Requirements for School Personnel in the United States,* 1967 Edition. Washington, D.C.: National Education Association, National Commission on Teacher Education and Professional Standards, 1967, Table 3, p. 22.

[6] Chester Harris (ed.) *Encyclopedia of Educational Research,* 3rd ed. New York: The Macmillan Company, 1960, 1,564 pp.

learning-on-the-job concept to college and university preservice preparation.

Members of the teaching groups contend that extended professional preparation is necessary to produce a competent teacher. This concept visualizes completion of a college or university curriculum, consisting of general, professional, and specialized education, of at least four years for the beginning teacher and, for the fully qualified teacher, preparation of at least an additional year after initial teaching experience. Yet this concept is not enforced universally among the states. In 1967 only forty-seven states required four college years of preparation for beginning teachers in the elementary schools (see Table 9, below). The requirements for be-

TABLE 9   *Minimum Number of College Years of Specified Preparation Required by States and Territories for Initial Certificates in 1967*

COLLEGE YEARS OF PREPARATION	NUMBER OF STATES AND TERRITORIES REQUIRING				
	Elementary School Teachers	High School Teachers	Elementary School Principals	High School Principals	Superintendents of Schools
Seven	0	0	0	0	1
Six	0	0	3	3	19
More than five but less than six	0	0	7	7	2
Five	1	3	34	37	27
More than four but less than five	0	0	3	2	1
Four	46	49	4	2	0
Three but less than four	0	0	0	0	0
Two but less than three	5	0	0	0	0
One but less than two	0	0	0	0	0
No Certificate Issued	0	0	1	1	2
TOTAL	52	52	52	52	52

Source: T. M. Stinnett, *A Manual on Certification Requirements for School Personnel in the United States*, 1967 Edition, *op. cit.*, Table 2, p. 19.

ginning high school teachers more nearly approach a professional concept. In 1967 two states (Arizona and California) and the District of Columbia required five college years of preparation for beginning high school teachers in academic fields, and in about 18 states completion of the fifth year of preparation during the life of the initial or probationary certificate is required; all states, the District of Columbia and Puerto Rico required at least the bachelor's degree for high school teachers. Of course, most states are issuing some emergency certificates below these levels of preparation.

By 1967, only 7 per cent of all employed public school teachers held no degree, while 69.6 per cent held bachelor's degrees and 23.3 per cent held master's or higher degrees. Among elementary teachers, 12.9 per cent held no degree whereas 71.4 per cent held bachelor's degrees and 15.7 per cent held master's or higher degrees. Among high school teachers, 67.7 held bachelor's degrees and 31.8 per cent held master's or higher degrees. These figures indicate that of the elementary teachers (996,031) in 1967 about 128,000 had preparation below the bachelor's degree and of the high school teachers (763,205) about 5,000 held no degree.[7] From the above figures it may be estimated that the average school teacher probably had as high as 4.5 years of college preparation and high school teachers as high as 4.7 college years.

Although it is true that, with the demands for teachers in new federal programs and other factors, the shortage of teachers became more acute in the school year 1966–67, the college-year's level of preparation will continue to climb. The vast increase in new knowledge, the need to keep abreast, will inevitably demand longer periods of preparation for teachers. Also, certain developments are imminent that will tend to increase the attractiveness and holding power of teaching. Some of these are higher salaries, fringe benefits, reorganization of the teaching job, and participation in policy making.

It is apparent that the trend is toward requiring the minimum of five college years of preparation for the fully qualified classroom teacher and six years (two years of graduate work) for special school service personnel.

The remarkable gains made in the preparation of employed teachers are reflected in Table 10.

Great progress has been made in recent years to elevate the minimum standards of admission for beginning teachers. For example, in 1946 only fifteen states required the bachelor's degree for regular certification of beginning elementary teachers. By 1967, as has been previously stated, the number of states with this minimum requirement increased to forty-seven.

It is impossible to make an accurate evaluation of the quality of teacher-preparing programs in the nearly 1,200 colleges and universities now offering such preparation, but there is little doubt that this quality varies from state to state and from institution to institution. Some teachers have had little more than a general college course, while others have had

[7] National Education Association, Research Division, *The American Public School Teacher, 1965–66,* Research Report 1967-R4 Washington, D.C.: The Association, 1966, p. 8.

TABLE 10   Per Cent of All Elementary School Teachers in Service in 32 States with at Least Four Years of College, and with Less Than Two Years, 1965–66

State	Teachers With at Least Four Years of College	Rank of State	Teachers With Less Than Two Years of College
Oklahoma	99.7%	1	...
New Mexico	99.5	2	...
Florida	99.3	3	*
California	98.2	4	...
Wyoming	98.0	5	0.1%
Texas	97.7	6	...
Delaware	96.7	7	1.9
Colorado	96.7	7	0.1
Georgia	96.6	9	...
Missouri	96.4	10	‡
North Carolina	96.2	11	0.1
Mississippi	95.2	12	0.2
South Carolina	94.0	13	0.4
Connecticut	93.9	14	0.1
Oregon	93.2	15	0.2
Arkansas	93.2	16	...
Kansas	93.1	17	...
Louisiana	91.8	18	0.4
Kentucky	91.1	19	0.1
Alabama	89.5	20	1.8
Wisconsin	85.0	21	0.1
Maryland	83.9	22	3.0
West Virginia	81.4	23	1.2
Tennessee	81.1	24	0.5
Virginia †	77.8	25	‡
Idaho	67.8	26	*
Iowa	66.9	27	3.3
Maine	65.8	28	5.1
Vermont	64.3	29	...
Nebraska	53.2	30	3.9
North Dakota	43.6	31	...
South Dakota	39.1	32	7.0

Source: NEA, Research Division, *Teacher Supply and Demand in Public Schools, 1966,* Research Report 1966-R16. Washington, D.C.: The Association, 1966, p. 54.

* Less than one tenth of 1 per cent.

† Data are for 1964–65.

‡ Data not available.

thorough, intensive, specific preparation for teaching. Many, it appears, did not plan their college work with the intent of preparing for teaching. They merely drifted into it at the tag end of their college work, taking only enough education courses to meet state certification requirements as a sort of job insurance in case they failed to get into more desirable occupations. There can be little doubt that teacher-preparation programs have increased in length and quality.

Contrast the present preparation requirements of other professions with those of teaching, as described above. Table 11 reflects the extent to which

TABLE 11   *Plans of Education and Training Covering Five or More Years, in Thirteen Professional and Technical Fields*

Field	General College Education, Years	Professional Curriculum, Years	Total College Years Required
Medicine	3	4	7
Dentistry	2	4	6
Osteopathy	2	4	6
Veterinary medicine	2	4	6
Chiropody	1	4	5
Optometry	1	4	5
Law	3	3	6
Architecture	0	5	5
Hospital administration	4	2	6
Library service	4	1	5
Public health	4	1	5
Social work	4	2	6
Theology	4	3	7

Source: Lloyd E. Blauch, *Education for the Professions,* a publication of the Office of Education, U.S. Department of Health, Education, and Welfare. Washington, D.C.: U.S. Government Printing Office, 1955, p. 14.

thirteen other professions require more preparation for beginning practitioners than does teaching. It should be emphasized that the data contained in Table 9 refer to minimum programs established by colleges and universities and do not necessarily reflect the minimum licensing requirements of the states.

A Profession Demands Continuous In-Service Growth

In this regard, teaching tends to show strong evidence of professional status. While there are no comprehensive, authoritative data available, there are good reasons for believing that increasing proportions of employed teachers are each year engaging in professional growth activities, either credit or noncredit. The chief clientele of college and university summer terms are teachers; and the proportion of graduate school enrollees who are teachers reaches in some instances as high as 75 to 80 per cent. Several factors have influenced this development. Perhaps the most effective one has been that of salary increments for additional college preparation. Many local school boards are now requiring the completion periodically of additional college preparation by their teachers. In many instances school boards provide part or all of the cost of such required added preparation. The certification requirements in many states mandate increased college preparation for renewal of certificates. This provision is general for certificates based on less than four years of college preparation and, in some instances, for certificates based on degrees. In fact, there is an evident trend among the states, as teacher certification requirements are revised, to issue a provisional or probationary initial certificate upon completion of the bachelor's degree and to mandate completion of a fifth year of preparation during the life of the initial certificate.

In-service growth activities of teachers, while perhaps still predominantly of the college-credit type, increasingly are emphasizing teacher needs, whether pursued for credit or not. Educational travel, participation in the work of professional organizations, workshops, clinics, research and writing, and school committee work are newer types of in-service activities being utilized. Teachers have become increasingly critical of mandated requirements that compel exclusive concentration upon the earning of additional college credits. The necessity for such requirements generally stems from the fact that no universal minimum preparation, at an adequate level, has been achieved for beginning teachers, as is the case with most other professions. When such a minimum becomes universal, then emphasis on continued professional growth doubtless will be placed on more informal and varied experiences. One justification often advanced for mandating in-service education for teachers is that teaching is to a great extent a noncompetitive profession. According to this view, teachers, lacking the stimulation of competition, tend to get into a rut, tend to fail to keep abreast of new developments, and yet are able to hold their jobs. In the private professions, where remuneration and clientele are based upon efficiency and performance, continuous professional in-service growth is essential to successful practice. It is extremely doubtful that this noncompetitive argument has the validity ascribed to it. It probably would obtain with teachers with substandard preparation. The professionally competent practitioner in any field is keenly sensitive to the necessity of keeping abreast of progress in his field. For fully qualified teachers, the problem of continuous growth should rest with them and local boards and not be enforced by certification.

A Profession Affords a Life Career and Permanent Membership

This is, perhaps, the weakest point in teaching's claim to professional status. While we do not know exactly the professional life expectancy of members of the teaching profession, we do know that on the average it is relatively rather low. There are no recent nation-wide data on the number of teachers who leave the profession each year or the average number of years that teachers remain in the profession. What data are available would indicate that the annual leaving rate ranges widely among the states, from 5 to 25 or even 30 per cent. Data obtained by NEA in a sampling survey in 1965–66 revealed that the mean years of teaching experience of the total staff in the public schools was 11.8. For women, the mean was 13.1 years; for men, it was 9.0 years. For elementary school teachers, the mean was 13.4 years; for high school teachers, it was 10.1. These are shocking figures, inasmuch as the mean age of all teachers was reported to be 36 years; of women teachers, 40 years; of men teachers, 33 years; of elementary teachers, 40; and high school teachers, 33 years.[8]

It is often pointed out, as a factor favorable to the teaching profession, that preparation for teaching provides competences that cause many other occupations to bid for the services of teachers. Also, it is often suggested that preparation for teaching provides superior background for home-making, child rearing, and the responsibilities of family life. These are, of course, favorable factors from many viewpoints. But this discussion is pointed solely at the causes of instability of the teaching staff.

The best guess, and it must be labeled only as a guess in the absence of accurate data, is that the average annual leaving rate for the teaching profession, for the nation as a whole, is from 7 to 10 per cent—more in some years and less in others, more in some states and less in others. Assuming that this rate is reasonably accurate, from 125,000 to 175,000 teachers leave the profession each year for all reasons, and the average length of time that teachers remain in the profession probably ranges from ten to fifteen years. Although, as has been stated, we do not have precise data to prove the point, there is good evidence that the leaving rate of teachers has been steadily declining in recent years and that the concept of teaching as a life career is growing.

Only a few years ago it was a fairly common practice for a young man to teach school for a year or two to earn money for a medical, dental, or law course, or for preparation for some other profession. This practice is not as common as it once was. Present certification laws and regulations of the states generally require professional preparation, a situation that did not obtain a few years ago. It is now almost impossible to secure the required preparation for teaching without losing valuable time, if one

[8] National Education Association, Research Division. *The American Public School Teacher, 1965–66* (February Report). Washington, D.C.: The Association, 1966, 16 pp.

really plans to prepare for another occupation. Furthermore, it is becoming increasingly difficult to secure a teaching certificate or a good teaching position without a college degree of preparation for teaching. There are exceptions to these general rules, of course. Although the trends are clearly in the directions indicated, the serious shortages of qualified teachers in recent years have forced school boards in many places to employ persons who, under normal conditions, would not be considered.

The assumption is that the chief reason for the high leaving rate is the preponderance of women, on whom the "family reasons" for quitting teaching jobs almost entirely fall. This assumption does not seem to be borne out by the experience figures quoted above. In a large number of cases, women teachers who marry quit teaching to establish homes and to rear families. Of course, a great many women continue to teach, but many do not, and this factor tends to reduce the holding power of teaching as a life career. In this respect, teaching is not much different from other occupations largely staffed by women. Nursing, stenography, social service, and dietetics seem to be in the same category. The once-common practice of school boards refusing to employ married women teachers has now been almost completely abandoned, and teaching does not now lose as many from its ranks because of marriage as it once did. If teaching is to be eliminated from the occupations that are not regarded as life careers, then apparently greater efforts will have to be made to retain in the profession a greater proportion of women teachers who marry; and salaries for both men and women will have to be made competitive with those in industry.

A Profession Sets Its Own Standards

Because teaching is, preponderantly, a public profession rather than a private one, its members have not been able to assume the degree of control of standards that members of other professions have exercised. While standards for licensing of most professions are fixed by state laws and regulations, generally the public has been willing to follow the recommendations of these professions in setting the standards for admission to practice and to vest other legal controls in these professional groups. The inclination of the public to accord the same rights to teachers has emerged more slowly, but the trend in that direction is pronounced.

Throughout our history, increased standards for the teaching profession have been achieved largely through the insistence of teachers themselves. Prior to 1946, however, the teaching profession had not established a national body charged with the responsibility of guarding and elevating its standards. In that year the National Education Association, which numbers in its own membership and that of its affiliated state education associations more than 90 per cent of the public school teachers of the nation, established the National Commission on Teacher Education and Professional

Standards. To this commission was delegated the task of carrying on a continuous program to bring about improvement in professional standards for teaching. The standards that the commission and its fifty-six parallel state commissions seek to raise to professional levels relate to selection, preparation, certification, and in-service growth of teachers; and to standards for institutions that prepare teachers. The effectiveness of this movement has in recent years drawn sharp criticism from some quarters but it is clear that teaching is at long last beginning to have the dominant role in setting the standards for its members, as is true of the other respected professions.

A Profession Exalts Service Above Personal Gain

That teaching is an occupation with a high potential social value is unquestioned. The effective teacher can vitally influence for the better the lives of adult citizens of tomorrow.

Teaching and the ministry are recognized universally as true professions in the sense that their members are motivated basically by their desire to serve others rather than for economic rewards. But such recognition does not mean that neither is entitled to fair rates of pay, and there is a growing public agreement with this view.

Within the profession itself, beginning about 1960, there has grown up an irritation with the concept that teachers should be paid in platitudes. They are demanding that they be paid professional salaries, at least in competition with those paid in industry for comparable preparation and experience. A growing number of teacher strikes and the invoking of sanctions between 1960 and 1968 are indicative of militancy of teachers regarding inadequate salaries and other working conditions. In other words, teachers have grown weary of public indifference to these matters and are now demanding that they be improved drastically. Many observers believe this upsurge of teacher aggressiveness is a major sign that teachers are maturing as professionals.

A Profession Has a Strong, Closely Knit Professional Organization

All recognized professions have strong professional organizations providing a means of determining unity of purpose and a unified voice for their members. In some respects the teaching profession fully meets this criterion, and in some it does not. There are education associations in each of the states and territories, and these more nearly approach the yardstick of a close-knit, all-inclusive membership than any other type. These associations contain more than 90 per cent of all employed public school teachers. There are several hundred special-interest associations, such as those for English teachers (National Council of Teachers of English), for science teachers (National Science Teachers Association), or for music teachers (Music Educators National Conference). In addition, there are many organizations for college teachers (for example, the American Association of University Professors, as an all-inclusive organization; the American Psychological Association, as a special-interest association) and for teachers in private schools. There is one large teachers' union whose membership is restricted to teachers. There is no one general organization, universally recognized as the teachers' organization, with authority to speak for the teaching profession.

The National Education Association of the United States is the largest all-inclusive, general organization for teachers in the United States. The NEA numbers in its members about 52 per cent of the teachers employed in the public schools of the United States. Its membership in June, 1967 was over 1,000,000. Since the NEA is a confederation of affiliated state education associations, actually it is the voice of almost 2,000,000 who are members of the state associations. The NEA membership is predominantly of public school teachers and administrators. Membership is open to teachers and administrators in colleges and private schools, and many of these do belong to the NEA. (After September 1, 1964, new members must have completed the bachelor's degree.) Here, many people think, is one of the weakest points in the claim that teaching is a profession (although many engaged in education would contend that it is not a weakness at all, but a strength)—the failure to achieve one universally acknowledged, all-inclusive parent organization, to which all teachers and administrators of whatever school level or subject belong. This leaves the organizational strength of teachers, to some extent, diffused and fragmented.

The American Federation of Teachers takes another viewpoint: that an exclusively classroom teachers' organization is necessary to speak effectively for them. AFT's membership in 1967 was about 140,000 (for further discussion, see Chapter 21).

It can be said that the teaching profession, through the National Education Association and its affiliated state education associations, has developed one close-knit, strong general professional organization, empowered to represent, reflect the views of, and speak for the preponderance of public school teachers. But it cannot be said at this point that such an organization presently exists for all engaged in education in the United States.

ADDITIONAL MARKS OF A TRUE PROFESSION

In the preceding pages an attempt has been made to appraise the status of teaching on the basis of eight criteria of a profession. On most of these criteria it was indicated that teaching does exhibit the characteristics of a profession; that on some criteria it has some weaknesses or deficiencies; and on a few criteria the evidence is mixed.

But these eight criteria do not denote all the yardsticks by which an occupation may be judged to be a profession. Let us examine some other factors that appear to be evident in the recognized professions.

Several authorities in the field have discussed the purposes and the characteristics of a profession. Carr-Saunders, for example, has described the role of the professional organization as threefold: (1) to guarantee professional competence, (2) to guarantee professional conduct of its members, and (3) to raise the status of the profession. He writes:

> As soon as a profession emerges, the practitioners are moved by the recognition of common interests to form a professional association. . . . What then are the motives common to the members of every profession which lead to the formation of professional association? . . . Of these, the first is that, as a profession emerges, the better equipped among the practitioners realize that they possess a certain craft. . . . But the public does not accord them an exclusive right to that description. Not only may the poorly equipped call themselves by these titles and obtain public recognition, but also may those without any equipment whatever. The better equipped desire that they should somehow be distinguishable, and to that end they form associations, membership of which is confined to those possessing certain minimum qualifications. . . . [Later these associations] come to desire that all practitioners should possess at least the minimum qualifications. . . . With a few unimportant exceptions, professional associations can now be said to be exclusive only in the sense that they exclude the unqualified. . . . [A second motive of the responsible members is that] a profession in fact desires to see a proper standard of professional conduct set up and maintained. Just as the qualified are not readily distinguished from the unqualified, so the scrupulous are not so readily distinguished from the unscrupulous. Thus professional associations define and enforce rules of professional conduct. The members, in other words, mutually guarantee not only their competence but also their honor. . . . There is a third motive . . . to raise the status of the profession.[9]

Other criteria for a profession that have been suggested by different writers are: [10]

1. Acceptance of personal responsibility and accountability by members, through adherence to a code of ethics.
2. Dedication to the derivation of new knowledge.
3. Aggressiveness in enforcing standards; a system of rewards—monetary and honorary.

[9] A. M. Carr-Saunders, "The Professions in Modern Society," as abstracted in *Readings in the Social Aspects of Education* (compiled by B. Othanel Smith, *et al.*). Danville, Illinois: Interstate Printers and Publishers, Inc., 1951, pp. 547–52.

[10] See Bernard Barber, "Some Problems in the Sociology of Professions," *Daedalus*, Fall 1963, pp. 669–688.

Flexner's comments on the role of organized professions.

There is, of course, always danger that the interests of an organization may conflict with those of the body politic. Organizations of physicians, lawyers, and teachers may find the personal interest of the individuals of whom they are composed arrayed against those of society at large. On the whole, however, organized groups of this kind are, under democratic conditions, apt to be more responsive to public interest than are unorganized and isolated individuals.[11]

Teachers' Salaries

Relatively high remuneration for services is a generally accepted characteristic of a profession. At least the compensation received by a practitioner indicates whether the public is willing to pay him as a skilled and responsible professional worker. Doubtless a basic reason why many individuals prepared themselves for professional service was their belief that they would achieve a higher-than-average economic status. Nevertheless, in some professions, such as nursing, the ministry, and social work, the financial returns have been no better and often not as good as those received by some categories of skilled labor.

How does the remuneration for teaching compare with other occupations? A comparison of average incomes of members of several occupation groups in 1965 follows: [12]

Occupation	Average Annual Salary	Per Cent Increase over 1955
Teachers	$6,845	163.5
All employed persons working for wages or salaries	5,705	148.3
Manufacturing employees	6,386	146.8

If high salaries are taken as the sole criterion of professional status, teaching does not rank very well. The average annual income of teachers

[11] Abraham Flexner, "What Are the Earmarks of a Profession?" as quoted in *Readings in the Social Aspects of Education*. Danville, Illinois: Interstate Printers and Publishers, 1951, p. 556.

[12] National Education Association, Research Division, *Economic Status of Teachers, 1966–67*, Research Report 1967-R8. Washington, D.C.: The Association, 1967. Table 19, p. 28.

looks even worse when compared to certain other professional workers. Here are some figures on annual average incomes for 1966: [13]

Teachers (all instructional personnel)	$6,897
Accountants	9,202
Engineers	12,022
Attorneys	14,751

The above figures demonstrate that teaching does not compare well in average income with most other professions. In terms of income, teaching is much more like manufacturing and government service.

There are, of course, some extenuating circumstances. In the first place teachers, as we have pointed out, have not had as much preparation, on the average, as the other professional groups. Only about 93 per cent of public school teachers of the United States are graduates of four-year college courses of study. One would find few, if any, physicians with less than six years of college preparation, few, if any, dentists with less than five, and few engineers with less than four.

Then, there persists in the public mind the traditional belief that teachers do not work as many weeks of the year as most professional groups; that schools are in session from thirty-six to forty weeks, while the other groups work from forty-eight to fifty weeks. The fact that most teachers actually are at work securing further college preparation during summer vacations, or seeking further increase of their effectiveness as teachers in other ways, has been slow in receiving general public recognition. The general concept that teachers have long vacations and should not be paid for the time not spent in actual classroom work has been very difficult to change.

Calculating average salaries for teachers, in all kinds of schools and from all over the United States, tends to distort the average salary in many of the more favorably situated school districts.

There are also some compensating factors in teaching that do not apply to some other professions, such as tenure, sick-leave provisions, and retirement benefits. Although teachers do not become rich, they are generally not as subject to the economic extremes—boom and bust conditions—as are workers in many other occupations.

[13] *Ibid.,* Table 18, p. 27.

Obstacles to the Professionalization of Teaching

The present status of teaching as a profession, as has been pointed out above, still leaves much to be achieved. It has been shown that in many respects teaching does exhibit the characteristics of a profession, in some it does not. It should be noted, too, that the status of teaching differs widely from place to place among teaching levels. In many modern school systems most of the marks of a profession are present. In others, few of these marks are evident. To sum up the case, it seems fairly clear that teaching can attain true professional status if a few obstacles are removed and a few conditions are improved. What are these obstacles and conditions?

Traditionally, the public concept of teaching has tended to view the occupation as an in-and-out, stopgap sort of general trade. In the early years of the public school movement in the United States, teaching was considered largely a matter of maintaining discipline and drilling on the skill subjects, such as reading, writing, and arithmetic. Professional preparation for these relatively simple tasks was not considered necessary. There has been a persisting belief by the public that just about anyone can teach if he has a little more general knowledge than his students. In the early years of our history, teaching was on a kind of welfare basis. Jobs were likely to be given to elderly women who had no other way of making a living, to ex-soldiers who had been crippled in military service and who, therefore, found it difficult to secure other positions, and to those who had been failures at other occupations. Such individuals would be "on the town" otherwise, so they were given teaching positions. Since anyone could teach, the schoolroom was an appropriate place for them to earn a living. Of course, there have been great changes in the public concept of teaching in modern times. However, too much of the old remains. Unfortunately, teachers themselves often contribute to this by an indifference about professional preparation. Repetition of persuasive statements to the effect that a teacher need only be a broadly educated person; that education courses are unnecessary; that student teaching is a waste of time because the best way to learn to teach is by teaching; all of these are appealing shibboleths for the person who wants to take short cuts to a teaching career. Granted that there may be some truth in such statements, especially in some situations, the basic fact remains that every profession is based upon the possession of specialized knowledge, skills, and techniques that are unique.

Haskew has stated this need as follows:

Professional education has three characteristics which distinguish it from unprofessional education. It does not leave to chance the cultivation of those attributes—ethics, disciplines, methods of thought, allegiances—which make the professional fit to assume the trusteeship with which society entrusts him. It has a unique focus upon the person, all of that person, who is to practice and seeks to change desirably that person as a person. Finally, professional education simply cannot stop short of performance; it cannot accept without unmistakable proof the dictum that knowledge alone is power.[14]

REFERENCES

AMERICAN ACADEMY OF ARTS AND SCIENCES, "The Profession," *Daedalus,* Fall, 1963, Vol. 92, No. 4, Kenneth Lyon, "Introduction," pp. 649–654; Everett C. Hughes, "Professions," pp. 655–668; Bernard Barber, "Some Problems in the Sociology of Professions," pp. 669–688; Alma S. Witten, "The Teacher," pp. 745–763.

ARMSTRONG, W. EARL, "Teacher Education," in Blauch, Lloyd E. (ed.) *Education for the Professions,* a publication of the Office of Education, U.S. Department of Health, Education, and Welfare. Washington, D.C.: U.S. Government Printing Office, 1955, pp. 221–29.

BAUER, W. W., NURSEY, H. J., and COREY, ARTHUR, "Professional Status: How It Is Achieved" (Symposium), *Journal of Teacher Education,* September, 1955, 6:206–32.

CARR-SAUNDERS, A. M., "The Professions in Modern Society," in SMITH, B. OTHANEL, STANLEY, WILLIAM O., BENNE, KENNETH D., and ANDERSON, ARCHIBALD W., *The Social Aspects of Education.* Danville, Illinois: Interstate Printers and Publishers, 1951, pp. 547–52.

CHANDLER, B. J., *Education and the Teacher.* New York: Dodd, Mead & Company, 1961., Chap. 10, "The Teacher as a Member of a Profession," pp. 234–264.

COGAN, MORRIS L., "Toward a Definition of Profession," *Harvard Educational Review,* Winter, 1953, 23:33–50.

CONANT, JAMES BRYANT, *The Education of American Teachers.* New York: McGraw-Hill Book Company, 1963, Chap. 1, 2, and 3, pp. 1–55.

FLEXNER, ABRAHAM, "What Are the Earmarks of a Profession?" in SMITH, B. OTHANEL, STANLEY, WILLIAM O., BENNE, KENNETH D., and ANDERSON, ARCHIBALD W., *The Social Aspects of Education.* Danville, Illinois: Interstate Printers and Publishers, 1951, pp. 553–56.

GILB, CORINNE LATHROP, *Hidden Hierarchies.* New York: Harper and Row, 1966.

HASKEW, L. D., and MCLENDON, JONATHAN C., *This Is Teaching,* 2nd ed. Chicago: Scott, Foresman & Company, 1962.

---

[14] L. D. Haskew, "Planning Institutional Programs," *The Education of Teachers: Considerations in Planning Institutional Programs.* Washington, D.C.: NEA, National Commission on Teacher Education and Professional Standards, 1960, p. 44.

LAMBERT, S. M., "Signs of a Maturing Profession," *NEA Journal,* December, 1966, 55:52–5.

LIEBERMAN, MYRON, *Education as a Profession.* Englewood Cliffs, New Jersey: Prentice-Hall, 1956, Chap. 1, "The Nature and Significance of the Profession," pp. 1–18; Chap. 2, "The Problem of Professional Function," pp. 19–48; Chap. 14, "Occupational Status," pp. 452–80.

————, *The Future of Public Education.* Chicago: University of Chicago Press, 1960. Chap. 5, "The Myth of the Teaching Profession," pp. 76–100.

LINDSEY, MARGARET (ed.) *New Horizons for the Teaching Profession.* Washington, D.C.: National Commission on Teacher Education and Professional Standards, National Education Association, 1961.

NATIONAL EDUCATION ASSOCIATION, National Commission on Teacher Education and Professional Standards, *Professional Imperatives: Expertness and Self-Determination,* Report of the Fort Collins Conference. Washington, D.C.: The Association, 1962, "Expertness in Teaching: Approaches to the Study and Definition of Professional Competence," pp. 87–113.

NATIONAL EDUCATION ASSOCIATION, Research Division, *Economic Status of Teachers, 1966–67,* Research Report 1967-R8. Washington, D.C.: The Association, 1966.

————, *Estimates of School Statistics, 1966–67,* Research Report 1966-R 20. Washington, D.C.: The Association, 1966.

————, *Teacher Supply and Demand in Public Schools, 1966,* Research Report 1966-R16. Washington, D.C.: The Association, 1966.

NATIONAL SOCIETY FOR THE STUDY OF EDUCATION, *Education for the Professions,* Sixty-first Yearbook. Chicago: The University of Chicago Press, 1962, Howard S. Becker, "The Nature of a Profession," Chap. II, pp. 27–46; John S. Brubacher, "The Evolution of Professional Education," Chap. III, pp. 47–67; Archibald W. Anderson, "The Teaching Profession: An Example of Diversity in Training and Function," Chap. VII, pp. 140–167; Earl J. McGrath, "The Ideal Education for the Professional Man," Chap. XIII, pp. 281–301.

RIVLIN, H. N., "Profession's Responsibility for Educational Change." *NCTEPS Official Report* 1963: 20–36.

STINNETT, T. M., *A Manual on Certification Requirements for School Personnel in the United States,* 1967 ed. National Education Association, National Commission on Teacher Education and Professional Standards. Washington, D.C.: The Association, 1967.

————, *The Profession of Teaching.* Washington, D.C.: Center for Applied Research in Education, Inc., 1962, Chap. 1 and 2, pp. 1–35.

4: Identification, Selective Admission, and Retention in Teacher Education

*T*he members of the teaching profession have not given the attention to the cluster of considerations discussed in this chapter that their importance merits. Because teaching *is* a profession, its members should be concerned with those who enter it. Why? Because professional groups are judged by their members.

Physicians are almost universally held in high esteem. The public generally regards them as being highly trained, competent, conscientious, and hard-working. Nearly everyone feels that his doctor is well qualified and that he will do the very best that can be done for his patients.

Much the same attitude is held by the public toward attorneys, dentists, pharmacists, nurses, and engineers. These professional groups have built up our confidence in them as competent practitioners and our esteem for them as individuals. We regard the individual members we know highly; hence, we hold the professions in high esteem.

Teaching, like the professions that we have been discussing, consists of individuals. The esteem with which the public regards teaching depends upon the regard it holds for the individual members, their personal and intellectual qualities, and the quality of their service.

Since we will be judged as a group by our members, we should be concerned with the type of candidates who are admitted to teacher-education institutions, the kind of preparation given to those who are selected, and the method of introduction into the classrooms of those who complete their preparation programs. We have examples before us of similar concern on the part of other professions. Physicians are very much interested in the type of candidates admitted to medical schools, in the quality of preparation provided by medical schools, and in how young doctors are assisted in securing satisfactory employment or in beginning private practice. Much the same concern is shown by architects, dentists, nurses, attorneys, and engineers. Should teachers be any less concerned about their future colleagues? Many competent observers believe that the basic approach to the improvement of teacher education as a process, improvement of teaching services, and the achievement of higher-quality education generally should be more careful attention to the identification and selective admission of teacher-education students. Bagley stated this viewpoint as follows:

I do not hesitate to say that if three-fourths of the time, energy, and money spent during the past fifteen years in carrying through elaborate programs of curriculum revision had been spent in a determined effort to raise the standards of selecting and training teachers, a far more significant contribution would have been made to the improvement of American education.[1]

Criticisms of Low Standards

A common criticism is that teaching has generally attracted college students of rather mediocre mental ability. This criticism has been based upon the results of several studies. There is evidence that this situation is rapidly being corrected now, but the past record tends to sustain much of the criticism. A Pennsylvania investigation some years ago indicated that students in teachers colleges were much lower in ability, as judged by a test of general culture, than were the students in engineering or liberal-arts curricula.[2]

The evidence gathered in connection with the Selective Service College Qualification Test in 1951 was also not encouraging.[3] College students taking the test ranked as follows:

Classification	Per Cent Passing
Engineering	68
Physical Science and Mathematics	64
Humanities	52
Education	27

Prospective teachers thus ranked lowest of all professional groups taking the test. In fairness, however, several aspects of these data that have led to erroneous interpretations should be pointed out. In the first place,

[1] William C. Bagley, "An Essentialist Looks at the Foreign Languages," *Educational Administration and Supervision,* April, 1939, 25:250.

[2] W. S. Learned and B. D. Wood, *The Student and His Knowledge,* Bulletin No. 29. New York: The Carnegie Foundation for the Advancement of Teaching, 1938, pp. 40–44.

[3] Educational Testing Service, *Annual Report to the Board of Trustees, 1951–52.* Princeton, New Jersey: The Service, 1952, p. 14.

the test was given only to men teacher-education students, and it should be borne in mind that at least two out of three of those preparing for teaching are women. Secondly, only a small proportion of men preparing for teaching in any given year are majors in education; most such students are classed as majors in some academic or special field. The classification "education," then, is inaccurate and overlapping. Although valid conclusions concerning the total teacher population or the total population preparing for teaching cannot be drawn from these data, they are rather telling in terms of needed improvement. Several other studies also tend to show that teacher-education students consistently rank lower than those preparing for other professions.[4] Two studies, however, reflect that most teachers colleges that give attention to high admission standards attract high-caliber students.[5]

North has analyzed the situation as follows:

When national samples of education students are compared with comparable samples of students in other curricular areas, they consistently fall below the liberal arts, science, and engineering groups, and most other groups as well. On the other hand, there is evidence that the teacher education students in certain colleges that maintain high admission standards compare quite favorably. . . . Under conditions now prevailing in the country as a whole, however, the field of education is not competing successfully with other professions in drawing the high caliber personnel that it so urgently needs.[6]

In the light of evidence—such evidence as has been given above—the conclusion has generally been drawn that education students (prospective student teachers) rank lower in mental ability, in terms of the usual measurements of such ability, than those who are in preparation for other professions. Perhaps it would be sounder to say that teaching has not as yet been enabled to compete on equal terms with other professions, rather than to draw the generalized conclusion that teaching attracts only the

[4] See Arthur E. Traxler, "Are Students in Teachers Colleges Greatly Superior in Ability?" School and Society, February 16, 1946, 63:103–107; and American Council on Education, Psychological Examinations for College Freshmen: Norms Bulletin, Princeton, New Jersey: Cooperative Test Bureau, 1955, 22 pp. Dael L. Wolfe and Toby Oxtoby, "Distributions of Ability of Students Specializing in Different Fields," Science, September, 1952, 116:311–14.

[5] Ben D. Wood and Robert D. North, "Teachers Colleges Can Select and Hold Superior Students," Journal of Higher Education, November, 1956, 27:419–27; and Ben D. Wood and Ruth A. Pederson, "Results of Selective Admission in Teachers Colleges," Teacher Education Journal, June, 1941, 3:12–22.

[6] Robert D. North, "The Teacher Education Student: How Does He Compare Academically With Other College Students?" The Education of Teachers: New Perspectives, Report of the Second Bowling Green Conference. Washington, D.C.: National Education Association, National Commission on Teacher Education and Professional Standards, 1958, p. 285.

inferior. Moreover, because of this fact, schools of education as a general rule have not as yet been enabled to apply as discriminating selective-admissions requirements as have most other professional schools. There are many exceptions to this general rule, and many schools of education are now making and publishing comparative studies of the records of their students with those in other professional schools on the same campus. Too, the data quoted above are old.

It should be pointed out, too, that such tests are not necessarily adequate measures of ability to teach. Mental ability certainly is a basic factor in success in teaching. We do not know all the answers about the qualities needed by a successful teacher, but apparently personality, social adjustment, liking for children, and willingness to work are of fundamental importance, along with mental ability. No significant studies have been made that compare these qualities for teacher-education candidates with those of other college students. Many people believe, and considerable evidence is available to support this belief, that students preparing for teaching do not rank as well in these respects as those who are planning to enter such professions as medicine, law, dentistry, and engineering. Certainly teaching wants the best possible candidates, not the leftovers. And there are some things that the profession can do to attract good candidates to teacher education. One of the basic things that can be done is for the profession to develop and apply discriminating selective procedures for teacher-education students.

The Role of Identification in Selection

Identification of potential candidates for admission to preparation for a given profession is an extremely difficult process, and a highly important part of the total selection process. The complexity stems from the fact that vocational (or professional) choices are not made at a given time or under a given circumstance. These choices might be called developmental, extending over a long period of time. A child changes his mind many times about what he wants to be, what career he wants. The process of identification of potential candidates for teaching, therefore, cannot be a one-year plan, but must be a continuing one. The process involves a series of evaluations and judgments by the candidate's teachers and counselors. Below are described some of the factors involved, negatively or positively, in the process.

Recruitment and Selection Needs

Obviously there are several ways of promoting teaching as an occupation, of assuring the flow of an adequate number of capable young people into preparation for teaching. One step in recruiting the young to prepare for teaching is a process that might be termed "informal identification." In the sense used here, this means that teachers seek to identify those pupils in their classes who *appear* to have the characteristics that would enable them to become good teachers. This process of informal identification can take place as early as the late years of the elementary school or the early years of high school. Some recent studies have shown that a number of children do make at least tentative decisions to become teachers before they reach the senior year of high school. Of course, identification is not enough. Once a pupil is spotted as a suitable prospect for a career in teaching, then opportunity should be provided for him to have some assisting-teacher or cadet experiences while still in high school. Such experiences involve the pupil's helping regular teachers with routine duties such as checking rolls, grading papers, caring for the physical comfort of children, distributing instructional materials, and supervising play periods. These experiences are, in themselves, very effective guidance devices, because they provide the pupil with firsthand contact with the active job of teacher, and permit him a tryout period in which he can decide whether he likes to work with children and what age level he prefers. As a result of such experiences, the pupil, by the time he is ready for college, has a rather definite conviction as to whether he wishes to become a teacher and, if so, for what level of teaching he wishes to prepare.

Schools are finding that one of the ways to lighten the nonteaching duties of teachers is to provide student assistants. Many schools are now paying these helpers on an hourly rate.

Another means of selective identification and recruitment is through the guidance given individual pupils by teachers and by the guidance department of the school. Another important means is through such organizations as the Future Teachers of America. Each of these means will be discussed in some detail.

Influence of Teachers' Attitudes

Teachers have opportunities in many classes and in some informal situations to say things about the various professions. Such opportunities occur in nearly every type of class. They also occur in conversations in the hall, before class, and in club meetings and other types of extracurricular activities. Of course, teachers should not emphasize the opportunties in teaching to the exclusion of other occupations. Certainly not everyone should become a teacher. It is the teacher's obligation to help pupils to choose the occupation for which each is best suited and in which he will find the greatest satisfaction. Teaching should be given a fair chance, along with other occupations, as a possible choice by those who have suitable endowments to be successful at it.

Role of the School's Guidance Program

In most modern high schools effort is made to guide pupils in the selection of suitable occupations to be followed when they enter the labor market. This is only a part of the usual guidance services that are offered, but it is a very important activity. Youngsters need assistance in choosing their lifework.

There is now a multitude of aptitude tests that aim to determine how well youngsters are likely to succeed in various vocations. Some of these appear to be of somewhat doubtful validity, but some give a degree of indication as to probable success. They are not the final word, as every counselor is quick to point out, because the intangibles, such as "drive," cannot so far be evaluated. In the hands of a skilled counselor, though, a great deal of good can be accomplished by these tests.

Guidance experts strive to be objective and impersonal. They present the data that they have gathered and encourage pupils to make their decisions in the light of the evidence, rather than as a result of personal influence. The basic purpose of skilled guidance is to reveal an individual to himself—his strengths and weaknesses—and to provide him with information about the requirements for and the opportunities in a given vocation. Through these factors the individual pupil can make an intelligent choice of a vocation.

The Future Teachers of America

This organization is designed to interest high school pupils in teaching, to present its good and bad points as an occupation, and to assist in the preparation of prospective teachers for their future work in the classrooms. Sponsored by the National Education Association, the FTA grew out of the Horace Mann Centennial in 1937.

The organization in 1966–67 had chapters in about 6,500 high schools, with some 250,000 members.

While the total membership in FTA organizations appears large, there is need for further expansion. Normal turnover in the teaching profession probably totals about 100,000 each year. This large turnover, coupled with increasing enrollments, indicates that the total demand for new teachers each year for perhaps the next decade will probably be nearly two times that number. Present enrollments in teacher-education institutions scattered among freshmen, sophomores, juniors, and seniors are not sufficient to supply the new teachers who will be needed each year for the next decade. Of course, at the present time, only a minor fraction of the total number of high school students needed to prepare for teaching is enrolled in FTA chapters.

While not necessarily a part of the work of the FTA, there appears to have been a growing tendency to give members experiences in actual classroom activities. They have been assistants to regular teachers, rather than assuming the function of teachers. This kind of activity is discussed in the paragraphs that follow.

TABLE 12   Growth of FTA and Student NEA

	LOCAL FTA CHAPTERS		LOCAL STUDENT EDUCATION CHAPTERS *	
Year	Number	Members	Number	Members
1938	62	1,061	14	278
1940	131	2,601	84	2,097
1942	118	1,838	127	3,129
1944	103	1,593	140	3,501
1946	155	2,912	176	6,003
1948	515	10,539	271	13,455
1950	926	19,829	413	20,948
1952	1,399	31,739	492	23,883
1954	2,441	62,134	562	29,504
1956	3,717	100,529	677	40,422
1958	4,461	134,458	745	51,782
1960	5,115	163,212	845	72,195
1967 †	6,500	250,000	1,000	135,000

Source: National Education Association, National Commission on Teacher Education and Professional Standards, office records of the Future Teachers of America and the Student National Education Association.

* From 1938 to 1957, college chapters of FTA.

† Estimates.

Helping-Teacher Experiences

One of the significant movements in the selective recruitment of teachers is that of giving high school pupils an opportunity to participate in some of the activities of actual classrooms in both elementary and secondary schools. These neophytes can help youngsters with their wraps, secure materials for units, assist with records, and do many other useful things. Not only does the teacher's helper assist the teacher, but he has an opportunity to find out whether he likes to work with children, to learn some of the characteristics of youngsters, and to observe what teachers do.

This assistance is always given on a volunteer, part-time basis. Instead of having study hall from ten o'clock to eleven, a high school pupil may be assigned to assist in the kindergarten. Many high schools are now providing helping-teacher experiences for pupils who are interested in preparing for teaching. Also, there is a rapidly increasing number of high schools offering a credit course in Introduction to Teaching, which includes helping-teacher activities as a part of the course.

SELECTIVE ADMISSION TO TEACHER EDUCATION

Role of High School Teachers

It is doubtful that high school teachers should exercise direct responsibility for the elimination of unlikely candidates for admission to teacher-education programs. The major responsibility here would seem to be that of the college or university where such preparation is sought.

No exact and unvarying accurate set of criteria for evaluating candidates for admission to teacher-education programs has been as yet established. There appears to be no yardstick by which probable success or failure in teaching can be measured. Several yardsticks are required to form any reasonably accurate judgment.

High school teachers and high school guidance programs, as has been pointed out, can assist materially in enabling pupils to discover whether they have the necessary qualities and aptitudes to become successful teachers. But such decisions must be purely voluntary on the part of the individual pupil. For those who reveal serious and obvious weakness, somewhere along the line a decision to reject them as candidates for teacher preparation must be made. In the final analysis, this decision probably must be made by the college where such preparation is sought. Mental ability is, of course, important. Liking for children, willingness to work hard, and good personality are essential. These qualities can hardly be evaluated by paper-and-pencil tests or even by academic marks. Much of what can be learned about candidates in preparation has to be learned in actual situations in which there is contact with children. Some candidates with average academic records do fine jobs in student teaching and on the job after graduation, while some good students may do equally as well and no better.

Role of Student NEA

The Student National Education Association serves an important co-curricular function in guidance and retention in teacher education. It is an organization for college students who are preparing to be teachers. The Student NEA is jointly sponsored by the National Education Association and the respective state education associations. Its purpose is to serve as a means of developing each prospective teacher's ability to perform as an efficient member of his profession. It provides preprofessional experience in participating in the work of professional organizations—local, state, and national—on the problems with which members of the teaching profession are constantly dealing, and orientation to t'ie procedure by which the profession seeks their solution. A student education association exists presently in nearly every eligible teacher-education college or university. In addition to preprofessional orientation, teacher-education students study the history and the ethics of their profession. The Student NEA serves as the all-inclusive general organization for teacher-education students. Many national professional associations in specialized teaching fields and subjects maintain student associations. The National Science Teachers Association, the Music Educators National Conference and the American Association for Health, Physical Education, and Recreation are examples. All of these perform important roles in guidance, screening, and retention of those in the process of preparing to be teachers.

Role of the Colleges

Final judgment on admission to preparation for teaching is, of course, a function of the colleges and universities. Sometimes admission to the college and to the teacher-education program is simultaneous, at the beginning of the freshman year. In most instances these are separate processes, the latter coming at the end of the sophomore year and involving requirements in addition to those for admission to the college. Stout, in a study of 785 regionally accredited colleges and universities, reported that 91 per cent of the institutions expressed the belief that there should be selective admission to teacher education; only one-tenth opposed selective admission.[7] But in actual practice only 189 of these institutions were found to have extensive programs of selective admission. The others had fairly good to indifferent programs.

Of the 189 institutions judged to have extensive programs of selective admission, the following practices appeared to be rather common: [8]

1. Applications of special requirements for admission to the teacher-education program, beyond those for admission to the institution.
2. Evaluation of emotional stability, personal-social-ethical fitness for teaching, and communications skills evaluated at three or more points in the student's preparation; also evaluation of academic ability and physical fitness.

[7] Ruth A. Stout, *A Study of Admissions and Retention Practices in College and University Programs of Teacher Education* (unpublished doctoral dissertation), University of Minnesota, 1957.

[8] Ruth A. Stout, "Selection of Teacher Education Students," *The Education of Teachers: New Perspectives,* Report of the Second Bowling Green Conference. Washington, D.C.: National Education Association, National Commission on Teacher Education and Professional Standards, 1958, p. 252.

3. Review of each student's case, at stated intervals, with interviews and faculty committee evaluations.
4. Efforts to relate the student's interests and abilities to job opportunities.
5. A continuing program of follow-up of graduates.

The task force of the special NCTEPS project on New Horizons in Teacher Education and Professional Standards recommended the following ingredients in a comprehensive program designed to get in teacher preparation candidates of high ability: [9]

1. That a co-operative process of selection and evaluation be carried on by the total profession so that a favorable climate is created for preparation, entrance into the profession, and continued effective performance in it.
2. That only those institutions be accredited for teacher preparation which have definable operating programs of continuous selection.
3. That the selective processes at least be based on evaluation of emotional maturity, moral and ethical fitness, health, demonstrated ability to work with children and youth, academic aptitude and intelligence, academic achievement, demonstrated competence in speech and basic skills, and professional interest and motivation.
4. That responsibilities for selection be clearly placed, that instruments and processes be well planned and diversified, and that sequential steps be sensitively applied and systematically followed.
5. That the staff in student personnel services be an integral part of the teacher education program, and that personnel from all faculties dealing with the education of prospective teachers be involved in the evaluation processes.
6. That the total profession, as defined above, accept recognition of the need and responsibility for helping develop and apply a continuing program of selection throughout the teaching careers of its members.
7. That programs of selection, admission, and retention for preparation and performance have as a primary goal securing qualified staffs for quality educational programs.

TEACHER EDUCATION

Varied Quality of Present Programs

The necessity for and nature of professional programs of teacher education are discussed in detail in Chapter 18. It is necessary, however,

[9] Margaret Lindsey (ed.) *New Horizons for the Teaching Profession.* Washington, D.C.: National Education Association, National Commission on Teacher Education and Professional Standards, 1961, p. 203.

that the diversity of programs be placed in perspective here to the identification and selection process.

There are vast differences in the existing programs of preparation for teachers. These vary not only from state to state but from institution to institution, even within the same state. There are great variations in quantity of offerings as well as in their quality.

Even a casual study reveals that there is no agreed-upon pattern of teacher education in the United States. There are, of course, some common elements in most of the programs. Beyond a few common elements, though, variations are so great as to make one almost believe that institutions are preparing workers for entirely different occupations. These variations present one of the major problems involved in teacher education.

Great differences will be revealed in comparative study of the programs of almost any two institutions selected. One would not find such differences in the programs of medical schools. Instead, the American Medical Association insists on a common pattern of courses and activities. While a fixed common pattern of teacher education would probably not be desirable, doubtless a reasonable degree of uniformity would prove to be more effective.

There should be, of course, opportunity for initiative and experimentation by colleges. But this opportunity could still be preserved within the framework of a more unified pattern of teacher education.

Teachers themselves should have a larger part in the establishment of such patterns of preparation, since they are the subjects of the process and are likely to discover the weaknesses and the strengths of such programs in the practice of their profession.

Many unjust and extreme criticisms have been recently aimed at the content of teacher-education programs. These have generally charged that there is too little concentration upon liberal arts or subject-matter courses and too much emphasis upon methods (education) courses. But not all recent criticisms of the preparation of teachers have been without justification. Doubtless, in some institutions there have been too many education courses and not enough general education. Teachers themselves are frequently very critical of the preparation they had for their work. They are able, from practical experience, to point out the courses and experiences that they found helpful and those that proved to be without much value. There is the prime reason why experienced teachers should have the opportunity to advise with colleges concerning the content of teacher-education programs.

The growing practices of the colleges and universities in consulting with their teacher graduates and with administrators and supervisors is a hopeful sign for the continuation of the improvement of teacher education, which has been in process for several years. The criticisms, if used to this end, can be constructive. Also, there has been a growing trend in recent years to involve college teachers of the liberal arts in planning the teacher-education programs of given institutions.[10] (See Table 13.) Recent efforts to strengthen teacher education in general have been in four broad areas: (1) improving the general education of teachers, (2) improving the specialization (mastery of teaching field or area), (3) efforts to telescope the necessary professional experiences for teachers into a smaller number of courses, and (4) efforts to broaden the range of laboratory experiences— the working with children in actual school situations. Recent efforts have also been made to involve liberal-arts professors in determining satisfactory programs of teacher education.[11]

TABLE 13 *Prevalence of Campus-Wide Committees or Councils for Teacher Education, June 1960*

Type of Institution	Number of Institutions Surveyed	Number Having All-Institutional Committee or Council
Liberal arts colleges	551	164
Teachers colleges	99	30
Public universities	93	37
Private universities	128	58
State colleges	154	69
Miscellaneous	49	2
TOTAL	1,074	360

Source: Adapted from John I. Goodlad and Howard R. Boozer, "Campus-Wide Committees on Teacher Education," *Educational Record,* October, 1961, *42*:349 (Table 1).

As is pointed out in Chapter 19, the legal authority for issuing certificates is now almost universally vested in the respective state departments of education. The governing bodies of the departments, usually a state board of education, have the authority to establish certification require-

[10] John I. Goodlad and Howard R. Boozer, "Campus-Wide Committees on Teacher Education," *Educational Record,* October, 1961, *42*:348–53.

[11] See reports of the Second Bowling Green, Kansas, and San Diego Conferences of the National Commission on Teacher Education and Professional Standards as follows: *The Education of Teachers: New Perspectives,* 1958, 399 pp., *The Education of Teachers: Curriculum Programs,* 1959, 453 pp., *The Education of Teachers: Certification,* 1960, 367 pp. Washington, D.C.: National Education Association.

Also see G. K. Hodenfield and T. M. Stinnett, *The Education of Teachers: Conflict and Consensus* (popularized report of the three cooperative conferences). Engelwood Cliffs, New Jersey: Prentice-Hall, Inc., 1961, 177 pp.; and T. M. Stinnett, "The Cooperative Teacher Education and Professional Standards Conferences in Retrospect," *Phi Delta Kappan,* November, 1960, *42*:61–66.

ments and policies. These governing bodies generally have established extra-legal advisory committees to assist with the formulation and enforcement of certification requirements.

While state boards of education have almost always provided for broad representation for all major segments of the teaching profession on these advisory committees, the group that is often charged with having wielded the greatest influence in certification has been the college group. Wherever this has happened, it probably was the result of one of two factors, or both: (1) default by teachers in their obligation and opportunity to participate in formulating the requirements, and (2) the greater competency, gained through years of experience, of college personnel. Teachers from the elementary and secondary schools, as has been said, have been only mildly interested in the past and have generally acquiesced in letting college personnel speak for them in matters relating to certification rules and practices of state departments of education.

Again, the college personnel that has been active in formulating certification requirements has largely been drawn from education staff members. College departments of education, however, have not always been able to have their way in respect to certification requirements. College teachers of education are a minority group on most campuses, being greatly outnumbered by professors of academic subjects. Moreover, recent studies reveal that in most institutions now the total staffs are being involved in planning the preparation programs for teachers; and now many state boards of education are including liberal-arts teachers on advisory committees that recommend certification requirements.

Teacher-Education Accrediting Agencies

The problem of accreditation of teacher-education programs is discussed in detail in Chapter 20. However, since the subject is so strongly related to the improvement of the preparation of teachers, it seems desirable to refer in a general way to the problem here. Colleges and universities that offer preparation for a number of vocations deal with a large number of accrediting agencies. There are, of course, general ones such as the North Central Association of Colleges and Secondary Schools, the Southern Association of Colleges and Secondary Schools, the New England Association of Colleges and Secondary Schools, the Middle States Association of Colleges and Secondary Schools, the Northwest Association of Secondary and Higher Schools, and the Western College Association. These strong regional agencies accredit colleges in terms of their general or over-all programs, but do not give as great emphasis to specific professional curricula as the professions themselves would like. The general agencies are concerned with such things as financial support, preparation and efficiency of faculties, staff loads, laboratory and library facilities, and academic standards.

Colleges and universities are thus rated in terms of such general criteria rather than in respect to adequacy in preparing physicians, dentists, attorneys, engineers, veterinarians, dietitians, journalists, and teachers. Generally, little attention is given to the professional curricula. All the agencies expect that there shall be adequate instructional staffs, suitable buildings and supplies, and acceptable academic standards for the courses that are offered. The general accrediting agencies are, therefore, not accrediting agencies for professional training.

In addition to these general accrediting agencies, there is a large number of associations and agencies that rate or accredit collegiate institutions with respect to the preparation given for specific occupations. Notable among these are the American Bar Association, the American Medical Association, and the National League of Nursing Education. Twenty-nine professions sponsor national professional accrediting agencies.

In 1967, out of a total of 1,200 institutions approved by state departments of education for teacher education, only 449 were accredited by the National Council for Accreditation of Teacher Education, the recognized accrediting agency for the teaching profession. But these 449 institutions prepared about 75 per cent of the new teachers graduated in that year. A total of 136 institutions held only approval of their state teacher-certification authority. More than 1,000 of these 1,200 institutions held accreditation by their regional associations, but such accreditation usually applies only to their general collegiate programs. In addition, about seventy institutions classed as technical, miscellaneous, or junior colleges had state approval to prepare teachers. In most other professions, institutions preparing their members must meet the national accrediting standards of these professions, or their graduates cannot be licensed.

Teaching is the last of the major existing professions to institute a professional accrediting process having profession-wide support and application. Despite the fact that it is, in terms of numbers engaged in it, the largest of all the professions, teaching has, unlike all other professions, continued to rely largely upon the evaluation of general collegiate programs as a measure of quality of preparation of its members.

The role that state departments of education have in certification has been previously described. All but a few of the states also grant to their state departments of education the right to approve institutions whose credentials will be accepted for this purpose; and in all the states and territories there is a legal provision for the approval of institutions whose credentials will be accepted for the issuance of teachers' certificates. Nevertheless, accreditation of institutions for teacher education by state legal agencies seems all too often to be little more than a formality. From 1927 to 1952 the American Association of Colleges for Teacher Education (AACTE), or its predecessor, the American Association of Teachers Colleges, was the only organization functioning as a national professional accrediting agency for teacher-education programs. In 1952, the accrediting function of the AACTE was taken over by the National Council for Accreditation of Teacher Education, which began actual accrediting in 1954.

An association such as the AACTE, representing as it does only college personnel, simply did not have the widespread professional and legal support necessary to secure general acceptance of its accrediting procedures. An organization composed entirely of teacher-education institutions tends to be isolated from the impacts of changing conditions in elementary and secondary schools. Sustained efforts have been made since NCATE was established to center its control in higher education, and divorce it from the practitioners.

A Professional Accrediting Procedure for Teacher Education

There appeared to be only one tenable solution to the problem of achieving satisfactory standards for teacher education. This was to establish a professional accrediting process that represents and is supported by all segments of the teaching profession, and not by only one segment of it. The National Council for Accreditation of Teacher Education which was established in 1952 and began actual accrediting of teacher-education institutions on July 1, 1954, appears to fit the criteria for a sound professional process. This is a joint national council composed of representatives of state legal agencies, teachers and administrators, boards of education, and teacher-education institutions. (The NCATE is described in Chapter 20.)

The functions performed by the NCATE are as follows: (1) to formulate standards for teacher preparation through continuous research and through consideration of the recommendations of all organizations concerned with the improvement of the preparation of teachers, (2) to devise ways and means of evaluating institutional programs of teacher education by the application of these standards on the request of an institution or state authority responsible for the accreditation desired by an institution, and (3) to publish lists of institutions accredited by this council.

One of the basic weaknesses of teacher education that the council is seeking to correct is that of selective-admission practices. The NCATE is insisting that every accredited institution should enforce admission requirements to the teacher-education program that are in addition to those for admission to the institution as a whole.

INDUCTION

The traditional ways of starting teachers in their first jobs are rapidly being abandoned. More and more teachers are assuming a part in the hiring, assignment, and orientation of beginning teachers.

Placement of Beginning Teachers

In the past, the superintendent of schools visited various teacher-education institutions to interview candidates for teaching positions. He bargained with the ones who, on the basis of credentials and interviews, seemed to be best qualified for the jobs that were open. He then presented his recommendations to the board of education. These were usually accepted without much question.

A different plan for employment is now rapidly finding favor. The superintendent, or director of personnel, still visits teacher-education institutions, goes over credentials, and interviews candidates. He selects several of the best-qualified prospective teachers for each position available in the school system. These candidates are then invited to visit the school to which they will probably be assigned. They spend at least a day in that school visiting various rooms, conferring with the principal and teachers, and going over supplies and curricula. Moreover, unlike the old days when teachers felt compelled to accept the first position they could get, candidates now ask searching questions about such matters as salary schedules, personnel policies, leaves, and non-wage benefits. At the end of the visiting period the candidates decide if they are still interested in teaching in that school. Growing, also, is the practice of school-staff participation in the evaluation of the candidates. The superintendent then makes his recommendations with the advice of the staff.

The thinking behind this procedure is that a group is better able to select personnel than is any one individual, that teachers should have a voice in the selection of the colleagues with whom they will work, and that candidates for positions should have an opportunity to decide if they will probably be happy and successful in a situation in which they will be placed.

Assignment of Beginning Teachers

The assignment of new teachers is also very much a concern of teachers already in service. Involved in assignment is the welfare of the schools as well as the happiness and success of some teachers.

New teachers are, of course, assigned to schools and instructional areas where there are vacancies. Usually these vacancies are not the original ones but have been created by teachers already in the system moving to more desirable positions and schools. This advancement process may take place several times because of one vacancy in a desirable position. New teachers are frequently assigned to the least desirable and most difficult positions in a school system for the simple reason that fairness would seem to dictate that teachers with several years of service to the school system should be given first choice of positions as vacancies occur. By the time the position for the newcomer to the system is established, it is often in a school in an underprivileged area where there may be many difficult problems to be met. Beginning teachers are sometimes called upon to cope with situations that would tax the resources of experienced teachers.

There are two basic considerations in the assignment of teaching duties among the school staff: the welfare of children and the seniority of teachers. The two are often somewhat antagonistic. For example, Miss Combs has taught for three years in the Elmwood School, located in a run-down section of the city. The neighborhood around the school is one of rooming houses, tawdry apartment houses, taverns, and dirty streets and alleys. It is an area of brief residence and many broken homes. Miss Combs had a hard time, at first, becoming adjusted to the situation, but has done splendid work for the past two years.

There is to be a vacancy in the Glen Rose School, which is located in a middle-class residential area near Miss Combs' home. Miss Combs has asked for this position and feels that she should have preference over the newcomer to the school system. She says, "I've served my time in a hard school. Let a new teacher start in there just as I did."

What Miss Combs loses sight of is that an inexperienced teacher may not be able to adjust to the situation, which is admittedly a difficult one. This may mean poor educational service to the children of that fringe area. The youngsters at Elmwood need good teachers, as do the children of Glen Rose. It may also mean that the budding career of a new teacher may be ruined because of a failure in a difficult situation. It is common for young teachers to become so discouraged over a situation like this that they quit teaching entirely.

Who shall receive priority? Miss Combs or the children of Elmwood School? Miss Combs or the beginning teacher? Teacher groups have usually contended that a seniority plan for teachers comes first. But should it? Is there a middle position?

Adjusting to the Position

Traditionally, administrative officials gave assistance to new teachers in the location of rooming and boarding places and in becoming adjusted to school situations. This was not too satisfactory a method, because teachers felt that there was some domination in respect to living arrangements and that it was hardly practical to turn to administrators when they needed help with their teaching activities. Administrators have to evaluate the work of teachers and to recommend them for retention or dismissal. This creates a bar that is hard for a teacher to hurdle when he needs help. He can hardly tell the administrator on whom his job depends that he doesn't want to rent one of the rooms that are on the list. The administrator may think he is fussy. The young teacher can hardly confess that he is having trouble with his job to the one who will appraise his work.

A growing practice is to have the local teachers' club or educational association handle all of the assistance needed by a beginning teacher. The local teachers' association has a committee to locate rooms and apartments, to meet new teachers upon arrival, and to see that they find satisfactory living quarters. The association arranges receptions and parties for the new members. The association appoints an experienced teacher in the building in which the new teacher is located to acquaint him with the rules and customs of the school, to give him needed information about the parents and children, and to extend assistance with any classroom difficulties that he may meet. This is a much more effective plan than to have such things done by administrators. It also reflects a growing professional attitude on the part of teachers.

REFERENCES

ARMSTRONG, W. EARL, "The NCATE in 1960," *Journal of Teacher Education*, March, 1960, *11*:9–14.

BURDIN, J. L., "Faculty Selection and Retention: A Quest for Quality," *Teachers College Record*, January, 1965, 36:185–7.

CHAMBERLAIN, LEO M., and KINDRED, LESLIE W., *The Teacher and School Organization*, 3rd ed. Englewood Cliffs, New Jersey: Prentice-Hall, Inc., 1958, "Recruitment and Selection," pp. 95–98.

CHANDLER, B. J., *Education and the Teacher*. New York: Dodd, Mead and Company, 1961, Chap. 7, "Who Should Teach?", pp. 159–184.

COOK, D. L., "Personal Data Form as a Predictor of Success in a Teacher Education Program and Entry into Teaching," *Journal of Teacher Education*, March, 1964, *15*:61–6.

COOK, WALTER W., and HOYT, CYRIL J., "The Predictive Validity of the Minnesota Teacher Attitude Inventory," *Journal of Teacher Education*, March, 1959, *10*:42–44.

DURFLINGER, G. W., "Recruitment and Selection of Prospective Elementary and Secondary School Teachers." *Review of Educational Research*, October, 1963, *33*:355–7.

EDSON, WILLIAM H., and DAVIES, DON, "Selectivity in Teacher Education," *Journal of Teacher Education,* September, 1960, *11*:327–34.

FORDYCE, JOHN W., "Admission to Teacher Education," *Journal of Teacher Education,* September, 1959, *10*:323–25.

GORDON, G. G., "Conditions of Employment and Service in Elementary and Secondary Schools," *Review of Educational Research,* October, 1963, *33*:381–90.

HALL, ROY M., and VINCENT, ANTONIO M., "Staff—Selection and Appointment," in Harris, Chester (ed.) *Encyclopedia of Educational Research,* 3rd ed. New York: Macmillan Company, 1960, pp. 1375–78.

HARRER, J. M., "Superior People Are Rejecting Classroom Teaching," *NEA Journal,* November, 1966, *55*:20–2.

KLEINMAN, L., "New Dimension in Teacher Selection," *Journal of Educational Sociology,* September, 1960, *34*:24–33.

KOERNER, J. D., "What Schoolmen Should Do to Attract Better Teachers," *Nation's Schools,* February, 1964, *73*:50+.

LINDSEY, MARGARET (ed.) *New Horizons for the Teaching Profession.* Washington, D.C.: National Commission on Teacher Education and Professional Standards, National Education Association, 1961, Chap. 7, "Identification, Selective Admission and Retention in Teacher Education," pp. 161–203.

LUECK, W. R., "Professional Insecurities of Prospective Teachers," *Teachers College Record,* December, 1965, *37*:119–25.

MACMINN, P., and BURNETT, C., "Comparison of Teacher Education Students and Non-Teacher Education Students on Measures of Academic Aptitude and Achievement." *Journal of Teacher Education,* Fall, 1966, *17*:312–16.

MOFFITT, F., "Click-Clack, Push-Pull; Teacher-Picker is Whirring," *Nation's Schools,* October, 1965, *76*:10.

NATIONAL EDUCATION ASSOCIATION, National Commission on Teacher Education and Professional Standards, *The Assignment and Misassignment of American Teachers.* Washington, D.C.: The Association, 1965.

———, *Competent Teachers for America's Schools: Lay-Professional Action Programs to Secure and Retain Qualified Teachers,* Report of the Albany Conference. Washington, D.C.: The Commission, 1954.

———, *The Education of Teachers: Certification,* Report of the San Diego Conference. Washington, D.C.: The Commission, 1961.

———, *The Education of Teachers: Curriculum Programs,* Report of the Kansas Conference. Washington, D.C.: The Commission, 1959.

———, *The Education of Teachers: New Perspectives,* Report of the Second Bowling Green Conference. Washington, D.C.: The Commission, 1958.

NATIONAL EDUCATION ASSOCIATION, Professional Rights and Responsibilities Commission, *Guidelines for Retention of Staff for School Districts Moving from Dual to Unified Systems.* Washington, D.C.: The Association, Leaflet.

PETTIT, M. L., "What College Graduates Say About Education Courses," *Journal of Teacher Education,* December, 1964, *15*:378–81.

REDFERN, G. B., "Teacher Selection," *Educational Leadership,* April, 1966, *23*:560–3.

RICHEY, ROBERT W., *Planning for Teaching,* 3rd ed. New York. McGraw-Hill Book Company, 1963, Chap. 1, "Looking Ahead: Why Teach?" pp. 2–33.

ROBINSON, J. J., "Recruiting Teachers With Care," *Journal of Teacher Education,* June, 1964, *15*:291–21.

STILES, LINDLEY J., and others, *Teacher Education in the United States.* New York: Ronald Press, 1960, Chap. 7, "Recruitment, Selection, and Admission of Prospective Teachers," pp. 134–55.

STINNETT, T. M., and CLARKE, CHARLES M., "Measurement and Prediction of Teaching Success," in Harris, Chester (ed.) *Encyclopedia of Educational Research,* 3rd ed. New York: Macmillan Company, 1960, pp. 1468–69.

STINNETT, T. M., and HASKEW, LAURENCE D., *Teaching in American Schools.* New York: Harcourt, Brace & World, 1962.

STOUT, RUTH A., "Selective Admission and Retention Practices in Teacher Education," *Journal of Teacher Education,* September, 1957, 8:299–317; December, 1957, 8:422–32.

SYMONDS, PERCIVAL M., "Interest Inventories Help Select Teacher Trainees," *Nation's Schools,* August, 1960, *64*:55–57.

WHITE, VERNA, "Selection of Prospective Teachers at Syracuse University," *Journal of Teacher Education,* March, 1950, *1*:24–31.

WOOD, BEN D., and NORTH, ROBERT D., "Teachers Colleges Can Select and Hold Superior Students," *Journal of Higher Education,* November, 1956, *27*:419–27.

WYNN, RICHARD, *Careers in Education.* New York: McGraw-Hill Book Company, 1960.

5: The Teacher's First Position

*T*he teacher's first position is all-important, because that first year's experience implants an image, good or bad, of what a teaching career will be like. If the experience is an unhappy one—and the record indicates that is the case with thousands of beginners—the likelihood is that the beginner will turn to other work. Therefore, the teacher-education student should approach the seeking and the acceptance of his first teaching job with the greatest of care, in the spirit that few other decisions will be more significant.

Proper approaches and right choices bring happiness, personal satisfaction, an adequate salary, success, and advancement. Wrong approaches and choices can result in dissatisfaction, disillusionment, and perhaps failure as far as one's chosen occupation is concerned.

Present graduates of teacher-education institutions are fortunate in that they usually have a choice among a large number of possible positions. Throughout the 1930's there was an oversupply of teachers in most fields, so that one was fortunate to have an offer of even one position. Today, and for the foreseeable future, there is such a shortage of teachers that employers compete for the graduates of teacher-education institutions. This is a happy condition for prospective teachers, because they need not accept positions in which happiness and success are doubtful.

The first purpose of this chapter is to discuss the kinds of positions that beginning teachers should seek and to describe some of the criteria that can be used to locate satisfactory jobs. It is hoped that the discussion will be helpful to education students who will soon be entering the ranks of teachers. It is hoped, also, that it will help save for the profession some of the thousands who have such unhappy, unsatisfactory first positions that either their effectiveness is lessened or they are so disgusted that they seek other means of earning a livelihood.

The second is that of discussing effective means of securing positions. In this connection, written applications, interviews, follow-up methods, use of references, ethics of acceptance and rejection of positions, and the importance of contracts and their observance will be discussed.

CERTIFICATION IS REQUIRED

A prerequisite in the search for a teaching job in the elementary and secondary schools is to secure either a teacher's certificate or assurance of eligibility for a certificate. All states require teachers in the public schools (some also require teachers in private schools) to hold a legal license issued by the state department of education. A few cities (Baltimore, Buffalo, Chicago, New York, and Portland, Ore., are examples) issue certificates to their teachers. Also state colleges and universities in a few states (Kansas and Missouri) are authorized to issue certificates to their graduates. In all other cases, the state agency must grant the license. A full description of teacher certification requirements is given in Chapter 19, but a few cautions and suggestions will be set forth here.

Legal licensure [1] is society's means of protecting its members from unqualified practitioners and is required for all the professions. This is the basic purpose of licensure, but it also serves incidentally to protect competent professionals from the competition of unprepared people. Thus, the qualified teacher should view certification as essential to the protection of children and as a protection of his own professional status, which he secured through a long period of preparation. All too often teachers tend to be irritated by this requirement. But this is a superficial reaction.

The graduating teacher, then, before accepting an apointment, should secure a teacher's certificate in the state where he is to teach. A few states issue a certificate of eligibility for a certificate, which authorizes the holder to seek a position and gives assurance that a certificate will be issued if employment is found. In fact, in most states it will not be possible to secure a certificate until after graduation, because official transcripts of college work completed cannot be issued until then, and state departments of education require transcripts to issue certificates. But college officers

[1] License (or licensure) and certificate (or certification) are usually applied interchangeably. All are terms applied to the issuance by a legal agency (usually the state) of authorization to engage in the practice of a given profession. In teaching, licensure generally means authorization to teach and to be paid from public funds. Certification confers such authorization but, in addition, specifies the level of preparation as well as the teaching levels or fields for which the holder's credentials qualify him.

can issue letters certifying to the candidate's meeting of requirements for certification.

It will be well to keep in mind the basic requirements of states. All but four states in 1967(Nebraska, North Dakota, South Dakota, and Wisconsin) and Puerto Rico require completion of the bachelor's degree for regular certification of beginning elementary school teachers. All states require completion of at least the bachelor's degree for certification of beginning high school teachers. Two states (Arizona and California) and the District of Columbia require five years of college preparation, with some variations. The precise requirements for all teaching positions can be found in the manual listed below,[2] a copy of which will be in most college libraries. In addition, there are certain general requirements for teachers' certificates, such as minimum age, U.S. citizenship, general-health certificate, and recommendation of the preparing institution; and a few states require a special course, such as state history and constitution.

To obtain a certificate, it is required that an application form from the state department of education be secured and filled out. Most teacher-education institutions keep these forms on hand for the use of their graduates. The form must be accompanied by the required fee charged in most states (ranging from $1 to $5), recommendation of the appropriate official of the graduating college, and such other certifications (health certificate, for example) as may be required by the state in which application is being made. Also, an official transcript of the candidate's college work must accompany his application or be sent by the registrar to the state department of education. Some states will accept the transcript directly from the applicant, but most require it to come from the registrar directly to the state office. Plenty of time (one to three months) should be allowed between application and receipt of the certificate. Remember that, if at all possible, you should have your certificate in hand when you seek a position, and by all means before you begin teaching. The employing school officer frequently satisfies himself from the college records or recommendations that a given applicant is eligible for a certificate and agrees to employ him, pending receipt of the certificate, but the school district cannot legally pay a teacher until the certificate has been filed with the district. Thus, much embarrassment can be avoided by making certain that legal licensure has been obtained before, not after, employment or the beginning of actual work.

Another caution should be observed. The certificates issued by virtually all states will certify eligibility to teach on a given school level: kinder-

[2] T. M. Stinnett, *A Manual on Certification Requirements for School Personnel in the United States* (1967 edition). Washington, D.C.: National Education Association, National Commission on Teacher Education and Professional Standards, 1967, 219 pp. (published biennially).

garten-primary, elementary school, junior high school or high school, or simply on the elementary or secondary school level. For high school teachers, most states also specify on their certificates the fields or subjects the holder is qualified to teach under the rules of the state. The beginning teacher should be careful about accepting teaching assignments for which his certificate does not show him qualified. It is true that several states issue a blanket or general high school certificate, but the teacher must meet the state's requirements to be assigned to teach a given teaching field or subject. Even though school employing officers are able to secure temporary legal approval of such misassignments, ultimately the teacher will be compelled to complete additional college work to continue to teach in the field or subject. Besides, the practice involves serious ethical questions. Only in extreme circumstances should a teacher accept an assignment for which he does not clearly meet the specified requirements of the state.

CRITERIA FOR EVALUATING POSITIONS

Do not rush in to take the first available job. List for yourself what you consider the minimum essentials of a satisfactory teaching job, and then make certain that the job you seek and accept meets these criteria. Rather than lessening your opportunities for employment, the chances are that a questioning attitude about the advantages and disadvantages of a given position in a given school district, if courteously expressed, will enhance the possibilities of satisfactory employment. Most progressive school systems now have published personnel policies. Secure a copy of these policy statements. If no policy statements are available, inquire of the school employing officer what the practices of the district are. Below are discussed some of the key factors about which you should inquire.

Salary

Certainly one basis for deciding on the desirability of a proffered position is that of salary. A teacher must eat and have a pleasant room or apartment. He must dress neatly. He should have a sufficient income for occasional lectures and concerts, purchase of reading materials, and some travel. He should carry life, sickness, and accident insurance. An automobile, a radio, and a television set are now almost necessities. It should be possible to set aside savings for the proverbial rainy day. The income should be sufficient, after some years of working upward on the salary schedule, to support a family on at least average or above-average American standards.

Salary *is* important, but there are a number of things to consider besides the starting pay. Living costs are usually higher in cities than they are in small towns. Rent, whether for an apartment or a room, is almost always considerably higher in a metropolitan center than elsewhere. Transportation to and from work is a considerable item in cities, but it is not generally much of a factor in small towns. Teachers who go to cities for the higher pay that is offered may find, after evaluating all factors, that they are pursuing a will-o'-the-wisp.

It is difficult to secure accurate data about the comparative living costs of cities and towns where positions are offered, but it is usually possible to make rough comparisons. One can investigate the cost of rooms and apartments that are available. He can estimate what transportation will cost. These criteria should permit a fairly accurate comparison of the purchasing power of the salaries that are offered.

Of much more importance than the initial salary is the provision for raises after the teacher is on the job. (This problem is discussed at some length in Chapter 7.) The teacher who intends to remain in the schoolroom for only one, two, or three years is interested almost entirely in the starting salary. He cares little for high maximums, because he does not expect to be around long enough to profit from provisions for the many and large increments that are awarded for experience and further preparation. On the other hand, those who expect to make a lifework of teaching are more interested in what they can earn after fifteen years of service and some additional preparation than they are in the salaries paid for the first year.

Let us illustrate by two hypothetical salary schedules: Tables 14 and 15. While neither schedule reflects typical practices now, they do indicate variations that still exist.

If one intends to teach for a year or so, the salary schedule of District A will look better to him than that of District B. On the other hand, if he expects to remain in the classroom during all his active years, he will much prefer the schedule of District B.

TABLE 14   Salary Schedule for District A

Years of Experience	Bachelor's Degree	Master's Degree	Master's Degree & 1 Year	Doctor's Degree
None	$4,800	$5,000	$5,200	$5,400
One	5,000	5,200	5,400	5,600
Two	5,200	5,400	5,600	5,800
Three	5,400	5,600	5,800	6,000
Four	5,600	5,800	6,000	6,200
Five or more	5,800	6,000	6,200	6,400

Some districts having trouble securing personnel make a play for the services of beginning teachers by offering a large initial salary. One district may offer $5,000 to beginning teachers. What is usually not mentioned is that $5,600 is the maximum salary for this district. Table 14 is an illustration of this booby trap.

No matter how many years of experience the teacher has had, and no matter how much preparation he secures, his salary is still not more than $6,400. This practice is more characteristic of rural and small-town schools than of those in cities.

Table 15, on the other hand, holds out inducements for the experienced teacher.

TABLE 15   *Salary Schedule for District B*

Years of Experience	Bachelor's Degree	Master's Degree	Master's Degree & 1 Year	Doctor's Degree
None	$4,600	$4,900	$5,200	$5,500
One	4,900	5,200	5,500	5,800
Two	5,200	5,500	5,800	6,100
Three	5,500	5,800	6,100	6,400
Four	5,800	6,100	6,400	6,700
Five	6,100	6,400	6,700	7,000
Six	6,400	6,700	7,000	7,300
Seven	6,700	7,000	7,300	7,600
Eight	7,000	7,300	7,600	7,900
Nine	7,300	7,600	7,900	8,200
Ten	7,600	7,900	8,200	8,500
Eleven	7,900	8,200	8,500	8,800
Twelve	8,200	8,500	8,800	9,100

Beginning teachers can very easily ascertain how much allowance is made for additional preparation and experience by asking employing officials for copies of their salary schedules. Nearly all town and city schools have such schedules. If there is no formal schedule, it is wise to inquire what the highest salary is in the district and how much experience and preparation the individual receiving it has had. One can also ask questions about the increments that are ordinarily given each year. Table 16 will be helpful in making comparisons of large city schedules.

Sick-Leave Provisions

Chapter 12 discusses present practices with respect to sick leave and other leave provisions. As has been noted, there are all sorts of provisions, from no days at all with pay to ten or fifteen days per year.

TABLE 16   *Salary Ranking of the Twenty-Six Largest Cities, 1966–67*

B. A. Degree Minima		B. A. Degree Maxima		M. A. Degree Minima		M. A. Degree Maxima	
Los Angeles	$6,220	New York	$9,950	New York	$6,900	New York	$11,450
San Diego	5,900	Montgomery Co.*	9,845	San Diego	6,844	Montgomery Co.*	10,890
Washington, D.C.	5,840	Prince George's Co.*	9,520	Los Angeles	6,600	Baltimore Co.	10,600
Detroit	5,800	Detroit	9,500	Washington, D.C.	6,385	Prince George's Co.*	10,120
Prince George's Co.*	5,600	Baltimore Co.	9,400	Detroit	6,300	Baltimore City	10,100
Baltimore Co.	5,500	Baltimore City	9,300	Prince George's Co.*	6,200	San Diego	10,027
Chicago	5,500	Dade Co., Fla.†	9,010	Baltimore Co.	6,100	Detroit	10,000
Milwaukee	5,500	Los Angeles	9,010	Montgomery Co.*	6,050	Indianapolis	10,000
Montgomery Co.*	5,500	Chicago	9,000	Baltimore City	5,900	Chicago	9,800
Philadelphia	5,500	Washington, D.C.	8,975	Chicago	5,900	Dade Co., Fla.†	9,750
Indianapolis	5,450	Milwaukee	8,810	Indianapolis	5,900	Los Angeles	9,540
Baltimore City	5,400	Philadelphia	8,800	Dade Co., Fla.†	5,830	Washington, D.C.	9,530
New York	5,400	Cleveland	8,717	Philadelphia	5,800	St. Louis	9,520
St. Louis	5,400	Indianapolis	8,700	Milwaukee	5,772	Cleveland	9,450
Cleveland	5,300	St. Louis	8,640	Columbus	5,700	Atlanta	9,329
Dade Co., Fla.†	5,300	San Diego	8,525	Atlanta	5,690	Milwaukee	9,265
Atlanta	5,200	Columbus	8,200	St. Louis	5,670	New Orleans	9,247
Columbus	5,200	New Orleans	8,200	Duval Co., Fla.‡	5,650	Philadelphia	9,100
New Orleans	5,200	Atlanta	8,040	Cleveland	5,504	Columbus	9,100
Dallas	5,050	Duval Co., Fla.‡	7,450	New Orleans	5,500	Duval Co., Fla.‡	8,700
Duval Co., Fla.‡	5,000	Dallas	7,200	Memphis	5,300	Houston	8,100
Memphis	5,000	Hawaii	7,054	Hawaii	5,264	Memphis	8,000
Hawaii	4,774	Memphis	7,000	Dallas	5,250	Dallas	8,000
Houston	4,590	Houston	6,991	Houston	4,781	Hawaii	7,900
							7,777

Source: Computed from National Education Association, Research Division, *Salary Schedules for Classroom Teachers*, 1966–67. Research Report 1966-R17. Washington, D.C.: The Association, October 1966, pp. 30–33.

* Maryland.
† Miami.
‡ Jacksonville.

Because of the nature of their work, teachers are particularly exposed to contagious diseases. Consideration should certainly be given to the item of sick leave in deciding on the desirability of a position. The amount per year is important. Certainly, this provision should be for at least ten days. Also of importance is the amount of time that can be accumulated over a period of years. One hundred days, or half a year, can be expected as reasonable. This will provide for most extended illnesses and major operations (see Chapter 12).

In this connection it is well to inquire if the leave-with-pay policies provide for funerals, illness in the family, jury duty, military service, maternity, and personal business. It is often just as necessary to be absent for a funeral or the illness of a parent or spouse, or for other reasons, as it is to be out of school because of personal sickness.

Maternity Leave

Women teachers who are married or expect to be married in the near future should ascertain of employing officials the district's policies with respect to maternity leave.

Length of School Term

This item is of relatively minor importance. Most teachers usually work many more days than are called for by their contracts. Teaching can hardly be placed on a so-many-hours-per-day or a so-many-days-per-year basis. The length of term may, however, for perfectly legitimate reasons, make a difference to some teachers. In most districts the school term runs from nine to ten months. In rural areas nine-month terms are common. This gives a long summer vacation during which some older children work on farms. City districts almost always have at least nine and a half months, while many have ten months.

There is some trend in urban districts toward year-round schools—not a compulsory twelve-month term, but keeping schools available the year round—and toward twelve-month employment of teachers. It is now recognized that the educational system has a responsibility to aid the growth and development of boys and girls during the entire year. Schools that have summer programs stress acceleration and enrichment in academic work, and provide programs in such activities as camping, playground, arts and crafts, music, and physical education. In districts providing a year-round program the trend is to employ and pay teachers on an annual basis, with one month of vacation allowed.

Professional Organizations

One of the signs of a professional, democratically operated school system is the presence and official recognition of professional organizations.

Is there a classroom teachers' organization? A local education association? A study club? A branch of the Association for Childhood Education International? All except the smallest school systems should have at least a teachers' club. Larger districts will have an education association, a classroom teachers' organization (union or association), and a number of others. Metropolitan districts will have a multitude of organizations, ranging from glee clubs and orchestras to mathematics and science clubs. Professional organizations provide an opportunity for professional growth and advancement, social contacts, and companionship.

Professional Opportunities

Closely connected to the previous topic is that of professional opportunities. Are there curricular or other professional committees upon which one may serve? Is one encouraged to attend professional conferences and conventions? Such opportunities help to give satisfaction in teaching, as well as chances for advancement. These are additional factors to evaluate in deciding on which teaching position to seek or accept.

Teaching Load

As pointed out in Chapter 11, no factor has more to do with success or failure than the teaching load. This has several facets, among which are the size of classes, the length of the school day, and the amount of co-curricular work that is expected. Some classes of forty are easier to teach than some groups of thirty. On the average, though, the larger the group, the more difficult it is to teach. Teachers have testified again and again that large groups demand more nervous energy, as well as longer hours of preparation, correcting papers, and keeping records.

The length of the school day is fairly well standardized. Most elementary schools are in session from five and a half to six hours a day. Teachers are usually expected to be on the job for about an hour a day longer. Thus, teachers spend at least seven hours per day at school. Many teachers, of course, take work home with them at night. Thus, in most school situations the working day is about the same, except for the work that must be taken home. Larger groups mean more papers to correct, more records to keep, more seat-work to plan, more plans to make, and more individual differences to meet. Thus, larger groups not only use up more nervous energy of the teacher, but require more time as well.

Perhaps the teachers with the longest day are those employed by schools that transport large numbers of pupils by buses. In such schools the teacher's day is likely to start when the first busload of children reaches the school. This may be as much as an hour before school begins. The teacher is often expected to supervise the youngsters assigned to him during the noon hour and recess periods and until the last busload departs in the late afternoon, often as much as an hour after school has been dismissed. Teachers in such schools are sometimes working with children for as long as nine hours a day. Such a schedule is a great burden on any teacher. The trend is toward relieving teachers of these noninstructional burdens.

Certainly beginning teachers should inquire about the school hours, the length of time that teachers are expected to be in the building, and what the provisions are for supervision during recess and noon periods. Any situation that calls for continual contact with children for more than six and a half to seven hours per day should be carefully examined. Such continuous contact is probably not good for the children and is almost certainly undesirable for the teacher.

Physical Conditions

This topic is also discussed in Chapter 11. As has been pointed out, a teacher has a right to expect a clean, well-ventilated building. It's no fun to work in a building permeated by offensive odors or one with dusty floors and dirty walls. A teacher has a right to expect that the lighting will be adequate and the walls decorated with pastel colors. He has a right to expect a good-size classroom equipped with attractive, functional furniture and all the books, audio-visual equipment, and supplies that he can use efficiently. These are minimum essentials. If there is a teachers' rest room, a library, a gymnasium, and a music room, the task of teaching is made easier. If there is a modern classroom with work space, room toilets, sink, workbench, tools, and an outside entrance to the playground, the teacher is indeed fortunate.

Obviously, a candidate cannot well visit all the schools of a large or even medium-size city that have offered contracts, but it is usually possible to visit some of them. In this connection it is best to do a little unescorted exploring. Every city has show schools to which it sends visitors. These probably are not typical of what exists. The only satisfactory plan is to visit some of the older schools, particularly those in blighted areas, as well as the newer ones. The beginning teacher is more likely to have his first assignment in an old school than in a new one.

Living Conditions

The happiness and success of teachers are greatly affected by their living conditions. If they have desirable rooms and apartments, good meals, and adequate transportation facilities, their adjustments are much more likely to be satisfactory.

Single teachers of today usually wish to share a small apartment with one or more other teachers. This type of living condition is usually much more satisfactory than having a room in a boardinghouse, hotel, or private home. A room is a rather restricted place to spend all one's spare time. Boardinghouse, hotel, and restaurant meals, even when they are the best of their kind, can become very monotonous. Apartment dwellers can prepare the kind of food they wish, keep the hours they desire, and have the kind of company they enjoy. An apartment thus permits a freedom of life that is impossible in even the best of single rooms.

When selecting a position, a visit to the community under consideration will reveal the availability of apartments for teachers. One can talk with the teachers in the community about their living conditions, check the classified advertisements in the local papers, and walk or drive through the sections of the city where such accommodations are found to see if there are signs advertising apartments for rent.

Transportation within a city and in and out of town is also of some importance. Teachers like to have good local bus service available, even if they have cars. They want to be able to get in and out of the city on weekends without long waits or frequent bus or train changes.

Associates and Friends

Most of our happiness and much of our success depends upon human factors. We can have the finest physical surroundings for work and play and still be unhappy and poorly adjusted. On the other hand, we can enjoy ourselves and be at least moderately successful in rather unpleasant surroundings if we are associating with those whom we enjoy. A teacher's associates are those with whom he works, eats lunch, and visits back and forth. They are the ones with whom he exchanges views on education, talks over trying problems, and secures assistance in instructional procedures.

Many a good beginning teacher has been handicapped and discouraged by having undesirable associates. A young teacher, for example, may be placed with a group of traditional, older teachers who deride all modern methods. They make fun of his efforts to decorate the classroom and laugh at dramatizations and choral readings. They tell him to stop worrying about individual differences and social maladjustments. "You'll soon learn," they will say, "that it doesn't pay to do all those extra things, because nobody appreciates them. All the people here want is for you to keep the kids quiet and teach them the three R's." Usually the young teacher in such an environment eventually loses all his drive toward doing things differently. Soon he is a routine teacher. It is unfortunate when beginning teachers find themselves so boxed in. Almost inevitably, they will be unhappy and unsuccessful.

Administrative Officials

It is fairly obvious that the school officials have a great deal to do with the happiness and success of beginning teachers. Principals, supervisors, and superintendents who are kindly and helpful mean much to any teacher, whether he is a beginner or experienced.

Every teacher wants administrators who are kindly but firm, who expect high standards of teaching but who realize that sometimes things go wrong for all of us, who regard teachers as colleagues in a common enterprise rather than considering themselves judges and taskmasters.

How does one make sure of such administrators? Again, the best way is to visit the schools of the community under consideration. An interview is seldom a good basis for spotting the insincere official. One can tell a great deal by the attitudes of the teachers of the community. If they are a fearful, depressed group who walk down the halls in silence and who watch the doors of their classrooms as though expecting an ogre to enter, it is time to exert caution. If, on the other hand, they talk pleasantly and freely to one another, to visitors, and to the principal and appear to be happy and unrepressed, the situation is probably a good one.

Sometimes a few judicious questions will give an accurate picture of the type of administrator. One cannot expect to learn much by asking if the principal is democratic or autocratic, encouraging or discouraging. It is possible, though, to inquire if curriculum committees are at work, what is done in teachers' meetings, whether there is a course of study that has to be followed, how many reports are required, if field trips can be taken, whether parent-teacher conferences are held, and whether the principal visits rooms on a schedule or upon invitation. Teachers will usually answer such questions quite frankly. Their answers will give an accurate idea as to the way the administrator operates in their school.

Job Security

The beginning teacher certainly should prefer, other things being equal, to secure a position in a school system where there is either tenure as a legal provision or the same degree of job security under personnel policies of the school board. Latest data indicate that about 85 per cent of the nation's public school teachers have job security of one form or another, contingent only upon satisfactory service (see Chapter 10). The beginning teacher should deliberate long and carefully before seeking or accepting a position in a district with a heavy teacher turnover or dismissal record.

Non-Wage Benefits

There are certain other provisions for the teacher's welfare that have now become rather common. These are usually granted together under the term "non-wage benefits." All states now have teacher retirement systems, and some twenty-four large cities have separate retirement systems for their teachers (see Chapter 9). Since retirement coverage is now virtually universal, the beginning teacher will want to look at the retirement benefits of districts and states in which he is offered employment.

These benefits vary widely. They are much too low in many states and adequate in others. It is extremely difficult for a young person to take this precaution, because retirement seems so far away as to be unreal. But it is real; it comes to all of us who live a normal lifespan. And the wise teacher will safeguard this eventuality. Next in importance is adequate insurance coverage. (See Chapter 12 for detailed description of school-district practices.)

SECURING THE FIRST POSITION

Applying for the First Job

There are recognized, legitimate ways of applying for teaching positions. There are also methods that are unprofessional and that bring discredit upon teachers as a group.

For most beginners, the initial contact is through the college placement bureau. Candidates file statements about their backgrounds of preparation and experiences. They furnish the names of references who can speak about their characters, personalities, academic abilities, and experiences with children or in general employment. The college adds statements about proficiencies in student teaching. These papers are bound together into a placement folder, usually prepared before the middle of the senior year.

Employing officials, usually the superintendent for small towns and cities and the personnel director for large communities, write the placement bureau describing their needs and stating the day that they will visit the campus. The placement bureau assembles a number of candidates and arranges an interview schedule. The bureau has the folders of all candidates ready for the employing official when he arrives. They are given to him along with the interview schedule. A small room is set aside for his use. He then interviews the candidates according to the schedule.

During the interview the employing official asks questions about preparation, experience, philosophy, personal life, and almost anything else that occurs to him. It is customary for him to guide the general trend of the conversation. This does not mean that the candidate should not ask questions. On the contrary, a much better impression is made on the employer if intelligent queries are made. A conference or meeting of any kind is a dead affair unless there is a two-way flow of conversation.

The candidate should look upon the interview as an opportunity to evaluate the desirability of becoming a teacher in the community represented by the employing official, as well as a means of careful selection of the right candidates for appropriate jobs. It is a time when one can find out how well the standards proposed in the first part of the chapter are met.

A number of things may result from the interview. The employing official may close it with a vague statement to the effect that he is not yet in a position to make an offer or that he has a number of other applications to consider. The candidate should recognize that this usually means that a position will not be offered.

If the employer is at least mildly interested and is of a rather cautious type, he will probably ask the prospective teacher to send him a letter of application. If this is done, the candidate may or may not hear further from the employer.

The official may ask the candidate to come to his community to talk things over. In this case there is almost sure to be real interest in the prospective teacher.

There are instances in which employers carry pads of contracts already signed by members of their boards of education. If they want to hire a teacher they simply fill in his name, have him sign, and give him one of the forms.

Accepting a Position

It is wise not to accept a position without some thought and gathering of information. In the previous section, the desirability of finding out everything possible about the community in which one is considering teaching was stressed. It would ordinarily be unwise to accept until one had visited the schools, talked with teachers, and secured every other bit of information that could be gathered. Then the pros and cons should be carefully weighed. One can then decide if a position will probably be satisfactory.

Should the first position that is offered be accepted? It is probably best to have several interviews and several files of information in order to have a basis for comparison. On the other hand, if the position that is tendered seems to be just what one is looking for, there is no point in waiting.

Ethics of Accepting

A teacher should not accept a position without due consideration, but after his word has been given, he should live up to his promise unless a very unusual condition arises. Not to do so brings discredit upon the individual, the institution from which he is graduating, and the teaching profession in general. An old saying is that one's word should be as good as one's bond. Society could hardly function unless most people kept their promises. (See Chapter 14 for descriptions of unethical practices.)

Admittedly, a few teachers have been careless about fulfilling their obligations. Some have been known to resign from one position in order to accept another only a few days before school begins. Others have quit at a moment's notice to go to a community nearer home or to one where friends are located. It is hard to justify such actions unless the officials of the district where the teacher has been serving are entirely willing to give releases.

When a beginning teacher, particularly, resigns from a contract signed in good faith, he labels himself as unreliable. He also casts a reflection upon his college, because employing officials may feel that he has not been taught proper ethics. He adds fuel to the charge that teachers are interested only in themselves and not in society.

Personal Interviews

There is much less concern about the dress of candidates for teaching positions than was true a few years ago. It is essential that one be neatly and appropriately dressed and well groomed. Today there is little emphasis upon the kind of dress that a teacher should wear, as long as it is in good taste.

In preparing for an interview, it is well to analyze one's strengths and weaknesses. If the candidate likes children, why not say so? If he feels that he is particularly good at art work, why not bring this out? If he is adept at promoting adequate social adjustments, why not mention it?

There is no need to mention weaknesses, although one should not attempt to conceal them. If he has trouble with classroom management, he should admit it if frankly asked, but it is not necessary to volunteer the information. If he is not good at reports, he should confess this fault when questioned about it. He does not need to bring up this topic himself.

A candidate does not want to sit like a dummy during an interview, but he should be careful not to talk too much. Being a good listener is sometimes difficult but essential. Probably more people have talked themselves out of jobs than lost them by talking too little.

In all that he does say, the teacher should be frank and honest. If he does not know the answer to a question, he should say so. If he has not had the training or experience about which the superintendent may inquire, it is not wise to give the impression that he has. He may, though, give reasons why he thinks that his qualifications more than outweigh any deficiencies that he has.

A Checklist for Securing a Teaching Job.   Here is a sequential checklist of things to do to assume employment as a beginning teacher.[3]

1. Register with your college placement bureau well in advance of graduation.
2. Fill out the placement forms, providing references, other required papers, and a photograph.
3. Talk with members of the placement staff about your desires regarding

[3] Adapted from Wilbur A. Yauch, Martin H. Bartels, and Emmet Morris, *The Beginning Teacher.* New York: Holt, Rinehart and Winston, Inc., 1955, pp. 55–61.

your first position, so that they can be alerted and in a position to suggest your name when an appropriate vacancy occurs.

4. Arrange to attend meetings of seniors, usually held by the placement bureau, to discuss job opportunities, salaries, certification, and interviews.
5. Check the placement bulletin board for schedules of interviews, so that you may arrange a meeting with the school employing officers of your choice.
6. Study the lists of jobs that have been filed with the placement office.
7. Write letters of inquiry or application, or telephone regarding the jobs in which you may be interested.
8. Respond immediately to notices of vacancies sent to you by the placement office. Do this whether interested or not in the job or jobs listed.
9. Apply for your teacher's certificate. Your placement office or faculty adviser will help with this.

Letters of Inquiry and Application

Sending out promiscuously a large number of letters of application is probably the least effective way of finding a suitable teaching job. A few letters of inquiry, brief and courteous, addressed to the superintendent of schools or director of personnel of districts in which you feel you would like employment is an acceptable and effective means of determining where vacancies exist. The following is an example of the type:

Dr. Charles E. Heath
Superintendent of Schools
Suburbia, Illinois

Dear Dr. Heath:

This will inquire whether your school system will have a position open for the ensuing school year in the teaching of mathematics.

I shall graduate from Central State College this June, with a Bachelor of Science degree and a major in mathematics. Upon graduation I shall meet all requirements for certification in Illinois in this field. In addition I shall have a minor in physical science.

My credentials are on file in the college placement-bureau office. I shall be pleased to have you request these for examination. Further, I shall be pleased to come for an interview at your request.

Cordially yours,

James Appleton

The formal letter of application may not be necessary. Your placement office may locate suitable vacancies, confer with the employing school officials, and arrange interviews. Also, most school districts now provide their own application forms, and may require only that you execute this form. If a letter of application is judged to be necessary, extreme care should be exercised in form and content. Even if you have to pay to have it done, send the letter in typed form. This is easier to read and makes a better impression upon busy school officials. Write your letter in first-draft form, then polish and repolish, checking words and their spelling until the letter is in correct form and conveys precisely what you want to say. Avoid the lengthy letter and the breezy or smart-alecky type of communication. Make the letter a personal one, addressed to the school official by name and position. Avoid at all costs the "To whom it may concern" salutation. Here is an example of a succinct, yet adequate, letter of application:

Dr. Charles E. Heath
Superintendent of Schools
Suburbia, Illinois

Dear Dr. Heath:

I submit herewith my application for the position of teacher of mathematics in the Suburbia High School. My interest in the position is based upon two considerations: (1) This is the teaching field for which I have prepared and in which I feel that I am competent. (2) I have studied carefully the policies and teaching climate in your school system and am convinced that they are superior.

My credentials are being sent to you, under separate cover, by the Central State College Placement Bureau. Should you desire additional references or other information, I shall be glad to supply them. Too, I shall be pleased to come for an interview if you desire.

Cordially yours,

James Appleton

The Letter May Be Important

The letter is the personal representative of the applicant. A misspelled, poorly written letter is likely to jeopardize chances of employment. No matter how many times it must be rewritten, and regardless of the amount of dictionary work that is involved, it is important that the letter be free of typographical errors, grammatical errors, and misspelled words.

At one time, school employing officials insisted that letters be written in the candidate's own handwriting. Many officials now seem to prefer typewritten letters because of their greater compactness and readability.

The important thing seems to be to present the best effect possible.

Commercial Agencies

Beginning teachers seldom have need to use a commercial teachers' agency. College placement bureaus feel responsible for helping all the current graduates to secure positions. The new crop is, therefore, sometimes pushed at the expense of the old. Experienced teachers sometimes find, although not often, that they get less consideration from their college bureaus than do the beginners. Commercial agencies are, therefore, more for those who have been teaching several years than for the ones seeking their first positions.

Beginners who wish to secure positions in states other than the one in which they received their training often find commercial agencies of value. Some college bureaus do not extend their efforts further than the borders of the state. The commercial agency is likely to operate on a regional or national, rather than a state, basis.

Cost is the chief disadvantage of the commercial agency. Ordinarily, 5 or 6 per cent of the first year's salary is charged.

Other Aids in Finding a Job

For making application to school districts in other states, superintendents' names and addresses can be obtained from the latest edition of *Education Directory*, Part 2, "Public School Systems." [4]

The United States Employment Service provides assistance, without cost, to applicants for teaching jobs. It maintains some 1,800 local and state offices and works closely with college and university placement bureaus and state school systems. Through its clearinghouse arrangement, teachers may be in touch with vacancies wherever they exist in the United States.

A number of state departments of education and state education associations maintain placement or listing services for teachers. Most of these charge placement fees. The following state departments of education maintain teacher-placement services (address is the capital city): Alabama, Alaska, Georgia, Idaho, Louisiana, Maine, Massachusetts, Minnesota, Mississippi, New Hampshire, New Jersey, New Mexico, North Dakota, Oklahoma, Pennsylvania, Utah, Vermont, and Wyoming.

The following state education associations maintain placement or listing services for teachers (address is the capital city, unless otherwise indicated): California (Burlingame; Los Angeles for southern section), Colorado, Illinois, Iowa, Kentucky (Louisville), New Hampshire, North Carolina, Oregon (Portland), South Carolina, Texas, Vermont, Washington (Seattle), and West Virginia.[5] Also, NEA has now established a teacher-position listing service called NEA*-Search.

Use of References

It is customary to list a number of references when writing a letter of

---

[4] See *Education Directory*, Part 2, "Public School Systems," published annually by the U.S. Department of Health, Education, and Welfare, Office of Education, and available from the U.S. Government Printing Office.

[5] National Education Association, Research Division, "Obtaining a Teaching Position in the Public Schools," Research Memo 1961-27. Washington, D.C.: The Association, June, 1961, 33 pp.

application and when registering with a college placement bureau or a commercial teachers' agency.

These references should, as far as possible, be persons who have observed the candidate's teaching or have watched him work with children in informal situations such as camp or scout work, recreation activities, or church schools. Next in value are the testimonials of employers or businessmen for whom candidates have worked. The recommendations of college or high school teachers have great weight. Of doubtful influence in employment are landladies, colleagues, and neighbors.

It is only common courtesy to ask permission of a person whose name is to be used as reference. He will feel much more like affirmative statements and will probably give a better recommendation if he has been consulted in advance.

The Contract Form [6]

A more complete discussion of contracts is included in Chapter 11. Here we shall consider only general contract procedures.

There can usually be no legal employment without a written contract. While in a few instances oral contracts have been upheld by the courts, oral agreements are difficult to enforce. Teachers should insist upon written contracts and should read them rather carefully before signing.

A contract need not be lengthy or complex. About all that it needs to do is to state the names of the parties, the times of beginning and ending work, the tasks to be performed, and the salary to be paid. To be valid, a contract must be signed by the teacher and by authorized representatives of the board of education.

Contracts that carry a clause permitting cancellation by either party on thirty days' notice are not satisfactory. Many teachers have them, though, and apparently are generally satisfied with such an arrangement.

It is best to watch for clauses such as, "The amount of salary paid may be reduced at any time if the district is short of funds." A statement like this is not good for the teacher, even if the district will probably never use this power.

It is also wise to be sure that no unexpected duties are specified. Teachers sometimes have had to coach senior plays or act as advisers to the school paper because they did not read their contracts. The duties were specified there but were not noted.

REFERENCES

ARCHER, CLIFFORD P., "Induction of New Teachers," in Harris, Chester

[6] A contract, as contrasted with a license, is a legal document, binding the school board and the teacher to certain conditions of employment. A contract is for the protection of the teacher and the employing school district against capricious action.

(ed.) *Encyclopedia of Educational Research,* 3rd ed. New York: Macmillan Company, 1960, p. 705.

"Beginning Teacher; Symposium," *NEA Journal,* October, 1965, *54*:16–31.

CHAMBERLAIN, LEO M., and KINDRED, LESLIE W., *The Teacher and School Organization,* 3rd ed. New York: Prentice-Hall, 1958, Chap. 6, "Securing a Position," pp. 106–33.

DROPKIN, S., and TAYLOR, M., "Perceived Problems of Beginning Teachers and Related Factors," *Journal of Teacher Education,* December, 1963, *14*:384–390.

HALL, ROY M., and VINCENT, ANTONIO M., "Staff—Selection and Appointment," in Harris, Chester (ed.) *Encyclopedia of Educational Research,* 3rd ed. New York: Macmillan Company, 1960, pp. 1375–78.

KAUFMAN, BEL, "Real World of the Beginning Teacher," *NEA Journal,* October, 1965, *54*:16–22.

NICHOLSON, J. C., "Placement Services of State Education Associations," *NEA Journal,* April, 1959, *48*:46.

NATIONAL EDUCATION ASSOCIATION, American Association for Health, Physical Education, and Recreation, *Fit to Teach.* Washington, D.C.: The Association, 1957.

NATIONAL EDUCATION ASSOCIATION, American Association of School Administrators, *Off to a Good Start: Teacher Orientation.* Washington, D.C.: The Association, 1956.

NATIONAL EDUCATION ASSOCIATION, Department of Classroom Teachers, *Thoughts for the New Teacher.* Washington, D.C.: The Association, 1965.

NATIONAL EDUCATION ASSOCIATION, National Commission on Teacher Education and Professional Standards, *The Assignment and Misassignment of American Teachers.* Washington, D.C.: The Association, 1965, 68 pp.

———, *The Real World of the Beginning Teacher.* Washington, D.C.: The Association, 1965.

———, *The Education of Teachers: Certification,* Report of the San Diego Conference. Washington, D.C.: The Commission, 1961.

NATIONAL EDUCATION ASSOCIATION, Research Division. "Assigning the New Teacher; Teacher Opinion Poll," *NEA Journal,* October, 1964, *53*:68.

"Orientation of New Teachers" (Symposium), *NEA Journal,* May, 1958, *47*:292–99.

RHODES, FRED G., and PECKHAM, DOROTHY R., "Evaluation of Beginning Teachers: Pointers and Opinions," *Journal of Teacher Education,* March, 1960, *11*:55–60.

STINNETT, T. M., *A Manual on Certification Requirements for School Personnel in the United States,* 1967 ed. National Education Association, National Commission on Teacher Education and Professional Standards, Washington, D.C.: The Association, 1967, Chap. III.

6: Opportunities for Advancement in Teaching

*T*he professional person is, of course, interested in advancement. However, different persons have different ideas as to what constitutes advancement. Some teachers want college teaching positions. Others want to advance to public school administrative positions such as principalships or superintendencies. There are many who prefer to remain classroom teachers but want to move into better-paying positions. There are many who do not want any positions other than the ones that they hold, but who wish to render better service to the children and the communities with which they are associated. This is especially true of classroom teachers, but presently salary schedules have not reached the levels where the pull of higher-paying jobs can be wholly ignored. As teaching acquires more and more of the characteristics of a profession, professional advancement will be considered more and more as growth in the ability to render high-quality services in the classroom, rather than as promotion to administrative positions, and salary schedules will tend to conform to this concept. We shall first be concerned with what each kind of teacher may do in order to advance professionally. Afterward we shall describe some general rules for securing advancement in almost any kind of position.

The Real Meaning of Professional Advancement

It is unfortunate that, among the teachers and the public, the concept is all too common that promotion, advancement, and success in the teaching profession depend solely upon the achievement of administrative positions. This concept has developed because of two factors. The first factor is that there has been too large a differential between remuneration for skilled teaching and that for skilled administration. The second factor is the imbalance that has been placed upon the relative value of the two in the educational process. The operation of an educational program has all too often, in the public mind, been considered as synonymous with that of a large business enterprise, where the top executives originate policy on which the enterprise prospers or fails and where, therefore, the top executives are paid fabulous salaries—fabulous in comparison to the average workers in the enterprise.

That concept for schools is not tenable, and is rapidly giving way to the cooperative plan in which all professional workers have a creative part. This newer concept will tend increasingly to dignify the work of the teacher, to lessen the gap between teaching and administrative salaries, and to assure satisfactory professional advancement within the teaching ranks. Thus, skilled teachers may concentrate more and more upon becoming still better teachers, rather than seeking the sense of success in administrative positions. Particularly will this development tend to be accelerated as the competence of all teachers reaches professional levels. Of course, schools will always require skilled administrators, and there will continue to be pay differentials for such positions, but the differentials for such positions will tend to grow smaller, and administration will tend to serve as a coordinator of staff resources rather than the exclusive determiner of policy.

To sit behind a desk, answer the telephone, and talk with visitors looks easy. It does not appear hard to dictate to a stenographer, give directions to the janitors, conduct teachers' meetings, scold youngsters, walk up and down halls, and visit classrooms. These are the usual things that teachers and students observe to be the duties of administrators. They often are not aware of such things as the many night meetings that must be attended, the weekends spent on budgets, correspondence, and reports, the stormy meetings with disgruntled parents, the criticism of board members and patrons, the worries over pupil delinquency, the multitudinous paper work, the fear of losing one's position, and the feeling of always sitting on a powder keg. The prestige, the salary, the lack of a fixed working schedule, and the opportunity to travel about to attend educational meetings are all fine. Some of the other things that accompany an administrative position are anything but play. Administration is not a job for a thin-skinned, emotional individual. It is not a task for a quick-tempered, prejudiced, narrow person. The job requires real emotional and intellectual balance.

In the final analysis, the most appropriate kind of professional advancement is that which makes the best use of the individual teacher's unique talents. Not all good teachers can become equally good administrators.

TYPES OF POSITIONS IN EDUCATION

To consider the many opportunities for advancement, it is necessary to look at the vast array of positions in education and the pay differentials. The following is a comprehensive list, although by no means all-inclusive, of positions in the field of education. Some overlapping will occur in the several categories.

Administration. Superintendent of schools, associate and assistant superintendent, director of personnel, director of research, curriculum director, director of guidance, director of counseling services, director of business management, director of public relations, attendance officer, high school principal, assistant principal, elementary school principal, assistant elementary school principal.

Supervisory (usually classified as administration). Supervisors of special subjects (music, art, physical education, vocation education), general supervisor (elementary or secondary), supervisor of academic fields (English, science and math, social science, foreign languages).

Special or Auxiliary School Services. School psychologist, school dental hygienist, school doctor, school nurse, guidance counselor, school dentist, librarian, child-welfare and attendance officer.

Special Teachers. Teachers of homemaking, industrial arts, lip reading (for hard-of-hearing children and adults), mentally retarded, music, nursing education, partially sighted children, physical education, public safety and accident prevention, speech arts, correction of speech defects, adult education, military service and tactics, exchange teacher.

Elementary Schools. Teacher in self-contained classroom, teacher of one or more subjects in a departmental school, teacher of special subjects (music, art, physical education), teacher of exceptional children (special education; see list under Special Teachers), librarian, speech correctionist, teacher of accelerated groups (talented), team teaching member.

Secondary Schools. Teacher of academic subject or field, head of subject or field department, coach, teacher of special fields (music, art, dramatics, journalism, physical education, vocational subjects, commercial subjects, driver training), guidance counselor, librarian, team teaching member.

College. President, vice-president, teacher (with ranks of lecturer, instructor, assistant professor, associate professor, professor), head of department (English, mathematics, etc.), supervisory teacher in campus laboratory school, director of laboratory school, director of student teaching, dean, dean of academic affairs, dean of a particular college, dean of students, dean of women, dean of men, provost, dean of admissions, registrar, business manager, director of research, director of public relations, director of placement, director of alumni relations.

State and National Education Agencies

State Departments of Education. Commissioner or state superintendent, deputy and assistant commissioner or superintendent, directors of divisions (instruction, school finance, teacher education and certification, vocational education, research, pupil accounting), supervisors (general), supervisor of subjects or fields (science, English), supervisor of vocational subjects, supervisor of guidance, supervisor of textbooks, supervisor of audio-visual instruction.

U.S. Office of Education. Commissioner of education, deputy commissioner, assistant commissioner (several categories: higher education, secondary education, elementary education, international education), directors (research, school statistics, school plants and facilities, counseling services), consultants and specialists (teacher education, science, mathematics, foreign languages, elementary education), specialized personnel to administer such federal programs as the National Defense Education Act, vocational aid to states, federally impacted areas aid. In addition, the federal government employs thousands of educators in its various units, largely recruited from colleges and universities.

Industrial, Commercial, and Noneducational Nonprofit Organizations. Because of the importance of education, a vast number of business and nonprofit organizations employ education experts, consultants, and advisers. In addition, industrial firms now are the chief competitors for skilled personnel in research.

Professional Organizations of Teachers. The NEA, state education associations, and local education associations, as well as several hundred national, specialized associations, employ many thousands of skilled people from education.

The National Education Association. Executive secretary, deputy executive secretary, six assistant executive secretaries (business, legislation, field service, information services, instructional services, and professional development and welfare); executive secretaries, associate and assistant secretaries, and directors of some thirty NEA commissions, departments, and divisions. And 35 independent departments employ executive secretaries, associate and assistant secretaries, consultants, and specialists.

The more than 50 state education associations employ personnel in categories to the NEA.

Federal legislation enacted in recent years has created thousands of new jobs—in the U.S. Office of Education, work with deprived children, Head Start programs, Job Corps, Teacher Corps, and Peace Corps.

OPPORTUNITIES FOR EMPLOYMENT

The Need for Public School Personnel

The shortage of teachers for the elementary and secondary schools has been serious since the early 1940's. The shortage continues and, from all evidence, will extend well into the next decade. Although it appears that a balance could be reached at the high school level soon if a larger proportion of those completing preparation each year took teaching jobs the following fall, the situation at the elementary school level is much more grave. In 1966, for example, a total of 124,615 high school teachers were graduated; only 76,304 were graduated in elementary education. The latter is just about one-half the number needed, even assuming that all of the graduating group took teaching jobs. We know from data in preceding years that, of the number of graduates prepared for teaching, about one-third will not go into teaching the September following their graduation. Thus, as a rough estimate, it may be assumed that only about 42,000 of the newly prepared high school teachers and about 25,000 of the newly prepared elementary school teachers will actually become teachers. It has been estimated that for the school year 1966–67 the total shortage of elementary and secondary school teachers is about 23,000, including all needs, and that for the two irreducible needs (to replace teachers leaving the profession for all reasons, and to staff new classrooms to handle increased enrollments) the minimum need is for 170,000 new teachers.[1] Thus, the opportunities for employment and promotion in public teaching appear to be extremely favorable for years to come.

The Need for College Teachers

With the drastically increasing enrollments in colleges and universities now in full swing, pronounced shortages of qualified teachers are in sight for the next decade in almost all fields. The present nature of the shortage is indicated by the declining levels of preparation of new teachers employed each year since 1953–54 by colleges and universities. These figures can only mean that new college teachers are being employed before they complete what is considered standard preparation, or that colleges are recruiting teachers from high schools.

In 1953–54 the NEA Research Division reported the preparation levels of the total full-time staff of colleges and universities (637 institutions) as follows: doctor's degree, 40.5 per cent; master's degree plus at least one year of graduate study, 20.9 per cent; master's degree, 28.2 per cent; less

[1] National Education Association, Research Division, *Teacher Supply and Demand in Public Schools,* 1966, Research Report 1966 R-16. Washington, D.C.: The Association, 1966, 80 pp.

than master's degree, 10.4 per cent. Some measure of the extent of the college teacher shortage, particularly of its impact upon the inability of colleges and universities to maintain accepted levels of preparation in the employment of new teachers, can be gleaned from Table 17 (p. 118). The percentage of new college teachers employed who possessed the doctor's degree declined from 31.4 in 1953–54 to 25.8 in 1960–61, while the percentage of the other categories, except one, increased. By 1964–65, this percentage increased slightly.

The Demand for New College Teachers

The best measure, however, of the opportunities for the future in college teaching is to be found in the unprecedented annual demands for the next decade. According to Table 18, a total of 346,800 new college teachers will be needed in the period 1959–60 to 1969–70; the average annual demand being about 30,000. The total production of university graduates with the doctor's degree in 1962–64 was 22,269, of which less than half continued or entered college teaching positions. These figures reveal how wide is the gap between college-teacher supply and the demand, if the doctor's degree is the criterion. While this is not the case, it is true that colleges and universities would prefer to employ persons with doctor's degrees. Thus, the gap between the number of new college teachers needed and the number available with doctor's degrees is a real measure of the potential demand.

Salary Differentials in Educational Positions

A key measure of advancement in any occupation or profession is the level of remuneration. This is not an infallible guideline to advancement, but it is an important one. Table 19 indicates the differentials in the mean maximum salaries of several categories of positions in the public schools for the school year 1966–67. The mean maximum pay for classroom teachers was $9,788, whereas that of supervisory and administrative personnel ranged from $13,295 to $26,017. As a general rule, teachers are paid on a nine or ten months' basis, administrative personnel on a twelve-month basis.

Although it ought not to be necessary for the skilled classroom teacher to leave the classroom and seek an administrative or supervisory post in order to advance to an adequate salary level, unfortunately that is still the case in most situations. The trend is quite definitely toward index salary schedules that provide salary maximums for teachers with the master's degree or above, which are equal to or in excess of some administrative salaries. But as long as this is not the universal practice, most teachers will consider administrative and supervisory positions as advancements. The same situation obtains at the college and university

TABLE 17 *Distribution of Total College and University Staffs in 1953–54 and of New Teachers in 1953–54 Through 1964–65, by Level of Preparation*

YEAR AND GROUP	DOCTOR'S DEGREE		MASTER'S DEGREE PLUS AT LEAST ONE YEAR		MASTER'S DEGREE		LESS THAN MASTER'S DEGREE		TOTAL	
	Number	Per Cent	Number	Per Cent	Number	Per Cent	Number	Per Cent	Number	Per Cent
Total staff in 1953–54[a]	23,768	40.5%	12,266	20.9%	16,582	28.2%	6,103	10.4%	58,719	100%
New teachers in 1953–54[b]	1,329	31.4	770	18.2	1,363	32.2	770	18.2	4,232	100
New teachers in 1954–55[b]	1,333	28.4	878	18.7	1,577	33.6	906	19.3	4,694	100
New teachers in 1955–56[c]	1,692	26.7	1,128	17.8	2,243	35.4	1,274	20.1	6,337	100
New teachers in 1956–57[c]	1,952	23.5	1,504	18.1	2,933	35.3	1,919	23.1	8,308	100
New teachers in 1957–58[d]	2,354	25.3	1,505	16.2	3,409	36.7	2,025	21.8	9,293	100
New teachers in 1958–59[d]	2,161	23.8	1,703	18.7	3,339	36.7	1,897	20.8	9,100	100
New teachers in 1959–60[e]	2,650	25.9	2,034	19.9	3,788	37.1	1,749	17.1	10,221	100
New teachers in 1960–61[e]	2,886	25.8	2,234	20.0	4,116	36.8	1,948	17.4	11,184	100
New teachers in 1964–65[f]	4,361	27.1	3,381	21.1	6,306	39.3	2,011	12.5	16,059	100

Source: National Education Association, Research Division, *Teacher Supply and Demand in Universities, Colleges, and Junior Colleges, 1959–60 and 1960–61 and 1963–64 and 1964–65,* Research Reports 1961-R12 and 1965-R4. Washington, D.C.: The Association, 1961 and 1965, Table 4, p. 15 and Table 2, p. 13, respectively.

[a] Based on reports from 637 universities and colleges.
[b] Based on reports from 656 universities and colleges.
[c] Based on reports from 827 universities and colleges.
[d] Based on reports from 936 universities and colleges.
[e] Based on reports from 1,085 universities and colleges.
[f] Based on reports from 1,084 universities and colleges.

level. Table 20 contains estimated median salaries of certain university teaching and administrative positions, with the teaching positions calculated on a twelve-month basis from the known figures for the academic year. This table will provide some rough comparisons of central tendencies in university salaries with those in the public schools as indicated in the preceding table.

OPPORTUNITIES FOR PROFESSIONAL ADVANCEMENT

After consideration is given to the many types of positions and the salary potentials, it is necessary to examine the advantages and disadvantages of the many areas.

College Teaching

Some students and many teachers look at college teaching through rose-colored glasses. It does have its good points, of course, but the job is not all "velvet" by any means. Before considering how a college teaching position may be secured, perhaps the advantages and disadvantages of college teaching should be analyzed.

In the way of advantages, college teaching has fairly short hours, although they are not as abbreviated as many people think. The teaching load in colleges and universities ranges from nine to eighteen hours per week. In the large universities, the usual load is from nine to twelve hours. In liberal arts colleges and teachers colleges the class load is somewhat heavier. The class load, however, is only part of the story. There are papers to be graded, marks to be assigned, and individual and group conferences to be held. In universities there are theses to direct, doctoral and master's examinations to conduct, and candidacy blanks to prepare. In all kinds of institutions of higher learning there is correspondence to answer and administrative details to handle. In all kinds of college positions, faculty personnel are expected to render service to the public and to the profession, to deliver speeches, to carry on research, and to publish articles and books. In every area of college teaching, considerable time is required to keep up with developments in one's field.

In other words, college teachers ordinarily lead busy lives; they are usually as occupied with required duties as are most professional workers, although they may not spend as many hours in the classroom with as many students. The desire for advancement to a college teaching position, on the assumption that the job is much easier than public school teaching, needs close examination.

TABLE 18 *Estimated Number of Full-Time University, College, and Junior-College Teachers Needed, by Field, 1959–60 Through 1969–70*

FIELD	PER CENT OF TOTAL	Full-time teachers 1958–59	ESTIMATED NUMBER OF				
			New full-time teachers needed, 1959–60 [a]	New full-time teachers needed, 1960–61 [a]	New full-time teachers needed, 1964–65 [a]	New full-time teachers needed, 1969–70 [a]	Total number of new full-time teachers needed 1959–70 inclusive [a]
Agriculture	4.4%	11,000	1,200	1,250	1,400	1,550	15,250
Biological sciences	5.9	14,750	1,600	1,650	1,850	2,100	20,450
Business and commerce	5.2	13,000	1,400	1,450	1,650	1,850	18,050
Education	7.5	18,750	2,000	2,100	2,400	2,700	26,000
Engineering	7.0	17,500	1,900	1,950	2,250	2,500	24,300
English	8.3	20,750	2,200	2,350	2,650	2,950	28,800
Fine arts (all)	10.8	27,000	2,900	3,000	3,450	3,850	37,450
Music	5.1	12,750	1,350	1,400	1,650	1,850	17,700
Speech and dramatics	2.7	6,750	750	750	850	950	9,350
Others	3.0	7,500	800	850	950	1,050	10,400
Foreign languages	5.2	13,000	1,400	1,450	1,650	1,850	18,050
Health sciences [b]	3.7	9,250	1,000	1,050	1,200	1,300	12,850
Home economics	2.4	6,000	650	650	750	850	8,300
Industrial and vocational arts	2.4	6,000	650	650	750	850	8,300
Library science	2.1	5,250	550	600	650	750	7,300

Mathematics	4.0	10,000	1,100	1,100	1,300	1,450	13,850
Philosophy	1.4	3,500	400	400	450	500	4,850
Physical and health education	5.3	13,250	1,450	1,500	1,700	1,900	18,400
Physical sciences (all)	8.1	20,250	2,150	2,250	2,600	2,900	28,100
Chemistry	3.8	9,500	1,000	1,050	1,200	1,350	13,200
Physics	2.6	6,500	700	750	850	950	9,000
Others	1.7	4,250	450	450	550	600	5,900
Psychology	2.5	6,250	650	700	800	900	8,650
Religion	1.4	3,500	400	400	450	500	4,850
Social sciences (all)	10.9	27,250	2,900	3,000	3,450	3,900	37,800
History	3.4	8,500	900	950	1,050	1,250	11,800
Economics	2.5	6,250	650	700	800	900	8,650
Political science	1.7	4,250	450	450	550	600	5,900
Sociology	1.7	4,250	450	450	550	600	5,900
Others	1.6	4,000	450	450	500	550	5,550
Others	1.5	3,750	400	400	500	550	5,200
All fields	100.0%	250,000	26,900	27,900	31,900	35,700	346,800

Source: National Education Association, Research Division, *Teacher Supply and Demand in Universities, Colleges, and Junior Colleges, 1959-60 and 1960-61*, Research Report 1961-R12. Washington, D.C.: The Association, 1961, Table 30, p. 55.

Note: The estimates offered in this table assume that (a) enrollments will increase at a consistent rate, (b) the number of teachers in service will increase at a slower pace, bringing about (c) steady increase in student-teacher ratio, and (d) the rate of annual replacements will remain constant.

[a] Presuming no change in the field-by-field distribution of all full-time teachers.
[b] Excluding dentistry and medicine.

Perhaps one of the principal advantages of college teaching is its security. Once established, college professors seldom lose their positions. Although somewhat higher, on the average, than that of his colleagues in the public schools, the college teacher's salary is not what it should be; it has not kept pace with the economic gains of many other groups of workers.

TABLE 19   *Mean Maximum Scheduled Salaries of Certain Public School Personnel, 1966–67*

Position	Mean Maximum Scheduled Salary
Classroom Teachers	$ 9,788
Supervising Principals	
Elementary	13,295
Junior High School	14,058
Senior High School	17,973
Counselors	10,960
Deans	11,764
Central Office Administrators	
Supervisors	13,572
Directors	16,011
Assistant Superintendents	19,246
Superintendents	26,017

Source: National Education Association, Research Division, *Salary Schedules for Administrative Personnel, 1966–67*, Research Report 1967-R3. Washington, D.C.: The Association, 1967. Adapted from Table 14, p. 32.

How does one become a college teacher? A high degree of scholastic achievement is expected of the person who enters college teaching. It is considered desirable for prospective candidates for positions in teacher education to have had several years of elementary or secondary school teaching experience, although this is not a mandatory requirement. The prospective college teacher should work for the completion of the doctor's degree as soon as possible, particularly if he hopes to advance to the higher ranks of college teachers. This amount of preparation is considered standard, at least for advancement to the best positions, by most of the larger colleges and universities and by many of the smaller ones. If the prospective teacher can do some professional writing, it will help him to secure a position.

While there is no set formula, as a general rule the first position of a young college teacher is that of instructor, particularly if he has not completed the doctor's degree. With the doctor's degree, the starting point may be assistant professor. Next higher ranks are associate professor and

TABLE 20   *Mean Average Salaries in Colleges and
Universities for the Academic Year 1966–67*

Position	Universities	Liberal Arts Colleges	Junior Colleges	Technical Institutions
Professor	$15,610	$13,037	$12,009	$14,369
Associate Professor	11,373	10,362	10,518	11,019
Assistant Professor	9,295	8,673	8,767	9,204
Instructor	7,173	7,062	7,330	7,080

Source: Appendix Table 6, "Further Progress: The Economic Status of the Profession," *AAUP Bulletin,* 53:2 (Summer, 1967), p. 150.

professor. As a general rule, full professorships carrying tenure and higher salary provisions are reserved for those with long years of teaching or those who have performed distinguished services to the institution. Among the administrative positions that are considered as top opportunities for college teachers, are heads of departments, directors of divisions, assistant deans, deans, and presidents.

ADVANCEMENT OPPORTUNITIES IN THE PUBLIC SCHOOLS

Moving to a Larger School System

At one time most teachers followed a regular plan of progression through school systems of various sizes. They usually started out in a rural school or in a school located in a small village. After two or three years they secured positions in large villages or small cities. Some eventually taught in large cities. Some teachers achieved their goals after only one change of position, while others worked their way to metropolitan centers by means of several steps. Teachers have sought positions in larger cities because of higher salaries, more cultural opportunities, less interference with their private lives, better working conditions, greater security, and increased prestige. Some of these advantages were more imagined than real. It is doubtful if the larger cities have ever had all the advantages that have been claimed of them.

At the present time this migration of teachers to cities has been somewhat checked. There has been such a shortage of teachers since the beginning of World War II that many beginners have been able to secure their first positions in the schools of large cities. With the general increase in state financial aid, smaller schools often have been able to pay about as good salaries as the school systems in large cities. Although the salaries paid in large cities, in general, continue to be above those in the small communities, the gap is closing; and all factors considered, the existing discrepancy is not as great as it seems.

Transferring from Elementary to High School Teaching

In the past there has often been a decided tendency on the part of public school teachers to select the high school field in preference to the elementary field. Furthermore, there has been a tendency to regard the shifting of an elementary school teacher to the high school as a promotion. This was due in some measure to an early policy whereby differentiated salary schedules existed. In part, this was because lower levels of preparation were formerly required for elementary teachers. Today the general rule is to require the same level of preparation for all public school teachers and to pay all teachers with equal preparation and experience the same salary. Since about 1946 or 1947 there has been greater demand for elementary school teachers than for high school teachers, and this condition will apparently continue for many years.

With the above factors for elementary and high school teachers rapidly becoming equalized, and with a growing appreciation by the public of the importance of the work of the elementary teacher, the old idea that professional advancement of teachers was involved in being transferred to high school teaching has become obsolete.

Securing Additional Preparation

Graduate work beyond the bachelor's degree is necessary today if a teacher hopes to secure advancement in salary and prestige, either by remaining within the system in which he is located, or by moving to a larger center of population or to another type of specialized job. For many years teachers for the elementary schools were certified on the basis of one or two years of normal-school preparation beyond the high school level. By the beginning of World War II the standards had risen to the point where most states granted certification to high school teachers only after the completion of a four-year college program of professional preparation, and at least nine states enforced this requirement for elementary teachers.

It has been pointed out that in 1967 a total of 47 states and territories (including the District of Columbia) were requiring completion of the bachelor's degree for the lowest regular elementary school teacher's certificate, and all of the states were requiring at least the completion of the bachelor's degree for high school certificates. Two states (Arizona and California) and the District of Columbia required five years of college preparation for beginning high school teachers. The time is not far off when all states will require a minimum of four years of college preparation for all beginning teachers, and there is some evidence that completion of the fifth year of preparation for permanent or full professional certification will eventually become a universal requirement among the states. The teacher who wishes to advance, therefore, cannot afford to stop after completing the four-year degree program. He must secure education above the minimum requirements specified by the state in which he serves.

The high school teacher who chooses to remain in classroom work rather than to enter the field of administration will ordinarily take his graduate work in some field of subject-matter specialty, although this is not necessarily standard. Some school systems prefer a master's degree in the subject matter taught. Others accept equally the degree in education. It is usually felt that the work in education is more helpful on the job than highly specialized courses in a subject-matter field. For this reason, many school systems willingly accept a master's degree in education, even though the teacher may be handling classes in such subjects as English, chemistry, a foreign language, or mathematics. The high school teacher who is preparing to start work toward a master's degree should probably inquire in his school system in order to find out the area of specialization that is expected. Also, it is desirable to check the certification requirements of the state in which he is teaching. There is a growing trend by states to specify the type of preparation required for certificates based upon the master's degree. If a subject-matter area is specified, the candidate can then take education as the minor field. Most elementary school teachers take the master's degree in education.

Administrative Positions in the Public Schools

There are many opportunities for advancement into administrative positions in the public schools. With estimated increases in school enrollments between 1960 and 1975, a proportionate increase in administrative and supervisory positions will result. If the present ratio of professional positions other than classroom teaching—administrative and supervisory positions—is maintained (about fourteen teachers to one administrative or supervisory official), there will be an increase of some 30,000 in the number of such positions. The number of superintendents will not, of course, increase, but may decline with the consolidation of school districts.

The administrative, supervisory, and special school service positions to which teachers may aspire are listed earlier in this chapter. Promotion to administrative positions may come from within a system or it may come as a result of transfer to another city. Formerly almost all school administrators secured advancement by beginning in small towns and making a series of changes until they achieved their desired goal. Today promotion from within the larger systems has become more common. In cities the elementary and high school principalships are frequently filled by promoting a teacher or assistant principal. It is not necessarily good practice, but many superintendents secure their positions as a result of promotion from the high school principalship to the superintendency. Because promotion comes more frequently from within the system, it follows that, in general, the larger the system, the greater the chances for promotion. This does not mean that a teacher who wishes to advance must enter service in a large city, but it does mean that one must be careful in choosing the place where he teaches. In almost every case, promotion to administrative position comes only after several years of successful teaching plus additional specific preparation.

Early in his career a teacher who decides upon the administrative field should also decide the direction in which he plans to go. He should decide whether he prefers a principalship or a superintendency, or some field of supervision. If a superintendency is his goal, then it is advisable to secure some elementary school teaching experience. For the teacher who plans to follow the administrative field, graduate work is even more important than it is for the teacher who plans to remain in classroom work. In most states now, superintendents and high school and elementary school principals must have earned at least the master's degree of preparation.

TABLE 21   *Minimum Number of College Years of Specified Preparation Required for Administrative Certificates by the States and Territories*

Number of College Years (or degrees) of Specified Preparation Required	NUMBER OF STATES AND TERRITORIES REQUIRING		
	Elementary School Principals	Secondary School Principals	Superintendents of schools
Seven	0	0	1
Six	3	3	19
More than five, but less than six	8	8	4
Five	35	37	26
More than four, but less than five	3	2	0
Four	2	1	0
No Certificate issued	1	1	2
TOTAL	52	52	52

Source: T. M. Stinnett. *A Manual on Certification Requirements for School Personnel in the United States,* 1967 ed. Washington, D.C.: National Education Association, National Commission on Teacher Education and Professional Standards, 1967, Table 2, p. 19.

Many of the larger city school systems now limit their choice of super-intendents to persons who have a doctor's degree. This is a new and rapidly growing trend. For persons in administrative work it is ordinarily better to secure the graduate degree in the field of education rather than in some subject-matter specialty. Not all teachers and school administrators should expect to secure the doctorate, but every person who expects to continue in school work should plan to complete the work for the master's degree within a reasonably short time after he has graduated from college. Many experienced and skilled teachers have found themselves barred from further promotion by virtue of their failure to acquire a graduate degree.

SOME GENERALIZATIONS ABOUT PROFESSIONAL ADVANCEMENT

It may sound axiomatic, but the first requirement for advancement in school work is that the individual should be a good teacher. This is a factor too often overlooked. Statements are sometimes made to the effect that such and such a man secured his promotion to a larger superintend-ency or to some other good position because of his activity in the Rotary Club or a similar organization. Generally such statements are motivated by jealousy. It is true that advancement may come as a result of an activity other than teaching, but outside work such as one does in Rotary Clubs merely attracts attention to the individual. If the attention attracted in this way is not backed up by good work on the job, the activity is not likely to lead to success. Leadership in social organizations comes largely as a result of having an attractive personality, but there must be a balance between personal popularity and actual success on the job. The teacher who wishes to advance will not neglect his teaching work in order to secure social recognition, nor should he devote so much attention to his teaching that he has no time for outside social activities. Of course, it is important to make community contacts. On the other hand, there are few, if any, instances where a person became a successful school administrator without first becoming a successful teacher.

More About Graduate Preparation. Attention has already been called to the need for graduate degrees both in the field of college work and in the field of school administration. The fact that, in teaching, the individual is now expected to complete more than a bachelor's degree cannot be over-emphasized. Teachers' salary schedules are now generally set up to provide differentials for additional college years of preparation. School administrators are generally required to have the master's degree for initial service, and six years of college work or completion of the doctor's degree will eventually come to be required for full professional qualification. In college work an individual without the doctor's degree works under a continual handicap.

Ordinarily the master's degree or a fifth year of college preparation may be acquired without the necessity of taking time off from the regular school work. The year of graduate work can be completed by attendance at summer sessions. It is also possible to secure some credit toward the master's degree by taking extension courses or courses in graduate centers. Most colleges and universities now arrange their graduate extension courses so that some of their work will be offered in the late afternoons, evenings, or on Saturdays. This permits those living within driving distance of the college to take further graduate work while they remain on the job. The person who wishes to acquire the Ph.D. or Ed.D. degree will ordinarily need to spend at least a full year in residence at a college accredited for graduate work. This means taking time off from the regular job.

Professional Affiliations. The advisability of teachers affiliating with one or more professional organizations and of attending meetings of these organizations has been previously stressed. Such membership applies to the local teachers' club or local education organization, to the state and national education organizations, and to the appropriate special-interest associations. The special-interest association that the teacher joins should, of course, represent the field of his specialty. Examples of special-interest associations are the National Council of Teachers of English, the National Council of Teachers of Mathematics, the National Science Teachers Association, the Modern Language Association of America, the American Industrial Arts Association, the American Association for Health, Physical Education, and Recreation, the Association for Supervision and Curriculum Development, the Council for Exceptional Children, Music Educators National Conference, National Association of Deans of Women, National Council for the Social Studies, National Business Education Association, or any one of many other similar organizations. For the superintendent, there is the American Association of School Administrators, and for the principal there are a number of organizations including the NEA Department of Elementary School Principals and the National Association of Secondary School Principals.

It has been pointed out that there are many educational organizations. Because there are so many, the teacher or administrator must exercise considerable judgment as to what organizations to join. Some persons make the mistake of affiliating with too many organizations, but more often the teacher merely affiliates with the state education association without giving consideration to other professional organizations that may be of great value. Activity in one or more so-called scholarly organizations is likely to attract attention to the teacher that may be of value at a later date. It is advisable for a teacher to affiliate with at least one professional education organization, other than the state and national teachers' associations, and to participate vigorously in its activities.

If the teacher has something to contribute, it is also advisable to write articles for the various professional educational magazines. By doing this, the teacher improves himself professionally and shares his professional experience with his colleagues. Almost every teacher does something that would be worth reporting in a magazine article. The report may cover a particular method of teaching a certain subject, or it may discuss some professional problem connected with teaching. In the field of administration, articles by school administrators are published in the *Nation's Schools, Overview* and the *American School Board Journal.* In elementary education, there are the *Elementary School Journal* and the *National Elementary Principal;* in the secondary field there are the *School Review* and the *Bulletin of the National Association of Secondary School Principals.* The *NEA Journal* and journals of the state education associations publish articles on all levels of teaching. *Phi Delta Kappan, School and Society, Educational Forum,* and *Saturday Review* publish general articles on education. Some of the journals for college teachers are *Higher Education, Liberal Education,* the *AAUP Bulletin,* and the *Journal of Teacher Education.* In addition, most of the special-interest or subject-field associations —mathematics, social studies, science—publish journals. These are only a few of the magazines publishing articles by teachers. Ordinarily there is no pay connected with this sort of writing. The reward comes in the form of personal satisfaction, the feeling of having made a contribution to one's profession, and, of course, a sense of increased prestige.

Do the Small Job Well. The teacher who wishes advancement should discharge with extreme care small tasks assigned as part of committee work or the preparation of a report. Most of us like to let the other fellow do these chores. But nothing so quickly attracts favorable attention as the careful execution of a thankless task. For example, a young teacher might be given a comparatively minor committee chairmanship in the local state teachers' association. If he did an unusually good piece of work, it would attract attention to him. Likewise, on a local level, doing a good job with a small assignment will lead to bigger and better assignments in the future. It is often possible to secure administrative experience while still a teacher by assisting a superintendent or principal with some piece of detail work.

Speech Training and General Appearance. Most teachers can profit by speech training. This may involve merely an effort to improve the speaking voice, or it may involve training in public speaking. Almost all successful public school administrators possess considerable ability in the field of public speaking. Obviously, the ability to speak effectively is very important to a teacher or school administrator. Teaching involves conveying your ideas to some other person. This cannot be done successfully unless the individual has a good speaking voice and knows how to present ideas in public. A pleasing appearance is important if a teacher wishes to succeed. In general, the women observe the advice better than the men. It is important for the teacher to dress well, maintain good posture, and otherwise make a good appearance in public.

Expanding Opportunities. It has often been said that this is a man's world, and to a certain extent this is true in the field of education. There are relatively few women school superintendents and high school principals. In the elementary field many of the principalships are now filled by men. College teachers are predominantly men, and in 1960–61, for the first time in recent years, more than half of the high school teachers were men. This does not mean that there is no possibility of advancement for women in education. The situation is changing. The number of women in administrative-supervisory and special school service positions has been increasing rapidly in recent years. Opportunity for advancement for women in the field of education is expanding significantly.

Other Areas for Professional Advancement. Space has prevented the providing of a detailed description of the highly specialized professional positions existing in state and national education legal agencies, in the several hundred professional organizations in education, and in educational posts with business firms, foundations, and religious and charitable organizations. These are significant and rapidly expanding fields for highly competent people, all of whom are drawn from the lower schools and the colleges and universities. There are also many important opportunities in foreign posts. The federal government, through the International Cooperation Administration, sends many American educators to help with the development of school systems in foreign countries. The federal government also maintains some 300 schools in thirty-six foreign countries for children of our military personnel stationed overseas. These are known as Overseas Dependent Schools, in which about 6,000 American teachers are employed.[2]

There is, moreover, a new cluster of professional-advancement opportunities now developing for teachers. This cluster includes TV teaching and programmed teaching, team teaching, new federal programs, and teaching the deprived.

---

[2] For a description of opportunities for teachers in foreign posts, see T. M. Stinnett, *A Manual on Certification Requirements for School Personnel in the United States.* National Commission on Teacher Education and Professional Standards, National Education Association, Washington, D.C.: The Association, 1967, Chap. III, pp. 175–185.

REFERENCES

BURDIN, J. L., "Faculty Selection and Retention: A Quest for Quality," *Teachers College Journal*, January, 1965, *36*:185–187.

CHANDLER, B. J., *Education and the Teacher.* New York: Dodd, Mead and Company, 1961, Chap. 15, "Professional Opportunities in Teaching," pp. 351–371.

CUMMINS, ROBBERT E., "Operation: Growth," *Journal of Teacher Education*, March, 1959, *10*:86–87.

EDINGER, L., "Continuing Education for Teachers," *Journal of Teacher Education*, March, 1965, *16*:3–4.

HANSEN, KENNETH H., *High School Teaching.* Englewood Cliffs, New Jersey: Prentice-Hall, 1957, Chap. 14, "Growth in Teaching," pp. 394–404.

HORNBOSTEL, VICTOR O., "Promotion and Reassignment Within Systems," in CHESTER HARRIS (ed.) *Encyclopedia of Educational Research*, 3rd ed. New York: Macmillan Company, 1960, pp. 1365–1366.

HUDSON, J. R., "On Becoming a College Teacher," *Educational Record*, Summer, 1966, *47*:410–415.

NATIONAL EDUCATION ASSOCIATION, National Commission on Teacher Education and Professional Standards, *The Development of the Career Teacher: Professional Responsibility for Continuing Education*, Report of the 1963–64 Regional TEPS Conferences. Washington, D.C.: The Association, 1964.

———, *Remaking the World of the Career Teacher*, Report of the 1965–66 Regional TEPS Conferences. Washington, D.C.: The Association, 1966.

NATIONAL EDUCATION ASSOCIATION, Research Division, *Economic Status of Teachers in 1966–67*, Research Report 1967-R8. Washington, D.C.: The Association, 1967.

———, *Inservice Education of Teachers.* Washington, D.C.: The Association, 1966.

NATIONAL EDUCATION ASSOCIATION, Research Division and American Association of School Administrators, *Policies and Procedures in the Selection of Personnel for Administrative Positions*, Educational Research Service Circular No. 6, 1958. Washington, D.C.: The Association, June 1956.

RICHEY, R. W., *Planning for Teaching*, 3rd ed., New York: McGraw-Hill Book Company, 1963. Chap. 5, "Opportunities in Education," pp. 118–145.

TURNEY, D. and L. W. STONEKING. "Professional Sequence for the Development of Career Teachers," *Journal of Teacher Education*, September, 1965, *16*:281–285.

Part Three
PROFESSIONAL PERSONNEL POLICIES AND WORKING CONDITIONS

7: Professional Salary Policies for Teachers

Of all the professional problems with which teachers will have to deal, that of salaries is the most persistent and, perhaps, the most complex. It is a continuing problem, year after year, as the price index fluctuates and employment conditions change. It is a problem for which there are no easy or permanent answers. It is, therefore, imperative that every teacher assume responsibility for becoming knowledgeable about sound practices and acceptable procedures.

Since the establishment of the public schools in the United States, the question of teachers' pay has been a continuing issue. The question has not only been "What is adequate pay for teachers?" but other related problems have been as widely debated and as controversial. Among these related problems are: How is adequate pay for the individual teacher to be determined? Shall there be equal pay for equal work without regard to sex, level or field of teaching, the number of dependents? Should there be formal salary schedules, officially adopted and published by school boards, or should there be individual bargaining with teachers? Should there be merit salary provisions? Should there be extra pay for extra duties? Who should participate in the development of teachers' salary schedules? These are some but not all of the intense issues involved in the problem of determining and implementing salary policies for teachers.

In this chapter some of these issues will be discussed, with indications of discernible trends regarding them as reflected by current practices and policies of school boards. An effort will be made, too, to evaluate current practices and policies in the light of procedures advocated by the teaching profession.

That the problem of adequate pay for teachers has been a persistent one is indicated in the following statement:

The first teacher in the town of Northampton, Massachusetts, was fined 20 shillings for cursing. Perhaps his lack of restraint arose from the meagre six pounds he was voted in 1664 provided he taught at least six months of the year. Or his indignation may have come from his efforts to collect tuition since part of his income was derived from his authority "to tacke [tax] the benefit of his scollers." [1]

The custom of paying teachers in produce from the farm developed early in New England; when the public school movement spread westward, it became a common practice to pay teachers, in part, with board and room, provided on a rotating basis by the parents of the children attending the school.[2]

Since that time we have come a long way in the development of professional salary policies for teachers. The "hired hand" concept of teaching services has slowly given away to the recognition of these services as being of professional caliber. The hit-or-miss, hand-to-mouth plans of paying as little as possible to teachers has generally been replaced by carefully planned schedules designed to provide remuneration at professional levels. Although, admittedly, present schedules are not considered adequate by the public or by the profession, and there are still great diversities in the methods employed in developing them, great progress has been made, especially in recent years. This discussion will attempt to delineate that progress and to identify the current issues regarding the means of still further progress in professional salary policies for teachers.

Reasons for Salary Schedules

The profession has long advocated the development and adoption of formal salary schedules for teachers by each school board. Not until after World War I did school boards generally begin to abandon the practice of individual bargaining in favor of an official salary schedule.

There are several reasons for the advocacy by the profession of official salary schedules. In the first place, the profession has contended that individual bargaining for the services of an employee, in which the employer seeks to exploit the meat-and-bread necessity of the worker for the job, is not characteristic of the profession—that such practices tend to cheapen the status of the profession. Secondly, professional services cannot be secured by hammering down the remuneration to subsistence levels, or by

---

[1] Frank W. Hubbard and Hazel Davis, "The Construction of Salary Schedules for Teachers." *Harvard Educational Review,* Spring, 1952, 22:83.
[2] *Ibid.*

a type of bargaining that awards a job to the lowest bidder and gives a salary increase to the most persistent claimant.

The profession has contended that salary schedules for teachers should be formalized and officially adopted, based upon the rewards commonly applied to other comparable professions. The profession, too, has felt strongly that schedules thus developed, adopted, and publicized will contribute greatly to staff morale and services. The argument here is that if schedules are developed on the idea of paying teachers for their services, with recognition being given to the extent of their professional preparation and to their years of successful experience, and if each knew his place on the schedule based on the factors, then suspicions, jealousies, and resentments would be eliminated.

Moreover, the profession has contended not only for the development of such salary schedules, but has insisted that these schedules should be developed cooperatively—that is, that teachers should participate in the formulation of the salary schedules under which they must work. (This aspect of the problem will be discussed in more detail below.)

In favor of definite salary schedules it may be said that they recognize and reward the professional group as a whole and avoid the necessity for individual bargaining, which is extremely distasteful to professional-minded teachers and administrators. If properly applied, schedules eliminate favoritism and "apple polishing." Also, if they are used properly, salary schedules prevent school officials from taking advantage of such groups as married or overage teachers or substitute teachers, who must accept what is offered because they cannot very well teach elsewhere.

Admittedly, the applications of definite salary schedules do not always produce equitable wage relationships. Some teachers contribute more to their pupils than do other teachers, but the uniform salary schedule recognizes no differences at all. Sometimes a school administration wants to pay more to a superior teacher to prevent losing him to a wealthier school district, but a definite schedule, scrupulously observed, prevents an individual exception. Some inequities and losses may be inevitable, but should be balanced by higher morale and efficiency when the salary policy is objectively administered.

DEFINITION OF TERMS RELATED . TO SALARY POLICIES

The following definitions of terms used in connection with salary schedules and policies will help in clarifying meanings.[3] The word "schedule"

[3] National Education Association, Research Division, *Analysis of Salary Schedules, 1957–58,* Research Report 1959-R1. Washington, D.C.: The Association, January, 1959, pp. 5–6.

is used to refer either to the salary policy (e.g., "the provisions of the schedule") or to the document in which the policy is recorded (e.g., "the schedule was mimeographed").

A *salary-schedule policy* is a written plan for the payment of school employees formally adopted by the board of education. A complete salary-schedule policy specifies the salary classes, the minimum salaries, the number and amount of annual increments, and salary steps in recognition of experience, the maximum salaries, and the principles and conditions governing the payment of salaries to various groups of school employees.

Salary class is one division of a basic salary schedule, for a group of teachers of equivalent preparation or equivalent assignment, showing the salary steps from minimum to maximum. In single salary schedules a salary class is ordinarily defined in terms of academic degrees or years of professional preparation.

Salary step is a specific annual salary within a salary class. The number of the step in the sequence of annual salaries is determined usually by the year of experience; that is, a teacher in his second year of experience is at the second step of his salary class.

An increment is the difference between two successive salary steps, the annual increase in salary needed to move forward within the salary class. It is related primarily to recognition of experience; ordinarily an increment is given each year until the maximum salary is reached.

Placement involves evaluation of a teacher's preparation and prior experience to determine his salary class and salary step; it is applied usually to new teachers, specifically to the crediting of prior experience for placement on a salary step above the minimum salary.

Reclassification involves transfer of a classroom teacher from one salary class to another, for example, transfer to a higher salary class in a single-salary schedule when a teacher has completed professional study or has met other prerequisites of the higher class. Such transfers ordinarily provide a salary increase in addition to the annual increment for experience.

Study requirement, barrier, hurdle, and training condition are used interchangeably to refer to a provision whereby a teacher is expected to submit evidence of professional growth at stated intervals of time in order to make normal progress on the annual steps of his salary class; sometimes this provision applies also as a condition for retaining the maximum salary. Requirements are usually stated in terms of college credits; some schedules permit the substitution of other educative activities for a part of the study requirement.

Supermaximum is reached by one or more salary steps beyond the normal maximum of a salary class. It can be granted for superior service, extra study, or extended service.

Superior-service maximum is reached by one or more salary steps beyond the normal maximum of a salary class and is granted by special action of the board of education to teachers judged to be rendering superior service.

Acceleration as a merit provision refers to the practice of giving either double increments or any larger-than-normal increment as the teacher advances from the minimum to the maximum salary, to reward above-average service.

Extra-study maximum is reached by one or more salary steps beyond the normal maximum of a salary class granted to teachers who submit evidence of the completion of additional professional study of specified types and under specified conditions as set forth in the salary schedule.

Extended-service maximum is reached by one or more salary steps beyond the normal maximum of a salary class, granted to teachers who have service for some specified number of years at the normal maximum; may be associated with requirements for extra study or may be granted on years of service alone.

TRENDS IN SALARY SCHEDULES [4]

Trends in Local Salary Scheduling

Table 22 reflects the trend toward mandated minimum salaries for teachers on a state-wide basis. Table 23 reflects the average salaries of teachers in the respective states in 1966–67. What are the trends in salary scheduling in urban districts? In 1966–67, the median starting salary for teachers in school systems with enrollments of 100,000 or more was $5,400; in systems with enrollments from 1,200 to 2,999, the median was $5,120. The median maximum salary for the highest preparation below the doctorate was $10,008 for the first, and $8,500 for the second. The average salary of elementary school classroom teachers in 1966–67 was $6,609; for high school teachers, $7,095; and for all classroom teachers, $6,821.[5]

The major trends in salary scheduling for teachers may be summarized as follows:

1. The *steady upward growth*. This growth is reflected in several ways:
   a. During the 10-year period from 1956–57 to 1966–67, mean annual salary of the public instructional staff increased by 63.7 per cent in the current dollar (from $4,350 to $7,119). In terms of purchasing power, the increase was 39.5 per cent.
   b. The gap in the disparity among the regions is closing. In 1939–40, the Far West average salary was 44.4 per cent above the national average; the Southeast was 42.9 per cent below. In 1966–67, the Far West was 20.8 per cent above and the Southeast 16.2 per cent below the national average.
   c. In 1956–57, some 35 per cent of all teachers received salaries below $3,500; in 1966–67 only 0.3 per cent of the teachers did. In 1956–57, 68 per cent of teachers received average salaries below $5,000; in 1966–67, only 5.6 per cent did. In 1966–67, more than three fourths of all teachers received average salaries of $5,500 and above; and 47.4 per cent received $6,500 and above. As reflected in the chart below, the aggregate increase in average salaries of all teachers, be-

---

[4] For an introduction to current economic trends that affect teachers, see National Education Association, Research Division, *Economic Status of Teachers in 1966–67,* Research Report 1967-R8. Washington, D.C.: The Association, 1967, 55 pp.

[5] National Education Association, Research Division. *Salary Schedules, Classroom Teachers, 1960–67,* Research Report 1966-R17. Washington, D.C.: The Association, October, 1966, pp. 5–6.

tween 1958–59 and 1966–67 was more than $2,000. For high school teachers, the increase in average salaries was just short of $2,000; and for elementary teachers, it was $2,002. The gap between average salaries of elementary and secondary school teachers has been steadily lessening in recent years.

d. Growth in the average salary of classroom teachers in current dollars:

Year	Elementary Teachers	High School Teachers	All Teachers
1958–59	$4,607	$5,113	$4,797
1960–61	5,075	5,543	5,275
1962–63	5,560	5,980	5,732
1964–65	5,985	6,451	6,195
1966–67	6,609	7,095	6,821

2. *Greater recognition of advanced preparation* through:
   a. Larger initial (step 1) differentials; typically, this differential is $400 for a year of college preparation, but many schedules exceed this amount.
   b. Provision for intermediate preparation level. Many schedules provide differentials for half years; for example, for bachelor's degree plus fifteen semester hours, or master's degree plus fifteen semester hours.
   c. More experience steps or larger annual increments as preparation progresses to higher levels.
   d. Additional levels beyond master's degree classification, typically recognizing up to the sixth year of preparation, with many schedules recognizing six and a half years, seven years, and the doctor's degree.

There are several other trends emerging. There is a definite trend toward fewer but larger annual increments; toward gradual decrease in the number of nondegree classifications; toward slight increases, especially in big cities, in the use of supermaximums or service increments; toward inclusion of supervisory and administrative personnel in the salary policy; and toward reduction in discriminatory practices, e.g., sex differentials, family differentials, paying secondary teachers more. As for merit-rating salary schedules, there are increased discussion and study of plans.

Theory of Salary Scheduling

The teaching profession, as represented by the NEA, has for many years strongly advocated salary schedules of the single salary type—that is, schedules based upon the factors of preparation, experience, and professional growth, without regard to sex, marital status, number of dependents, teaching level, or type of school. The growth of the trend toward this type of salary scheduling is reflected by the fact that in 1921, when the NEA first recommended the single salary schedule, only a few cities had such schedules. Presently, almost all schedules are of the single salary type. AFT also advocates the single salary schedule.

But the principle of single salary scheduling limited to preparation and experience is not universally accepted even among members of the profession, and many lay people have expressed dissatisfaction with the principle on the grounds that it does not properly reward teachers who are deemed to be rendering superior service, and conveys undeserved rewards upon mediocre and inferior teachers.

Detailed discussion of the arguments for and against the single salary schedules and those for and against the merit-rating plan of salary schedules will be found in Chapter 8.

TABLE 22   States with Minimum Salary Laws and Date of Original Adoption

Before 1915	1915–1924	1925–1934	1935–1944	1945–1954	After 1954
West Virginia, 1882	Vermont, 1915	Tennessee, 1925	California, 1937	South Carolina, 1945	Florida, 1955
Indiana, 1901	Wisconsin, 1915		Georgia, 1937	Texas, 1945	Arkansas, 1957
Pennsylvania, 1903	Kentucky, 1918		Washington, 1937	Illinois, 1946	
Maryland, 1904	Massachusetts, 1918		Alaska, 1939	Virginia, 1946	
Rhode Island, 1909	Delaware, 1919		Oklahoma, 1939	Idaho, 1947	
	New Jersey, 1919		Maine, 1943	Louisiana, 1948	
	New York, 1919			Ohio, 1951*	
	Oregon, 1919			Mississippi, 1953†	
	North Carolina, 1923				
(5 states)	(9 states)	(1 state)	(6 states)	(8 states)	(2 states)

Source: National Education Association, Research Division, *State Minimum-Salary Laws and Goal Schedules for Teachers, 1966–67*, Research Report 1966–R18. Washington, D.C.: The Association, November, 1966, p. 5.

* An earlier minimum-salary law was in effect from 1927–28 through 1934–35.

† A minimum-salary law enacted in 1924 became obsolete almost immediately because of the extremely low salary specified.

TABLE 23 *Estimated Average Annual Salaries for Teachers in the U.S., 1966–67*

| State | Instructional Staff | CLASSROOM TEACHERS | | |
		Elementary	Secondary	All
Alabama	$5,675	$5,285	$5,685	$5,480
Alaska	9,200	NA	NA	8,923
Arizona	7,410	7,065	7,645	7,230
Arkansas	5,140	4,804	5,224	5,013
California	9,000	8,075	9,025	8,450
Colorado	6,850	6,500	6,700	6,625
Connecticut	7,850	7,325	7,648	7,460
Delaware	7,700	7,225	7,600	7,450
Florida	6,600	NA	NA	6,430
Georgia	6,075	5,845	5,970	5,895
Hawaii	8,092	7,850	7,950	7,902
Idaho	6,050	5,500	6,174	5,875
Illinois	7,525	7,125	7,825	7,400
Indiana	7,650	7,200	7,600	7,377
Iowa	6,531	6,115	6,778	6,396
Kansas	6,270	5,925	6,275	6,100
Kentucky	5,600	5,250	5,675	5,400
Louisiana	6,587	6,257	6,560	6,388
Maine	5,850	5,575	6,160	5,825
Maryland	7,710	7,153	7,483	7,308
Massachusetts	7,575	7,125	7,500	7,300
Michigan	7,650	7,250	7,400	7,300
Minnesota	7,050	6,675	7,175	6,910
Mississippi	4,782	4,530	4,803	4,650
Missouri	6,400	6,163	6,411	6,250
Montana	6,100	5,725	6,550	6,000
Nebraska	5,800	5,233	6,098	5,619
Nevada	7,763	7,274	7,560	7,390
New Hampshire	6,200	5,930	6,210	6,050
New Jersey	7,647	7,175	7,625	7,356
New Mexico	6,720	6,650	6,625	6,630
New York	8,600	7,600	8,200	7,900
North Carolina	5,763	5,512	5,780	5,604
North Dakota	5,500	4,850	6,050	5,280
Ohio	6,750	6,300	6,900	6,534
Oklahoma	6,180	5,900	6,100	6,000
Oregon	7,253	6,850	7,135	7,000
Pennsylvania	7,050	6,755	6,880	6,815
Rhode Island	6,900	6,575	6,675	6,625
South Carolina	5,486	5,080	5,527	5,343
South Dakota	5,025	4,450	5,675	4,800
Tennessee	5,775	5,460	5,950	5,625
Texas	6,190	5,920	6,140	6,025
Utah	6,750	NA	NA	6,490
Vermont	6,000	5,500	6,200	5,700
Virginia	6,600	6,150	6,650	6,400
Washington	7,550	7,095	6,670	7,330
West Virginia	5,900	5,320	5,600	5,450
Wisconsin	6,860	6,375	7,000	6,700
Wyoming	6,600	6,400	6,500	6,450
50 States & D.C.	7,119	6,609	7,095	6,821

Source: National Education Association, Research Division, *Estimates of School Statistics, 1966–67*, Research Report 1966-R20. Washington, D.C.: The Association, 1966, Table 8, p. 30.

Relationship of Salaries to Those of Other Groups

One of the bases used in seeking periodic readjustment of teachers' salaries is to compare them with remuneration provided other types of employment. According to figures compiled by the NEA Research Division, teachers' salaries clearly have not kept pace with advances accorded to most other occupations. It cannot be assumed, either, that teachers' salaries were on an equitable comparable basis in 1939. Comparisons of advances are indicated in Table 24.

Some Salary Comparisons

Figures released by the Bureau of the Census in 1958 reflect the comparative disadvantage of teachers' salaries with other professional groups. These are shown in the following chart: [6]

Average Earnings in 1958

Lawyers, physicians, and dentists	$13,457
Engineers	9,647
Seventeen selected professions	9,439
Public school teachers	4,827

Teachers also compare unfavorably in starting salaries. For example, in 1960 engineers were able to command starting salaries of $6,120; accountants, $5,352; chemists, $5,800; and teachers, $3,900. Another comparison of the disadvantage of teachers, in terms of starting salaries, is shown in Table 26.

Analysis of Salary-Schedule Practices

According to the NEA Research Division, from an analysis of the schedules of 1,704 school districts, the following practices were reported: [7]

About 51 per cent of the schedules provided specific salary provisions for both administrators and classroom teachers. There has been an increase in this trend in recent years. More than one-fourth of the 1,704 schedules included sick-leave regulations, and in excess of 20 per cent included other leave-of-absence provisions. Less than 4 per cent included sabbatical-leave provisions.

The size of annual increments varied from $350 to less than $50, with the median being $149. The median number of increments (steps from

[6] National Education Association, Committee on Educational Finance, *Professional Salaries for Professional Teachers*. Washington, D.C.: The Association, February, 1961, p. 8.

[7] National Education Association, Research Division, *Analysis of Salary Schedules, 1957–58*, Research Report, 1959-R1. Washington, D.C.: The Association, January, 1959, 32 pp.

TABLE 24 Average Annual Earnings of Teachers and Certain Other Groups, 1939 and 1959

Year	Teachers (Calendar-Year Estimated Average Salary)	All Persons Working for Wages or Salaries	Employees in Manu-facturing	Civilian Employees of Federal Government	Nonsalaried Professional Practitioners			
					Dentists	Lawyers	Physicians	Average
1939	$1,420	$1,264	$1,363	$1,843	$3,096	$4,391	$4,229	$4,053
1959	5,013	4,573	5,212					
Percentage increase 1939–1959	253	261.8	282.4					

Source: National Education Association, Research Division, *Economic Status of Teachers in 1959–60*, Research Report 1960-RB. Washington, D.C.: The Association, May, 1960, adapted from Table 26, p. 37.

TABLE 25 *Rank of States on Average Teachers' Salaries, 1966–67*

Rank	State	Estimated Average Salary, 1966–67
1	Alaska	$8,923
2	California	8,450
3	Hawaii	7,902
4	New York	7,900
5	Connecticut	7,460
6	Delaware	7,450
7	Illinois	7,400
8	Nevada	7,390
9	New Jersey	7,356
10	Indiana	7,337
11	Washington	7,330
12	Maryand	7,308
13	Massachusetts	7,300
13	Michigan	7,300
14	Arizona	7,230
15	Oregon	7,000
16	Minnesota	6,910
	UNITED STATES and District of Columbia	6,821
17	Pennsylvania	6,815
18	Wisconsin	6,700
19	New Mexico	6,630
20	Colorado	6,625
20	Rhode Island	6,625
21	Ohio	6,534
22	Utah	6,490
23	Wyoming	6,450
24	Florida	6,430
25	Virginia	6,400
26	Iowa	6,396
27	Louisiana	6,338
28	Missouri	6,250
29	Kansas	6,100
30	New Hampshire	6,050
31	Texas	6,025
32	Oklahoma	6,000
32	Montana	6,000
33	Georgia	5,895
34	Idaho	5,875
35	Maine	5,825
36	Vermont	5,700
37	Tennessee	5,625
38	Nebraska	5,619
39	North Carolina	5,604
40	Alabama	5,480
41	West Virginia	5,450
42	Kentucky	5,400
43	South Carolina	5,343
44	North Dakota	5,280
45	Arkansas	5,013
46	South Dakota	4,800
47	Mississippi	4,650

Source: National Education Association, Research Division. *Estimates of School Statistics, 1966–67*, Research Report 1966-R-20. Washington, D.C.: The Association, 1966, Table 8, p. 30.

the minimum to the maximum) was 12. Salary differentials based on sex alone appear to be on the decline. Only about 6 per cent of the 1,704 provided salary differentials for men. This is a decline of nearly 30 per cent since 1935.

TABLE 26   Average Starting Salary Paid to Men College Graduates With Bachelor's Degree, Class of 1967

Field	Average Starting Salary
Men graduates, paid by industries that recruit on college campuses*	
Engineering	$8,544
Accounting	7,344
Sales	6,996
General business	6,864
Other fields	7,248
Chemists, inexperienced graduates	
Bachelor's degree	7,896
Master's degree	9,408
Teachers in public schools †	
Largest school systems	5,400
Smaller school systems	5,120

Sources:
* National Education Association, Research Division. *Economic Status of Teachers, 1966–67,* Research Report 1967-R8. Washington, D.C.: The Association, 1967, Tables 39 and 40, pp. 44–45.
† National Education Association, Research Division, *Salary Schedules for Classroom Teachers, 1966–67,* Research Report 1966-R17. Washington, D.C.: The Association, p. 5.

About one-fourth of the schedules required that teachers furnish evidence of continued professional growth as a prerequisite to progress on the experience steps of their salary classes. Less than 1 per cent of the schedules required teachers at the maximum of their schedules to continue professional studies in order to remain at the maximum.

TYPES OF SALARY SCHEDULES

The Single Salary Schedule

Virtually all salary schedules for teachers are now of the single type. This term originated some thirty years ago when there were separate schedules for elementary and high school teachers, for men and women, and sometimes for different types of teaching jobs at the same school level. The demand for elimination of differentials based on school levels or sex eventually resulted in the "single salary schedule," in which the only differentials recognized were levels of preparation and years of experience. All of the specimen schedules (Tables 27, 28, 29, and 30) are of this type.

Preparation Schedules

This is the same as the single salary type, the prime factor in placement of a given teacher on the schedule being the college years of preparation achieved by the teacher. Such schedules usually provide differentials in starting pay for the bachelor's degree, the master's degree, six years of preparation, and the doctor's degree (see Connecticut schedule, Table 30). Many however, provide differentials for fractional years of preparation above the bachelor's degree.

Merit Pay Schedules

There is no commonly accepted definition of a merit salary schedule. In general, it is based on a single salary schedule, with provisions to reward teachers above the regular schedule who have been judged to be rendering superior service. The extra incentives or rewards may take the form of acceleration of increments, where some teachers reach the maximum ahead of the majority, or it may include superior-service maximums, where the judged superior teacher gets additional increments that the average teacher does not, or it may include preferred placement of some teachers on a multiple-track schedule.

Index or Ratio Salary Schedules

The index salary schedule for teachers has come into use only within the last decade. For a decade or more this type of schedule has been used for administrative and supervisory personnel. Its use for teachers seems to be growing.

The basic idea of such index-ratio schedules is that they express annual increments as per cents of a base salary rather than in terms of dollar amounts. Typically the base is the bachelor's degree with no experience, expressed as 1.00 on the schedule (preparation of less than the degree is figured at proportionately less than the degree). Increments for preparation and experience beyond the bachelor's degree are figured as per cents above the base. Though in some schedules fractional years of preparation are recognized, typically only the degree levels or year equivalents are recognized: bachelor's, master's, six years, and doctor's degree.

The schedule advocated by the Connecticut Education Association (Table 30) illustrates how the index or ratio principle works. Note that the base is the bachelor's degree with no experience. The base salary is

TABLE 27 *Teacher's Salary Schedule Effective 1967–68*
Westhampton Beach, New York, Public Schools

		COLUMN A B.A. 100%	COLUMN B B.A. + 15 103	COLUMN C B.A. + 30 106	COLUMN D B.A. + 40 or M.A. 109	COLUMN E B.A. + 50 M.A. + 10 112	COLUMN F B.A. + 60 M.A. + 20 115	COLUMN G B.A. + 70 M.A. + 30 118
100	1	$ 6,400	$ 6,592	$ 6,784	$ 6,976	$ 7,168	$ 7,360	$ 7,552
104.5	2	6,688	6,888	7,089	7,289	7,490	7,691	7,891
104.5	3	6,988	7,197	7,407	7,616	7,826	8,036	8,246
104.5	4	7,302	7,521	7,740	7,959	8,178	8,397	8,617
104.5	5	7,630	7,858	8,087	8,316	8,545	8,774	9,004
104.5	6	7,973	8,212	8,451	8,690	8,929	9,168	9,409
104.5	7	8,331	8,580	8,830	9,080	9,330	9,580	9,832
104.5	8	8,705	8,966	9,227	9,488	9,749	10,010	10,274
104.5	9	9,096	9,368	9,641	9,914	10,187	10,460	10,736
104.5	10	9,505	9,790	10,075	10,360	10,645	10,930	11,219
104.5	11	9,932	10,229	10,527	10,825	11,123	11,421	11,723
104.5	12	10,378	10,689	11,000	11,312	11,623	11,934	12,250
104.5	13	—	—	—	11,821	12,146	12,471	12,801
104.5	14	—	—	—	—	—	13,032	13,377
*D.O.B.	20	10,878	11,189	11,500	12,321	12,646	13,532	13,877
*D.O.B.	25	11,378	11,689	12,000	12,821	13,146	14,032	14,377

* D.O.B.–Discretion of the Board of Education.

148

TABLE 28   Index Schedule of Springfield, Michigan Public Schools

Below is the 1966–67 index schedule of the Springfield, Michigan public schools, a 12-step schedule with 5.5 per cent increment at successive steps, with the maximum at 1.725 times the minimum in each salary class, or preparation level.

Steps	Years	B.A.	M.A.	M.A. + 30	Ratio
1	0	$5,600	$ 5,936	$ 6,272	1.000
2	1	$5,908	$ 6,262	$ 6,617	1.055
3	2	$6,216	$ 6,589	$ 6,962	1.110
4	3	$6,524	$ 6,915	$ 7,307	1.165
5	4	$6,888	$ 7,301	$ 7,715	1.230
6	5	$7,252	$ 7,687	$ 8,122	1.295
7	6	$7,616	$ 8,073	$ 8,530	1.360
8	7	$8,036	$ 8,518	$ 9,000	1.435
9	8	$8,456	$ 8,963	$ 9,471	1.510
10	9	$8,876	$ 9,409	$ 9,941	1.580
11	10	$9,269	$ 9,854	$10,411	1.660
12	11	—	$10,240	$10,819	1.725

$5,000 (1.00), the first step after one year of experience is 1.10, or $5,500. Similarly, each successive step is 10 per cent above the preceding one. The base for five years' preparation ($5,500) is 1.10, or 10 per cent above that for the bachelor's degree, and each successive step for experience is 10 per cent above the base for this preparation level. The base ($6,000) for the sixth year of preparation is 10 per cent above that for five years' preparation (or 1.20 of the bachelor's degree base), and each experience increment is 10 per cent above the preceding one. The base for the doctor's degree with no experience ($6,750) is 15 per cent above the preceding preparation level, and each successive experience increment increases by 15 per cent. Note that this schedule is several years old. The $5,000 no longer obtains, but the principle can be applied to a new base each year.

DETERMINATION OF SALARIES

There are a number of ways of determining the salaries of teachers, but none of them is exactly scientific. As far as that goes, there is probably no wholly objective way of determining the wages or salaries of any occupational group. No one knows the percentage of the national income that should go to the workers. No one knows how much of the returns of each business should go to the labor group. No one knows how much a teacher is worth in comparison to a plumber, bricklayer, or physician.

TABLE 29 Chicago Public Schools Salary Schedule for Elementary and High School Teachers, Based upon Ten Month School Term, 1967

STEPS (Years of Service)	LANE I Bachelor's Degree	LANE II Master's Degree	LANE III Master's + 36 Sem. Hrs. of Approved Graduate Credit
1st year	$ 6,000	$ 6,400	$ 6,600
2nd year	6,350	6,750	6,950
3rd year	6,700	7,100	7,300
4th year	7,050	7,450	7,650
5th year	7,400	7,800	8,000
6th year	7,750	8,150	8,350
7th year	8,100	8,500	8,700
8th year	8,450	8,850	9,050
9th year	8,800	9,200	9,400
10th year	9,150	9,550	9,750
11th year	9,500	9,900	10,100
12th year	9,500	10,250	10,450
13th year	9,500	10,250	10,800
14th year	9,500	10,250	10,800
15th year	9,500	10,250	10,800
16th through 20th years	9,750	10,500	11,050
21st through 25th years	10,000	10,750	11,300
26th through 30th years	10,250	11,000	11,550
31st through 35th years	10,500	11,250	11,800
36th year and thereafter	10,750	11,500	12,050

LANE IV—$25.00 per school month is added to LANE III at appropriate step for completion of doctor's degree.

To date, wages and salaries have been generally determined by bargaining, by supply and demand, by competition, by fluctuations in commodity-price indices, and by trends. One has only to read accounts of wage meetings between management and labor to realize the importance of bargaining. It seems to be the accepted way of fixing wages and salaries at present. Supply and demand always affect wages and salaries, as they do the price of any commodity.

In a short labor market, one business, industry, or agency competes with others for available workers. Thus, teachers are likely to leave the schoolroom, factory, store, or office during times when labor is in great demand. There is competition, too, within each type of enterprise. Thus, schools compete against other schools, factories against other factories, offices against other offices, and stores against other stores.

TABLE 30 *Connecticut Education Association's Suggested Structure and Principles of Teacher-Salary Scheduling*

Total Years of Teaching Experience	Step on Schedule	Bachelor's Degree		Five Years' Preparation		Six Years' Preparation		Doctorate Degree	
0	1	1.00	$5,000	1.10	$ 5,500	1.20	$ 6,000	1.35	$ 6,750
1	2	1.10	5,500	1.20	6,000	1.30	6,500	1.50	7,500
2	3	1.20	6,000	1.30	6,500	1.40	7,000	1.65	8,250
3	4	1.30	6,500	1.40	7,000	1.50	7,500	1.80	9,000
4	5	1.40	7,000	1.50	7,500	1.60	8,000	1.95	9,750
5	6	1.50	7,500	1.60	8,000	1.70	8,500	2.10	10,500
6	7	1.60	8,000	1.70	8,500	1.80	9,000	2.25	11,250
7	8	1.70	8,500	1.80	9,000	1.90	9,500	2.40	12,000
8	9	1.80	9,000	1.90	9,500	2.00	10,000	2.55	12,750
9	10			2.00	10,000	2.10	10,500	2.70	13,500
10	11					2.20	11,000	2.85	14,250
11	12							3.00	15,000

All steps of each salary schedule are based on the four-year preparation starting salary.

Source: *Connecticut Education Association Salary Policies.* Reproduced by permission.

151

When the wage trends are upward, any employer finds it difficult not to follow the trends. The pressures of the workers and of the public are in that direction. These kinds of pressures are hard to resist.

Teachers' salaries tend to rise as the wages paid to labor rise. They should, or teachers will continue to leave the field. All of us have seen promising teachers secure positions in business or industry when teachers' salaries lag.

How, then, should teachers' salaries be determined? Is there a scientific method? These are debatable questions. Some would contend that there is no more objective way of determining teachers' salaries than there is of fixing the wages of workers. Under present conditions, according to this viewpoint, teachers' salaries tend to be fixed just as are those for other workers: bargaining, supply and demand, competition, price indices, and trends all enter the picture, and of these the only ones that the teacher can do much about are bargaining and supply and demand.

Balancing Supply and Demand

It is certain that supply and demand in a service field such as teaching will, as is true of any other commodity, affect the price of that commodity in the markets. An undersupply will tend to raise prices. An even balance between the two will tend to place the emphasis in salary fixing upon bargaining and other factors.

It is, therefore, imperative to the economic welfare of any group of skilled or professional workers that a reasonable balance be maintained between the supply of qualified workers and society's demand for such workers. Serious imbalance in either direction tends to work to the unjustifiable disadvantage of one or the other, i.e., either the economic group or society as a whole. The proper interests of each should receive consideration. This element in the determination of remuneration is sometimes misunderstood by the public and severely criticized. For example, some professions and trades are accused of enforcing strict quotas of new persons admitted to preparation each year in order to further the selfish economic interests of the group. The enforcement of arbitrary quotas designed for such a purpose and without due regard for the welfare of society might justly be condemned. However, the teaching profession has not advocated the fixing of such quotas. It has, from time to time, advocated the achieving of a fair balance between teacher supply and demand, not by the establishing of rule-of-thumb quotas, but by raising the standards of preparation required for admission to the profession and by adhering to discriminating standards of admission to teacher education. The teaching profession contends that such procedures are, first, in the interests of society and, second, for the welfare of teachers themselves.

The teaching profession has an obligation to seek to bring about a reasonable balance between the number prepared for teaching each year and the number that can reasonably be expected to find employment at adequate salaries. Moreover, the teaching profession has the same fundamental right to self-regulation that has been granted to the so-called "private professions." That this principle will be increasingly accepted by the public is evident.

Participation of Teachers in Salary Scheduling

What is to be the role, in the future, of teachers themselves in the determination of teacher salary schedules? Will they be consulted through their salary committee and teachers' association? Or will they be resented, resisted, and forced into a minor role? While, presently, there remains some public sentiment against the participation of teachers in the determination of the salary schedules under which they are to work, the trend toward such participation through their own professional associations is unmistakable and growing. It is clear that we shall see more of such participation in the future.

Procedures in Salary Scheduling for Teachers

The growth in negotiation between teachers and boards of education will necessarily make certain demands on teachers. These should be foreseen so that adequate preparation can be made. Some of the probable demands are as follows:

1. Teachers will need to become better informed on general economic problems. Several state education associations employ specialists to investigate such problems for them and to help local members present the issues locally. Teachers themselves will also have to possess a basic understanding of economics.

2. Teachers will need to be well informed about the finances of school districts. Some teachers have surprised their school boards with their knowledge about their school district's ability to pay, about tax rates, about budgets, about instructional and noninstructional costs, and about building needs.

A good example of the value of such knowledge is the case of a large city school district where the teachers had been denied cost-of-living raises for several years on the ground that the district did not have the money to provide such raises. A teachers' committee made an intensive study of the financial affairs of the district and discovered that the annual budget was setting aside, from current operating funds, several hundred thousand dollars annually to amortize the construction of a football stadium. With this information the teachers were enabled to point out to the board that this procedure was not only bad financial practice but a clear violation of its legal power. The board finally conceded the soundness of the teachers' contention, proceeded to transfer the amortization of the stadium to capital outlay, and granted the requested increase in teachers' salaries. Only in the largest districts would it be practical to hire experts to find out these things for teachers. Even in metropolitan areas it would be better for teachers to do their own investigating. Boards of education are not as likely to be resentful about examination of school-district records by teachers as they would be toward "snooping" by outsiders.

3. Teachers will need to be informed about changes in cost of living and about other economic trends. The Bureau of Labor Statistics price indices should become as familiar to teachers as attendance reports and cumulative records. Figures on employment, wage rates, per-capita income should be available and understood by them. Teachers will have to know what they are talking about when they discuss the need for a raise with the members of the board of education.

4. Teachers will need to learn how to work together democratically and cooperatively. In all bargaining procedures a united front is essential. Teachers need to learn how to reconcile their differences in committee, how to accept the will of the majority, and how to support what has been established by the group.

Teachers Should Have a Part

A good case can be made for teacher participation in developing salary policies. Pupils will receive better service from teachers who are well prepared and who are reasonably happy, secure, and adequately paid than from those who are emotionally upset, poorly prepared, and have financial worries.

On this point the NEA Department of Classroom Teachers has said:

Teacher participation in school administration has been advocated for many years and to an increasing extent is being practiced. Perhaps in no field of administrative action have teachers rendered a larger service than in the thorny patch represented by the drafting of salary schedules. In many communities children are being benefited by heightened efficiency and morale of teachers, resulting from improved salary schedules that teachers themselves helped to prepare.[8]

Teacher participation in the formulation of salary schedules should help in securing and maintaining an adequate staff that will be primarily concerned with the growth and learning of boys and girls, and not with the teachers' personal problems.

[8] National Education Association, Department of Classroom Teachers and Research Division, *Salary Scheduling*, Discussion Pamphlet No. 8. Washington, D.C.: The Association, April, 1956, p. 1.

Hubbard and Davis assert:

Prior to World War I the characteristic pattern in public school systems was either to have no official salary schedule or to have the schedule worked out entirely by the board of education and the superintendent of schools.

One of the significant contributions of the NEA Research Division since 1922 has been to provide the profession with information on current practices so that salary scheduling could be a joint activity of school administrators and classroom teachers. Not until classroom teachers were informed on practices and trends were they able to take their places at the conference table. . . .

The availability of information alone did not establish the principle of teacher participation in the making of salary schedules and policies. Many local associations had to demonstrate that they could make concrete and practical suggestions and, in many instances, had to appeal to the public before recognition was given. Even today there are school boards and administrators who resist cooperative planning of salary schedules, but they are clearly in the minority. Approved practice involves committees, conferences, workshops, and hearings whereby the views of the employees can be freely given.[9]

How Far Should Participation Go?

This question is a delicate one to answer on a theoretical basis, just as it is in connection with workers in industry. Involved in the extent of participation by teachers in the establishment of salary schedules are such factors as collective bargaining or professional negotiation, tax rates, the legal responsibility of school boards, state aid, and general budgetary considerations, as well as the willingness of teachers to assume responsibility for participation in such a process. The making of salary schedules is a complex matter. The desirable kind and extent of participation are not easy to determine. Boards of education, as direct representatives of the people, generally have legal responsibility with respect to the expenditure of money for schools. But such boards can exercise this authority in a cooperative manner.

In the last analysis the community must decide how much it wishes and can afford to spend for schools. Teachers have a responsibility in respect to presenting the needs of children, but the final voice on total expenditures cannot and should not be theirs. The people, or their duly chosen representatives, must settle that question.

In the matter of allocation of funds, too, the boards of education have legal control of school funds, but teachers should have a more influential voice than in the determination of total school costs. Teachers are better able than anyone else to determine the educational needs of children. Certainly they should be heard with much consideration when funds are allocated.

This matter has been before the NEA Representative Assembly for years. In 1960 the Assembly directed the NEA Board of Directors to

[9] Frank W. Hubbard and Hazel Davis, *op. cit.*, pp. 87–88.

appoint a special committee to study the matter. The report of the committee was adopted by the Board in March, 1961, and amended by the Representative Assembly in June, 1961. The statement follows:

TEACHER-BOARD OF EDUCATION RELATIONSHIPS
As Amended by the Representative Assembly
NEA Convention
Atlantic City, New Jersey
1961

Since boards of education and the teaching profession have the same ultimate aim of providing the best possible educational opportunity for children and youth, relationships must be established which are based upon this community of interest and the concept of education as both a public trust and a professional calling.

Recognizing both the legal authority of boards of education and the educational competencies of the teaching profession, the two groups should view the consideration of matters of mutual concern as a joint responsibility.

The National Education Association believes, therefore, that professional education associations should be accorded the right, through democratically selected representatives using appropriate professional channels, to participate in the determination of policies of common concern including salary and other conditions for professional service.

The seeking of consensus and mutual agreement on a professional basis should preclude the arbitrary exercise of unilateral authority by boards of education and the use of the strike by teachers as a means for enforcing economic demands.

When common consent cannot be reached, the Association recommends that a Board of Review consisting of members of professional and lay groups affiliated with education should be used as the means of resolving extreme differences.

SALARY POLICY STATEMENTS OF THE PROFESSION

NEA Salary Policy Statements

The National Education Association and several of its units have, from time to time, adopted salary policy statements enunciating what they consider justifiable bases for remunerating teachers.

The NEA adopted in 1967 the following policy statements:

The Association believes that teachers' salaries should compare favorably with income in other professions and occupations requiring comparable preparation. Starting salaries for qualified degree teachers should be at least $8,000, and salaries for experienced teachers with masters' degrees should range at least to $16,000 followed by continuing scheduled increases for career teachers of advanced qualifications.[10]

[10] National Education Association, *NEA Handbook, 1967–68*, Washington, D.C.: The Association, 1967, p. 71.

A professional salary schedule should: (a) be based upon preparation, teaching experience, and professional growth; (b) provide a beginning salary adequate to attract capable young people into the profession; (c) include increments sufficient to double the beginning salary within ten years, followed by continuing salary advances; (d) be developed cooperatively by school-board members, administrators, and teachers; (e) permit no discrimination as to grade or subject taught, residence, creed, race, sex, marital status, or number of dependents; (f) recognize experience and advanced education, through the doctor's degree; (g) recognize, by appropriate salary ratios, the responsibilities of administrators and other school personnel; and (h) be applied in actual practice.

The most recent resolution of the AFT, adapted at its August 1967 convention reads as follows:

WHEREAS, public school teachers' salaries are scandalously low throughout the United States, causing a tremendous exodus from teaching, and extensive moonlighting by teachers, therefore be it

Resolved: that the AFT cause federal legislation to be introduced granting massive federal aid for increase of public school teachers' salaries.

NEA announced in January 1968 that it would sponsor legislation in the Congress to appropriate $5 billion for general federal aid to schools, including $2.5 billion for aiding teachers' salaries.

The Future in Teachers' Salaries

The pressures of demands for professional personnel in the future will compel society to raise the remuneration of teachers to competing levels. It has been pointed out that the average salary of instructional staff in 1960–61 was $5,389; that of seventeen other professions was $11,100, more than twice that of teachers.

Based on the expected rise in the price index and national income, the U.S. Office of Education estimates that teachers' salaries, on the average, will advance to $8,213 (in terms of 1959 dollars) by 1968–69.

COLLECTIVE BARGAINING VS. REPRESENTATIVE NEGOTIATIONS

Collective bargaining in salary matters is a term which, by law and in the public mind, has come to be associated with organized labor. The principle is written into federal law in the Wagner Act and the Taft-Hartley Law. Briefly stated, the principle concerns the obligation of the employer and representatives of employees to meet and confer with regard to wages, hours, and other working conditions, usually ending in agreement and a signed contract. The principle has emerged as a result of the increasing complexity of modern industrial society, in which the single worker is ineffectual in negotiating for his individual wages. Alone, he is practically helpless because he must have the job to live. But the loss of one worker is inconsequential to the industry employing thousands of workers. Only when the full weight of the total working force is pooled does the single worker have a powerful weapon in wage negotiations. In fact, the weapon is so powerful that the reasonable balance in bargaining as between the employer and employee is often upset. This condition has both advantages and disadvantages, and it calls for statesmanship and a sense of fairness on both sides. Whatever shortcomings or excesses may be inherent in the principle, it is an accepted fact of life in our society, and it is here to stay, with modifications and adaptations from time to time.

As a general rule, professions have not invoked the principle, preferring to use other methods of securing reasonable pay for their members. Inherent in collective bargaining are certain factors that professions are reluctant to accept. In the first place, it involves the designation of a bargaining agent to represent the mass of workers. This is the labor union. Secondly, there must be a weapon with which to enforce the demands of the bargaining agent. This is the strike. In the past, both have been unacceptable to members of the professions, for the most part, although there have been exceptions to this general rule.

Public employees, especially, have been slow in demanding and achieving the right to collective bargaining. The basic reason is that often (not always) public-welfare considerations of a vital nature are involved. The famous edict of former President Calvin Coolidge in 1919, when, as governor of Massachusetts, he overruled the right of the Boston police to strike, set a pattern of public thought that has only in recent years begun to give way to a more reasonable concept. He said, "There is no right, at any time or place, to strike against the public welfare."

But the public attitude has changed, and many public employees now do have the right to bargain collectively. In the early days of the administration of President John F. Kennedy, a bill was introduced in the Congress (HR-12) spelling out the rights of federal employees to bargain collectively, but it did not pass. In January, 1962, President Kennedy issued an Executive Order directing agencies of the federal government to recognize employee organizations and to issue appropriate policies, rules, and regulations for implementing the Order. Employee organizations under the Order means any lawful association, labor organization, federation, council, or brotherhood, a primary purpose of which is to improve working conditions among federal employees. Organizations which assert the right to strike against the federal government or its agencies, which advocate the overthrow of the constitutional form of government, or which permit discrimination in conditions of membership with respect to race, color, creed, or national origin are excluded by the Order.

In brief, this Executive Order recognizes the right of civilian employees to join and participate in the work of employee organizations (association, federation, brotherhood, or society), and recognizes the right to consultation between management officials and employee groups regarding working conditions, pay regulations, promotion and demotion policies, grievances, etc. The Order, obviously, is aimed at spelling out the right of civilian employees of the federal government to collective representation in relations with the government, but rules out the right of such employees to strike. The Executive Order has the force of law and, in time, such principles doubtless will be spelled out in law. These are significant harbingers of new viewpoints about the rights of public employees.

This changed public attitude toward the rights of public employees to bargain collectively arose from several factors. Perhaps the chief one was the basic principle of simple justice and the fact that the majority is not engaged in occupations of vital necessity to the public welfare. Teachers, being members of a profession and public employees, have traditionally kept aloof from collective bargaining. Yet the conditions of modern life have compelled them to demand the right to negotiate as groups on salary matters. They have insisted upon the right to "representative negotiations." There are fine lines of distinction between this principle and that of collective bargaining, although it is often contended that no difference exists. What are the factors involved that makes representative negotiation generally acceptable to teachers and collective bargaining generally unacceptable? There is the matter of representation. Teachers want to represent themselves, through elected committees of their local associations. They do not look with favor upon assigning this function to an outside organization. There is the concept of "one profession": people engaged in education have common goals and interests—administrators as well as classroom teachers. Teachers see clearly that to accept the principle and techniques of collective bargaining means that somewhere, sometime in the future, either by court interpretation or by law, administrators (employers) and teachers (employees) will be enjoined from membership in the same organization. In addition, there is the historical reluctance of teachers to use the ultimate weapon of collective bargaining, the strike. (For fuller discussion see Chapters 21 and 22.)

What of the future? Will teachers be forced by the facts of life to adopt collective bargaining? The evidence seems to point in this direction, but no one can predict the future with certainty. The NEA was compelled to consider carefully a revision of its professional negotiation policy statement by the developments in New York City and elsewhere.

COMPARISONS OF SALARIES OF TEACHERS AND NONTEACHING PROFESSIONAL PERSONNEL

In the summer of 1967, the NEA Research Division released data on salaries paid professional employees of the public schools. The following are salient points of the estimates for the school year 1966–67:

Average salary of classroom teachers was $6,905.

One per cent (less than 20,000) of classroom teachers received less than $4,000 for the year.

A total of 6.4 (nearly 120,000 per cent) were paid $10,000 or more. In the largest school systems (enrollment of 25,000 or more) 13.3 per cent of all classroom teachers received $10,000 or more.

The mean salary paid in 1966–67 to elementary school supervisory and teaching principals was estimated to be $9,757; for junior high school principals, $11,226; and for senior high principals, $10,507. The larger average salary for junior high school principals, as compared to senior high school principals, is explained by the predominance of junior high schools in the largest and typically higher salaried districts, whereas senior high schools exist in more districts.

For assistant principals, the estimates of mean salary for 1966–67 were for elementary schools, $10,470; for junior high school, $10,435; and for senior high, $10,643. The closeness of these salaries is explained by the fact that only the largest and higher paying school districts have assistant principals.

Estimated mean salary in 1966–67 for counselors was $8,630; for directors of guidance or head counselors, $8,934; for librarians, $7,006; for social workers and visiting teachers, $7,884; for school psychologist, $9,547; for school nurses, $6,664.

The mean salary for all superintendents was $12,975. Of the 14,671 superintendents, only 6.8 per cent received less than $8,000, whereas 7.7 per cent received $20,000 or more.

Salary Schedule for Administrative Personnel

There is a growing trend to derive salary schedules for administrators by using an index or ratio relationship to the salaries scheduled for classroom teachers. In 1966–67, the NEA Research Division found such type schedules for administrators obtained (in 667 school systems, with enrollment of 6,000 or more) as follows: In 40.2 per cent of the reporting systems with enrollments of 25,000 or more; in 57.4 per cent of the reporting systems with enrollments of 6,000 to 11,999. The next most frequently reported type of salary schedule for administrative personnel is the inde-

TABLE 31   *Estimates of the Number of Professional Employees in the Public Schools in 1966–67 (Total Instructional Staff)*

Classroom Teachers	1,813,382	
Subtotal		1,813,382
Administrative and Supervisory		
Elementary School Supervising and		
Teaching Principals	46,451	
Assistant Elementary School Principals	3,337	
Junior High School Principals	7,097	
Junior High Assistant Principals	3,843	
Senior High School Principals	15,413	
Senior High School Assistant Principals	8,337	
Local District		
Superintendents of Schools	14,671	
School Counselors	27,621	
Directors of Guidance	5,093	
Full-Time Librarians	27,520	
School Nurses	15,209	
Subtotal		174,592
GRAND TOTAL		1,987,974

Source: Research Division, National Education Association, *23rd Biennial Salary Survey of Public School Professional Personnel, 1966–67: National Data,* Research Report 1967-R11. Washington, D.C.: The Association, 1967, p. 7.

pendent type; that is, schedules that have no specified relationship to the schedules for classroom teachers. A third type of salary schedule for administrative personnel is the dollar differential. Ranging from the largest to the lowest districts, in terms of the enrollments listed above, the percentages of the independent schedules were 41.7, 29.7, and 29.9 per cents respectively. The most common bases for deriving schedules for administrative personnel, based on index or ratio of the schedule for classroom teachers are (1) to use the highest salary a given administrator would earn if he were a classroom teacher; and (2) to use the maximum of the teacher salary for the master's degree. Many school systems do not have an administrative salary schedule. In the index or ratio type of schedule, in which the salaries of administrative personnel are related to the schedules of classroom teachers, the preparation levels specified for reaching the maximum salaries are usually the same as for classroom teachers. The independent schedules for administrative personnel often specify no preparation levels for administrators. The median index relationship of maximum salaries for administrative and supervisory personnel to maximum salaries for classroom teachers in 1966–67, as reported by the NEA Research Division from the largest school districts (with enrollments of 100,000 or more) to the smallest (6,000–11,999) reporting systems were as follows:

	LARGEST	SMALLEST
Supervising Principals		
Elementary School	1.40	1.30
Junior High School	1.47	1.37
Senior High School	1.52	1.50
Counselors	1.03	1.10
Central Office		
Supervisors	1.34	1.17
Directors	1.72	1.38
Assistant Superintendents	1.98	1.65
Superintendents	2.99	1.97

The mean maximum salaries for classroom teachers and for supervising and administrative personnel in 1966–67, in reporting systems with enrollments of 100,000 or more were as follows:

Classroom teachers	$ 9,788	
Elementary School Principals	$13,295	1.36
Junior High School Principals	$14,058	1.43
Senior High School Principals	$14,973	1.53
Supervisors	$13,572	1.38
Assistant Superintendents	$19,246	1.95
Superintendents	$26,017	2.66

Of course, the above salary comparisons are based on maximums. The picture is not so rosy when the ranges in administrative salaries are considered. The ranges are: from $5,960 to $19,455 for elementary principals; for junior high school principals from $6,716 to $20,900; for senior high school principals, from $6,495 to $22,000.

How to Evaluate a Teacher Salary Schedule

Beginning in 1965, the NEA Research Division and Salary Consultant Service began experimenting with the development of a rating scale by which teachers could evaluate their own salary schedules in relation to national norms. The 1967–68 scale ("Tests for the Evaluation of School District Policies on Teachers Salaries") contains 10 tests and a maximum scale value of 1,000 points. Table 32 is an explanation of the ratings plan.

Since the weighted score bases used by NEA for evaluation of salary schedules will change year by year, an up-to-date document evaluation form can be secured from NEA, as indicated in the footnote below.[11]

[11] National Education Association, Research Division and Salary and Negotiation Consultant Service. Tests for the Evaluation of School District Policies on Teachers' Salaries. Washington, D.C.: The Association, 1967. 24 pp. (Request latest publication.)

TABLE 32   Evaluation of Teacher Salary Schedules, 1967–68

TEST	MAXIMUM POINTS
Part A—Scheduled Dollar Amounts	
Test 1—Dollar amount of the minimum scheduled salary for the bachelor's degree salary class	100
Test 2—Dollar difference between scheduled minimum and step 11 of the bachelor's degree salary class	100
Test 3—Dollar amount of scheduled salary for the master's degree salary class at step 11	100
Test 4—Dollar differential between bachelor's degree and master's degree salary classes at step 11 or highest step recognized on the bachelor's degree class if fewer than 11	100
Test 5—Dollar amount of maximum scheduled salary for the highest preparation salary class not requiring an earned doctorate degree	100
Subtotal, Part A—Tests 1 to 5	500
Part B—Structure of the Schedule	
Test 6—Ratio of minimum scheduled salary for the master's degree salary class to the minimum for the bachelor's degree class	100
Test 7—Ratio of the amount scheduled for the master's degree salary class at step 11 to the minimum scheduled for the bachelor's degree class	100
Test 8—Ratio of the maximum scheduled salary for six years of preparation to the minimum scheduled salary for the bachelor's degree	100
Test 9—Increments in the master's degree salary class: Subtest (a)—Number of increments Subtest (b)—Average increment (dollar amount) for the master's degree salary class as a per cent of the bachelor's degree minimum scheduled salary	100
Test 10—Recognition of advanced preparation beyond the bachelor's degree: Subtest (a)—Recognition of advanced preparation requiring advanced degrees or full-year academic training Subtest (b)—Recognition of intermediate advanced preparation requiring less than a full year of academic training	100
Subtotal, Part B—Tests 6 to 10	500
TOTAL SCORE—Tests 1 through 10	1,000

REFERENCES

CHAMBERLAIN, LEO M., and KINDRED, LESLIE W., *The Teacher and School Organization,* 3rd ed. Englewood Cliffs, New Jersey: Prentice-Hall, 1958, Chap. 7, "Salary," pp. 134–57.

COONS, E. L., "Salary Justice for Career Teachers," *NEA Journal,* October, 1965, 53:34–5.

DAVIS, H., *et al.*, "Economic, Legal and Social Status of Teachers; Selected Research Studies," *Review of Educational Research,* October, 1963, *32*: 400–1.

EASTMOND, JEFFERSON N., *The Teacher and School Administration.* Boston: Houghton Mifflin Company, 1959, Chap. 17, "Teachers' Salaries and Economic Status," pp. 359–88; Chap. 18, "Professional Performance as a Factor in Teachers' Salaries," pp. 389–409.

GROSS, E., "Sociological Aspects of Professional Salaries in Education," *Educational Record,* April, 1960, *41*:130–37.

HASKEW, L. D., and McCLENDON, JONATHAN C., *This Is Teaching,* 2nd ed. Chicago: Scott, Foresman and Company, 1962, "Salaries and Economic Benefits," pp. 503–506.

HECHINGER, FRED M., "The Story Behind the Strike," *Saturday Review,* May 19, 1962, *45*:54, 56, 58.

LIEBERMAN, MYRON, *Education as a Profession.* Englewood Cliffs, New Jersey: Prentice-Hall, 1956, Chap. 11, "Collective Barganing and Professionalization," pp. 334–72.

"Moonlighting? Me Too," *NEA Journal,* September, 1963, *52*:48–50+.

"NEA Unveils New Series of Tests for Comparing Teacher Salary Scales," *Nation's Schools,* August, 1965, *76*:63–4.

NATIONAL EDUCATION ASSOCIATION, Research Division, "Adequacy of Salary; Teacher Opinion Poll," *NEA Journal,* October, 1966, *55*:29.

———, *Analysis of Salary Schedule Provisions, 1965–66.* Washington, D.C.: The Association, 1966.

———, *Economic Status of Teachers, 1966–67,* Research Report 1967-R8. Washington, D.C.: The Association, 1967.

———, *Estimates of School Statistics, 1966–67,* Research Report 1966-R20. Washington, D.C.: The Association, 1966.

———, *Evaluation of Salary Schedules for Classroom Teachers,* 1966–67. Washington, D.C.: The Association, 1966.

———, *Instrument for Evaluation of Teacher Salary Schedules, 1966–67.* Washington, D.C.: The Association, 1966.

———, "Lifetime Earnings," *NEA Research Bulletin,* February, 1964, *42*: 28–30.

———, "NEA Works for Teachers' Salaries," *NEA Journal,* October, 1963, *52*:11–14.

———, *Salary Schedules for Administrative Personnel, 1966–67.* Washington, D.C.: The Association, 1967.

———, *State Minimum-Salary Laws and Goal Schedules for Teachers, 1966–67,* Research Report 1966-R18. Washington, D.C.: The Association, 1966.

———, *Twenty-Second Biennial Salary Survey of Public School Employees, 1964–65: Individual School Systems.* Washington, D.C.: The Association, 1965.

————, *Twenty-Second Biennial Salary Survey of Public School Employees, 196–65: Summary Data for All School Systems.* Washington, D.C.: The Association, 1965.

REEDER, WARD G., *Fundamentals of Public School Administration,* 4th ed. New York: Macmillan Company, 1958, pp. 158–73.

Richey, R. W., *Planning for Teaching,* 3rd ed. New York: McGraw-Hill Book Company, 1963, Chap. 9, "Salaries of Educators," pp. 258–278.

RHODE, E., "What Index Scheduling Means," *Phi Delta Kappan,* May, 1965, *46*:459–60.

STIEBER, G. N., "Teacher Salary Trends," *NEA Journal,* September, 1965, *54*:20–21.

WOODRING, PAUL, "The New York Teachers' Strike," *Saturday Review,* May 19, 1962, *45*:51–52.

8: Teacher Evaluation
and Merit Pay

One of the most intense, continuing controversies regarding salary policies for teachers is that of merit-pay schedules, providing rewards for superior performance. The profession in the public schools has rather consistently opposed the idea on the grounds that no satisfactory measures of merit have been developed. The demand from certain segments of the public for merit-pay schedules is equally vigorous and persistent. In fact, educators themselves divide on the issue.

Since the ideas of teacher ratings and evaluation are so often associated with salary scheduling for teachers, the two chapters are placed in proximity, with special emphasis on evaluation in this one. The meaning of the terms evaluation, rating, and merit pay, as applied to teachers and their salary schedules, have become greatly confused. Their distinctions tend to be lost in semantics. In fact, the terms are often and erroneously used interchangeably, while their meanings are quite clearly different.

Evaluation is basic. Its purpose is to improve instruction. And it can be used with or without merit pay. Rating is a part of the evaluative process, involving subjective judgments of the teacher's degree of success in measuring up to certain standards of good teaching. Rating can be used with or without merit pay. Evaluation, on the other hand, does not involve measuring a given teacher's work in terms of comparisons with other teachers or on the basis of certain criteria. Its emphasis is upon discovering strong and weak points in the teacher's performance, as a means of contributing to and improving the teacher's service and continuous professional growth.

Merit pay, in other words, generally presupposes both evaluation and rating. The rating of a teacher usually involves comparisons with other

166

teachers, or an appraisal of the teacher's proficiency in meeting certain criteria. However, there are some salary plans that require certain professional growth activities in order for a teacher to qualify for upper salary levels. It may or may not be employed in connection with the teacher's place on the salary schedule. If it is related to salary, the term "merit rating" is usually applied to the process.

Since any discussion of evaluation and rating of teachers must be put in proper perspective with merit pay, definitions of the different types of salary schedules should be repeated here. A single salary schedule is based on and governed by two factors: preparation and experience. The term "single" arises from the fact that no salary differentiations are made for sex (as between men and women), marital status (whether married or single), family size (the number of dependents), teaching level (elementary or high school), or teaching field (subjects taught).

The merit salary schedule generally uses a single schedule as a basis, but differentials are provided for individuals judged to merit additional pay on the basis of superior quality of service. The devices used for rewarding merit are acceleration of increments, merit bonuses, superior-service maximums, and assignment to higher levels of a multiple-track schedule. It is not always easy to identify a merit schedule or the precise meaning of merit rating. It is quite common for school districts to claim that they have a merit salary schedule when, upon examination, there is only a provision that "the school board reserves the right to withhold increments in cases of unsatisfactory service." Further examination often reveals that this provision is rarely or ever used. Thus, in practice, these districts actually have a single salary schedule.

The extent of the difficulty and confusion of interpretation of terms has been indicated by Davis: [1]

There is still no real consensus on the meaning of the term *merit schedule*. In the [NEA] Research Division we have always shied away from the phrase *merit ratings*. If a salary schedule has any kind of device, negative or positive, for varying the salary to recognize teaching efficiency, as judged subjectively, we call it a *quality-of-service salary provision*.

If the schedule says that increments will be withheld if a teacher's services are unsatisfactory, or that no increments will be given except for satisfactory service, or that a teacher's salary may be reduced if his rating becomes unsatisfactory, we call it a *penalty provision*. By such plans, a few are held back, the majority are treated alike.

If the schedule provides that double increments may be given to recognize superior service, so that the teacher reaches the maximum ahead of others, we call that *acceleration;* it is a *reward provision*. A few go ahead; the majority are treated alike. If the schedule provides that having reached the maximum, a superior teacher gets additional increments that the average teacher does not

[1] Hazel Davis, "Merit Rating: Facts and Issues," Address before NEA Second National Salary School, November 11–14, 1959, 8 pp. (mimeographed).

receive, we call that a *superior-service maximum;* it is another reward provision. If the schedule is divided into tracks on the basis of quality of service, with larger increments and higher maximums for the superior teachers, there is both acceleration and a superior-service maximum.

What is Rating and What is Evaluation?

Here are some definitions. The Commission on Teacher Evaluation of the Association for Supervision and Curriculum Development has defined the terms *rating, merit rating,* and *evaluation* as follows: [2]

Rating. A subjective, qualitative judgment of a teacher given by a rater (principal, supervisor, superintendent, or board of education) without the participation of the rated person. It may or may not determine salary.

Merit Rating. A subjective, qualitative judgment made by a rater without the participation of the person rated for purposes of determining salary, promotion, or reward.

Evaluation. A broad term covering all forms of judgment, even rating. Often used to review the process by which individuals or groups, through active and mutual participation by all persons concerned, are enabled to make choices and come to decisions in planning for growth.

The NEA Department of Classroom Teachers has developed definitions as follows: [3]

Merit Rating is a subjective qualitative judgment of a teacher made administratively by one or more persons, with or without the participation or the knowledge of the person rated, for purposes of determining salary.

[Evaluation is] a continuous process by which individuals and groups cooperatively make choices and come to decisions in planning for the improvement of instruction.

Evaluation and Rating

As a general rule, the teaching profession has opposed ratings for salary purposes (merit rating) and has as vigorously endorsed and supported evaluation. Why?

Evaluation is considered a requisite of good supervisory practices. It is considered essential to the operation of a good school system and to continual progress toward still better programs of instruction. It is considered a reasonable expectation of all who work in a salaried or group status. Evaluation is applied both to teaching service and to the individual teacher. As for the first—teaching service—evaluative factors would include such items as the methods used, outcomes of the teaching, conduct and

[2] Association for Supervision and Curriculum Development. *Better Than Rating: New Approaches to Appraisal of Teaching Services.* Washington, D.C.: The Association, a department of the National Education Association, 1950, pp. 8–9.

[3] National Education Association, Department of Classroom Teachers, *Classroom Teachers Speak on Merit Rating,* Report of Study Conference. Washington, D.C.: The Association, 1957, pp. 4–5, 9.

attitudes of pupils, use of standardized tests. Evaluation of the teacher would involve the concept of the role of the teacher, the teacher's personality, amount of professional study completed, cooperation in school and community activities.

What is the purpose of evaluation? First, as has been stated, is the improvement of instruction. It is aimed at securing constant growth of the individual in order to fulfill the role of the teacher. This is quite different from ratings, which seek to measure different levels of success.

A sound program of evaluation is essential to every school system; otherwise, there is no coordinated plan to keep the instruction moving steadily toward perfection. It is extremely unfortunate that so many evaluation plans have been developed only to carry out the provision of a merit salary plan. The use of evaluation for this exclusive purpose often is an admission of failure to develop an effective program for improving instruction and the constant in-service growth of the teaching staff.

Rating establishes comparative classifications of teachers, whereas, in evaluation, a teacher can be given an appraisal of success in meeting certain standards of achievement, can be apprised of points of weakness and strength, without conversion of this information into a comparative score or classification. In rating, it is essential that the teacher be given a score or a verbal label that establishes his status in comparison to other teachers. This is not the case with evaluation. Many research studies have tried to develop rating instruments or procedures by which relative levels of teacher success could be predicted. These studies have had only limited success. The big problem is defining valid criteria for such measurements.

HISTORY OF RATING [4]

The idea of rating workers is an old one, the origin probably dating back to antiquity. For example, a philosopher of the Wei Dynasty in China (about 200 A.D.) is quoted as saying, "The Imperial Rater of Nine Grades seldom grades men according to their merits, but always according to his likes and dislikes. It is difficult to judge men and I do not blame him." [5] Sir Francis Galton, in England (1869), rated his employees on a normal distribution curve. And in the United States, Robert Owens earlier used a set of character books for rating cotton mill workers.

Not until after World War I did any considerable number of industrial firms in the United States begin the use of systematic rating of employees. The United States Civil Service Commission began employee ratings in

[4] For an extensive treatment, see National Education Association, Research Division, "Review of Literature on Personnel Rating in Business and Industry," Research Memo 1961-11. Washington, D.C.: The Association, February, 1961, 17 pp.

[5] *Ibid.*, p. 1.

1923 to determine whether each employee would be eligible for promotion to the maximum of his grade, continued at existing rates of pay, demoted one salary step, dismissed, or reassigned. In 1950 the Performance Policy Act (for civilian employees of the federal government) reduced the ratings from five to three: (1) outstanding performance, (2) satisfactory performance, and (3) unsatisfactory performance. Actual operation of the ratings resulted in 99.8 per cent of the employees receiving a satisfactory rating, with only 0.2 per cent receiving outstanding or unsatisfactory ratings. Currently, less than half of industrial or business firms use ratings for salary determinations.

POLICY STATEMENTS OF EDUCATIONAL ASSOCIATIONS

Both the National Education Association and the American Federation of Teachers, as well as other important national organizations, oppose merit rating. The National Education Association statement is as follows: [6]

The National Education Association believes that it is a major responsibility of the teaching profession, as of other professions, to evaluate the quality of its services. To enable educators to meet this responsibility more effectively, the Association calls for continued research and experimentation to develop means of objective evaluation of the performance of all professional personnel, including identification of (a) factors that determine competence; (b) factors that determine the effectiveness of competent professionals; (c) methods of evaluating effective professional service; and (d) methods of recognizing effective professional service through self-realization, personal status, and salary.

The Association further believes that use of subjective methods of evaluating professional performance for the purpose of setting salaries has deleterious effect on the educational process. Plans which require such subjective judgments (commonly known as merit ratings) should be avoided. American education will be better served by continued progress in developing better means of objective evaluations than by expanded use of subjective ratings.

Of course, the above statement, reflecting the official position of the National Education Association, has been vigorously and repeatedly attacked by segments of the lay public and some educators, especially those in higher education. Generally, the charge is that the preparation-experience salary schedule puts a premium on mediocrity and discounts superior service. Some go so far as to denounce the idea of what they term "equal pay for all" (which the single salary schedule does not provide) as pinkish, if not communistic. But this kind of emotional response tends to ignore the difficulties involved in merit-rating pay schedules. The National Education Association statement endorses evaluation

[6] National Education Association, *NEA Handbook, 1960–61*. Washington, D.C.: the Association, 1960, pp. 59–60.

of teachers for improvement of teachers' performances, but rejects differentials in pay based on subjective ratings.

From the criticisms of the single salary schedules, it might be assumed that school administrators would be the first to denounce them and the first to advocate merit pay, especially if the alleged ease with which merit-rating salary schedules could be applied, according to the critics, were valid. But this is not the case. Superintendents themselves are opposed to rushing into the merit-rating plans, as reflected by a policy statement of their own national professional organization, the American Association of School Administrators.

This Association believes that teachers and other school personnel should be paid what they are worth. The science of teacher evaluation, however, has not yet developed a sufficiently valid instrument of procedure which justifies general adoption of salary schedules based on individual merit ratings. To attach merit pay to invalid and unreliable evaluations would deter by a generation progress toward true merit pay. The Association strongly urges accelerated systematic experimentation in teacher evaluation to the end that professional pay can be attached to professional rating and merit. The Association cautions those in the profession who adamantly oppose such experiments lest they place the supposed interests of the profession above those of the public. We also caution those lay groups who use a concept of merit pay as a subterfuge by which they oppose paying any teacher what he is worth.[7]

The AASA statement, in effect proposes that the teaching profession itself should take the lead in sponsoring research and experimentation, looking toward deriving sound pay plans for teachers.

To Rate or Not to Rate

The emotionalism that usually accompanies a discussion of merit pay affecting teachers' salaries has been mentioned. The opinions about ratings that do not affect salaries are less unanimous. Experienced teachers are likely to react unfavorably to ratings given—as they frequently are—after very brief periods of classroom observation. Many teachers do not want any ratings at all to be made. Some apparently feel that it is a necessary evil. A few welcome an evaluation, provided it includes a personal conference with the rater and is used solely as a constructive device to promote teacher growth. Data from studies of teachers' attitudes toward rating can be somewhat explained by its historical origins and developments. These will be traced briefly in an effort to present an understanding of the reactions of teachers toward rating.

The idea of efficiency rating was borrowed in part from business and industry and in part from the practices of governmental civil service. The fallacies in the idea, which mislead many businessmen, are the notion

[7] National Education Association, American Association of School Administrators, *Your AASA in 1957–58*, Official Report for the Year 1957. Washington, D.C.: The Association, 1958, pp. 269–70.

that teaching and skilled labor are analogous and the belief that teacher competence can be evaluated in measurable units that justify corresponding differences in pay.[8]

During the early days of this country, evaluation of teachers was conducted by the town selectmen or some other governmental body. The reader has probably read accounts of the visits of such groups. Seated at the front of the schoolroom, the group watched the lessons, examined the copybooks, and sometimes asked questions of the class to determine its progress. Everyone who has studied the history of education recalls a famous school examination held at Quincy, Massachusetts, in 1873. On that occasion the school committee, of which Charles Francis Adams was a member, not only took over examining, but conducted it in an unexpected manner. The result was a calamitous exposure of the schools. Pupils might be able to give grammatical rules, but they could not write a simple sentence. They could read passages from books that they had practically memorized, but they could not cope with any kind of new material. They could add, subtract, multiply, and divide when a problem was set before them, but they could not do practical things such as getting the number of board feet in a pile of lumber or computing the number of tons of hay in a mow. The school committee was so shocked that the "Quincy New Departure," an effort to make education useful, was originated. In connection with his movement, Colonel Francis Parker formulated many of the ideas that brought him such fame in connection with his work at Boston, the Chicago Normal School, and the University of Chicago.

By the latter part of the nineteenth century, communities had become too large, curricula too expanded, and teaching methods too complex to permit laymen to evaluate the work of the teacher. By this time professional school administrators were employed by most school districts. This group inherited the task of rating teachers.

Rating of teachers by professional educators has generally been of two kinds: an evaluation of the teaching process and of the teacher as an individual, and an evaluation of the progress the pupils have made. Sometimes, although not commonly, the two have been combined.

By far the most common rating method in the past was one of evaluation of the teaching process. The rater noted the discipline, interest, respect for the teacher, and methods of presentation. Often order was the primary item judged. A veteran superintendent some years ago phrased this basis of rating: "I can tell you how good a teacher is just by walking down the hall by his room. If there is a lot of noise, I know that he isn't any good. If it is quiet, I know that he is a good teacher."

Probably the next item most likely to have received attention was the actual methods of presentation. Some administrators wished teachers to

[8] Frank W. Hubbard and Hazel Davis, "The Construction of Salary Schedules for Teachers," *Harvard Educational Review*, Spring, 1952, 22:83–96.

use the five formal steps advocated by Herbart. Others advocated a review period, either oral or written, then presentation of the material assigned for that day and, finally, the next day's assignment. There were many other organization plans advocated by administrators.

Most of the efforts to rate teachers by means of pupil progress came in the 1920's as a corollary to the testing movement. At that time many educators believed that they could accurately judge pupil progress by means of standardized tests covering such subjects as reading, arithmetic, spelling, grammar, writing, geography, and history. These were given at the beginning of the year to measure status before instruction. At the end of the semester or year, similar tests were given. The differences in the results indicated the gains. Some administrators assumed that teaching was wholly responsible for whatever gains were made. If this assumption was correct, then the efficiency of the teacher could be judged by standardized tests. Completely disregarded, of course, were the variations in the natural abilities to learn, the influence of external conditions (attendance rates, classroom environment, etc.), and the growth that had taken place in some of the intangibles such as social adjustment, character, and personality.

It is not too difficult to understand why teachers have come to feel that ratings are unfair. The selectmen or the school committee, obviously, were unable to make an accurate judgment in respect to the efficiency of the teacher. This fact, perhaps, started the distrust of ratings. When administrators took over the evaluation of teaching, the process was still far from being an objective one, as each administrator had his own ideas as to effective teaching. Teacher rating by means of measuring pupil progress was also not to be trusted, because it neglected incidental learning such as took place in the home and in the community, and disregarded entirely some of the important outcomes of good teaching. Teachers have rather generally distrusted the ratings of administrative officials because of the feeling that the process is too subjective and too susceptible to favoritism. Numerous research studies have upheld the teachers' judgment.

The critics of the single salary schedules, those who vehemently advocate merit pay schedules in the public schools, generally tend to think in terms of private employment. They are not sensitive to the difficulties of arbitrary decisions about teachers' salaries. They cannot visualize the havoc caused by a community squabble arising from the complaint of a single teacher.

There are several basic needs here, all difficult to achieve. One of these is a definition of what constitutes good teaching, and the other is the development of some objective means of evaluation of teaching in accordance with the definition formulated. Also, there is the need for an agreement on the values to be gained by the rating. At the present time we have none of these—at least, none that is generally acceptable.

Certainly there is presently no agreement in respect to what constitutes good teaching. To some teachers and parents, good teaching involves only drill upon skill subjects. Others think in terms of growth and development of the whole child. These are the extremes; there are almost numberless variations in between. Even when there is agreement on the objectives to be attained, there are countless differences about the teaching methods that should be used to attain these objectives.

An accurate method of evaluation seems to be just as difficult to achieve. Teaching is a social process and shares the complexity of all social processes. One can test the strength of steel, the thickness of lumber, the accuracy of watches, and the finish of steel castings. He cannot easily evaluate teaching, social service, and statesmanship.

BASES FOR TEACHER EVALUATION

Some of the bases for teacher rating have already been briefly discussed. The following are some common bases for evaluation, which may or may not involve ratings.

Pupil Progress. If we can define what we want pupils to get out of school in the way of skills and knowledges, and if we can isolate the portion that they may learn in school, then we should be able to rate teachers by means of pupil progress. The trouble is that we cannot agree on the definition of education, and we cannot separate the school portion from that of the home, community, and other influences. Efforts during the twenties to measure pupil progress by means of achievement tests have been discussed. Certainly it would not be desirable to base teacher ratings upon this one factor alone. As yet we have no other instruments by which we can measure progress in schools.

Methods of Teaching. Perhaps the most-used rating plan has been an evaluation of the methods used in the classroom. This has been almost the standard method. The supervisor or administrator visits the classroom and judges such factors as planning, interest, management, pupil participation, general methods, and relationships. At one time notes were taken during the visit. Often a copy of these notes was left with the teacher upon departure. Always there was supposed to be a conference after the visit.

The weaknesses of this plan are apparent. There is no one best method of teaching. Probably no two teachers carry on classroom activities in exactly the same way. Sometimes, though, the supervisor or administrator has one method that he regards as being the best. This places the rating of teaching entirely on a subjective basis. Here are some illustrations:

Mr. Frye, principal of the Henry Barnard Elementary School, is an administrator of the old school. Quiet is his fetish. He cares little about what takes place in the room, as long as he "can hear a pin drop."

Mr. Carlson, principal of the Horace Mann School, has more modern ideas. He is suspicious of the unnaturally quiet room, because it indicates to him that there is no pupil activity and that it is entirely dominated by the teacher. He likes to see youngsters working in groups and committees, even though they may be a bit noisy. The same teacher could be rated as excellent by him but as a failure by Mr. Frye. Until we have commonly accepted standards in respect to what constitutes a good teacher, it will be very difficult to evaluate teaching by the methods that these principals are using.

Relationship with School and Community. With the present emphasis upon community-school relationships and upon school use of community resources, teachers are likely to be somewhat judged by the services that they render to various groups in the school environment and by their relationships with parents and patrons. They are also probably somewhat evaluated by the extracurricular activities that they sponsor, by the school committees upon which they serve, and by their general leadership in their own situations and in the profession in general. Records can be kept of these community and professional services. These contributions to the school and community should be used as one basis for the rating of teachers, but must be used in proper relation to the teacher's work in the classroom.

The Teacher's Growth. Most evaluation plans take into account indications of the professional growth of teachers. College courses, educational travel, committee work on special school assignments, publication of professional articles or books, outstanding service in teachers' professional associations are some of the commonly accepted evidences. Such activities should help the teacher to improve.

Tests of Teachers' Abilities. Scientifically devised paper-and-pencil tests of such factors as intelligence, attitudes, and aptitudes are available. At the present time no one knows what their exact relationships are to teaching success. They should have some bearing, but we can't be sure just what it is. Perhaps at some time in the future, tests of this kind can be used as a part of the rating of teachers, but as of now data gathered in this way should not be used to any great extent for such a purpose. Such tests are commonly used as a selective employment device.

A Composite Evaluation Plan. Apparently no completely satisfactory formal evaluation plan has been worked out as yet. Instead, they are much like baseball umpires, of whom one manager remarked, "They are all bad, but some are worse than others." A composite plan is probably the best that has been developed, and probably would be the most acceptable of any yet worked out to teachers, administrators, and the general public.

The composite plan requires a cumulative personnel folder for every employee. Into this folder go all sorts of information about the teacher. The file starts when the teacher is employed. The college placement folder, notes on the employment interview, letters of recommendation, and physical-examination reports are all placed in the folder. If tests of intelligence, personality, social attitudes are given, their results would, of course, be included. The teaching assignments for each year are an integral part of the personnel record. The information given should consist not only of grade and class assignments, but should also include a listing of number of pupils taught and any peculiar conditions, such as street noises, lack of equipment, or faulty attendance due to epidemics, that may have existed. The results of tests of pupil achievement in various areas of instruction should have a place, but care should be exercised that test results not be misused. The committee assignments the teacher has had and the extracurricular duties he has performed should be listed with notes in respect to the efficiency with which they have been carried out. Periodically, teachers should be asked to supply data as to their participation in professional organizations and in community affairs.

Official evaluations of classroom activities are an integral part of the personnel record. This is true whether or not a definite rating scale is used. In large cities such evaluations are usually made by the building principals, although supervisors are involved in some school districts.

Self-ratings should by all means be included. Some of us rate ourselves too highly and others not highly enough, but self-rating forms are at least useful for comparison with the ratings made by school officials.

In colleges, evaluations of teachers by students are much in vogue. There is considerable question as to their validity in higher education, although they probably do give the instructor considerable worthwhile data as to his mannerisms, personality, and social relationships. In high schools the value of pupil ratings is even more questionable, because the raters are more immature. There is some evidence that considerable good can result from occasional ratings of high school teachers by their pupils.

Letters from parents and patrons in regard to a teacher's work are frequently included, along with notes on conferences in which the work of an instructor is discussed. Unfortunately, parents and patrons are less likely to commend than to criticize. Thus, such comments must be evaluated with great care .

The composite plan is certainly not perfect. But it is perhaps the most satisfactory plan that has been proposed. The profession still needs to develop a better plan.

Rating Forms. Almost all the school districts that rate teachers use some kind of rating device. There are a number of kinds of rating forms.

These are (1) the check scale, in which lists of qualities are rated, (2) the guided comment, which asks questions for which sentences are expected in reply, (3) the total impression, in which the one doing the rating merely gives an over-all judgment as to whether the teacher is superior, average, or poor, and (4) the descriptive report, in which the observer writes a paragraph in essay style about the work of the teacher. Many districts use two or more of these types in combination.

One study [9] reported the types and extent of use of rating forms in 1,007 urban school districts, as follows:

TYPE OF FORM	EXTENT OF ALL DISTRICTS USING	
	No.	Per Cent
An appraisal form on which each teacher is evaluated on several qualities but no composite score is made for the basis of comparison	471	47
A comparison scale, setting up several levels of proficiency	307	30
A comparative scale with only two levels, satisfactory and unsatisfactory	157	16
Other type	72	7

As to the uses made of these ratings of teachers, a given district may use it for more than one purpose; 1,064 districts reported as follows: [10]

USE MADE OF TEACHER RATINGS	EXTENT OF USE	
	Districts No. of	Per Cent of Districts
In deciding on reappointment of teachers not on tenure	755	71
In recommending probationary teachers for permanent appointment	593	56
As a supervisory aid	824	77
In selecting teachers for promotion	386	36
In paying regular increments on the salary schedule	174	16
In selecting teachers to receive super-maximum salaries	73	7
In fixing size of the salary increment	47	4
Other uses	11	1

[9] National Education Association, Research Division, *Teacher Personnel Practices: Urban School Districts, 1955–56,* Special Memo. Washington, D.C.: The Association, June, 1956, p. 29.
[10] *Ibid.*

Merit Pay

Most controversial of all ratings is the issue of merit ratings of teachers for salary increments. It isn't the merit rating itself that makes the trouble but the use of the ratings to determine salary differentials, when tied to extra increments, bonuses, superior-service maximums, and assignment to higher levels on a multiple-track schedule. If rewards for high rating were confined to some other form of recognition, few would object.

On the one hand, there are those who feel that superior teachers deserve to be rewarded, just as are superior dentists, physicians, and attorneys. This attitude is more commonly held by parents and businessmen than it is by teachers. In almost any community one can hear remarks like this: "We don't pay good teachers like Miss Smith anywhere near enough, but those like Miss Jones and Miss Miller already get a lot more than they are worth." It has often been said that teaching, as it is now evaluated and remunerated, tends to perpetuate mediocrity. What this statement means is that teachers who are on the job, going through the motions of teaching, but who are doing a very uninspired, traditional job, receive the same financial rewards as those who are recognized as rendering outstanding service. There seems to be little question about how some segments of the public feel. They contend that they want to reward good teachers properly and eliminate or pay much lower salaries to the poor ones. Teachers, as we have indicated, are somewhat divided in opinion, but there are more who disapprove of merit increments than approve of them. Why do such large numbers of teachers oppose any kind of merit rating to determine salary differentials?

First of all, it is contended that there are no accurate instruments for evaluating the relative worth of individual teachers. Teaching efficiency, as we have said, cannot be measured quantitatively at the present time.

Secondly, many contend that a plan of merit rating accompanied by salary increments to the able would lower the general morale of teachers. Teachers are aware of the unreliability of present rating plans, and they fear purely subjective judgments. Many teachers feel that the merit increments would go to the "apple polishers" and to those with local influence. If this happened, it would certainly lower the general morale of teachers.

In the third place, some teachers argue that merit rating is inconsistent with the nature of the work of the teacher. At the present time we are stressing teaching as a cooperative, social process in which teachers work together for the welfare of children. Merit ratings would introduce an element of competition that would be inimical to cooperation. Merit rating would tend to destroy the service motive of teachers and supplant it with the money motive. Education is a group project, not an individual one, and anything that institutes attitudes of rivalry and competition is likely to reduce concern with the growth and development of youngsters.

Finally, some teachers insist that teaching is an occupation in which employees merge their contributions into the general whole. They receive a salary that is dependable but not related to individual efforts. The ultimate goal of all teaching must be educational service to children. No individual teacher is the sole cause of the success of a given pupil. The impact of any one teacher on a given pupil is not likely to be clearly discernible until years later. Perhaps the school system is most likely to receive maximum service for its tax contributions when the morale of teachers is high and they work together cooperatively. The proponents of this view hold that merit rating is not conducive to either high morale or cooperative effort.

Winnetka Rejects Merit Schedule

These objections are largely sustained by a school board committee in Winnetka, Illinois. In 1958 a citizens' advisory committee recommended adoption of a new salary schedule for the Winnetka School District, with salary maximums ranging from 7,000 to $9,000, and the progressive adoption of a schedule with maximums from $7,000 to $12,000. The committee, made up largely of business executives, rejected merit rating as a part of the salary schedule. Salient points in the committee's rejection were stated as follows:

> If it is our purpose, and we believe it is, to design compensation policies that will produce a better product, a better program, a better educational design for Winnetka, we do not believe this would be achieved by merit rating. We do not feel that good teachers, now giving all the energy they can offer to children, will somehow discover more energy under a merit system. Nor do we feel that teachers with less devotion and concern will necessarily struggle to do better for reasons of such limited financial differential as can be incorporated in a merit salary device.
>
> We do not feel that the competitive implications of merit awards are consistent with the cooperative and mutually helpful practices which now characterize our faculty. We do not think that the role of the superintendent as a leader and stimulator and object of faith and good will would be enhanced if he were also the rater, the distributor of financial awards, the judge and jury, as well as counsel.[11]

CURRENT STATUS OF MERIT PAY PLANS

The continued demand for some plan of differentials in teachers' salaries, arising largely from sources outside the profession, has created great pressures upon school administrators and legislators in recent years. There have been in many school districts and in some state-wide programs

[11] James C. Worthy (chairman), *Report on the Citizen's Advisory Committee on Teacher Salaries*. Winnetka, Illinois: The Committee, 1958, 73 pp.

earnest efforts to make merit plans work. How successful have the plans been?

The NEA Research Division has surveyed the history of such efforts in school districts of 30,000 population or more as far back as 1938–39 and has published results.[12] In 1938–39, of 225 (out of a total of 325) such schedules examined, 46 (20.4 per cent) included a superior-service maximum. In 1958–59, of 529 (out of a total of 724) such schedules examined, only 33 (6.2 per cent) included provisions for rewarding superior service. In 1960–61 only 58 (8 per cent) of the 701 city school systems analyzed reported salary schedules designed to reward superior service.

During the period from 1938–39 to 1958–59, for which studies were made (usually in alternate years), 170 different districts were reported as having schedules including superior-service maximums. The largest number for any given year reporting such provisions was 49; and this number had dropped to 33 in 1958–59. In July, 1960, 91 of the districts, which in the two different years during the twenty-year period had reported superior-service maximum plans in operation, were queried as to why the plans were abandoned. Replies were received from 71 of these 91 districts. The replies were as follows: 18 per cent of the districts (13) denied ever having had such plans; 20 per cent (14) indicated that the adopted plan had never been put into effect; 9 per cent (6) reported that the plan had not been dropped; 11 per cent (8) admitted that the plan had been abandoned but gave no reason. Thirty districts (42 per cent) gave specific reasons for abandoning the superior-service maximums. The reasons varied, but the following were the major ones reported: evaluations unsatisfactory, dissension created, ratings not based on merit, sense of injustice created, opposition by teachers' organizations, quota system restrictive, burden on raters, resentment caused by partial financing, discontinuance recommended by survey, plan poorly inaugurated, services of principals damaged, teacher opposition, board opposition.

Since most districts gave more than one reason, it is difficult to indicate in exact proportions the causes of abandonment. But two factors were predominant: unsatisfactory evaluations, and creation of dissension among the staff.

THE FUTURE OF TEACHER SALARY SCHEDULING

Despite overwhelming opposition by teachers to merit salary schedules, public pressures for the adoption continue. What is the answer to this

[12] National Education Association, Research Division, *Why Have Merit Plans for Teachers' Salaries Been Abandoned?* Research Report 1961-R3. Washington, D.C.: The Association, March, 1961, 51 pp.

dilemma? Obviously there is no single or simple answer. Not all teachers oppose the idea, and if workable plans could be devised, more teachers would favor the idea.

A summary of the future possibilities in salary scheduling for teachers might be stated as follows:

1. The demand for some plan of pay differentials for teachers will probably continue. But school boards and districts, aware of past experiences and failures, will seek sounder approaches to experimenting with merit-rating schedules.
2. Strong efforts will be made to strengthen the administration of existing single salary schedules by better selection of teachers, elimination of inferior teachers, and the development of more effective in-service growth devices.
3. Evaluation of teacher performance, aimed at improved services and professional growth rather than bases for pay differentials, will receive increasing attention of school districts.
4. Teacher organizations will assume an increasing role in research and experimentation on the problems of merit pay schedules, teacher evaluation, and in-service growth programs.

Precautions About the Inauguration of Merit Plans

The first prerequisite for the school board and administration considering the possibility of installing a merit pay schedule is to study carefully the experience of districts that have tried it. Many of the mistakes and failures can be avoided. A second step is to involve the staff in a cooperative, democratic study of the problem. The major mistake some boards have made has been the arbitrary imposition of a plan on the staff or the issuing of an arbitrary directive to the staff to "come up with a plan." Neither approach is designed to secure the sympathetic consideration of the teachers. There must be cooperative agreement upon criteria. Inclusion of too many classifications (perhaps not more than three classifications are workable: the poor teacher, the average teacher, and the above-average or superior teacher) is a certain omen of failure of the plan. The extra pay must be sufficient to justify the work of developing and administering a merit pay plan. Providing piddling amounts in differentials, experience has shown, invites the contemptuous dismissal of such plans by teachers. Ratings of individual teachers should involve at least three raters, and the ratings should be made each year, with a sufficient number and length of observations to give some reliability to the ratings. There should be included a formalized plan for reconciling disputes regarding the ratings of a given teacher. The plan itself must be constantly reviewed and modified in the light of experience. A static plan will fall under its own weight.

Improving the Operation of Single Salary Schedules

Likewise, static single salary schedules are likely to invite increasing criticism and attack. The key to their continuance as the predominant practice is to improve their administration, structure, and operation so that quality service and staff morale are enhanced.

First of all, this involves the strengthening of the school system's recruitment and employment policies, to the end that few inferior or below-average teachers are employed. There must be an orderly plan for eliminating the few weak teachers who slip by any recruitment system. And there must be a definite plan for evaluating the work of each teacher, to the end that each member of the staff is constantly growing in effectiveness of performance. Teachers welcome this kind of rating—not tied to pay differentials but to teacher growth. The administrator of a non-merit plan must be willing to move for the dismissal of inferior teachers through the established and understood policies, observing the "due-process" procedures. Nothing holds up a single salary schedule to attack so quickly as the retention of inferior and inept teachers on the staff. There must be a carefully planned and continuing program of in-service growth for the staff. Finally, there must be a carefully planned system of nonmonetary recognition of outstanding service by teachers.

The Role of Teachers' Organizations

It is not unfair to observe that, in all too many instances, teachers' organizations have in the past been on the defensive regarding innovations in salary scheduling. Their posture has tended to be one of seeking to maintain the status quo and of resisting experimentation with new plans.

In the future, teachers' organizations cannot, for the sake of preserving and continuing their own influence and for the sake of improving education, avoid taking vigorous leadership in two significant areas of teacher salary plans. First, they must lead, not reluctantly follow, frontier research toward achieving improvement in teacher salary scheduling. Second, they must take increasing leadership in the development of professional growth programs for teachers, the objective being the ever-growing competence of members of the profession.

Differentiated Staff Positions

The most likely future development is the institution of pay differentials based on position and responsibility and not on the rating of teachers for merit pay differentials. With the growth of team teaching and the reorganization of the teaching job, using inexperienced professionals, paraprofessionals, teachers' aides and technological aids, several categories of teaching positions may be developed.

One suggestion is that the following job differentiation may develop.[13] There would be these positions: (1) academic assistant; (2) staff teacher; (3) senior teacher; (4) teaching curriculum associate; (5) teaching research associate. The preparation of these teachers would range from the bachelor's to the doctor's degrees, with differentiated assignments, length of work year, and pay.

REFERENCES

AMERICAN ASSOCIATION OF SCHOOL ADMINISTRATORS, *Who's A Good Teacher?* Washington, D.C.: The Association, 1961.

BARR, ARVIL S., and JONES, ROBERT E., "Measurement and Prediction of Teacher Efficiency," *Review of Educational Research*, June, 1958, 28: 256–64.

"The Bay City, Michigan, Experiment: A Cooperative Study for the Better Utilization of Teacher Competencies" (symposium), *Journal of Teacher Education*, June, 1956, 7:99–153.

BENNETT, M., "Matter of Merit," *Phi Delta Kappan*, January, 1965, 46:225–6. Same condensed, *Education Digest*, March, 1965, 30:32–4.

BRAIN, G., "Evaluating Teacher Effectiveness," *NEA Journal*, February, 1965, 54:35–6.

CALABRIA, F. M., "Characteristics of Effective Teachers," *Educational Research Bulletin*, April, 1960, 39:92–100; Reply, E. G. GUBA, September, 1960, 39:157–59.

CASSEL, RUSSELL N., and JOHNS, W. LLOYD, "Critical Requirements of an Effective Teacher," *Bulletin of the National Association of Secondary-School Principals*, November, 1960, 44:119–24.

CHAMBERLAIN, LEO M., and KINDRED, LESLIE W., *The Teacher and School Organization*, 3rd ed. Englewood Cliffs, New Jersey: Prentice-Hall, 1958, "The Appraisal of Teaching," pp. 252–59.

COLLISTER, LAREW M., "A Better Way than Merit Pay," *NEA Journal*, May, 1964.

DAVIS, H., "What Teachers Say About the Evaluation of Teachers," *NEA Journal*, February, 1965, 54:37–9.

FILBIN, R. L., "Merit Salary: A Realistic Approach to Upgrading the Teaching Profession," *American School Board Journal*, April, 1965, 150:11–12.

FORBES, J. E., "You Can Measure Teaching Quality, Even If It Hurts," *Grade Teacher*, September, 1965, 83:54+.

GRIEDER, CALVIN (moderator), "Satisfactory Pay Should Precede Merit

[13] M. John Rand and Fenwick English. "Toward a Differentiated Teaching Staff," *Phi Delta Kappan*, January 1968, 44:8, pp. 264–268.

Rating" (roundtable discussion), *Nation's Schools,* February, 1961, *67*: 114–17.

HOAR, G. W., "Community Service and Nonschool Activities Replace Merit Rating," *Nation's Schools,* July, 1964, *74*:32.

HOLLOWAY, GEORGE E., JR., "Objective Look at the Merit Pay Issue," *School Executive,* April, 1959, *78*:19–21.

HOWSAM, R. B., "Teacher Evaluation: Facts and Folklore," *National Elementary Principal,* November, 1963, *43*:6–18. Same condensed *Education Digest,* March, 1964, *29*:12–15.

KINGSTON, A. J. and GENTRY, H. W., "Criteria Which Teachers Believe Should Be Evaluated in Merit Rating," *Peabody Journal of Education,* May, 1964, *41*:338–42.

KLEINMANN, JACK H., *Merit Rating: Past, Present and Perhaps.* (Paper presented to a panel meeting at the American Association of School Administrators Convention, February 20, 1963). Washington, D.C.: The Association, 1963.

LEWIS, GERTRUDE M., *Evaluation of Teaching.* National Education Association, Elementary-Kindergarten-Nursery Education. Washington, D.C.: The Association, 1966.

MCKEOWN, L. W., "On Merit Rating," *Phi Delta Kappan,* October, 1966, *48*:77.

"Merit Pay Sounds Better Than It Works," *Nation's Schools,* February, 1967, *79*:82+.

MICHAEL, C. B., "Teachers Attitudes Toward Merit Rating as a Function of Conflict of Interest," *Journal of Teacher Education,* June, 1964, *15*: 210–18.

MILLER, L. K. *et al.,* "Suggested Research Model for the Investigation of Classroom Teachers' Effectiveness," *Journal of Educational Research,* May, 1965, *58*:405–8.

MITZEL, HAROLD E., "Teacher Effectiveness," in HARRIS, CHESTER (ed.) *Encyclopedia of Educational Research,* 3rd ed. New York: Macmillan Company, 1960, pp. 1481–86.

NATIONAL EDUCATION ASSOCIATION, Department of Classroom Teachers, *Classroom Teachers Speak on Professional Salary Schedules.* Washington, D.C.: The Association, 1958.

NATIONAL EDUCATION ASSOCIATION, Research Division, *Arguments on Merit Rating,* Research Memo 1959-30. Washington, D.C.: The Association, 1959.

———, *Evaluation of Classroom Teachers,* Research Bulletin, October, 1964, *42*:83–8, 108–11; February, 1965, *43*:12–18. Same condensed, *Education Digest,* April, 1965, *30*:22–4.

———, *Merit Ratings in Business and Industry: Fact or Fancy?* Research Memo 1964–6. Washington, D.C.: The Association, 1964.

————, "Methods of Evaluating Teachers," *Education Digest,* September, 1965, *31*:22–4.

————, *Quality-of-Service Provisions in Salary Schedules, 1958–59,* Research Report 1959-R24. Washington, D.C.: The Association, 1959.

————, *Report of Merit Study Committee in Public Schools in Hamden, Connecticut,* Research Memo 1965-7. Washington, D.C.: The Association, 1965.

————, *Selected References on Merit Salary Schedules,* ARL 63-6. Washington, D.C.: The Association, 1963.

————, *Superior-Service Maximums in Teachers' Salary Schedules, 1962–63,* Research Memo 1963-14. Washington, D.C.: The Association, 1963.

————, *Why Have Merit Plans for Teachers' Salaries Been Abandoned?* Research Report 1961-R3. Washington, D.C.: The Association, 1961.

NATIONAL EDUCATION ASSOCIATION, Salary Consultant Service and Department of Classroom Teachers, *Professional Growth Recognition,* Guidelines No. 12. Washington, D.C.: The Association.

REDFERN, GEORGE B. *How to Appraise Teaching Performance.* Columbus, Ohio: School Management Institute, 1963.

REEDER, WARD G., *Fundamentals of School Administration,* 4th ed. New York: Macmillan Company, 1958, Chap. 9, "Evaluating Teaching Efficiency," pp. 189–96.

ROSE, G. W., "Performance Evaluation and Growth in Teaching," *Phi Delta Kappan,* October, 1963, *45*:48–53.

————, "Preparation Unlocks the Door to Successful Merit Rating," *Nation's Schools,* October, 1959, *64*:51–53.

RYANS, DAVID G., "Assessment of Teacher Behavior and Instruction; Observation and Assessment of Teaching," *Review of Educational Research,* October, 1963, *33*:423.

————, *Characteristics of Teachers, Their Description, Comparison and Appraisal.* Washington, D.C.: American Council on Education, 1960.

————, "Prediction of Teacher Effectiveness," in HARRIS, CHESTER (ed.) *Encyclopedia of Educational Research,* 3rd ed. New York: Macmillan Company, 1960, pp. 1486–91.

STINNETT, T. M., "Merit Rating for Teachers?" *Instructor,* January, 1961, *70*:20, 93.

STIRLING, THOMAS, "What Is the Case for and Against Merit Rating for Teachers?" *Bulletin of the National Association of Secondary-School Principals,* April, 1960, *44*:92–95.

SYMONDS, PERCIVAL M., "Characteristics of the Effective Teacher Based on Pupil Evaluations," *Journal of Experimental Education,* June, 1955, *23*:289–310.

TATE, MERLE W., and HAUGHEY, CHARLES F., "Teachers Rate Merit Rating," *Overview,* February, 1960, *1*:41–44.

VAN ZWOLL, JAMES A., *The Domain of the School Administrator in the Merit Rating of Teachers,* (Address presented at the annual convention of the American Association of School Administrators, February 18, 1962). Research Memo 1962-13. Washington, D.C.: The Association, 1962.

WILSON, CHARLES H., "The Case Against Merit Pay," *Saturday Review,* January 20, 1962, 45:44, 62–63.

————, *Merit Pay and Teacher Evaluation,* (Paper presented at the Fifth National School for Teacher Salary Scheduling, September 24–28, 1962). Washington, D.C.: The Association, 1962.

9: Retirement Systems
for Teachers

Retirement always seems, to the young teacher or prospective teacher, like a remote subject. No young person about to launch upon a life career ever seems to think of himself in terms of reaching retirement age. It is a very human trait to feel that some extraordinary streak of good fortune will provide the means of livelihood in old age. The accumulation of sufficient savings or investments for comfortable living after active working days are over is, for most workers, not easy. Consequently, retirement plans have become general for workers in industry; and the federal government, through social-security legislation, has inaugurated a compulsory plan that applies to millions of workers. Adequate retirement provisions for teachers are extremely important, especially so because of the moderate annual incomes they receive. Together with good salaries and tenure, adequate retirement systems provide a well-rounded program of reasonable security, which contributes to the attractiveness of teaching as a life career. One of the first things the enlightened teacher will examine, when seeking employment, is the retirement system under which he will work.

Average life expectancy is constantly increasing. According to the 1937 Standard Annuity Mortality Table, a man who attains age sixty has a remaining life expectancy of seventeen and a half years. Preparation for retirement should be an important consideration from the very beginning of teaching service.

Teacher retirement systems are of comparatively recent origin. Pensions for policemen and firemen were started in some cities at about the time of the Civil War. In most cases these early pensions were paid entirely from public funds. On the other hand, early teacher retirement systems were frequently without public support and were financed by

187

member contributions. The New York City teachers founded an Old Age and Disability Annuity Association in 1887. Similar associations were established soon after that in Baltimore, Boston, Cincinnati, Philadelphia, and Washington, D.C. New Jersey adopted the first state-wide teacher retirement system in 1896. At present, all states have in operation state-wide retirement systems for teachers.

At first, the teacher retirement movement developed almost entirely in the larger cities. In 1895 New York City teachers secured the enactment of permissive legislation that provided for the establishment of a city teachers' retirement system. This system was financed by deductions from the salaries of teachers absent from their teaching duties. The money so deducted was turned into the pension fund. The plan of operation for the early systems was later placed on a sounder basis, and many have continued in operation to the present time. In general, the adoption of state-wide teacher retirement systems has resulted in the absorption of local plans into the state-wide systems, but there are notable exceptions. Twenty-four cities (Chicago, Detroit, Milwaukee, New York, Los Angeles, San Francisco, District of Columbia, Denver, Wilmington, Atlanta, Des Moines, Kansas City, Kansas, and Kansas City, Missouri, New Orleans, Baltimore, Boston, Duluth, Minneapolis, St. Paul, St. Louis, Omaha, Knoxville, Memphis, and Portland) still operate retirement plans entirely separate from their respective state's system.

Early in the twentieth century there commenced a rapid increase in the adoption of state-wide teacher retirement systems. This movement, however, was first confined almost entirely to the northeastern part of the United States. Until the late 1930's only eleven states west of the Mississippi had state-wide teacher retirement systems; only two were operating in the southeast. In 1930 there were only twenty-two state-wide retirement plans for teachers in the whole United States. By 1950 all states had provided for teacher retirement. In almost every case the early systems were of an unsound nature, but most were later replaced by plans that are now adequately financed.

Federal social-security legislation, as amended in 1950 and 1954, has caused certain states to amend or repeal their retirement laws. South Dakota abolished its state retirement system for teachers in 1951 and put its teachers under social security only, but reinstated its state system in 1959. Presently all but 12 states have worked out programs for combining social security with the states' retirement systems. (Social security will be discussed in more detail in another part of this chapter.)

Benefits to Public and to Teachers

A teacher retirement system benefits the public by affording an enlightened system of removing from service teachers who, because of age or disability, are no longer able to give efficient service. In the absence of retirement benefits, a board of education would be reluctant to remove a teacher who had given years of faithful service. Thus, the primary reason for teacher retirement plans is to serve the welfare of children. A retirement system also benefits the teacher by affording him a degree of economic security in his old age. The existence of retirement systems tends to attract competent people into teaching, to retain them in the profession, and to improve teacher morale by alleviating worries concerning old age. The public has come to accept the soundness of the idea of providing all employees with old-age protection.

The National Council on Teacher Retirement

As early as 1887 the NEA began advocating pensions for teachers. In 1911 the association established a committee on teachers' salaries, tenure, and pensions. In 1936 its successor, the Committee on Retirement Allowances, was merged with the National Council on Retirement Systems to form the National Council on Teacher Retirement. The NCTR is a joint council of the National Education Association, the executive officers and board members of state and local teacher retirement systems, and the state education associations. Teachers have representation in the council through the six members of the Executive Committee appointed by the NEA, as well as the executive officers and board members of retirement systems and the representatives of the state education associations. A total of forty-four state and sixteen local retirement systems and twenty-six state education associations were members of the NCTR in 1967.

The NCTR has two main objectives: to safeguard and strengthen legal provisions for retirement income of teachers, and to disseminate information on current trends and on proposed or newly enacted legislation affecting teachers' retirement systems and in sponsoring amendments to social-security legislation to include teachers. It also, from time to time, works for federal legislation to improve the tax status of retired teachers.

GENERAL PROVISIONS OF RETIREMENT SYSTEMS

Age and Service Requirements

Almost all teacher retirement systems now contain a minimum-age requirement—the earliest age at which a member of the system can retire and be eligible for benefit payments. Age sixty is the commonly accepted figure for regular retirement, though there are plans with age sixty-five as the minimum for full benefits and still other systems that permit retirement at fifty-five or fifty with or without reduction in benefits. There are some systems that permit retirement after a specified number of years of service, regardless of age. In general, it is reasonable for a retirement plan to set a minimum age. Plans that permit an individual to draw a retire-ment allowance after a certain number of years of service without regard to age may be expensive to maintain. The number of persons eligible to retire is thereby increased, and the individuals who do retire early live for a much longer period and, therefore, draw more benefits from the fund. Both of these factors increase the cost. It is obvious that it will cost more to pay retirement allowances throughout the remainder of life to a person who retires at age fifty or fifty-five than to a person who retires at sixty or sixty-five. It is advantageous to the individual to be able to retire after a certain number of years of service, but there is no particular benefit to the public in permitting retirement at an early age. Ordinarily there is no need for removing the teacher from service until he has become at least sixty years old, unless, of course, he is disabled.

Teachers like an arrangement whereby they are permitted to retire at an early age. This is true even though they may continue in service long after meeting the minimum qualifications. To offset the excessive cost of earlier retirement, some states have adopted a provision whereby a person may retire at an earlier age and accept the actuarial equivalent of what he would receive had he continued in service to the normal retirement age, which is ordinarily sixty. The following figures for women employees of the Michigan public schools indicate the way such an arrangement oper-ates. Because of difference in life expectancy, the allowance of men would not be reduced on exactly the same basis.

Age of Retirement	Per Cent of Benefits Allowable at Age 60
55	71.896
56	76.524
57	81.590
58	87.142
59	93.260
60	100

The reason for reducing the allowance is that consideration is given to the greater life expectancy of a person retiring at an earlier age; also, two other factors are involved: shorter period for paying into the system by the teacher, and shorter period such payments earn interest. This is what is meant by taking the actuarial equivalent.

Deferred Benefits

Another way of taking care of persons who wish to retire from service at an early age is by provision for deferred benefits. The principle of deferred benefits is sometimes known as maintenance of membership. Under such an arrangement an individual is allowed to retire from service after satisfying service requirements with the understanding that benefits will be paid from age sixty forward. For example, some systems permit retirement after a designated number of years of service, but benefits do not begin until age sixty. The deferred-benefit or maintenance-of-membership arrangement also serves to protect the individual who might be forced out of service prior to the attainment of the regular retirement age. If a school superintendent or a school teacher were dismissed at age fifty-seven or fifty-eight, and if one of the requirements of the law was continuous service to age sixty, he would then lose retirement rights entirely. Obviously, this is unfair for persons who have spent a lifetime in service.

Compulsory Retirement

In addition to setting a minimum age for retirement, 34 states include in their laws a maximum age beyond which the teacher is not permitted to serve. The first is permissive, the second mandatory. This figure is generally fixed at seventy (22 states), with eight states at age 65, and a few in which the mandatory age is above seventy. The purpose of specifying a mandatory retirement age is to make certain that the retirement system accomplishes its objective of removing from service those who are no longer able to teach effectively. Chronological age, to be sure, is not always a measure of effectiveness, since some individuals maintain their effectiveness up to an advanced age. However, the number of persons in this category beyond the age of seventy is comparatively small.

When the state law does not fix a compulsory retirement age, local employers frequently do. The question of adopting a compulsory retirement age for school employees comes before almost every board of education at some time or other.

One board-of-education policy with respect to compulsory retirement reads as follows: "Retirement of all employees shall be at the age of sixty-five years, effective on June 30 of the fiscal year during which they reach their sixty-fifth birthday."

In some instances provision is made for extending the retirement age for an individual employee when the best interests of the pupils and the schools so require. Such extensions of the age limit are sometimes made contingent upon the passing of a satisfactory physical examination.

The difficulty of the problem is indicated in the replies of two superintendents of schools in a recent survey.

One said: "Personally, I think my biggest problem in a system this size is the overagedness of some of our teachers to the extent that they are in such a 'status quo' state of mind that there isn't anything I can do to pry them loose or any activity I can lead them into that would indicate professional growth." A somewhat different attitude was expressed by the second superintendent, who said: "Age, of course, is not the complete answer in so far as retirement is concerned. I have some people who could go on to seventy years of age without too much difficulty, but I have others who ought to retire at the age of fifty-five." The main difficulty in adapting a flexible retirement age is the lack of an objective measure for determining who should be retired and who should not at a given age.

Another difficulty is that some school districts make the mistake of attempting to solve a current problem by adopting a permanent policy. Some cities have adopted a specified compulsory-retirement age because they wanted to get rid of some teachers who had reached that age. This is not a sound principle upon which to base a retirement policy, because it may later work a hardship on other individuals.

Ordinarily it is advisable that there be a difference between the compulsory-retirement age and the minimum retirement age prescribed by the state retirement system. Just because state law permits a person to qualify for a retirement allowance at the age of sixty does not mean that sixty is a desirable compulsory-retirement age.

In general it may be stated that the interests of the schools are best served by the adoption of a compulsory-retirement age. The adoption of such a policy may work hardships in some cases, and occasionally a good teacher will be removed from service prematurely. However, in many more instances the compulsory age limit will remove from service persons who are no longer able to deal effectively with boys and girls.

The general tendency toward increased life expectancy raises problems that conflict with the adoption of a compulsory-retirement age. The American Experience Table of Mortality, which was in use for many years, calculated that a man at age sixty had a life expectancy of fourteen years. The 1937 Standard Annuity Mortality Table, which is now widely used by insurance companies, gives a man aged sixty a life expectancy of seventeen and one-half years. More recent studies of mortality by actuaries show a constant improvement in the life expectancy of older people. Thus, we now know that the number of older people who make up our population will continue to increase, and some way needs to be found to keep them occupied. Without some sort of occupation, either in the form of a vocation or an avocation, old people become very unhappy and dissatisfied. Thus the adoption of compulsory-retirement ages, based on life-expectancy rates of several years ago, conflicts with the fact that people are now living much longer than they formerly did. A partial solution of this problem lies in making arrangements for part-time employment on the part of retired school employees. Generally, this would call for a modification of the state retirement law. In a number of states the retirement law has been amended recently to permit a retired teacher to earn up to a designated amount of money per year in school employment or to serve a designated number of days as a substitute without loss of retirement benefits.

As we have said, there is a trend for school boards to adopt a compulsory-retirement age, and sixty-five is a very commonly accepted figure for use in this connection. Further, the interests of the schools are best served by the establishment of some compulsory-retirement age. Schools should not try to solve a current problem by hurriedly adopting a permanent policy. The adoption of compulsory retirement should be preceded by a careful study of the problem.

Service Requirements

Great variation exists from state to state in service requirements, with a range from a low of ten years to a high of thirty-five. Common requirements for normal retirement are ages 60 or 65, with a specified number of years of service. Most states require that at least fifteen years of the school service be performed in that state, although in a few instances this requirement is as low as ten years. The amount of the allowance is generally related to the number of years of service. Disability retirement allowances are paid after a certain minimum period of service regardless of the age of the individual. The minimum-service requirement for disability allowance is ordinarily ten or fifteen years.

Computing Benefits

It is customary to refer to a teacher's retirement pay as a retirement allowance, rather than as a pension or an annuity. However, all three terms are sometimes used with the same meaning, though not technically correct. In general, the term "pension" refers to an outright grant from public funds to a retired person. The "retirement benefits" refer to annuities built up for the retirement years of the worker by joint contributions of the individual and his employer. In one state, Delaware, retired teachers receive a straight pension paid entirely from state funds. Teachers contribute nothing to this plan. The remainder of the states have what is commonly known as joint-contributory retirement systems financed by funds collected from the teachers and from some public source, either state or local or both.

Many formulas exist for computing the benefits payable at time of retirement. One plan bases the allowance primarily on the amount of the accumulated contributions of the member together with interest thereon. Under this system an individual contributes 4 per cent or more of his salary throughout his period of membership, and at the time of retirement his allowance is fixed by determining what his contributions would secure in the form of an annuity, and then this is matched with an equal allowance from public funds. Some recognition is given to prior service, by which is meant service performed before the retirement law went into effect. The part of an allowance paid for prior service is usually paid out of public funds. This type of benefit is called a money-doubled formula, because the annuity purchasable by the member's accumulated contributions is doubled by the addition of an equal amount from public funds for membership service.

Ordinarily, the retirement allowance is computed in three separate parts: an annuity based on the member's own contributions, the pension for membership service, and the pension for prior service. The membership-service pension equals the annuity in a money-doubled formula. Under a more commonly accepted arrangement, the membership-service pension equals a certain fraction (frequently 1/140, 1/160, or 1/120) of average compensation multiplied by the number of years of service, regardless of the amount of the annuity purchasable by the member's own contributions.

The prior-service pension is usually paid at a higher rate to take into account the fact that during the period of prior service (service before the enactment of the law) the teacher was not accumulating contributions for an annuity. Some systems do not separate prior and membership service, but instead pay a pension including the years served both before and after the law was passed.

A third general type does not divide the allowance into annuity and pension, but pays 1/60, 1/70, or 1/80 of average compensation multiplied by the number of years of service, and public funds must make up the difference between what the member's accumulated contributions will buy in the form of an annuity and the total allowance promised.

Although the specific formula used in computing retirement allowances is not particularly important, benefits and costs differ according to these three general types of formulas. For no particular reason there has been a general acceptance of the idea that people should retire on an allowance of half pay. Average compensation used in the formula for benefits is ordinarily based on the last five or ten years' salaries, or the best five in the last ten, or it may be based on the best five years' salaries, consecutive or nonconsecutive. Lifetime earnings are seldom used as an average, as this would work a hardship on the retiring teachers, most of whom earned low salaries until the past ten years. The reason for using 1/60 in the computation formula is that such an arrangement provides an allowance of approximately half pay after thirty years of service (30/60). In states where the fraction is 1/70 or 1/140, it is because the individual is expected to serve for thirty-five years in order to attain an allowance of half pay (35/70).

Theoretically, the member is expected to pay for half the cost of his retirement allowance based on membership service, but only in the money-doubled plans does this expectation result. In all other types of formulas, public funds may pay more than half the cost for membership service.

In almost all cases there is a maximum placed on the number of years of service that will be used in computing the pension. It is important for teachers to understand the formula used, if they are to be satisfied that the allowance is reasonable. A reasonable allowance is ordinarily accepted to be half of average salary based on the best five-year average if the individual has worked for thirty or thirty-five years.

Refunds

Teachers who leave the service before qualifying for a retirement allowance are entitled to a return of the payments they have made. A number of different plans exist for taking care of the withdrawal privilege of members who terminate their service prior to retirement. The most common arrangement is to return to the teacher the total amount that he has contributed to the fund. It is generally agreed, and practiced, that since the contributions represent deductions from the teacher's salary, he is entitled to interest on his deposits. There are, however, some systems under which a member leaving service after ten or more years of work may elect a deferred annuity to be paid him when he reaches retirement age. Under this arrangement the individual leaves his funds on deposit instead of taking a refund. Sometimes the state's matching funds also remain.

Optional Benefits

To permit a retiring teacher to protect his dependents, all but one or two states allow him an optional method of settlement at the time of retirement. Under this arrangement the retiring teacher elects a full benefit that terminates with his death, or he may elect instead a reduced benefit with the understanding that it will be continued for as long as he or his beneficiary survives. The amount of the reduction in allowance depends upon the age of the named beneficiary as related to the age of the retiring teacher. There is also an arrangement whereby the retiring teacher elects a reduced allowance with the understanding that half of his allowance will be paid to the surviving beneficiary. In this case, the allowance is not reduced as much, because only half of the benefit will be paid the survivor. It is customary to provide that no option election shall be effective in case a member dies within thirty days after the date of his retirement. This is to prevent so-called "deathbed" elections. Ordinarily, no change in an option election is permitted after the first retirement payment has been made. Option payments work on the theory that there is no additional cost to the state. The idea is that on the basis of life expectancy it is possible to predict the amount that is likely to be paid to a retiring teacher. When an option is elected, this amount is then divided upon the basis of the combined life expectancy of the two individuals.

The amount of the reduction in the allowance depends upon the age and sex of the beneficiary. Each individual case must be figured separately. As an example, a man sixty years old, whose wife is also sixty and whose salary record entitles him to a retirement allowance of $1,000 per year, may elect Option 2, in which case he will receive $739.11 per year as long as he lives, and his wife will receive the same amount per year after his death as long as she lives. Or he may elect Option 3, in which case he will receive $849.66 per year as long as he lives, and his wife will receive $424.98 per year after his death as long as she lives.

There is a refund option, in which the money on deposit for the benefit of the teacher is guaranteed to be paid as a minimum benefit. This means that for a teacher who, upon retirement, has a total deposit of $20,000, and who dies after having received only $5,000 in benefits, the remainder will be paid out to his beneficiary.

Summary of Certain Provisions in One State Retirement Law

The great range of variations and practices among the state teacher-retirement systems makes it impossible to describe any particular system as typical. The following summary [1] of the provisions of one of the state systems will indicate the general nature of these systems and many common features, although this state system is probably among the most liberal.

Retirement Age: Maximum benefit at age sixty; reduced benefit at age fifty-five.

Minimum Length of Service Required. Ten years in the state for age benefit at age fifty-five, or for permanent disability; three years for death benefit; military-service credit to five years; state service to ten years counted.

Amount Paid by Teacher: Six per cent of total salary, matched by state. An additional ¼ per cent of teacher's salary required for survivors' benefits.

Formula for Determining Teacher's Benefit: Multiply .02 times average annual salary for ten highest of last fifteen years times years of service. This product is reduced by 5 per cent for each year below age sixty (retirement year). Example: For a teacher who has thirty years of service and whose average annual salary for the ten highest of the last fifteen years is $5,000—.02 times $5,000 times 30 equals $3,000 annual or $250 monthly benefit.

Disability Benefits: Permanent disability computed on same formula

[1] Adapted from "Important Items in Teacher Retirement Systems" (summary of state plans). Springfield: Research Department, Illinois Education Association, April, 1961, 14 pp. (planographed).

as age benefit at age sixty, except that it cannot exceed benefit projected to age fifty-five. Minimum of $75 a month or 25 per cent of average final salary.

Monthly Survivors' Benefit: For death in service after three years of service in the state, benefits for dependents are: spouse and child under eighteen, or child alone, $165; $200, if more than one child; parent sixty-five or spouse age fifty, $100. For spouse alone, ten years of service in the state are required.

Death Benefit, Lump Sum: After three years' service in the state, upon death of teacher a lump sum of $500 is paid to the beneficiary.

Refunds: Contributions of the teacher may be withdrawn with interest. The beneficiary receives contributions plus interest, or for death after retirement, the balance of contributions.

TABLE 33   Monthly Age Benefit Based on Above Formula

MONTHLY BENEFITS ACCORDING TO AGE AND LENGTH OF SERVICE				
Average Annual Salary	Age 60, 20 Years' Service	Age 55, 31 Years' Service	Age 62, 38 Years' Service	Age 65, 41 Years' Service
$7,800	$260.00	$302.25	$494.00	$533.00
7,200	240.00	279.00	456.00	492.00
6,000	200.00	232.50	380.00	410.00
4,800	160.00	185.00	304.00	328.00
4,200	140.00	162.75	266.00	287.00
2,400	80.00	93.00	152.00	164.00

Post-retirement Employment: A retired teacher may do substitute teaching in the state without loss of age benefit.

Financing the Retirement System

Retirement systems are ordinarily financed jointly by the employer and employee. In the case of teacher retirement systems, this means that they are financed jointly by the teacher and by the state or local school district.

Teachers contribute or deposit 4 or 5 per cent of their salary, or the percentage to be deducted from the member's salary may be determined by an actuary. Members' deposits are segregated and credited to each individual teacher's account. The deposits accumulate interest and remain the property of the teacher.

It is necessary, at the start of a retirement system, to provide a larger amount from public revenues than the aggregate of the members' contributions. This is to take care of accrued liabilities that have been built up over a period of years, especially for prior-service pensions. Various procedures are used to build up the public's part of the retirement allowance. In operation, retirement plans are of three main types: full reserve systems, partial reserve systems, and pay-as-you-go or cash disbursement plans. Under the cash disbursement plan the appropriations are spent as rapidly as they are received, and appropriations are not made in amount larger than the expected need for a biennium or a year. The reserve plans are just as the name implies—an arrangement whereby reserves are built up to the point that, when a teacher is ready to retire, enough money has been accumulated to pay the allowance throughout the remainder of the teacher's life. Appropriations are large enough to take care of the allowance due for each year of membership service at the time the service is being rendered, and the accrued liability for prior service is amortized over a period of years. The advantage of such an arrangement is that it affords an almost complete guarantee to the individual that money will be available to pay his retirement allowance at the time of retirement; and those taxpayers who received the teacher's services pay their rightful share of the cost. The objection to such a plan is that it calls for accumulating very large reserves, and for that reason some systems now proceed on a partial-reserve plan. Under this arrangement the state's share is appropriated in the full amount needed for life at the time of the retirement of each teacher. Thus the state would have on hand at all times a reserve sufficient to make all future payments to persons already retired.

An important thing to note is whether or not the cost of benefits promised is recognized. In the early days of pension funds it was common to promise benefits far beyond those that could be paid on the basis of the financing it provided. It is possible for an actuary to predict with a fair degree of accuracy the cost of financing any particular set of benefits. There is always a tendency on the part of teachers to seek liberalization of their retirement plan without noting the increased costs that are involved. Mention has already been made of the difficulties encountered with the lowering of age limits. The payment of a retirement allowance for the remainder of a person's life is always an expensive procedure. For example, an insurance company requires a payment of about $150 to guarantee an annuity of $1 per month for the remainder of life to a man aged sixty. Applying this to a single retirement allowance of $1,200 per year (or $100 per month) to a man aged sixty, it would be apparent at once that a reserve of about $15,000 is required to finance such a single retirement allowance. When, in any state, this is multiplied by several thousand retired teachers, the cost becomes clear. It would seem apparent that existing plans should be liberalized only after reserves have been accumulated to take care of the already promised benefits.

Teachers are sometimes concerned over the soundness of their retirement system. They will frequently ask, "What assurance have I that I will be paid when I am ready to retire?" or they may ask, "Isn't it possible that the legislature will abolish the retirement system before I am ready to retire?" The answer to the first question lies largely in seeing that the fund is on a sound basis and that reserves are accumulated to meet the future demands. The second question may be answered by stating that the courts have held that a pension or retirement system is a contractual obligation that cannot be eliminated for present members of the system, although changes can be made in the plan for future teachers. It is unlikely that any legislature would take such action except for the purpose of enacting a new and better law. The courts have generally held that persons already retired have a vested right in the retirement allowance and that the legislature must make some arrangements for continuing payments to them. With respect to persons not yet retired, the opinion is divided, but it has generally been held that the retirement plan could be changed or even done away with for those who are still in service. It should again be noted that it is highly unlikely that any state legislature would treat teachers in such an unfair manner. In an attempt completely to guarantee the retirement rights of public employees and teachers, New York State has inserted the following section in its constitution:

Membership in retirement systems; benefits not to be diminished nor impaired. Section 7. After July first, nineteen hundred forty, membership in any pension or retirement system of the State or of a civil division thereof shall be a contractual relationship, the benefits of which shall not be diminished or impaired.

This affords complete protection to the members, but it must be recognized that the constitutional amendment could be repealed. Or the legislature could close the membership to future employees without impairing the rights of members of the system.

Reciprocity

One other matter requires consideration: namely, reciprocity among states. As matters now stand, the successful teacher or school administrator may find that after he has served in one state for a period of years, he has an opportunity to advance professionally by accepting a position in some other state. Such a teacher immediately sees that by making a change he may find himself without retirement benefits or he may suffer a reduction in retirement rights. Presently, the lack of reciprocity among states in retirement benefits is probably the chief barrier to the free flow of qualified teachers across state lines. A solution to the problem of the migrant school teacher lies in the adoption of some form of reciprocity among state retirement systems. Some state retirement systems permit a teacher coming from another state to purchase credit for past service in another state. The most satisfactory proposal calls for a system of deferred benefits. This would require persons leaving school employment in one state to leave their accumulated payments in the fund, and would permit such teachers to draw a retirement allowance at a later date. Probably a specified number of years of service, such as ten or more, should be required before a member would be eligible for a deferred allowance. Under this arrangement, the retired teacher might receive partial allowances from two or more states. This plan is called vesting.

Retirement Needed by All School Employees

This discussion has centered around teacher retirement. That is because this book was written primarily for teachers. However, it should be recognized that, in addition to teachers, schools have many nonteaching employees such as clerks, janitors, engineers, and bus drivers. All school employees are entitled to the protection of a retirement system, but this fact has not been generally recognized. There are still many states in which no provision is made for the retirement of nonteaching public school employees. According to the National Education Association,[2] twenty-four state retirement systems cover all school employees, including custodial and clerical help. In a few other states nonteaching employees are cared for by a separate system. There is no real basis (except tradition) for providing for the retirement of one group of school employees—namely, teachers—without providing at the same time for nonteaching employees. It is unfortunate that the distinction has developed between teaching and nonteaching school employees. The unity of the whole school staff should be stressed. All school personnel, whether teachers, custodians, or clerks, should be considered as agents in the facilitation of instruction. The only basis for the employment of any school personnel is that the individual employed will contribute to the educational process. If instruction is to be successfully accomplished, children need to be adequately housed and cared for. This requires custodians and engineers. Clerks are also needed to free teachers for instruction, and an enlarged school program often includes other types of personnel, such as nurses, bus drivers, and cafeteria workers. When they satisfy the statutory age and service requirements, all these nonteaching employees are entitled to retirement allowance on the same basis as teachers. Further, the inclusion of all school employees in the retirement system serves to unify the whole school staff and to bring teachers and non teachers together.

Social-Security Provisions for Teachers

The federal program for old-age and survivors' insurance benefits is now available to teachers under designated circumstances. Being a na-

---

[2] National Education Association, Research Division, "Public-School Retirement at the Half Century," *Research Bulletin*, December, 1950, 28:120.

tion-wide program, it avoids the weakness in many retirement laws that do not provide for reciprocity. It has no compulsory-retirement age, but does limit the amount an individual can earn after he begins to draw OASI benefits up until he is seventy-two years of age. The survivors' benefits are usually considered more liberal than those of retirement systems. In fact, many teacher retirement systems do not provide any benefits for the survivors of members who die before they retire, although amendments to retirement laws in the recent years have been enacted to accomplish this objective in at least sixteen states.

The Social Security Act, originally passed in 1935, was then a part of President Roosevelt's so-called New Deal program. Several of the New Deal measures had been declared unconstitutional. There was a question as to whether including public employees under the Social Security Act might make it unconstitutional. The constitutionality question centered around the fact that OASI benefits are financed by a tax upon the employee and a tax upon the employer. It was doubtful whether a tax on the states or local government agencies or their employees would be legal. For that reason government employees were excluded from the original act. Subsequently, the federal government found the right legally to collect income tax from state and municipal employees, implying a right to impose the social-security tax, but the constitutional question remained with regard to the social-security tax on public employers.

In 1940 Senator Wagner of New York introduced a bill to extend social-security coverage to state and municipal government employees. This bill met with strong opposition from policemen and firemen, from municipal and state employees, and from teachers. Most of the above-mentioned groups were covered by existing retirement systems and were opposed to the extension of social security, because they felt that it was a threat to their existing systems and that the benefits were more liberal under their systems than under social security. A ten-year battle followed. Included in the groups that actively opposed the extension of social security to public employees and teachers were the National Education Association, the International Firefighters' Association, the Fraternal Order of Police, the Municipal Finance Officers Association, and the National Conference on Public Employee Retirement Systems. These organizations formed the Joint Committee of Public Employee Organizations. The NEA and other organizations were successful in the 1950 campaign in opposition to the extension of social security to public employees by having section 218(d) of the act exclude employees in positions covered by a retirement system on the date an agreement is made applicable to any coverage group.

The "agreement" was the device used by the federal government to get around the constitutional question of taxing states and local subdivisions. The 1950 amendments to the Social Security Act permitted states to make an agreement with the Social Security Administration to cover its public employees. Since the state voluntarily entered into an agreement for the social-security coverage of some or all of its public employees, the payment of the employer's share of the cost could not be called a tax, technically. Therefore, the federal government was not taxing a state or its agencies.

Since section 218(d) of the act, as incorporated in 1950, excluded public employees in positions covered by a retirement system *on the date of an agreement*, South Dakota repealed its retirement law in 1951 so that teachers would no longer be in positions covered by a retirement system. Thereafter they were eligible for social-security coverage, and coverage was effected by an agreement between South Dakota and the federal government. By the end of 1953, Delaware, Iowa, Mississippi, Oregon, Utah, Virginia, and Wyoming had followed suit, except that these seven states immediately enacted new state-wide retirement laws after obtaining social-security coverage, for which the teachers were eligible after repeal of their former retirement laws, and South Dakota took this action in 1959. The exclusion from social security referred only to positions covered by a retirement system on the date the agreement for social-security coverage was executed.

Congress undertook to amend the Social Security Act again in 1954, liberalizing benefits in a number of ways. The Joint Committee of Public Employee Organizations proposed an amendment to section 218(d) that would permit public employees to obtain social-security coverage without the necessity of repealing their existing retirement laws; in fact, they sought language that would preserve their existing retirement benefits intact in the event that a state placed members of retirement systems under social security. These amendments became law on September 1, 1954, and permitted OASI coverage of members of public-employee retirement systems as of January 1, 1955, provided the members voted in favor of coverage in a referendum of which they would have had ninety days' notice. Certain other procedural prescriptions were included in the law, along with a statement of policy that it was not the intent of Congress that inclusion in the social-security program would impair the over-all benefits to which public employees would have had a right under existing retirement systems.

A total of twelve states took almost immediate advantage of the 1954 social-security amendments. In 1956 further amendments to the Social Security Act permitted the divisional method, that is, the covering of those members voting for social-security coverage. Eighteen states have entered through this plan.

Again, in 1961, the Social Security Act (Public Law 87–64) was amended—broadened and liberalized. The major changes were as follows:

1. Increased the minimum benefits from $33 to $40 per month.
2. Lowered retirement age for men from sixty-five to sixty-two, with reduced benefits.
3. Increased the benefits of widows and widowers of insured workers from 75 per cent to 82.5 per cent of the insured's primary benefit.
4. Reduced the quarters of coverage required to be fully insured from one quarter for each three quarters since 1950 to one quarter for each calendar year since 1950.
5. Increased the contribution rate for employee and employer by one-eighth of 1 per cent beginning January 1962.
6. Liberalized the earnings limit. Previously, those who earned more than $1,200 lost their social-security benefits. Under the amendments, those who earn between $1,200 and $1,700 will lose one dollar for each two dollars earned.

Provisions Applicable to "Divided" States

Several states have provided a divided system for their teachers. In these states, at the time of the social-security referendum, those teachers voting for coverage were covered, and those voting against coverage were not covered. All new entrants into the retirement system are covered by social security.

The 1961 amendments extended the time in which those who voted against coverage at the time of the referendum could transfer to the covered group. This provision now permits such transfers prior to 1963.

In order for a retirement system (to which teachers belong) to be divided in the manner described above, the state must be named in the Social Security Act. The 1961 amendments added New Mexico to the list of those states permitted to use the divisional method. The state must pass an enabling act providing for such division before it may be accomplished.

The Congress amended Social Security in 1965 and in 1967. The 1967 amendment, effective February 1, 1968, increased benefits by 13 per cent, and the minimum monthly benefit was raised from $48 to $55. The maximum benefits, which by the year 2000 will reach $218 per month for an individual or $323 for a couple at age 65, were raised correspondingly. Also, the earnings base of taxation was increased to $7,800 (from $6,600).

The highest benefits to be paid during 1968 will be $156 per month for an individual, and $234 for a couple, at age 65.

Also, Medicare is now available through Social Security providing, at the cost of $48 annually per person, comprehensive medical and hospital care. Both Social Security and Medicare will significantly contribute to adequate retirement income for teachers.

STATE	SYSTEMS RESTRICTED TO TEACHERS		PUBLIC EMPLOYEE SYSTEMS INCLUDING TEACHERS	
	With Social Security	Without Social Security	With Social Security	Without Social Security
Alabama	X			
Arizona			X	
Arkansas	X			
California		X		
Colorado				X
Connecticut		X		
Florida		X		
Georgia	X			
Hawaii			X	
Idaho	X			
Illinois		X		
Indiana	X			
Iowa			X	
Kansas	X			
Kentucky		X		
Louisiana		X		
Maryland	X			
Massachusetts		X		
Michigan	X			
Minnesota	X			
Mississippi			X	
Missouri		X		
Montana	X			
North Dakota	X			
Nevada				X
New Hampshire	X			
New Mexico	X			
New York	X			
North Carolina			X	
Nebraska	X			
Ohio		X		
Oklahoma	X			
Oregon			X	
Pennsylvania	X			
Rhode Island				X
South Carolina			X	
South Dakota	X			
Tennessee	X			
Texas	X			
Utah	X			
Vermont	X			
Virginia			X	
Washington	X			
West Virginia	X			
Wisconsin	X			
Wyoming			X	
Puerto Rico		X		
TOTALS	25	10	9	3

Source: "School Law Summaries (Retirement)," prepared by the NEA Research Division and the National Council on Teacher Retirement, December, 1965 (Multilithed).

Does not include classifications for Alaska, Delaware, Maine, or New Jersey.

RETIREMENT PLANS FOR NONPUBLIC SCHOOL TEACHERS

Many private schools, especially in higher education, have their own retirement system or cooperate in the Teachers Insurance and Annuity Association, which was an outgrowth of the Carnegie Foundation Pensions. The 1950 amendments to the Social Security Act permitted coverage of the employees of these schools, but here, too, there were certain limitations. Nonprofit institutions are tax-exempt. They feared the imposition of the social-security tax on the school, as the employer, might open the door to other tax inroads, impairing their tax-exempt status. Congress avoided this difficulty by providing that the institution may elect coverage by filing a certificate indicating the desire for coverage and the vote of at least two-thirds of the institution's employees. Employees who do not vote for coverage are not included, but all thereafter employed are covered automatically. Under these provisions many colleges under the TIAA plans have adopted social security in addition to, or coordinated with, their institutional retirement system. As social-security coverage becomes more prevalent in both private and public schools, transfers from private to public employment or vice versa will be facilitated.

Summary

A retirement system benefits the public by removing from service teachers who, because of advanced age, are no longer able to give good service. A retirement system benefits the teacher by affording him protection in his old age. Most present-day retirement laws contain a minimum-age requirement. Age sixty has been widely accepted as the minimum, though lower limits exist in a few states. Service requirements vary from a low of ten years to a high of thirty-five. The benefits paid are generally related to the years of service and the salary earned. It is rather common practice to provide a retirement allowance of half pay after thirty or thirty-five years of service. There are generally stated minimums and maximums fixed for the allowance.

Teachers who leave service before reaching retirement status are ordinarily entitled to a refund of their payments with interest. Modern retirement systems include option elections that permit a retired teacher to protect his dependents.

A combination of state retirement systems and social security will tend to move benefits to teachers toward the goal of 75 per cent of salary during the five highest years of service. Moreover, there is a trend toward retirement systems to provide fixed and flexible annuities, to permit escalation of benefits to keep abreast of the price index.

REFERENCES

BLANCHARD, B. E., "Mobile Teacher Pensions for Migratory Teachers," *High School Journal,* October, 1959, *43*:23–27.

CHAMBERLAIN, LEO M., and KINDRED, LESLIE W., *The Teacher and School Organization,* 3rd ed. Englewood Cliffs, New Jersey: Prentice-Hall, 1958. Chap. 9, "Retirement," pp. 184–208.

DAVIS, H., *et al.,* "Economic, Legal, and Social Status of Teachers: Retirement," *Review of Educational Research,* October, 1963, 33:405–6.

ELSBREE, WILLARD S., and REUTTER, E. EDMUND, JR., *Staff Personnel in the Public Schools.* Englewood Cliffs, New Jersey: Prentice-Hall, 1954, Chap. 13, "Retirement," pp. 332–66.

"Forward to Retirement," *Times Educational Supplement,* February 18, 1966, *2648*:464.

HORNBOSTEL, VICTOR O., "Pensions and Retirement," in HARRIS, CHESTER (ed.) *Encyclopedia of Educational Research,* 3rd ed. New York: Macmillan Company, 1960, pp. 1364–65.

KLEINMANN, JACK H., *Fringe Benefits For Public School Personnel.* New York: Bureau of Publications, Teachers College, Columbia University, 1962, Chap. 6, "Retirement," pp. 87–119.

KRAFT, L. E., "Teachers Must Leave Retirement Benefits Behind," *NEA Journal,* February, 1966, 55:50+.

LILLYWHITE, R. L., and WARE, M. L., "Retirement Benefits and Teacher Mobility," *NEA Journal,* April, 1966.

NATIONAL EDUCATION ASSOCIATION, Department of Classroom Teachers, *Plan Now—Retire Later.* Washington, D.C.: The Association, 1963.

NATIONAL EDUCATION ASSOCIATION, Educational Research Service, *Mandatory Retirement Regulations for Classroom Teachers, 308 Local School Systems.* Washington, D.C.: The Association, 1965.

NATIONAL EDUCATION ASSOCIATION, National Council on Teacher Retirement, *Proceedings of the Forty-Fourth Annual Meeting, 1966.* Washington, D.C.: The Association, 1966.

———, *Retirement: School Law Summaries.* Washington, D.C.: The Association, 1965.

NATIONAL EDUCATION ASSOCIATION, Research Division, *Retirement Income Series* (Prepared for the National Council on Teacher Retirement). Washington, D.C., published periodically.

———, "Tax-Sheltered Annuities," Research Bulletin *44*:29–30, February, 1966.

RICHEY, ROBERT W., *Planning for Teaching,* 3rd ed. New York: McGraw-Hill Book Company, 1963, "Teacher Retirement," pp. 291–296.

WARE, M. L., "Higher Income for Retired Teachers," *NEA Journal,* February, 1964, 53:14.

10: Tenure and Continuing Contracts for Teachers

Presently thirty-seven states and the District of Columbia have tenure laws for teachers in effect, on a state-wide basis or in certain specified areas. In the remaining thirteen states, either continuing contract laws or annual or long-term contracts for teachers are authorized by law. In 1920 only five states had provided any such legal protection for the job rights of teachers. The NEA Commission on Professional Rights and Responsibilities estimates that at least 75 per cent of all public school teachers are now covered by tenure laws, whereas in 1930 not more than 22 per cent were covered. When teachers covered by continuing contracts are added, perhaps as high as 85 per cent of all public school teachers have job equity by virtue of one or the other type.

The Need for Job Security for Teachers

Teaching in the United States has traditionally been an itinerant occupation. Like many clergymen, teachers did not remain long in one position; at least, this practice was common up to the beginning of this century. Roughly, their instability was like that of the hired hands who helped farmers for a few weeks during planting or harvesting periods.

Until this century, many teachers worked on an off-season basis. During the farming season, men teachers assisted in the fields. In winter, when there was no outside work, they taught in the district schools. Women taught during the outdoor season, when there were no big boys enrolled. They were not thought to be competent to teach during the winter term when husky young men attended. Thus, a century ago, only in rare cases did teachers remain in the same school during the entire year or carry on indefinitely in the same location.

During these earlier times, contracts were issued for the term or month only. There were very few agreements for more than a few months' duration. Gradually, as the nation changed from a rural to an urban economy, schools changed to a different type. Children attended for the entire school year rather than for a few months at a time. Contracts began to be issued on an annual basis.

Even after the shift to the longer school year of from eight to ten months, teaching continued to be widely regarded as a relatively itinerant occupation. While contracts for a single term gradually vanished, the annual election of teachers has continued to be a common practice. Such practice has been one of the chief barriers to teaching's becoming a true profession, and it has been a major cause of continuing instability in the profession. Industry has found that, generally, the providing of job continuity for its workers has a twofold advantage: it gives workers a feeling of security and permanence in their positions, and it results in greater efficiency on the job. The traditional practice of requiring teachers to apply for their jobs again each spring, even though they may have rendered many years of splendid service to the school district, is a deplorable custom that tends to withhold from teachers the dignity that professional workers ought to possess.

The one-year term of employment has had particular application in rural areas and in small-town schools. City teachers, while often employed on an annual basis, have usually been able to hold their positions indefinitely. Urban boards of education have generally followed more enlightened personnel policies that have permitted teachers, if they have acceptable service, to hold their positions throughout their professional careers.

Part of the briefness of the tenure of teachers was due to the formerly held idea that anyone can teach and to the meager professional preparation of many teachers. About all the teacher was expected to do was to drill on the skill subjects. He himself had to be able to read, write, and do arithmetic problems. That was about the extent of professional competence for teachers. Obviously, if no particular preparation was necessary for teaching, it should be possible to employ a teacher at a moment's notice,. Why keep one after some of the parents were "down on him"? Why run the risk of the teacher's taking things easy because he knew that he would probably be rehired? Why not bring in someone who has fresh ideas? Such was the status of the teacher almost everywhere until well into this century. It still prevails in many rural and small-town communities.

Protection Given by Annual Contracts

Many teachers in the United States are still teaching on annual contracts. These merely guarantee the teacher employment in the district for the duration of the school year. Annual contracts do not place any obligation upon boards of education to employ teachers for the ensuing year. If a contract is not renewed, the teacher technically should consider himself to have been dismissed. Boards of education, as a rule, are not required to state reasons why an annual contract is not renewed. A teacher simply has no legal redress if he is not given a new contract when the old one expires. Recent legislation and court decisions have changed this situation significantly.

The Continuing-Contract Principle

One way of providing greater stability and job security in teaching has been through the use of continuing contracts. A continuing contract is an agreement that remains in effect for an indefinite period. As has been noted, an annual contract covers only one school year; if the teacher is rehired, another contract is issued.

The least valuable kind of continuing contract states only that the teacher is employed for an indefinite term unless notified by a given date of any year (often March 1) that his services are not to be retained after the close of that school year. These laws are often called "spring-notification continuing-contract laws." A contract of this kind lessens some of the anxiety inherent in annual contracts, because boards of education must take the initiative in terminating the contract. The board cannot merely fail to elect the teacher for another year. Instead, it must take positive action to dismiss the teacher. A continuing contract of this kind, while better than an annual contract, does not give the kind of protection that teachers should have.

A much more desirable kind of continuing contract, from the point of view of teachers, is issued after a probationary period of two or three years. It states that the teacher will be employed by the district for an indefinite term. Usually provision is made for supplementary yearly contracts that state the rate of pay for the next year and carry agreements in respect to such things as sick leave, leaves of absence, and special duties.

If the contract is violated, the teacher can appeal to the courts. Samples of a continuing contract and supplementary annual contract are cited on succeeding pages.

The Values of Continuing Contracts for Teachers

There are a number of valid reasons why teachers should be permitted to hold their positions indefinitely. These may be summarized as follows:

1. *Eliminates Emotional Stress.* Anyone who has been through the stress of an annual election of teachers, of the type that formerly prevailed everywhere and even now is followed in some communities, can testify that teachers are under emotional stress for several days before the board meeting that may result in the loss of jobs for some. For some days after the election the halls buzz with gossip, and those who have not been re-employed are receiving condolences and looking for new positions. Dur-

ing such times teachers cannot function effectively as guides and counselors of students. There can thus be little question but that annual elections of teachers, unless they are a mere formality, weaken the work of schools. Even when these elections are largely a matter of form there is usually some anxiety on the part of teachers.

2. *Value of Continuity of Service.* It is important for school efficiency that good teachers remain in their positions for a relatively long period of time. Teaching is like every other occupation: it requires time for the beginner to become proficient in it. One has to be on the job for an extended period, if he is to become acquainted with pupils, teachers, and administrators and if he is to learn about local community matters, before he can reach anything like maximum efficiency.

It is not possible for any teacher to render his best service the first year in a school. Other things being equal, efficiency increases for a number of years on the same job. There may be a point of diminishing returns in this principle, but that assumption is doubtful in the case of professionally competent teachers who continue to grow on the job.

3. *Better Community Leadership.* Teachers with indefinite tenure can give much better community service. If they are freed of the fear of unjustified dismissal, they can participate in all kinds of civic enterprises. It is even possible for them to hold political offices and to work actively in community-betterment programs. Since teachers are better educated and have had more experience in group dynamics than most people in many communities, they can thus provide some of the socially minded leadership that is needed in every school district.

4. *Benefits of Professional Security.* Teachers should expect greater security than the usual laissez-faire plan that gives only year-to-year protection in positions. Civil service for government employees is now widely accepted. Labor unions insist that their members not be discharged unless there is a real reason for such action. Surely teachers are as deserving as other workers.

Can Boards "Freeze Out" Teachers?

At one time or another, boards of education of districts that use continuing contracts have tried to eliminate unwanted teachers by reducing their salaries to such low figures that it was practically impossible to live on what was paid. By this method such teachers could be "frozen out." The courts, though, have not supported this kind of tactic but have ruled, instead, that boards must pay teachers according to the law or school code of the state. Teachers, therefore, have little to fear in the way of prejudiced cutting of salaries.

Contract Provisions for Teachers

What are essential provisions in a good contract for teachers? What are some of the provisions that have been found to be undesirable in teachers' contracts? First, let us consider the bad features. Thomas has listed what he considers defects that frequently occur in teachers' annual contracts, although they could occur in any type.

Defects in Annual Contracts.   According to Thomas, a poor contract may have the following defects: [1]

1. It may include many unnecessary clauses covering matters now provided for by school law.
2. The opening date may be designated, but the length of the school term may have been omitted.
3. The yearly salary may not be specified, nor dates or methods of payment.
4. Services as a teacher may not be specified.
5. There may be no provision for assignment by superintendent or school board.
6. The regular duties of a teacher, provided for by school law, may be unnecessarily included in the contract.
7. Details of child accounting, included in the child accounting law, may be in the contract needlessly.
8. Unnecessary details may be included. School boards are required by law to provide a building, heat, light, water, and sanitary conditions. Therefore, it is not necessary to write these into the teacher's contract.
9. Ambiguous or inadequate wording may be used. If a rural teacher is to do janitorial duties, a sufficient amount should be added to the salary to compensate for this service.
10. Specific reasons for dismissal may be included in the teacher's contract unnecessarily. The courts will determine the rights of both parties and the reasonableness of the causes for dismissal.
11. The contract may not include a sick-leave plan.
12. The contract may include considerable blank space where unnecessary and inconsequential items may be written in. If the contract includes such a space and it is not used, it should be crossed out with ink so that no items may be listed after the signing of the contract. This is a protection to the board of education as well as to the teacher.

Good Contract.   The desirable features of the contract form may be summarized as follows:

1. It is simple. It does not include clauses, terms, and phrases that are unnecessary.
2. The length of the school year and the opening date are clearly stated.

[1] Wesley E. Thomas, "Form and Essentials of Good Contracts," *Michigan Education Journal,* November, 1950, 28:215–19.

TABLE 35 *Use of Written Contracts for Teachers*

PRACTICE	PER CENT OF SCHOOL DISTRICTS GROUPED BY POPULATION						TOTAL	
	Group I	Group II	Group III	Group IV	Group V	Group VI	Number of Districts	Per cent
Which teachers sign contracts for their services?								
No teachers sign contracts	41%	7%	7%	3%	2%	3%	81	4%
All teachers sign every year	0	42	60	59	67	66	1,187	61
All teachers sign on first employment only	18	12	13	14	12	12	247	13
Probationary teachers only	12	17	5	10	6	8	153	8
Probationary teachers and teachers when first placed on tenure	23	22	14	13	12	10	252	13
All first teachers sign at every salary change	0	0	1	1	1	1	18	1
When teachers are first placed on tenure only	6	0	*	0	0	*	3	*
	100%	100%	100%	100%	100%	100%	....	100%
Number of districts reporting	17	100	305	579	561	379	1,941	....

Source: National Education Association, Research Division, *Teacher Personnel Practices, Urban School Districts, 1955–56, Special Memo.* Washington, D.C.: The Association, June, 1956, Table 19, p. 13.
* Less than one-half of 1 per cent.

3. The salary and method of payment are clearly stated.
4. The services as a teacher are stated.
5. The rights of the school board or superintendent, relative to assignment or transfer, are definite.
6. The sick-leave plan is stated clearly.
7. Provision is made for signatures by authorized officers of the school district and the teacher.
8. The contract does not contain a detailed list of teaching duties.
9. It does not contain a thirty-day or other cancellation clause.
10. It does not include a list of causes for dismissal. These usually are hard to define and difficult to enforce. The courts will uphold any just and reasonable cause for dismissal.

The following is an example of a good contract form:

THIS CONTRACT, made the _____ day of _____, 19_____, BETWEEN _____ of _____ County, State of _____, hereinafter called the School District, and _____ of _____ hereinafter called the Teacher.

WITNESSETH: Said Teacher being certificated to teach in the Public Schools in said County and State hereby contracts with said School District for the school year of _____ months commencing the _____ day of _____, 19_____, and said School District hereby contracts to hire said Teacher to teach as herein set forth, in consideration for which the School District will pay to said Teacher the sum of _____ Dollars payable in _____ equal installments as follows: _____

The services of the Teacher shall consist of teaching in the Public Schools of said School District; the Teacher shall not be required to perform any other services not connected with the Public Schools.

The Teacher is subject to assignment and transfer at the discretion of the Superintendent of Schools or the Board of Education.

It is further agreed that the said Teacher will be allowed leave of absence, in accordance with the rules and regulations of the Board of Education, for _____ days during the school year covered by this contract, the unused portion of the leave of absence to accumulate to _____ days.

IN WITNESS WHEREOF the parties hereto have hereunto set their hands and seals this day and year above written.

_____
(Legal Name of School District)

By _____   By _____
  (Name)   (Official Position)   (Name)   (Official Position)

By _____   By _____
  (Name)   (Official Position)   (Signature of Teacher)

Thirty-Day Clauses

During the depression period of the 1930's some boards of education inserted thirty-day clauses, providing that the contract could be canceled by either party by giving thirty days' notice to the other. This provision was adopted because of the doubtful ability of some districts to pay teachers for the usual school years. In those years it was never certain just how many months a school district could operate.

The thirty-day clause is still often used, but for a different reason. This provision has sometimes boomeranged. Teachers, of course, also have the right to cancel the contract on thirty days' notice.

The thirty-day clause would seem to be indefensible, especially in times of balance between teacher supply and demand, for if a teacher's contract is canceled during the school year, the chances of securing another position for the year would be small. Such clauses would tend to destroy the basic purpose of a contract, in that there would be little, if any, actual job security. However, any contract can be terminated by mutual consent of the parties involved.

Continuing-Contract Form

The following is a good example of a continuing contract for teachers, as contrasted with the annual contract form.

THIS CONTINUING CONTRACT made the _____ day of _____, 19_____.
BETWEEN _____ Board of Education (hereinafter called the Board) and _____ (hereinafter called the Teacher).
WITNESSETH: Said Teacher being the holder of a permanent or life certificate and having been employed at least two (2) consecutive years by said Board, hereby contracts with said Board for the school year of _____ school months, commencing the _____ day of _____, 19____, and said Board hereby contracts to hire said Teacher to teach in the Public Schools of _____
_____, such appointment to continue in full force and effect until the said Teacher resigns, elects to retire, is retired, or is dismissed for a reasonable and just cause after a fair hearing before the Board. For and in consideration of such services for the school year 19____–19____ the said Board will pay to the said Teacher the sum of $_____, payable as follows: _____
_____. Said Teacher shall annually, hereafter, so long as employed by said Board, receive a supplementary contract stating the salary and leave of absence for the ensuing school year to which said Teacher is entitled under the rules of the Board.

Said Teacher shall be subject to assignment and transfer at the discretion of the Superintendent of Schools or the said Board. The services of said Teacher shall consist of teaching in the Public Schools of the school district administered by said Board and the Teacher shall not be required to perform any other services not connected with the Public Schools.

In Witness Whereof the parties hereto have respectively set their hands and seals this day and year above written.

_____
(Legal Name of School District)

By _____   By _____
   (Name)   (Official Position)   (Name)   (Official Position)

By _____   By _____
   (Name)   (Official Position)   (Signature of Teacher)

A Recommended Supplement to Continuing Contract

To _____ Date _____

You are hereby notified that your salary for the school year 19____–19____ beginning _____, 19____, will be $_____ payable as follows: _____ to teach in the _____ Public Schools.

You are assigned to the following position, _____ in the _____ School for the year of _____ school months, ending _____, 19____.

It is further agreed that you will be allowed leave of absence, in accordance with the rules and regulations of the Board of Education, for _____ days during the school year covered by this contract supplement.

If you accept the terms of this continuing contract supplement, please date, and sign, and return the same to the Board of Education within _____ days of this notice.

	_____
	(Legal Name of School District)

By _____   By _____
   (Name)   (Official Position)   (Name)   (Official Position)

By _____   By _____
   (Name)   (Official Position)   (Signature of Teacher)

THE TENURE PRINCIPLE FOR TEACHERS

There are many different kinds of tenure, so the term may mean different things to different individuals. Probably a fairly commonly accepted definition would be as follows: Tenure is the right of a teacher, after a period of successful probationary experience, to hold his position for as long a time as he renders efficient service. The probationary period is not ordinarily of more than three years' duration. A description of the various kinds of tenure in existence will be given below.

Unfortunately, the word "tenure" is charged, for many people, with considerable emotion. It seems to be one of those things that most of us are either strongly for or rather violently against. This unfortunate emotionalism often obscures the real issues in tenure legislation and enforcement. The reasons for this emotionalism will be discussed later on in this chapter.

The Kinds of Tenure

There are two main types of tenure. These are continuing contracts of a certain type, and what is commonly called tenure.

A continuing contract that provides that teachers may hold their positions indefinitely, unless notified by a designated date, such as March 1 of any school year, that their services are to be terminated at the end of the school year, does not give adequate tenure protection.

Tenure itself goes considerably further than continuing contracts. It is not a question of "either/or," because tenure often uses continuing contracts. Tenure adds features that continuing contracts do not usually have. Almost always a dismissed teacher has a right to a hearing before the local board of education. At this hearing he may be represented by an attorney. In many tenure states the teacher may appeal from the board-of-education ruling to some higher body or individual, such as the county superintendent of schools, the state superintendent of public instruction, or a special appeal board. After exhausting the various methods of appeals that are provided, a dismissed teacher can always ask the intervention of the courts.

Which Type Is Best?

Teachers are entitled to the best protection, assuming good service on their part to the public, that can be had. Certainly, teachers who have the right to a hearing before their boards of education and the privilege of an appeal to higher bodies or individuals have more protection than those with simon-pure continuing contracts alone. Tenure provisions would appear, therefore, to have advantages over the continuing contract. It should constantly be kept in mind that teachers can only expect protection in their positions if it will result in better educational service to the children. They are not entitled to tenure for their own welfare alone.

Classification of Tenure Provisions

In the remainder of this chapter there will be included under the term "tenure" all forms of teacher protection that give the teacher, after a reasonable probationary period, the right to hold his position indefinitely. Continuing contracts that do not include a cancellation clause are not included. This broad classification is necessary in order to make any kind of adequate generalizations.

What States Have Tenure Laws?

The tenure picture is constantly changing as additional states adopt laws. According to Table 36, thirty-one states and the District of Columbia have state-wide tenure laws (covering all teachers subject to local adoption in some specified districts). Six states have tenure laws that apply only to specified school districts. In the remaining districts in these six states the continuing-contract principle is generally used. In the nontenure-law states six have continuing-contract laws, and seven states provide for either annual or long-term contracts for teachers.

Arguments for Tenure

The arguments for tenure have already been covered to some extent. It was stated that more security for teachers contributes to the emotional stability of teachers, makes for greater continuity in service, and provides better community service and leadership as well as professional security for teachers. All these contribute to better schools. Tenure is simply a way of giving more effective educational service to children. If it did not do this, tenure could not be justified. The welfare of teachers is not nearly as important as the welfare of children. The two aims, of course, are not inimical; they tend to be synonymous. When better security for teachers is provided, it almost inevitably results in better service to children.

TABLE 36   Types of State Tenure or Contract Provisions in Effect

STATES WITH TENURE LAWS State-Wide		STATES WITHOUT TENURE LAWS State-Wide Continuing Contract of Spring Notification Type
Alabama[a]	Maine	Arkansas
Alaska	Maryland	Nevada
Arizona	Massachusetts	North Dakota
California[b]	Michigan	Oklahoma[g]
Colorado	Minnesota	South Dakota
Connecticut[c]	Montana	Virginia[gh]
Delaware	New Hampshire	
District of Columbia	New Jersey	Annual or Long-Term Contracts
Florida[c]	New York[f]	
Hawaii	New Mexico	Mississippi
Idaho	Ohio	North Carolina
Illinois[e]	Pennsylvania	South Carolina[h]
Indiana[d]	Rhode Island	Texas
Iowa	Tennessee	Utah
Kentucky	Washington	Vermont[h]
Louisiana	West Virginia	Wyoming
In Certain Places Only		
Georgia	Nebraska	
Kansas	Oregon	
Missouri	Wisconsin	

Source: National Education Association, Research Division, "Tenure and Contracts," November, 1965, (Mimeographed).

[a] Special local acts in eight counties take precedence over state tenure law.
[b] Optional in districts with average daily attendance under 250.
[c] Special local tenure laws govern certain cities or counties.
[d] Applies to township schools effective July 1, 1967.
[e] Excludes district under a board of directors.
[f] Excludes certain rural districts.
[g] Subject to local adoption.
[h] Statute silent on length of contract term.

Arguments Against Tenure

The principal arguments advanced against tenure are as follows:

1. Tenure Is Unnecessary. It is often contended that no teacher loses his job unless he is hopelessly inefficient. This is probably generally true in urban areas, except for teachers whose political and social activities are locally unpopular. But there are flagrant exceptions to this general rule, which constantly point up the need for protection of professional workers against capricious action by individual school boards or pressures from elements in the community who do not like some viewpoints of a given teacher and, thus, seek to have him dismissed. Also, the condition of teacher supply and demand will affect the operation of this principle. When positions are plentiful, there is little employment favoritism shown local teachers. When work is scarce, nepotism and local influence are likely to enter the picture. Anti-nepotism laws to the contrary, there have been many cases of teachers being dismissed to make places for relatives of school board members. Relatives of influential local citizens have even greater opportunities. Such things happened often during the depression of the 1930's. There is on record the case of the city of 50,000 population in which, in 1932, all teachers who had not graduated from the local high school were dismissed to make places for youngsters with the ink still wet on their certificates. Some of the casualties were successful, highly regarded teachers who had been in the city for years. Many owned their own homes. Tenure is designed to prevent such injustices.

Another type of teacher who may lose his position unjustly is the one who is active in politics or in causes that are unpopular with most of the citizens. Some people do not feel that teachers should run for or hold political office or engage in any sort of political campaign. The thinking behind this attitude seems to be that teachers, who serve all the people, should not engage in any kind of partisan activity. The other side of the picture, though, is that teachers should have the small political rights as any other citizens, including the privilege of holding office. Furthermore, teachers are potentially some of the best leaders of any community. Should this leadership be wasted?

2. Tenure Interferes with Authority. There are those who hold that the proper powers of the superintendent of schools and board of education are interfered with if tenure laws are adopted. Presumably this means the traditional right to fire teachers. But what is overlooked in this argument is that school boards and school employing officials have no powers or rights except those conferred by state laws. If such laws provide for teacher tenure, then local school officials have no arbitrary power of dismissal.

Tenure does not, and cannot, interfere with legally constituted authority in any legitimate activity, since the powers of local school officials are defined in the law. It merely assures that teachers who render efficient service may have security in their positions. It provides that dismissal must be an orderly process in accordance with the rules laid down in the law.

From one important viewpoint, tenure is not a means of freezing incompetents in their jobs; it is a legal statement of the terms of fair dismissal, because, bear in mind, tenure does not mean that a teacher cannot be dismissed from his job. He can, but he can be dismissed only for causes enumerated in the law. From this viewpoint, tenure is a fair-dismissal provision and, furthermore, not a legal blanketing of teachers in their jobs without regard to their competency or efficiency. The teaching profession has never insisted upon the right of the incompetent to his job. It does insist that the rules under which a teacher can be dismissed should be fair, should be spelled out in law, and that there be means of redress in case of unjust dismissal.

3. Poor Teachers Are Blanketed In. Some administrators, patrons, and teachers feel that tenure works against the welfare of children because, after the probationary period, it is difficult to remove poor teachers from their positions. It *is,* of course, more difficult to discharge a poor teacher who is under tenure than one who has only an annual contract. In the case of the teacher who is employed from year to year, the only action required is simply not to renew the annual contract. If a tenure teacher is to be discharged, there are a number of formalities such as the filing of charges and arranging for a hearing. Usually, too, it is very difficult to prove inefficiency. There almost has to be either overt neglect of duty or insubordination. Philosophies of method vary so greatly that it is virtually impossible to prove inefficiency in classroom activity. So it is commonly conceded that poor teachers are more difficult to remove if they have attained tenure status.

Poor teachers, of course, should not be permitted to attain tenure status but should be removed during the probationary period. This procedure works better when there is an ample supply of teachers than when there is a scarcity of qualified classroom personnel. When there are not enough good teachers available, the tendency is to keep the ones who are on the job, if they are not too satisfactory, rather than risk securing others who may be even more inefficient.

There is no question but that some poor teachers have been retained in areas that have tenure. On the other hand, there are inefficient teachers where tenure is not in force. It is doubtful that conditions are worse in tenure areas than they are in areas where teachers do not have this protection, except in rare cases.

4. Tenure Kills the Incentive to Improve. Probably the most serious charge against tenure is that teachers, sure of its protection, make no effort to improve. It is difficult to refute such a charge. Undoubtedly there are some teachers in tenure areas who are content to "rest on their oars."

On the other hand, there are teachers in nontenure areas who do exactly the same thing. The testimony of administrators who have served in both kinds of situations is that there is as much effort toward in-service improvement under tenure as when it is not in force.

Perhaps the answer to the self-improvement of teachers will be found quite outside the areas of tenure. It may be inherent in a greater professionalization of teaching. As we advance toward higher standards of service, in-service improvement may become so universally accepted that teachers everywhere will constantly strive to render ever better educational service to children.

Moreover, the continuing development of professional leadership will have profound influence upon stimulating the professional growth of teachers, giving them the feeling that their work is of such critical importance that they will want to improve.

Private-School Teachers

The employment and retention of teachers in private schools are not matters of statute, as is the case usually for teachers in the public schools. Arrangements as to how much time is to be devoted to teaching, the duties, and the length of service—semester, summer-school session, or full school year—are worked out in the negotiations preliminary to employment. Not all private schools use a formal contract form for the employment of teachers, but usually a letter is sent by the president or other appropriate authority informing the teacher that he is employed and stating the conditions of his employment. Although some private-school teachers continue in service with the same school for many years, most are subject to release at the end of any term, session, or school year because their appointment has been for a limited period. Dismissal before the end of the term for which a private-school teacher has been appointed, however, gives the dismissed teacher the right to sue for breach of contract unless the dismissal is justified. The employment rights of private-school teachers are bound by the common law of contracts.

Provisions of an Adequate Tenure Law

The NEA Committee on Tenure and Academic Freedom, which has been working since 1919 to stimulate the adoption of tenure legislation for teachers by the states, has defined what the provisions of an adequate tenure law should specify, as follows.[2]

1. A probationary period: three years is most common.
2. Length of tenure: should be effective as long as the individual exhibits good behavior and efficiency, and should continue until retirement or resignation.

[2] National Education Association, Committee on Tenure and Academic Freedom, *Tenure—What and Why.* Washington, D.C.: The Association, 1960, p. 4.

3. Causes for dismissal: should relate to personal attributes and conduct that militate against competent service. Necessary reduction in staff is justifiable cause.
4. Procedures for dismissal: a written statement of charges with a record of criticisms, evaluations, and deficiencies; a hearing before a constituted board or commission; benefit of witnesses and counsel, and opportunity to cross-examine; a record of hearings and decisions to be supplied to the dismissed teacher.
5. Machinery for review: should be established for use of either party, and should include the courts.
6. Recognition of seniority: in the event of reduction of staff and consolidation of school districts, seniority should be recognized.
7. Coverage: the law should apply to all school districts and to all properly certificated personnel.

Tenure Brings Responsibilities

If teachers are to be protected from unjust dismissal, they must show that they are worthy of such protection. Tenure brings responsibilities as well as privileges. Teachers can help to make tenure bring better educational service to boys and girls in the following ways:

1. If requested, they can assist in the initial selection of candidates. Often, teachers can secure information denied to administrators. A great deal of the success of tenure rests upon careful selection of teachers new to the school system.
2. Teachers can assist newcomers to become adjusted to the community situation. It means a lot to a comparative stranger to be helped to find individuals and groups with whom he will be congenial. It helps to be informed about community mores and customs and the attitudes of various groups.
3. Help can be given in methods, routine, and other problems faced by the probationary teacher. The beginner often needs an older teacher who can give suggestions in respect to relations with pupils, other teachers, and administrative officials, and in regard to successful teaching procedures and ways of maintaining order.
4. Professionally minded members of the staff can help in the building up of an *esprit de corps* that will frown on such unethical actions as "jumping" contracts, gossiping, and unwarranted criticism of the administrative officials of the school district. Prevention of such actions will convince administrators, boards of education, and patrons that teachers are worthy of job security.
5. Tenure teachers can advise and support the administration in the evaluation of the worth of the services of teachers. This holds true for those with tenure status as well as for those serving probationary periods.

Adequate educational service to children requires that the efficiency of teachers be judged by recognized and acceptable means. This cannot be adequately done by the administration alone.

6. Tenure teachers can advise and assist the administration when the welfare of the school system requires that probationary teachers not be retained or that charges be made against permanent members of the staff. If teaching is ever to become a profession, its members must have a part in policing it. No one else can do this as fairly and as effectively as teachers themselves.

Older teachers in a building are much more aware of the efficiency of probationers than anyone else, because they have constant opportunity to judge their effectiveness. Principals, supervisors, and superintendents must depend upon casual visits to the rooms, occasional incidents, and other informal means. Classroom teachers can observe the probationers in all their failures and successes.

Tenure teachers who have "gone to seed" admittedly present a more serious problem. They have become recognized colleagues, which makes it difficult to recommend their dismissal. Furthermore, careful evidence will need to be presented if they are to be removed from their jobs. It is difficult to serve as accuser in the trial of a colleague. If pupils are to be adequately served, though, and if tenure is to be a success, teachers must assume greater responsibility in this area.

All this, of course, demands the assumption of greater responsibility by teachers. It also requires better professional attitudes than we have ever had. Teachers must emancipate themselves from pettiness, jealousy, and gossip. They must give support when it is due, and censure when it is deserved. If this seems impossible, we shall have to admit that teaching can never be a profession like medicine and law. Granted that teachers still have a long way to go in building attitudes of helpfulness toward one another and toward rendering the best possible service to children, there is no good reason not to believe that teachers can achieve the same degree of professional competence and experience, the same degree of professional responsibility, as the other recognized professions.

•

REFERENCES

"Administrators Agree: Give Us Contracts for at Least Three Years; School Administrators Opinion Poll." *Nation's Schools,* August, 1965, 76:47.

CHAMBERLAIN, LEO M., and KINDRED, LESLIE W., *The Teacher and School Organization,* 3rd ed. Englewood Cliffs, New Jersey: Prentice-Hall, 1958, "Tenure Legislation," pp. 177–81.

DAVIS, H., *et al.*, "Economic, Legal, and Social Status of Teachers: Certification, Tenure, and Autonomy," *Review of Educational Research,* October, 1963, *33*:402–3.

EDWARDS, NEWTON, *Courts and the Public Schools,* rev. ed. Chicago: University of Chicago Press, 1955, "Rights of Teachers Under Tenure Statutes," pp. 468–73.

GARBER, LEE O., "Boards Bound by Powers Specified in Statutes," *Nation's Schools,* July, 1959, *64*:62.

———, *Yearbook of School Law, 1960,* Danville, Illinois: Interstate Printers and Publishers, 1960, "Tenure," pp. 108–15.

HAMILTON, ROBERT R., and MORT, PAUL R., *Law and Public Education,* 2nd ed. Brooklyn, New York: Foundation Press, 1959, Chap. 11, "Teacher Tenure and Retirement Legislation," pp. 466–505.

HANEY, J. H., "How to Stop Contract Jumping by Teachers," *Nation's Schools,* March, 1965, *75*:16.

MACHLUP, F., "In Defense of Academic Tenure," *AAUP Bulletin,* June, 1964, *50*:112–24.

NATIONAL EDUCATION ASSOCIATION, *Developing Personnel Policies.* Washington, D.C.: The Association, 1967.

NATIONAL EDUCATION ASSOCIATION, Professional Rights and Responsibilities Commission, *Fair Dismissal Procedures for a School System.* Washington, D.C.: The Association, 1963.

———, *Practical Personnel Policies Essential for Good Schools.* Washington, D.C.: The Association, 1963.

———, *Tenure—What and Why.* Washington, D.C.: The Association, 1963.

NATIONAL EDUCATION ASSOCIATION, Research Division, *Tenure and Contracts: School Law Summaries.* Washington, D.C.: The Association, 1966.

———, *Trends in Teacher Tenure Thru Legislation and Court Decision.* Washington, D.C.: The Association, 1957.

NOLTE, M. C., "Tenure Teacher Entitle to a Hearing When One District Merges with Another," *American School Board Journal,* March, 1964, *148*:11–12.

REMMLEIN, MADALINE KINTER, "Staff—Tenure," in HARRIS, CHESTER (ed.) *Encyclopedia of Educational Research,* 3rd ed. New York: Macmillan Company, 1960, pp. 1382–85.

RICHEY, ROBERT W., *Planning for Teaching,* 3rd ed. New York: McGraw-Hill Book Company, 1961, "Teacher Tenure," pp. 279–287.

"Schools Should Be Firm About Teacher Contracts; School Administrators Opinion Poll." *Nation's Schools,* December, 1967, *74*:36+.

STOVER, WILLIAM R., "The What and Why of Tenure," *NEA Journal,* March, 1961, *50*:47–48.

11: Professional Working Conditions for Teachers

I. THE WORK CLIMATE

This chapter deals with working conditions for teachers apart from matters of tenure, salary, retirement, leaves, and political rights, which are discussed in separate chapters. Included in this chapter are discussions of personnel policies, work load, class size, personal considerations, teaching and extracurricular loads, and physical conditions. A discussion of political rights and various types of leaves for teachers will be given in Chapter 12.

The Need for Written Personnel Policies

The NEA Tenure Committee, from its experience in investigating cases of dismissals of teachers and the consequent unrest and low morale that are the usual aftermaths of dismissals, has found that the lack of clearly stated personnel policies often is the basis of the difficulty. Equally important is for all members of the staff to know precisely what the policies are when such exist. If policies have been formulated but have not been made known to the school staff, this is only half of the need.

It is difficult to delineate in a precise order of importance all of the factors that enter into the achievement of an educational program of high quality, but certainly a sound set of personnel policies, cooperatively developed, written out and published, and available to every teacher, is high on this list. The personnel policies of a given school district not only reflect its philosophy, but indicate how it proposes to deal with its professional employees. Such a statement spells out orderly procedures for dealing with human beings and adds a sense of dignity to the members of the staff. Absence of carefully developed personnel policies is indicative of a haphazard, hit-or-miss approach, which all too often results in arbitrary, hasty, or capricious personnel actions by school boards and administrators. Of course, clearly spelled-out personnel policies will not solve all problems of staff and morale. But this is an essential factor, without which the solution of such problems are extremely difficult, if not impossible.

Factors in Developing Personnel Policies for a School District

An analysis of existing personnel-policy statements of school districts throughout the country reveals certain common elements. Among those that have come to be considered as basic principles are:

1. The agreed-upon policies should be written and distributed to all members of the staff.
2. The policies should be developed cooperatively, through participation of all those affected by them—the administrators, the school board, the teachers.
3. The policies should be officially adopted by the school board (or the legal policy-determining body).
4. The policies should reflect the philosophy of education and the objectives of the school system.
5. Responsibility for initiation of action to develop written personnel policies for a school system is basically that of the school board and administration, but may originate with the staff.
6. Policies should be definite enough to be a guide to action, yet flexible enough to permit adjustment based upon good judgment.
7. Personnel policies should seek to implement those spelled out in school law, such as tenure and minimum salaries.

What items should be included in a set of personnel policies? The NEA Tenure Committee has enumerated the following items, based upon its analysis of existing codes: [1]

ITEMS GENERALLY COVERED IN A HANDBOOK OF POLICIES, RULES, AND REGULATIONS FOR SCHOOL PERSONNEL

A. Statement of Philosophy of Purpose and Function of the School System.
B. Principles and Processes of Selection.
    1. Preparation and certification requirements for teachers
    2. Qualifications for administrative and supervisory personnel
    3. Qualifications for nonteaching personnel
    4. Selection
    5. Re-employment
    6. Eligibility lists
    7. Health examinations
C. Duties and Responsibilities.
    1. Administrative personnel
    2. Teaching personnel

[1] National Education Association, Committee on Tenure and Academic Freedom, "Developing Personnel Policies," Washington, D.C.: The Association, 1958 (packet).

      3. Building personnel
      4. Food-service personnel
      5. Secretarial and clerical personnel
  D. Policies Covering Employment Conditions of Certificated Personnel.
      1. Contracts
      2. Salary schedules
      3. Time schedules
      4. Assignments
      5. Transfers
      6. Promotions
      7. Evaluation
      8. Retirement
      9. Substitutes
    10. Tenure
    11. Resignations
    12. Absences:
        a. Sick leave
        b. Maternity leave
        c. Leaves of absence for study, travel, political activity, military service
        d. Excusing teachers for professional meetings or conferences
  E. Policies Covering Teaching Conditions.
      1. School buildings and property
      2. Instructional materials
      3. Teacher load
      4. School contests
      5. Teaching current public problems
      6. Extracurricular duties
      7. Working routine
      8. Guideline re courses of study
  F. Policies Covering Pupil Administration.
      1. Admission of pupils
      2. Attendance
      3. Control
      4. Enrollment
      5. Records
      6. Reporting to parents
      7. School boundaries
  G. Policies for Handling Public Information.
      1. Organization
      2. Procedures

CONDITIONS OF WORK

It has long been recognized that there is a high correlation between good working conditions and a high level of performance by workers. Satisfactory, stimulating working conditions are important in all lines of endeavor, but, because of highly specialized skills of professional workers, perhaps they influence performance more in the professions. Members of professions endure relatively long, rigorous periods of preparation before they are permitted to begin practice. These periods of preparation are generally in congenial environments with adequate equipment and materials essential to efficient performance of the particular professional task. Increasingly, professional workers are demanding that they be provided the working conditions in which they can perform the tasks for which they have been trained. Anything less tends to be frustrating and, in a large degree, nullifies the arduous periods of preparation. Thus, doctors, for example, are extremely reluctant to settle in communities unable or unwilling to provide clinic and hospital facilities. This reluctance is not, as some conclude, due to an unwillingness to live and work in small communities. It is simply a recognition of the realities: that a physician, however good his preparation, cannot use his professional knowledge fully, cannot serve his patients to the degree that he is capable, without modern facilities.

These conditions obtain also for the competent teacher, perhaps not as dramatically, perhaps not to the same degree as in medicine, but the situations are roughly analogous. Adequate working conditions involve not only appropriate welfare provisions, but also the tools and environment for maximum performance.

Aware of these factors, the NEA Department of Classroom Teachers has sponsored two special studies on working conditions and time to teach.[2] The first study delineated the conditions necessary for good teaching. The second considered relieving teachers of nonteaching duties.

The most common causes of poor teacher morale, revealed by several studies, are inadequate salaries, large classes, poor administration, lack of a free period during the school day, unsatisfactory plant and buildings, and lack of equipment and materials. Related factors are lack of democratic administrative procedures, lack of sharing in policy making, lack of cooperation of school boards and the public, lack of social and recreational facilities, and inadequate provisions for teacher tenure.

The Basic Proposition of the Study

The DCT study on conditions of work states:

Everywhere . . . there should be introduced and sustained those conditions of work under which fully prepared educators can render professional service to each new generation of citizens. If this proposal were put into effect, large numbers of the most able and talented people would seek to enter school service. Once they had prepared for and entered into teaching or school administration, these career educators would find their efforts so rewarding and so satisfying that only unusual circumstances could induce them to leave teaching. Real satisfaction would be the result of their high quality educational work and of their professional standing and economic recognition.

[2] See National Education Association, Department of Classroom Teachers, *Conditions of Work for Quality Teaching* (Kenneth R. Brown, Director of the Project). Washington, D.C.: The Association, 1959. 160 pp., and *Innovations for Time to Teach.* Washington, D.C.: The Association, 1966, 147 pp.

The nation has long indicated that the operation of the public-school system demands the services of professional practitioners. In response to this requirement, members of the teaching profession have prepared themselves for lifetime careers. They know that they must succeed in advancing the purposes for which schools are maintained. In their turn, citizens have an initial obligation to establish those conditions in the schools which will make successful teaching possible. When both the public and the profession agree upon the objectives of education, then the provision of satisfactory working conditions will take on the nature of quasi-rights. The profession deserves to work under favorable conditions, not only as a dedicated, self-respecting group, but also because only in this way can our teachers best serve America's children and youth.[3]

The study specifies desirable conditions of work in five major areas, in terms of rights of teachers in a professional climate, as follows:

1. The right to professional status.
2. The right to a manageable task.
3. The right to personal consideration.
4. The right to leadership opportunities.
5. The right to economic satisfaction.

Only the first three areas will be dealt with in this chapter, since the other two are treated in other chapters.

THE RIGHT TO PROFESSIONAL STATUS

Recognition of teaching as a profession rather than a trade, and of the individual teacher as a competent professional rather than the mere holder of a job, are essential to maximum performance. Such recognition implies certain rights and responsibilities for the school staff. The two—rights and responsibilities—are not easily distinguishable. On almost every consideration each shades into the other. Some of the basic rights and responsibilities that are germane to professional status are the prescribing of conditions to assure competence of the members, such as preparation, certification, and assignment.

Involved in this principle is the recognition of the profession's responsibility for defining adequate preparation programs, identified by an authorized accrediting process. Also involved is acceptance and maintenance of certification standards to undergird the preparation program. Recognition of professional status implies that the professional, competent teacher should be protected against the callous use of emergency certification, the widespread employment of substandard teachers. During undoubted shortages of teachers, the profession has accepted this practice as a necessary expedient. But abuse of the practice is galling to career teachers who have invested years of their lives in preparing for their life's work.

[3] *Conditions of Work for Quality Teachers, op. cit.,* p. 12.

This principle, also, implies that the ethics of teaching assignments be scrupulously observed both by the school administration and the individual teacher. There are many specialties in teaching, and the assignment of a teacher to subjects, fields, or school levels for which he has not had adequate preparation is indefensible. Most cases of this misassignment probably arise from the teacher shortage, the inability of the school administration to find qualified teachers for a given position. But there have been many cases where this was not the reason. There have been some cases of tenure teachers who, because the district wanted to get rid of them, were assigned to teaching areas for which they had no preparation at all. One such teacher was assigned to teach two Latin classes without ever having had a course in Latin. But the teacher who accepts such misassignments has a responsibility, too. The sense of professional ethics requires that the teacher who is asked to take a teaching assignment out of his field of qualification should have the right not only of protest but of refusal. Of course, in most states the teacher's certificate reflects the fields of competence, and, legally or theoretically, teaching assignments are to be made in accordance with the certificates. But there are many loopholes in this arrangement. Misassignment is primarily an offense against the children involved; it is also an offense against the teaching profession, which suffers a loss of public respect for such indefensible practices. Professional recognition involves the opportunity for in-service growth and advanced study; it involves the opportunity to participate in policy making and in the planning of the local school program; it involves the enforcement of high standards of ethical and professional conduct; and it involves the exercise of the right to academic freedom.

THE RIGHT TO A MANAGEABLE TASK

The right to a manageable task refers, for the most part, to time and means that will enable the teacher to function with maximum efficiency. A manageable task is dependent upon a number of factors and can be precisely defined only in a given school situation. There are, however, common elements that should obtain in any situation. These common elements can be more easily identified in a school system whose goals have been clearly defined.

There should be a written statement of the educational plan of the system; then the professional staff can do those things necessary to carry it out.

Staff Load and Class Size

In the problem of teaching load the teacher is concerned with seven principal factors: (1) the size of classes, (2) the presence of problem children, (3) the number of teaching periods per day, (4) the amount of clerical work required, (5) the extracurricular duties expected, (6) the number of professional duties assigned, and (7) the amount of outside preparation required. All of these factors will be discussed in this section.

Class Load

One of the most difficult of all educational problems is that of defining adequacy of staff size and desirable class load for each teacher. The Educational Policies Commission has suggested that there should be a minimum of fifty professionals on the staff of a school system for each 1,000 pupils.[4] Not all of these fifty would be classroom teachers; some would be specialists in school services, such as counselors, curriculum directors, and supervisors.

The question of defining class size or teacher load is one on which there is no unanimity of opinion or scientific evidence that has general acceptance. The best class size or teacher load varies, of course, with a number of conditions involved: the teacher, the subject, the maturity and ability of the children, teaching materials and aids. As a rule of thumb, based on some research but more on experience, a class size not to exceed thirty in the elementary and twenty-five in the high schools has been generally accepted. But in recent years these yardsticks have been vigorously attacked.

Eurich, for example, has stated:

Because so much in education depends upon it, the first shibboleth that requires critical examination is the fixed teacher-student ratio. . . . It is usually assumed that the all-important ratio must be maintained at any cost: 1 to 30 at the elementary level, 1 to 25 for high schools, and 1 to 13 for colleges. Yet a half century of experimental work does not support this fixation in American education. . . .

For many years, I have wondered where the fixed teacher-student ratio came from. Finally, with the aid of a Talmudic scholar, I learned that in the Babylonian Talmud, the rule was established by Rabbi Raba, an authoritative sage of the 3rd century, A. D.: "Twenty-five students are to be enrolled in one class. If there are from 25 to 40, an assistant must be obtained. Above 40, two teachers are engaged." [5]

There have been many research studies on the subject, but their results have not been uniform. Preponderantly, these studies have favored small classes.[6]

---

[4] National Education Association and American Association of School Administrators, Educational Policies Commission, *An Essay on Quality in Public Education.* Washington, D.C.: The Association, 1959, 31 pp.

[5] Alvin Eurich, Address Before the Fifty-Second Annual Governors' Conference (Glacier National Park, Montana, June 27, 1960). New York: Fund for the Advancement of Education, 1960, 18 pp.

[6] For summaries of the class-size issue and studies, see National Education Association, Research Division, "Class Size and Quality of Instruction," Research Memo 1958–28. Washington, D.C.: The Association, December, 1958 (multilithed); and Donald

But frequently experience and observation, even though these may be subjective in evaluation, are as valid evidence on a general problem as statistical studies. The elementary teacher who has taught classes of twenty-five to thirty children, in what would generally be considered a normal-size classroom, and who has also taught classes varying from thirty to fifty children, rarely needs any statistical evidence to decide under which circumstance the most effective teaching can be done.

The general studies in class load have been able to evaluate comparative growth of children only on the matter of achievement in subject matter. From these studies the proposition is often advanced that the teaching profession cannot justify the contention that class size should not run beyond twenty-five to thirty pupils, and that each teacher could instruct forty or fifty children with as good results as would be obtained in the smaller classes. These conclusions are generally based on the concept of education as the acquisition of knowledge alone. They tend to overlook the necessity for education of the whole child.

In the Department of Classroom Teachers study previously referred to, teachers responded on two measures of load, as set forth in the table below:

TABLE 37   Teachers Evaluation of Loads

Teacher Evaluation of Teaching Load by Per Cent of Reporting Teachers	Elementary School Teachers (by Size of Class)			Secondary School Teachers (by Number of Pupils/Day)		
	Less than 25	25–29	30–45	Less than 115	115–119	150–184
Reasonable Load	73.6	74.0	55.5	72.6	65.1	55.6
Heavy Load	21.6	21.2	38.9	23.0	29.3	36.5
Extremely Heavy Load	4.8	4.8	5.6	4.4	5.6	7.9

Source: National Education Association, Research Division. *The American Public School Teacher*, 1965–66, Research Report 1967-R4. Washington, D.C.: The Association, 1967, p. 28.

In the above study, 62.3 per cent of the teachers reporting felt that their load was reasonable; 31 per cent felt it was heavy; and 6.7 per cent felt it was extremely heavy.

Teacher Aide Proposal

As a result of the critical shortage of teachers and classrooms in recent

Ross and Bernard McKenna, *Class Size: The Multi-Million Dollar Question*, Study No. 11. New York: Institute of Administrative Research, Teachers College, Columbia University, 1955.

years, the Fund for the Advancement of Education has financed an experiment in the Bay City, Michigan, schools with large-size classes, in which the work of a qualified teacher is supplemented by that of a "teacher aide." In the Bay City plan, elementary school classrooms enrolled from forty-five to fifty-two children with one qualified teacher and an aide, the idea being that the aide, by relieving the teacher of clerical and nonprofessional duties, frees the teacher to spend more time in direct instruction. The report of the fund [7] claims greater efficiency for this plan. In recent years, great impetus has been given to reducing the work load of teachers by extensive use of technology, aides, and paraprofessionals.

Too Many Problem Children

There are differences in definition of what constitutes a problem child. Those of a psychologist, mental hygienist, and social worker might differ greatly. The teacher would probably have a still different definition from these three groups, because to him a problem child is one who causes trouble in the classroom. Mischievous youngsters are problem children to many teachers, but they would not necessarily be thus classified by experts in psychology, mental hygiene, and social work. However, most teachers would agree that real problem children are those who are either so physically and mentally retarded as to be uneducable in the regular classroom, or who are so poorly adjusted socially that they cannot adapt themselves to the usual group of children.

Experts agree that most children can and should be taught in regular classrooms, but that there are some children who simply cannot make satisfactory progress in growth and development in a regular classroom. Such children also are a detriment to other children and to the teacher.

Problem children place an extra burden on the teacher. The mentally retarded are often guilty of antisocial behavior because they do not understand the work of the class and hence are bored by it. The socially maladjusted child brings disturbing influences into the schoolroom. Those with a severe physical handicap often have emotional problems that are difficult to handle.

Problem children, wherever possible, should be placed in special classes with teachers having special preparation for teaching them. Such grouping works out to their advantage as well as to that of the other pupils and teachers.

Too Many Teaching Periods

Some teachers have too little time for rest and relaxation during school hours. Fifteen minutes of rest entirely away from children in the middle of the morning and afternoon is of great value to teachers; a half hour is

[7] The Fund for the Advancement of Education, *Teachers for Tomorrow*. New York: The Fund, 1955, pp. 42–43.

much better. It is usually not intensive effort that wears the teacher down; it is continuously working with children throughout the day.

The NEA Research Division reported on teacher load in terms of class periods taught for the school year 1965–66.

TABLE 38   Number of Class Periods Taught Per Week

Number of Periods	Per Cent of Teachers Reporting
Fewer than 20 periods	4.1
20–24 periods	17.2
25–29 periods	51.5
30–34 periods	21.8
35 or more periods	5.4

Source: National Education Association, Research Division, *The American Public School Teacher, 1965–66,* Research Report 1967-R4. Washington, D.C.: The Association, 1967, p. 24.

According to the data in Table 38, about 79 per cent of all teachers reported in the sampling survey had class period loads of 25 or more. More than half of the teachers had 25–29 periods per week, and more than one fourth had 30 or more class periods.

In addition, the teachers surveyed reported as follows on load as a factor in strain: 22.1 per cent of the teachers reported little or no strain, 61.7 per cent reported moderate strain, and 16.2 per cent reported considerable strain.

Because elsewhere in these pages it is reported that the hour work load of teachers per week is about 48 and that nearly eighteen hours are devoted to work outside class periods, it may be assumed that a significant part of the overloading of teachers results from nonteaching duties.

Too Much Clerical Work

School reports and records seem constantly to increase in number and complexity. The day when a teacher could keep all of the required data in his attendance book is past. Now the clerical work expected of teachers in many schools is almost a full-time load in itself, at least so it seems to the teachers involved. The need for data has greatly increased. The number of days absent, number of times tardy, and academic marks are no longer enough. We now need medical, dental, and health records, family history records, personal data, records of psychological and achievement tests, statements regarding social and emotional adjustments, behavior incidents, and emotional outbursts.

The loads of teachers are greatly increased by the clerical work they are required to perform. The record keeping and the reporting should be held to a lowest possible minimum consistent with furnishing adequate service to youngsters. And, if possible, adequate clerical assistance should be provided. A little money spent for clerical help lightens the teacher's burdens considerably. Many schools are seeking to provide relief for teachers in routine clerical work by providing nonprofessional clerical helpers and high school students. Also, many schools are now installing computer record keeping.

The Work Week

Studies consistently report the typical teacher work week as ranging from forty-two to fifty hours. In the study referred to above, the teacher's work week was reported as 47.4 hours, divided as follows: 63 per cent (30 hours) was spent with pupils, and 37 per cent (about 18 hours) in other duties. Also, 23 per cent (11 hours) was spent in unpaid work after the school day.[8]

What is a reasonable work week for teachers? There is no definitive answer to this question. Professional people tend to spend whatever hours are required to render adequate service. The prevalence of the forty-hour week (and the trend is downward) in industry and for government employees, in fact in most occupations, points up the need for reasonable standards for teachers. One study recommended a work week for teachers not to exceed forty-five hours, with a maximum of thirty hours to be spent in classroom instruction. Teaching is not and should never be a clock-punching job, but reasonable limitations should be observed.

A Free Period for Teachers

A major dissatisfaction of teacher working conditions is the sustained nature of the daily schedule. As a general rule, elementary teachers have classroom assignments straight through the school day and, in addition, supervise playground and lunchroom periods. In the DCT study, teachers overwhelmingly expressed the need for a free lunch period (freedom to eat, as some expressed it) and additional rest periods or preparation periods.

Clerical Help

In at least one study, the burden of clerical duties was listed by teachers as the chief obstacle to good teaching. Other studies included these burdens as contributing to teacher overload and did not rank them so high.[9] Such duties include personnel record keeping, results of testing programs, reports to parents, anecdotal evaluations of pupils, and a variety of public-relations material. All of these are essential to a good educational pro-

[8] *Ibid.*, p. 27.
[9] Robert E. Jewett, "Why the Able Public School Teacher is Dissatisfied," *Educational Research Bulletin*, October 19, 1957, 36:224.

gram, but some means should be found to relieve the teacher of most of them. There are several means of relieving the teacher of this load, the most common being the employment of clerical workers or nonprofessional aides.

Other important factors in teacher load—or in relieving it—are those related to instruction, such as preparing materials, duplicating lesson materials, preparing displays; subject variations (time required in preparation, grading of papers, etc.), which differ both with subject and between the elementary and secondary schools; and individual differences in pupils. In the DCT study, 68 per cent of the elementary school teachers and 62 per cent of the high school teachers judged some degree of homogeneous grouping as vital to improved teaching.

Too Many Extracurricular Duties

Elementary school teachers have little asked of them in the way of extracurricular activities, but many high school teachers are almost overwhelmed by the duties performed outside class hours. In most high schools, athletics of all kinds, preparation of the school paper and the school annual, and dramatic and forensics rehearsals are performed on after-school time. The same is true for clubs of all sorts. Such activities must be coached, sponsored, or supervised by teachers.

Unfortunately, the load is not always equally distributed. The talented and able teachers draw the assignments. Some teachers carry a very heavy burden of extracurricular activities; others have practically nothing of this kind to do.

Some of the former extracurricular load has now been placed in some schools within the regular school day, but much of it still takes place during after-school hours. Those who must carry this extra burden should certainly have their class loads reduced accordingly. There is no justification for assigning a teacher a full load of classes and then expecting him to put in much added time working with extracurricular activities.

Heavy Professional Duties

A recent favorable development is the movement toward democracy in school administration. Democratic administration inevitably places additional burdens upon teachers. There must be many more committee meetings, faculty meetings, and individual assignments than commonly exist under a centralized administration. Some teachers ordinarily draw more than their share of such assignments. These staff members need to have class loads lightened during the times they are heavily engaged in such activities.

Teachers who sponsor such activities as glee club, orchestra, dramatics, and band often need protection from excessive community demands for appearances of their organizations. The same is true of the teacher who is

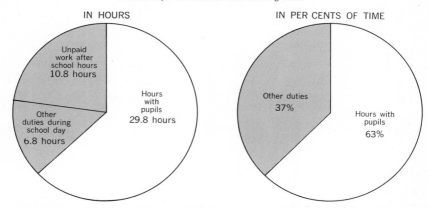

THE TEACHER'S WORKING WEEK – DUTY
HOURS EXTEND FAR BEYOND HOURS "ON DUTY"
Mean hours per week devoted to all teaching duties

Source: National Education Association, Research Division, *The American Public School Teacher 1965–66*, Research Report 1967-R4, 1967, p. 27.

a good vocal soloist, speaker, or reader. These teachers, if expected to engage in a large number of community programs, should have their teaching loads lightened accordingly.

The trend toward in-service growth programs for teachers, by means of extension classes, curriculum projects, and experimentation with teaching methods, is becoming more popular. School systems must be careful, though, that teachers do not become overloaded with such activities. Teaching is an exacting occupation, hard on the nerves and the emotions. There is a limit to what teachers can carry above their regular classroom activities.

Technological Aids

In addition to the teacher-aide plan, several significant experiments in the use of technological aids have been sponsored in an effort to demonstrate that larger classes can be handled effectively by teachers without increasing the work load. These experiments have involved the use of closed-circuit TV teaching, with the regular classroom teacher having the benefit of a master TV teacher, a specialist in a given subject, presenting basic materials. They have involved team teaching, where a cluster of teachers work as a team to improve the quality of instruction. Also, the teaching machine, which is designed to relieve the teacher of much of the task of drill on the fundamentals, has had wide experimentation and use. The extent to which these aids will relieve the excessive loads of teachers, and the most effective means of using them in the teaching profession, remain debatable questions to be resolved by sustained experimentation and research.

PHYSICAL CONDITIONS

In this section will be discussed the surroundings in which teachers work. These include the general attractiveness of the buildings and grounds, the adequacy of buildings, rooms, furniture, and equipment, the noise outside the classroom, the amount of books and instructional materials provided, the kind of rest rooms and toilets provided, and the work and storage facilities.

The Attractiveness of School Surroundings

Psychologists tell us that monotony and boredom are responsible for a great deal of fatigue and that attractive surroundings help to prevent these. This being the case, drab, unattractive buildings and grounds may add to the teacher's load.

Teachers themselves can help to create attractive surroundings. Shrubbery can be planted as pupil projects. Perhaps the outside of a building is beyond the efforts of teachers in most instances, but the inside walls can sometimes be decorated with the help of the pupils, if no other method is readily available.

There is no excuse for the barren, drab classrooms and halls that exist in some schools. Any teacher with a little gumption and the desire to make them more pleasant can do so. Likewise, there is little excuse for dingy, run-down exteriors or muddy, unattractive grounds. Surely any board of education can afford paint, grass seed, and a few ornamental shrubs. The rest should not be too difficult.

The Adequacy of the School Plant, Furniture, and Equipment

Studies in industry have repeatedly shown that output increases if the workers have comfortable surroundings, sufficient working space, efficient equipment, and adequate heat, light, and ventilation. Like industrial workers, teachers cannot do their best if they do not have physical surroundings that will help them in their work.

Four decades ago Averill wrote as follows: [10]

The fact should not be lost sight of . . . that cheerful and harmonious surroundings, comfortable chairs and desks, ample illumination, and a general cleanliness, exert no small influence over the quality of work done in the schoolroom. Buildings in which the temperature is not permitted to climb over 65 to 68°, that are well ventilated at all times, and whose individual rooms are made homelike and attractive by subdued color tones, beautiful pictures, and fresh flowers or plants are large factors in the promotion of good mental hygiene in those who spend their days within their walls. The school is the only really

[10] Lawrence A. Averill, *The Hygiene of Instruction*. Boston: Houghton Mifflin Company, 1928, p. 57.

beautiful environment within the experience of many children (and, unfortunately, although it should not be so, it may often be more pleasant than the teacher's living quarters), and from it they must absorb whatever standards of refinement and beauty they acquire. The day will come when the schoolroom appointments will be at least as attractive and withal as comfortable as, say, the moving-picture theatre and the club house. . . . Any reasonable equipment, in short, which would help to make the school premises physically comfortable and mentally appealing should be forthcoming. They have been bare and uncomfortable too long. Factories and business offices have long since felt the need of providing attractive quarters and lounging rooms for their employees.

The marked influence of school housing conditions on the attitude of teachers toward their work was brought out in a phase of another DCT study. "The group of teachers who reported fewest injurious housing conditions on the average enjoyed teaching most. Unquestionably, a teacher's success in and enjoyment of teaching is largely conditioned by pleasant and healthful school buildings." [11]

Adequate Heating and Ventilation

Only occasionally today does one find cold, drafty schoolrooms. Usually they are too hot, if anything! We do sometimes find poor ventilation, as indicated by offensive odors, excessive warmth, and dust from chalk boards.

It should be pointed out that authorities do not now believe that a blower system for heat and ventilation is necessary. Instead, the trend is toward unit heat and ventilation with radiators and intakes and outlets in each room. Health authorities do not feel that open windows are bad, as long as there are no drafts directly upon the children. Given sufficient heat, teachers should be able to keep their rooms ventilated if they are provided with glass or boards set on a slant in the window so that the cold air will be directed upward. Ventilation is mostly a matter of teacher consciousness and responsibility.

Cleanliness

It is difficult, of course, to keep a school building as clean as it should be. There is so much tracking in of mud by little feet and so many dirty hands to be washed. At some times of the year it is just about impossible to keep the halls clean and the washbowls spotless. Really, though, there is no excuse for dirt in the school. Seldom does a man custodian sweep or dust to suit women teachers, but children can be trained to help with the housekeeping. The development of attitudes of responsibility and cleanliness is a task of the school. The help of the children may even be extended to the halls and toilet rooms if necessary.

Teachers get a "lift" from clean surroundings and are depressed by

[11] National Education Association, Department of Classroom Teachers, *Fit to Teach*, Ninth Yearbook. Washington, D.C.: The Association, 1938, p. 125.

dirty, smelly school buildings. Schools with toilet-room odors permeating the building, muddy halls, dusty furniture, and dark wooden floors are not conducive to the best work of pupils or teachers. Such things indicate careless or lazy custodians, weak administration, and a lackadaisical public attitude. They also indicate teachers who are indifferent to proper learning climate.

The Adequacy of Buildings

This is a difficult topic upon which to generalize, because the teacher is so much more important than the surroundings. Splendid teaching can take place in small rooms and poor buildings, and poor teaching in the finest of buildings and the most adequate of rooms. Still, teachers are helped to do good work if they have favorable buildings and rooms. Functional surroundings make the teaching burden easier to carry.

The classrooms themselves should be large enough to permit all the usual activities that normally take place. We no longer believe in the "standard" classrooms of a decade ago. Those 22-by-30-foot classrooms were too small. They were barely large enough for a sitting, listening type of school. For pupil activity such as we have at the present time the rooms must either be much larger or else there must be separate workrooms. Modern schoolrooms are equipped with a sink and running water, workbenches, and a great deal of cupboard space for storage purposes. The older building with the 22-by-30 classrooms can be made functional only by extensive alterations.

Newer buildings feature outside entrances and toilet rooms for each classroom. Lunchrooms, particularly in consolidated schools, are almost a necessity. Without them, pupils must usually devour a cold lunch and eat in the classrooms. Neither of these procedures is good.

A school library for the elementary as well as the secondary school contributes greatly to the learning situation of children. By means of this storehouse of information and pleasure, pupils can carry on more diversified units and projects than is otherwise possible. If the school is not too crowded, a classroom can always be converted into a library.

Laboratories for art, music, and science should be available in elementary schools as well as in high schools. Equipped with the diversified materials needed by pupils and staffed with consultants who can help with various units and projects, these laboratories are of great assistance in pupils' worthwhile activities.

Teachers' Rest Rooms

Teachers also need to have a place to rest and relax in privacy. A room or rooms decorated in pastel colors and furnished with a cot, easy chairs, magazines, and books is a necessity. Preferably, the rest rooms should be connected with the toilet rooms for teachers.

What Kind of Furniture?

Fixed furniture has been almost completely abandoned in new elementary school buildings. Fixed furniture retards the modern educational program. It cannot be altered to vary the deadly monotony of fixed rows. It cannot be moved into circles for committee meetings. It cannot be pushed together to make worktables. With fixed furniture, the whole climate is such that it is difficult to use the unit- and project-type of modern instruction. Movable furniture need not be confined to new buildings. The oldest structure can be equipped with tables and chairs.

How Much and What Equipment?

Modern teaching demands much more equipment than was needed in the formal school. A few decades ago about the only articles thought to be necessary for elementary classrooms were a set of blocks for the kindergarten, reading charts for the primary grades, and a large dictionary, a globe, and a set of maps for the later elementary grades. The usual high school room had literally nothing in it except a teacher's desk and chair and fixed seats; only the science, home-economics, and manual-training departments had any considerable amount of equipment.

Elementary classrooms now have a great variety of more or less permanent articles that are used in their activities. One usually finds hammers, saws, planes, and drawknives. Typewriters and hectographs are not at all uncommon. Aquariums, canaries, and even rabbits are found in many rooms. Science kits and planetariums are far from rare. Maps are of the latest and finest. Most rooms have dictionaries and encyclopedias. Some rooms have musical instruments, toys, and many other articles that children use in their homes.

High school classrooms generally do not reflect the same progress in supplying equipment as do elementary schoolrooms, but they are improving. Social-studies teachers are now usually supplied with a variety of the best maps, reference books, library books, and globes. English rooms have a great deal in the way of reference materials. Science, home economics, and shop rooms have added a great deal of additional equipment. Teachers are assisted in their work by sufficient equipment. Like craftsmen, they need tools with which to work.

Supplies

Such things as wood, nails, screws, cloth, paper, crayons, pencils, scissors, and paste cost so little in comparison to the total school budget that it would seem to be poor economy to restrict their purchases, unless they are being wasted or used unwisely. It would be about as sensible to tell a carpenter to acquire his nails by extracting them from old lumber or by picking them up around construction projects.

It also seems like poor economy to restrict the purchase of supplies for science laboratories, music and instruments for the music classes, wood, metal, and other supplies for the shops, and food and cloth for the home-making laboratories. Good workmen are entitled to all the tools that they can use efficiently.

Books are needed in every classroom. School libraries, valuable as they are, cannot care for all the book needs of classrooms. Instead, every room should have its own small library of books pertaining to the daily work of the pupils. The central library can supplement, but it cannot wholly replace.

Noise

Over 27 percent of all the teachers who replied to the *Health Questionnaire* . . . mentioned noise outside the classroom as a factor detrimental to their health. . . . These facts emphasize a rapidly growing problem of the machine age—one that comes from the "speeding up" processes of the modern world. This mechanical age subjects the teacher, as it does all others, to increased nerve strain, as communities become more and more congested and people rely increasingly on noisy modern conveniences.

Noise reacts on the health of the teacher in more than one way. It is not only a source of direct nervous irritation but also a hindrance to effective teaching. Noise distracts the attention of pupils, makes it difficult for them to hear, and in numerous other ways adds to the burden of classroom work.[12]

Newer schools are being located in quiet neighborhoods and are being placed on ample sites that do not permit traffic close to the building. Cities are shifting away from streetcars and elevated railways to buses and subways. Noise campaigns are being conducted in many localities.

Wall materials of a deadening type can help a great deal in cutting down noise. Noiseless floor coverings in the rooms and halls also help considerably. Wooden floors, from the standpoint of noise, are the worst type that can be used.

THE RIGHT TO PERSONAL CONSIDERATION

Fair Treatment

The DCT study enunciates the rights of teachers to fair and humane treatment, to which Americans believe every person is entitled. For teachers, these rights are usually embodied in the personnel policies of a school district. In enumerating the principles upon which fair treatment is founded, the study lists the following: [13]

1. School systems should establish and maintain modern personnel procedures.

[12] *Ibid.*, p. 129.

[13] National Education Association, Department of Classroom Teachers, *Conditions of Work for Quality Teaching, op. cit.,* p. 74.

2. Personnel policies should be cooperatively developed by school board and staff and made available in written form.
3. Employment should be based upon professional qualifications.
4. New staff members should be thoroughly and sympathetically oriented to the school system and its educational program.
5. The professional staff should be protected from unwarranted dismissal, demotion, or transfer.
6. Professional staff members should have the same personal freedoms granted to citizens generally.
7. Personnel policies should provide procedures for settling individual grievances.
8. School facilities should be provided for the personal comfort and health of the staff.
9. Comprehensive and dependable personnel records should be maintained as a part of official school records.
10. The organized profession should be recognized as rightfully concerned with the welfare of its members, and as their official spokesman in all welfare matters.

Personal Freedom

Personal and academic freedom are somewhat confused by both laymen and teachers. An effort will be made, therefore, to clarify these terms. Under the head of personal freedom we shall include the right of the teacher to engage, without undue criticism, in the activities that respectable citizens make a part of their lives. Such activities are not a part of the professional or business lives of either teachers or other citizens of the community. Normally, instead, they are leisure-time activities. Academic freedom means the right of the teacher to present material in his classes that is pertinent to the topics being considered. This has to do entirely with his professional life and is not connected with activities outside of school hours.

Dress

Formerly, teachers were expected to dress conservatively. Then, teachers could often be distinguished by their appearance. The women wore dresses of dark hue that were longer than those of ladies engaged in other occupations. Makeup was frowned upon, or even forbidden. Now, of course, teachers cannot be distinguished by their dress from any other group.

Church Attendance

Not too many years ago teachers in small towns were expected to attend church and assist in its activities. Now, even in the most remote hamlets, there seems to be little discrimination because of religious faith; a teacher can choose his church with only his own conscience as a guide.

Teachers are also not generally required or expected to assist in church work. They are welcome, of course, but their jobs do not depend upon religious activities.

Drinking

During the early days of this country drinking in moderation by teachers seems not to have been particularly frowned upon. During the nineteenth century and first decades of this century, though, teachers were expected to lead somewhat puritanical lives. Drinking was one thing that was absolutely forbidden to teachers. The prohibition against all use of intoxicating beverages seems to be waning; apparently the public attitude is changing in general toward drinking. Few communities would condone drunkenness in teachers or approve drinking in public by teachers, but there seems to be a growing attitude toward permitting teachers to drink in moderation as long as it is done in private. A study sponsored by the NEA Committee on Tenure and Academic Freedom found that school-board rules, in areas reported by 16.1 per cent of teachers answering the questionnaire, prohibited drinking in public and that it was essentially prohibited by community pressure in communities represented by 47 per cent of other teachers. This means that a total of almost two-thirds of the school districts employing the reporting teachers frown upon drinking in public. Drinking in private was prohibited by school-board rules in the districts employing 4.8 per cent of the teachers and by community pressure in another 13.7 per cent.[14] Thus, a total of only about one-fifth of the communities frown upon drinking in private. More and more the public is beginning to take the attitude that teachers may do anything that respectable citizens do.

Smoking

Except in isolated instances, there has been no great amount of displeasure over smoking in private by men teachers. Until the twenties, women seldom smoked cigarettes. It was not respectable during the early days of this century for a woman to smoke. Now, smoking by women is almost universally accepted. Most people would object to teachers smoking at school or before the children in their rooms, but would place no other prohibition upon this practice.

In the study just referred to, 4.8 per cent of the teachers reported that smoking in public is forbidden by school-board rules, while another 18.5 per cent indicated that community pressure forbids it. There seems to be no pressure at all against smoking in private. Apparently, again, teachers can do just about anything that any respectable citizen can do. Only 6

[14] National Education Association, Committee on Tenure and Academic Freedom, *The Freedom of the Public-School Teacher*. Washington, D.C.: The Association, 1951, p. 60.

per cent of the teachers felt any restriction on dancing, and but 4 per cent on playing cards.

Living Outside the Community

There is still objection in some areas to teachers living outside the community where they teach. The study referred to indicated that some 7 per cent of teachers felt that they were under obligation, because of either school-board rules or community pressures, to live in the district where they were teaching. The study found, for example, that 5 per cent of the teachers (almost as many as felt pressure to live in the community) felt under some obligation to do their buying locally.

It is doubtful that any such pressure will ever again become at all common. The NEA Research Division found in 1965–66 that 38 per cent of teachers did not live in the school district where they were employed.

Living in Apartments

Time was when women teachers were not permitted to live by themselves in an apartment. Instead they were compelled to room in a home. This, too, was a remnant of the days when teachers were expected to maintain standards of conduct quite different from those of the general population. Not only were they expected to maintain higher standards, but they were surrounded with such walls that they found it almost impossible to violate community ideas about teachers' conduct and morals. The study quoted above indicated that only about 3 per cent of the teachers now have such prohibitions placed on their residence.

Part-Time Employment

Although the profession deplores the necessity of moonlighting to supplement salaries, most recent data indicate that 32 per cent of all teachers engage in work other than teaching: 58 per cent of the men and 20 per cent of the women are employed outside the profession in the summer. During the school year, 57 per cent of the men and 15 per cent of the women engage in outside work. Many teachers feel that the placing of restrictions upon part-time employment outside school hours is a violation of personal freedom. The problem is not entirely one of personal freedom. Other issues are involved. The principal ones are as follows:

1. Can teachers do justice to their school duties if they have part-time outside jobs?
2. Are teachers' salaries low enough to justify some married men's complaint that they cannot support their families on the take-home pay that the schools provide?
3. Does the holding of part-time outside jobs by some teachers tend to hold down the salaries of all? Does it hold back improvement in working conditions for everybody?

4. Granted that the holding of outside, part-time jobs is generally harmful to children and to other teachers, should the practice be prohibited by board-of-education rules?

ACADEMIC FREEDOM

A large number of teachers and some lay citizens are concerned about the academic freedom of school staffs. By academic freedom is usually meant the right of the teacher to present the truth as he sees it.

Initial consideration would leave little doubt as to the right of the teacher to present the truth. Unfortunately, people do not agree upon what the truth is, and there are still many individuals and organizations who are intolerant in respect to views or beliefs that do not agree with theirs. What is the truth to some may be rank heresy to others.

Historically there have been many cases of insistence that teachers present certain attitudes or beliefs held by a dominant group, or at least refrain from inculcating contrary attitudes or beliefs. In some school systems there have been pressures to glorify our free-enterprise system as an absolute, and to discount the aims and principles of labor organizations. Teachers have sometimes lost their positions because of their refusal to teach certain beliefs or attitudes held by dominant groups of school patrons.

Certainly the schools should not be dominated by any group to such an extent that a teacher who dared to present a differing political, religious, racial, or economic viewpoint would be denied promotion or even might be dismissed. A democratic form of government can exist only when minority groups are protected in their right of life, liberty, happiness, and freedom of speech. Emphasis upon freedom to learn, the freedom of pupils to search for the truth, cannot be denied at one point without endangering the search at all points.

And yet there must be one exclusion. No one has the right to use a public school to advocate the overthrowing or changing of our government by force or by any other means except that of the ballot box. No American has the right, under the guise of freedom of speech, to advocate something which would destroy freedom of speech. Recent incidents of preventing high government officials from speaking come close to denying freedom of speech.

At the present time, resistance to the principle of academic freedom seems to be tied up with fear of communism. The fear of infiltration of Communists and communistic ideas, which has been prevalent in the United States in recent years, is real. But that fear, while doubtless alerting the people to subtle tactics of some subversives among us, has had some adverse effects on the freedom of teachers and students to search for truth. One unwholesome result has been the inclination of groups and individuals to label any idea not expressed by them as "subversive." Thus, such a label has frequently been applied to loyal and devoted Americans who were liberal thinkers or who freely discussed in the classroom ideas that some group didn't like. A peculiar twist to this dangerous trend has been the labeling of persons so accused, even after their complete loyalty has been proved, as "controversial." And some have been dismissed from positions because, as a result of unfounded charges, they had become controversial figures. This, of course, is a perversion of freedom—freedom of inquiry, freedom to teach and learn. And, long sustained, it would destroy the idea of freedom of inquiry and speech.

Communism, of course, causes us great concern. Most citizens are frightened by its insidious efforts to indoctrinate and to plant its representatives in key positions. Teachers should have academic freedom, but how far should this go? What are the justifiable limitations on academic freedom? These questions are of grave concern.

Few Communistic Teachers

All available evidence indicates that there are very few teachers in American schools who are communistic or even socialistic.

The type of young person who goes into teaching has a lot to do with this. Most prospective teachers come from the middle classes: farmers, merchants, and professional people. The middle classes, from which most teachers come, are perhaps as little likely as any group to embrace communistic or socialistic doctrines.

The National Education Association has set forth its views on teaching *about* communism and the employment of Communists in the following language:

As a measure of defense against our most potent threat, our American schools should teach about communism and all forms of totalitarianism, including the principles and practices of the Soviet Union and the Communist Party in the United States. Teaching about communism does not mean advocacy of communism. Such advocacy should not be permitted in American schools. At the same time the National Education Association condemns the careless, incorrect and unjust use of such words as "red" and "communist" to attack teachers and other persons who in point of fact are not communist, but who merely have views different from those of their accusers.

Members of the Communist Party should not be employed in our schools.[15]

Children Need the Facts

Social-studies teachers and all others need to present the facts to children. They cannot work effectively with "bogeymen" complexes. Children cannot be trained to think scientifically on the one hand and, on the

[15] National Education Association, "The Platform of the National Education Association," *NEA Handbook for Local and State Associations, 1954–55.* Washington, D.C.: The Association, 1954, pp. 370–71.

other hand, to believe in fairies and demons. The modern generation is accustomed to forming conclusions based on the available evidence. We should not expect them to believe in the evils of communism without presenting to them the facts about the principles and practices of communism. We need not fear for the future of our form of life as long as it is given a fair chance for full discussion along with other political and social systems.

The facts should be set forth as objectively as possible. Teachers should not twist them in any direction or use their influence to cause an interpretation not justified by the data. This poses a difficult problem for teachers, but most of them meet it successfully. Social-studies teachers have the most difficult problem of any instructors. Inevitably an occasional teacher slips in one direction or the other. We should not be too critical when there is not a deliberate intent back of their actions.

The public, too, needs to understand the problems faced by the school in connection with teaching the facts about communism. They should realize that schools cannot work in a vacuum, nor can they be expected to withhold pertinent data. Democracy will not suffer if its principles and accomplishments are presented fairly in comparison to the various "isms." The National Education Association has expressed itself on this point as follows: [16]

The Association advocates . . . the right to unfettered teaching, which will aid the child to adjust himself to his environment and to changing social conditions through the development of habits of sound thinking. The fundamental principles of American democracy and world cooperation demand that students be informed concerning controversial issues.

Loyalty Oaths

There has been considerable discussion of the pros and cons of the so-called loyalty oaths now often being exacted of teachers in public elementary and secondary schools and colleges. Except for New York City teachers, most of the controversy has come in college circles, although only a relatively few colleges and universities have taken such action. The Board of Regents of the University of California ordered its instructional staff to take such an oath. A number refused, and their dismissal was ordered. An appellate-court decision ordered their reinstatement. This decision was appealed to the state Supreme Court by the Board of Regents. While the case was still before the Supreme Court, the Board of Regents on October 19, 1951, rescinded the loyalty-oath requirement. Several states have passed laws requiring the loyalty oath of all state employees.

The requirement of a loyalty oath is much more common for public elementary and secondary teachers. A study made in 1949 by the National

[16] *Ibid.*, p. 365.

Education Association Committee on Tenure and Academic Freedom found that twenty-five states and Alaska, Hawaii, Puerto Rico, and the District of Columbia required, either by statute or by board regulations, that teachers take an oath of allegiance or otherwise satisfy the employing agencies that they are loyal to the government of the United States.[17] In 1967 a total of twenty-three states and the District of Columbia and Puerto Rico required, as a prerequisite to the issuance of a teacher's certificate, that the applicant take an oath of allegiance or loyalty.[18] The number of states requiring such oaths has been declining in recent years, as a result of court decisions.

The texts of the loyalty oaths are so varied as to make generalization impossible. Some are simply statements that the applicant will support the Constitution of the United States and of the state in which the applicant is to teach. Others require the teacher to swear that he is not and has not been a member of the Communist Party of the United States. These oath requirements have caused great controversy. Why? For several reasons.

In the first place is the question whether an oath has any real value in rooting out subversives. President Warner of Carnegie Tech, while testifying before a committee of the Pennsylvania Legislature, had this to say:

> I do not know of a single subversive engaged in the Communist conspiracy who has been weeded out by an application of the non-communist oath. . . . Our colleges and universities can keep their own houses in order.[19]

Teachers generally feel that they are singled out to take an oath not required of all government employees or private citizens in leadership positions. To some teachers the oath seems like an insult, although the lawmakers purport to feel that it is necessary from teachers because they are the ones who have the real opportunity to influence defenseless and impressionable children.

Barring of Communists from Teaching

Closely connected with the loyalty oath is the question of eliminating from public school teaching positions all who are or have been members of the Communist Party of the United States.

At the 1949 Representative Assembly of the National Education Asso-

[17] National Education Association, Committee on Tenure and Academic Freedom, *Teachers' Oaths and Related State Requirements.* Washington, D.C.: The Association, 1949, p. 5.

[18] T. M. Stinnett, *A Manual on Certification Requirements for School Personnel in the United States,* 1967 ed. Washington, D.C.: National Commission on Teacher Education and Professional Standards, National Education Association, 1967, Table XIII, p. 55.

[19] National Education Association, Department of Higher Education, "Concerning Academic Freedom," *College and University Bulletin,* November, 1951, 4:2.

ciation, held at Boston, July 3–7, the Educational Policies Commission presented a report including the following statement:

Members of the Communist Party of the United States should not be employed as teachers. Such membership in the opinion of the Educational Policies Commission involves adherence to doctrine and disciplines completely inconsistent with the principles of freedom on which American education depends. Such membership, and the accompanying surrender of intellectual integrity, render an individual unfit to discharge the duties of a teacher in this country.[20]

Although the report was attacked in a discussion-group hearing and again on the floor of the convention, all but five of the 2,822 delegates voted not only to receive and file the report, but to approve it.

REFERENCES

"Academic Freedom and the Public School Teacher," *Journal of Teacher Education,* September, 1963, *14*:231–3.

ANDERSON, R. A., "Organizational Character of Education: Staff Utilization and Deployment; Subprofessional and Paraprofessional Personnel," *Review of Educational Research,* October, 1964, *34*:458–9.

"Bay City, Michigan, Experiment: A Cooperative Study for the Better Utilization of Teacher Competencies," *Journal of Teacher Education,* June, 1956, *7*:100–153.

BELOK, M. V., "Teacher Freedom: How Much?" *Journal of Teacher Education,* December, 1965, *16*:450–2.

BISSES, HENRY S., "Newton Plan Challenges Traditions of Class Size," *Nation's Schools,* March, 1960, *65*:60–64.

BRANICK, J. J., "How to Train and Use Teacher Aides," *Phi Delta Kappan,* October, 1966, *48*:61.

CARR, W. G., "International Magna Carta for Teachers; UNESCO Intergovernmental Conference on the Status of Teachers," *NEA Journal,* December, 1966, *55*:42–4.

"Conditions of Work for Quality Teaching," *NEA Journal,* March, 1965, *54*:33–40.

DENEMARK, G. W., "Teacher and His Staff," *NEA Journal,* December, 1966, *55*:17–19+.

FIELD, J. T., "What the Books Don't Tell You," *NEA Journal,* October, 1964, *53*:38–9.

"Hell Breaks Loose in Paradise," *Teachers College Record,* May, 1964, *65*:651–3.

[20] National Education Association and American Association of School Administrators, Educational Policies Commission, *American Education and International Tensions.* Washington, D.C.: The Commission, June, 1949, p. 39.

"Improving Teachers' Status World-Wide," *NEA Journal*, April, 1966, 55:45–6.

KLEINMANN, JACK H., *Fringe Benefits for Public School Personnel*. New York: Bureau of Publications, Teachers College, Columbia University, 1962.

LANTOS, T. P., "Free Profession in a Free Society," *National Elementary Principal*, September, 1966, 46:40–5.

LIEBERMAN, MYRON, *Education as a Profession*. Englewood Cliffs, New Jersey: Prentice-Hall, 1956, "Loyalty Oaths," pp. 102–104.

MILLER, W. W., "Clerical Help," *NEA Journal*, November, 1963, 52:32.

NATIONAL EDUCATION ASSOCIATION, Department of Classroom Teachers, *Conditions of Work for Quality Teaching*. Washington, D.C.: The Association, 1959, 157 pp., Summary: *Toward Better Teaching*.

————, *Innovations for Time to Teach*. Washington, D.C.: The Association, 1966.

————, *Time to Teach Action Report*. Washington, D.C.: The Association, 1966.

NATIONAL EDUCATION ASSOCIATION, Professional Rights and Responsibilities Commission, *Developing Personnel Policies*. Washington, D.C.: The Association, 1963.

PROVUS, M. M. and DeLAUTER, A., "Self Direction for Teachers: the Time to Teach Project," *NEA Journal*, January, 1966, 55:49–51.

ROGERS, V. R., "Minnesota's Famous (Infamous) Sibley Letter: Case Study in Academic Freedom," *Phi Delta Kappan*, June, 1964, 45:467–9.

STINNETT, T. M., KLEINMAN, JACK H., and WARE, MARTHA L., *Professional Negotiation in Public Education*. New York: The Macmillan Company, 1966.

WEST, A. M., "What's Bugging Teachers?" *Education Digest*, February, 1966, 31:32–3.

12: Professional Working Conditions for Teachers

II. TEACHER LEAVES, NONWAGE BENEFITS, POLITICAL RIGHTS

*I*nvolved in the problems of providing professional working conditions for teachers are many factors that are indirect and incidental. Nevertheless, they are important ones; in fact, they are essential to rounding out a total climate in which the professional teacher can function with maximum effectiveness. The factors recommended in this chapter are not easily classified. Some are frequently called "fringe benefits," and some involve human rights. All are a part of the conditions under which teaching is done.

This chapter, therefore, will include treatment of several factors more or less peripheral to actual working conditions, such as leaves of absence of several types, group-insurance programs, and political rights of teachers.

Fringe benefits are defined as all payments to or for an employee as wages for time not actually on the job, and related benefits given as a service, product, or cash payment that improves the employee's security or well being. In industry, fringe benefits tend to be about 25 per cent of salary payments.

LEAVE-OF-ABSENCE PROVISIONS

Workers who are paid on an hourly basis often have no sick-leave allowances. They are paid for the actual number of hours they work. If they are sick, take time off for private business or to attend a funeral, or are sent home because there is no work to be done, they are not paid for the time missed. On the other hand, they receive time-and-a-half for hours worked in excess of the standard forty-hour work week on Saturdays and Sundays, or even double-time for work on legal holidays.

Salaried workers are those who receive a fixed amount per week or per month. Professional workers are paid a salary. Professional employees, as a rule, are not paid extra if they work more hours than the standard amount, even if this extra labor involves time put in on Saturdays, Sundays, or holidays, the theory being that professional employees are paid to perform the duties of a given job and that they will perform the required services without regard to the time element or other factors. Generally, there is no reduction in their salaries for a reasonable amount of absence because of personal illness, sickness in the immediate family, personal business, or funerals.

Teachers are salaried, professional workers. Universally, they receive an annual salary paid on a monthly, semimonthly, or weekly basis. Until relatively recent times, though, they were often not paid if they were absent from school for even such an unavoidable cause as personal illness. In addition to sick-leave provisions, some other types of leave such as absence for personal business, sabbatical leave, and vacations will also be described.

Justifications for Sick-Leave Provisions for Teachers

Trade, industry, and government have two justifications for sick-leave allowances. The first is humanitarianism. It is felt only fair to pay employees when they miss work because of illness. Illness is inevitable, and the only fair thing seems to be to prevent employees from worrying about loss of salary. Sick-leave provisions have become a part of enlightened labor policies of the twentieth century. The employer has some degree of responsibility for the welfare of his employees. The second reason is economic: employees with adequate sick-leave allowances are happier and better satisfied and hence do better work. Sick leave, thus, can be justified on a dollars-and-cents basis.

In teaching there is a third reason for adequate sick-leave provisions— the welfare of the children. Youngsters should be protected from teachers who have colds or other communicable diseases. Furthermore, if pupils are to have adequate educational service, they must have teachers who are at their physical, social, and emotional best. Teachers who are ill cannot furnish such service.

There is still another reason for sick-leave provisions for teachers: that is the probability that teachers may catch many of the colds, viruses, and other communicable diseases carried by the children with whom they come in contact in school. Teachers are constantly exposed to a considerable number of children who seem to have every conceivable form of communicable disease, from the common cold to the mumps, whooping cough, measles, and diphtheria. It is doubtful if factory, store, or office workers run this risk to such an extent. For one thing, they do not come into such close contact with other human beings. For another thing, most of them are not exposed to as many different individuals as are teachers.

Illness thus seems to be much more of an occupational hazard for teachers than for most occupational groups.

Teachers are now much concerned with the problem of proper sick-leave provisions. Largely because of their interest and efforts, constant improvement has been made in recent years in the conditions under which sick leave is granted and in the protection that is afforded.

A study made of practices of school districts in 1965–66 regarding sick leave estimated that 98.7 per cent of all districts with enrollments of 300 or more grant paid sick leave to teachers. The median number of days of sick leave with full salary per year was 12.3, cummulative to 69.2 days.[1] As a general rule, school districts require proof of illness in cases of absence lasting longer than five days. A few systems now have no limit on the cumulative sick leave. Also some systems, in cases of extended illness, advance sick leave allotments when a teacher has exhaused his accumulated time.

In the past, there have been complaints that some teachers used sick leave for other purposes, pretending to be ill but actually being absent for other reasons. Such use of sick leave raises serious ethical questions. The provision of leaves for a variety of purposes has had great influence on stopping this practice. Such leaves for other purposes are reasonable because it becomes necessary for a teacher to be away from his school to look after pressing matters. Quite often only the teacher in person can attend to these matters.

Rogers has classified five types of sick-leave provisions for teachers as follows: "(1) sick leave with full pay; (2) sick leave with full pay, cumulative; (3) leave with full pay with additional days at reduced pay; (4) leave at full pay, cumulative, with additions at part pay; and (5) leave at part pay."[2] In practice, there are still other plans in operation, but a description of the aforementioned plans will suffice.

Sick leave with full pay means just what the name implies: that the teacher will be paid in full for absences due to illness up to a certain number of days. Whether or not such an arrangement is satisfactory depends to a large extent upon the number of days of absence for which the school board will grant pay. A common practice in city school systems is to allow sick leave with full pay up to ten days in any one year. There are, however, many districts that allow only three or five days of leave.

In the past few years there has been a tendency on the part of boards of education to adopt cumulative plans. As indicated in the above survey, the most common cumulative allowance at present is from thirty to ninety

[1] National Education Association, Research Division. *Leaves of Absence for Classroom Teachers, 1965–66.* Research Report 1967-R5. Washington, D.C.: The Association, 1967, p. 14.

[2] James F. Rogers, *The Welfare of the Teacher,* U.S. Department of the Interior, Office of Education, Bulletin 1934, No. 4. Washington, D.C.: U.S. Government Printing Office, 1934, p. 67.

days, although some districts provide for cumulative leaves with pay ranging as high as from ninety to two hundred days. For example, the Board of Education at Port Huron, Michigan, has adopted the following policy: "An employee absent from duty on account of personal illness or injury shall be paid his full salary for the period of such absence, not to exceed five days in any one year, excepting where additional time has accumulated. Each employee shall have placed to his credit the number of days sick leave not used during the year. The maximum number of accumulated days shall be 30."

There are many variations on the cumulative plan. Some cities have a schedule whereby the number of days that a teacher can accumulate depends upon the years of teaching experience. An example of this sort of arrangement is afforded by the City of New York.

The advantages of the cumulative plans are quite apparent. They permit a longer period of protection for the teacher. There is at least one disadvantage in a cumulative system: the cumulative plan gives a reward in the form of cumulative benefit to those who are not absent. This may easily encourage teachers to remain in their classrooms when they are not well. When this happens, children may suffer.

Another arrangement for illness provides leave with full pay for a certain number of days with additional days at reduced pay. For example, the board may allow full pay for ten days of illness and half pay for an additional twenty days of sickness. Or the board may pay in full for ten days and then allow the difference between the teacher's pay and the pay of the substitute for an additional period of days. The additional period ranges from ten days to as high as ninety days, or indefinitely.

A variation of the above plan provides that the leave at full pay may be cumulative, although the additions at part pay may not be so regarded. For example, a school board may allow ten days at full pay, cumulative up to thirty days, with an additional sixty-day period in which the teacher receives his salary less the pay of the substitute.

There are still school systems that allow half pay up to a certain maximum number of days. The trend, though, is away from this sort of practice.

But studies indicate that there is no one sick-leave plan that has been accepted everywhere. In practice, there are hundreds of variations from the ones that have been discussed.

Criticisms of Sick-Leave Plan

The cumulative sick-leave plans now in existence are criticized by some teacher groups on the ground that they afford insufficient protection to the beginning teacher who is unfortunate enough to be ill for several weeks during the first year of his employment. Thus, a beginning teacher might contract diphtheria, which would mean an absence of several weeks. He could be paid for only part of the time lost, whereas a teacher who had been in the system for several years would probably have enough days accumulated to carry him over such a period of illness.

A more frequent and valid criticism is that teachers are often not protected against loss of time because of serious illness and death in the family. With the exception of quarantine, some plans do not permit teachers to be paid if their wives, children, or parents are so ill that it is necessary to remain out of school, or if attendance at a funeral is necessary. Certainly teachers should be protected from loss of pay because of absences due to such causes.

To cover such situations, there is a growing trend toward income protection insurance for teachers. Recent figures indicate that about 10 per cent of urban school districts of 30,000 population and above pay part of the premiums for such insurance for teachers.[3]

Leave for Personal Business

Some plans also provide that teachers can be paid for a limited number of days per year (usually two to five) required for personal business. For

TABLE 39   *Weighted Estimates (Per Cent) of School Systems with Enrollments of 300 or More Granting Leaves of Absence with Pay, 1965–66*

Reasons for Which Leave May be Granted with Pay	Per Cent of Systems
Sick leave	98.7
Death in the immediate family	93.5
Attending professional meetings	88.5
Illness in the immediate family	82.2
Professional organization work	76.9
Visiting other schools	68.5
Jury duty	64.0
Court summons	59.5
Personal business leave	49.3
Military reserve duty	35.6
Religious holidays	35.2
Sabbatical leave	18.7
Other	1.4
Number of School Systems Reporting 12,130	

Source: National Education Association, Research Division. *Leaves of Absence for Teachers, op. cit.,* p. 12.

[3] National Education Association, Research Division, "School Districts That Pay Part of the Premiums for Certain Insurance Programs Covering School Employees," Research Memo 1961-23. Washington, D.C.: The Association, June, 1961, 13 pp. (multilithed).

example, it may be necessary to go to another city to sell a house, settle an estate, or attend a court case or hearing. Often, in such cases, if the teacher is to be paid while away from the school, he is required to write a letter setting forth the cause of the absence in advance of the days that he is to be out of school.

As a general rule, such leave is charged to the sick-leave allotment of the teacher.

Teachers' Obligations

Obviously, teachers are obligated not to abuse sick-leave allowances. The purpose of a sick-leave plan is primarily to protect children from a teacher who is ill or from one whose morale is low because of the threat of loss of pay constantly hanging over his head. If teachers report being sick and are then seen shopping or attending shows or social events, the plan may be placed in jeopardy. Exceptional cases of this sort are not unknown, where the inconsiderate actions of a few tend to discredit the idea of sick leave. Best of all is the development of high professional attitudes that reject any thought of using sick leave for any purpose other than the one for which it is intended.

Leaves of Absence for Civic Reasons

In the study [4] referred to leaves for certain civic reasons with or without pay were found to be quite common among the larger school districts as follows: military service (63 per cent of the systems), court summons (82.9 per cent of the systems), jury duty (72.1 per cent of the systems), and military reserve duty (63 per cent of the systems). Other reasons for which many systems provide some leave plans are government service, such as service in the Peace Corps and election or appointment to public office.

Leaves of Absence for Professional Reasons

In addition, leaves are provided for professional reasons as follows: professional study (88.4 per cent of the systems), professional meetings (86 per cent), exchange teaching abroad (82.2 per cent), extended leave for professional organization work (67.4 per cent), visiting other schools (65 per cent), paid sabbatical (60.5 per cent), Department of Defense Schools (60 per cent), research (58.9 per cent), travel (58.9 per cent), and exchange teaching in the United States (53.5 per cent).[5]

Sabbatical leave, of course, is found most frequently in the largest school systems. Sabbatical leave for further professional study is the most commonly used purpose. A majority of the largest systems require seven full years of service for a teacher to be eligible for a sabbatical. The

[4] *Ibid.*
[5] *Ibid.*

minimum period granted for a sabbatical with full or partial pay is one semester in the great majority of school systems.

The basic purpose of the sabbatical is to allow respite from the routines of teaching, with their great tensions. Secondly, the sabbatical provides opportunities for further study and professional growth in a variety of ways. The assumption is that the school system will benefit from the new vigor of the rested teacher, and that he will return with new viewpoints and enlarged vision. The sabbatical also gives the experienced teacher opportunities to observe other schools, to compare his teaching and courses with other skilled teachers, as well as to do research and writing in his specialized field.

The Twelve-Month Salary Plan

Teachers rightly expect a salary large enough to permit them to live throughout the year without the necessity of taking a part-time job during the summer. The occupational strains of teaching require long periods for sustained rest and for additional studying and planning. A few school systems expect teachers to work throughout the year. During the time between the closing of school and August 1, they may assist with the summer recreation program, prepare curriculum materials, or improve themselves by travel or attendance at summer school. If a three-year cycle is established for these activities, boredom should be avoided and work distributed equally.

There have been in recent years, largely because of the serious shortage of teachers, proposals to conduct twelve-month schools on the assumption that one staff of teachers could serve up to one-half more children by staggering the terms. These proposals assume that teachers should work throughout the year, as do employees in other fields. This assumption overlooks the severe strains received in teaching that are not experienced in other occupations. The twelve-month term has been tried in a number of places and generally has not found favor with parents, children, or teachers.

Superintendents and other administrative personnel sometimes take vacations during the school year. In such cases the officials usually work on a twelve-month basis with the understanding that they shall take vacations at times when their duties are comparatively light. Superintendents of large cities may find that they must be on the job in the summer to look after repairs, purchasing supplies, and the employment of new teachers. The winter months may be the time that they can most readily be spared.

Sabbatical Leaves

These are granted to teachers for the purpose of further study or professional-growth activities. The term comes from the practice of requiring beforehand at least seven years of service to the school system or college, and the leave may recur only at seven-year intervals of service. The practice originated with colleges and universities, but is beginning to be employed extensively by public school systems. A sampling study of practices of 133 institutions was made in 1959.[6] The sample included twenty-four urban school districts (of 500,000 population and over), thirty-one colleges and universities, thirty-seven state departments of education, and forty state education associations. Three-fourths of the school systems and colleges, 22 per cent of the state departments, and 12 per cent of the state associations reported the existence of sabbatical leave plans.

Procedures and regulations governing sabbatical leaves vary rather widely according to the type of institution, but there are many commonalities. Some of the typical provisions are:

1. Seven years of service to the school system or six years to colleges is prerequisite to eligibility.
2. Substitute teachers and college teachers of instructor's rank are not eligible.
3. The length of the leave is either a semester (half calendar year) or school year (calendar year).
4. In school systems typical pay is half salary; in colleges (71 per cent) it is full pay.
5. The obligation to return to service after the sabbatical is recognized and observed almost without exception.
6. Advance approval of the program of activities to be carried on during the sabbatical year is virtually a universal requirement.
7. The normal salary increment and other benefits, such as retirement and life insurance, are guaranteed the person on leave.
8. A majority of the schools and institutions permit the person on leave to accept employment or fellowships to supplement income.
9. The purposes for which leave is granted are typically study, travel, restoration of health, research, writing, teaching in other institutions.

Professional-Service Leaves for Teachers

Teachers are sometimes elected to important state and national educational positions that require almost full-time service for a year or two. Examples would be the presidency of a state education association, the National Education Association, the NEA Department of Classroom Teachers, a state department of classroom teachers, or such an organization as the Association for Childhood Education International.

Some school systems have so valued professional recognition in the election of one of their teachers that they have freed the teacher from all

---

[6] National Education Association, Research Division, "Sabbatical Leave Practices of Representative Educational Agencies," Research Memo 1960-22. Washington, D.C.: The Association, July, 1960, p. 53 (multilithed).

classroom service while paying his salary in full. Others have provided substitutes for the days that the teacher must be absent without any deduction in salary. Some professional organizations, the NEA Department of Classroom Teachers, for example, pay the salary of their presidents during the year that they must be almost completely away from their regular jobs.

The National Education Association suggests the following as desirable features of extended professional-leave plans: [7]

1. Teachers must have rendered service in the district for seven consecutive years before being eligible for the extended professional-improvement leave.

2. Numbers of teachers on leave for study and travel are limited to 1 per cent of the professional staff.

3. Applications outlining the plans of the teachers for the periods of absence must be submitted to the superintendent for consideration, suggestion, and approval.

4. Some part of the regular salary, but not exceeding a specified amount, is to be paid during the year of leave.

5. The teacher retains seniority, retirement, and tenure rights as if he were in regular employment.

6. The teacher is required to prepare and submit to the superintendent monthly and final reports describing the work or travel and the benefits received.

7. The teacher agrees to return to service for a period of three years following the leave or else must return all or part of the amount received from the board of education while on leave.

Attendance at Conventions, Leave Provisions for Teachers

In the past, teachers have enviously watched superintendents leave on a week's trip to the annual convention of the American Association of School Administrators, usually with expenses paid by the local school district. Teachers observed that superintendents also attended a number of other state and national meetings.

Not only were superintendents enabled to attend such meetings, but so were principals, supervisors, business managers, and other administrative personnel; but provisions for classroom teachers to attend conventions were the exception rather than the rule. That situation, however, is changing rapidly. More and more it is becoming the practice among school districts to allow teachers time off with pay, occasionally with expenses paid out of school funds, to attend state and national conventions of associations to which they belong. Of course the great difficulty here is the cost of financing the leave and travel expense. Particularly does this trend apply to teachers who have been chosen as members of important state or national committees and commissions, as officers of professional organiza-

[7] National Education Association, Department of Classroom Teachers and Research Division, *Teacher Leaves of Absence*, Discussion Pamphlet No. 7. Washington, D.C.: The Association, 1945, pp. 15–16.

tions, or who are to appear on programs of these organizations. If it is important for administrators to get new ideas, it is worthwhile for teachers to get them, too. The classroom is where most educational service is given. A chief function of administration is to stimulate the improvement of classroom procedures. Hence, the practice is growing of making provisions for classroom teachers to attend the meetings of their professional associations on school time and with some reimbursement of expense. This growing practice is justified on the basis of improved instruction for the school system involved; it is really an in-service growth device for teachers, from which children reap great benefits. In seeking proper working conditions, teachers feel it proper to emphasize acceptance of the principle of the right of participation in the activities of state and national conventions of their professional organizations.

Other Types of Leave

Other types of teacher leaves for which many school districts are now making some provision are professional study, travel, and exchange teaching. The majority of districts probably make no provision for any salary payments during these leaves, but a few pay full salary and many provide half salary, or full salary less pay of a substitute. In practically all such leaves the teacher retains his place on the salary schedule, retirement, and other fringe benefits, as though he were actually performing his normal services in his school district.

INSURANCE FOR TEACHERS

The increasing complexity of life, population growth, and other factors have given increasing emphasis in recent years to protective services for employee groups, including teachers. These are fringe benefits, usually in the form of group insurance of one type or another. As a general rule, group-insurance plans are considerably cheaper than individual ones; and this helps to explain the growing use of the former. Types of group insurance that are now available to most teachers, through their school districts or professional organizations or both, are accident, health, hospitalization, surgical, life, and personal liability (against damage suits due to pupil injuries). Table 40 indicates the extent to which these types of insurance were provided in the 426 largest school districts of the United States. Table 40 indicates the extent to which these types of insurance are paid for in part or wholly, among 583 reporting school districts. It is not surprising that the largest number of districts tend to support medical and hospital insurance for teachers. All types of insurance except personal liability are most frequently paid for by the teacher.

TABLE 40   Number and Per Cent of School Systems in Which Employers Pay All or Part of the Cost of Group Insurance 1964–65

TYPE OF INSURANCE	TOTAL SYSTEMS REPORTING, 12,000 AND OVER IN ENROLLMENT		SELECTED SUBURBAN SYSTEMS OF LESS THAN 12,000 ENROLLMENT	
	Number	Per Cent	Number	Per Cent
Life	99	25.4	61	31.6
Hospitalization	131	33.6	77	39.9
Medical-surgical	128	32.8	74	38.3
Major medical	115	29.5	86	44.6
Disability	16	4.1	5	2.6
Occupational liability	48	12.3	51	26.5
Fidelity	93	23.8	60	31.1
Auto	89	22.8	78	40.6
Number of school systems reporting	390		193	

Source: National Education Association, Research Division. *Employer Cooperation in Group Insurance Coverage for Public School Personnel 1964–65.* Research Report 1966-R4. Washington, D.C.: The Association, 1966, Adaptation of Table 2-B, p. 8.

While data are not available, it is known that many teachers, perhaps a majority, carry such insurance through their state education associations. In 1961, for example, certain state education associations made available to their members the types of insurance indicated in Table 41.

Since 1961–62 NEA has inaugurated low cost group term life and accident insurance for its members who are also members of their state education associations.

INCOME TAX DEDUCTION FOR EDUCATIONAL EXPENSES

The Internal Revenue Service in its interpretation of the Internal Revenue Code (income tax law passed by Congress) ruled in 1958 that teachers were entitled to deduct certain expenses for further study, under the provisions of business expense allowed to individuals and firms engaged in private business. For the first two years of the application of this ruling, there was great confusion among teachers and, indeed, among the various district offices of the Internal Revenue Service, regarding the meaning of the interpretation. In 1960, this ruling was clarified as follows:

TABLE 41 *Types of Insurance Made Available to Members of State Education Associations in 1960*

States	Life	Hospital and Surgical	Income Protection	Automobile	Teacher Liability
			TYPES OF INSURANCE AVAILABLE*		
Alabama	X	X	X	X	
Alaska					
Arizona					
Arkansas	X	X	X	X	
California	X	X	X	X	
Colorado	X	X	X	X	X
Connecticut	X	X	X		
Delaware	X			X	X
District of Columbia					
Florida					
Georgia					
Hawaii					
Idaho	X	X	X		
Illinois	X	X	X	X	X
Indiana	X	X	X	X	
Iowa	X	X	X	X	X
Kansas		X	X		
Kentucky	X		X		
Louisiana		X	X		
Maine			X		
Maryland	X	X		X	X
Massachusetts			X		
Michigan					
Minnesota	X	X	X	X	X
Mississippi					
Missouri	X	X	X	X	
Montana	X	X	X	X	X
Nebraska	X	X			
Nevada					
New Hampshire					
New Jersey	X†		X	X	
New Mexico	X	X	X	X	X
New York					
North Carolina		X	X		
North Dakota		X	X		

TABLE 41 (*Continued*)

| States | TYPES OF INSURANCE AVAILABLE* | | | | |
	Life	Hospital and Surgical	Income Protection	Automo-bile	Teacher Liability
Ohio				X	X
Oklahoma		X	X		
Oregon	X	X	X	X	X
Pennsylvania					
Puerto Rico					
Rhode Island					
South Carolina					
South Dakota	X	X	X	X	X
Tennessee	X	X	X	X	
Texas					
Utah	X	X	X	X	X
Vermont	X†		X		
Virginia		X	X	X	X
Washington		X	X	X	X
West Virginia		X	X	X	X
Wisconsin		X	X		
Wyoming	X	X	X	X	X
TOTALS	24	29	32	23	16

Source: National Association of Secretaries of State Teachers Associations, from un-published survey made in 1960 by the central office of the Association.

* X indicates states offering each type.

† Provided as a part of state teacher-retirement system.

1. *Deductible Expenses of Teachers.* Expenses of attending classes, workshops, and other educational meetings (during sabbatical leave or otherwise) are deductible if the teacher incurred them in order to meet requirements of his employer or the state as a condition for retaining his salary, status, or employment, or if the teacher incurred them voluntarily in order to improve his professional skills.

2. *Nondeductible Expenses of Teachers.* Educational expenses are not deductible if the teacher incurred them for any one of the following reasons: (1) to prepare for the profession (that is, preservice education); (2) to meet minimum qualifications for a position; (3) to obtain a promotion;

(4) to fulfill his general educational aspirations; or (5) to satisfy any other personal purpose.

The meaning of the above regulations caused much confusion and frustration among teachers. After a ten-year effort to clarify and liberalize the regulations governing the deductibility by teachers of education expense, the Internal Revenue Service amended existing regulations on May 2, 1967, and made the new regulation retroactive to the Calendar year 1964.

The new regulations retain two standards of deductibility: (1) the maintenance or improvement of skills, and (2) meeting the express requirements of the employer. Under the new regulations teachers who have not received permanent state certification will not be deprived of the deduction. A teacher meeting the minimum education normally required of an individual initially being employed in such a position will be entitled to deduct the expenses of further education. For example, if a state requires a bachelor's degree for initial employment, and a master's degree for permanent certification, the expense of securing the master's degree will now be deductible. Also, educational expense in meeting the requirements for an administrative position may be deducted by teachers. The new regulations also have liberalized the deduction of expense for educational travel.

These new regulations should prove a great benefit to teachers as they seek additional education at the graduate level.

THE TEACHER AS A POLITICAL CITIZEN

For most people, including members of the teaching profession, the idea that teachers should set a good example in politics, as in other aspects of citizenship, is a relatively new concept. The generally accepted viewpoint has been that schools should divorce themselves from politics and that teachers should keep out of political activity. In 1956, teachers polled in a study by the NEA Research Division reflected in overwhelming numbers that they believed teachers should stay aloof from politics, except for the act of voting. Of those questioned, 77 per cent felt that a teacher should *not* make speeches or give other services on behalf of the teacher's candidate in a presidential election, even outside of school hours.[8] In 1960 another poll revealed that this percentage had apparently dropped to 50 (see Chart I).

Stirred by this poll, the NEA Citizenship Committee adopted what it called "a new focus," for developing a stronger concept of the teacher as a political citizen. The committee adopted the viewpoint that teachers

[8] National Education Association, Research Division, "The Status of the American Public-School Teacher," *Research Bulletin*, February, 1957, 35:34.

should set a good example in politics in participating in the machinery of government, as in other aspects of citizenship.

Despite the prevailing conservatism of teachers regarding their role in politics, the committee found much support for its convictions. A former president of the National Education Association said in 1942: "It is of the utmost importance that teachers, who must train our youth to exercise the full rights of citizenship, have all the rights of citizens and

CHART I   Teacher-Opinion Poll

Should teachers on their own time work actively as members of political parties in national elections? Half of the nation's 1.4 million classroom teachers think they should, according to a recent NEA Teacher-Opinion Poll. Only one-third of those polled think teachers should not; 1 in 8 is undecided.

Opinions were almost identical when the same question was asked regarding teachers' working actively as members of political parties in state elections.

Here are the responses to the two questions:

	National elections	State elections
Yes	50%	51%
No	34	33
Uncertain	16	16

A higher proportion of teachers in large school districts than in small districts believe they and their colleagues should work as members of political parties. The opinion trends were similar for national and state elections.

Opinions regarding national elections were distributed as follows:

	Districts with 500 teachers or more	Districts with fewer than 500 teachers
Yes	59%	47%
No	28	36
Uncertain	13	17

Regarding state elections, opinions were divided as follows:

	Districts with 500 teachers or more	Districts with fewer than 500 teachers
Yes	58%	48%
No	29	35
Uncertain	13	17

These results indicate there is a substantial body of opinion in the teaching profession that teachers, as private citizens, should actively participate as members of political parties in both national and state elections.

Source: National Education Association, Research Division, "Teacher-Opinion Poll," *NEA Journal*, October, 1960, 49:64.

participate fully in political life. The efficiency and expansion of our schools are dependent upon the political approval of states and local communities. Their progress up to date has been dependent largely upon the efforts of teachers to inform the public of school needs and present the cause of education to voters, candidates for office, and public officials . . . the Hatch Act would in many states and communities muzzle the teachers and permit the control and financial starvation of our schools by those organized minority groups who have consistently fought educational support." [9] At the moment, the NEA was fighting for an amendment to the Hatch Act—to exempt teachers from the provisions of this act, and to give them freedom to participate in politics. This amendment was passed and signed by the President on October 24, 1942.

President John F. Kennedy, while he was still a senator, in an address to the American Association of School Administrators in 1957, said:

It is disheartening to me, and I think alarming to our Republic, to realize how poorly the political profession is regarded in America. Mothers may still want their favorite sons to grow up to be President, but, according to a famous Gallup Poll of some years ago, they do not want them to become politicians in the process. . . . *Unfortunately, this disdain for the political profession is not only shared but intensified by the educational profession.* . . . This disdain for the political profession in our schools and communities did not matter quite as much in the days when active participation in the political affairs of the nation was limited to a select few. *But today, the implications of national policy necessarily make politicians of all of us.*[10]

President Dwight D. Eisenhower wrote in 1959:

I am particularly impressed by the NEA Citizenship Committee's program to encourage our teachers to play a more active role in the political life of our nation. By their training and experience they are not only entitled to this role, they have a clear duty to perform in it. Our government—at every level—requires the support as well as the constructive criticism of an educated citizenry.

The chairmen of the Republican and Democratic National Committees endorsed the drive of the Citizenship Committee to induce teachers to exercise their political rights in the following respective statements:

As a nation, we can ill afford either the voluntary or the enforced disenfranchisement of large groups of responsible citizens. This is particularly true of our teachers and our other more highly educated groups. Teachers have a responsibility, yes, a duty, to set an example of mature citizenship by participating fully in politics. . . . I believe the teacher should enjoy complete political freedom once he steps out of the shadow of his official duties and environs. . . . To the

[9] Donald DuShane, "The Hatch Act," *Addresses and Proceedings, 1942.* Washington, D.C.: National Education Association, 1942, p. 89.

[10] John F. Kennedy, "The Education of an American Politician," *Schools on the Threshold of a New Era,* Official Report. Washington, D.C.: American Association of School Administrators, National Education Association, 1957, pp. 158–59.

teacher who today stands alongside the political pond, tentatively dunking a toe, I have this word: Come on in, the water's fine.

The power of example is the teacher's greatest influence. The teacher who runs for office at any level involves his students inevitably in the political process. Any sensitive teacher who becomes a candidate (and we want no insensitive people either in teaching or in politics) does not have to involve his students in any partisan way. But the very fact of his candidacy both enlivens student interest and makes him much more aware of community views about the schools. This in turn should make him a better teacher.

The Fears of Teachers

These viewpoints were not enthusiastically embraced by many members of the profession. Even those who, in general, endorsed the committee's efforts were highly dubious about particulars. For example, does a teacher have a right to participate in a school-board election? The NEA Ethics Committee has said that he does, provided that, in making his influence felt, he does not use the facilities of the school or his relationship with his pupils. However, when *Nation's Schools*, in a nation-wide sampling of superintendents' opinions, asked the question, "Is it ethical for teachers to engage actively in school-board election campaigns?" 49 per cent said no, only 47 per cent said yes, with 4 per cent checking "neither." Following these close percentages, reported *Nation's Schools*, came answers that were poles apart: "Teachers never have been and never can be normal people" (i.e., shouldn't campaign); "Teachers are American citizens, aren't they?" (i.e., they should campaign)! In this poll some respondents suggested that "in the majority of cases teachers would probably defend purely selfish interests" if they participated in school-board elections.[11]

In other places some citizens were doubtful about teachers holding public office, suggesting a conflict of interests if teachers were members of city councils, boards of supervisors, or state legislatures.

In response to these apprehensions and to those teachers who expressed fear of reprisals if teachers assumed full political citizenship, the NEA Citizenship Committee argued that, whereas there is danger in anything that is partisan and teachers would doubtless meet obstacles, the greater danger is to the nation when teachers hold themselves aloof from politics. The committee's stand was expressed as follows: "The Committee urges teachers to assume the obligations of full political citizenship. . . . Communities will benefit when all teachers accept the rights and responsibilities of political citizenship. In so doing, teachers will be contributing that which every citizen owes to our self-government. And, in strong likelihood, teachers who are themselves active participants in government will be more competent and effective teachers of citizenship."

[11] "Teacher Ethics in Board Elections: Opinion Poll," *Nation's Schools*, December, 1957, *60*:52.

Restrictions Loosen

Teachers were exempted from the Hatch Act in 1942. A recent study by the NEA Research Division of legal restrictions in states revealed almost none. In Hawaii, where there had been a prohibition against teachers' activity in politics, citizens won a ten-year campaign when in 1956 the board of commissioners adopted a ruling saying: "Certified personnel are permitted to exercise those political rights and responsibilities which they share in common with other citizens, such as electioneering for candidates, accepting positions in political campaigns, holding office in political party organizations, and serving as delegates to political party conventions."

Provisions were made in the Hawaii statement to enable teachers to be candidates for and hold public office.

In Oregon, where the state Supreme Court had ruled that teachers could not be members of the state legislature, citizens amended the state constitution in 1958 to provide that teachers could serve.

In Newport, Rhode Island, an amendment to the city charter, proposed in 1959, would have had the effect of barring teachers from membership on the city council. The local teachers' association, the state education association, and the NEA combined to defeat the amendment.

Examples of Political Activity

Political activity by teachers, as could be expected, met both success and difficulty. Teachers of Omaha have been politically active for years. One report from this group states:

In cooperation with parents and other interested persons, we [help] choose the members of the board of education whom we can support. We do not work for them as teachers but as participants in the friends of the schools group. . . . This group always runs on an orange ticket which is widely disseminated throughout the community. We have used the plan for twenty years, always as a joint effort of parents and teachers with teachers providing much of the manpower.

The Personnel Standards Commission of the California Teachers Association was asked to look into teacher participation in the 1957 Pasadena School Board election. Many Pasadena teachers had participated in the formation of "Citizens Supporting Good Education," an organization that had selected three candidates who were elected by a landslide vote. However, during the campaign it had to come to light that one teacher had exploited pupils in her campaign efforts. This prompted the school board to order an investigation of political activity within the professional staff. The result was that the board sought and obtained the superintendent's resignation, and demoted the assistant superintendent for instruction and the president of the Pasadena Education Association. The two demotions were later reversed by the newly elected board. There were demands that disciplinary action against the teachers be taken by the board. Then the board appealed to the California Teachers Association for an investigation of unprofessional conduct by teachers.

In the report of its investigation, the CTA Personnel Standards Commission says:

Pasadena teachers exercised their civil rights and fulfilled their professional obligation in supporting the principles in which they believed and the candidates who seemed to represent those principles. They acted largely within the traditions of Pasadena City Board of Education elections, but the increased enthusiasm led to errors in judgment and to a few unethical acts.

In this atmosphere it is difficult to condemn individuals for past acts where direction and precedent were lacking, but it is highly important that these mistakes be the basis for a greater wisdom which will preclude future errors.

Resulting from this controversy, the Pasadena Board of Education adopted the following policy concerning political activities:

The Board of Education recognizes and encourages the right of its employees, as citizens, to engage in political activity. However, the Board of Education also recognizes that school property and school time, paid for by all of the people, shall not be used for political purposes except as provided under the Civic Center Act. It therefore enacts the following rules in regard to political activity:

1. No employee shall engage in political activities upon property under the jurisdiction of the Pasadena City Board of Education. . . . However, outside of on-duty hours employees have the same right as all other persons to participate in political activities permitted under the Civic Center Act.

2. Except as permitted under the Civic Center Act, the following activities upon property under the jurisdiction of the Pasadena City Board of Education are specifically prohibited: posting of political circulars or petitions on bulletin boards; the distribution to employees, whether by placing in their school mailboxes, or otherwise, of political circulars or petitions. United States mail being excepted; the collection of and/or solicitation for campaign funds; solicitation for campaign workers; the use of pupils for writing or addressing political materials or the distribution of such materials to pupils.

3. Elections to determine membership on the Board of Education shall be considered to be political within the meaning of these Rules.

·   ·   ·

5. Violation of any of the foregoing rules shall, at the discretion of the Pasadena City Board of Education, constitute cause for reprimand, demotion, suspension, discharge, or dismissal.

6. Nothing in these rules shall prevent: the dissemination of information concerning school tax and/or bond elections; the discussion and study of politics and political issues, when such discussion and study are appropriate to classroom studies, such as history, current events and political science; the conducting of student and employee elections, and campaigning connected therewith.

The California report is quoted in such detail because it emphasizes that good judgment and professional ethics must be a part of the teacher's equipment if his political activity is to lend prestige to the profession and strength to the nation.

Teacher Citizenship and Teacher-Education Experiments

Evidence of the growing emphasis upon teachers' knowledge and participation in citizenship is reflected in certain teacher-education courses.

At Jersey City State College, a practicum in politics inaugurated for prospective social-studies teachers won such high approval that the president now endorses the extending of the program throughout the college so that all prospective teachers studying at the college may have the benefit of it.

In New York an in-service course on "The Law of the Bill of Rights," first contemplated as an offering to social-studies teachers, was opened to all teachers and proved highly popular and highly successful. It is now being promoted by the Civil Liberties Educational Foundation, Inc., with the school administrations of other cities.

In Maryland, a state-wide in-service credit experiment, "Institutes on Maryland Public Affairs," promoted by the Maryland State Teachers Association and the State Department of Education, has grown in influence and strength.

Positions of Teachers' Organizations

As one of its goals, the National Education Association has for several years accepted the following statement: [12]

Understanding and support of the teacher's right to participate fully in public affairs.

   a. Informed participation by teachers in the consideration of all legislation that would affect the quantity or quality of education either directly or indirectly.
   b. Recognition of teachers' political rights and responsibilities, including the right to seek public office.
   c. Recognition of the right of all teachers to join organizations of their own choosing, except those which advocate changing the form of government of the United States by unconstitutional means.

This statement is in line with the "planks" of the "platform" that the NEA Citizenship Committee approved and publicized in 1958: Every teacher should register, should inform himself on the issues before the voters and their representatives, should study the candidates and their records, should vote regularly in both primary and regular elections, should seek to make his influence felt through all the avenues open to him within the framework of the law, should have the privilege of participating in the political party of his choice, and should have the privilege of running for public offices to which he is eligible by law.

Progress has been made toward these goals, but problems connected

[12] National Education Association, *NEA Handbook for Local, State, and National Associations, 1960–61*. Washington, D.C.: The Association, 1960, p. 53.

with them are still far from solved. The Citizenship Education Project, Teachers College, Columbia University, phrases teasing questions when it asks, Is it proper or improper for a teacher: To discuss politics and candidates in his social life in the community? To affiliate himself with a political party? To serve as a checker at the polls? To assist in getting out the party vote in the ward? To circulate a nominating petition for a candidate? To solicit for campaign funds? To make campaign speeches in his own community for the candidate of his choice? To run for political office? To promote a pre-election forum in his school for political candidates of opposing parties? To encourage students to work with political parties on a nonpartisan basis to get out the vote? To support the candidate or party of his choice in debate with a fellow teacher before a school gathering? To accept an invitation to take part in a student-organized political rally? To wear a campaign button in the school? To make a statement in the classroom on his political convictions? To encourage students to work on a partisan basis for his candidate or party during a campaign? To post propaganda for his party or his candidate on a students' bulletin board? On a teachers'-lounge bulletin board? To distribute political propaganda via students?

In an "Institute on the Teacher as a Citizen," the Maine Teachers Association asked: "Should school boards grant leave to a teacher, who, every other year, is absent much of the time in order to serve in the legislature? Who should pay the salary of the substitute? What if a substitute is unavailable? Should a teacher, after school, convey voters to the polls in the interest of his party? Should a teacher be granted leave to attend the state party convention? It was said of one highly competent teacher that no one in his classes could tell whether he was a Democrat or a Republican. Is this necessarily a high compliment? Is it possible for a deeply committed member of a political party not to indoctrinate his pupils? How can a conscientious teacher avoid indoctrination? Is it enough to present both sides of all questions?"

Public opinion and teacher opinion is changing on the subject of political participation of teachers, but opinion must change still more if teachers are to fulfill successfully their role in politics.

Summary

That teachers' salaries have not kept pace with advances of most other groups is well known. What is not well known is that teachers have lost even more ground in nonwage or fringe benefits. Since 1930, all salaries have increased about 500 per cent; fringe benefits for all workers have increased by 3300 per cent. Obviously, teachers' salaries must be increased if teaching is to compete successfully in the tight labor market, and much greater emphasis must be placed upon nonwage benefits.

REFERENCES

BRINEY, ANDRENA CROCKETT, "Should Teachers Be Politically Active?" *Journal of Teacher Education*, March, 1958, 9:7–11.

CROWE, S. G., "Teacher's Role in Politics," *NEA Journal*, October, 1964, 53:30–1.

"Ethics Opinion 42: Political Solicitation," *NEA Journal*, November, 1963, 52:30.

GARBER, L. O., "Political Zeal Can Bring Litigation to Schoolmen," *Nation's Schools*, May, 1966, 77:76+.

HANNAN, C. J., "Teachers: A Political Force," *NEA Journal*, November, 1965, 54:49.

KLEINMANN, JACK H., *Fringe Benefits for Public School Personnel*. New York: Bureau of Publications, Teachers College, Columbia University, 1962.

————, "Group Insurance is Growing," *NEA Journal*, May, 1966, 55:48–9.

LANTOS, T. P., and BAIN, H., "Should Teachers Form Their Own Political Groups? Opinions Differ," *NEA Journal*, December, 1966, 55:58–60.

NATIONAL EDUCATION ASSOCIATION, Educational Research Service, *Extended Leaves of Absence for Classroom Teachers*. Washington, D.C.: The Association, 1966.

————, *Maternity Leave Provisions for Classroom Teachers in Larger School Systems*. Washington, D.C.: The Association, 1966.

NATIONAL EDUCATION ASSOCIATION, Research Division, "Expanded NEA Life Insurance Plan," *NEA Journal*, October, 1964, 53:16–17.

————, "Group Insurance Coverage Increasing; Summary of Employer Cooperation in Group Insurance Coverage of Public School Personnel," *NEA Research Bulletin* 43:84–5, October, 1965.

————, "Groups Health Insurance for Teachers; Summary of Group Health Insurance Programs for Public-School Personnel, 1964–65," *NEA Research Bulletin* 44:85–9, October, 1966.

————, "Group Life Insurance for Teachers: Summary of Personnel Administration in Urban School Districts, 1961–62," *NEA Research Bulletin* 42:5609, May, 1964.

————, "Leaves of Absence for Teachers," *NEA Research Bulletin* 44:72–9, October, 1966.

RICHEY, ROBERT W., *Planning for Teaching*, 3rd ed. New York: McGraw-Hill Book Company, 1963, Chap. 10, "Other Economic Benefits," pp. 279–298.

ROACH, S. F., "Liability Insurance; Social Law," *School Management*, June, 1966, 10:126+.

Part Four
DEVELOPING RESPONSIBILITIES AND RIGHTS OF TEACHERS

13: Autonomy for
the Teaching Profession

A basic mark of any recognized profession is that it is self-determining; that is, it manages its own affairs. It sets standards—and sees to it that they are enforced—to assure competence of those admitted to membership. It defines ethical conduct and standards of professional practice, and sees that these are enforced. Moreover, it sets standards for treatment of its members and establishes machinery to see that these are enforced. This cluster of responsibilities and rights is termed professional autonomy.

Thus, every teacher must function in a dual role: he is a practitioner, and he is a responsible member of his profession. In the first role, he functions in the daily routine of instruction and related endeavors. In the second, he participates in the development of programs designed to improve education; he participates with his professional colleagues to improve the profession. And the latter involves a complex of responsibilities such as selection, preparation, certification, accreditation, enforcement of ethical standards and practices, and defending colleagues against unjust treatment. To function in one role, however effectively, and not in the other may be compared to a citizen who performs his particular job well, supports his family adequately, but refrains from voting or actively participating in the operation of his government. The big issue, as Kinney and Thomas have pointed out, is not whether education is a profession, but rather how to bring all the individuals and groups in the profession to accept their professional obligations.[1]

[1] Lucien B. Kinney and Lawrence G. Thomas, *Toward Professional Maturity in Education*, Bulletin No. 5. Burlingame: Commission on Teacher Education and Professional Standards, California Teachers Association, 1955, p. 29.

The Meaning of Autonomy

What is professional autonomy? What does it involve as applied to teaching? It is a highly controversial and highly emotional term because of the erroneous connotations ascribed to it by many.

Autonomy for a profession means, essentially, the recognized right and responsibility of a professional group to manage affairs of a strictly professional nature. The term is often used to denote complete independence or sovereignty. Autonomy does not quite mean that. Plenary or sovereign powers with respect to education actually are vested in the respective state legislatures. But a certain degree of autonomy with respect to the school districts are vested in local school boards. Or, to use a political analogy, cities and states are vested with autonomy in regard to certain matters. Neither is completely independent. The city gets its grant of powers from the state, and the state is circumscribed by the limitations of the federal Constitution. The city, because of its closeness to certain problems such as police and fire protection, sanitation, and traffic regulations, is autonomous. But its powers can be modified or even withdrawn, in extreme circumstances, by the state. It is not independent or sovereign, but it is autonomous. The principle of autonomy is to localize responsibility where it can be efficiently performed.[2]

The rationale for localizing of responsibilities is based not only upon proximity to the problems involved, but also upon specialized competence and concern to do the job. And the extension of autonomy implies that the recipient will be free to perform the assigned task so long as it is performed competently and in the interests of society. Of course, the granter of such authority (in the case of professions, the state legislature) may withdraw the authority if it is incompetently performed or performed in a selfish, monopolistic manner.

The delegation by state legislatures of authority to state boards of education to fix and enforce teacher certification requirements (which is virtually universal among the states) is another example of the conferral of autonomy. As Lieberman has pointed out, an indispensable need of a democracy is to identify and to vest power of action in expert groups, otherwise the people make the absurd mistake of attempting to settle the most complex problems by popular vote.[3]

Professional autonomy, then, is really a diffusion of authority in a free society among expert groups by the sovereign or independent source. This is the free society's answer to the divine-right-of-kings philosophy—a symbol of rebellion against the idea that one or a few are endowed with

---

[2] Walter E. McPhie, and Lucien B. Kinney, "Professional Autonomy in Education," *Journal of Teacher Education*, September, 1959, *10*:285–90.

[3] Myron Lieberman, *Education as a Profession*. Englewood Cliffs, N.J.: Prentice-Hall, 1956, p. 88.

supernatural powers to rule all men and direct all affairs of a heterogeneous society.

Our free society has discovered by trial and error that expert occupational groups, professions in particular, can regulate their own internal affairs with greater efficiency and with greater profit to the people, in terms of better services, than can legal bureaucracies. This is a concept that could exist only in a free society. But it is a concept that must safeguard possible abuses of such power in the hands of private groups. Such power is granted by state legislatures, and these bodies can modify the grants at will or withdraw them if the necessity arises.

The Necessity of Autonomy for Teaching

The rash of criticisms of education following the Sputnik hysteria of 1957 has served to point up the need for vesting authority in an expert group to determine matters relating exclusively to the internal affairs of the teaching profession. Suddenly education became "everybody's business." Tycoons, politicians, admirals, plumbers, and busboys rushed in with proposed panaceas for American education. Quick-acting miracle drugs were prescribed for many of the fancied ills of education. New gimmicks and fads were described in almost every issue of the daily press and the slick magazines. Curriculum making by headlines assumed alarming proportions. Of course, in this rash of remedial pronouncement was a basic urge to find a scapegoat for the failures of our society, and this is understandable. But the widespread nature of the willingness of the general public to prescribe cures for professional problems, problems to which many devoted and competent members of the profession have spent their lives seeking sound solutions, borders on the incredible. Only the looseness of organization, the schisms within education itself, and the profession's confusion regarding the responsibility for leadership can explain these phenomena.

Professional Autonomy: A Well-Established Principle

For almost all professions except teaching, control over internal matters (those involving expert ability and opinion) are vested by law in the respective groups. The chief evidence of this is to be found in the controls of admission to the profession and continuance in practice. Control of admission and continuance in practice are, of course, centered in a cluster of standards including admission to preparation, prescribed preparation programs, licensure, employment, ethical and professional conduct, working conditions, admission to the professional organization, the power to expel from membership, and the power to revoke licensure.

The key to the extent of the delegation of most of these powers to a profession is the make-up of the licensing boards and the authority for selecting the board members. It would be meaningless to prescribe that a board be made up of members of a given profession, unless the profession is given the power to determine the membership. A survey made in 1952 by the Council of State Governments revealed that, in the membership of licensing boards for the professions, all or a majority of board members were members of the profession or occupation involved in the following number of states (there were then forty-eight states): lawyers, 48; doctors, 48; dentists, 48; pharmacists, 46 (2); optometrists, 46 (2); nurses, 44 (1); barbers, 42 (3); accountants, 41 (5); beauticians, 38 (4); architects, 34 (6); chiropractors, 34 (4); chiropodists, 31. (Number in parentheses represents number of states in which composition of the board is not known.) [4]

It must come as a shock to teachers that barbers and beauticians have much greater controls, controls given by legal sanction, over their own standards than do teachers. The obvious answer to this situation is that these are private occupations, and teaching, for the most part, is a public profession. But this is far from a satisfactory answer.

Obstacles to Autonomy for Teaching

There are several obstacles to the achievement of autonomy for the teaching profession. The first and most compelling is the fact that teaching, largely, is a public profession; that is, most of its members are employed in public schools and paid from public funds, which, of course, are derived from taxes. This fact seems to intimidate teachers to the extent that they tend to be obsessed with the role of subservience at every point to the public. This is a false notion of their status, their rights, and their responsibilities. Of course there are public concerns, but there are also professional concerns. The great problem is to separate the two into hemispheres of primary responsibility. The public owns the public schools. It is the public right to determine policy concerning the kind of schools it wants and what it is willing to pay for them. But when public policy making gets over into the hemisphere of defining competent teachers, preparation (what content and how much will provide competence), standards for admission to and continuation in practice, the details of the curriculum, teaching methods, textbooks, etc., it is preempting areas of primary professional concern and competence. This is going far afield from the principle of vesting decisions on expert matters in expert groups. It is analogous to a public decision to build a bridge, with the public insisting upon drawing the plans, specifying the materials, and making decisions that appropriately belong to expert groups such as architects

[4] Council of State Governments, *Occupational Licensing in the States*. Chicago: The Council, 1952, pp. 84–87; and information from the American Medical Association and American Dental Association, as cited by Lieberman, *op. cit.*, p. 95.

and engineers. The problem here is, probably, a vacuum created by the timidity of the teaching profession itself. Dealing as it does with problems so complex as to defy categorical treatment, the profession naturally tends to be reserved in its pronouncements. The public often mistakenly interprets this reserve as indecisiveness and even incompetence. Thus, it tends to accept cocksure prescriptions, or to take over from the teachers and make its own decisions.

A second obstacle is division within the teaching profession itself. Talk of autonomy for the profession probably irritates more people within the profession than without. Some teachers count it an impossible dream. Some vaguely sense that the notion threatens an infringement upon their own domain of vested interest or status. Others are blunt about their contempt for what they designate as mob rule and their worship of the "man-on-the-horse" idea of leadership. Thus, there have been many proposals to vest the fixing and dictating of standards for education and teachers in the hands of a self-elected professional hierarchy or in the hands of a few scholars.

The role of leadership in education must somehow be reconciled or synchronized with the consent-of-the-governed principle. This does not mean transferring full policy decisions from wherever they now reside to a nebulous mass of one and a half million or more teachers. It does mean participation in policy making, much as the people in a democracy do in making laws. Within each area, the essential roles of leadership and responsibility will not be diminished. Teacher education may be used as an example. The roles of planning and executing programs will still reside in the respective institutions. But such roles will be exercised within the framework of certain judgments and recommendations of the total profession—exercised through the accrediting process. These are the consumers of the product, and their demands and needs can be ignored only by facing the same hazards the producer of any other marketable product faces. As for the "public profession" caution, this has been debated so often it hardly seems profitable to discuss it further. As previously stated, there are public concerns and there are professional concerns, as there are in the services of any professional group. How to assure the quality of services the public wants and expects obviously involves decisions and policy that only the profession can decide. To pursue any other track is to ignore practices and precedents by which other professions achieved status.

In the drive for professional autonomy, the expert and expert groups will be given assignments according to their area of special competences. A major problem in the drive for professional autonomy is to achieve appropriate and effective machinery for policy making that will have the full support and sanction of the profession as a whole. A second major problem is to find appropriate and effective means of delegating the execution of specialized functions to competent organizations, institutions, and groups. Failure to solve these problems inevitably means that these functions will be assumed by vested-interest groups.

In the future the teaching profession will rely less and less upon other-directed techniques and more and more upon professional competence, self-discipline, and ethics. The spectacle of professionals being driven back to college campuses periodically by legal mandates, and of legal clubs being held over the administrators and teachers in the making of teaching assignments, is neither wholesome nor healthy for a dignified and responsible profession. Careful selection through scholarly preparation of competent professionals and their functioning as such are the best safeguards of the public interest in the long look.

Some Fruits of the Lack of Autonomy in Teaching

Recently a bill was introduced in one state legislature to modify the curriculum in the elementary schools of the state. The bill was defeated on the ground that this was an educational rather than a legislative matter. Contrast this action with that of another state legislature: Goaded by charges in a current book on subversive or left-wing treatment in textbooks, the state legislature repealed a long-existing law providing for the designation of a multiple list of high school textbooks by a committee of the teaching profession, from which each school could select its choice, and enacted new legislation placing authority for selecting textbooks in a lay committee appointed by the governor of the state.

RECENT MOVEMENTS TOWARD AUTONOMY

Two organized major thrusts toward achieving a self-determining status have been made by the teaching profession since the close of World War II. The first was the creation of the National Commission on Teacher Education and Professional Standards in 1946. The second, "New Horizons in Teacher Education and Professional Standards," was a special two-year study project by the commission (1959–61), in which a selected task force projected new goals for the future in terms of higher standards for the profession. Both thrusts were toward implementing the idea of a self-governing profession.

Origin of the Professional Standards Movement

One of the basic marks of any profession is that it sets its own standard, standards designed to assure society that its members are competent practitioners in the particular field. This effort to achieve this essential characteristic of a profession in teaching has been called the Professional Standards Movement. As an organized movement, it came into being with the establishment of the National Commission on Teacher Education and Professional Standards (NCTEPS) by the NEA Representative Assembly at its annual meeting in Buffalo in July, 1946. The movement is popularly known as the TEPS Movement, and the National Commission and the parallel state commissions as TEPS commissions.

Of course, there have been throughout the history of the teaching profession in the United States continuous efforts to elevate its standards. But these efforts, prior to the creation of NCTEPS, had been informal and diffused. The profession in 1946 decided upon a formally organized movement, with a specific charge to NCTEPS to represent it in a continuing drive to elevate and protect standards for admission to practice.

The resolution creating NCTEPS reads as follows:

That the National Education Association shall establish a Commission on Teacher Education and Professional Standards, composed of nine members to be selected by the Executive Committee. . . .

That the Commission on Teacher Education and Professional Standards shall be charged with the responsibility . . . of developing and carrying forward a continuing program for the profession in matters of recruitment, selection, preparation, and advancement of professional standards, including standards for institutions which prepare teachers.[5]

These were events and ideas that came to focus in the creation of NCTEPS as the beginning of the organized Professional Standards Movement. Back of these were certain developments, mostly adverse, that helped to solidify professional thought in this direction. What really brought the idea to full growth was the devastating effect that World War II had upon the stability of teaching staffs throughout the country, and the alarming lowering of standards that was almost universal during that period. During the war, with insatiable manpower demands of defense industries and of the armed forces, teaching became a rather forgotten area. As was natural, the American people, obsessed as they were with the cost, the sacrifices, and the tensions of the war, tended to ignore their public schools. While salaries, wages, and incomes in almost every line of endeavor skyrocketed, while prices of goods and commodities soared to new peaks, tax structures were not overhauled to provide the needed additional revenues for the schools. Obsolete school buildings and equipment were not replaced, teachers' salaries remained at static levels,

[5] National Education Association, *Proceedings of the Eighty-fourth Annual Meeting, 1945–46.* Washington, D.C.: The Association, 1946, Vol. 83 and 84, p. 239.

and teachers who remained in the profession suffered unusual hardships in meeting the rising costs of living.

Thousands of teachers were compelled by the pinch of the economic situation to migrate to other lines of endeavor. Standards were lowered almost everywhere in an effort to recruit somebody to assume charge of classes. Toward the end of the war, about 15,000 classrooms were actually closed because of the lack of teachers. Thousands of emergency, substandard teachers were employed, and the stability of teaching as a profession was seriously threatened. At one time during the war, at least one of every six teachers was an "emergency" teacher. It has been estimated that as many as 600,000 teachers came into and went out of teaching between the years 1939 and 1945. This has been called the greatest professional migration in the history of the world.

At the close of the war it was generally assumed that the situation would quickly right itself, that thousands of teachers employed in defense plants and other industries would return to teaching and force out the unqualified personnel employed during the war. It was assumed that college enrollments would quickly produce annually the number of new teachers needed to fill normal replacements. But exactly the opposite happened. Instead of the expected economic recession, the backlog of shortages of consumers' goods arising from the war resulted in boom economic conditions. Therefore, instead of manpower demands in industry being lessened, actually they expanded. Again the American people were slow to recognize the tragic conditions that had overtaken the public schools and to become aroused sufficiently to correct the situation. Conditions finally became so deplorable that, for the first time, strikes by teachers became fairly common. In the year 1946–47 serious strikes of teachers occurred in Flint, Michigan; Saint Paul and Minneapolis, Minnesota; Norwich, Connecticut; and other places.

It was in the midst of such unrest among teachers and apparent indifference of the public to the plight of the schools that the NEA Representative Assembly created the National Commission on Teacher Education and Professional Standards. The basic idea behind the work of the commission and of the Professional Standards Movement is that any profession worthy of the name fixes the standards that will be enforced on its own members. Of course, it is a basic premise that any profession will enforce standards the intent of which is to improve services to its clientele, rather than selfishly fixing them solely to obtain a monopoly or to create new economic, political, or social advantages for its members. In reality the two go together, because in the final analysis the welfare of children and the welfare of teachers are inseparable. As the welfare of teachers is increased, they are enabled to render more competent services to children.

DEVELOPMENTS IN THE PROFESSIONAL STANDARDS MOVEMENT

The creation and work of NCTEPS are good illustrations of how professional autonomy works. The basic step is for the profession to establish policy-making machinery (in this case, the NEA Representative Assembly was the policy-making body). The next step is to assign specific responsibility for implementing policy to an expert group (in this case, NCTEPS). Many people, even members of the profession, tend to be apprehensive about professional autonomy because of apprehension that all powers and controls will be vested in a huge mass of teachers, and, according to this mistaken motion, this would eventually lead to chaos. From its inception NCTEPS has sought to implement, through cooperative processes, the charge given to it.

Although NCTEPS is the one national body given the specific assignment by the profession of spearheading efforts to bring about the adoption of acceptable standards, this does not imply that the work in this area of professional endeavor is the exclusive province of NCTEPS or, indeed, that the great progress achieved is to be attributed to the commission. The fact is that many organizations have been working over long periods of time to bring about better standards. This discussion is intended only to point up the fact that the organized teaching profession has, at long last, established a national organization which, with its parallel state bodies, can serve as a focus of efforts by organizations and individuals to achieve standards at professional levels.

The commission, although given the responsibility of policy declaration in the areas of its charge, derives its chief powers from concert of opinions and actions among the rank and file of the teaching profession. The commission's first efforts, therefore, were to form an effective, cooperative partnership among the major segments of the teaching profession. In the creation of NCTEPS and in its work since, the NEA Department of Classroom Teachers, representing those engaged in actual classroom instruction in the public schools, has vigorously supported the Professional Standards Movement. Staff members of teacher-education institutions joined enthusiastically in the movement to raise standards for the profession all along the line. The legal authorities, representatives of the state departments of education in the fifty-two state and territorial jurisdictions, charged with the responsibility of administering the legal provisions for teacher education and certification, welcomed the new movement. These officers had for years been struggling almost alone in their efforts to achieve reasonable standards for admission to the profession and reasonable standards for the preparation of teachers. School administrators, principals, supervisors in the public schools, teachers in many private schools at the elementary and secondary levels, and staff members of higher-education institutions joined in the movement.

Parallel State Commissions

One of the first acts of NCTEPS after its formation was to call upon the respective state education associations to establish parallel commissions or committees on teacher education and professional standards to carry out the same objectives within the states as were assigned to the commission at the national level. (There are commissions in all states except Alaska, and several states have two commissions.) The state commissions in turn requested local education associations to establish local committees on teacher education and professional standards as parallel bodies to the state commissions. Hundreds of local TEPS committees have been formed to push vigorously at the local level the study of the standards that the profession must achieve.

The basic strength of the Professional Standards Movement depends upon involving directly about two million teachers in the study of the relationship between professional standards on the one hand and child and teacher welfare on the other, in the forming of intelligent opinions about the standards the profession needs, and in the exercising of unified support for the respective state legal authorities in developing and enforcing standards at professional levels. As a general rule, the acceptance and support of autonomy for the professions by the public has resulted in continuous improvement of professional service to the public. Teaching, the last of the major professions to move to assume the responsibility of autonomous management of its affairs, is now moving vigorously toward the goals of setting its own standards and seeing that they are enforced for admission to and continuation in practice.

Goals of the Professional Standards Movement

The original goals of the movement, as defined by NCTEPS, were as follows: [6]

1. Discriminating selection of candidates for teacher preparation.
2. A balanced supply of qualified teachers.
3. Effective, thorough programs of preparation for teaching.
4. Adequate certification requirements: minimum of four college years for beginning teachers, minimum of five years for fully qualified teachers.
5. Continuous and effective professional growth in service.

[6] "Building A Profession" (Annual Report of NCTEPS for the year 1949–50), *Journal of Teacher Education*, September, 1950, 1:175–83.

6. Professional accreditation of all teacher-education programs.
7. A professional concept of teaching.

A recent restatement of these goals, most of which have been wholly or partially achieved, is contained in the "New Horizons in TEPS" project, described later in this chapter.

PROGRESS IN THE PROFESSIONAL STANDARDS MOVEMENT

Substantial gains have been made since 1946 in all of the areas of endeavor assigned to NCTEPS. The progress may be summarized as follows:

Certification

The legal expression of standards for admission to the profession is found in the requirements for teachers' certification, which are applied by the respective state education legal authorities. In this area the Professional Standards Movement shows extraordinary progress since the creation of NCTEPS in 1946. In 1946 the idea of full professional preparation of at least the bachelor's degree for elementary school teachers had made so little headway that only fifteen states of the fifty-two state and territorial jurisdictions of the United States were enforcing the degree requirement for beginning elementary school teachers. This concept, that only a little learning is needed to teach little children, had become so embedded in our traditions that this has, perhaps, been the greatest single obstacle to the Professional Standards Movement and to the professionalization of teaching. This tradition, of course, arose out of pioneer conditions in our early history as a nation, where in sparsely populated rural areas one-room schools predominated. State legislatures made an effort to locate schools within walking distance of the children. This principle, sound in the economy and geography of the times, led to the multiplication of one-room school districts. At one time approximately 150,000 such small school units existed in this country. The type of education given in this simple society was exclusively that of the fundamentals, of the three R's. Thus, there became ingrained in our tradition the idea that teachers in these schools needed only the competency of mastery of the three R's. As the nation grew, population increased and society became more complex, but this tradition concerning the meager preparation of elementary school teachers persisted. The overcoming of this tradition and the placing of the preparation of elementary school teachers on the same professional levels as that of high school or college teachers has been most difficult. The extent to which this traditional concept is being overcome is one of the great fruits of the Professional Standards Movement, as indicated in the figures given below.

TABLE 42   Number of States Requiring Completion of the Bachelor's Degree for the Lowest Regular Certificate for Beginning Elementary School Teachers, in Selected Years

Year	Number of States Requiring
1937	5
1940	9
1946	15
1951	17
1953	27
1955	31
1957	37
1959	40
1961	44
1967	47

Source: T. M. Stinnett, *A Manual on Certification Requirements for School Personnel in the United States.* Washington, D.C.: National Education Association, National Commission on Teacher Education and Professional Standards, 1967 edition. Table 3, p. 22.

Preparation of Employed Teachers

Despite the continuing teacher shortages, the average preparation of employed teachers has continued to show rapid increases in recent years. Each year, in conection with the national study of teacher supply and demand made by the NEA Research Division, sampling data are collected on the preparation of employed elementary teachers. The comparison of the preparation requirements for the 1948–49 and 1959–60 school years shows the extent of the increase in the average preparation of employed teachers. In 1948–49 only 49.1 per cent of the employed elementary school teachers had completed the bachelor's degree. In 1966–67 the percentage of holders of the degree was 93.[7]

Accreditation

One of the major gains in the Professional Standards Movement has been the establishment of the National Council for Accreditation of Teacher Education. This is the first national professional accrediting body for teacher education in which the total profession has had representation. The NCATE is now the recognized accrediting body for teacher education.

[7] National Education Association, Research Division, *The American Public School Teacher, 1965–66,* Research Report 1967-R4. Washington, D.C.: The Association, 1967, p. 8.

TABLE 43 *Progress in Selected Factors in the Professional Standards Movement Between 1946 and 1967*

Item	STATUS		
	1946	1967	Change
Number of states requiring a degree for beginning elementary school teachers	15	47	+32
Per cent of employed elementay school teachers possessing a degree	45%	93%	+48
Average annual teacher's salary	$2080	$6821	+4,741
Number of teachers possessing only an emergency certificate	123,000 (1 in 6)	90,500 (1 in 20)	−32,500
Number of degree teachers graduated from college	41,000	200,919	+159,919
Number of teaching positions	875,000	1,759,236	+884,236
Number of teachers belonging to their state education association	735,804	1,700,000+	+400,000
Number of teachers belonging to the National Education Association	340,973	1,000,000+	+659,027

Source: Data compiled from several publications of National Education Association, especially *Milestones, Teacher Supply and Demand, The American Public School Teacher,* and *Manual on Certification Requirements* for years involved.

THE NEW HORIZONS REPORT

By 1958, as previously mentioned, many of the goals set by NCTEPS in 1946 had been achieved or were well on the way to achievement. By 1958, however, the impact of events at home and abroad sparked a critical reappraisal of their schools by the American people and a general demand for higher quality in education.

Several factors were involved in a new and intense concern of the American people regarding education. The unprecedented rate of acceleration in the accumulation of new knowledge, resulting from an upsurge in scientific research following World War II; the impacts of the discovery of new weapons—the atomic and hydrogen bombs, intercontinental missiles; space exploration and startling new developments in industrial research; the continuing cold war with communism; the upsurge of new nations—all these tended to focus attention upon new and more demanding emphasis in education.

In the resulting searching analysis of education, many obsolescences both in the curriculum and in teaching procedures were revealed. It became evident that the demands of society for trained manpower would focus increasingly in the future upon preparation for the professions. These demands inevitably dictated education of greater complexity at higher levels of quality, and higher standards of preparation for teachers. "Quality education," "quest for excellence," "demand for teachers of higher standards of competence" became almost universal slogans of the American people.

As a result of this public apprehension and clamor, American schools throughout the 1950's were in a dynamic ferment of change and groping for improved procedures. The launching of the first Sputnik by the Russians in 1957 sparked anew a public concern for adequacy in education that at times reached almost the point of frenzy. In 1957 NCTEPS sensed that the goals defined earlier for the Professional Standards Movement were inadequate to meet the new conditions in society. Thus, with a special appropriation from the NEA, a two-year special study was authorized. This study was titled "New Horizons in Teacher Education and Professional Standards." A task force of thirty-five leading educators was established in a cluster of five committees to study emerging needs and to develop proposed new goals in the areas of responsibility of NCTEPS, viz., selection, teacher education, certification, accreditation, and advancement of standards.

The task force was directed to project an image of the teacher and teaching services a decade or two decades into the future, to define goals to achieve this image, and to suggest means by which the profession could implement the new goals.[8]

The sweep of the recommendations of this task force is inexorably toward achieving an inner-directed profession of teaching, toward achieving a greater degree of autonomy for the profession. Many of the recommendations are challenging and controversial. For example, the report attacked the problems of "What is the teaching profession?" and "Who constitutes its membership?" At first glance these seem to be simple, innocuous questions. But they are not. Perhaps the greatest weakness of teaching as a profession is its diverse nature, its fragmentation into many interest groups, its greatest problem how to achieve unification as a professional group and yet retain the pluralism that has admittedly been one of the great and cherished strengths of American education.

The task force, in effect, called for one profession of teaching and defined the members as including all who are engaged in endeavors of a

[8] See Margaret Lindsey (ed.), *New Horizons for the Teaching Profession.* Washington, D.C.: National Commission on Teacher Education and Professional Standards, National Education Association, 1961. 243 pp.

professional nature, from the kindergarten through the graduate school of the university, in professional organizations, in legal education agencies, and in related professional work. Its analysis of membership in 1961 was as follows:

Job Category	Members Engaged
Teachers in public elementary and secondary schools	1,400,000
Teachers in private elementary and secondary schools	220,000
School administrators, supervisors, consultants, researchers, and state specialists in elementary and secondary schools	130,000
Professional personnel in higher education institutions	350,000
Professional staff members in professional organizations, government offices of education, private agencies with educational programs	25,000
TOTAL in 1961	2,125,000

On the question of seeking unification of the teaching profession, the task-force report states:

Within this body there exists differentiation in function and consequent variation in specialization, but such differentiation does not entail differences in status, prestige, or quality of contribution to the central purpose. The work of the first-grade teacher who opens wide new vistas for groups of children year after year is not more or less important than that of the research scientist who confines his teaching to tutoring two advanced doctoral students each year; it is different in kind. The contribution to the improvement of the educational program made by the school superintendent who succeeds in securing a large allocation of funds for a new junior high school is not greater or smaller than that made by the faculty planning the program for that new school; it is different in kind. So it might also be said of the work of college teachers, of staff members of state departments of education, and of executive secretaries of state teachers associations.[9]

Public and Professional Responsibilities

The New Horizons Report recognizes that there are concerns about education that belong wholly, or primarily, to the public; that there are concerns that belong wholly, or primarily, to the teaching profession; and that there are concerns that blend into both areas of responsibility. The preceding chart depicts these concepts.

Specific Goals for the Professional Standards Movement

The New Horizons task force recommended major goals [10] that the

[9] *Ibid.*, pp. 6–7.

[10] National Education Association, National Commission on Teacher Education and Professional Standards, *New Horizons in Teacher Education and Professional Standards,* Preliminary Report. Washington, D.C.: The Association, 1960, p. 2–4.

CHART II   The Profession's Leadership Responsibility for the
Quality of Education in Schools and Colleges

The Profession's Responsibility   *The Public's Responsibility*

Joining with the Public in	Establishing Public Policy Regarding Education Determining Purposes of Education Providing Working Conditions Conducive to Productivity	Joining with the Profession in
Assuming Autonomy for	Determining and Utilizing Best Means for Achieving Agreed-Upon Purposes Ensuring Competent Professional Personnel	Granting the Profession the Right to Make and Carry out Decisions in
Joining with the Public in	Evaluating Achievement of Purposes Appraising Public Policy Regarding Education	Joining with the Profession in

Source: Margaret Lindsey (ed.), *New Horizons for the Teaching Profession.* Washington, D.C.: National Commission on Teacher Education and Professional Standards, National Education Association, 1961, p. 23.

teaching profession should strive to achieve. Essential to achievement of these goals is a climate in which:

1. A united profession moves forward assuming responsibility for the competence of its members.
2. Standards are co-operatively developed by the total profession and applied to all members and groups within it.
3. The profession has autonomy in matters requiring expertness.
4. Each member of the profession is committed to active participation in the development and enforcement of standards.

The proposed goals are that:

1. Standards of selection be rigorously applied, from early identification of able students throughout the professional careers of all educators.
2. Preparation of professional scholars be a continuous process in which:
Preservice preparation of all personnel is purposefully planned with appropriate emphasis on broad general education, depth in specialization, and study of educational theory and practice
Essential preservice preparation of elementary- and secondary-school teachers requires a minimum of five years

Essential preservice preparation of college teachers and other leadership personnel requires a minimum of three years beyond the baccalaureate degree

Inservice educational growth—with appropriate emphasis on general education, specialization, and study of educational theory and practice—is an obligation of all professional personnel throughout careers in education.

3. The profession's agency [National Council for Accreditation of Teacher Education] for accrediting preparatory programs be adequately supported, financially and morally, and the agency assume its full responsibility.

4. Only those professional preparatory programs (both graduate and undergraduate) accredited by the professional accrediting agency be recognized by licensing agencies.

. . . .

6. There be one standard license to teach, endorsed by area of specialization and obtained on the basis of graduation from an accredited program, satisfactory passing of a comprehensive examination of background information, institutional recommendation of fitness to begin to teach, and satisfactory performance during one year of full-time responsible teaching. Fulfilling requirements for this license will require six years generally.

7. Only those teachers be employed who have been prepared in accredited programs requiring demonstrated competence to practice, and, beyond the first year of teaching, only those who hold the standard license.

8. Appropriate assignment of professional workers be disciplined by specialized groups within the profession.

9. The profession establish state professional standards boards with affiliated commissions on (a) preparation of teachers for elementary and secondary schools, (b) preparation of college teachers, (c) preparation of educational leadership personnel, other than teachers, (d) accreditation of preparatory programs for all professional personnel, (e) licensure of all professional personnel, and (f) professional practices; the profession work toward the attainment of legal sanction for such boards.

10. Professional standards and procedures of enforcement be subject to continuous, systematic evaluation by the profession.

THE NEW HORIZONS PROGRAMS AND PROFESSIONAL AUTONOMY

Summarizing the sweep of the report of the New Horizons in TEPS task force, the director of the project analyzed its implications for developing an inner-directed profession of teaching as follows: [11]

I. The center of this profession is the teacher; other educational specialists complement the teacher and his work.

II. The core of the Professional Standards Movement is the profession's commitment to the central purpose of providing the best possible educational opportunity for all.

[11] Lindsey, *op. cit.,* Chap. 9, "The Teaching Profession in the Decades Ahead," pp. 231–43.

III. The center of the professional standards program is the continuous selection and preparation of all professional personnel.

IV. The three essential processes of professional standards are accreditation of preparatory programs, licensure of professional personnel, and rigorous application of standards of practice.

V. The chief requisition to success in the Professional Standards Movement is leadership by the National Education Association.

VI. Within this total image of a profession moving vigorously toward self-discipline and the attendant autonomy, the National Commission on Teacher Education and Professional Standards and its affiliated state TEPS commissions continue to have fundamental leadership responsibility.

Is Professional Autonomy for Teaching Possible?

It not only is possible, it is imperative. There is no other route to competent service by the teaching profession or to recognized professional status. On this point Corey has stated: "We cannot expect society to evaluate the significance of our work any higher than we ourselves do. As long as we, without protest, permit anyone to teach, society will assume that anyone can teach." [12]

It must be borne in mind that autonomy for the teaching profession does not involve disdain for public concerns or the flouting of public authority in its rightful controls over education. Nor does it imply any measure of contempt for public opinions concerning education. Rather, professional autonomy means a strengthened partnership with the public toward better service by teachers and a higher quality of education.

And in the drive for autonomy, the puzzling problems lie within the teaching profession rather than with the public. Medicine faced the same problems, different only in degree, when it began to move in the first two decades of this century toward self-government. The introduction to the Flexner report, by Henry Pritchett, sets forth the basic ones:

> The development which is here suggested for medical education is conditioned largely upon three factors: (1) The creation of a public which shall discriminate between the ill-trained and the rightly trained physician, and which will also insist upon the enactment of such laws as will require practitioners of medicine . . . to ground themselves in the fundamentals upon which medical science rests; (2) upon the universities and their attitudes toward medical education standards and support; and (3) upon the attitudes of members of the medical profession toward standards of their own practice and upon their sense of honor with respect to their own profession. [13]

All of these elements and factors are involved in the task of developing the teaching profession into a self-regulating one, except that those in

[12] Arthur F. Corey, "Let's Be Done With Compromises," *Nation's Schools*, May, 1959, *61*:49–50.

[13] Abraham Flexner, *Medical Education in the United States and Canada*, Bulletin No. 4. New York: The Carnegie Foundation for the Advancement of Teaching, 1910, p. xiii.

teaching are, perhaps, more complex. The sheer weight of numbers is one: there are about ten times as many teachers as doctors. The diversity and number of institutions preparing teachers is another: there are about fifteen times as many as there are medical schools. The lack of unification of teaching, which tends to fragment into as many professions as there are specialties in education, is a third—perhaps as many as fifty, contrasted with one for medicine.

This fragmentation leads to status and prestige levels, real or fancied, that are real barriers to unity of purpose and concert of action. The proliferation of professional organizations is another barrier that divides the teaching profession. There are several hundred education associations, contrasted with, typically, one national organization with affiliated local and state associations for most of the other professions.

How to find a center of common interest, a focus for common concerns —these are the crucial problems for the teaching profession and the chief barriers to the development of autonomy.

REFERENCES

AMERICAN ACADEMY OF ARTS AND SCIENCES, "The Professions," *Daedalus,* Fall, 1963, 92:4, 647–865, Bernard Barber, "Some Critical Problems in the Sociology of Professions," pp. 669–688.

CONANT, JAMES B., *The Education of American Teachers.* New York: McGraw-Hill, 1963, Chap. 1, 2, and 3, pp. 1–55.

FLEXNER, ABRAHAM, *Medical Education in the United States and Canada,* Bulletin No. 4. New York: The Carnegie Foundation for the Advancement of Teaching, 1910.

KINNEY, L. B., "Certification and Professional Autonomy; Excerpts from *Certification in Education,*" *School and Society,* December 28, 1963, *91*:434–9.

———, *Certification in Education.* Englewood Cliffs, N.J.: Prentice-Hall, Inc., 1964.

LIEBERMAN, MYRON, *Education as a Profession.* Englewood Cliffs, New Jersey: Prentice-Hall, 1956, Chap. 4, "Professional Autonomy," pp. 87–123.

———, *The Future of Public Education.* Chicago: University of Chicago Press, 1960.

LINDSEY, MARGARET (ed.) *New Horizons for the Teaching Profession.* Washington, D.C.: National Commission on Teacher Education and Professional Standards, National Education Association, 1961.

MAYOR, JOHN R., *Accreditation in Teacher Education.* Washington, D.C.: National Commission on Accrediting, 1965.

NATIONAL EDUCATION ASSOCIATION, National Commission on Teacher Education and Professional Standards, *Guidelines for Professional Standards Boards.* Washington, D.C.: The Association, 1967.

———, *Professional Practices Regulations.* Washington, D.C.: The Association, 1965.

———, *Professional Imperatives: Expertness and Self-Determination,* Report of the Fort Collins Conference. Washington, D.C.: The Association, 1962, "Self-Determination and Self-Regulation in the Profession of Teaching," pp. 37–59.

———, "Professional Position on Professional Standards," *Physical Education Record,* May, 1964, 35:40–1.

NATIONAL EDUCATION ASSOCIATION, Research Division, *Teacher's Day in Court: Review of 1966.* Washington, D.C.: The Association, 1967.

STINNETT, T. M., *Golden Years Upcoming—Maybe.* National Commission on Teacher Education and Professional Standards, National Education Association, Washington, D.C.: The Association, 1967. Also, in *Journal of Teacher Education,* September, 1967.

———, "New Horizons Project: USA," *Yearbook of Education 1963:*513–20.

———, "The Meaning of Autonomy" (editorial), *Journal of Teacher Education,* September, 1960, *11:*325–26.

———, *The Profession of Teaching.* Washington, D.C.: Center for Applied Research in Education, Inc., 1962.

14: Developing and Enforcing
A Code of Ethics for
the Teaching Profession

ROLE OF ETHICS IN THE PROFESSIONS

*T*he adoption, general observance, and enforcement, where required, of a professional code of ethics are basic characteristics of all professions.

The necessity for such a code, self-imposed, is obvious. In the first place, the average layman is not in a position to pass judgment upon the quality of professional services. He must depend upon the integrity of the professional practitioner for a fair appraisal of what he is buying to a much greater extent than would be the case in the purchase of ordinary goods and services in the marketplace. The public, therefore, has a great stake in the development and enforcement of ethical rules of conduct and practice by the members of a profession.

In the second place, the application of such codes by the professions tends to make them self-regulating and self-governing and prevents the imposition of rules by government agencies, whose knowledge of the complex problems of a given profession necessarily would be limited.

The formulation and enforcement of a code of ethics by a profession, then, has a twofold purpose: to derive a set of rules under which its members will be enabled to provide better service to society and under which the profession can provide better protection for its members, and to assume responsibility for assuring the competence of its members; and to prohibit the type of conduct that will bring the profession into disrepute.

The need for a code of ethics by a profession and its observance or enforcement has been stated by Tawney: [1]

A profession is not simply a collection of individuals who get a living for themselves by the same kind of work. Nor is it merely a group which is organized

[1] R. H. Tawney, *The Acquisitive Society*. New York: Harcourt, Brace & World, Inc., 1920, p. 91.

exclusively for the economic protection of its members, though that is normally among its purposes. . . . Its essence is that it assumes certain responsibilities for the competence of it members or the quality of its wares, and that it deliberately prohibits certain kinds of conduct on the ground that though they may be profitable to the individual, they are calculated to bring into disrepute the organization to which he belongs.

This chapter will attempt to trace the efforts of the teaching profession to derive a workable code of ethics for its members and to secure universal compliance.

Ethical Codes of Other Professions

The idea of the imposition of ethical standards upon a given professional group is an ancient one. The idea in medicine, which has perhaps the oldest code among the professions, goes back 2,500 years to the Oath of Hippocrates. In the United States the American Medical Association adopted its first written ethical code in 1848. This code of the American Medical Association, *Principles of Medical Ethics*, has undergone several revisions since.[2] The American Bar Association adopted its *Canons of Ethics* in 1908. Other professions have adopted codes: the American Institute of Accountants did so in 1917; the American Institute of Architects adopted *A Circular of Advice—Relative to Principles of Professional Practice and Canons of Ethics* in 1909, revised this document in 1912 and again in 1918, and the present code of the AIA was adopted in 1947 and revised and adopted in 1954 under the title *The Standards of Professional Practice;*[3] the Engineers' Council for Professional Development formulated a code in 1947 from a consolidation of existing codes of several engineering societies.

Development of Codes of Ethics for Teachers

Currently one code of ethics—Code of Ethics of the Education Profession—is applicable to the preponderance of members of the teaching profession. This new code, adopted by the NEA in 1963, has also been adopted by all of the state education associations and 15 of the NEA affiliated departments.

Thus its applicability, although not universal, is binding upon perhaps as high as 95 per cent of public school personnel.

The first ethical codes for teachers were developed by state education associations. The first of these was the one adopted by the Georgia Edu-

[2] William T. Filts, Jr., and Barbara Filts, "Ethical Standards of the Medical Profession," *The Annals of the American Academy of Political and Social Science,* January, 1955, 297:17–36.

[3] George Bain Cummings, "Standards of Professional Practice in Architecture," *The Annals of the American Academy of Political and Social Science,* January, 1955, 297: 8–16.

cation Association in 1896. The California Teachers Association adopted a code in 1904, and the Alabama Education Association in 1908.

Evolution of NEA Codes of Ethics

In 1924 the National Education Association appointed a committee, consisting of fifty-six members of the association, to develop a code of ethics for teachers.[4] The work of this committee had been preceded by work in various states dating back as far as 1896. The first NEA code was officially adopted in 1929. Based largely upon the results of a questionnaire sent to several thousand NEA members, the code contained twenty-one ethical principles. The committee recommended that all state education associations set up ethics committees to interpret the code and that the code be used by teacher-education institutions. Revisions of the original code were adopted by the Representative Assembly of the National Education Association in 1939, 1941, and 1952. NEA membership requirements now include the obligation to abide by the Code of Ethics of the Education Profession.

The new code, together with annotations of interpretations by the Ethics Committee, reads as follows: [5]

The Code of Ethics of the Education Profession

PREAMBLE

We, professional educators of the United States of America, affirm our belief in the worth and dignity of man. We recognize the supreme importance of the pursuit of truth, the encouragement of scholarship, and the promotion of democratic citizenship. We regard as essential to these goals the protection of freedom to learn and to teach and the guarantee of equal educational opportunity for all. We affirm and accept our responsibility to practice our profession according to the highest ethical standards.

We acknowledge the magnitude of the profession we have chosen and engage ourselves, individually and collectively, to judge our colleagues and to be judged by them in accordance with the applicable provisions of this Code.

Opinions 2, 10. The term *teacher* as used in Opinions 1 through 41 includes school administrators.

Opinion 4. The Code has no application to members of boards of education.

Opinion 14. The official actions of a local association are the collective actions of its membership, and therefore, a local association is bound by the pertinent provisions of the Code.

PRINCIPLE I—COMMITMENT TO THE STUDENT

We measure success by the progress of each student toward achievement of

[4] National Education Association, *NEA Handbook for Local, State, and National Associations, 1966–67*. Washington, D.C.: The Association, 1966, p. 133.

[5] National Education Association Ethics Committee. *Interpretations of the Code of Ethics of the Educational Profession.* Washington, D.C.: The Association, 1966.

NOTE: New interpretations were submitted to the NEA Representative Assembly in the summer of 1968.

his maximum potential. We therefore work to stimulate the spirit of inquiry, the acquisition of knowledge and understanding, and the thoughtful formulation of worthy goals. We recognize the importance of cooperative relationships with other community institutions, especially the home.

In fulfilling our obligations to the student, we—

1. Deal justly and considerately with each student.

Opinion 13. It is improper for an educator to make remarks in public reflecting on a student's abilities and family background. However, an educator has the right and often the duty to confer in confidence with colleagues or authorized agencies regarding a student's problems in conduct and adjustment.

Opinion 37. It is improper for an educator deliberately to assign a grade that reflects factors irrelevant to the performance or progress of that student.

Opinion 39. A principal has an obligation to disclose confidential information about a pupil to a school counselor if access to the information is essential to the counselor's performance of his professional duties.

2. Encourage the student to study varying points of view and respect his right to form his own judgment.

Opinion 30. An educator may properly identify and express his own point of view in classroom discussion, but in doing to assumes certain correlative responsibilities.

3. Withhold confidential information about a student or his home unless we deem that its release serves professional purposes, benefits the student, or is required by law.

Opinion 24. It is improper to reveal confidential information about the family background of a student who is causing difficulty in the classroom, even though the motive is to secure the cooperation of fellow students during the period of the child's adjustment.

Opinion 28. It is improper for an educator to reveal confidential information to parents about the disabilities of students in his class.

See also Opinions 13 and 39.

4. Make discreet use of available information about the student. See Opinions 13, 24, and 39.

5. Conduct conferences with or concerning students in an appropriate place and manner. See Opinion 13.

6. Refrain from commenting unprofessionally about a student or his home. See Opinion 13.

7. Avoid exploiting our professional relationship with any student.

Opinion 9. While the right to augment teaching income by outside employment is recognized under the Code, solicitation by an educator of parents of students under his immediate jurisdiction is improper.

Opinion 18. While the right to augment teaching income is recognized under the Code, an educator who solicits parents of students in his class to purchase musical instruments is acting improperly.

Opinion 19. There is no provision of the Code which governs the selection and use by an educator of instructional materials. Good practice permits comparison of branded products, but no recommendation by an educator of a particular brand.

Opinion 40. It is improper for an educator to try to convert to his religious faith the parents of students to whom he has the relationship of teacher.

8. Tutor only in accordance with officially approved policies.

Opinion 6. Tutoring for compensation, including one's own students, is proper if in accordance with approved policies. In absence of board policies on tutoring, local associations should take initiative in their formulation.

Opinion 27. A director of a school band may properly give private lessons to members of the band and to students in his music classes, providing the arrangements conform to policies of the school board. In the absence of board policies the arrangements should be approved by the chief school officer or the local professional association.

9. Inform appropriate individuals and agencies of the student's educational needs and assist in providing an understanding of his educational experiences.

Opinion 31. It is improper for an educator in a report to parents to give a false impression as to the student's general adjustment in the classroom.

See also Opinions 24 and 37.

10. Seek constantly to improve learning facilities and opportunities.

Opinion 29. There is no provision of the Code which governs the selection and use by an educator of instructional materials. Good practice requires that commercially sponsored materials be selected on a basis of their instructional value and that students be protected from exploitation by any special interest group.

PRINCIPLE II—COMMITMENT TO THE COMMUNITY

We believe that patriotism in its highest form requires dedication to the principles of our democratic heritage. We share with all other citizens the responsibility for the development of sound public policy. As educators, we are particularly accountable for participating in the development of educational programs and policies and for interpreting them to the public.

In fulfilling our obligations to the community, we—

1. Share the responsibility for improving the educational opportunities for all.

2. Recognize that each educational institution may have a person authorized to interpret its official policies.

Opinion 7. It is improper for educators to consult members of the governing board regarding the dismissal of a professional associate without first presenting their views to the appropriate administrative authorities.

Opinion 38. It is improper for a minority group of a local association to submit a salary proposal directly to a board of education without advance consultation with the superintendent and notice of its intentions at the meeting when the majority proposal is adopted.

3. Acknowledge the right and responsibility of the public to participate in the formulation of education policy.

4. Evaluate through appropriate professional procedures conditions within a district or institution of learning, make known serious deficiencies, and take any action deemed necessary and proper.

Opinion 4. It is improper to accept a position made vacant by the application of unjust personnel practices and procedures.

Opinion 22. A local association may properly report its loss of confidence in the integrity of a colleague to the school authorities provided professionally accepted procedures are followed and the report is made through proper channels.

5. Use educational facilities for intended purposes consistent with applicable policy, law, and regulation.

Opinion 26. Educators may properly urge friends and acquaintances to support a school bond issue and candidates in a school board election who favor its passage.

Opinion 32. It is improper for educators to distribute campaign literature supporting individual candidates in a school board election on school property and on school time.

Opinion 42. It is improper to use school facilities to solicit funds in behalf of candidates for public office on school property during school time.

6. Assume full political and citizenship responsibilities, but refrain from exploiting the institutional privileges of our professional positions to promote political candidates or partisan activities. See Opinions 26, 32, and 42.

7. Protect the educational program against undesirable infringement.

Opinion 21. An offer by a commercial organization to pay the cost of an association banquet on condition that the association accept as main speaker a person of the donor's selection may properly be accepted by the association.

Opinion 33. An educator, in the exercise of his professional judgment, must decide for himself the kind and extent of his community activities.

See also Opinions 19, 29, and 30.

PRINCIPLE III—COMMITMENT TO THE PROFESSION

We believe that the quality of the services of the education profession directly influences the future of the nation and its citizens. We therefore exert every effort to raise educational standards, to improve our service, to promote a climate in which the exercise of professional judgment is encouraged, and to achieve conditions which attract persons worthy of the trust to careers in education. Aware of the value of united effort, we contribute actively to the support, planning, and programs of our professional organizations.

In fulfilling our obligations to the profession, we—

1. Recognize that a profession must accept responsibility for the conduct of its members and understand that our own conduct may be regarded as representative.

Opinion 36. It is improper for a chief school officer to give verbal assurance of a favorable recommendation and later issue an unfavorable recommendation.

2. Participate and conduct ourselves in a responsible manner in the development and implementation of policies affecting education.

Opinion 2. An educator's refusal to cooperate in an investigation being conducted by a professional association is not contrary to the Code, but in the absence of a satisfactory explanation it is a disservice to the profession.

Opinion 14. A local association may properly express its views to the press on the action by a governing board against a professional colleague following rejection of its appeals by appropriate school authorities.

Opinion 41. Sick leave is to be used for the purpose for which it was granted. It is unethical to misuse sick leave time.

Opinion 47. Members of the profession who participate in reporting false attendance figures are in violation of ethical practice. Educators, as public officials, have an obligation to observe the laws relating to state financing of public schools.

3. Cooperate in the selective recruitment of prospective teachers and in the orientation of student teachers, interns, and those colleagues new to their positions. See Opinion 36.

4. Accord just and equitable treatment to all members of the profession in the exercise of their professional rights and responsibilities and support them when unjustly accused or mistreated.

Opinion 20. There is no provision in the Code which governs an administrator's use of an intercommunication system without the knowledge of an educator, but such use can cause tension and resentment on the part of the educator and is contrary to good practice.

Opinion 45. The practice of monitoring a classroom without the knowledge of the teacher is unethical. The practice of criticizing teachers via the intercommunications system is clearly in violation of this section.

See also Opinions 36 and 38.

5. Refrain from assigning professional duties to nonprofessional personnel when such assignment is not in the best interest of the student.

6. Provide, upon request, a statement of specific reason for administrative recommendations that lead to the denial of increments, significant changes in employment, or termination of employment.

Opinion 10. An administrator should consult with an educator about parents' complaints before taking administrative action. While it may be advisable for an administrator to discuss parents' complaints, he is not required to do so where no administrative action is contemplated.

Opinion 16. It is improper for a chief school officer to recommend a transfer because of complaints of parents without notice to and prior consultation with the educator and an opportunity for the educator to state his side of the case.

See also Opinion 36.

7. Refrain from exerting undue influence based on the authority of our positions in the determination of professional decisions by colleagues.

Opinion 48. Professional organizations, to be effective and meaningful to their members, must be voluntary and emphasize the improvement of service. The administrator who coerces his subordinate to join an association by threatening or implying professional retaliation has acted improperly.

Opinion 49. Professional autonomy involves the principle that the best results in education are obtained when decisions are left to the people who are best informed about them. Alteration of a professional decision can properly stem only from clear evidence of incompetence, the presence of bias, or indications of unethical behavior.

8. Keep the trust under which confidential information is exchanged.

9. Make appropriate use of time granted for professional purposes.

10. Interpret and use the writings of others and the findings of educational research with intellectual honesty.

    Opinion 46. Those who produce instructional materials for sale purposes to earn a profit should not be expected to subsidize a school district program that does not elect to provide audiovisual materials in sufficient measure. "Standards of fair use" should be observed by educators.

11. Maintain our integrity when dissenting by basing our public criticism of education on valid assumptions as established by careful evaluation of facts or hypotheses.

12. Represent honestly our professional qualifications and identify ourselves only with reputable educational institutions.

13. Respond accurately to requests for evaluations of colleagues seeking professional positions.

    Opinion 11. While there is necessarily a wide margin for individual judgment in the formulation of references, it is improper for an administrator to withhold in a reference information about unresolved, current difficulties which affect an educator's competence.

    Opinion 23. An administrator may properly withhold in a letter of reference information about past difficulties which have been resolved and which do not affect an educator's present competence.

    Opinion 25. It is improper for an administrator to imply in a letter of reference that he had some reservation about an educator's competence if the educator's record has been outstanding.

    See also Opinion 36.

PRINCIPLE IV—COMMITMENT TO PROFESSIONAL EMPLOYMENT PRACTICES

We regard the employment agreement as a solemn pledge to be executed both in spirit and in fact in a manner consistent with the highest ideals of professional service. Sound professional personnel relationships with governing boards are built upon personal integrity, dignity, and mutual respect.

In fulfilling our obligations to professional employment practices, we—

1. Apply for or offer a position on the basis of professional and legal qualifications.

    Opinion 44. Insofar as the responsibility for the content of employment applications is that of educators, it is unprofessional to include on such forms questions concerning the race and/or religion of applicants.

2. Apply for a specific position only when it is known to be vacant and refrain from such practices as underbidding or commenting adversely about other candidates.

    Opinion 1. Although it is permissible to circulate mimeographed inquiries about vacancies, it is improper to file a formal application based on the indiscriminate circulation of a mimeographed application prepared for general distribution.

3. Fill no vacancy except where the terms, conditions, policies, and practices permit the exercise of our professional judgment and skill and where a climate conducive to professional service exists.

    Opinion 4. It is improper to accept a position made vacant by the application of unjust personnel practices and procedures.

4. Adhere to the conditions of a contract or to the terms of an appointment until either has been terminated legally or by mutual consent.

Opinion 12. An educator may properly resign from his position after an administrator has imposed material modifications in a contract. All the details of an educator's duties cannot be incorporated in a contract, and reasonable adjustments in teaching assignments are often necessary and desirable.

Opinion 15. If an educator has entered into a contract with one school district, it is improper for him to initiate or continue negotiations for a contract with another school district without the consent of the district to which he is obligated. By the same token, it is improper for a chief school officer knowingly to negotiate with an educator already under contract without the approval of the school district to which the teacher is obligated.

Opinion 17. If an educator has conducted oral negotiations with a school district but has made no final commitment, he may properly conduct negotiations and accept a contract with another school district.

Opinion 34. It is improper for an educator to resign to accept a new position after his contract has been automatically renewed and the governing board has refused to release him.

Opinion 43. It is improper for an administrator to make a firm offer to an educator on a continuing contract of a position that requires service to begin within less than thirty days without first securing the assent of the administration of the district holding the educator's current contract.

5. Give prompt notice of any change in availability of service, in status of applications, or in change of position. See Opinions 12, 15, and 43.
6. Conduct professional business through the recognized educational and professional channels. See Opinions 2, 7, 10, 14, 16, 22, and 38.
7. Accept no gratuities or gifts of significance that might influence our judgment in the exercise of our professional duties.
8. Engage in no outside employment that will impair the effectiveness of our professional service and permit no commercial exploitation of our professional position.

Opinion 3. Solicitation and sale of commercial products to professional associates is looked upon with disfavor by the profession under certain circumstances.

Opinion 5. The operation of a private teacher-placement agency in competition with a placement office operated by the university which employs him is inconsistent with a faculty member's obligation to the university and to his students.

Enforcement of Teachers' Codes of Ethics

Machinery for disciplining teachers who violate their ethical codes is maintained by some local associations, practically all state associations, and by the National Education Association. The NEA Committee on Professional Ethics (commonly called the Ethics Committee) is the body charged with development, enforcement, and interpretation of its Code of Ethics. It seems apparent that most of the violations among teachers result from a lack of knowledge of the Code or of the interpretation of specific provisions that have been made by the profession. The Committee on Professional Ethics is composed of five members. Its functions, as defined by the NEA Representative Assembly, are to study the Code of Ethics and make recommendations for improving it, to publicize and promote its use by the profession, to render opinions interpreting its provisions, and to hold hearings on cases involving alleged violations and to take disciplinary action against violations by members. The committee emphasizes its informative function by printing the code and distributing it widely among the profession. It is empowered after hearings to censure, suspend, or expel any member for violation of the Code subject to review by the NEA Executive Committee. A member may within 60 days after a decision by the Ethics Committee file an appeal of the decision. The Executive Committee may affirm, reject, or modify the decision rendered by the Ethics Committee.

The Ethics Committee, in holding a hearing on Code violations, must give the accused a hearing in which judicial procedure is closely followed. The accused has the right to be represented by counsel and to cross-examine witnesses. Judicial procedure must be observed because the accused always has the right of appeal to the Executive Committee and the courts.

Developing a Body of Professional Opinions Regarding Teacher Ethics

The drafting and adoption of a law are legislative functions. The interpretation of the law, what its meaning is, and its application to a variety of cases is a judicial function. And the enforcement of the law is entrusted to an executive agency. The NEA structure is used here to illustrate how these principles apply to the adoption, interpretation, and application of the Code of Ethics for teachers. The NEA Representative Assembly is the legislative body of the NEA, acting for the teaching profession in a way somewhat analogous to the Congress in the realm of government. It adopts a code of ethics for its members. The Committee on Professional Ethics acts as the interpretive body or judiciary. The NEA Executive Committee is given power to review decisions of the Committee on Professional Ethics.

Any law is without substantive meaning until it is tested in the courts and opinions are rendered as to its meaning in given situations. As someone has phrased it, "The law is what the courts say it is."

A primary function of the Ethics Committee of the NEA, at least at this stage of development and application of a professional code of ethics for teachers, is to develop from actual cases reported to it a body of opinions interpreting the Code of Ethics for teachers that will serve as a guide to teachers as to the meaning of a given principle in the Code, and as a guide to interpretation and enforcement bodies before which actual cases of alleged violations are brought.

As has been previously stated, it is believed that most cases of alleged violations of the Code by teachers arise from their lack of knowledge of the Code or the absence of authentic interpretation of its meaning—in other words, that most violations are unwitting or unintentional. The Ethics Committee is, therefore, currently engaged in building up not only a sound, comprehensive set of laws for the profession, contained in a constantly revised code of ethics, but developing a body of professional opinion interpreting the meaning of the Code in specific cases.

The committee has issued a compilation of opinion in forty cases.[6]

The following section will describe some of the common types of code violations by teachers and the interpretation of the committee of the meaning of the Code regarding such cases.

WAYS IN WHICH TEACHERS MAY VIOLATE THE PROFESSIONAL CODE OF ETHICS

Breaking Contracts

Once a contract for his services is signed, a teacher should expect to fulfill it, unless he is released willingly by his employer. The truly ethical person takes great pride in strict observance of a written agreement or oral pledges.

In business, the person who fails to observe commitments is not likely to be successful. We like to deal with the individual whose word is as good as his bond, whose commitments are fulfilled regardless of the difficulties that may arise after the commitment is made. We avoid the individual who is undependable and whose word, whether written or oral, is not good. The contract jumpers among teachers are a continuous source of embarrassment to their colleagues, who often are judged on the basis of unethical conduct by a few.

Most teachers live up to the contracts that they have signed. It is the exception, the one in a thousand, who brings disrepute upon the profession. For example, there is the case of a teacher who applied to a superintendent for a position in August. After discussing the teacher's qualifications, the superintendent asked, "How does it happen that you don't have a job, when there are so many openings in your field?"

"Well, I do have," the young woman replied, "but I'd like to get a better one. To be frank, I have three contracts now." Reaching in her purse, she pulled out three signed contracts. Each of the school systems was apparently expecting her to teach for it. She was on a shopping tour and would take the best position available when school opened.

[6] National Education Association, Committee on Professional Ethics, *op. cit.*, pp. 9–73.

Ethics Committee Interpretation. *If a teacher has entered into a contract with one school district, it is improper for him to initiate or continue negotiations for a contract with another school district without the consent of the disrict to which he is obligated. By the same token, it is improper for a superintendent knowingly to negotiate with a teacher already under contract without the approval of the school district to which the teacher is obligated.*

Case Example. A teacher was negotiating for a contract with two school districts, A and B, for the ensuing year. She signed a contract without a cancellation clause with District A and the superintendent thereupon notified placement bureaus that the vacancy no longer existed. Unknown to the superintendent of District A, the teacher continued negotiations with District B. Shortly before school opened she orally agreed to accept a position with District B at a higher salary. She then asked to be released from her contract with District A. At this point it was doubtful that a replacement could be secured. The superintendent of District A asks whether the conduct of the teacher was contrary to the Code.

Committee Opinion. It is the opinion of the Committee that on the facts presented the conduct of the teacher was contrary to Principle IV, Sections 6 and 7 of the Code. . . .

Obviously, there was no issue as to the binding nature of the contract between the teacher and District A. It was unethical for her to continue negotiations with District B without the knowledge and consent of the superintendent in District A. Because of her conduct, the superintendent was faced with the dilemma of either recommending release of a teacher who probably could not be replaced or refusing to recommend the release, thereby having a teacher on his staff who might be dissatisfied. In either case the level of professional service of District A would be adversely affected. It does not appear in the facts whether the superintendent in District B knew that the teacher had signed a contract with District A; if he did his participation in the negotiations was also unethical.[7]

The reverse of this situation—one that is also a violation of ethical practice—happens when a school employing official holds out the promise of employment to one teacher while waiting for another to accept a proffered position.

Ethics Committee Interpretation. *If a teacher has conducted oral negotiations with a school district but has made no final commitment, he may conduct negotiations and accept a contract with another school district.*

Case Example. A few weeks before the opening of the school year the superintendent of schools in District A telephoned a teacher in another city, who was not presently employed, regarding a position. He had received her credentials through an employment agency. The teacher says she indicated definite interest in the position, but told him that due to the time factor she would have to insist on a signed contract at an early date. The superintendent replied that, while several teachers were under consideration, he was confident that a contract would be offered and agreed to seek board approval for her employment as soon as possible. A period of two weeks elapsed without further word from the superintendent. Meanwhile, the teacher had received an offer from District B at a higher salary which she accepted. She telephoned the superintendent of

[7] *Ibid.*, Opinion 15, pp. 32–33.

District A, expressing regrets and explaining the various reasons why the position in District B was more desirable. The superintendent advised the teacher that her contract offer was in the mails and claimed she was unethical because in his opinion she had made a final commitment to District A. The teacher denied having made any such commitment.

Committee Opinion. The Ethics Committee does not presume to pass on what transpired in the conversations referred to in this case. However, on the basis of the facts presented, the Committee is of the opinion that the teacher had made no final commitment to District A and, therefore, under the sections cited, could properly enter into a contract with District B. A superintendent and a schoolboard may initiate or continue negotiations with several teachers for a given position pending a final commitment. A teacher may likewise, in the absence of a final commitment, negotiate for another position without notice to the superintendent. . . .[8]

This is an extreme case, of course, but there are many instances of teachers resigning just before school starts in the autumn or even during the school year. Positions are usually difficult to fill on short notice, and often good candidates are not available at such times. As a usual thing, teaching in the system is weakened by last-minute resignations or those that occur during the school year, and the schools are put to considerable work and some expense to fill such vacancies.

The day before school opened, a home-economics teacher in the school system walked into the superintendent's office. Opening her purse, she extracted her contract and threw it on the desk. "Here you are," she said. "I'm quitting. I have another job that pays $300 more a year."

The superintendent inquired, "Are you willing to teach for a couple of weeks until we can get someone to replace you?"

"No, I'm quitting as of now," the teacher retorted. "I've told them that I'd be there tomorrow, and I'm going to do it."

"Wait just a minute," said the superintendent. "I want to call your new superintendent. Perhaps we can work out a solution that is satisfactory to everyone." When the connection was made, the second superintendent was amazed to find that the teacher had not secured release from her contract with the first district. When he was assured that no prior arrangements had been made for the teacher's release, the superintendent said, "Then you tell her that we don't want her. I won't hire anyone who hasn't been released. Besides, there's a falsehood involved. And I don't want her now, anyway, because I was told that a release had already been secured."

Some school administrators deserve to be censured for their part in contract jumping. Teachers are not always the ones at fault. There have been cases in which teachers were goaded into breaking a contract by unethical action of employing officials.

[8] *Ibid.,* Opinion 17, pp. 35–37.

One superintendent of a city employing about one hundred teachers took his vacation each summer from July 15 to August 15. During his absence several resignations from teachers usually piled up. He released, without question, the teachers who requested it, but then he had to have replacements. He always had some candidate on tap. Sometimes these were hopefuls who had applied for positions the previous spring; sometimes they were teachers whom the superintendent had met or perhaps just heard about.

The superintendent was entirely ruthless in his methods. He simply contacted, by telephone if possible, the teachers that he wanted. He knew exactly the salaries being paid in the surrounding areas, and he offered the teachers $300 to $400 more per year than they were receiving. He also told them that he had to know at once whether they would accept. Most of the teachers thus pressured accepted, hoping that they could make peace with their own superintendents and boards of education. The unethical practices of this superintendent represent an isolated case rather than the rule.

The Ethics of Resignations

Teachers should exercise extreme care and observe strict ethics in resigning from a position after having signed a contract. There are instances of teachers who left one position only a few days before the beginning of the school year to accept another one that paid more. A high school teacher jumped his contract to accept a position paying exactly the same salary but requiring the teaching of one less class per day.

On the other hand, there are conditions justifying resignations. A teacher is justified in asking to be released from a contract if he will materially better himself, provided the request is made well in advance of the opening of school, or if his place can be satisfactorily filled, or if the terms of his contract have been altered without his consent. Some examples of ethical practice in resignations are as follows:

A high school teacher of biology received, on the sixth of August, an unsolicited offer from another high school. The salary offered in the new position was $500 more. The teacher felt that the salary differential was too great to turn down without some attempt to secure a release, so he talked the situation over with his superintendent. The superintendent was cooperative and readily agreed to recommend to the board of education that the teacher be released. The teacher then suggested the name of a friend, also a biology teacher, who did not yet have a position and who would be glad to fill his place. The teacher's friend was employed, and both parties to the contract felt satisfaction over the transaction. The teacher had acted in a professional and ethical manner, and the school board was pleased to help him secure a deserved promotion.

Ethics Committee Interpretation.   A teacher may properly resign from his position after an administrator has imposed material modifications in a contract. All the details of a teacher's duties cannot be incorporated in a contract, and reasonable adjustments in teaching assignments are often necessary and desirable.

Case Example.   A teacher's contract was renewed in May. It provided for specific teaching responsibilities at a given salary. In accepting the contract, the teacher, who was president of a state association, was assured by the superintendent that a fixed number of days of leave would be allowed him during the school year for carrying on professional organization work within the state. He was also assured that if it proved necessary to increase the teaching load, additional salary would be granted. In August, the superintendent advised the teacher that his teaching load would be materially increased at no change in salary and the amount of leave for professional work would be reduced. The teacher requests advice as to whether under the circumstances he could ethically resign from his position.

Committee Opinion.   It is the opinion of the Committee that the teacher could resign from his position without acting contrary to [Sections 6 and 7 of Principle IV of the Code].[9]

Blind Applications

A second type of poor professional ethics is applying for positions that are not known to be open. Many teachers are guilty of this practice.

For some types of positions, at some times of the year, it is proper to make a blind application. Large cities are almost sure to have vacancies in many types of instructional positions during the hiring season in the spring. There can be no objection to teachers applying for these.

Where there is only one high school principal, one head of the guidance department, one supervisor of the elementary grades, and one director of visual aids, there is not likely to be a vacancy in one of those categories.

Probably all educational workers see the dangers to the profession that are involved in blind and wholesale applications. For one thing, it may appear that there is a surplus of teachers or administrators, many of whom are without positions. Actually, most, if not all, of the shotgun applying is done by teachers or administrators who have positions but who wish to better themselves. Administrative officials or boards of education, if they think there is a surplus of personnel, may not have quite the incentive to press for pay raises and better working conditions for employees. Furthermore, there may not be as much inclination to assist the personnel to adjust to the local situation if they know that they can replace doubtful ones without any particular difficulty.

Gossiping About Pupils and Parents

In the matter of passing out professional information that should not be revealed and in discussing characteristics of a given child or incidents at school, teachers have obligations of a delicate nature, as is the case with

[9] *Ibid.,* Opinion 12, pp. 28–29.

physicians. Here are two examples of the harm that can result from such thoughtlessness:

Example 1: Miss Gregory told her landlady that Bobby Reynolds, who lived across the street, had an IQ of about eighty. "Why, he is a regular dumbbell," she said. The landlady told a friend, and soon the information was all over the neighborhood. How Bobby's parents felt toward Miss Gregory and the school can be easily imagined. The parents never forgave the teacher or the school.

Example 2: Miss Karen, a kindergarten teacher, was told in confidence by a mother that her daughter, Jeanne, was at the state home for the mentally handicapped. The mother was very anxious about her boy Jimmy, who was just entering kindergarten. She asked Miss Karen to watch Jimmy as closely as possible so that she could make a judgment about his mental ability. Unfortunately, Miss Karen told her bridge club about Jeanne's being in an institution. In a few days it was all over town. The mother did not come to school again that year and developed a hatred for all teachers.

The teacher's violation of professional confidence may be compared to the physician telling everyone a patient has a bad heart, or to the lawyer revealing that a client has just made his will, or to the pharmacist who tells his friends that a customer is taking digitalis, or to the pastor who reveals the family troubles of his parishioners. Physicians regard everything patients tell them as strictly confidential. Equally reticent about their patients and clients are dentists, pharmacists, nurses, and attorneys.

Ethics Committee Interpretation. *It is improper for a teacher to make remarks in public reflecting on a child's abilities and family background. However, a teacher has the right and often the duty to confer in confidence with colleagues or authorized agencies regarding a child's problems in conduct and adjustment.*

Case Example. Teacher A discussed one of his students with Teacher B in a school hallway within the hearing of a classmate of the student in question. The teacher commented adversely on the student's mental ability and personal integrity, attributing these deficiencies to the pupil's family background. Teacher B reported the incident to the local association.

Committee Opinion. It is the opinion of the Committee that the conduct of Teacher A was contrary to Section 2 of Principle I and Section 3 of Principle II of the Code. . . .

Under Principles I and II of the Code, respectively, a teacher is entrusted with the obligations of helping children to develop into "happy, useful, self-supporting citizens" and of furthering "cooperative relationships with the home." These obligations cannot be fulfilled in terms of Sections 2 and 3 when a teacher makes disparaging remarks reflecting on a child's abilities or family background in such circumstances as are herein presented. It must be presumed that in repetition such criticisms will generate malicious gossip which will get back to the student and to his parents.

The Committee recognizes that on occasion a teacher has not only the right but the duty to confer in confidence with appropriate professional colleagues or authorized agencies regarding a child's problems in conduct and adjustment. However, casual criticisms made indiscriminately, especially in the presence of other students, are clearly improper.[10]

Appealing to Higher Authority

It is unethical to go over a superior to higher authority unless other means of redress have failed. Teachers should be able to appeal to the highest authorities if necessary, but immediate superiors should have the first opportunity to act.

Example 1: Smith Burnham, a teacher in Wynnville High School, joined a community discussion club. The club met one night a week to discuss national and local problems. Eventually the group discussed the inefficiency of local government. The mayor, the public-works department, the police, and the firemen all came in for criticism. Word of the criticisms leaked out. Soon there were whispers that the discussion group was a communist organization.

Mr. Burnham's principal heard some of the rumors and suggested to Mr. Burnham that he resign from the club. Mr. Burnham protested that the club was not communistic, but that it was trying to inform its members about current affairs and hence to promote good citizenship. The principal was adamant. "You've got to drop out," he said. "We can't have teachers belonging to organizations that are questioned in any way."

"Then I shall carry an appeal to Superintendent Forsythe and to the Board of Education if necessary," Mr. Burnham stated.

"I suppose that is your privilege, but I still think that it would be better to just drop out and keep still," was the principal's reply. "I don't want my teachers mixed up in anything the public questions."

"I feel that I have to carry this case to the highest authorities," Mr. Burnham stated. "It seems to me that there is a question of infringement of freedom of thought and action. I do not believe that anyone who advocates overthrow of the government by force should be allowed in the schools. But I think that teachers should have the right to discuss vital questions and to take part in the usual activities in which citizens engage." The principal was not too happy about an appeal being made, but he raised no further objection.

Mr. Burnham decided that the best way to appeal to Superintendent Forsythe was by writing a letter explaining his side of the controversy.

A few days later, Mr. Burnham received a note requesting him to call at the superintendent's office. The superintendent sided with the principal and insisted that Mr. Burnham get out of the club. The teacher refused and requested that he be given an opportunity to present the matter to the

[10] *Ibid.*, Opinion 13, pp. 29–30.

school board. The superintendent agreed to place the issue on the agenda of the next board meeting.

When Mr. Burnham appeared at the meeting, the few spectators glanced at him seriously. Mr. Forsythe nodded to him courteously, if in a somewhat cool manner. The same thing was true of the greeting given him by his principal. The board members did not seem to be aware of his presence. As far as Mr. Burnham knew, they did not even know who he was.

Mr. Forsythe explained the circumstances that had led to Mr. Burnham's appeal. The high school principal was asked to explain why he had asked Mr. Burnham to drop out of the Forum Club. He stated his reasons in much the same way as he previously expressed them to Mr. Burnham. Mr. Burnham was then given an opportunity to state his case. The president asked the board how they wanted to dispose of the issue.

There was a moment or two of silence, then one board member said: "Our schools must be kept free from any taint of communism. Our teachers must not associate with any group that is in any way suspected of having communistic leanings. I think that this teacher should have given up his membership in the Forum Club when he was requested to do so by his principal."

Another member said: "Gentlemen, it is about time that everyone recognized that teachers have the same rights as anyone else. I happen to know some of the members of the Forum Club. They are not the least bit communistic. I don't see any reason why Mr. Burnham should not belong to the Forum Club the same as anyone else. As far as I can see, the rumors were started by some of our local government officials whose toes were being stepped on. If the Forum Club can make our city officials improve services, then I'm all for them. Perhaps the rest of us ought to join in and try to help them make this a better community in which to live. I move that Mr. Burnham be not only allowed to keep his membership in the Forum Club, but be commended for his activity in that group, and that all teachers be permitted and encouraged to join or associate with any groups that are composed of decent, law-abiding citizens." The motion was seconded and carried unanimously.

Teachers should always have the right of appeal from capricious, injudicious decisions. They should be able to secure decisions on matters of policy that affect the teaching staff. Appeals should always be cleared through the proper channels and should not be made for minute, unimportant issues.

Contrast the way that this was handled with another actual instance. The participants and school systems have been given hypothetical names.

Example 2: John Lockwood, superintendent of schools at Smith Center, issued a short bulletin concerning the handling of the recess period for the elementary grades. The contents of the bulletin had previously been worked out at teachers' meetings in the various buildings. Everyone had had a chance to express himself; in fact, the bulletin embodied suggestions made by a majority of the teachers.

Because of a number of accidents on the playground, the bulletin asked each teacher to go with her group whenever they were dismissed from the building for recess or any other purpose, and to remain with the children throughout the period. This decision, as we have said, was not made arbitrarily. The majority of the elementary teachers of the system had agreed that this was the only procedure that could well be followed.

At one building there was considerable dissatisfaction when the bulletin was given out. Miss Black was particularly outspoken. She had attended the teachers' meeting at which the issue was discussed but had said little. She expressed herself at the first teachers' meeting after the bulletin was issued as follows:

"Teachers need to rest," she exclaimed. "We should have time off just like the high school instructors. It is too much to ask us to be with the children every moment from early morning to late afternoon. Children need to learn to take care of themselves. If they can't do it, then the Board of Education should hire a policeman for the playground. They shouldn't expect us to keep order."

The other teachers soon noticed that Miss Black was not complying. She escorted her children to the door at recess time and then went back to her room until it was time for them to come back to the building. Miss Black's children were a burden on the other teachers. They had to look after her group as well as their own.

The principal asked for an explanation, to which Miss Black replied, "I'm not being paid for police duty, and I don't intend to do it. I'm standing up for my rights."

The president of the Board of Education one day informed Superintendent Lockwood that Miss Black had called on him the night before to protest the rule. "I think that she will call on the other members," he advised. "You'd better be ready for this to come up at the next board meeting."

At the next board meeting, one of the members said that he had something to bring up. He related the details of a visit from Miss Black, during which she made about the same contentions that she had expressed at the teachers' meeting.

The superintendent explained about the injuries on the playground and the complaints from parents. "There did not seem to be any other satisfactory solution," he stated. "I'd like to permit the teachers to have this time free, but I do not see how it can be done with our present teaching force."

"Couldn't two or three teachers handle the children?" queried the board member. "By changing around, each teacher would have to be on duty only about one week in four."

"We've tried that," the superintendent replied, "but it didn't work out very well. There were far too many children for two or three teachers to manage, and some of the children didn't feel that they had to mind anyone but their own teachers. Besides, we feel that recess should be a constructive activity during which children learn how to play together. It can't be that, if a teacher has two or three hundred children under her direction."

The board agreed. Finally a member moved that Mr. Lockwood be supported in the plan. Another member added an amendment that the teachers be requested thereafter to bring any complaints or suggestions through the superintendent's office. "We don't want teachers running to us every time they feel that they have some little complaint," he asserted. "They should talk with Mr. Lockwood first, and then if they aren't satisfied they can ask him to bring the complaint to our attention." The amendment and amended motion both carried unanimously.

Teachers should have the right to carry complaints or suggestions to the board of education, but these should be routed through the superintendent. Only if he "sits on" these appeals are teachers justified in going around or over him. And only a real problem merits an appeal over the heads of administrative officials.

Although dealing with a different matter, Opinions 7, 10, 14, and 16 of the NEA Committee on Professional Ethics bear on the ethics of teachers observing proper channels. Also, Opinions 26 and 32 interpret the rights of teachers as involved in Example 1, described above, to exercise the rights of citizenship. Opinion 7 is cited below as applying to the observance of proper channels in appeals from the decisions of administrative officers.

Ethics Committee Interpretation. *It is improper for teachers to consult members of the school board regarding the dismissal of a professional associate without first presenting their views to the appropriate administrative authorities.*

Case Example. Members of a school faculty became concerned over rumors that a competent principal with many years of service would not be recommended by the superintendent for re-employment. Subsequently a local newspaper announced that the principal had resigned, implying that the resignation was forced. Without discussing the matter with either the superintendent or their local association, several teachers consulted a member of the school board. They told him their purpose was to express concern over the alleged resignation, to state their opinion that the principal was able and well liked, and to seek information as to his status. The superintendent charged that the teachers were unethical in going to the board member.

Committee Opinion. It is the opinion of the Committee that the teachers who consulted the schoolboard member acted contrary to Principle IV, Section

1 of the Code which provides that a teacher will: Conduct professional business through the proper channels.

. . . They should have first discussed the question of the principal's re-employment with the superintendent. If they felt the issue had not been satis-factorily resolved by the superintendent, they could properly have asked the board of education, rather than an individual board member, to meet with them after notifying the superintendent of their intention.[11]

Outside Employment

One other opinion of the NEA Committee on Professional Ethics will be cited, because it involves a problem with which many teachers are con-fronted. That problem is, under what conditions is it unethical to accept part-time or summer employment in order to supplement the regular in-come from teaching? Below is described Opinion 9 of the committee.

Ethics Committee Interpretation. While the right to augment teaching in-come by outside employment is recognized under the Code, solicitation by a teacher of parents of children in his class to purchase encyclopedias is improper.

Case Example. A number of parents, after discussion at a PTA meeting, complained to a local association regarding the activities of two teachers who were seeking to sell encyclopedias for profit to the parents of children in their classes. Several of these parents reported that they had admitted one teacher to their homes as a friend only to find she had come to sell books. The parents were concerned over whether their failure to buy encyclopedias might adversely affect the grades of their children. The request asks whether or not such solicita-tion by teachers constitutes a violation of the Code.

Committee Opinion. The Ethics Committee has pointed out in previous opinions that many teachers, in order to remain in the profession, have found it necessary to supplement their teaching salaries by outside employment. The right to augment teaching income is specifically recognized in the Code. Out-side employment is permissible if it does not fall within the provisions of Prin-ciple IV, Sections 9 or 10. These sections require that a teacher will:

Section 9. Accept no compensation from producers of instructional supplies when one's recommendations affect the local purchase or use of teaching aids.

Section 10. Engage in no gainful employment, outside of his contract, where the employment affects adversely his professional status or impairs his standing with students, associates, and the community.

.   .   .

There is agreement among parents and teachers generally that encyclopedias can be useful educational materials. Obviously no professionally minded teacher would be influenced in grading a child by the attitude of his parents toward purchasing an encyclopedia. Moreover, there is no doubt that some teachers can solicit parents of their pupils in such a way as to give no offense and raise no question of propriety. However, in the case presented such factors are not the test of ethical practice under Section 10. The test is whether the special nature of the student-teacher relationship tends to affect adversely the response of par-ents to the solicitation and, in turn, the teacher's standing in the community.

[11] *Ibid.*, Opinion 7, pp. 20–21.

TABLE 44 *Practices Considered Unethical by Nine in Ten of the Respondents, by Per Cent of Each Group*

Practice	Elementary School Teachers	Secondary School Teachers	Administrators	Others	Total
For an official to dismiss a teacher or recommend him for dismissal without giving him ample notice or an opportunity to be heard	99.0	97.8	96.0	98.2	98.0
For a school official to fail to recommend one of his teachers for a position in another community because he does not want to lose the teacher	97.9	98.0	96.9	97.3	97.7
To show favoritism	97.9	95.8	96.5	91.0	96.3
To disclose to unauthorized persons official correspondence or conversation among teachers	96.9	96.6	96.0	91.0	96.2
To permit pupils to make derogatory remarks about other teachers	97.1	95.2	95.6	92.8	95.8
To use sick leave for purposes other than that for which it was intended	96.9	94.5	96.5	91.0	95.5
To discuss deficiencies of pupils in a way that embarrasses them or their parents	96.1	93.4	94.3	94.6	94.7

In this case there is a factor of implied pressure not unlike that which arises when a teacher is asked to purchase a product by his supervisor.[12]

Proper Application Channels

At the present time there seems to be no reason for any teacher, except those in school districts so small that an administrative officer is not employed, to apply for a position directly to the school board.

Personal Conduct

Discussions of professional ethics are likely to become confused with the matter of standards of personal conduct. For this important reason,

[12] *Ibid.*, Opinion 9, pp. 23–24.

TABLE 44   (Continued)

Practice	Elementary School Teachers	Secondary School Teachers	Administrators	Others	Total
To be careless of one's personal appearance	95.6	93.4	92.4	91.9	94.0
To try to get or to keep a position by innuendo, exploitation, complimentary press notices, or advertising	95.4	90.9	93.3	94.6	93.4
To accept compensation for helping another teacher obtain a position	95.4	91.8	89.8	89.2	92.7
To make derogatory remarks about the teaching profession	95.0	90.7	90.6	86.5	92.1
To apply for a position which one is unqualified to fill	95.0	93.6	91.5	72.1	92.0
To bid or underbid for a position	93.8	90.3	92.4	86.5	91.7
To fail to defend members of the profession when they are unjustly attacked	90.8	92.5	91.5	87.4	91.2

Source: National Education Association, Research Division, "Teachers' Opinions on Ethics in the Teaching Profession." Washington, D.C.: The Association, 1950, Table 2, pp. 10–11 (mimeographed).

teachers should study Principle III of the code, which defines the relationship between ethics and conduct.

Commonly, in the past, the public has required teachers to adhere to standards of conduct above those required of the general population. In the early days of this country, teachers were closely associated with churches. Prospective teachers had to be satisfactory to clergymen, and many a teacher was a sort of assistant minister. Like clergymen, teachers have been expected to live exemplary lives, as they are supposed to serve as models of conduct for young people. Following this concept, teachers have often been expected to refrain from drinking cocktails, smoking, playing cards, and associating with persons of bad reputation.

Except in isolated communities, teachers seem no longer to be expected to maintain standards of conduct vastly different from those of decent members of the community. Card playing, smoking, and drinking in moderation at private homes and parties are not generally considered cardinal sins for teachers, as was once the case.

These things are not strictly matters of professional ethics; they are questions of personal conduct. However, the two are often considered as synonymous.

Teachers have a right to oppose any attempt to subject their group to puritanical standards. Competent young men and women will not enter teaching unless they can live normal lives free from undue censorship. On the other hand, teachers must recognize that they are in the public eye and, therefore, must meet accepted standards of conduct. Doctors, lawyers, and other professional workers must do the same.

REFERENCES

AMERICAN ASSOCIATION OF SCHOOL ADMINISTRATORS, *AASA Code of Ethics.* Washington, D.C.: The Association, 1966.

AMERICAN ASSOCIATION OF UNIVERSITY PROFESSORS, Committee on Professional Ethics, "Statement on Professional Ethics," *AAUP Bulletin,* September, 1966, 52:290–91.

CHANDLER, B. J., and PETTY, PAUL V., *Personnel Management in School Administration.* Yonkers-on-Hudson, New York: World Book Company, 1955, Chap. 16, "Responsibilities of Teachers to the Profession," pp. 429–38.

"Ethical Standards and Professional Conduct," *Annals of the American Academy of Political and Social Science,* January, 1955, 297:76–82.

"Local Association Studies Ethics Case," *NEA Journal,* February, 1964, 53:24–5.

LIEBERMAN, MYRON, *Education as a Profession.* Englewood Cliffs, New Jersey: Prentice-Hall, 1956, Chap. 13, "Professional Ethics," pp. 417–51.

MITCHELL, M. M., "Implementing the Code of Ethics," *NEA Journal,* December, 1964, 53:41.

NATIONAL EDUCATION ASSOCIATION, Ethics Committee, *Code of Ethics of the Education Profession.* Washington, D.C.: The Association, 1963.

———, *Implementing the Code of Ethics of the Education Profession and Strengthening Professional Rights.* Washington, D.C.: The Association, 1964.

———, *Interpretations of the Code of Ethics of the Education Profession.* Washington, D.C.: The Association, 1963.

———, *Opinions of the Committee on Professional Ethics.* Washington, D.C.: The Association, 1966.

NATIONAL EDUCATION ASSOCIATION, National Commission on Teacher Education and Professional Standards, *Professional Imperatives: Expertness and Self-Determination*, Report of the Fort Collins Conference. Washington, D.C.: The Association, 1962, "Maintaining Standards of Ethical and Competent Practice: Professional and Legal Procedures," pp. 200–234.

RICHEY, ROBERT W., *Planning for Teaching*, 3rd ed. New York: McGraw-Hill Book Company, 1963, "Code of Ethics for the Teaching Profession," pp. 239–244.

TYNER, C., "Neglected Landmark: California's Jack Owens Case," *Phi Delta Kappan*, March, 1964, 45:270–7. Reply: Williamson, J. M., *Phi Delta Kappan*, April, 1964, 45:339–41.

"When Ethics Matter," *Teachers College Record*, January, 1964, 65:342–4.

WOLLMAN, H. J., "What Happens If Teachers Break Contracts," *Nation's Schools*, December, 1966, 78:62.

15: Protecting and Disciplining Members of the Profession

A profession sets up machinery to protect its members from unjust treatment, and to protect the public from incompetent or unethical practice by its members. For many years these functions have been performed for the teaching profession by these NEA agencies: the Defense Commission, the Tenure Committee, and the Ethics Committee.[1]

In July, 1961, the NEA Representative Assembly created the National Commission on Professional Rights and Responsibilities. The new commission was created by merging the National Commission for the Defense of Democracy Through Education (commonly called the Defense Commission) and the Committee on Tenure and Academic Freedom (commonly called the Tenure Committee). The Ethics Committee will retain its separate identity, but will continue to work in close cooperation with the new commission.

Thus, these two agencies, established by the teaching profession to safeguard popular education against unwarranted attacks, to protect its members from unfair practices, and (in conjunction with the Ethics Committee) to discipline members who fail to serve competently and ethically, were merged into a larger unit (12 members) to improve services and to provide a more efficient operation.

The history of these separate organizations and their record of achievement should be preserved as a developmental stage in the thrust of the teaching profession to achieve maturity. Some of this record is recorded below.

---

[1] The American Association of University Professors (AAUP) maintains machinery for examining unfair dismissals of teachers in higher-education institutions. It issues an annual list of "censured colleges and universities."

A Professional Responsibility

Throughout this book the self-regulating aspect of voluntary professional organizations has been stressed. It has been noted several times that a clear mark of the acknowledged professions is the tendency to fix and to enforce the standards under which members are admitted to and continued in practice. It has been pointed out, too, that the teaching profession has found it more difficult to observe this principle than have most of the other professions, chiefly because it is a public profession and many people continue to view self-regulation for teaching as a means of serving self-interests.

But in exercising control over their own standards, the professions have a dual responsibility. They have an obligation to improve the welfare of their members and the obligation to serve the welfare of their clientele—the public. This dual responsibility may be stated in another way. The professions have the obligation to protect their members against unjust treatment and to discipline those of their members who are guilty of incompetence or of unethical conduct.

The regulation of a voluntary association, to which society has entrusted broad powers, cannot ignore the welfare of the people it serves, cannot be a one-way street. If an occupational group is to command the respect and consideration usually accorded a competent profession, it must be prepared to accept the responsibilities that go with such status. Certainly, it has the right to demand fair treatment for its members and to protect them from unjust treatment. But, at the same time, it must be prepared to protect the public from the occasional member whose acts or services are below professional levels.

Nothing can so quickly destroy public respect for a given professional group than the failure to move quickly and aggressively to discipline members guilty of flagrant violations of standards of ethical practice.

The teaching profession has exercised both of these obligations in the past with perhaps greater emphasis upon the protective feature than upon the disciplinary function. The discharging of both obligations has varied in effectiveness among professional organizations. Some have had aggressive programs for years; other have made only token efforts.

The trend presently in the NEA and among state education associations is toward developing the necessary procedures and machinery to move promptly and vigorously into cases involving either alleged unfair treatment or alleged unethical conduct of teachers, or both. This chapter will attempt to describe the developing procedures and machinery, and will cite case examples illustrating the application and enforcement of ethical codes.

PROFESSIONAL MACHINERY FOR PROTECTING AND DISCIPLINING MEMBERS OF THE PROFESSION

As has been pointed out, the National Education Association has maintained three agencies whose functions are to protect the members of the teaching profession from unjust attacks or unfair treatment, and to assure the integrity of teaching services. The three are so interrelated that it is sometimes difficult to distinguish the services of one of them from the others. Also, it is often difficult to classify a given action of either as protecting or disciplining the members of the profession; both functions are frequently involved.

A description of the three agencies and the functions assigned to them will be followed by a description of their working procedures, and finally some examples of cases that they have handled will be given. Since the work of the Committee on Professional Ethics (the Ethics Committee) has been described in detail in the preceding chapter, its work will be mentioned here only as it involves cooperative action with one or both of the other agencies.

The three NEA agencies charged with the responsibility of protecting its members against unjust treatment and the public against incompetent and unethical practices of its members are the Committee on Professional Ethics, the Committee on Tenure and Academic Freedom (Tenure Committee), and the National Commission for the Defense of Democracy Through Education (Defense Commission).

The reader should keep in mind that while the history, procedures, and case examples that follow are those of the Defense Commission and the Tenure Committee, these two bodies now operate as the National Commission on Professional Rights and Responsibilities.

The Ethics Committee, as described in the previous chapter, has really three basic functions: to promote understanding and acceptance of a general code of ethics, to interpret the meaning of the Code of Ethics in abstract or real cases reported to it, and to render decisions in actual cases brought before it involving members accused of unethical conduct. With reference to the first function, these interpretations really constitute a body of interpretive law, in somewhat the same manner that court decisions define the precise meaning of laws. With regard to the second function, the Ethics Committee may hand down a decision which may clear the member or censure, suspend, or expel him from NEA membership. The member may appeal the decision to the Executive Committee.

The Tenure Committee and the Defense Commission are authorized to conduct investigations. In a sense, therefore, they serve as the police and prosecuting attorney in cases involving alleged violations of the Code of Ethics or of proper professional conduct, and as defense attorney in cases involving alleged mistreatment of a member of the profession. The analogies to the civil government suggested above are not exact ones. If a case involving what appears to be an unfair dismissal of a teacher is reported to the NEA, it may follow one of two possible courses: If the case involves only alleged unfair dismissal, or threat of dismissal, the Tenure Committee is empowered to handle the case. Cases involving broader conditions and circumstances that threaten general harm to the school system—for example, partisan political interference with the administration of the school system, or intimidation of the school board by a pressure group—would be referred to the Defense Commission. These cases often arise in states without tenure-law protection for teachers. Where there are tenure laws, legal processes are usually resorted to by teachers who feel they have been unjustly and illegally dealt with, with the state or local education association, or both, assisting them in securing redress from the courts. Details of how the Defense Commission operates are described in case examples below.

The Work of the Tenure Committee

The Tenure Committee consists of five members appointed by the NEA president for terms of three years. The responsibilities of the committee are as follows: (1) to provide protection to teachers in their relationships with employers, (2) to encourage the use of personnel policies that develop competent school personnel and prevent difficulties that lead to unnecessary dismissals, (3) to aid in improvement and extension of tenure legislation throughout the states, and (4) to foster a favorable climate in which teachers may safely teach the full truth without fear or favor.[2]

When a teacher requests assistance, the Tenure Committee makes a preliminary inquiry through correspondence to determine whether the facts justify an investigation. No case is investigated unless the teacher involved requests it or gives his consent. The committee will not enter a case being handled by another educational organization, unless requested to do so. Also, concurrence of the appropriate state and local education association in the request for an investigation is usually required. If preliminary inquiry indicates that the teacher has just cause for grievance, the committee attempts first to negotiate a settlement. If this attempt fails, an investigation is launched.

The investigation may be made by the Tenure Committee and its staff, or a special investigating committee from its membership may be appointed. The investigation consists of collecting the facts, evaluating the

[2] National Education Association, *Annual Report of the Committee on Tenure and Academic Freedom*. Washington, D.C.: The Association, 1954, p. 5.

findings, formulating recommendations, and issuing a report. Copies of the report are submitted to the employers and the teacher involved, and are given public release. The great instrument at the command of the committee to secure redress for unjust treatment of a teacher is, as in the case of the Defense Commission, an aroused public opinion.[3]

FORMATION OF THE DEFENSE COMMISSION

The NEA Representative Assembly created the National Commission for the Defense of Democracy Through Education (the Defense Commission) at its annual meeting in Boston, on July 3, 1941. At that time the United States was edging toward participation in World War II. Rising prices and defense preparations were beginning to increase taxes. These were troubled times, and tempers were flaring among the American people. Influential organizations were growing more vehement about rising taxes. As so often happens in times of strain, school costs and procedures were among the first targets of the critics. There were extreme criticisms of textbooks, school expenditures, and teachers. The most destructive attacks were those upon the loyalty and patriotism of teachers. Many of the attacks were by honest, well-meaning citizens; others transcended the bounds of reason and fair play.

The rationale for the creation of a body by the profession to combat the extremity of these attacks was set forth by the president of the NEA:

Believing as we do that effective education of all our people is the only sure and ultimate protection of democracy, we must seek and win from the public a new and more understanding loyalty to education. We must protect teachers from fear, intimidation, and unjust discharge. We must so protect our schools and teachers that the youth of today may be prepared to live effectively in a changed but democratic world of tomorrow.[4]

The Defense Commission was charged with the responsibility of creating public understanding and support of education by informing the public concerning educational purposes and need; of investigating criticism and movements against education, school systems, teachers colleges, textbooks, teachers' organizations, and members of the teaching profession, and pub-

---

[3] For examples of the work of the Tenure Committee see *Dismissals in Cherokee County, South Carolina* (1956); *Wisconsin State College* (1958); and *Chicksaha, Oklahoma* (1960). Washington, D.C.: The Nationla Education Association, Committee on Tenure and Academic Freedom.

[4] Donald DuShane, "A Challenge to the Teaching Profession," *Addresses and Proceedings, 1941*. Washington, D.C.: National Education Association, 1941, p. 33.

lishing results of investigations; of investigating alleged subversive teaching and to expose any teacher whose attitude is found to be inimical to the best interests of our country. These were the major responsibilities of the Defense Commission.

Work of the Defense Commission

In the twenty years between its creation (1941) and its merger (in 1961) into the Commission on Professional Right and Responsibilities, the Defense Commission conducted twenty-eight full-scale investigations and published reports. The names of the cases and the titles of the published reports are listed below. For a list of cases of the PR & R Commission since 1961, see References, page 368.

INVESTIGATIONS OF TWENTY-EIGHT CASES BY THE NEA
DEFENSE COMMISSION AND TITLES OF REPORTS ISSUED,
1941–1961

New York City; February, 1944: *Interferences with the Independence of the New York City Board of Education.*

Chicago, Illinois; May, 1945: *Certain Personnel Practices in the Chicago Public Schools.*

McCook, Nebraska; March, 1947: *An Example of Some Effects of Undemocratic School Administration in a Small Community.*

North College Hill, Ohio; November, 1947: *An Example of Some Effects of Board of Education Interference with Sound Administration of Public Education.*

Chandler, Arizona; October, 1948: *An Example of Need for Fair Dismissal Procedures.*

Grand Prairie, Texas: September, 1949: *A Case Involving the Civil Rights of Teachers and the Ethical Responsibilities of Boards of Education.*

Kelso, Washington; June, 1950: *Report of the NEA-WEA Investigation Committee on Kelso, Washington.*

Newport, New Hampshire; August, 1950: *Report of the Professional Investigation Committee on Teacher Dismissals in Newport, New Hampshire.*

State Education Agency, Utah; August, 1950: *An Inquiry into the Organization and Administration of the State Education Agency of Utah.*

Twin Falls, Idaho; September, 1950: *An Example of Unfair Dismissal Practices When Supervisory Responsibilities Are Indefinite.*

Polson, Montana; April, 1951: *Report of an Investigation of a School Controversy in Polson, Montana.*

Oglesby, Illinois; May, 1951: *A Case Involving Unfair Dismissal Practices and Unethical Conduct on the Part of Teachers.*

Pasadena, California; June, 1951: *An Analysis of Some Forces and Factors that Injured a Superior School System.*

Mars Hill, North Carolina; October, 1951: *A Case Involving the Coercion of Teachers Through Political Pressures.*

Miami, Florida; October, 1952: *An Example of the Effects of the Injection of Partisan Politics into School Administration.*

Houston, Texas; December, 1954: *A Study of Factors Related to Educational Unrest in a Large School System.*

Kansas City, Missouri; October, 1955: *A Study of Some Problems Arising Out of the Failure to Clarify the Respective Responsibilities of a Board of Education and Its Administrative Staff.*

Bridgewater Township, New Jersey; May, 1956: *A Study of Difficulties Growing Out of Misunderstanding Between a Board of Education and Its Chief Executive Officer.*

Gary, Indiana: June, 1957: *A Study of Some Aspects and Outcomes of a General School Survey.*

Bethpage, New York; February, 1958: *A Study in Faulty Human Relations.*

Monroe, Michigan; March, 1958: *A Study of a Dismissal Involving Responsibility for Criticism of Proposed School Policies.*

Hawthorne, New Jersey; April, 1958: *A Study in Ineptness and Apathy.*

Missoula County High School, Montana; July, 1958: *A Study of Ineffective Leadership.*

Ambridge, Pennsylvania; May, 1959: *A Study of Deteriorating Relationships in a School System.*

West Haven, Connecticut; September, 1959: *A Study of Community Inaction.*

Hickman Mills, Missouri; January, 1960: *A Study of Conflict Between Administrative and Policy-Making Agencies in a School System.*

Indianapolis, Indiana; May, 1960: *A Study of the Sudden Forced Resignation of a Superintendent.*

Santa Fe, New Mexico; January, 1961: *A Study of Turmoil Resulting from Ill-Advised Practices Affecting School Personnel.*

Its first major investigation was of the New York City school system in 1944. Its published report exposed the interference of the mayor into the affairs of the city schools.

In 1945, in conjunction with the NEA Ethics Committee (see below), it investigated the personnel practices of the Chicago school system. Its report was instrumental in securing reform in the procedures for selecting members of the board of education. Prior to the investigation, board members were selected by the mayor, and they were strictly political appointments with consequent political patronage and meddling. In 1946 Chicago instituted, as a result of the commission's recommendations, a plan by which possible appointees to the board are screened by a commission consisting of university presidents in the Chicago area and representatives of eleven civic organizations. The screening commission submits a list of persons judged to be suitable for appointment to the board, and the mayor makes the final selection from this list.

Legal Services

The Defense Commission also provided legal services for members of the teaching profession threatened with unfair treatment. A legal counsel and an assistant counsel are members of the commission staff.

One example was the Butte, Montana, case in which eight tenure teachers were denied salary increases by the school board when they refused to join the local teachers' union. The Defense Commission provided legal counsel in carrying the teachers' appeal to the Montana Supreme

Court which upheld the right of the eight teachers to equal treatment on the salary schedule.

Another example of legal service rendered by the Defense Commission was the case of a college teacher in Wisconsin. The teacher, director of personnel of Stout College (a state college) had, in the course of his official duties, counseled a student who later committed suicide. The parents of the student filed suit against the personnel director, on the grounds that he was derelict in not recommending psychiatric treatment for the emotionally disturbed student. On behalf of the NEA, legal counsel for the Defense Commission filed an *Amicus Curiae* brief on the case before the Wisconsin Supreme Court. The court's decision was in favor of the director of student personnel.

How the Commission Protects Members of the Profession

It is not possible to give detailed descriptions of the cases that the Defense Commission has investigated. A few case examples will be described to illustrate how the commission serves both to protect and to discipline members of the profession. Because of space limitations, the case descriptions given below will necessarily be vignettes of each case investigated by the Defense Commission.

West Haven Case.[5] An unprecedented action of the Connecticut Education Association in the spring of 1958 led to an investigation by the Defense Commission of the West Haven Case. The action of the Connecticut Education Association Board of Directors declared it a violation of professional ethics for any member not already employed in the county to accept a position in the West Haven school system.

Back of this action was a series of frustrations in efforts to secure adjustments in teachers' salaries in the district. For three years prior to the CEA's action, increases in teachers' salaries proposed by the West Haven Board of Education were reduced by the Board of Finance. In Connecticut teachers are eligible for tenure status after three years of teaching, when they sign a permanent contract. Each year they sign a written salary agreement, specifying the amount of the salary for the ensuing year. In June 1957 and again in June 1958, dissatisfied with salary arrangements, a majority of the West Haven teachers refused to sign salary agreements. Instead they submitted signed statements of their intention to teach the following year with the understanding that salary negotiations were still open. The Board of Education accepted this substitute form in 1957 but refused to do so in 1958, and notified teachers that only those who returned signed salary agreements would receive salary increases for the coming year.

[5] For detailed description, see National Commission for the Defense of Democracy Through Education, *West Haven, Connecticut—A Study of Community Inaction.* Washington, D.C.: The Association, 1959, 38 pp.

The teachers then appealed to the CEA, requesting the drastic action, referred to above, of placing a boycott (withholding of services) by its members (not already employed in the school system) of the West Haven school district as long as the controversy remained unsettled. At the same time, the West Haven teachers requested the Defense Commission to send a fact-finding committee to study not only the salary problem but all phases of the educational situation in the district. Back of these developments was an involved system of budget responsibility, which frustrated efforts to adjust school costs and teachers' salaries to needed levels. The Board of Education prepares the two school budgets: the School District Budget (capital outlay, maintenance and operation of school plant) and the Town Account Budget (current expense, including teachers' salaries). The first is financed by a separate school tax, while the support of the latter comes from the town tax. In addition, the complex governmental structure made settlement of the controversy difficult. The Board of Education prepares the school budgets, but they are subject to the review of the Town's Board of Finance and final approval by the Representative Town Meeting (an elected body of forty-five members). Following the adoption of the budget by RTM, the Board of Finance fixes the tax rate to yield the needed funds. In 1956 the Board of Education submitted a budget that was substantially reduced by the Board of Finance. Appeal was made to the courts, but the action was sustained. In other words, the school board is charged with operating a satisfactory school system, but has no powers to levy the necessary taxes, resulting in obsolescence in buildings and equipment, and inability to adjust teachers' salaries to rising prices. Again in 1957 the school board's budget, which included a proposed raise of $500 per teacher, was reduced to allow only a $200-per-teacher increase. Despite protests of citizens, the reduction stood. At this point the teachers refused to sign the annual salary agreement and substituted a statement declaring their intention to serve on the assumption that salary negotiations would continue. In the spring of 1958 the Board of Education again submitted a budget including a proposed raise of $600 for each teacher. Again the Board of Finance drastically cut the school budget to a point that permitted only a $200 raise per teacher. At a meeting of the West Haven teachers on May 13, a motion to submit a mass resignation at the end of the school year was rejected, but they did vote to withhold signatures from salary agreements as they had done the previous year.

By June 2, 1958, 14 teachers had resigned, 91 had returned signed salary agreements, and 233 had withheld agreements but had submitted signed statements of their intention to return with the understanding that salary negotiations were still open. On June 4 the Board of Education voted to notify teachers that if they did not return signed salary agreements by June 18, they would receive no increases at all.

This was too much for the teachers to take, so they appealed to the

CEA to take the action described above. The CEA Board of Directors, in addition to interceding with the West Haven Board of Directors on the teachers' behalf and calling upon the members of the association not to apply for jobs in the West Haven system, invited the Defense Commission to conduct an inquiry into the situation. Subsequently, meetings involving the CEA, the West Haven teachers and Board of Education, and the state commissioner of education resulted in the following actions: The West Haven Board of Education agreed to accept substitute forms in lieu of the annual salary agreements; the board also agreed to rescind its action denying raises and increments to teachers who refused to sign the board's salary contract form; the CEA Board of Directors voted to rescind the action that declared it unethical for CEA members to accept positions in West Haven.

Defense Commission recommendations: The report of the investigation contained sweeping recommendations involving state law, citizen responsibility, board and administrative responsibilities, and teacher participation. The heart of the recommendations, however, was for a resurgence of citizen interest and support of their schools, and a clarification to appointed and elected officials of their demand for improved educational programs. It recommended the amending of state laws so that authority for determining the total school budget and tax rate for support of schools be vested in boards of education.

The Chicago Case. During the summer of 1944 the Defense Commission was requested by several lay and professional organizations in Chicago to investigate the administration of the Chicago school system. The resulting investigation centered largely on the personnel practices of the system. The investigating committee, appointed by the commission, found "ample evidence of intimidation and punishment of capable, independent teachers who were unwilling to submit to domination, insistence upon blind loyalty to the administration rather than upon loyalty to the children and the cause of education, attempts to dominate or to divide teachers or organizations, use of transfers to punish some individuals and to intimidate others, dependence upon domination of teachers rather than upon leadership and integrity to secure necessary teacher unity and compliance." [6]

The report condemned certain personnel practices of the administration, condemned the tie-in with the political administration of the city, and submitted a list of nine recommendations for improving the situation.[7]

[6] National Education Association, National Commission for the Defense of Democracy Through Education, "Defense Commission Completes Fruitful Decade of Service to the Profession," *Defense Bulletin No. 41.* Washington, D.C.: The Association, December, 1951, p. 6.

[7] National Education Association, National Commission for the Defense of Democracy Through Education, *Report of An Investigation: Certain Personnel Practices in the Chicago Public Schools.* Washington, D.C.: The Association, 1945, pp. 64–66.

Results of the investigation: Several of the commission's recommendations have been followed, and the superintendent of the Chicago schools was expelled from membership in the National Education Association for unethical and unprofessional conduct. The superintendent was later removed from his position.

The story of disciplining the superintendent of the Chicago schools at the time of the above investigation was reported as follows:

In spite of the injuries done to the Chicago schools by the present management, the educational basis of the Chicago schools was found to be essentially sound. This is due primarily to the fact that a great majority of the teachers are well-prepared and are able because of the tenure law to devote themselves to the welfare of their children, altho sometimes under very great handicaps.[8]

With respect to the Chicago situation as it existed in 1944 and 1945, it was stated:

Intimidation of teachers, financial irregularities, use of a "spy system," improper use of teacher transfer, nepotism, the domination of teacher organizations, a "one-man school-board," and undemocratic management are some of the conditions uncovered by the investigation of personnel practices in the Chicago schools, conducted by the NEA Commission for the Defense of Democracy Through Education.[9]

On October 10, 1945, the chairman of the Professional Ethics Committee of the NEA wrote to Superintendent William H. Johnson as follows: [10]

Dear Superintendent Johnson:

At the October 5 meeting of the Ethics Committee of the National Education Association at the NEA headquarters in Washington, D.C., the following motion was made and unanimously carried:

"Moved: That a letter be sent to Mr. William H. Johnson informing him that the Ethics Committee, in light of the findings of the Defense Commission in *Certain Personnel Practices in the Chicago Schools,* invites him to appear before the Ethics Committee of the NEA on January 18, 1946, and show cause why he should not be dropped from the membership of the NEA in accordance with Article IV of the NEA Code of Ethics for teachers which reads as follows: 'The Committee is further vested with authority to expel a member from the NEA for flagrant violation of the Code.' "

If this date is not convenient for you to appear before the Committee, will you kindly advise the Committee at NEA headquarters in Washington?

Very truly yours,
Virgil M. Rogers, Chairman
Ethics Committee

[8] "NEA Investigates Chicago Schools," *NEA Journal,* November, 1945, *34*:162.
[9] *Ibid.,* p. 162.
[10] "Ethics Committee Expels Chicago Superintendent from NEA Membership," *NEA Journal,* March, 1946, *35*:161.

Mr. Johnson did not reply to this letter, nor did he appear before the NEA Ethics Committee to deny the charges. A hearing was held in Washington on January 18, 1946. At this hearing various teachers in the Chicago school system appeared. It was brought out that much political favoritism had been shown in the appointment of principals and that the superintendent had arbitrarily interfered with the grading of pupils. It was alleged that the superintendent operated a "spy system," transferred teachers and principals as a punitive measure, intimidated those who opposed him, and failed to promote worthy teachers. After this hearing the chairman of the NEA Ethics Committee wrote to Superintendent Johnson on January 18, 1946, as follows: [11]

Dear Mr. Johnson:

In compliance with our letter of October 10, 1945, the Ethics Committee of the National Education Association has met at the headquarters office of the Association today to consider action in connection with your membership in the Association. We regret that you did not accept our invitation to meet with us in order that we might have had your side of the case presented at the hearing. On the basis of the evidence presented at the hearing, our Committee passed the following motion unanimously:

"That on the evidence presented by the investigating committee of the National Commission for the Defense of Democracy through Education of the National Education Association and on the evidence presented at the public hearing held at the headquarters office of the Association in Washington, D.C., January 18, 1946, the Ethics Committee finds William H. Johnson, superintendent of schools in Chicago, Illinois, guilty of flagrant violation of the Code of Ethics of the Association and in compliance with the authority vested in the committee by the Code of Ethics of the Association hereby expels him from membership in the National Education Association."

In view of the above action will you kindly discontinue further use or display of the Life Membership card, certificate, and key issued to you in November 1935.°

Very truly yours,
Virgil M. Rogers, Chairman
Ethics Committee

The Oglesby, Illinois, Case. This case illustrates the two-edged aspect of the Defense Commission's work: to protect teachers where they have been unjustly treated, and to censure teachers guilty of unethical practices. The case arose from the resignation of four members of the Oglesby Board of Education in a dispute over the re-employment for a third year of a probationary teacher. The Board alleged that threats of violence by "an angry mob of union leaders and followers which invaded the school

[11] *Ibid.*, p. 161.
° N.B. At that time, the Ethics Committee had authority to expel a member for cause. Since 1957 it can only render judgment and recommend expulsion action to the NEA Executive Committee.

board's meeting" had caused them to reverse a decision made on six previous occasions to discharge the teacher.

The investigating committee, in its report, was equally harsh in its criticism of the way the Board had handled the situation and of the conduct of the teachers who supported the dismissed teacher. The board and superintendent were commended for recommending an action that they sincerely believed to be in the best interests of the school system. The board was judged, however, to have violated sound professional practice in not giving the dismissed teacher, who would have been entitled to tenure with another year of probationary employment, prior notice of alleged shortcomings and an opportunity to correct the weaknesses. The supporters of the teacher involved in the dispute were judged as being unprofessional in participating in a work stoppage in protest and in joining in undue pressures on the board.

The Hickman Mills Case.[12] In February, 1959, the Defense Commission received a letter signed by several attorneys requesting an investigation of the strife existing between the Board of Education and the administrative staff of the Hickman Mills, Missouri, school district, a fast-growing suburb of Kansas City. This request was subsequently endorsed by the Board of Education, the PTA, and the Missouri State Teachers Association. The commission's analysis of the problem revealed that the district had had three superintendents during the period from 1952 to 1959, that there was constant division and bickering among the members of the board, and that the senior member of the board, who had served since 1952 and who, prior to this period, had been employed by the Hickman Mills district as a principal and teacher, who was currently employed in an adjoining school district, and whose wife was on the staff of the Hickman Mills schools, seemed to be a major cause of division in the board. The board constantly usurped or interfered with the administration of the schools. The board constantly split up into factions, with the senior member being the dominating factor in board decisions, and even in the election of school-board members. The board was without written policies for operating the schools. The results were lack of strong administrative leadership, instability in the position of superintendent of schools (one superintendent was fired, another denied a vote of confidence by the board, and a third resigned under similar circumstances), and confusion and discontent among the faculty and citizens in general. At one time the district had been without a superintendent for about six months—from September, 1956, to February, 1957.

[12] For a detailed account, see National Education Association, National Commission for the Defense of Democracy Through Education, *Hickman Mills, Missouri: A Study of Conflict Between Administrative and Policy-Making Agencies in a School System.* Washington, D.C.: The Association, 1960, 37 pp.

As a result of its investigation, the Defense Commission found that the central focus of the trouble was the Board of Education, but did not spare the three superintendents, the teachers, or the citizens for certain failures. The Board of Education was charged with failure to follow established lines of procedure, failure to maintain decorum at board meetings, failure of board members to maintain impersonal and objective attitudes, failure to observe propriety in the reporting of board meetings, failure to eliminate an important divisive factor in the school controversy (the membership on the board of a man whose wife was engaged as a teacher), and failure to follow proper procedure in requesting resignation of one of the superintendents.

One of the superintendents was criticized for failure to insist upon an appropriate administrator-board relationship. Another of the superintendents was criticized for failure to insist upon adherence to basic administrator-board relationships, for failure to establish an effective school public-relations program within the community, and failure to establish an effective working relationship with the staff. The teachers were criticized for failure to assume professional responsibility and for failure to protect members from unfair treatment. While praising the citizens of the community for their attitude of strong support of the schools, the report criticized citizens for failure to demand cooperation among board members, failure to conduct themselves properly at board meetings, and failure to follow up on the presentation of petitions.

Recommendations: The published report of the investigation recommended that the Board of Education (1) serve primarily as a policy-making unit, (2) develop a handbook of school policies in cooperation with the school staff and make it available to all members of the staff, (3) abolish all standing committees and act as a committee of the whole, (4) improve its employment and dismissal policies, (5) approve and support a consistent program of public relations, (6) consider the value of a self-survey of the school system, (7) limit the school board minutes to issues discussed and action taken at board meetings, (8) inform the superintendent who was forced to resign in 1956 that the board's decision was unduly influenced by rumor and unfounded charges, (9) expect and accept the resignation or retirement of the senior member of the board.

Outcomes of the investigation: Although other recommendations were made regarding responsibilities of the superintendent, teachers, and citizens, those to the board were keys to resolving the divisiveness in the school. The report was presented to a mass meeting of citizens, by TV, and in the local press. Plans were begun immediately to implement the recommendations. The center of the controversy, the senior board member, resigned, and the school board has developed and adopted a set of written policies.

The Hickman Mills Case is a good example of the constructive value of an investigation of unsatisfactory school conditions in a community by an outside, competent, and objective body. Because it is an agency of the NEA, a national organization of teachers, the Defense Commission is viewed by some critics as existing only to protect teachers. The Hickman Mills report sought out and identified all the factors and groups entering into the confused situation. It did not spare board members, administrators, teachers, and citizens any criticism of failure to perform at levels necessary to assure a satisfactory program. Perhaps this even-handedness explains the favorable reaction of the community.

How the Defense Commission Operates

The effectiveness of the NEA Defense Commission depends not upon enforcing powers, but largely upon exposure of conditions and the pressures of public opinion among the general public and the teaching profession. An aroused public opinion, resulting from revelations of unwholesome, unprofessional, or unethical administrative practices in a given school system, is the most powerful weapon at the command of the Defense Commission. The second weapon, rarely used, is to request members of the teaching profession to boycott the school system that has been guilty of unfair treatment of teachers, that is, a request that members of the profession not seek employment in the school system.

The NEA Defense Commission can investigate conditions in a given local school system when a specific case arises in which a teacher has allegedly received unjust treatment, or in cases involving problems of concern to the profession. While its investigations, generally, are undertaken upon request of the local and/or state education association involved, an individual teacher may request that an investigation be made. The NEA Ethics Committee may refer charges of unethical conduct to the commission for investigation.

The commission itself does not constitute the investigating committee. A special committee is appointed, one that is carefully selected to assure impartiality and fairness. Such special committees often include lay persons—usually school board members.

SOME CASE EXAMPLES OF HOW STATE EDUCATION ASSOCIATIONS PROTECT AND DISCIPLINE THEIR MEMBERS

All the state education associations have some form of machinery for protecting and disciplining their members. While the most flagrant cases tend to be referred to the NEA Defense Commission, by far the bulk of the cases are handled within states. Most state education associations have committees to deal with defense and discipline of their members. These committees vary in name from state to state. Some of the committees are the Teacher Welfare Committee, Public Relations Committee, Defense Committee, Professional Relations Committee, and Ethics Committee. The procedure followed, once a case is reported to the state association and a request made for an investigation, is to refer the case to the Ethics Committee or Defense Committee. Usually the committee appoints a special investigating group, although sometimes the committee itself carries out this function. A staff worker is sent to the scene to collect all pertinent information and to arrange meetings with the local school board and teachers involved. Then a formal hearing is held by the committee, at which evidence is presented by those concerned. The committee then renders its decision, usually addressing it to the controlling board of the state association of which the committee is an agent. The controlling board, if it concurs, proceeds to take the actions necessary to carry out the decision. The actual means of enforcing the decision varies. In most cases involving unjust action by a school board regarding teachers the chief weapon is to give publicity to the committee's findings. This is a powerful weapon, since the people are sensitive to unwise, harsh, arbitrary actions by their elected representatives. The exposing of an unwholesome condition to the light of public scrutiny and study is a powerful instrument in the formation of a body of public opinion to which a school board is answerable. If public opinion does not cause the board to adjust its policies, the association may advise its members not to seek or accept employment in the school district.

In cases involving the legal rights of teachers, the state association may take the case to a court to secure redress for the teachers involved, furnishing legal services and providing court costs. In many instances state associations have provided suspended teachers financial assistance during the period when they are off the job and while a trial is pending. (See DuShane Defense Fund for similar aid by NEA, p. 366.) In cases involving censure of teachers, sometimes a reprimand will effect the desired change in attitude and conduct, but if this fails, the association may expel the members.

These are a few of the means that state associations may use to enforce observance of ethical practices.

Discipline Through Consultation

A member of the Connecticut Education Association, an elementary teacher, submitted her resignation to the school board with the following comment: "The help I had every reason to expect from the elementary supervisor has not been forthcoming, and I am not in sympathy with the aims and methods of the local teachers' association, which, it seems to me, is more interested in personal gains than in the gains of children. I am resigning my position to accept another in a community where the children come first and where I can have the kind of professional supervision that will lead to real growth and development."

This letter was read at the school board meeting and publicized in the press. This action was adjudged by the teacher's colleagues as a probable violation of the CEA Code of Ethics, Article III, Section 14, which states: "The teacher avoids disseminating unfavorable criticism or injurious hearsay concerning his associates."

The CEA staff investigated the incident and found that the teacher's colleagues were concerned about the criticism of the supervisor and of the teachers' association. They felt that there was a lack of professional responsibility on the part of the teacher. The supervisor believed that she had given ample guidance to the teacher and recommended that the CEA staff talk with the teacher and give her professional guidance and counsel. This the staff did, and found that the teacher had never heard of the Code of Ethics. The changed attitude of the teacher after these consultations was such that the CEA staff recommended that the matter be dropped and that the teacher not be asked to appear before the CEA Ethics Committee.[13]

Case of a Teacher Falsely Accused of Being a Communist

A case illustrating how teachers' organizations can protect their members from unwarranted and unjust accusations, accusations that would tend to destroy a teacher's reputation and his usefulness as a member of the profession, was the Fern Bruner case in California.

Fern Bruner was a social-studies teacher in a small town near San Francisco from 1947 to 1950. In 1949–50 some of the high school students formed a student unit of United World Federalists and asked Miss Bruner to serve as adviser. Permission to do so was granted by the principal and the school board. Then a housewife in the community, obsessed with the idea that the United World Federalists was a subversive organization, protested the student club. The school board supported the teacher in the matter, but requested that the group not meet in the school building because of the community uproar. The students, rather than be a party to division in the community, disbanded their club. The housewife demanded that the board fire Miss Bruner. The board refused, and subsequently Miss Bruner took a high school position in another school district.

At this point a radio commentator in San Francisco, having received a letter from the housewife accusing Miss Bruner of being a subversive, began to attack Miss Bruner on his radio program. Without any evidence other than the letter from the housewife who had been thwarted in efforts to have the teacher fired by the school board, the commentator accused

[13] Connecticut Education Association, "A Case Study in Ethics." Hartford: The Association, 1953 (typewritten).

Miss Bruner of being a Communist. In her new position, unknown to her new colleagues and to her students, Miss Bruner found herself powerless to refute the charges constantly made by the radio commentator. She has summarized the situation she faced in the first months in her new position as follows:

I found myself surrounded by a wall of silence and it was erected wherever I approached. In the new community I had no way of clearing this up. My students didn't know me, wouldn't come to me—or even accept me—until I had earned their confidence. I had no opportunity to dispel their suspicion. After all, they had heard it on the radio. I was in a state of nervous exhaustion, trying to clear my name and do justice to my teaching.

Then the California Teachers Association entered the case. Its Tenure and Ethics Committee made a thorough investigation, cleared Miss Bruner of the ugly charges, and declared her to be an outstanding teacher of exceptionally high moral character and unqualified loyalty to her country. But this did not stop the radio commentator. With no further evidence, he delivered two more broadcasts attacking the report of the CTA's Tenure and Ethics Committee and the California Teachers Association for its "whitewash" of Miss Bruner. The California Teachers Association immediately filed a libel suit in Miss Bruner's behalf against the radio commentator and the radio station over which the broadcasts were made, and assumed all the expense involved in this suit.

After a dramatic trial in which the radio commentator was proved to be without any information about Miss Bruner other than the letter, and in which he was unable to substantiate any of his charges or show any valid grounds for having called Miss Bruner a Communist, the jury found in favor of Miss Bruner and ordered the radio commentator to pay her damages in the amount of $25,000. The radio station was ordered to pay an additional $25,000, and the manager of the radio station $5,000 to Miss Bruner.

The *San Francisco Chronicle* commented on the case as follows: "This case presented one uncommon and welcome aspect. The accused woman found willing and competent defenders. The California Teachers Association, having investigated and disproved the charges against Miss Bruner, came to her defense. The Association is to be commended for its intelligent and courageous conduct." [14]

A Tenure Violation Case

Many years ago Miss X was granted tenure status by the California high school in which she taught. For several years she had been the subject of parent complaints, and her work had been considered unsatisfactory by all who had observed her.

[14] Harry A. Fosdick, "A Victory for Every Teacher," *NEA Journal*, October, 1953, 42:397–98.

Her high school district was unified with other districts to form a new district in 1949. In 1952 the superintendent devised a scheme by which he thought he could dismiss Miss X. Without following the tenure procedures for dismissal of a permanent incompetent employee, he assigned her to teach fourth grade in an elementary school for the 1952–53 school year. At the conclusion of that year he notified her that she was not being re-employed. He claimed that she had relinquished her tenure status by accepting an assignment in the elementary school, whereas she had been granted tenure by the old school district.

California law provides that permanent teachers in districts included in any newly unionized or unified districts must retain their permanent status in the new district. The superintendent and board were advised that the California Teachers Association would not inject itself into the case if they followed legal procedures, but that the association would back the teacher in mandamus action if this illegal dismissal were attempted.

The advice was not accepted. The CTA provided legal counsel for Miss X in a suit for reinstatement, back pay, court costs, and legal fees. The court ruled that the dismissal was illegal, ordered the district to reinstate Miss X, and ordered the district to pay court costs and to reimburse Miss X for legal expenses. She also was awarded back pay for the months she had not been teaching.[15]

Professional Action Against Unfair Dismissal of a Principal

A Connecticut board of education voted in October not to renew the contract of the principal of its high school after the current school year. The principal, who had been employed by the local schools for sixteen years, was not given specific reasons for the dismissal. Connecticut's statutes do not provide for tenure or continuing contracts for administrative personnel, although they do provide that a board may enter into a three-year contract with administrators. They do not provide, as is the case with teachers, for public hearing in case of dismissed administrative personnel.

The Connecticut Education Association established a fact-finding committee to investigate the case. The only evidence of friction between the dismissed principal and the administration that the committee could find was that there were charges of untidy housekeeping in the high school and that the principal and his staff felt that their plans for a new high school building were not given proper consideration. The investigating committee reported to the board of directors of the Connecticut Education Association as follows: "The principal involved had served continuously in his position for sixteen years; during that time the school board had never censured or warned him of unsatisfactory service."

The high school faculty, upon learning of the dismissal notice, sent the

[15] California Teachers Association, "The San Lorenzo Case," mimeographed release, February 25, 1955.

principal a written expression of unanimous confidence; the band boosters' club issued a written statement protesting the board's action; the home-school association went on record as being vigorously opposed to the board's decision. The board refused the discharged principal a public hearing at which he could have an opportunity to defend himself.

Failing to get any constructive action from the school board, the CEA board of directors issued the following declaration: [16]

1. That the school board acted without regard for fair dismissal practices.
2. That all active members of the CEA employed elsewhere be notified that in its judgment acceptance of employment in public schools of this district would be professionally inadvisable.
3. That when the school board gives adequate assurance to its present school staff or to the CEA that it has adopted professional personnel policies consistent with the accepted good practices, this notice will be publicly withdrawn.

The Carver School Case

In March, 1952, the Carver (Michigan) School District Board of Education notified five tenure teachers that their contracts would not be renewed, despite the fact that the State Tenure Act provided that "a tenure teacher is entitled to a hearing (private or public, as the teacher chooses) and is entitled to counsel." The teachers asked for a hearing within the time limit, and no hearing was provided by the Board of Education. The board stated that the teachers did not set a date for the hearing. Contending that it was the board's responsibility to provide for a hearing within the thirty to forty-five day period after application, and further contending that the board had violated the State Tenure Act, the teachers applied to the Michigan Education Association for assistance. Legal assistance was provided, and an appeal to the State Tenure Commission was filed.

The Tenure Commission of the Michigan Education Association handed down a decision in favor of the teachers as follows: [17]

1. Teachers are not required by the Tenure Law to provide a hearing.
2. The Board of Education is required by law to provide a hearing when requested and to set a date.
3. That the Board acted illegally in the matter, the teachers were not dismissed legally, and the Board must return these teachers to their teaching positions.

Results: The school board failed to act on the recommendation, and the Tenure Committee of the Michigan Education Association filed a man-

[16] Connecticut Education Association, "New Building, New Principal (How One Board of Education Rewarded Sixteen Years of Service)," report of a fact-finding committee of the CEA, March 5, 1954.

[17] "The Carver School Case," *Michigan Education Journal*, September 15, 1953, 31:78.

damus suit in circuit court to compel the school board to reinstate the teachers. The case dragged on in the courts for several months, during which time the Michigan Education Association provided financial assistance for the teachers during the time of unemployment. The circuit court finally ordered the school board to reinstate the five dismissed teachers and to pay them back salary.[18] After failure of the board to observe the court order, the case was carried to the supreme court, which sustained the position of the circuit court. Thus the five teachers were restored to their positions and paid for the time they were suspended from service.[19]

A Case Involving Unprofessional Conduct by a Teacher

The Y unified school district in California employed Mr. X as teacher, coach, and assistant superintendent in May. Less than a month later the board demanded Mr. X's resignation, charging him with "conduct unbecoming a teacher or administrator." Failing to secure Mr. X's resignation, the board requested that the Ethics Commission of the California Teachers Association investigate the charges.

The commission found a disrupted and disunited school district in which the school board seemed to divide among themselves most of the functions of a superintendent of schools, that the board had apparently condoned or encouraged various teachers to consult with members of the school board about complaints and decisions. The assumption of administrative duties by the five board members and the district having an assistant superintendent led the California Teachers Association to dub this case "The Valley of Seven Superintendents."

The Ethics Commission of the CTA found that the board had charged Mr. X with about a dozen violations of professional ethics. Among these were the following: the use of profane language, exhibitions of uncontrolled temper, the use of the personal confidence approach to create friction among the staff, failure to meet his class schedules on time, undermining of his superior, overemphasis of competitive athletics, assumption of duties not delegated to him, failure to observe general regulations of the school, showing of partiality to students whose parents had political influence, failure to build respect for the teaching profession, inconsiderateness of fellow teachers, ridiculing students, and lack of responsibility to the teaching profession.

In its investigation the commission found many extenuating circumstances, including the divided authority in the school district and testimonies of many good qualities of Mr. X. However, it found him in vio-

---

[18] "The MEA Victory: Carver Teachers Reinstated," *Michigan Education Journal*, December 15, 1953, *31:*223.

[19] "The MEA Victorious in Carver Equity Case," *Michigan Education Journal*, November 15, 1954, *32:*165.

lation of the Code of Ethics for California teachers in many significant respects. The commission recommended:

1. That the school board remain firm in its demand for the resignation of Mr. X.

2. If Mr. X did not resign, since he had a contract for the ensuing year, that Mr. X make every effort to redeem and re-establish himself in a situation he had helped to create. That his future as a teacher be based largely on the recommendations of the new superintendent.

3. That the board establish an administrative code, and publicize it—one which would clearly define the relationship between the board and the administration of the teachers in the community.

Legislation Placing Responsibility on the Profession

The California State Legislature in 1955 passed a bill recognizing the California Teachers Association as the official representative of the teaching profession in that state, and assigning to the CTA the responsibility of assisting governing boards of law in defining competence, unfitness, and unprofessional conduct. The bill provides that, in the dismissal of a permanent teacher on charges that involve unfitness, incompetence, or unprofessional conduct, the California Teachers Association shall, upon request, nominate a panel of teachers to investigate the charges and render a written report. The written report of the representatives of the profession would then become a part of the record of the case and be considered as evidence. The request for the panel of educators to investigate the charges could be made either by the school board or the employee involved, and the expenses would be paid by the school district.

In the first case investigated under this law by the CTA, the investigation committee found the teacher guilty of unprofessional conduct and recommended dismissal of the teacher. The school board did fire the teacher. When the case was taken to the courts, the ruling sustained the school board. The decision cited the judgment of the teacher's colleagues (a "jury of peers") and sustained the board's action largely on this basis. On appeal, the California Supreme Court reversed the lower court on the grounds of infringement of freedom of speech.

In commenting upon this progressive legislation, the executive secretary of the California Teachers Association said: "This proposal is a natural step in the evolution of a profession which is slowly building machinery to assume self-determination of the qualities of its own service to society. This program is grounded in the belief that if teaching is to be a quality profession, it must have certain standards of ability, preparation, ethics, and competence, and that the profession itself should be vocal in determining what these standards should be. Therefore, these panels do not contain laymen. The report of the panel must be considered as expert and professional opinion. On no other basis can it be admitted as competent evidence. The plan will succeed or fail in terms of the wisdom and ability of the professionals who comprise the panel." [20] Since 1963, about eight states have adopted professional practices acts vesting broad powers in the profession regarding standards of competence and practice.

THE DUSHANE FUND FOR TEACHER RIGHTS

Closely allied to the principle of a profession protecting its members against unjust treatment and the establishment of machinery to do so is the need to provide financial assistance to the individuals involved in hardship cases. The NEA maintains a special fund for this purpose—the Dushane Fund for Teacher Rights. The fund was originally sponsored by the NEA Department of Classroom Teachers and the Defense Commission, and grew out of the unfair dismissal of a teacher. A fund was raised from voluntary contributions to provide subsistence for the teacher during the period she was fighting for reinstatement. When reinstatement was accomplished, the balance remaining in the fund became the nucleus for the Donald Dushane Memorial Defense Fund (named in honor of the first executive secretary of the NEA Defense Commission). Until 1962 the fund was sustained by contributions of NEA members, and assistance to individual teachers was restricted to subsistence grants. In 1962 the NEA Executive Committee directed that the fund be supported by annual appropriations by the NEA and contributions, that the fund be built up to $100,000, and that assistance grants be authorized to provide legal assistance to teachers in cases having import for the welfare of the profession.[21]

Summary

The case examples in this chapter deal with cases handled by the Defense Commission, the Tenure Committee, and the Ethics Committee. Since 1961, when the National Commission on Professional Rights and Responsibilities replaced the first two groups, added responsibilities have been given to the PR&R Commission. The adoption (in 1962) of the use of professional sanctions vested responsibility for investigating cases that may result in invoking sanctions in the Commission. Notable cases resulting in sanctions are Utah, Oklahoma, Baltimore and Florida. (See Chapters

[20] Arthur F. Corey, "The Profession Moves Forward With Tenure" (editorial), *CTA Journal*, March, 1955, 51:3.

[21] An appropriation of $10,000 was provided by the NEA for the 1962–63 school year and provision made to match the appropriation each year with the estimated need. Also, funds were transferred from the surplus to bring the fund up to the recommended $100,000. In 1965, NEA enlarged the goal of this fund to $1,000,000 to come from voluntary contributions of members.

21 and 22. Also see published reports of investigations of the PR&R Commission in references below.)

REFERENCES

BUTLER, J. T., "Approach to Professional Practices Legislation," *NEA Journal,* February, 1967, 56:43–4.

CARR, W. G., "Discriminatory Dismissals of Negro Teachers," *School and Society,* October 2, 1965, 93:338.

DAVIS, H., *et al.,* "Economic, Legal, and Social Status of Teachers; Legal Status," *Review of Educational Research,* October, 1963, 33:401–2.

DAVIS, J. L., "NEA and Teacher Welfare: Defense of Teachers," *NEA Journal,* December, 1955, 44:564–65.

EASTMOND, JEFFERSON N., *The Teacher and School Administration.* Boston: Houghton Mifflin Company, 1959, "Operational Aspects of Tenure Legislation," pp. 417–21.

ELSBREE, WILLARD S., and REUTTER, E. EDMUND, JR., *Staff Personnel in the Public Schools.* Englewood Cliffs, New Jersey: Prentice-Hall, 1954, "Enforcement of Codes," pp. 402–404.

FIRST, J. M. "When You Need Help," *Michigan Education Journal,* November, 1959, 37:225–27.

FIRTH, G. R., "Teachers Must Discipline Their Professional Colleagues," *Phi Delta Kappan,* October, 1960, 42:24–27.

GARBER, L. O., "Can You Fire a Teacher for Unprofessional Conduct?" *Nation's Schools,* April, 1964, 73:90+.

———, "Cause and Procedures for Dismissing a Tenure Teacher," *Nation's Schools,* December, 1956, 58:73–74.

———, "Where the Courts Took Public Schools in 1964," *Nation's Schools,* March, 1965, 75:50–1+.

GORDON, G. G., "Conditions of Employment and Service in Elementary and Secondary Schools; Evaluation, Retention and Dismissal," *Review of Educational Research,* October, 1963, 33:385–6.

HAMILTON, ROBERT R., and MORT, PAUL A., *The Law and Public Education,* 2nd ed. Brooklyn: Foundation Press, 1959, Chap. 10, "Discharge of Teachers," pp. 394–448.

LEIPOLD, L. E., "Teachers in the Courts," *Clearing House,* January, 1966, 40:280–2.

"NEA an Negro Teacher Displacement Problem," *School and Society,* October 6, 1965, 93:365+.

NATIONAL EDUCATION ASSOCIATION, Department of Classroom Teachers, *Conditions of Work for Quality Teaching.* Washington, D.C.: The Association, 1959, pp. 83–86, 114–15.

NATIONAL EDUCATION ASSOCIATION, Ethics Committee, *Opinions of the Committee on Professional Ethics.* Washington, D.C.: The Association, 1966.

NATIONAL EDUCATION ASSOCIATION, Professional Rights and Responsibilities Commission, *Developing Personnel Policies.* Washington, D.C.: The Association, 1963.

————, *Guidelines for Professional Sanctions.* Washington, D.C.: The Association, 1966.

————, *Report of an Investigation.* Washington, D.C.: The Association. Baltimore, 1967. Detroit, 1967. Bellville, New Jersey, 1966. Kenosha, Wisconsin, 1966. Florida, 1966. Louisville, Kentucky, 1965. Manchester, New Hampshire, 1965. Oklahoma, 1965. Idaho, 1965. Rio Arriba County, New Mexico, 1964. Cleveland, Ohio, 1964. Utah, 1964. Carter County, Kentucky, 1963. Springfield, Missouri, 1963. Knoxville, Tennessee, 1967. Warwick, Rhode Island, 1962. Jefferson County, Idaho, 1963. Waterbury, Connecticut, 1963. Conway, Arkansas, 1964.

————, *Tenure—What and Why.* Washington, D.C.: The Association, 1963.

PICOTT, J. R., "Displacement of Experienced Teachers Without Due Process," *NEA Journal,* December, 1965, *54*:41.

PUNKE, H. H., "Immorality as Grounds for Teacher Dismissal." *Secondary School Principal Bulletin,* January, 1965, *49*:53–69. Same condensed, *Phi Delta Kappan,* March, 1965, *46*:268.

ROACH, S. F., "Scope of Board Authority to Dismiss Teachers," *American School Board Journal,* March, 1957, *134*:50.

STINNETT, T. M., "Million Dollar Fund for Teachers Rights," *NEA Journal,* October, 1965, *54*:38–9.

————, KLEINMANN, JACK H., and WARE, MARTHA L., *Professional Negotiation in Public Education.* New York: Macmillan Company, 1966, Chap. 6, pp. 121–151.

"Teachers to Police Their Own Ranks," *School and Society,* October 2, 1965, *93*:336.

WILLIAMSON, J. M., "Court Calls Expert Panel to Testify on Teacher Conduct," *CTA Journal,* March, 1960, *56*:15–16.

————, "Teacher's Right to Speak," *CTA Journal,* April, 1960, *56*:24–25.

16: The Role of Teachers as Educational Leaders

Several times it has been stated in this book that every member of a profession has a dual role: that of a practitioner and that of a responsible member of his profession. To perform only the daily routine of his technical tasks is not enough; he must involve himself in the affairs of his profession. Thus the job of the teacher is more than teaching; it also involves the job of improving the profession and education, and there is a third role—the role of educational leader. This third role for teachers is, perhaps, unique among the professions. Because the member of no other profession is so intimately involved in the lives of almost all the people of the community—so involved in the task of improving the community, its economic, political, social, and cultural life—as is the teacher.

The doctor, for example, deals largely with the individual patient, the lawyer with the individual client, the minister with a segment of the community. The teacher is involved with the aspirations of the total community.

But before proceeding to discuss each of the above roles in detail, perhaps it will be well to define the concept of leadership as applied to education. One influential professional association has defined it as "that action or behavior among individuals and groups which causes both the individual and the groups to move toward educational goals that are increasingly mutually acceptable to them." [1]

A related question is, what separate functions does the teacher perform in his leadership role? Raths has enumerated thirteen functions as fol-

[1] Association for Supervision and Curriculum Development, *Leadership for Improving Instruction*. Washington, D.C.: The Association, a department of the NEA, 1960, p. 27.

lows: [2] (1) initiating, managing, directing, and taking charge; (2) modifying the curriculum; (3) informing, explaining, and showing how; (4) security-giving operations; (5) the clarifying process, moving from opinion to fact or truth; (6) group-unifying operations; (7) community-enriching operations; (8) diagnostic and remedial work; (9) evaluating, recording, and reporting; (10) school-wide functions; (11) homeroom aesthetics; (12) professionalizing own career; and (13) functioning as a citizen.

Although it is extremely difficult to categorize all of the aspects of the teacher's role as an educational leader, the following encompass the major ones: the role of the teacher in the development of the community's educational program, the role of the teacher in community and public relations, and the role of the teacher in professional policy making and execution.

ROLE OF TEACHERS IN DEVELOPING THE COMMUNITY'S EDUCATIONAL PROGRAM

A slight noise from the doorway caught her attention. She saw the burnished knob turn and watched the door swing open slowly and silently on its well-oiled hinges. Her heart leaped in her breast as she recognized him. Softly he stepped into the room and, careful to make no disturbance, made his way noiselessly along the left wall. He chose his vantage point carefully, and from it his eyes seemed to miss no detail. She watched him tensely, trying to pull her scattered thoughts together, but was shaken anew as his hand went to his pocket and withdrew the black, flat object he habitually carried there. With a great effort of will she tore her eyes from him. . . .

An episode from a mystery thriller? No, simply a description of a principal making a routine supervisory visit in the manner recommended by some authorities a decade and a half ago or more. Even today it is characteristic of practice in many schools.[3]

Administration of school systems as a cooperative enterprise, involving all members of the professional staff, is a relatively new but rapidly growing trend in American public education. The classroom teacher is rapidly coming into his own, in the sense that increasing recognition is being given to the creative potentials of the teacher to make valuable contributions to the effective administration of schools. This trend is one of great significance, in that it tends to give to teachers the sense of belonging to a democratic team, tends to give them a real part in a creative enterprise of great power and promise. Conversely, this trend toward involving all

[2] Louis E. Raths, "What is Teaching?" *Educational Leadership*, December, 1955, 13:146–49.

[3] Willard S. Elsbree and Harold J. McNally. *Elementary School Administration and Supervision*. New York: American Book Company, 1951, p. 397. (Second edition of this title published in 1959.)

the professional staff in policy making and policy decision, in running the total affairs of a given school system, tends to remove one of the chief obstacles to the development of good staff morale: the discouraging feeling on the part of teachers that they are but cogs in a complex machine, where they are not permitted to operate as true professionals, but are permitted to do only as they are directed by higher authority. The development has been slow in coming, but it is definitely on the way. The development has lagged behind the adoption of truly democratic procedures in the classroom, and indeed it has lagged behind the general acceptance of the democratic, cooperative philosophy concerning the goals and methods of education.

This trend toward participation of the total school staff in administration and supervision opens up new and promising vistas of power, power heretofore largely unused, in the continuous improvement of the quality of education.

Such a trend is, of course, pleasing to teachers. But like any other privilege or right, as one may choose to view the development, it confers as well great responsibilities and great challenges to teachers. If the promise of the movement is to be fully realized, then the preparation of teachers must be altered accordingly, to the end that each may be equipped to function as a member of a great, cooperative team, to the end that the role and the responsibility of administration be fully understood. However, if administration and supervision are to be made truly cooperative processes, teachers must not only be equipped with technical know-how in these fields; they must be willing to share the responsibility with all of the headaches inherent in policy making and policy decisions.

To demand and get a privilege or a right is one thing; to measure up to that right or privilege is another. Thus, the new trend in policy making for the school systems demands teachers fully equipped both in professional competence and in professional spirit and devotion to be able to make constructive contributions to these ends.

The new trend demands that teachers have the ability and the will to participate in the process of decision making, but to distinguish this from the authority for making the final decision.

Evolution of Democracy in School Administration

The history of public education in the United States reveals two (a third is now emerging) eras in the administrator-teacher relationship. Roughly stated in another way, there have been two eras of administrative philosophy. The first era was one in which the lay administrator was dominant, in which the school visitor, or committeeman, or selectman, or school-board members assumed responsibility for directing the school and for executing school policy.

The second era saw the assumption of these responsibilities by professional school administrators. This was the period of the "line and staff" philosophy of administration, wherein decisions were made at the top of the executive team and handed down "through channels" to the teachers in the classrooms. In such a scheme the teacher generally held a second-rate place in the hierarchy of command. The determination of objectives of the school program, selection of materials, methods of teaching, and lesson planning were vested in the administrator. Teachers had little voice in such matters of vital concern to them. In such a scheme an obviously autocratic arrangement existed in the framework of an avowed devotion to democracy in education. Such a plan was analogous to the teacher who professes great devotion to the principles and the concepts of democracy, who gives fervent lip service to the power of the democratic process, but who nevertheless fails to observe any of these beliefs in the handling of his classroom.

The above description is obviously a bit harsh; it states the case in extremes. But the practice, as a general rule, is not overdrawn. There were, to be sure, many exceptions to this general rule. Administrator-teacher teamwork during this period was evident in many school systems in varying degrees.

The Emergence of a New Era

For the last decade or so the "line and staff" philosophy in administration has been rapidly giving way to the teamwork idea, involving all members of the professional staff in the determination of school policies. And the trend is a fortunate one. For if education is to be democratic, that process must start with those who staff the schools.

Evidences of the trend are to be found in the changing nature of teachers' professional organizations. Only a decade or so ago, state and national organizations tended to be dominated by administrators, with participation of classroom teachers all too often a token gesture. Teachers are now assuming their rightful role of leadership in these associations under the impact of the new trend.

The Emerging Trend in Supervision

Most of what has been said above has reference to the administrative procedures of school systems. Closely paralleling the dominant practices in administration were those relating to supervision. Bartkey classifies the eras or types of supervision through which we have gone in seven categories: [4]

1. *Autocratic Supervision.* Implies that the top official in the line of command knows the answers and passes these on to subordinates as absolutes.

[4] John A. Bartkey, *Supervision as Human Relations.* Boston: D. C. Heath and Company, 1953, pp. 14–21.

2. *Inspectional Supervision.* Began with inspection by school committees and later became a technique of professional administrators, in which the official hunted for judged strengths and weaknesses of the individual teacher, on which decisions to retain or dismiss were made. The process became popularly and contemptuously known as "snoopervision."

3. *Representative Supervision.* Attempted to mimic political practices in our society by selection of supervisory officials by those to be supervised. The plan gave no voice to parents and pupils in the selective process, and it never became a popular practice.

4. *Cooperative-Democratic Supervision.* Placed emphasis upon group dynamics to determine teaching methods and procedures. It tended to ignore, as was the case with representative supervision, the role of parents and pupils and to discount the role of the expert in contributing to the improvement of instruction.

5. *Invitational Supervision.* Developed to offset tensions of inspectional supervision. It placed emphasis upon supervisory visits and assistance only upon request of the individual teacher. The weakness is the tendency of teachers to invite supervision only when they have some strong point to be observed.

6. *Scientific Supervision.* Stresses classroom observation and objective measurement of results in the improvement of instruction. It uses elaborate check sheets and rating tools, and aptitude, diagnostic, and achievement tests.

7. *Creative Supervision.* Opposed to scientific type of supervision. Supervision acts as catalytic agent in the growth of teacher and supplements the child-centered curriculum philosophy.

The last named, creative supervision, is clearly the emerging trend in supervision, in which the creative powers of the individual teacher are given full play.

These types of supervision, as defined by Bartkey, are not, of course, mutually exclusive; all are aimed at the common purpose of improving instruction.

How Cooperative Teamwork Begins

The starting point in teamwork in teacher-administrator relationships, in the sharing by all the staff in the school policy making, is the determination of a common goal for the school program. Once cooperatively defined and accepted by the group, the common goal becomes the chart and compass for effective teamwork. Then each has had a part in a decision of immeasurable importance. To each the task is his very own. If it fails, each has his measure of a sense of failure. If it succeeds, each has his measure of a sense of achievement, and there is glory enough for all. The power of the group process is comparable to that of a great democratic nation geared to the task of winning a war. Each somehow surpasses himself in his zeal and self-motivation.

Some Disadvantages of Cooperative Administration

Of course, in any type of administrative procedure some decisions must be made by individuals. In other words, some decisions can best be made by individuals, while some are best met through group action.

The trend away from authoritarian administration quite naturally brings into play some hazards. Any democratic process always is subject to certain abuses and certain dangers. Cooperative administration generally results in a proliferation of committees, which often is so extreme as to be time-consuming and, therefore, burdensome. But this is an inevitable part of the democratic process. Frequently we hear teachers grumble about too many meetings and conferences that they are expected to attend. They are inclined to revolt against what they term "talk, talk, talk." But we must never forget that a lot of conferring, a lot of palaver, is essential to the democratic process. If some higher authority is to hand down decisions, then such meetings and talk are not necessary. We must never forget, either, that the democratic process is usually slow, time-consuming, and seemingly time-wasting. But we treasure something above efficiency, and that something is the right of all to participate in decision making and in the determination of the rules under which we live.

Another hazard of the cooperative process in administration is that there may develop a sort of blind faith in the infallibility of a group decision. Groups can err as individuals can err, and the wise group will consider its decisions as tentative and will revise these in the light of experience and new evidence.

Staff Organization for Cooperative Policy Making

As has been already implied, the "line and staff" arrangement was necessary in a period when the professional preparation of the teaching staff was meager. Teachers with little or no preparation for their jobs were hardly in a position to meet their teaching responsibilities adequately, let alone exercise the difficult additional duties of policy making. Even today about one-fourth of the nation's elementary school teachers have had preparation below the degree level. But that situation is rapidly changing. Only in small rural school districts, or in isolated cases in larger districts, and in a few states will school-system staffs be found with average preparation of less than the bachelor's degree. The trend, typically, will be toward staffs with full professional preparation, ranging from four to six college years, and with competences, therefore, to function effectively as skilled teachers and as skilled members in administrative and supervisory teamwork. Thus the authoritarian administrative arrangement is no longer necessary—indeed, will no longer work efficiently and satisfactorily.

A type of staff organization designed to utilize the resources and the full participation of the total professional personnel has been adopted in the Westport, Connecticut, school system. Rast has described the basic principles of that organization as follows: [5]

The work of the teacher in the classroom with the pupils is the key to a strong educational program. The teacher has full freedom, within the framework of general building, system wide, and community policies to exercise initiative and judgment in meeting his responsibility.

The building unit is next in importance in a successful educational program. The principal, the office staff, the committee system, building meetings, custodians, PTA group, and special services all exist to assist the teacher in carrying out his responsibility for the growth of the pupils toward intellectual, physical, social and emotional maturity. The building unit is allowed much autonomy in the conduct of its work. Responsibility for productivity goes hand in hand with decentralization of control.

The central office of the school system, with its entire staff, exists to support the teacher through the building unit. Such support comes through the determination of the general aims or desired outcomes of the educational program by cooperative action; the provision of general program, staff, materials, facilities, and finances to carry out these aims; the development of evaluative criteria; and the conduct of a broad community relations program.

The community, through its official representatives, the members of the Board of Education, exists also to assist the teacher's work in the classroom. General policies are established with this goal in mind. In addition to the Board of Education the community contains many organized and informal groups whose power and influence can be used to assist the teacher in the job of educating the community's children.

Such a program, Rast points out, requires:

1. An exceptionally well-prepared staff, with a growth drive toward intellectual, social, and emotional maturity.
2. Recognition of the roles of leadership, followership, and cooperation in their proper perspective, depending upon the exact situation and personnel resources available.
3. Freedom to make reasonable mistakes. The staff will make mistakes and must be prepared to face up to them, knowing that there will be no reprisals.
4. The critical importance of decision making. Since authority to make decisions is not lodged in a few top officials, but is widely dispersed, the quality of the decision-making process becomes of crucial impor-

[5] G. E. Rast, "Cooperative Teamwork in Administration," *Competent Teachers for America's Schools: Lay-Professional Action Programs to Secure and Retain Qualified Teachers*, Report of the Albany Conference. Washington, D.C.: National Commission on Teacher Education and Professional Standards, National Education Association, 1954, p. 235.

tance, and effort constantly to improve the process is an obligation of the total staff.

5. Effective communication. The numbers of persons involved in a co-operative process of teamwork make effective communication among the members of the team essential if misunderstandings, lack of information, and duplication of effort are to be avoided.

ROLE OF TEACHERS IN POLICY MAKING IN SCHOOLS

In 1962, in recognition of the emerging demand of teachers for a significant role in policy making, the NEA adopted a resolution calling for the adoption of professional negotiation agreements (see Chapter 22).

The AASA in 1966 gave support to the process of professional negotiation in the following statement: [6]

New patterns of staff relationships require many changes in local school administrations; old, established traditions and processes no longer suffice. It avails little to debate the desirability of these changes in relationships or bemoan either their existence or their speed. Changes are here, and their pace will quicken rather than abate in the years ahead. New processes and new insights into the nature and means of policy formulation are needed not only to upgrade the professional status of teachers but to improve the conditions under which they work, thus enhancing the quality of education.

. . . written negotiation agreements which carefully delineate the roles and responsibilities of the superintendent, the board, teachers, administrative and supervisory staff, and professional organizations are essential to the smooth and efficient operation of the schools.

Many observers believe that the emerging participation of teachers in policy making will inevitably add to the status of teaching and to the quality of educational programs. School superintendents and boards incline to view these developments with apprehension. They protest that they impinge upon their legal authority. Indeed they do, but state legislatures have power to change by legislation existing powers in the governance of the school. This is happening in a number of states.

Support of Administrative Leadership

The emergence of democratic participation of the total staff in the development of the community educational program is having many wholesome by-products. Chief among these is, of course, the sense of responsibility by individual members of the staff for the quality of the total program. This is an inevitable and powerful outcome of participation, the value of which we are just beginning to recognize and to exploit.

[6] American Association of School Administrators, "School Administrators View Professional Negotiation." Washington, D.C.: The Association, 1966, 58 pp.

Another concomitant is the sense of responsibility of the total staff for the security and welfare of the competent administrator. There is a growing insistence upon the creation of a climate in which the good administrator will be free to lead and free of extraneous and capricious pressures.

A good example of this emerging trend is the emphasis that the NEA Department of Classroom Teachers gave to the necessity for such a climate in its study of working conditions. In a chapter devoted to "Good Administration" are guidelines for assuring competent administration.[7] These guidelines, which were primarily concerned with working conditions for classroom teachers, were as follows:

The school administrator should be recognized as the executive officer of the school board; should be the leader of the professional staff; should have the status of a professional adviser on educational policy; should have the support of those responsible to him in the execution of established policy; should have reasonable freedom from political duress or community factionalism; should be protected from unwarranted termination of his contract; should be provided with adequate staff and facilities to perform his duties; should be assured of sufficient time away from his duties to maintain health and normal family life; and should have opportunities to extend his professional preparation and to assist in maintaining high standards among school administrators.

THE ROLE OF TEACHERS IN COMMUNITY AND PUBLIC RELATIONS

The concept that teachers themselves really are the key persons in developing good community or good public relations is a relatively new one. Until recently, "public relations" was thought to be a job for administrators, because the task was principally one of furnishing a continuous flow of effective publicity. Teachers, it was assumed, could have little part in this process. The change from "public relations" to "community relations" has very definitely brought classroom teachers into the picture.

During the past few years there has been a decided trend in teacher-education institutions toward courses in community study. Such courses have stressed the school as an integral part of the social order, the use of community resources, and better correlation between the school and the community. Both administrators and teachers have taken such courses.

The emphasis in the community study and curriculum courses, though, has been upon better educational service. There has not been too much stress upon building better understanding between school and community or in acquainting the public with the goals, methods, and activities of the

[7] See National Education Association, Department of Classroom Teachers, *Conditions of Work for Quality Teaching.* Washington, D.C.: The Association, 1959, Chap. 4, "Good Administration," pp. 103–19.

school. It seems to have been assumed that these goals will be accomplished indirectly through better relationships between the school and the community. The direct approach is also needed. This is an age of advertising. The school needs constantly to keep its product before the public if it is to receive its share of the tax dollar, and if it is to render the service it should.

Teachers, as has been indicated, have not in the past been called upon to do very much with public relations. They have been expected to maintain good relations with the parents of children in their classes, but that has been the extent of their responsibilities. School officials have done the rest. Now, though, we are entering a new era in which teachers will need to have a part in establishing and maintaining satisfactory community relations.[8]

The Larger Task

There is now plenty of evidence that something different must be done in community relations. No longer will publicity suffice. Schools are under fire almost everywhere. There have been a number of flare-ups, including widespread and intensive attacks on the schools in many cities. There are doubtless organizations that exist for the sole purpose of discrediting public schools. But it must be assumed that much of the criticism arises from sincere friends and supporters of the schools who have not been kept informed properly of the work of the schools, or who have not been provided with the opportunity of participating in developing school policies.

Much of the criticism is to the effect that the three R's, the academic subjects, are being neglected. But there are also those who feel that the schools are excessively subject-matter centered and hopelessly behind the times. And, in recent years, there have been waves of criticism in many communities regarding liberal teaching, particularly of the social studies. Often one finds these antagonistic criticisms within the same community. Some boards of education even wage internal warfare over them.

No school, of course, can walk a chalk line between the several opposing groups. In the first place, the chalk line is not well defined and shifts constantly. In the second place, the fence sitter pleases no one. It is thus impossible to keep peace with the opposing factions.

No solution is in sight unless everyone—parents, pupils, and teachers—can be organized into a group that works as a unit. There has to be a common purpose, or peace can never be achieved. There have to be the

[8] For an excellent description of the role of teachers in public relations, see *It Starts in the Classroom* (A Public Relations Handbook for Classroom Teachers). Washington, D.C.: National School Public Relations Association, National Education Association, 1951.

adjustments and compromises that come from across-the-table working for a common cause.

The Role of Teachers

As has been previously stated, school administrative officials formerly carried the entire task of maintaining adequate relationships with the community. That day appears to be over. Unless teachers assume a portion of the burden we shall inevitably have more upheavals such as have been described.

These considerations make community relations a professional problem. As they are with tenure, retirement, and other issues, teachers need to be concerned about community relations. The strivings to make teaching a profession will otherwise be futile; there will exist no proper bases upon which to build.

Schools formerly looked upon their so-called "public relations" as a means of informing the people in respect to the objectives and accomplishments of the schools. Publicity was supposed to be entirely complimentary. Mistakes and questionable practices were often not brought into the open. Various media were used in this kind of sales program. Among the important onces were radio and television, newspapers, school publications, parents' nights, school programs, and extracurricular events. These were all used to portray the school in a favorable light to the public. We still need these media of publicity, but we also need more than these.

The concept of the community school furnishes a new base and a different approach. If it is to be effective, the school must be a part of the society in which it functions. It cannot be a separate entity, any more than the arm can be a separate whole. The public is not willing to judge the school entirely by handouts. Unless we make an active partner of the public, we are doomed to endless criticism and many upheavals. In this section we shall be concerned with means by which teachers can not only keep the people informed, but make the public into an active participant in a true community school. Besides, effective educational service can only be achieved with the united effort of everyone.

TEACHERS' ACTIVITIES AND PERSONAL RELATIONSHIPS

The Curriculum

At one time the curriculum was made largely by administrators. Perhaps we should say "course of study" rather than "curriculum." The distinction is that a course of study lists the subjects to be taught without giving any particular attention to the content of the subjects, while a curriculum describes the activities to be undertaken as well as the areas to be considered. In former days the administrator listed the subjects to be taught and the amount of time to be devoted to each. The textbooks largely determined the content of the courses. Now, of course, we try to build curricula rather than courses of study.

It is widely recognized that adequate curricula can only be built by the united efforts of many people. No one person, sitting in an office, could possibly come up with anything like an adequate one. Instead, there must be cooperative efforts by every person who is in any way equipped to contribute to the process.

Teachers can do much to further good community relationships by participating in curriculum meetings. They can impress parents and community leaders by their knowledge of school needs and curriculum resources. By their fair-mindedness and willingness to listen, they can create good will for the school organization. By their friendliness and interest in pupils, they can help to establish a belief that the school really wants to give the best possible educational service to children.

Good Teaching

Although there is no clear-cut, universally accepted definition of good teaching, and although the public is not united on what it wants the school to accomplish, different groups do have some very definite ideas on that subject. Teachers are rated by the popular mind just as physicians, dentists, lawyers, and clergymen are rated. All anyone has to do to find out how certain teachers in the neighborhood school are regarded is to ask parents who have children attending that school. They will be able to give an evaluation without much delay. Of course, not all parents will agree on an evaluation of any teacher, any more than the public will agree upon the effectiveness of a given physician, dentist, or attorney. All of this points up the necessity for the teaching profession to work intensely and intelligently to define good teaching. This is admittedly an extremely difficult task. But it is not an insoluble one. And if the teaching profession cannot identify good teaching, the public becomes skeptical of its expertness.[9]

Desirable Qualities

It is difficult to put one's finger on the qualities in a teacher. There are some identifiable traits that the public has built into its concept of the good teacher, but these are not always reliable criteria by which good teaching can be measured. They tend to be personality traits that are

---

[9] For a clear treatment of this difficulty, see *Who's A Good Teacher?* Washington, D.C.: Joint publication of the American Association of School Administrators, Department of Classroom Teachers, and the National School Boards Association, 1961, 64 pp.

pleasing to parents and pupils, such as fairness, friendliness, a sense of humor, interest in others, etc. The Department of Classroom Teachers of the National Education Association has issued a check list [10] to assist teachers in establishing good public relations. Under the heading "In My School," they include the following questions:

1. Does each pupil feel that I am interested in him personally?
2. Do I make a pleasing appearance before my pupils?
3. Do my pupils like me, respect me, and have faith in my judgments?
4. Are my pupils convinced of the value of the learning activities in which we engage?
5. Do I use democratic procedures in my relationships with pupils?
6. Do I value and cultivate the friendships of the parents of my pupils?
7. Do I take an active part in the parent-teacher work of my school?

Under the heading "In My Community," the same organization lists the following:

1. Are my teachings reflected in the lives of my pupils in the community?
2. Does my own conduct bear evidence that education ennobles and enriches our daily lives?
3. Am I friendly toward my neighbors and welcome at community gatherings?
4. Am I active in some nonteacher group in my community?
5. Do I help with some community improvement project or campaign?
6. Do I use the advice and ability of laymen in improving and enriching my instructional program?
7. Do I assist my local teachers' group in fulfilling its public-relations obligations?

MEDIA FOR PUBLIC RELATIONS

The preceding section has dealt with community relations as they concern the individual teacher. Attention will now be given to the media that a teacher or group of teachers may use to secure satisfactory public relations. Most of these avenues of approach to the public are used under the direction of the school administrative officers. However, this is not necessarily the case. The principal media for public relations are the radio, the newspapers, and the various school publications. School publications include, among others, annual reports, house organs, school programs, and school papers.

[10] National Education Association, Department of Classroom Teachers, *Am I Plus or Minus?* Washington, D.C.: The Association, 1947, 4 pp.

Radio and Television

The exent to which radio and television are available as means of familiarizing the public with the work of the school depends upon the size of the community. In almost every good-size community now there are both radio and TV stations. Both radio and television expect to devote a part of their program time to noncommercial programs. It has not been difficult for local schools to secure generous time on both.

Educational television is just now beginning to be widely used. A number of universities and local and state school systems are developing their own UHF stations, and the number is growing. Also, the schools are making wider use of commercial TV stations. Some boards of education have already appointed television directors to arrange for and produce programs over local facilities. Educators have here a marvelous medium for public relations in the wider use of television, both for direct public-relations programs and for the offering of formal courses for students and adults.

Newspapers and Other Publications

Newspapers vary all the way from metropolitan dailies with circulations up to a million copies per day, down to rural weeklies with circulations of three or four hundred copies. Almost every city of ten thousand population or more has a daily newspaper. In outstate areas many cities of five or six thousand have a daily paper. Virtually every town of any size has some kind of a newspaper. Thus, every school administrator must deal with the press, and almost every teacher meets newspaper reporters in the course of his work. The newspaper carries the story of the school's activities into the home daily or weekly. It is, therefore, important to know how to treat news.

News means change. The newspaper story must tell of something that happened or is about to happen. Further, there is an old axiom that "names make news"—the names of pupils participating in the event or the names of the teachers who developed the project. Thus the school news story may tell about some action on the part of the board of education, or it may actually report something that happened in one of the schools. Dramatic programs, music programs, debates, and athletic contests are always good for a story.

In large cities there are generally two or three daily papers, morning and afternoon. In such cases care must be taken to treat all papers impartially. No newsman likes to be scooped by another paper. If possible, news should be released so that the morning papers will get the "break" one time and the afternoon papers the next time. Also, it is generally possible to give different approaches to a story so that when the afternoon paper reports a story previously printed in the morning paper they can give some new details.

Newspapermen do not like to have their stories written for them. It is much better to call in the newspapermen and to give them the facts orally. They will then ask questions and write their own stories. It is true that under such a system there will be occasional mistakes, and people will sometimes be misquoted; this, however, is usually not serious.

The School Page. Both metropolitan dailies and rural weeklies frequently make use of the school page. In the case of the large city papers this is sometimes a part of the Sunday edition, or it may appear in Saturday night's issue. Village weekly papers frequently permit the schools to publish a sort of paper of their own as a page in the weekly. In such cases the copy is generally prepared at the school. In either case the school page represents an excellent community-relations medium. Through this page it is possible to keep the public informed concerning all the activities of the school.

Other School Publications. Other school publications include the annual report, house organs, school annual, school programs, and school papers.

In some states, schools are required to file an annual report. For many years annual reports were of a dry, statistical nature, and they were seldom read by the people. In recent years many school systems have used a popular type of annual report containing many pictures about the work of the schools. The purpose of this pictorial type of report is obviously to impress parents and taxpayers favorably with the work of the schools. On the other hand, there are many examples of creditable mimeographed or dittoed reports issued by small school systems. Probably the most satisfactory answer is an annual report that combines the statistical treatment of the old type of report with the pictorial features of the newer reports.

School Newspapers and School Programs. Almost all city high schools now publish a school newspaper. In some of the larger cities the junior high schools also have a paper. Many schools also publish a magazine, and almost all high schools issue a yearbook or annual. All these go into the homes; hence, they are all avenues for public relations. The annual is a pictorial publication covering the various activities of the school, with emphasis upon the senior-class program.

School programs are printed or mimeographed dozens of times during the school year. There is a program every time a play or musical entertainment is presented, and frequently a program is produced for athletic contests. The program always contains the names of the participants, but it may also be used to convey other information to parents and patrons. For example, the program for a musical entertainment might include a short account of the music courses offered by the school. Similarly, an athletic-contest program might contain a story of how athletics are supervised.

ROLE IN PROFESSIONAL POLICY MAKING AND EXECUTION

The third broad area of responsibility of teachers as educational leaders is their leadership roles in organizations of their profession. Basically, professional organizations in any profession exist, or *should* exist, to attest to the public the competence of its members. There are related purposes, of course, the major ones being: to advance the cause of the profession as a whole and extend and raise the level of its service, and to protect and advance the welfare of its members. These are, or should be, subsidiary to the first.

Such purposes require the searching out and developing of potential leadership. It is an interacting relationship. Associations cannot exist as effective units without capable leaders, and capable leaders are dependent upon associations as the means of emerging and as the vehicle for the exercise of new powers. Spot any organization in which leadership year after year is centered in a continuing few or a hierarchical segment, and you can identify a stagnant institution.

This thesis runs counter to some popular notions. Presently there are vociferous demands in some quarters for a small group of scholars to be designated to define and impose national standards for education and teachers, even their certification. Apparently, the NEA began with some such concept. Women were excluded until 1866. From 1857 to 1920 the dominant elements were college presidents, normal-school presidents, and school superintendents. The breakup of this hierarchical leadership has been described as follows:

> Unfortunately, the period of the "great names" on committees directing the country's educational policy was relatively short. It ended about 1905. The pressure of new problems apparently scattered the small groups of national leaders; partly also these problems were of a kind for which the old guard was no longer competent. As a matter of fact, even before the period of the great committees, issues appeared far beyond the orbit of education, if understood inthe merely scholastic sense of the word. Women, admitted in 1866, entered the NEA in larger numbers and asked for equal rights; there was the desire for the discussion of teachers' salaries; the relation between education and the government became increasingly complicated. Labor tried to increase its influence on the public school system; the assimilation of minorities became more and more urgent; there was the conflict between nationalism and internationalism; various reform movements asked for consideration; the new technological society in America was no longer satisfied with schools dating from earlier times.[11]

As the teaching profession has moved toward greater maturity, the func-

[11] Howard Mumford Jones, Francis Keppel, and Robert Ulich, "On the Conflict Between the Liberal Arts and the Schools of Education," *Newsletter* of the American Council of Learned Societies, V, 2:17–38, 1954.

tion of the various professional organizations has become increasingly important. Indeed, the professional organizations make up a major segment of the teaching profession today, where once they occupied a position of little importance in the mainstream of American education. Several examples will illustrate the growing significance of professional organizations. The professional association has served as the medium by which group aspirations are expressed. The implementation of those aspirations has generally been affected through designated small bodies, committees, commissions, councils, and agencies, whose membership, as a rule, is made up of individuals who have emerged as capable, articulate, thoughtful leaders.

The Commission for the Defense of Democracy Through Education is a good example of the small group exercising a mandate from the total profession. The creation of the Defense Commission and the Tenure Committee [12] was an expression of the aspiration of the great body of teachers for dignity and respect and fair treatment, as accorded other recognized professions. There are several ways in which an occupational group becomes a profession and gains status, strength, and dignity. It gains these through raising the quality of its services to its clients. It gains these through developing a reputation for reliability through the use of well-established research techniques and careful interpretations of research. It gains these through establishing and maintaining high standards for entering into and continuing in the profession. It does not gain full status until it sets up the machinery and the techniques and gains the strength to see to it that its members are treated with respect and consideration and accorded the rights, privileges, and immunities that should be given to members of an honorable profession.

Much of the very basic policy governing American education is established within and among the great plurality of professional organizations that we now have in the United States. Since it is true that these organizations have taken on such important functions, and more and more are becoming the focus of policy formation and coordinating activities for American education, it is of particular importance that an appropriate leadership for these professional organizations be deliberately developed.

It seems apparent that there are two major categories of leadership required for professional organizations. The first we might classify under voluntary leadership. In this group, of course, would fall all of the various professional voluntary workers, whether it be a building representative for a local teachers' association, or whether it be a commission member for the Educational Policies Commission. Obviously, the type and variation in the realm of required leadership with regard to volunteers is almost

---

[12] In June, 1961, these two units were merged into a new agency, becoming the National Commission on Professional Rights and Responsibilities.

unlimited. Research minds are needed, as is the professional evangelist who can generate enthusiasm for constructive action.

The other major category of needed professional leadership for organizations is that of the staff member of such organizations. Certainly no professional organization can adequately function without a strong corps of both employed and volunteer leaders.

Let us consider some of the problems of staff leadership of professional organizations. One of the most important, if not the most important, function of staff leadership in a professional organization is to locate, nurture, and develop volunteer leadership from within the confines of the professional organization. And since this is such an important responsibility of the staff member of a professional organization, it is imperative that one in such a role be so secure himself and in his mind so thoroughly committed to the larger task before him that he is able to freely permit the aspirations of those who would be his subordinates or volunteer helpers to be fulfilled.

The whole matter of locating outstanding people to play the leadership role from among the voluntary workers is closely related to the need for establishing policies for any given organization. To be sure, this is true of every educational endeavor and institution, but it may be even more subtle in the case of educational organizations, since so often there is both distance and a time factor that may well interfere with the policy-formation process. At any rate, it is important to reflect on the idea that the policy of most educational organizations is made by the voluntary member in the field, and this means that the voluntary leaders are representing the wishes and desires of the constituency to whom they are responsible.

A policy is a reasoned procedure that affords the greatest promise for solving existing and anticipated problems. Policy formation requires the ability to identify, delineate, and anticipate problems. And this phenomenon requires a particular kind of mind. Therefore, a staff member must be very determined to lead in such a way that the time of volunteer workers responsible for policy is spent in policy formation. It is this policy forming that improves the chances for the decision makers, administrators, and leaders to make more productive and intelligent judgments in their day-to-day practical situations. Moreover, adequate policy will avoid the pitfall of inconsistency in decision making and will facilitate the type of planning that avoids exigencies of the moment to dictate the behavior patterns of leadership. In short, adequate policy should avoid crisis types of situations. Or, at least, it should cut down on the number of crises that arise in an institution or organization.

Developments in the last few years compel consideration of still another leadership role of teachers. This is the area of negotiation regarding salaries and working conditions. As indicated in Chapter 7, the 1962

NEA Representative Assembly adopted the resolution demanding that teachers must be given the legal right to participate in such negotiations with boards of education. This simply means that teachers have become more aggressive regarding the conditions under which they are to work. They are demanding the right to participate in the formulation of school board policy in these areas. Such participation opens up a relatively new role of leadership of great significance, requiring new insights, new concepts, and new techniques.

Summary

The trends in administration and supervision in educational leadership and in professional organizations are to provide larger roles of democratic participation in decision making by the total staff or group rather than by a few at the top. What do such trends imply for the competences that the rank and file of teachers must possess? The trends imply, first of all, an ever-increasing background of initial preparation. They imply that each teacher must be a skilled performer in his job. They imply that every teacher must be a well-rounded person, secure in himself, tolerant in his attitudes, and generous in his evaluation of his colleagues. Moreover, they imply the possession of great art in human relations and the process of group dynamics.

Satisfactory community relations are of great importance to the teacher. To secure good relations, it is advantageous for the teacher to get to know the child and the parent. Knowledge of the child may be obtained in part by reference to school records, but knowledge concerning the parents must come from actual contacts. Acquaintances with parents may be made through encouraging parents to visit the schools and parents' nights at the school, although they also may be made through social engagements in the community or by means of home visits. Home visits should be on a voluntary basis.

The teacher needs to work cooperatively with other teachers and other members of the school staff. The successful teacher takes a normal part in community affairs and makes an effort to become an integral part of the community in which he serves. The parent-teacher association is a valuable means for establishing satisfactory relations between the home and the school.

REFERENCES

BUCK, R. C., "Extent of Social Participation Among Public School Teachers," *Journal of Educational Sociology*, April, 1960, 33:311–19.

CHAMBERLAIN, LEO M., and KINDRED, LESLIE W., *The Teacher and School Organization*, 3rd ed. Englewood Cliffs, New Jersey: Prentice-Hall,

1958, Chap. 19, "Participating in School Administration," pp. 421–39; Chap. 21, "Engaging in Public Relations," pp. 460–86.

DYKES, A. R., "Democracy, Teachers, and Educational Decision-Making," *School and Society*, April 4, 1964, 92:155–6.

HILLS, R. J., *New Concept of Staff Relations*. Chicago, Illinois: University of Chicago Press, Midwest Administration Center, 1960.

LAUX, D. M., "New Role for Teachers?" *Phi Delta Kappan*, February, 1965, 46:265–8.

LIEBERMAN, MYRON, *Education as a Profession*. Englewood Cliffs, N.J.: Prentice-Hall, 1956.

LIEBERMAN, MYRON, and MOSKOW, MICHAEL H., *Collective Negotiations for Teachers*. Chicago: Rand McNally and Company, 1966.

LITTRELL, J. H., "When Teachers Evaluate Curriculum Study," *Educational Leadership*, December, 1964, 22:173–6.

NATIONAL EDUCATION ASSOCIATION, Department of Classroom Teachers, *Classroom Teachers Speak on Opportunity for Responsibility*. Washington, D.C.: The Association, 1966.

NATIONAL EDUCATION ASSOCIATION, National School Public Relations Association, *Public Relations Gold Mine*, 9 Volumes. Washington, D.C.: The Association, 1967.

————, *The Schools and the Press*, Washington, D.C.: The Association, 1967.

NATIONAL EDUCATION ASSOCIATION, National School Public Relations Association and Department of Classroom Teachers, *Public Relations Ideas for Classroom Teachers*. Washington, D.C.: The Association, 1964.

RAST, G. E., "Cooperative Teamwork in Administration," *Competent Teachers for America's Schools: Lay-Professional Action Programs to Secure and Retain Qualified Teachers*, Report of the Albany Conference. Washington, D.C.: National Commission on Teacher Education and Professional Standards, National Education Association, 1954, pp. 232–39.

RICE, A. H., "Teacher Unrest Has Damaged School Public Relations," *Nation's Schools*, March, 1965, 75:46–7+.

RICHEY, R. W., Planning for Teaching, 3rd ed. New York: McGraw-Hill, 1963, Chap. 6, "School and Community Responsibilities of Teachers," pp. 166–197.

SCHOOLING, H. W., "Teacher–Administrator Relations." *NEA Journal*, February, 1965, 54:32–4.

SOUTHWORTH, W. D., "Teamwork is the Answer: Teachers Seek a Bigger Voice," *American School Board Journal*, September, 1966, 153:65–6.

STINNETT, T. M., KLEINMANN, JACK H., and WARE, MARTHA L,. *Professional Negotiation in Public Education*. New York: The Macmillan Company, 1966.

Part Five
SAFEGUARDING
TEACHING
AS A PROFESSION

17: Professional
Organizations of Teachers

Young physicians do not face the problem of selecting a general professional organization to join; for them it is the American Medical Association. There is no competing national group. State, county, and regional organizations of doctors are integral parts of the American Medical Association. Beginning dentists and attorneys also have no problem of selection; nor do nurses, architects, and most other professional groups. To be sure, there usually are, in these professions, other special-interest associations or associations for specialists in the profession, but the national, all-inclusive association represents the total profession.

Young teachers, though, can easily be confused by the number of competing organizations in education. Teachers have not as yet achieved one all-inclusive, general national association that all those engaged in teaching in the United States belong to or recognize as "the organization" of the profession. And there are so many special-interest associations in education that the beginning teacher may find it difficult to make choices among them.

TEACHERS' PROFESSIONAL
ORGANIZATIONS

The Number of Organizations

No other profession comes even close to teaching in the number of professional organizations to which its members belong. According to the 1965–66 *Education Directory* (Part 4, "Education Associations") of the U.S. Office of Education, there are over 1,400 separate educational associ-

367

ations. Table 45 gives a listing by categories and numbers from the directory.

TABLE 45   *Education Associations*

TYPE	NUMBER OF ASSOCIATIONS
National and Regional Education Associations	586
College Professional Fraternities, Honor Societies, and Recognition Societies (National)	152
State Education Associations (all-inclusive organizations of teachers)	57
Other State-Wide Associations, usually affiliated with state education associations	537
Foundations (national and regional, primarily educational in purpose)	39
Religious Education Associations	53
International Education Associations	19
TOTAL	1443

Source: U.S. Department of Health, Education, and Welfare, Office of Education, *Education Directory, 1965–66.* Washington, D.C.: U.S. Government Printing Office, 1966, Part 4, "Education Associations," 133 pp. (issued annually).

There are some duplications in the directory listings, as some organizations qualify for listing in more than one category. However, it is safe to say that there are at least 1,200 educational membership associations. This does not include several thousand local education associations. The exact number is not known, but there are about 9,000 affiliated with the National Education Association.

This statement needs clarification. Of course, a teacher in one state will not likely hold membership in organizations in another state. On the average there are about ten associations per state (not to be confused with the all-inclusive associations that exist in every state, such as the Alabama Education Association), ranging from two in Alaska and Puerto Rico to twenty in Pennsylvania. Thus, five in each state would be the maximum number of associations a given teacher is likely to hold membership in (including his state and local education associations). At the national level a teacher might be a member of a much larger number of associations. The number of specialized associations in some fields is relatively large. Here are some examples: in the field of higher education there are 38 separate organizations; in administration there are 25 separate associations; 27 in the social sciences; 23 in secondary education; 23 in guidance and placement; 22 in business education; 20 for women in education; 16 in language arts; 16 in childhood education; 17 in research; 16 for librarians; 15 in journalism; 15 in physical education; 15 in teacher education; 13 in industrial arts; 13 in music; and 12 in history.

These are the fields with the largest number of separate associations. There are, of course, one or more specialized associations for all teaching levels and fields. In how many of these educational associations does a teacher, typically, hold membership? Naturally, the number will vary with the individual teacher, according to his interests and his teaching level or field. For example, an elementary school teacher probably will belong to his local education association, the state education association, the department of elementary education of the state association, the state unit of the Association for Childhood Education International, and the state department of classroom teachers. At the national level, the elementary school teacher probably will belong to the AFT or NEA, the Department of Classroom Teachers (NEA), the Department of Elementary-Kindergarten-Nursery Education (NEA), and the Association for Childhood Education International.

The secondary school teacher, typically, will belong to the local education association, the state education association, the subject-field department of the state education association, and the state department of classroom teachers. At the national level he is likely to be a member of the AFT or NEA, the Department of Classroom Teachers (NEA), and his special subject-field association (for example, the National Council of Teachers of English, if that is his teaching field). The total annual membership fees for the typical teacher would probably be about $75 and in some instances may be as high as $100.

The college teacher, typically, will not be a member of his state education association and the NEA, or the AFT and its local, although many do hold such memberships. He is likely to belong to a local chapter of his national subject-field organization and, frequently, to the department of higher education of the state education association. At the national level he is likely to belong to the American Association of University Professors (all-inclusive organization) and to one or more scholarly societies, depending upon his teaching fields. For example, a college teacher of science might belong to the American Association for the Advancement of Science, the National Academy of Sciences—National Research Council, the National Association of Biology Teachers, and the National Science Teachers Association.

Are There Too Many Teachers' Organizations?

The fact that there is such great diversity in numbers and types of teachers' voluntary associations in the United States is good evidence that there are differences of opinion on this question among the members of the teaching profession. One viewpoint is that ours is a pluralistic society, that one of our great strengths as a nation is that we respect and nurture individual differences. Those who hold this viewpoint contend that teachers ought to avoid a unified pattern, either of opinion or organization. Others contend that the failure of teachers to achieve one association to which all members of the profession can belong results in diffusion of strength and effort. As reasons for this view they assert that teacher groups sometimes pull in different directions, thereby wasting effort; that the strength of teachers as a group is often so diffused that little can be accomplished; and that the public tends to be confused by so many groups purporting to speak for the profession.

The overlapping that takes place in the 586 national and regional special-interest, teaching-field, or specialized organizations is not a serious handicap. Because of overlapping and duplication, these organizations may not be as effective as they could be, but no great amount of harm is done, because most of these groups do not purport to speak for teachers and for education in general. They may issue pronouncements about educational content and methods in their areas of special interest—and many of these pronouncements have great influence on education in their specialty, especially those of national groups—but they do not attempt to represent teachers before legislative groups or to speak for the profession in matters such as the need for improved provisions for sick leave, tenure, retirement, salaries, working conditions, and accreditation of teacher-education institutions.

It is the number of general educational organizations that causes serious concern. There have sometimes been several such groups working for different objectives before Congress and the various state legislatures. This, at least, has caused confusion and impaired achievement. A very natural position for a member of a legislative group to take is that he will not do anything until the teachers get together on what is desirable educational legislation. Somewhat the same reaction is often found in PTA groups, service clubs, and other civic organizations that are asked to work for educational causes.

Perhaps the most serious drawback of the multiplicity of general organizations of teachers is the confusion that is caused in the public mind. All these groups periodically issue statements regarding educational policies, and often these statements are at odds with one another. Unfortunately, the public cannot well discriminate between the recommendations of a group to which 60 per cent of the teachers of the United States belong and an organization that has but a few thousand members. Newspapers, radio, and television reports seldom describe the size or the general type of membership of the group making a recommendation; they simply give the name of the organization and describe its recommendations. Thus a group that is relatively unimportant in size or influence may secure wide publicity for a position that represents the viewpoint of a relatively small segment of teachers.

How Many Organizations Should a Teacher Join?

This is a difficult question to answer. This much may be said: Every teacher should belong to a local, a state, and a national organization that is general in nature and that deals with all kinds of pupil and teacher problems, and that seeks constantly for improved education for all American children and youth. It is desirable that every teacher and administrator should also belong to his special-interest or teaching-field association, such as the National Council for the Social Studies, the National Council of Teachers of English, the Association for Supervision and Curriculum Development, or the American Association of School Administrators. There is also an over-all organization for classroom teachers, the Department of Classroom Teachers, with which teachers belonging to the NEA should affiliate since NEA dues entitle them to such membership.

TYPES OF GENERAL TEACHERS' ORGANIZATIONS

Local Associations

The foundational or grass-roots general organization for teachers is the local education organization. Without teachers' clubs or local associations, state or national teachers' organizations would not be very effective. General recognition of this principle is reflected in the efforts of state and national organizations to keep their local organizations functioning effectively. They recognize that without strong support on the local level their own effectiveness is impaired.

The importance of local associations is fourfold: they are the instrument for concerted action for improving local school systems, they furnish membership and financial support for state and national associations, they give assistance in the campaigns and projects that state and national groups conduct, and they are the media by which the opinions and desires of teachers are channeled into the action programs of state and national associations. The stimulation of membership and the collection of membership fees through a national office are difficult. Both can be better accomplished by fellow teachers who are in daily association with each other.

Local groups and individual members are of great assistance in legislative campaigns. It is a generally accepted fact that members of Congress and of the state legislatures hear a whisper from back home much more loudly than a shout within the capital city.

Types of Local Associations. The National Education Association in 1946 listed the following types of local teachers' organizations: [1] county-unit type, city-unit type, county rural teachers' association, city or village with surrounding rural areas, and groups of villages or small towns.

With rapid changes in school-district organization and in other factors, the NEA's latest statement on types of local organizations reads as follows: [2]

Since conditions vary widely in the United States, there is no prescribed pattern of local organization required for affiliation with the NEA. It is for the teachers of state and local communities to decide the type or types of organization which will best meet local needs. Some communities prefer an all-inclusive organization; others prefer a department of classroom teachers, principals, etc., within the all-inclusive organizations; still others prefer a separate classroom teachers organization.

Activities of Local Associations. Local teachers' organizations have at least four objectives: social fellowship, better salaries and improved working conditions for teachers in the system, service to school and community, and general advancement for the profession.

In some communities the local teachers' club is largely a social organization, devoting most of its attention to teas, dinners, and other forms of fellowship. In few local associations is the social function entirely neglected.

This is an important function of local associations. Social events for teachers serve to unite the group and to make teaching a pleasant occupation. Moreover, as teachers become acquainted with one another, individual reserve disappears and sympathetic attitudes are developed for fellow workers. Teachers work much better together for the welfare of children and community and the improvement of the profession when they get to know one another outside the classroom. Yet the social function can be, and often is, overemphasized. The real effectiveness of a local group and its challenge to teachers to participate goes far beyond the social aspects. In fact, overemphasis upon this function tends to repel the serious, dedicated teacher who wants his professional group to be more than a club.

Local teachers' organizations seek to improve working conditions for their members. They conduct studies comparing local salary schedules and working conditions with those of other communities. Their members inform themselves regarding tax rates, budgets, and community ability to support schools. They seek collective action in these matters through professional negotiation.

---

[1] National Education Association, *Manual for Local Associations,* 1946 ed. Washington, D.C.: The Association, 1946.

[2] National Education Association, *NEA Handbook for Local, State and National Associations, 1967–68.* Washington, D.C.: The Association, 1967, p. 22.

Recent developments have added significantly to the functions of local teachers' associations. It is now common for such associations to serve as effective orientation agencies for new or beginning teachers in the local school system. Professional help and advice are provided for new teachers by their experienced colleagues. Another area of local-association work of great importance is the emphasis upon recruiting capable young people from the local school system to enter preparation for teaching.

Activities of Local Teachers' Associations

AIMS OF LOCAL TEACHERS' ASSOCIATIONS	To Promote the Professional Welfare
	To Contribute to the Cultural Growth of Members
	To Foster a Spirit of Good Will and Fellowship Among Members through Social and Recreational Facilities
	Social
GENERAL OBJECTIVES	Better Salaries and Improved Working Conditions
	Service to School and Community
	General Advancement of the Profession

Sources: David M. Hoffman, *Status of Voluntary Teachers Associations in Cities of 100,000 Population or More,* U.S. Department of Interior, Office of Education, Bulletin 1930, No. 36. Washington, D.C.: U.S. Government Printing Office, 1931, pp. 1–5; and T. M. Stinnett, *The Teacher and Professional Organizations,* third edition. Washington, D.C.: National Commission on Teacher Education and Professional Standards, National Education Association, 1956, pp. 89–90.

More and more it is being recognized that teachers have the desire and the ability to improve the communities whose schools they serve. Local groups often assist with such activities as UGF, Red Cross, blood banks, Boy and Girl Scout troops, recreation programs, and health projects.

Finally, local groups support state and national teachers' organizations in their drives for increased school funds and better professional standards. Teachers' clubs can be particularly effective with local members of the state legislature and Congress. Members of legislative bodies listen much more to their own constituents than they do to the most eloquent representatives of state and national organizations.

State Education Associations

Because public education in the United States is a function of the states, state education associations are in key positions to influence progress perhaps more than any other teachers' organizations. Certainly it may be said that the state education associations in partnership with the NEA have exercised key leadership roles, both in state and national legislation and in creating a public climate for educational purposes.

It is within the respective states that programs for the improvement of schools and the welfare of teachers must be largely achieved. State legislation can vitally affect progress in the public schools. Federal legislation has had great influence through the Morrill Act, the several vocational education enactments, the NDEA; federal influence will be greatly enhanced by enactment of 30 school laws by the Kennedy and Johnson administrations, 1961–1967. The impacts of the increased funds and special needs to which they are directed will be significant. State education associations are the cutting edge of organized efforts to bring about better schools, enriched services to children, and increased welfare provisions for teachers. They have been instrumental in securing steadily increasing financial support for public schools, for creating larger, more effective administrative school units, for securing general acceptance of the principle of equalization of educational opportunity, and for bringing about the enactment of improved teacher salary, tenure, and retirement laws.

The actual and potential influence of state education associations is reflected in their membership. Of an estimated 1,855,573 public school teachers in the United States in 1965–66, a total of 1,639,083 (about 90 per cent) were members of their respective state education associations. The National Education Association (NEA) is largely an outgrowth of the state education associations. Eighteen of these were in existence at the time of the founding of the NEA in 1857. The presidents of ten of these state associations joined in issuing the invitation to the meeting on May 15, 1857, at which the NEA was born.

The state associations combined enroll a much larger proportion of teachers than the NEA. The NEA depends to a large extent upon the state associations to further its membership campaigns and its various types of activities. Without the state associations the NEA would not be nearly as influential or as active as it is. All the states, the District of Columbia, and Puerto Rico have associations affiliated with the NEA. Table 46 gives the dates of organization of the state education associations in chronological order.

Rapid Growth of Membership. Before 1910 few of the state associations maintained staffs or permanent headquarters. Until that time they were principally concerned with the holding of annual conventions.

By 1967 all the state associations and those of the District of Columbia and Puerto Rico had a full-time executive secretary and staff, and virtually all owned their headquarters buildings.

Until well into this century, membership in the state associations was

TABLE 46   Dates State Associations Were Organized, in Chronological Order

State	Year	State	Year
Alabama	1840; Reorg. 1856	Maryland	1866
New York	1845	Georgia	1867
Rhode Island	1845	Nebraska	1867
Ohio	1847	Arkansas	1869
Connecticut	1848	Colorado	1875
District of Columbia	1849	Texas	1880
South Carolina	1850	Montana	1882
Vermont	1850	Mississippi	1884
Kentucky	1851; Reorg. 1852	South Dakota	1884
Michigan	1852	Florida	1886
Pennsylvania	1852	New Mexico	1886
Illinois	1853	North Dakota	1887
New Jersey	1853	Nevada	1888
Wisconsin	1853	Oklahoma	1889
Indiana	1854	Washington	1889
Iowa	1854	Idaho	1890
New Hampshire	1854	Arizona	1891
Missouri	1856	Louisiana	1892
North Carolina	1857; Reorg. 1884	Wyoming	1892
Maine	1859; Reorg. 1902	Utah	1892–93
Minnesota	1861	Oregon	1899
California	1863	Puerto Rico	1911
Kansas	1863	Massachusetts	1911
Virginia	1863; Reorg. 1905	Delaware	1919
West Virginia	1863	Hawaii	1921
Tennessee	1865	Alaska	1922

Source: National Education Association, *Handbook for Local, State, and National Associations, 1956–57*. Washington, D.C.: The Association, 1956, p. 212.

relatively small. Beginning in the mid–1920's it increased rapidly as is shown in Table 47.

The range in annual dues in 1967 of state and territorial associations was from $4 in Missouri to $96 in Puerto Rico. Forty associations charge a flat rate ($10 in ten states; $15 in seven states; above $20 in 18 states), while about twenty charge varying rates depending upon salaries, six of which charge 0.3 to 0.6 per cent of the teacher's annual salary.

Meetings. A rather common feature of state-association activity is the annual meeting open to all members. The states that are relatively small in area and population are able to do this on a state-wide basis, but in the states that are large in population and geographical area it would be very difficult to hold such a convention because of the long distances that many members would need to travel, the lack of large auditoriums, and

TABLE 47 *Membership in State Education Associations in Selected Years*

Year	Number of Teachers Employed	Number of Teachers Enrolled as Members	Per Cent Enrolled
1907	477,457	65,993	14
1916	553,309	188,730	34
1925	779,954	572,182	73
1930	907,625	697,775	77
1940	928,499	790,705	86
1950	967,602	856,502	89
1952	1,040,578	952,577	92
1960	1,468,502	1,317,696	93
1966	1,855,573	1,639,083	90

Source: T. M. Stinnett, *The Teacher and Professional Organizations.* Washington, D.C.: National Commission on Teacher Education and Professional Standards, National Education Association, 1953, p. 70; and National Education Association, *NEA Handbook for Local, State, and National Associations, 1966–67.* Washington, D.C.: The Association, 1966, p. 373.

the lack of adequate housing accommodations. In such states the trend is toward holding annual regional or district meetings in various parts of the state.

The annual meetings of state education associations have little part in the administration or government of most associations. In the states with large populations it would be impossible to get all the teachers together under a single roof. Even in the states with smaller populations the number of teachers is so large that it would be difficult to conduct business efficiently. Most state associations now have a delegate or representative assembly (comparable to state legislatures or the Congress) composed of representatives elected by the total membership, or the total membership of component divisions, to formulate policies and to act upon important items of business.

Annual meetings are designed to acquaint teachers with the conditions prevailing in schools generally, with trends in teaching methods, and with problems that need to be solved. A few sentences cannot possibly summarize all the activities undertaken by meetings sponsored by state teachers' associations. Smaller meetings of special-interest groups are conducted to discuss trends in content and methods in the subject fields or grade levels. Discussion groups on such professional problems as tenure, retirement, insurance, and working conditions are common. General sessions schedule outstanding speakers on a diversity of subjects.

Administrative Machinery. Delegate assemblies under varying names (delegate assembly, council, representative assembly, and house of delegates) usually establish policies and act upon important business affecting the association. The actual executive machinery is run by a board of directors elected by the delegate assembly, or by an executive committee named in the same way or chosen by the board of directors.

Personnel. The executive secretaries of the state education associations are the chief executive officers and they carry on the day-to-day administrative functions. They are assisted in some states by as many as thirty or forty full-time employees. Among the professional positions usually maintained are executive secretary, assistant executive secretary, editor, director of field services, director of publications, director of research, director of public relations, director of professional relations, and field workers.

The Services of State Education Associations. The services that the state education associations attempt to provide their members, of course, vary widely according to size, income, and other diverse conditions. These are common clusters of service that result from a common philosophy about the nature and purposes of a teacher's voluntary professional association. Corey has stated that there are five areas in which state associations should function:

1. Developing and maintaining high ethical standards.
2. Developing and maintaining high professional standards.
3. Developing and maintaining high educational standards.
4. Developing and maintaining high standards of community service.
5. Developing and maintaining high standards of working conditions for teachers.[3]

[3] Arthur Corey, "The Purpose of the California Teachers Association," *Competent Teachers for America's Schools: Lay-Professional Action Programs to Secure and Retain Qualified Teachers,* Report of the Albany Conference. Washington, D.C.: National Commission on Teacher Education and Professional Standards, National Education Association, 1954, p. 295.

Publications. All the state associations publish a journal, and several publish a newspaper. A subscription to the journal is ordinarily provided as part of the state association dues so that all members receive the publication. Early school journals were devoted almost entirely to discussion of school administration, teaching methods, school management, moral and religious instruction, and current educational news. More recently the journals have become the house-organ type, with a primary purpose of keeping the members informed concerning the activities of the association. Articles treating professional problems such as tenure, retirement, sick leave, salaries, financial support, and working conditions now share space with discussions of teaching methods and newer techniques of teaching.

Legislation. Legislation is a very important part of the program of every state education association. The action of the fifty state legislatures controls to a large degree education in the United States. This means that if the interests of the schools are to be adequately served, it is necessary for teachers to maintain an active representation during legislative sessions. The terms "lobby" and "lobbyist" sometimes carry bad connotations. However, the practice is well established in our democratic society, and teachers are as entitled as other groups to have representatives observe proceedings of the legislature, to attempt to influence the passage of good legislation, and to prevent the passage of laws that are undesirable from an educational point of view. Generally, the executive secretary or a designated member of his staff assumes this function. The state associations have greatly influenced the passage of legislation providing for more adequate financial support for the public schools. They have also been influential in opposing proposals to divert money from the schools to other agencies. On the whole, the legislative programs of the state education association have been kept on a high level in the public interest, and they have been extremely effective.

Fact-Finding or Research. Research is now a part of the program of every state association. At least twenty-five associations employ a full-time director of research. In the smaller states the executive secretary or some other professional employee performs this work along with his other duties. The department of research makes available facts relative to educational costs and other matters. Frequently the research division of state education associations is the source of the latest data on state school systems. The findings of these research divisions form the basis for formulation of needed legislation.

Field Service and Public Relations. Field-service and public-relations departments also exist in the larger state education associations. In most cases these are separate divisions. All state associations, except Nevada and Puerto Rico, maintain field-service programs. Twenty-nine associations have established field-service divisions. The purpose of the field-service division is to provide direct contact with the membership. The field-service representative meets with the local units or groups to assist them in carrying on their work. The public-relations division of state associations seeks to develop public awareness of the work and needs of the school.

Teacher Welfare. The improvement of teacher-welfare provisions is one of the most important services rendered by state education associations. The state associations attempt to help teachers receive more favorable consideration in the matter of tenure, retirement, salary, and working conditions. The teacher-welfare division of state associations also affords legal service or other assistance to teachers who have received unfair treatment from school boards. Through the efforts of state associations, teachers have often been protected from unfair dismissal or have been able to collect the full amount of their salaries as specified in the contract. Where a teacher, or a group of teachers, has a welfare problem, it is customary for the state association to furnish assistance upon request. This assistance generally includes a visit from a field representative, and it may include legal service. Frequently a field representative, meeting with the board of education and the aggrieved teacher or teachers, is able to act as an arbitrator and often works out a solution agreeable to both sides.

Professional literature is provided by some state associations. This is in the form of a professional library from which teachers may withdraw books on various phases of education. A few states maintain "reading circles" from which books may be purchased at reduced prices.

Other Services. Most state associations maintain, in addition to the broad areas described above, many other miscellaneous services for their members. Among these are such services as legal counseling on professional problems, group insurance, discount purchasing plans, library service, credit unions, educational films, radio programs, recreational camps or resorts, and homes or colonies for retired teachers.

Special-Interest Groups. To enable teachers with special interests to receive help with their problems, the various state associations encourage subdivisions, usually called departments. Common among such departments are those for superintendents, classroom teachers, high school principals, elementary school principals, and departments for classroom teachers for health and physical education, art, science, social studies, vocational education, foreign languages, English, mathematics, audio-visual education, business education, home economics, library, industrial arts, and music education. Most state associations will permit any legitimate special-interest group to be a department. These departments have their own constitutions, bylaws, and officers. Their work is largely financed by funds from the state association, although they sometimes collect a supplementary membership fee.

NATIONAL EDUCATIONAL ASSOCIATIONS

The National Education Association

The National Education Association of the United States, organized in 1857 and chartered by an act of Congress in 1906, is the largest teachers' organization in the world, indeed the largest of all professional organizations. In June, 1967, its membership exceeded 1,000,000, about 52 per cent of the employed public school teachers of the United States. There are affiliated with it about 55 state and territorial education associations and more than 9,000 local associations. The NEA is the all-inclusive, national professional organization of the teaching profession in the United States. Actually, the NEA is a confederation of affiliated state and local education associations. It numbers among its seventy-four departments, divisions, commissions, and committees special-interest or subject-field associations for almost every teaching interest.

History of the NEA

The National Education Association was founded in Philadelphia in 1857 as the National Teachers' Association. The organization meeting was attended by forty-three educational leaders representing twelve states and the District of Columbia. The meeting to form the National Teachers' Association was called by the presidents of ten state education associations as follows: New York, Massachusetts, Missouri, New Hampshire, Indiana, Pennsylvania, Vermont, Iowa, Wisconsin, and Illinois. The invitation to attend the meeting to form a national teachers' organization stated:

> The eminent success which has attended the establishment and operations of the several State Teachers' Associations in this country, is the source of mutual congratulations among all friends of popular education. . . . Believing that what has been done for states by state associations may be done for the whole country by a National Association, we, the undersigned, invite our fellow-teachers throughout the United States to assemble in Philadelphia on the 26th day of August, next, for the purpose of organizing a NATIONAL TEACHERS' ASSOCIATION.
>
> We cordially extend this invitation to all practical teachers in the North, the South, the East, and the West, who are willing to unite in a general effort to promote the educational welfare of our country, by concentrating the wisdom and power of numerous minds, and by distributing among all the accumulated experiences of all, who are ready to devote their energies and contribute of their means to advance the dignity, respectability, and usefulness of their calling. . . .[4]

[4] National Teachers' Association, *Proceedings, 1857.* Syracuse, New York: The Association, 1857, p. 11.

It is interesting to note that this national teachers' organization came after the establishment of similar organizations for at least three other major professional groups. The American Medical Association was formed in 1847, the American Pharmaceutical Association in 1852, and the American Institute of Architects in 1857.

Until about 1920 the NEA was largely a men's organization and was dominated by school administrators and college personnel. Between 1857 and 1866 its membership actually was restricted to men. In the latter year the NEA (then the National Teachers' Association) charter was amended to permit women to become members.

In 1870 the National Association of School Superintendents (now the American Association of School Administrators, a department of NEA) and the American Normal School Association (now the American Association of Colleges for Teacher Education, a department of NEA) merged with the National Teachers' Association to form the National Education Association. This merger, together with the existing membership of the NEA, made it an all-inclusive organization embracing in its membership the major segments—public school teachers, administrators, and college personnel—of the teaching profession. The two organizations merging with the NTA became the first two departments of the new association. Since 1870 additional departments, divisions, committees, and commissions have been added to the NEA structure, and now practically every professional interest in education is represented.

National Education Association service and office building, Washington, D.C.

In 1906 the NEA was chartered by an act of Congress, and its name was changed to the National Education Association of the United States. Not until 1919 did the NEA own its own headquarters building. A full-time secretary (Irwin Shepard) was employed in 1898. In 1917, with the election of J. W. Crabtree as executive secretary, permanent headquarters of the NEA was established in Washington, D.C., in two rented rooms. In 1919 the association purchased a four-story private residence at 1201 Sixteenth Street, N.W. (site of its present headquarters building), and converted it into an office building. In 1930 a seven-story building was added, and additional land and buildings adjoining the headquarters were purchased. In 1953 the NEA announced a new building program on the present site, which, when completed in 1962, formed a great national educational center for the teaching profession in the United States. Four executive secretaries have served the NEA since 1917: J. W. Crabtree from 1917 to 1935, Willard E. Givens from 1935 to 1952, William G. Carr from 1953 to 1967, and Samuel Lambert, the incumbent.

Previously it was stated that until about 1920 the NEA was largely a men's organization. In 1920 the association was reorganized along more democratic lines to provide for participation of all members in the determination of its policies. The Representative Assembly was created to provide representation from affiliated local and state associations on the basis of membership. Prior to 1920 NEA membership was relatively small, but, with the democratization of the organization, membership has steadily increased.

In 1961 the Representative Assembly, meeting in Atlantic City, New Jersey, approved an amendment to the NEA Bylaws to require that beginning September 1, 1964, "any person who is actively engaged in educational work of a professional nature" shall be eligible for active membership in the association only if he has an earned bachelor's, or higher, degree.

Membership of the NEA

The NEA has had, in recent years, a remarkable growth in membership. This is shown in Table 48.

Annual membership dues of the NEA are $15. This includes subscription to the *NEA Journal*, a monthly magazine published throughout the school year, and the general services of the association, including the services of the divisions, commissions, and committees, and in some instances membership in the department of one's special interest—for example, the Department of Classroom Teachers and the Association for Higher Education, neither of which requires dues beyond those required for NEA membership. Most NEA departments, as will be indicated later, require membership fees. The NEA has consistently advocated unified dues: one annual fee that covers membership in local, state, and national associations.

The NEA Representative Assembly

Like most state associations, the NEA is governed by a representative assembly. The NEA Representative Assembly contains about 8,000 members. Delegates are allotted to state and local associations on the following bases: local associations are allowed one delegate for each 100 of its NEA members or major fraction thereof; state education associations are allotted representation on the basis of one for each 100 members, up to 500 members (thereafter one delegate is allowed for each 500 NEA members or a major fraction thereof). The NEA Representative Assembly meets annually during the last week in June or the first week in July in a city selected by the Board of Directors. The Representative Assembly is a legislative body that establishes broad policies for governing the association.

The NEA Board of Directors

The Board of Directors interprets and puts into effect the legislation passed by the Representative Assembly. The board is composed of at least one NEA director from each state (states having more than 20,000 NEA members are allowed an additional director for each 20,000 members), nominated by state associations and elected by the Representative Assembly, and several ex-officio members. In 1967 the board numbered ninety-two members. The Board of Directors performs the following functions: approves bills incurred by the Executive Committee, appropriates from current funds the amounts of money authorized by the Representative Assembly for the support of the various units and activities of the association, determines the place of the annual meeting of the Representative Assembly, and elects four members of the Board of Trustees and two members of the Executive Committee.

There are two other executive bodies of the NEA: the Board of Trustees and the Executive Committee. The Board of Trustees consists of five members. Its duties are to serve as trustee of the association's permanent fund and to select the association's executive secretary. The Executive Committee consists of eleven members, four of whom are elected by ballot for two-year terms by delegates to the Representative Assembly, two are chosen by the Board of Directors, and five are the officers of the association who are ex-officio members. Major functions of the Executive Committee are to serve as the interim policy-making body between sessions of the Representative Assembly, to carry out the policies adopted by the Representative Assembly, to receive and print reports of committees, to fill vacancies in offices of the association, to appoint members of the NEA

TABLE 48   *Membership of the National Education Association in Selected Years*

Year	Number of Classroom Teachers in Public Schools	NEA Membership	Per Cent of Classroom Teachers Belonging to NEA
1870	200,515	170	0.1
1880	286,593	354	0.1
1890	363,922	5,474	1.5
1900	423,062	2,332	0.6
1910	523,210	6,909	1.3
1920	679,533	52,850	7.8
1930	854,263	216,188	25.3
1940	875,477	203,429	23.2
1948	860,678	441,126	51.3
1952	956,458[a]	490,764[b]	51.3
1955	1,169,298[c]	612,716[c]	52.4
1960	1,468,502[d]	713,994[d]	49.0[d]
1967	1,966,239[e]	1,028,456[e]	52.0[e]

Classroom Teachers
In Public Schools

NEA
Membership

Sources: Column 2 (with footnoted exceptions) is from U.S. Department of Commerce, Bureau of the Census, *Statistical Abstract of the United States,* 1951. Washington, D.C.: U.S. Government Printing Office, 1951, p. 112.

Column 3 (with footnoted exceptions) is from National Education Association, *Proceedings,* 1950. Washington, D.C.: The Association, 1950, pp. 366–71.

[a] National Education Association, Research Division, "Advance Estimates of Public Elementary and Secondary Schools for the School Year 1952–53." Washington, D.C.: The Association, November, 1952, p. 9.

[b] National Education Association, *NEA Handbook for Local, State, and National Associations, 1952–53.* Washington, D.C.: The Association, 1952, p. 31.

[c] *Ibid.,* 1955–56 ed., p. 25.

[d] *Ibid.,* 1960–61 ed., p. 305.

[e] *Ibid.,* 1967–68 ed., p. 386.

commissions and committees, and to confirm appointments to the NEA staff.

The Staff of the NEA

The executive secretary is elected by the Board of Trustees for a four-year term. There are over 1,100 employees on the staff of the NEA and its affiliated departments. The executive secretary is the administrator charged with the responsibility for directing and supervising the NEA staff proper—about 500 employees. In this he is assisted by a deputy secretary and six assistant executive secretaries who constitute the cabinet and who have general administrative supervision over major organizational areas of the NEA structure. The executive secretary also furnishes professional advice and leadership to the Board of Directors, Board of Trustees, the Executive Commitee, and to the profession.

The National Meeting

The Representative Assembly is the only national meeting held by the NEA. While it is essentially concerned with the conduct of business, some of the time is used for general speeches and for entertainment. Many of the seventy-seven NEA departments and other units also conduct large separate national meetings. The largest of these is the annual convention of the American Association of School Administrators, attended by about 15,000 persons.

NEA Units

The NEA organizational structure consists of seventy-seven units as follows: seventeen headquarters divisions, thirty-four departments, thirty-five committees and commissions, and one council. The divisions are permanent organizations, with full-time staffs, financed by the NEA. The eighteen divisions are those of Accounts, Adult Education, Affiliates and Membership, Business Service, Center for Instruction, Educational Technology, Educational Travel, Federal Relations, NEA Journal, Organization Relations, Press, Radio and TV, Publications, Research, Records, Rural Service, Special Services, and Urban Services.

As a general rule, NEA departments are independent organizations supported by the dues of their members and having their own executive committees as policy-forming bodies. Membership in NEA, in some instances, includes membership in departments (Department of Classroom Teachers, and Association for Higher Education), with no further fee required. For most departments, however, a separate membership fee is required. And, except for the two departments mentioned, only the executive committees are required to be NEA members.

NEA departments are created by the Representative Assembly to deal with some special phase of educational interest and concern. Most departments receive relatively small financial support from the NEA, being supported by dues from their membership, while two departments are supported entirely from NEA funds. The departments of the NEA, with dates of organization as NEA departments, annual dues, and membership as of 1966 are as follows:

ORGANIZATION CHART

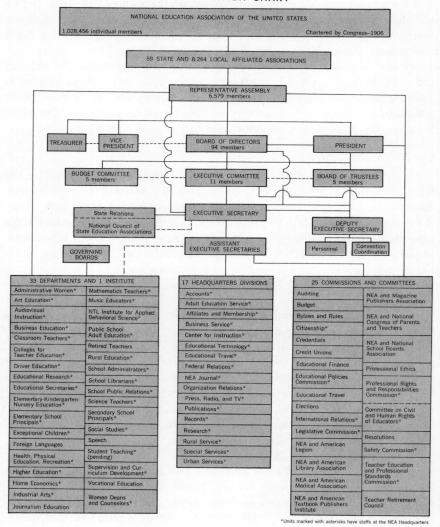

Source: National Education Association, *NEA Handbook,* 1967–68. Washington, D.C.: The Association, 1967.

American Association for Health, Physical Education, and Recreation (1937); $10; 49,000

American Association of Colleges for Teacher Education (1948); dues (institutional) $150 to $375 according to enrollment; 734

American Association of School Administrators (1870); $20; 18,000

American Association of School Librarians (1960); $6 to $50 based on salary; 9,000+

American Driver and Traffic Safety Education Association (1960); $5; 2,250
American Educational Research Association (1930); $15; 4,800
American Industrial Arts Association (1942); $10; 10,000
Association for Higher Education (1942); membership dues included in NEA
  membership; 22,300
Association for Student Teaching (1967); new
Association for Supervision and Curriculum Development (1929); $10; 14,820
Council for Exceptional Children (1922); $8.50; 26,000
Department of Audiovisual Instruction (1923); $10; 6,000
Department of Classroom Teachers (1913); dues included in NEA membership;
  includes approximately 85 per cent of NEA membership (changed in 1967 to
  Association of Classroom Teachers)
Department of Elementary-Kindergarten-Nursery Education (1927); $3; 4,000
Department of Elementary School Principals (1921); $12; 22,460
Department of Foreign Languages (1961); $5; 12,000
Department of Home Economics (1927); $2; 4,000
Department of Rural Education (1919); $5; 1,600
Department of Vocational Education (1875); no dues; no estimate of member-
  ship
Journalism Education Association (1939); $5; 1,300
Music Education National Conference (1907); $10; 53,797
National Art Education Association (1948); $10; 7,400
National Association for Public School Adult Education (1953); $10; 4,958
National Association of Educational Secretaries (1946); $7; 3,500
National Association of Secondary School Principals (1916); $15; 30,000+
National Association of Women Deans and Counselors (1918); $20; 2,500
National Business Education Association (1892); $8; 11,068
National Council for the Social Studies (1925); $9; 15,465
National Council of Administrative Women in Education (1932); $3; 1,800
National Council of Teachers of Mathematics (1950); $5; 43,000
National Retired Teachers Association (1951); $2; 180,000
National School Public Relations Association (1950); $10; not reported
National Science Teachers Association (1895); $8; 32,000
Speech Association of America (1939); $10; 8,000

Committees and commissions are created by the Representative Assembly to deal with special problems and are financed by the NEA. Usually committees do not have full-time staffs, but commissions do. The twenty-seven committees and commissions maintained by the NEA are: Standing committees (7)—Citizenship (1944), Credit Union (1940), Educational Travel (1959), International Relations (1920), Professional Ethics (1924), Educational Finance (1941), Tenure and Academic Freedom (1944). Joint committees (8)—NEA and American Legion (1921), NEA and American Library Association (1944), NEA and American Medical Association (1921), NEA and American Teachers Association (1928), NEA and American Textbook Publishers (1960), NEA and National Congress of Parents and Teachers (1924), NEA and National School Boards Association (1957), NEA and Magazine Publishers Association (1954). Convention committees (6)—Auditing, Budget, Bylaws and Rules, Credentials, Elections, and Resolutions.

The five NEA commissions are the Educational Policies Commission (1935), Legislative Commission (1920), National Commission for the Defense of Democracy Through Education (1941—changed to National Commission on Professional Rights and Responsibilities in 1961), National Commission on Safety Education (1943), and National Commission on Teacher Education and Professional Standards (1946).

The National Council on Teacher Retirement is the one joint council maintained by the NEA, although several of the departments have "council" in their titles.

Services of the NEA

A detailed description of the multiplicity of services provided for the teachers of the United States by so large and complex an organization as the NEA is impossible here. Only a skeleton outline of these services can be given. The titles of the divisions, departments, committees, and commissions listed above will indicate the general nature of their work. In general, the divisions of the NEA perform services of a general nature for the entire membership in broad designated areas. The departments are the special-interest associations, serving the major teaching-field interests and instructional areas, with services generally available to those who join the departments. It will be noted that, with few exceptions, every special or teaching-field interest of teachers is encompassed in the work of these departments. The work of committees and commissions deals with special problems or areas, and is available to the entire membership of the NEA. Some of the broad areas of service of the NEA, available to all members, are as follows:

Publications. The NEA and its various units publish more than a score of professional journals and more than two hundred other publications annually. These include books, research abstracts, pamphlets and bulletins dealing with special problems, and yearbooks. The NEA publishes more professional materials than any other educational organization in the world, totaling more than a half-billion printed pages annually.

Research. The NEA Research Division makes available to the profession up-to-date data on all phases of public education. Its studies have stimulated improvement in the field of teacher welfare (salaries, tenure, retirement, and sick leave) and school financing. In many areas the NEA Research Division is the only source of the most recent national data on education.

Defending Teachers. Both the National Commission for the Defense of Democracy Through Education and the Committee on Tenure and Academic Freedom serve to promote and defend the professional status of teachers.[5] They defend teachers who have been unjustly dismissed

[5] These two were merged by a resolution of the NEA Representative Assembly in July, 1961, into the National Commission on Professional Rights and Responsibilities.

from their positions, and defend school programs against unwarranted attacks.

Public Relations. One of the important services that the NEA performs for its membership is the creation of a favorable public opinion for education. Although all units emphasize public-relations work, the Press and Radio Relations Division is charged directly with this responsibility. This division provides a continuous flow of materials about schools to newspapers, periodicals, and radio and television outlets. In addition it produces an annual series of films for TV showings, which are televised by TV networks and hundreds of local TV stations.

Legislation. The NEA Legislative Commission works to achieve federal legislation affecting education that has been approved by the Representative Assembly. The Division of Legislation and Federal Relations helps in the formulation of legislative policy, analyzes legislation affecting the schools of the nation, and reports to the NEA membership on the implications of proposed federal legislation for the schools.

Teacher Welfare. A large part of the work of the NEA is devoted to improving welfare provisions for teachers and to improving their working conditions. Through continuous research and publicity the association has been instrumental in bringing about steady improvement, nation-wide, in the areas of teachers' salaries, tenure provisions, retirement provisions, and professional standards. The NEA Office of Professional Development and Welfare includes three salary consultants and a consultant on teacher welfare.

NEA Accomplishments

The NEA has been able to secure a great deal of legislation favorable to the schools. It has done this by assisting state and local associations and by working directly with members of the Congress. By encouraging and assisting its various units, the NEA has been instrumental in improving instructional methods. Through its commissions it has improved professional standards and working conditions. By sponsoring articles in general publications, it has helped to interpret schools and school needs to the public.

General Organizations of the NEA

Three units of the NEA serving the general organizational interests of teachers are the Future Teachers of America (FTA), the Student National Education Association (Student NEA), and the Department of Classroom Teachers (DCT). The latter is open to all classroom teachers who are members of the NEA, without additional dues. The FTA, as its name implies, is designed to serve high school students who want to explore the possibility of becoming teachers. The Student NEA is a professional organization for college students who are preparing to be teachers.

Future Teachers of America and Student NEA

The FTA organization was founded in 1937 under the leadership of Joy Elmer Morgan, who served as editor of the *NEA Journal* and director of the Division of Publications from 1920 to 1954. The founding of FTA grew out of the Horace Mann Centennial, and represents a joint project of local, state, and national education associations. The purpose of FTA is to provide exploratory, prevocational experience for high school students with an interest in becoming teachers. At the college level, the Student NEA provides an orgnization for teacher-education students to pursue mutual interests regarding their future profession and to learn the mechanics of professional organizations through active participation as student members.

The college units are called local student education associations. Members pay annual dues of $2 to the NEA, plus a similar fee to their respective state education associations. Individuals receive the *NEA Journal*, the journal of their state education association, and the *Student NEA News*; and copies of the *Student NEA Handbook*, the *Journal of Teacher Education*, the *TEPS Newsletter*, and other publications are distributed to the student associations. High school FTA chapters are chartered jointly by the NEA and the state education associations. Charters are issued by the NEA for a $3 charter-and-service fee and are renewable each year thereafter for a fee of $2. Each chapter regularly receives the *NEA Journal*, *The Future Teacher* newsletter, and a number of other publications.

In 1967 there were approximately 6,500 high school FTA chapters, with a total membership of about 250,000. There were, in 1967 about 1,000 local student education associations with a total membership of about 135,000.

The Department of Classroom Teachers

The NEA Department of Classroom Teachers comprises membership estimated at about 85 per cent of the NEA membership. As previously stated, its services and membership are available to any classroom teacher who is a member of the NEA. The department was created in 1913 and reorganized in 1922. Until 1941 it was a part of the Division of Elementary School Service, as the Division of Classroom Service. In 1941 it became a department of the NEA, with a full-time staff being added in 1942. In 1967, the name was changed to the Association of Classroom Teachers.

The Department of Classroom Teachers provides a medium for the mutual exchange of information and experience among classroom teachers. Its activities have provided superior in-service opportunities for teachers, and these activities have served as effective laboratories for the development of professional leadership. The department conducts annual regional conferences in six regions of the United States. It holds an annual national conference, following the NEA Convention, which is conducted as a college-credit, in-service workshop. These national conferences of the department are training grounds for future professional leaders. While there is no formal legal provision for such a practice, traditionally the NEA alternates the presidency among men and women. As a general rule, therefore, a member of the department becomes president of the National Education Association in alternate years, rising through the ranks as a result of participation in the work of the department.

In summary, the NEA Department of Classroom Teachers is the chief medium for teachers to learn and participate in the work of professional organizations, from the local association to the NEA and its affiliated international educational organization.

TEACHERS' FEDERATION

The American Federation of Teachers

The A.F. of T. was organized April 15, 1916, and affiliated with the American Federation of Labor May 9, 1916. A few locals, already affiliated with the A.F. of L., met in Chicago, drew up a constitution, and applied to the A.F. of L. for a charter as an international union of that body.[6]

Plan of Organization

The American Federation of Teachers consists of state federations in a majority of the states and approximately 600 locals in the United States and the Canal Zone. These units are affiliated with their state and local labor organizations. Groups of seven or more teachers in public schools or colleges may apply for charters. Dues in each local federation are determined by the members of the local, which must include local, state, and national affiliation. National dues per member, which are remitted by the local federation, average fifty cents per month. National dues entitle members to affiliation with A.F. of L.-C.I.O., subscription to the *Changing Education* magazine and the *American Teacher* newspaper, and services of the national office of the A.F. of T. The initial membership of the A.F. of T. in 1916 was about 3,000. In 1967 the A.F. of T. membership was about 140,000.

The governing body of the A.F. of T. is its annual convention. Repre-

---

[6] Material concerning the American Federation of Teachers was obtained from "Questions and Answers About the American Federation of Teachers." Chicago: The American Federation of Teachers, 1955, 10 pp. For a comprehensive history of the American Federation of Teachers, see *Organizing the Teaching Profession* (prepared by the Commission on Educational Reconstruction). Glencoe, Illinois: The Free Press, 1955, 320 pp.

sentation is apportioned as follows: each affiliated local is entitled to one delegate for the first 25 or fewer members, one delegate for each 25 additional members up to 500, an additional delegate for each 50 members beyond 500 up to 1,000, and one for each 100 members beyond 1,000. The administrative body, the Executive Council, consists of the president, who is a full-time officer, and sixteen vice-presidents. The president and vice-presidents are subject to election every two years.

Superintendents Not Admitted

The constitution of the A.F. of T. states that "this organization shall consist of associations of public-school teachers and of other educational workers organized in conformity with the provisions of this Constitution." Further provision is made for the admission, under certain conditions, of "associations of public-school principals, assistants to principals, heads of departments, or other supervising officers, except superintendents." The A.F. of T. contends that there can be no democracy in an educational organization that admits superintendents, because the teachers are afraid to oppose administrative officials. This, the A.F. of T. contends, produces in effect a "company union." The AFT Constitution was amended in 1966 to exclude administrative personnel from the "principal on up." The provision was not made retroactive.

Goals of the A.F. of T.

The long-range objectives of the A.F. of T., as stated in the publication cited above, are as follows:

1. To bring associations of teachers into relations of mutual assistance and cooperation.
2. To obtain for them all the rights to which they are entitled.
3. To raise the standards of the teaching profession by securing the conditions essential to the best professional service.
4. To promote such a democratization of the schools as will enable them better to equip their pupils to take their place in the industrial, social, and political life of the community.
5. To promote the welfare of the children of the nation by providing progressively better educational opportunity for all.

Other general objectives adopted by the A.F. of T. include federal aid to education for school construction, teachers' salaries, scholarships; adequate state aid to education, teacher tenure laws, compulsory attendance, and free textbooks.

Specific objectives to improve conditions for teachers are a starting salary of $6,000, reaching $14,000 in eight annual increments; better retirement pensions, including social security; adequate accumulative sick-leave pay, hospitalization and medical insurance paid from school funds; severance pay; and recognition of the rights of teachers to organize, negotiate, and bargain collectively.

The No-Strike Pledge

The A.F. of T. has often been commended for having a no-strike policy and the NEA condemned for not having such a policy. Actually, the positions of both organizations in the past have been somewhat ambiguous. A 1955 document of the A.F. of T. (cited above) declares:

The Constitution of the American Federation of Teachers contains a no-strike policy. There have been a few times when the members of locals have been faced with unreasonable and unbearable conditions and felt it necessary to vote a work stoppage.

There seems to be no reference to this policy in the current constitution of A.F. of T. A resolution passed at the A.F. of T. 1952 Convention reads, in part, as follows:

Whereas, we believe in a national no-strike policy for AFT; and whereas, locals are occasionally forced into emergencies with which they are unable to cope; and whereas this is a federation of unions designed for mutual aid and assistance in such emergencies; therefore be it resolved that . . . the national office offer its services and aid to such a local immediately and directly in accordance with the no-strike policy of the Executive Council adopted in December 1951.

Also, the 1958 Convention of the A.F. of T. adopted a resolution urging the repeal of state no-strike legislation for public employees, and for the enactment of legislation guaranteeing public employees protection against injunctions in labor disputes.

The foregoing statements do not indicate a categorical no-strike policy. They seem to say that strikes are not advocated but that they may sometimes be necessary. It is true that the NEA, until 1961, had no official statement concerning the use of strikes by teachers. Actually, the NEA has taken the position that it was not necessary for a professional group to state the obvious: that strikes are not an appropriate weapon for the professions. The executive secretary of the NEA in 1947, following a series of teachers' strikes, did put the NEA on record in opposition to the strike. But the NEA Representative Assembly did not formally adopt a resolution on the subject until 1961, a resolution made stronger by the 1962 Assembly.

The NEA 1961 and 1962 resolution, that part dealing with the strike, reads as follows:

The seeking of consensus and mutual agreement on a professional basis *should preclude* the arbitrary exercise of unilateral authority by boards of education and the use of strikes by teachers.

It would be as difficult to read a categorical no-strike policy into this statement as it would be in the A.F. of T. statements, although many, perhaps most, NEA members would so interpret the statement.

The words *should preclude* would seem to express the hope that teacher strikes will not happen or be necessary. Faced with the reality of an increasing number of teacher strikes, AFT in 1963 endorsed strikes "under certain circumstances." NEA in 1967, although not endorsing strikes, adopted a resolution to offer its assistance to affiliates that are on strike. Many people will find little difference between the two positions.

Professions and Unionization

The professions have seldom unionized their members or resorted to strikes. There are exceptions to both, for example, the American Newspaper Guild and the Musicians Union. Examples of strikes by the professions are the strike by about 1,000 doctors in Saskatchewan, Canada, in the summer of 1962, against the province's medical plan; and the strike petition signed by 200 doctors in a New Jersey community in the summer of 1962, if the Kennedy administration's medical plan became law.

Unionization is largely a characteristic of skilled, semi-skilled, and unskilled labor groups. The two major labor organizations in the United States are the American Federation of Labor and the Congress of Industrial organizations. (These two powerful, influential unions, the C.I.O. and A.F. of L., formed a merger in the spring of 1955, thus creating one unified organization of labor.) The first is a federation of guilds, that is, a federation of unions of specialized workers in given fields. Within a given industry like the railroads, for example, the A.F. of L. may have many separate unions. The Congress of Industrial Organizations, on the other hand, operates throughout an entire industry, such as automobiles, clothes, or electrical goods, with one over-all union.

Where does teaching stand with reference to the best type of organization for its members? Over all, teachers prefer the professional association to labor-affiliated federations, as membership figures will imply. However, in large cities there is a mixed picture. AFT holds representation rights in New York, Chicago, Cleveland, Detroit, Baltimore, Philadelphia, Boston, and Washington. The American Federation of Teachers was organized in 1916, and by 1967 its membership had grown to approximately 140,000. This is less than 15 per cent of the membership of the National Education Association, organized in 1957, and about 7 per cent of the total number of public school teachers in the United States.

Presently, NEA membership exceeds 50 per cent of the total number of public school teachers and is increasing each year by 40,000 to 50,000.

Strikes Not Acceptable

It has been previously stated that members of recognized professional groups rarely resort to strikes to obtain their demands. The labor groups, on the other hand, have used the strike with great effectiveness in securing higher salaries and better working conditions. But this is not a discussion of the ethics of strikes; such a subject should be considered elsewhere. This is merely an attempt to analyze the prevailing attitudes toward teachers' organizations.

Professional groups such as physicians, attorneys, and dentists hold that strikes may be all right for labor groups but, as a general rule, they are not acceptable for the professions. Their reasons for this attitude are that professional work cannot well be standardized, and that a strike would be unthinkable against people who are sick or whose welfare requires the constant personal service that professions furnish.

There would seem to be no reason to argue that the work of the teacher is as immediately crucial as that of the physician, dentist, pharmacist, policeman, fireman, utility worker, or nurse. It could be argued that a few weeks' delay in the services of teachers would have no permanent effect upon the growth and development of children. But a few hours of neglect of medical, nursing, or prescription services, or of absence from the job of a policeman, fireman, or utility worker, could easily cause serious impairment of bodily functions or even death.

Argued from this viewpoint, the question of strikes by teachers possibly becomes more one of policy than of ethics. Too, strikes by public employees are illegal in virtually every state.

There are, of course, strong arguments on both sides of this complex question. Both positions have advantages and disadvantages. Teachers' professional organizations have uniformly declared against the strike as a means of securing the adjustment of unsatisfactory conditions.

Yet there have been teacher strikes. It is estimated that there have been more than 140 in the United States since 1941. A rash of such strikes occurred in the school year 1946–47 in twelve states, involving about 5,000 teachers. The concentration of so many strikes in one school year probably may be explained by the impatience of teachers with neglect of the schools during the war years and with the apparent lack of evidence that the public attitude had changed after the war had ended. Apparently the long-suffering patience of teachers exploded in overt action. In 1946–47 teacher strikes occurred in Connecticut (Norwalk: actually this was not a strike in the usual sense; contracts had been signed, and teachers withheld service for eight days), Iowa (Coolville), Maine (Sabattus),

Minnesota (St. Paul), New Jersey (Hawthorne), New York (Buffalo), Ohio (Austintown: five strikes), Pennsylvania (Coal Township, East Conemaugh, Rankin, West Potts Grove, and Wilkes-Barre), Rhode Island (Pawtucket), Tennessee (McMinnville, and a lockout of teachers at Shelbyville), and Wisconsin (Muscoda).

The largest of these strikes was the one in Buffalo, involving more than 2,400 teachers. The smallest was the one in Sabattus, Maine, involving only one teacher, who got tired of being the teacher and the janitor, too.

The 1960–62 New York City strikes involved 40,000 teachers, not all of whom participated in the walkouts. Whether strikes will eventually come to be widely used by teachers is, of course, impossible to predict. Extreme conditions of hardship and unrest such as result from a callous attitude of the public toward reasonable economic returns for teachers in times of depression or rapidly advancing living costs, have impelled a growing number of teacher strikes in recent years. (For further discussion on this point see Chapters 7, 21, and 22.)

SPECIAL-INTEREST NATIONAL ASSOCIATIONS

In this section only a few of the national special-interest associations for teachers can be described. The ones in which beginning teachers are likely to be interested have been selected for description. (See pp. 416–17 for special-interest departments affiliated with the NEA.)

The Association for Childhood Education International

The ACEI, as it is called, is composed of members interested in the growth and development of children of ages two to twelve. The organization is largely made up of classroom teachers, although some principals and supervisors as well as a few parents are members.

There are about 100,000 members of the ACEI in the United States and foreign countries. There are three classes of membership: branch, international, and life. By far the bulk of the membership is composed of branch members who have joined a local group affiliated with the ACEI. There are some 3,000 international members, and only about 300 persons are life members of ACEI.

The ACEI official magazine *Childhood Education* is outstanding in articles on child growth and development, the needs of children, and effective teaching methods. *Childhood Education* is included in all life and international memberships. Branch members pay a subscription fee of $4.25, and all others $4.50. The ACEI publishes some thirty bulletins and other publications. Some titles are *Discipline; Kindergarten Teachers Portfolio; Continuous Learning; How Do Your Children Grow?;* and *Space, Arrangement, Beauty in School.*

The National Council of Teachers of English

The NCTE was organized in 1910 with the major purpose of improving English at all levels. Membership is open to persons interested in the improvement of English teaching, and includes elementary, secondary, and college teachers. In addition to publishing three professional journals for its sections—*Elementary English* (for elementary school teachers), *English Journal* (for high school teachers), and *College English* (for college teachers)—the NCTE publishes research studies, teaching aids, instructional materials in its field, and the journals *College Composition and Communication, Abstracts of English Studies,* and *Research in the Teaching of English.* It conducts regional spring institutes and holds an annual national convention. Membership fee is $7, including a subscription to one of the section journals. In 1968 membership was 41,595 and the number of subscribers 83,307, or a total of 124,902.

The American Council of Learned Societies

The ACLS is a federation of thirty national scholarly organizations concerned with the humanities and the social sciences. The ACLS was organized in 1919. Its purpose, as defined in its constitution, is "the advancement of humanistic studies in all fields of learning and the maintenance and strengthening of relations among the societies devoted to such study." Its membership is institutional rather than individual. The major portion of its support is provided by philanthropic foundations. There are approximately 70,000 members of its constituent societies; they are predominantly college teachers, but not exclusively. Qualifications for membership vary among the societies; in general, interest in or teaching the field are basic criteria, and some require certain scholastic attainment and recommendation for membership. The constituent societies, dates of founding, membership, and dues are as follows ("S" indicates that the society has student membership):

American Philosophical Society, 1743; 575
American Academy of Arts and Sciences, 1780; 2,000; $10 and $20
American Antiquarian Society, 1812; 218
American Oriental Society, 1842; 1,490; $10; S
American Numismatic Society, 1858; 1,575; $20.00 and $10.00 (associate)
American Philological Association, 1869; 2,000; $8
Archaeological Institute of America, 1879; 4,215; $15; S
Society of Biblical Literature, 1880; 2,362; $7.50

Modern Language Association, 1883; 24,500; $15; S
American Historical Association, 1884; 16,793; $15; S
American Economic Association, 1885; 15,229; $10
American Folklore Society, 1888; 1,750; $8.50; S
American Dialect Society, 1889; 520; $3
Association of American Law Schools, 1900; 115 (institutional membership)
American Philosophical Association, 1901; 2,546; $7.50
American Anthropological Association, 1902; 5,970; $12
American Political Science Association, 1903; 1,500; $15; S
Bibliographical Society of America, 1904; 1,379; $10
Association of American Geographers, 1904; 4,500; $15; S
American Sociological Association, 1905; 9,500; $20; S
College Art Association of America, 1912; 5,000; $15
History of Science Society, 1924; 950; $12; S
Linguistic Society of America; 1924; 5,305; $8; S
Mediaeval Academy of America, 1925; 2,207; $10
American Musicological Society, 1934; 2,200; $10; S
Economic History Association, 1940; 878; $6; S
Society of Architectural Historians, 1940; 3,100; $10; S
Association for Asian Studies, 1941; 3,500; $15; S
American Society for Aesthetics, 1942; 850; $10
Metaphysical Society of America, 1950; 700; $3
American Studies Association, 1950; 2,300; $6; S
Renaissance Society of America, 1954; 2,707; $8
Society for Ethnomusicology, 1955; 800; $5

The American Association for the Advancement of Science

The AAAS, founded in 1848, is considered the all-inclusive membership association in the fields of science. Its work and membership cover all fields in science. Its membership in 1968 was 115,000 and includes both professional scientists and laymen who are interested in the advancement of science. The purposes of AAAS, as stated in its constitution, are to further the work of scientists, to facilitate cooperation among scientists, to improve the effectiveness of science in the promotion of human welfare, and to increase public understanding and appreciation of the importance and promise of the methods of science in human progress. Annual membership dues are $12.00, including a subscription to *Science*, a professional journal published weekly. The AAAS is not only an individual membership organization but also a federation of 300 scientific societies, academies (including forty-six state academies), and other organizations. The AAAS publishes symposium volumes on science. It sponsors a Commission on Science Education which, during the past five years, has developed a program in science for elementary schools known as

Science—A Process Approach. The Commission sponsors annual seminars on science in cooperation with the American Association of School Administrators and publishes anually, with the assistance of the University of Maryland Science Teaching Center, a report of curriculum developments in science and mathematics. The 1967 report included 100 projects in other countries and 90 projects in the United States.

Modern Language Association of America

Founded in 1883, it is among the largest of the learned societies. Its membership consists largely of college teachers of English and modern foreign languages. Its basic purpose is to advance literary and linguistic studies in modern foreign languages. It is a constituent organization of the American Council of Learned Societies. In 1968 its membership was 25,000. Dues are $15.

The American Association of University Professors

Founded in 1915, it serves exclusively the interests and welfare of all college teachers and research scholars. It is, therefore, considered the all-inclusive or general professional organization of college teachers (much as the NEA is considered the general organization of public school teachers). Its membership in 1968 was 87,754; annual membership dues are $15, $12, or $8 depending upon salary. The AAUP is open to those with faculty status in a college or university, or to junior members ($3) who are ineligible for active membership but are graduate students. Administrators are eligible only for associate memberships. The AAUP defines and defends principles of professional ethics, academic freedom, and tenure for college and university teachers. It seeks to improve faculty salaries, stimulate faculty participation in college and university government, and defend members against unfair dismissal.

In activating its concern for academic freedom and tenure, the AAUP has no power in and by itself, but it can often secure significant results by means of publicity. It cannot investigate every case of apparently unjustified discharge or the muzzling of its members that is reported to it. But it can do so with the most flagrant cases. When a case is once chosen, a committee is appointed to make an investigation. Every possible bit of evidence is gathered. The professors' colleagues and students are interviewed and statements are taken from college officials. The committee then publicizes its findings. This is done through newspaper releases, as well as through the association publications. Institutions that violate tenure rights and academic freedom of members of their teaching staffs find themselves placed before the public in an unfavorable light. No college or university can stand very much of this because appropriations, donations, and enrollments may be adversely affected, and the institution may find it difficult to attract good teaching personnel.

INTERNATIONAL EDUCATIONAL ORGANIZATIONS

It is probably natural that educators should seek to unite in one organization all the teachers of the world. There have been a number of attempts of this kind.

The International Federation of Teachers Associations (IFTA), composed of elementary school teachers, was organized in 1912, and the International Federation of Secondary Teachers (FIPESO, from the letters of its French name) was founded in 1912. World War II left them in a seriously weakened condition. The World Federation of Education Associations was organized in 1923 at a conference called by the NEA in San Francisco. Sixty nations were represented in this conference. The primary purpose of WFEA was to bring together teachers from all nations for exchange of information about their school systems. Before World War II biannual meetings were held. During the war, meetings were suspended and WFEA has been inactive since. Under the sponsorship of the National Education Association, the World Organization of the Teaching Profession (WCOTP) was organized at Endicott, New York, in 1946. The WCOTP was regarded as the successor of the WFEA.

In the summer of 1952, IFTA, FIPESO, and WOTP merged to form the World Confederation of Organizations of the Teaching Profession (WCOTP). A fourth organization, the World Federation of Teachers Unions (FISE), including teachers largely from the Soviet Union and the Russian satellite nations, opposed the formation of WCOTP and took no part in its formation.

WCOTP membership consists of national, associate, and international members. A total of 148 national teachers associations belong to WCOTP, all with voting rights. There are 68 associate members consisting of regional, provincial state, local associations, and education societies which may send nonvoting members to the annual Assembly of Delegates. There are 3 international members of international organizations in education. WCOTP membership represents over 5,000,000 teachers in 95 countries.

Purposes of WCOTP are to foster a conception of education directed toward the promotion of international understanding, to improve teaching methods, to foster educational organizations and the training of teachers so as to equip them better to serve the interests of youth, to defend the rights and the material and moral interests of the teaching profession, and to promote closer relationship among teachers in different countries.

Summary

The purpose of this chapter was to present information regarding the various teachers' organizations, so that the beginning teachers might have valid bases for forming judgments as to the organizations that can best serve their interests. We live in a democracy where each citizen is privileged to make his own choice of associational groups. That is true of teachers. It is a choice reserved for each individual. The objectives, procedures, and organization of several types of teachers' organizations have been described in this chapter. Perhaps the following criteria, developed by the NEA Educational Policies Commission, will be helpful in the evaluation of national teachers' organizations.[7]

1. *Purposes*—The purpose of a national professional organization in the field of education is the maintenance and improvement of the educational service. In order to achieve this purpose, it is essential that there should be: continuous study and research with respect to the process of education, the conditions under which the process is carried on, the results achieved, and the means of its improvement; promotion of all movements which will give stability and professional character to educational undertakings; provision which will insure the continued professional growth of those engaged in the service of education; and the maintenance of such relations with the public as will secure economic welfare, social security, and civil liberties for those who serve the public in carrying on education.

2. *Membership*—Membership in professional organizations should be voluntary.

3. *Socio-economic activities*—A professional organization should be concerned with programs calculated to improve the quality of educational service. Although avoiding partisanship on general social questions, the national professional organization should call public attention to the educational aspects and implications of existing socio-economic conditions and of proposed social, economic, or governmental changes.

4. *Protection of members*—The national professional organization should define and publicize the civic and professional rights and obligations of teachers. It should also in certain important cases, investigate or assist state and local associations in investigating apparent infringements and engage in efforts to secure judicial rulings in defense of these rights.

5. *Branches of educational service*—The national professional organization should provide a department for each important branch of educational service. Membership in a department should require and carry with it membership in the general organization. The departments and affiliated organizations (to which latter group the requirement of individual membership may not apply) should be integrated thru representation in the governing machinery of the general organization or in some other effective way.

6. *Local, state, and national membership*—Membership in any local and state or territorial organization should, so far as possible, be made co-inclusive with membership in the national organizations so that membership in one would carry membership in the other.

7. *Lay organizations*—The national professional organization should welcome the active cooperation of lay groups in measures designed to inform the public on educational matters and to improve educational conditions. In no case should it enter into organic affiliation with any lay organization which has as its primary purpose the promotion of interests outside the field of education.

[7] National Education Association and Department of Superintendence, Educational Policies Commission, *A National Organization for Education.* Washington, D.C.: The Commission, 1937, p. 47.

REFERENCES

AHLERS, E. E., "Professional Affiliations," *National Association of Secondary School Principals Bulletin*, January, 1966, *50*:70–4.

American Federation of Teachers, Commission on Educational Reconstruction, *Organizing the Teaching Profession.* Glencoe, Illinois: Free Press, 1955.

CALIGURI, J., "Do Associations and Unions Have the Same Goals?" *American School Board Journal*, December, 1963, *147*:9–10.

CAPEN, SAMUEL P., "The Case Against Affiliation," in STANLEY, WILLIAM O., SMITH, B. OTHANEL, BENNE, KENNETH D., and ANDERSON, ARCHIBALD W., "The Educational Profession and Organized Labor," *Social Foundations of Education.* New York: Dryden Press, 1956, pp. 616–18.

CARR, W. G., "Assault on Professional Independence," *Phi Delta Kappan*, September, 1964, *46*:17–18.

EBY, KERMIT, "The Case for Affiliation," in STANLEY, WILLIAM O., SMITH, B. OTHANEL, BENNE, KENNETH D., and ANDERSON, ARCHIBALD W., "The Educational Profession and Organized Labor," *Social Foundations of Education.* New York: Dryden Press, 1956, pp. 618–20.

ELAM, S., and GARVUE, R., "Professional Organizations and Education," *Review of Educational Research*, February, 1964, *34*:101–11.

HUBBARD, FRANK W., "Teachers' Organizations," in HARRIS, CHESTER (ed.) *Encyclopedia of Educational Research*, 3rd ed. New York: Macmillan Company, 1960, pp. 1491–96.

LIEBERMAN, MYRON, *Education as a Profession.* Englewood Cliffs, New Jersey: Prentice-Hall, 1956, Chap. 9, "Education Associations," pp. 257–96; Chap. 10, "Teachers Unions," pp. 297–333; Chap. 11, "Collective Bargaining and Professionalization," pp. 334–72.

———, *Future of Public Education.* Chicago: University of Chicago Press, 1960, Chap. 9, "Teachers' Organizations: A Look at the Record," pp. 179–98.

———, "Some Reflections on Teachers' Organizations," *Educational Forum*, November, 1959, *24*:71–76.

"Local Associations; Symposium," *NEA Journal*, May, 1965, *54*:26–37.

"Local Associations Build Professional Strength; Symposium," *NEA Journal*, February, 1964, *53*:18–32.

MOSKOW, M. H., "Teacher Organization: An Analysis of the Issues," *Teachers College Record*, February, 1965, *66*:453–63.

NATIONAL EDUCATION ASSOCIATION, Department of Classroom Teachers, *Classroom Teachers Speak on the New Teacher and the Professional Association.* Washington, D.C.: The Association, 1964.

NATIONAL EDUCATION ASSOCIATION, Research Division, "All-Inclusive vs.

Restricted Local Associations; Teacher Opinion Poll," *NEA Journal,* December, 1965, 54:58.

————, "Status of Local Education Associations; Summary of Status of Local Education Associations, 1964–65," *NEA Research Bulletin,* May, 1966, 44:46–9.

NEWLON, JESSE H., "Local Conditions and Affiliation," in STANLEY, WILLIAM O., SMITH, B. OTHANEL, BENNE, KENNETH D., and ANDERSON, ARCHIBALD W., "The Educational Profession and Organized Labor," *Social Foundations of Education.* New York: Dryden Press, 1956, pp. 620–22.

RICHEY, ROBERT W., *Planning for Teaching,* 3rd ed. New York: McGraw-Hill Book Company, 1963, Chap. 8, "Professional Organizations and Publications," pp. 225–244.

STINNETT, T. M., *The Profession of Teaching.* Washington, D.C.: Center for Applied Research in Education, Inc., 1962.

————, "Qualifications for Membership in Education Associations," *Journal of Teacher Education,* December, 1958, 9:338–39.

————, KLEINMANN, JACK H., and WARE, MARTHA L., *Professional Negotiation in Public Education.* New York: The Macmillan Company, 1966.

U.S. DEPARTMENT OF HEALTH, EDUCATION AND WELFARE, Office of Education, *Education Directory, 1965–66.* Washington, D.C.: U.S. Government Printing Office, 1966, Part IV, "Education Associations," Part III, "Higher Education."

WEAVER, J. F., "Professional Organizations and Education," *Review of Educational Research,* February, 1967, 37:50–6.

18: The Professional Education of Teachers

*F*oremost among the factors to which any profession must give interest and sustained attention is that of programs for the preparation of its members. Virtually the exclusive route into all professions now is the completion of prescribed college and university curricula and, for most professions, the passing of an examination for licensure. Except for teaching, both the prescribing of curricula and the administration of the examination are vested wholly or largely in the respective professions.

In the early part of this century, admission to practice in the professions was gained through a combination of informal study, usually in the office of a licensed practitioner, an internship under a licensed practitioner, and an examination for licensure. There are still some remnants of these and other informal procedures remaining for a few professions in some states, but they are fast disappearing; and for all practical purposes the main requirement is completion of prescribed courses in professional preparation in higher education, that is, courses in addition to those required for a liberal-arts degree.

The reasons for this development are two. First, the members of any profession must possess certain knowledges, skills, and techniques not possessed by members of any other occupational group. Of course, there are many commonalities of knowledge, but these areas are unique to a given profession. Second, the professions have learned from long experience that the only way—if not the only way, certainly the most effective way—to assure that persons admitted to practice are competent is through a formal, rigorous, scholarly, prescribed program of preparation. This is why any profession must be constantly concerned with the collegiate and university programs that prepare its members. It is the only way that reasonable standards can be enforced for admission to practice, and it is the only way the members of a recognized profession can be protected from the competition of unqualified persons.

The same conditions pertain to teaching, and the reasons given above indicate why the professional education of teachers is of prime concern to every member of the profession, and why this chapter is placed in the section of this book that deals with protecting and safeguarding the profession.

THE EVOLUTION OF TEACHER EDUCATION IN THE UNITED STATES

Special preparation for teachers was extremely slow in developing in the United States. Two centuries elapsed between the time Massachusetts ordered schools to be established and the time the state founded its first school for preparing teachers. This was due partly to the slowness in developing schools and the long period during which only a small proportion of children received any schooling at all. During the philanthropic period of education, schools were almost entirely private or church-administered. This period extended, alongside the emerging free schools, from the founding of the country to the establishment of state systems of public schools, roughly from 1607 to 1830. Once schools began to be made available to all children through the common schools (the free public schools), the need for special training for teachers became a pressing problem. Prior to this time the traditional concept was that the only qualifications a good teacher needed were knowledge of the subject matter to be taught and the physical strength to enforce discipline. Not only was this concept held true of teaching in the lower schools, but it also applied to medical schools, engineering schools, and other professional schools.

The concept of the low status of teaching as a profession is reflected in a recommendation in 1850 of the Committee of Education of the Massachusetts Legislature to abolish the normal schools:

Academies and high schools cost the Commonwealth nothing; and they are fully adequate to furnish a competent supply of teachers. . . . Considering that our district schools are kept, on the average, for only three or four months in the year, it is obviously impossible, and perhaps it is not desirable, that the business of keeping these schools become a distinct and separate profession, which the establishment of the normal schools seem to anticipate.[1]

The founding of the first normal school at Lexington, Massachusetts,

[1] Charles A. Harper, *A Century of Public Teacher Education*. Washington, D.C.: American Association of Teachers Colleges, National Education Association, 1939, pp. 35–36.

marks the first public institution dedicated exclusively to the preparation of teachers. Horace Mann, who had studied normal schools in Germany and the work of the German teachers, was instrumental in the founding of the Lexington normal school. Back of the founding of this school was a growing dissatisfaction, beginning about 1825, with a system that seemed to concentrate upon high-quality education in private schools for the well-to-do and neglect of schools for the masses. In the latter, the common schools, where three-fourths of the children got their only chance at schooling, conditions in the schools were growing worse rather than better; sessions were for three or four months a year, poorly attended, and teachers were woefully unprepared for their tasks. The growing dissatisfaction is reflected in the writings of the period and in certain other developments. In 1823 a private academy for the preparation of teachers was opened in Concord, Vermont. Here Samuel R. Hall began his famous series of lectures on "school keeping," later incorporated into a book, *Lectures on School Keeping*, which became a standard text in the normal schools.[2] Also in 1823 Governor Dewitt Clinton of New York recommended to the legislature that it concern itself with finding a source of competent teachers. In the same year Thomas H. Gallaudet proposed that an institution be established in every state for training teachers. The writing of James G. Carter had such influence that he came to be called the "Father of the American Normal School." The establishment of a state-controlled system of education in Prussia in 1819 eventually led to the development of normal schools to provide teachers. The success of the Prussian and French normal schools had much to do with their founding in the United States. Horace Mann made a crusade of establishing the normal schools. At the dedication of one of them, he said:

I believe Normal Schools to be a new instrumentality in the advancement of the race. I believe that without them, Free Schools themselves would be shorn of their strength and their healing power and would at length become mere charity schools and thus die out in fact and in form. Neither the art of printing, nor the trial by jury, nor a free press, nor free suffrage, can long exist, to any beneficial and salutary purpose, without schools for the training of teachers; for, if the character and qualifications of teachers be allowed to degenerate, the Free Schools will become pauper schools, and the pauper schools will produce pauper souls, and the free press will become a false and licentious press, and ignorant voters will become venal voters, and through the medium and guise of republican forms, an oligarchy of profligate and flagitious men will govern the land; nay, the universal diffusion and ultimate triumph of all-glorious Christianity itself must await the time when knowledge shall be diffused among men through the instrumentality of good schools. Coiled up in this institution, as in a spring, there is a vigor whose uncoiling may wheel the spheres.[3]

[2] *Ibid.*, pp. 12–14.
[3] As quoted in Charles A. Harper, *op. cit.*, pp. 21–22.

So the first normal schools were born by an act of the Massachusetts Legislature, signed by the governor on April 19, 1839, authorizing the establishment of three schools, with an appropriation of $10,000 to match a similar sum provided by a private donor. This was the beginning of teacher education as a professional process in the United States. The normal schools spread rapidly. By 1860 twelve such schools had been founded (see Table 49). Several normal-school departments had been

TABLE 49   *Normal Schools Established as of 1860*

Place	Date Opened
Lexington, Massachusetts*	July 3, 1839
Barre, Massachusetts	September 4, 1839
Bridgewater, Massachusetts	September 9, 1840
Albany, New York	December 18, 1844
New Britain, Connecticut	May 15, 1850
Ypsilanti, Michigan	March 29, 1853
Salem, Massachusetts	September 13, 1854
Providence, Rhode Island	May 29, 1854
Trenton, New Jersey	October 1, 1855
North Bloomington, Illinois	October 5, 1857
Millersville, Pennsylvania	December, 1859
Winona, Minnesota	September 3, 1860

Source: Charles A. Harper, *A Century of Public Teacher Education*. Washington, D.C.: American Association of Teachers Colleges, National Education Association, 1939, p. 8.

* Moved to West Newton, Massachusetts, in September, 1844, and moved again to Framingham in 1853.

organized in high schools, and a normal department had been established at the University of Iowa.

Normal-school students were graduates of the district (common) schools, and few, if any, were denied admission. Instruction was in the elementary school subjects that they were to teach, plus study of the principles of teaching. Students attended for a few weeks or months.

The period between 1860 and 1890 brought rapid increases in the number of normal schools. By 1895 there were probably as many as 350 private and public normal schools.[4] And by this date the normal schools had become recognized as institutions for the chief source of teachers for the common schools. Still these institutions were a hodgepodge of types and

[4] Newton Edwards and Herman G. Richey, *The School in the American Social Order*. Boston: Houghton Mifflin Company, 1947, p. 777.

differing practices. Some were normal departments of high schools; some were one-year colleges, some two-year colleges; and some were simply normal departments of universities; but their offerings were still predominantly at the secondary school level. The importance of their development cannot be minimized, however. Their establishment represented a break with tradition and the first evolutionary step in the emergence of teacher education as a recognized professional endeavor, the beginning of the acceptance of education as a discipline and teacher education as a part of the mainstream of higher education. As such, then, they symbolized also the beginning of the emergence of teaching as a recognized and respected profession.

EMERGENCE OF TEACHERS COLLEGES

After 1890 the normal schools began slowly to evolve into degree-granting teachers colleges. And this movement marked a struggle to convert the teacher-preparing institutions from secondary schools to ones of higher education caliber. The period of transformation lasted, roughly, from 1890 to 1950, when another transformation was in full swing; the conversion of state teachers colleges to state general colleges. Then during the 1950's another transitional step got under way: many of the state colleges became state universities.

Many factors influenced the change of normal schools to degree-granting teachers colleges. Among these were the growing demands for more education, the rapid growth of public high schools, the rise of accrediting associations, which enforced higher standards for high school teachers, and the need to keep the educational level of teachers above that of the general population. In 1895, at the summit of the normal-school era, only 37 per cent of the staffs of these institutions held degrees,[5] which indicates the great struggle the succeeding teachers colleges had to lift themselves on a par with recognized colleges. Actually, the conversion of normal schools to state teachers colleges began in 1882, when the state teachers college at Livingston, Alabama, was created. Four state teachers colleges, according to Hughes,[6] began as such, and did not evolve from normal schools. Hughes found that 139 normal schools became state teachers colleges between 1881 and 1950.[7] The switch did not really gain momentum until 1920, while 69 transitions occurred in the succeeding decade. Beginning in 1930, while the conversion from normal schools to teachers colleges was in full swing, the latter began the change to state colleges. From

[5] *Ibid.*, p. 285.
[6] Rees H. Hughes, "Changing Status of Teacher Education Institutions," *Journal of Teacher Education*, March, 1951, 2:48–52.
[7] *Ibid.*, p. 48.

1930 to 1950 a total of 33 became state colleges, and from 1950 to 1960 a total of 73 state teachers colleges became state colleges or universities. In 1967 only 9 public and 11 private teachers colleges were in existence.[8]

PROFESSIONAL EDUCATION IN COLLEGES AND UNIVERSITIES

The emergence of professional education in the universities was also slow to begin and gradual in development. The first efforts were in the East, but it was in the West that the practice really took hold. New York University established a chair of the philosophy of education "for educating teachers for the common school" in 1832, but it was short-lived.[9] A normal department was instituted at Brown University in 1850, but was dropped when the state of Rhode Island established a normal school in 1854. In the East the established colleges and universities were satisfied to leave the preparation of teachers for public schools to the normal school. But in the West, where the founding of the normal school was slower, there developed early pressures upon the state universities to supply trained teachers. Normal departments or classes were established at the University of Indiana in 1852, the University of Iowa in 1855, the University of Wisconsin in 1856, the University of Missouri in 1868, the University of Kansas in 1876, and in 1881 at the state universities of Utah, North Dakota, and Wyoming. Some of these subsequently discontinued the work temporarily when state normal schools were established in their states, but later resumed the work.[10] And then departments, classes, or chairs in education rapidly evolved in schools or colleges of education in the universities. Liberal-arts colleges also began establishing departments of education. Thus, by 1967, there were 1,200 institutions of higher education maintaining schools, colleges, or departments of education, or offering approved programs of teacher education. Included in the 1,200 were 299 universities (146 public and 153 private); 808 general or liberal-arts colleges (207 public and 601 private); 20 teachers colleges (9 public and 11 private); and 71 teacher preparatory schools of other types.

From the above figures, it is clear that the low estate of professional preparation of teachers, which existed throughout the normal-school period, has evolved into a respected and recognized endeavor of all types of higher-education institutions.

[8] T. M. Stinnett, *A Manual on Certification Requirements for School Personnel in the United States,* 1967 edition. Washington, D.C.: National Commission on Teacher Education and Professional Standards, National Education Association. 1967.

[9] Edwards and Richey, *op. cit.,* p. 786.

[10] *Ibid.,* p. 787.

CURRENT STATUS OF TEACHER EDUCATION

Among the 1,200 colleges and universities that are now engaging in teacher education there are, naturally, varied programs for the preparation of teachers. Much of the recent criticism of teacher education stems from such wide variations and from the fact that in isolated cases the requirements in education courses, as compared to academic courses, have been found to be excessive. These criticisms, which have implied that excessive requirements in methodology were typical, have been difficult to answer because data were lacking. In 1959, for the working papers of the Kansas Conference, the National TEPS Commission was able to profile offerings of 294 institutions accredited by the NCATE. The analysis [11] includes the following information:

Type of Institution	Number of Institutions
Institutions primarily teacher preparatory (teachers colleges)	72
Liberal-arts colleges	112
Universities with two or more professional schools	102
Unclassified institutions	8
TOTAL	294

For the first time on so large a scale—a sampling comprehensive enough to suggest typical practices—a true national picture was available.

Table 50 (p. 411) reflects a composite of the 294 programs, as to the basic requirements in professional education, general education, and specialization in a teaching field.

According to the data in Table 50, the 294 institutions tend to require (in the bachelor's-degree program of 120–124 hours) about 46 semester hours in general education for both elementary and secondary school teachers, with a range from 11 to 97 hours. The course work in general education includes English and communication arts, the humanities, social studies, the physical and biological sciences, religion and philosophy, physical education, American history, general psychology, foreign languages, and literature. All institutions do not include all of these areas in their required general-education work, but these are the basic ones from which specific requirements are derived.

For the teaching field or subject requirements—specialized education—the median requirements of the 294 institutions range from 25 semester

[11] For the complete analysis of the 294 institutions, see National Education Association, National Commission on Teacher Education and Professional Standards, *The Education of Teachers: Curriculum Programs,* Report of the Kansas Conference. Washington, D.C.: The Association, 1959, pp. 173–92.

TABLE 50 *Composite of Central Tendencies and Ranges of Semester-Hour Requirements in the Teacher-Education Programs of NCATE-Accredited Institutions*

	PROGRAMS FOR ELEMENTARY TEACHERS				TOTAL NUMBER OF INSTITUTIONS REPORTING	PROGRAMS FOR SECONDARY TEACHING MAJORS		TOTAL NUMBER OF INSTITUTIONS REPORTING
	Mean	Median	Mode	Range		Median	Range	
Professional education	34.8	34	36	18–68	287	23	10–51	275
General education*	—	46	—	11–97	292	46	11–97	292
Teaching major								
Agriculture						43	24–99	58
Art						36	12–93	207
Business						36	18–75	215
English						30	18–64	249
Foreign languages						25	18–68	210
History						30	18–64	155
Home economics						40	24–78	189
Industrial arts						37	18–79	149
Mathematics						27	18–64	251
Music						40	24–99	227
Physical education						34	18–99	221
Science						31	18–81	257
Social science						35	18–62	152

Source: National Education Association, National Commission on Teacher Education and Professional Standards, *The Education of Teachers: Curriculum Programs,* Report of the Kansas Conference. Washington, D.C.: The Commission, 1959, p. 178.
* Report is for elementary and secondary teachers.

hours in foreign languages to 43 in agriculture. The study also threw needed light on the oft-repeated charge that most or too much of teacher preparation was in methods courses (education). This analysis found that the median requirements of these 294 institutions in professional courses for elementary school teachers was 34 semester hours, the range being from 18 to 69, with only three institutions requiring 60 hours or above; 85 required below 30 hours, and 154 required from 30 to 40 hours.

For high school teachers the median requirement in professional courses was 23 semester hours; the range was from 10 to 51 semester hours, the latter required in only one institution. About 85 per cent of the institutions required from 15 to 30 hours. The professional work for elementary school teachers contained three main clusters: special methods (median requirement, 8 semester hours), student teaching (median requirement, 8 semester hours), and professional content courses (median requirement, 6 semester hours). The other courses for elementary school teachers tended to be three-hour courses in such subjects as curriculum, guidance, history and philosophy of education, human development, general methods, and orientation to education. For high school teachers the largest single cluster was student teaching or laboratory experience, the median requirement being 6 semester hours. Other courses required by a preponderance of the institutions, typically 3 semester hours each, were: history and philosophy of education (216 institutions), psychology (228 institutions), general methods (126 institutions), special methods (124 institutions), human development (84 institutions), orientation to education (82 institutions), and measurement and evaluation (67 institutions).

Student Teaching Requirements

The 294 institutions, as a typical practice, conducted student teaching off campus, with the use of a combination of off-campus and campus schools as the second most-used procedure, and the exclusive use of campus schools as the least-used procedure.

As to the length of the student practice period, the practice most commonly used was a semester, less a few weeks for orientation and examination (fifteen to nineteen weeks). The second most-used period was from five to nine weeks, as a trisemester, bisemester, or quarter period. The student teaching period tended to use the five-day week and three hours each day.

THE CRITICISMS OF TEACHER EDUCATION

Since the establishment of the normal schools for the preparation of teachers for the common schools, there have been severe critics of teacher education as such. So long as the normal schools and their successors, the state teachers colleges, were restricted to the preparation of elementary school teachers, the critics were not unduly concerned or alarmed; they were for the most part only indifferent to or contemptuous of these institutions and their programs. But when they entered the field of preparing high school teachers, the feuding between the liberal arts and education professors began to emerge into the open and to appear in the public prints.

With the close of World War II, during the decade 1950–1960, and especially after Russia threatened the security of the United States with the launching of the sputniks in 1957, the feud became intense and bitter. Here was internecine warfare at its bitter best (or worst). Education was split into hostile camps, with the professors of the academic fields in one group and the professors of education in the other. The elementary and secondary school teachers and administrators in the beginning were innocent bystanders. They could not, however, remain so for long, because the attacks were aimed at what the critics called their inferior preparation and, as a consequence, their incompetence. Eventually they were ranged alongside the professors of education.

What was the essence of the differences, the cause of the feuding? This question can be answered in a sentence, but that would be an oversimplification. Boiled down to a common denominator, the fighting was over the content of teacher education: whether there should be any professional courses, and if so, how many. Involved in this, of course, are many philosophic and pragmatic viewpoints. On the one hand, many college people believe that a broad liberal education is the only justifiable content in the education of teachers, that inclusion of professional courses is unnecessary and inevitably dilutes the real education of teachers. Many of the members of both camps took a middle ground. This middle-ground position acknowledged that the teacher must be broadly and liberally educated, but he must be more—he must be prepared professionally; and that there are serious weaknesses in existing programs of teacher education, but the solution is a remedial one, not abandonment. The middle grounders, the moderates, seem to be on the road to a reconcilement of the struggle, which the extremists were unable to effect. Beginning in 1958, eight large and influential associations of the scholars and of professional education joined with the National Commission on Teacher Education and Professional Standards in sponsoring a series of three cooperative national conferences in an effort to work together toward strengthening the education of teachers.[12]

[12] For reports of these three conference, see *The Education of Teachers: New Perspectives*, 1958, *The Education of Teachers: Curriculum Programs*, 1959, and *The Education of Teachers:* Certification, 1960, Reports of the Second Bowling Green,

Concurrently, many of the scholarly societies began to concern themselves with the refinement of the secondary school curriculum and with the improvement of the preparation of high school teachers in their respective fields. These efforts point toward growing partnership endeavors to upgrade teacher education, and toward an ending of the long-time warring over the problem.

Some of the expected and hoped-for outcomes of these joint efforts are indicated in the following section.

EMERGING TRENDS IN TEACHER EDUCATION

In what direction is teacher education heading? What are probable future trends and developments in the process? The following seem to be pretty well defined or in prospect.

1. There will be teacher education as such. There appears to be little or no evidence to support the idea that the professional preparation of teachers will be abandoned. There will be many changes made in existing patterns, but they will be changes to improve the quality. Chiefly these changes will center on strengthening the academic, or liberal, education of teachers, strengthening the content and instruction in professional courses, upgrading the teaching field preparation, updating the content in the teaching fields of experienced teachers, and more rigorous selection of candidates for teacher education.

2. There will be professional units—departments, schools, or colleges of education—in all institutions recognized for the preparation of teachers. The fight to establish and gain recognition for these units has been a long and bitter one. As long as teacher education was confined largely to the single-purpose teachers colleges, the resistance to recognition of these units continued. Now that teacher education is becoming a function of all types of higher-education institutions, the need for retaining and strengthening such units is receiving increasing support.

3. Teacher education will increasingly become a matter of all-institution concern. The trend toward this practice is a significant one. One of the basic causes of the warfare between the liberal-arts and education professors in the past has been the feeling on the part of the former that they were denied any real part in planning programs for the education of

---

Kansas, and San Diego Conferences respectively. Washington, D.C.: National Commission on Teacher Education and Professional Standards, National Education Association. Also, for a popularized version of these conferences see G. K. Hodenfield and T. M. Stinnett, *The Education of Teachers: Conflict and Consensus*, Englewood Cliffs, New Jersey: Prentice-Hall, 1961, 177 pp.

teachers. Since the professors of the academic fields provide at least three-fourths of the courses taken by prospective teachers, it seemed unfair to them to be denied some voice in determining what courses and the content of the courses that make up the major part of the preparation of teachers. A recent study [13] revealed that 360 colleges and universities preparing teachers now have all-institution committees or councils for planning teacher-education programs, and another 150 institutions indicated that some kind of such machinery was under consideration. Perhaps one of the greatest needs for the strengthening of teacher education is for colleges and universities to view the task of preparing teachers as one of first-rate importance, rather than as one with which the institutions, and some segments of their staffs, are ashamed to be associated.

4. There will be major changes in the content and length of teacher-education programs. States are already beginning to mandate the completion of a graduate year of preparation for teachers who were admitted to practice upon completion of the bachelor's degree. The New Horizons Project of NCTEPS proposes a five-year preservice program of preparation as a prerequisite to admission to practice. These two procedures (the four-plus-one and the five-year plan) will develop alongside each other. The predominant pattern for perhaps a decade will be the four-plus-one. But during the decade an increasing number of states will mandate the five-year preservice program, and an increasing number of colleges and universities will provide such programs. Especially will this be true for high school teachers.

In content and quality, teacher-education programs in the future will become more alike, with present prescriptions for the preparation of elementary and secondary school teachers moving toward each other, and with common general education and professional cores, the chief differentiation in the latter being in student teaching. Elementary school teachers will be required to complete an area of concentration in an academic field, and the teaching field and subjects for high school teachers will be upgraded significantly. Graduate programs for teachers will give major emphasis to further preparation in the teaching fields of the teachers involved.

The preparation of special school service personnel (administrators, supervisors, counselors, nonteaching professional personnel, etc.) will require a minimum of six years of college preparation, with specialization being built upon that required for the classroom teacher. The action of the American Association of School Administrators of setting the prerequisite of two years of graduate preparation in institutions accredited by NCATE for new members admitted after 1964 will accelerate the trend toward the six-year preparation requirement for special school service personnel.

[13] John I. Goodlad and Howard R. Boozer, "Campus-Wide Committees on Teacher Education," *Educational Record,* October, 1961, 42:348–53.

Eventually the doctor's degree will become standard preparation for these specialized fields, whether by voluntary action of individuals or by membership requirements of the professional associations. Legal requirements will follow these standards.

5. *There will be discriminating selective-admission standards for teacher-education students universally applied by accredited institutions.* Here is a major instrument by which the teaching profession can strive to guarantee the competence of its members to the public. This development must be concurrent with that of achievement of a thorough, scholarly program of preparation. The latter can only be effective to the extent that highly capable people are admitted to study. No amount of tinkering with the teacher-education curriculum or reshuffling of courses and hours, as important as these may appear, is likely to result in the needed quality in teacher education. Inevitably, academic politics on individual campuses—the power struggle by departments for increased courses and hours in the total program—will blunt the effectiveness of rearranging the teacher-education curriculum. The basic approach to quality and excellence in teacher education is the application of carefully developed and honest enforcement of rigorous criteria for admission to teacher education, as a means of making certain that teacher education will secure its fair share of the best students. Moreover, such criteria must be universally applied in all institutions and in all states; otherwise, by the Gresham's Law analogy, the indifferent institutions, in their search for enrollments, will dilute the effort to the point of defeating it.

A concerted effort to upgrade the caliber of students admitted to teacher education must be undergirded by sanctions of the teaching profession and by an enforcing agency. The profession has long rankled under the charges, arising from a series of studies, that those preparing to be teachers are inferior scholastically and intellectually to college students in general or those preparing for the other professions.

The National Council for Accreditation of Teacher Education, in an effort to correct this situation, now is requiring in its accrediting standards that institutions securing national accreditation must enforce admission requirements to teacher-education programs, in addition to those for admission to the institution as a whole.

6. *The number, functions, and quality of professional units in teacher education will undergo marked change.* It seems undesirable and unlikely that the present rather heterogeneous group of 1,200 institutions will continue to be recognized for the preparation of teachers. Such a huge number—more than the total number approved by all other major professions for the preparation of their members—is not likely to provide uniformly good programs. On the contrary, the very diversity of programs seems likely to defeat any great improvement in the preparation of teachers. In time, the number of accredited institutions probably will be

halved. This drastic reduction will come about as the result of two factors: the enforcement of increasingly high standards of accreditation, and the voluntary abandonment of teacher education as such by many undergraduate colleges. The trend toward graduate preparation of teachers is too pronounced for any doubt to remain that teaching is moving toward the preparation levels of other professions. As this trend accelerates, the undergraduate colleges will rapidly cease to try to compete in the professional areas, and will, instead, concentrate upon the liberal-arts degree. This development will have a twofold advantage: The liberal-arts college will be released from an obligation that to many of them is distasteful and for which they are often not well equipped: the obligation to provide professional training. It will enable them to provide the liberal foundations, which they are well equipped to do, leaving the professional training to graduate schools of education. The second advantage is that many professional schools and colleges will be enabled to become graduate institutions.

This latter development should stimulate greater concentration of the professional schools upon research in the processes and motivations of learning, perhaps the greatest single need of teacher education and teaching. The most vulnerable spot in teaching's claim to professional status is the relative paucity of validated research. There is, of course, a substantive body of such research, but it is, as yet, not enough. Too much of what we presume to know about the art and science of teaching we don't actually know. Too much of what we claim to know are merely slogans, catchwords, observation, subjective guesswork, and cliches. The remedy for this situation is for the teaching profession to develop a group of first-class graduate research centers, with a competent corps of research specialists, to advance the horizons of knowledge about the human animal and his learning potentials and processes. In time, too, there should be at the apex of this effort a national center for research in education, similar in nature, purpose, and resources to the National Institutes of Health, established to probe the frontiers of medical practice.

ROLE OF TEACHERS IN TEACHER EDUCATION

If, as has been the history of other professions, teacher education is to take on more and more the image of the teaching profession, then teachers must exercise a greater, more influential role than they have done in the past. If teacher education is to contain more of intellectual content and training, teachers committed to these objectives must insist upon them. If teachers believe in a balance of theory and practice in the preparation program, their insistence upon such balance can do much to settle the violent arguments on college and university campuses. If teachers insist that ethical conduct be a concomitant of preparation, or that commitment to teaching be a goal of preparation or that orientation to responsibilities as members of a profession be also inherent in preparation, this insistence will have ultimate and powerful impact upon the nature and content of teacher education. For teachers to remain aloof from these issues is to assure that the field of battle will be surrendered by default to the traditional and ineffectual combatants, college professors. The professors, of course, are essential to the development of a teaching profession, but, left alone, they will be indifferent to or luke-warm about its achievement.

REFERENCES

AMERICAN ASSOCIATION OF COLLEGES FOR TEACHER EDUCATION, *Conceptual Models in Teacher Education.* Washington, D.C.: The Association, 1967.

————, *Teacher Education Looks to the Future.* Washington, D.C.: The Association, 1965.

————, *Excellence in Teacher Education.* Washington, D.C.: The Association, 1967.

————, *Frontiers in Teacher Education* (Proceedings of the 1966 annual meeting). Washington, D.C.: The Association, 1966.

ANDREWS, L. O., *Student Teaching.* New York: Center for Applied Research in Education, Inc., 1964.

ARMSTRONG, W. EARL, "The Teacher Education Curriculum," *Journal of Teacher Education,* September, 1957, 8:230–43.

BEGGS, WALTER K., *The Education of Teachers.* New York: Center for Applied Research in Education, Inc., 1965.

BORROWMAN, MERLE L., *The Liberal and Technical in Teacher Education.* New York: Teachers College, Columbia University, 1956.

———— (editor), *Teacher Education in America.* New York: Teachers College Press, Columbia University, 1965.

BRUBACHER, JOHN S., "Teacher Education—Development," in HARRIS, CHESTER (ed.) *Encyclopedia of Educational Research,* 3rd ed. New York: Macmillan Company, 1960, pp. 1452–53.

CHANDLER, B. J., *Education and the Teacher.* New York: Dodd, Mead and Company, 1961, Chap. 8, "Preparation for Teaching," pp. 185–210.

COLEMAN, DOROTHEA A., METHENY, ELEANOR, and SKUBIC, VERA, "Liberalizing the Professional Curriculum," *Journal of Teacher Education,* March, 1960, *11*:41–44.

CONANT, JAMES B., *The Education of American Teachers.* New York: McGraw-Hill Book Co., 1963.

COTTRELL, DONALD P. (ed.) *Teacher Education for a Free People.* Washington, D.C.: American Association of Colleges for Teacher Education, National Education Association, 1956.

EDWARDS, NEWTON, and RICHEY, HERMAN G., *The School in the American Social Order,* 2nd ed. Boston: Houghton Mifflin Co., 1963, Chap. 16, "Changing Patterns of Teacher Education," pp. 576–619.

GOODLAD, JOHN I., "The Professional Curriculum of Teachers," *Journal of Teacher Education,* December, 1960, 11:454–59.

———, and BOOZER, HOWARD R., "Campus-Wide Committees on Teacher Education," *Educational Record,* October, 1961, 42:348–353.

HANGARTNER, C. A., "Teacher Education: A Concern of the Total College," *Liberal Education,* December, 1966, 52:434–41.

HARRIS, CHESTER W. (ed.) *Encyclopedia of Educational Research,* 3rd ed. New York: Macmillan Company, 1960, "Teacher Education," pp. 1452–81.

HASKEW, L. D., *Discipline of Education and America's Future.* Pittsburgh: University of Pittsburgh Press, 1959.

———, "Planning for the Education of Teachers," *Journal of Teacher Education,* Summer, 1966, 17:257–61.

———, "The Teaching Profession and Professional Education," *Educational Forum,* November, 1957, 22:21–29.

HAZARD, WILLIAM R., *The Tutorial and Clinical Program of Teacher Education.* Evanston: Northwestern University Press, 1967.

HODENFIELD, G. K., and STINNETT, T. M., *The Education of Teachers: Conflict and Consensus.* Englewood Cliffs, New Jersey: Prentice-Hall, 1961.

KOERNER, JAMES D., *The Miseducation of American Teachers.* Boston: Houghton Mifflin Company, 1963.

LIEBERMAN, MYRON, *Education as a Profession.* Englewood Cliffs, New Jersey: Prentice-Hall, 1956, Chap. 7, "Teacher Education as Professional Training," pp. 185–213.

LINDSEY, MARGARET (ed.) *New Horizons for the Teaching Profession.* Washington, D.C.: National Commission on Teacher Education and Professional Standards, National Education Association, 1961, Chap. 4, "Preparation of Professional Personnel," pp. 27–108.

NATIONAL EDUCATION ASSOCIATION, National Commission on Teacher Education and Professional Standards, *Changes in Teacher Education: An Appraisal,* Report of the Columbus Conference. Washington, D.C.: The Association, 1963.

———, *Professional Imperatives: Expertness and Self-Determination,* Report of the Fort Collins Conference. Washington, D.C.: The Association, 1962, "Some Basic Issues in Teacher Education," pp. 3–21.

NATIONAL SOCIETY FOR THE STUDY OF EDUCATION, *Education for the Pro-*

fessions, Sixty-first Yearbook: Brubacher, John S., "The Evaluation of Professional Education," Part 11, Chap. III. Chicago: University of Chicago Press.

RUDY, S. W., "America's First Normal School: Formative Years," *Journal of Teacher Education,* December, 1954, 5:263–70.

STILES, LINDLEY J., *Teacher Education in the United States.* New York: Ronald Press, 1960.

STINNETT, T. M., and CLARKE, CHARLES M., "Teacher Education—Programs," in HARRIS, CHESTER (ed.) *Encyclopedia of Educational Research,* 3rd ed. New York: Macmillan Company, 1960, pp. 1461–73.

TAYLOR, H., "Need for Radical Reform; Teacher Education," *Saturday Review,* November 20, 1965, 48:74–6+.

WOODRING, P., "Challenge for Excellence," *AACTE Yearbook,* 1963, 16:24–31.

19: Professional Certification of Teachers

The certification of teachers is a legal function exercised by each of the fifty states and the territorial jurisdictions of the United States. For over a century the certification of teachers in the public schools of the United States has existed in some form in the states. In the New England states, teachers have been required to have certificates since colonial times. Oddly enough, Massachusetts was the last state to pass a general certification law, in 1951. The first certification standards were low, and enforcement perfunctory. Indeed, the fact is that until recent years, the public has had too little real protection from unqualified teachers.

The purpose of this chapter is to discuss the general significance of licensure for all professions and of certification for teachers. As it has long been for other professions, the licensing of teachers is now regarded as being of vital concern to those who have made the classroom their life-work and who have the right to be protected against the licensure of those who have not subjected themselves to the extended preparation necessary for the work. Teachers have a stake in the standards that are set up and enforced, as well as in their own certification.

What Is Teacher Certification?

Certification is the process of giving legal sanction to teach.[1] It includes all types of licenses, whether permanent or temporary in character, whether short-term or long-term, and whether issued on the basis of

---

[1] As indicated in footnote 1, Chapter 5, the terms license, licensure, certificate, and certification are used interchangeably. Certificate and certification are used predominantly in this chapter because (1) they have achieved common usage when referring to teacher licensure; and (2) they are more comprehensive than the other two terms implying inclusion of levels of preparation and fields of specialization.

several years of study or as a result of a few weeks or months of preparation, or even on the basis of having passed an examination. It includes those of an emergency nature as well as those that meet regular requirements.

THE PURPOSES OF CERTIFICATION

Teachers' licenses or certificates have for their purpose the protecting of pupils from unqualified persons. To put the matter in a positive way, teacher certification is the state's means of attempting to assure that only qualified persons will be permitted to teach. In this sense, certification is a privilege extended by the state and not a right. The public is thus supposed to be protected from charlatans, quacks, and other unfit people in the classroom in the same way that it is protected from unqualified physicians, dentists, lawyers, pharmacists, barbers, hairdressers, clergymen, realtors, and insurance agents. The trend is in the direction of licensing more and more occupational groups. Such workers as electricians, plumbers, morticians, and chiropodists are now usually required to obtain licenses.

It is almost impossible for the public to tell the difference between a qualified professional worker and a quack. This is particularly true for the complex society in which we live. It thus becomes increasingly necessary for occupational groups to be licensed.

Physicians were probably the first professional class to be licensed. At one time anyone could practice medicine, just as anyone could start a bank. All that was necessary in either case was to secure a place of business and to make an announcement of availability. The rest was up to the public. Finally it was realized that people had to be protected from those who had no preparation in medicine, so states passed laws requiring anyone wishing to practice medicine to secure a license.

Other professions took a similar step. It was realized that people need protection from unqualified workers in all aspects of professional, personal, and skilled labor service.

EVOLUTION OF LICENSURE FOR
THE PROFESSIONS

Licensure as a means of assuring the public of the competence of practitioners, as well as a means of protecting such practitioners from competition of the unqualified, goes back to ancient times.[2] In ancient

[2] See Harry J. Carman, "The Historical Development of Licensing for the Professions," *Journal of Teacher Education*, June, 1960, *11*:136–46. This issue of the *Journal* contained the working papers for the San Diego TEPS Conference on certification, and is a valuable source for students of certification.

Greece there were no professions as we know them today, but there were priests, lawyers, and physicians, all with little formal training for their speciality and with no licensure identifying them as competent to practice. In the Middle Ages the church was the predominant agency for training and licensing for the professions, sharing these functions with associations or guilds. And from the latter arose the universities that provided training in theology, medicine, and law. A degree from a university was a certificate to practice a given specialty. At first under the domination of the church, these professions gradually became independent and established their own associations. For example, the Royal College of Physicians of London was founded in 1518. These associations evolved into guilds and later into professional associations, which became the training and licensing agencies. With the decline of the guilds, the state began to enter into both training and licensure in order to protect both the public and the members of the professions. In Germany and France state licensure for the professions became exclusive. In England some professions are regulated by the government, but most are not; rather, the professions regulate themselves. In early America, because of the varied European backgrounds of the colonists, a patchwork of practices prevailed. Our early colleges were under church control, with the ministry dominating the faculties and, therefore, controlling training and licensure for the professions. This was not the case in the medieval universities. Standards were low, and specific training in the professions (theology, medicine, and law) was meager. Dogma, rather than scientific inquiry, was the rule. Teacher education as such did not exist. In the United States, by 1750, law was well along toward professional status through establishment of bar associations and legal requirements for licensure, and by 1800 at least four states had established by law training and licensure requirements. Although attempts had been made by a few colonial governments to regulate the practice of medicine, it was not until 1770 that the first Medical Practices Act, administered by a lay board, was passed in New Jersey. By 1800 thirteen of the sixteen states had adopted such acts, placing administration in the hands of the state medical societies.[3]

HISTORY OF TEACHER CERTIFICATION IN THE UNITED STATES

As to the training and licensure of teachers in colonial times, procedures were haphazard or nonexistent. According to the colony, procedures for licensure varied, with authority in the hands of towns, churches, royal commissioners or governors, or even the Bishop of London. The teacher and his period of employment were at the mercy of local officials. Tenure was unknown, and the term of employment hinged largely upon judged

[3] *Ibid.*, p. 141.

orthodoxy. With independence, the state governments tended to follow the *laissez-faire* colonial practices by placing authority for the training and licensure of teachers in the hands of local school officials. Teacher licenses were valid only in the school employing the teacher. The results were far from satisfactory. Examination of applicants was haphazard, nepotism was prevalent, standards were disgraceful, teachers rejected or failing in one town could find employment in another. Charges of intemperance, immorality, and incompetence were common.

By 1850 these central facts were clear, if the free public schools were to survive: some system of preparing competent teachers had to be devised, and the decentralization of the chaotic system of licensure had to be abolished. After 1850 and especially following the Civil War, trends toward these two corrective measures developed rapidly. The movement was led by local, state, and national societies of teachers. Many such local associations were in evidence by 1860, ten state education associations had been founded, and the National Teachers Association (now the National Education Association) was formed in 1857. Other professions had established national bodies in the following years: medicine, 1847; pharmacy and engineering, 1852; architecture, 1857; and dentistry, 1859.

The contributions of these associations and those subsequently established were incalculable in the establishment of standards for preparation, licensure, and practice, standards that were gradually and legally adopted by the respective states. The professional associations accomplished these things through the pressures of standards for membership: the kind and extent of preparation, professional conduct and practices, codes of ethics. And they backed these with authority to expel from membership. Legal licensure served to support these standards; moreover, it gradually gained for the professions representation in the execution of legal policies of licensure.

As to the other imperative that had become apparent by 1850—the devising of a formal system of preparation for teaching—the establishment and development of the normal school were of great significance. Until 1839, when the first normal school was established at Lexington, Massachusetts, teacher education as we know it today had not existed in the United States. Prior to 1839 the private academies and general colleges were the sole source of supply of teachers. By 1860 twelve normal schools had been established, and by 1900 the number had grown to more than three hundred. The establishment of these schools with prescribed curriculums for teacher preparation created pressures for legal licensure to support the type of preparation. Here was the beginning of the evolution of teaching into a profession. The first step was a state law in New York, passed in 1849, prescribing that a diploma from the state's normal school (Albany) should be deemed evidence that the holder was a qualified teacher.[4]

In the early years, because they produced such a small proportion of the teachers needed for the public schools, the normal schools did not materially affect certification practices. But they did establish the principle of gaining certification upon completion of a prescribed professional curriculum, which by now has become a universal practice among the states.

Steps Toward State Systems of Licensing

By 1850 the establishment of state school systems had become general. By 1861 twenty-eight of the then thirty-four states had provided for a "chief state school officer" (now called state superintendent of public instruction, or state commissioner of education). The movement toward state certification of teachers began to get under way. The first step was to delegate to local or county school officials authority to license teachers. New York (1841) and Vermont (1845) were the first states to pass such legislation. Between 1860 and 1910 the following developments in teacher certification took place: gradual shifts of the certification authority from local to state control; the appearance of graded certificates (first, second, and third grade); the issuance of life certificates; shift to written examinations, as contrasted with oral, first written and administered by local authorities and later prepared by state authorities, but administered locally; gradual emergence of licensure based upon completion of a prescribed course rather than upon examination; gradual emergence of the state-wide certificate; issuance of specialized certificates (endorsed for given positions or teaching fields); and beginning of efforts to bring about interstate reciprocity.[5]

The shift to centralize certification in state departments of education had several facets. Laws passed in New York between 1864 and 1894 vested authority in the state superintendent to revoke certificates, to grant certificates upon examination or upon graduation from college and three years of experience, and to validate normal-school diplomas from other states. In 1865 Illinois passed a law authorizing the state superintendent to issue state-wide life certificates on the basis of examination. By 1898 in only three states was certification completely centralized in the state department of education; in thirty-six states there existed a combination of state and county authority; and in four states the authority still resided exclusively in the county.

At the turn of the century there were some 3,000 governmental units

[4] This section has drawn extensively upon Anthony C. LaBue, "Teacher Certification in the United States: A Brief History," *Journal of Teacher Education*, June, 1960, 11:147–72.

[5] *Ibid.*, p. 153.

(largely county) with authority to certify teachers. By 1911 a total of fifteen states issued all certificates, with twenty-seven states dividing authority between state and county officials. Currently (1967) there is virtually complete centralization of licensing authority in state departments of education; in only nine states is any portion of this authority shared with other agencies.

Perhaps the most significant change in teacher-certification procedures, in terms of the evolution of the teaching profession, has been the shift from examinations based upon meager schooling as prerequisites to completion of prescribed college and university curriculums. This development was slow, but is now almost universal. It has been pointed out that New York recognized normal-school diplomas as a basis of certification in 1849. California, in 1863, recognized such diplomas as certificates; and by 1900 one-half of the states waived the prescribed teacher examinations for normal-school graduates, forty-one states issued certificates to normal-school graduates who had completed prescribed curricula, and ten did not specify any professional preparation to be included. A diploma that is accepted as a license is often called a diploma certificate.

Prior to 1900 little attention was given to issuing specialized certificates except for separate certificates for elementary and secondary school teachers. In all but six states a certificate to teach was a certificate to teach any and all grades and subjects. Currently, in all but twelve states, which issue general high school certificates, the specialized certificate restricting the holder to teach at a school level (elementary or high school) or to a specified teaching field or subject is universal. And in the twelve states with blanket high school certificates, a teacher must meet the prescribed preparation requirements to be assigned to teach a given subject or field.

A concept of the progress that has been made since 1921 in upgrading preparation requirements for entrance into teaching can be gained from Table 51.

How Centralization of Certification Authority Developed

The trend toward centralization of certification in the hands of state departments of education has been mentioned briefly. It is interesting to trace the successive steps in this significant development. By the beginning of this century most states had taken the first step in the direction toward centralization. At the start of this trend toward centralization, the usual procedure was for the state department of education to make out examination questions to be used by local authorities. The county and city officials gave the examinations, corrected the papers, and issued the certificates. Certificates were often of first, second, or third class, depending upon the marks achieved. The distinction in type was mostly in duration of term of validity, although there were many variations. A third-

TABLE 51   Scholastic Requirements for Licensure of Beginning Elementary School Teachers in 1921 and 1967

PREPARATION REQUIREMENTS	1921	1967
None specified	30	0
High school graduate	14	0
High school graduate plus	4	0
One year college	0	0
Two years college	0	5
Three years college	0	0
Bachelor's degree	0	47
TOTALS	48	52

Source: Anthony C. LaBue, "Teacher Certification in the United States: A Brief History," *Journal of Teacher Education,* June, 1960, *11*:159, for 1921 requirements. For 1967 requirements, see T. M. Stinnett, *A Manual on Certification Requirements for School Personnel in the United States,* 1967 edition. Washington, D.C.: National Commission on Teacher Education and Professional Standards, National Education Association, 1967.

For high school teachers in 1967, all states required a minimum of the bachelor's degree; three states (Arizona, California, and the District of Columbia) required five years of college preparation.

grade certificate generally was valid for six months, a second-grade for one year, and a first-grade for two years. Sometimes a third-grade certificate was given first, to be followed by one of higher grade if acceptable marks were made on ensuing examinations. Life certificates sometimes were achieved by high examination marks earned in a succession of tests taken for the various grades of licenses.

During the middle part of the nineteenth century not more than 5 or 10 per cent of the candidates for teaching positions could be prepared by the normal schools then in existence. Gradually more facilities for teacher education were added; better transportation made the normal schools accessible to more students.

The trend toward the centralizing of certification authority in one state agency is indicated by the following: Between 1898 and 1940 the number of state systems in which the issuance of teachers' licenses was vested in the state increased from three to forty-two.[6] By 1967 all states exercised legal authority over teacher licensing, although that authority was shared with other agencies to some degree in ten states; two states (California and Pennsylvania) share minor authority with county superintendents. In two of these ten states (Kansas and Missouri) state colleges and/or

[6] Benjamin W. Frazier, *Education of Teachers as a Function of State Departments of Education,* U.S. Office of Education, Federal Security Agency, Bulletin 1940, No. 6, Monograph No. 6. Washington, D.C.: U.S. Government Printing Office, 1940, p. 87.

universities are authorized to issue certificates to their graduates who have completed teacher-education curricula; in five of these states (Delaware, Illinois, Maryland, New York, and North Dakota) certain cities are authorized to issue certificates to their teachers.[7]

Decline of the Examination System

Eventually it became apparent that those who had attended an accredited teacher-education institution did not need to take the licensure examinations. They were obviously much better prepared to teach than were those who had merely graduated from high school and had then "boned up" on the subject matter ordinarily taught in schools. The practice of exempting normal-school graduates from the examinations became common. Instead, certificates were issued on the basis of a transcript listing prescribed courses that had been completed. By 1898 twenty-eight states recognized graduation from normal schools and universities as evidence of qualification for certification. At the present time all states except Florida, North Carolina, and South Carolina grant certificates to the graduates of their own teacher-education institutions without further examination. These three require passage of the National Teachers Examination.

The once-prevalent examination system, as the exclusive basis for issuing teachers' certificates, by 1967 had been virtually discarded by all states. Some sixteen states make some use of examinations in connection with certification, but these examinations are in addition to basic college preparation requirements. In some instances examinations are used to permit experienced teachers to qualify for additional teaching fields, in some instances, to demonstrate proficiency in a required course. Florida, the District of Columbia, North Carolina, and South Carolina use national examinations to issue initial certificates to college graduates.

CURRENT STATUS OF TEACHER CERTIFICATION

Who Must Be Certified?

The legal licensing of teachers is generally thought of as being applied only to teachers in the public schools. Since states have compulsory school laws and levy taxes for the support of the public schools, teacher licensing is essential for the states to safeguard children against incompetent teachers and to assure the efficient spending of public monies. The argu-

[7] T. M. Stinnett, *A Manual on Certification Requirements for School Personnel in the United States,* 1967 edition. Washington, D.C.: National Commission on Teacher Education and Professional Standards, National Education Association, 1967, pp. 21–22.

ment for state licensure of public school teachers is that children and their parents have little to do with the choice of teachers, compulsory school laws enforce attendance (unless they elect to attend a nonpublic school), and children attending these schools are a captive audience; therefore, the state is obligated to assure the employment of competent teachers.

In 1967 nineteen states required nursery school teachers and forty-two states required kindergarten teachers to hold state certificates, if public funds were involved in support of the schools. All states and territorial jurisdictions required public elementary and high school teachers (and administrative, supervisory, and special school service personnel) to hold state certificates. Ten states required teachers in public junior colleges to hold state certificates and three states required teachers in state teachers colleges to be certified.

With reference to teachers in nonpublic schools, the traditional practice of the states has been to require state certificates only in case the schools seek accreditation by the state department of education. This is done, of course, to apply the same standards of instruction in both types of schools. Eighteen states have limited legal requirements for the certification of teachers in some types of nonpublic elementary and secondary schools. In addition, twenty-seven states require such certification for teachers in some types of nonpublic schools, if these schools seek state accreditation. In twelve states there is no provision for certification of teachers in private and parochial schools.[8]

Lack of Uniformity

While all states require that teachers obtain a license, certificate, or permit to teach, there is still a striking lack of uniformity in regulations. There is still too much diversity in the amount of training required for a teaching certificate, in the number and types of certificates granted, in the conditions for the renewal of licenses, and in the extent to which they are valid.

Not only do states differ from one another, but there is great complexity within each state. Most states have a multitude of certificates of different kinds for the teachers of normal children in the regular courses of study; these various certificates differ one from another in the qualifications required, the scope of teaching positions and types of schools in which they may be used, and the length of the period during which they are valid. Although there still exist great differences, remarkable progress has been made toward the bachelor's degree as a basic requirement.

Table 52 reflects that, for the lowest regular certificate for beginning elementary school teachers, one state requires five college years of prep-

[8] *Ibid.*

TABLE 52 *Minimum Requirements for Lowest Regular Teaching Certificates for Preparing Teachers (as of January 1, 1967)*

State	ELEMENTARY SCHOOL			HIGH SCHOOL		
	Degree or Number of Semester Hours Required	Professional Education Required, Semester Hours (Total)	Directed Teaching Required, Semester Hours (Included in Column 3)	Degree or Number of College Years Required	Professional Education Required, Semester Hours (Total)	Directed Teaching Required, Semester Hours (Included in Column 6)
1	2	3	4	5	6	7
Alabama	B	27	6	B	21	6
Alaska	B	24	C	B	18	AC
Arizona	B	24	6	5[a]	22	6
Arkansas	B	18	6	B	18	6
California	5[a]	20	180CH	5[a]	15	120CH
Colorado	B	AC	AC	B	AC	AC
Connecticut	B	30	6	B	18	6
Delaware	B	30	6	B	18	6
District of Columbia	B	15	AC	5	18	AC
Florida	B	20	6	B	20	6
Georgia	B	18	6	B	18	6
Hawaii	B	18	AC	B	18	AC
Idaho	B	20	6	B	20	6
Illinois	B	16	5	B	16	5
Indiana	B	27	8	B	18	6
Iowa	B	20	5	B	20	5
Kansas	B	24	5	B	20	5
Kentucky	B	28	8	B	17	8
Louisiana	B	24	4	B	18	4
Maine	B	30	8	B	18	6
Maryland	B	26	8	B	18	6
Massachusetts	B	18	2	B	12	2
Michigan	B	20	5	B	20	5
Minnesota	B	30	6	B	18	4
Mississippi	B	36	6	B	18	6
Missouri	B	20	5	B	20	5
Montana	B	AC	AC	B	16	AC
Nebraska	60	8	3	B	18	AC
Nevada	B	18	4	B	18	4
New Hampshire	B	30	6	B	18	6
New Jersey	B	36	6	B	24	6
New Mexico	B	24	6	B	18	6
New York	B	24	10	B	18	80CH
North Carolina	B	24	6	B	18	6
North Dakota	64	16	3	B	16	3

TABLE 52 (*Continued*)

	ELEMENTARY SCHOOL			HIGH SCHOOL		
State	Degree or Number of Semester Hours Required	Professional Education Required, Semester Hours (Total)	Directed Teaching Required, Semester Hours (Included in Column 3)	Degree or Number of College Years Required	Professional Education Required, Semester Hours (Total)	Directed Teaching Required, Semester Hours (Included in Column 6)
1	2	3	4	5	6	7
Ohio	B	28	6	B	17	6
Oklahoma	B	21	6	B	21	6
Oregon	B	20	AC	B	14	AC
Pennsylvania	B	36	6	B	18	6
Puerto Rico	68	23	6	B	29	5
Rhode Island	B	30	6	B	18	6
South Carolina	B	21	6	B	18	6
South Dakota	60	15	3	B	20	6
Tennessee	B	24	4	B	24	4
Texas	B	18	6	B	18	6
Utah	B	26	8	B	21	8
Vermont	B	18	6	B	18	6
Virginia	B	18	6	B	15	4–6
Washington	B	AC	AC	B	AC	AC
West Virginia	B	20	6	B	20	6
Wisconsin	64	26	8	B	18	5
Wyoming	B	23	AC	B	20	AC

Source: T. M. Stinnett, *A Manual on Certification Requirements for School Personnel in the United States, op. cit.,* 1967 edition, Table VIII, p. 20.

Legend: AC means approved curriculum; B means bachelor's degree of specified preparation; 5 means bachelor's degree plus a fifth year of appropriate preparation, not necessarily completion of master's degree.

[a] Arizona and California allow variations from the 5 year requirement.

aration but is not presently enforcing this requirement, forty-six states (and territories) require completion of the bachelor's degree, five states require two college years, and one state requires one college year. For beginning high school teachers, three states require five college years of preparation (for academic fields—only two are now enforcing), and forty-nine states require four college years. The above requirements do not apply to certain trade and vocational teachers.

The great diversity in requirements for teachers' certificates among states is reflected, too, in the course requirements specified. For example, the states requiring completion of the bachelor's degree for beginning elementary school teachers show a range in required education courses from fifteen in one state to thirty-six in three others. In these same states the requirements in student teaching range from two hours in Massachusetts to ten in New York. The range in course requirements for high school teachers, although not quite so great, is pronounced. This great diversity in course requirements among states, although the number of years of required college work may be the same, serves as an effective barrier to the free flow of qualified teachers from one state to another. A similar diversity also exists in the requirements for administrative certificates (see Table 53). There are certain trends toward removing these obstacles, though, which will be discussed in the following section.

TABLE 53 *Summary of Minimum Preparation Requirements of States for Administrative Certificates (as of January 1, 1967)*

NUMBER OF COLLEGE YEARS (OR DEGREES) OF PREPARATION REQUIRED	NUMBER OF STATES REQUIRING		
	Elementary Principal	Secondary Principal	Superintendent of Schools
7 years or doctor's degree	0	0	1
6 years plus	0	0	1
6 years	3	3	18
Master's degree plus, but less than 6 years	7	7	3
Master's degree	34	37	26
Bachelor's degree plus, but less than 5 years	3	2	1
Bachelor's degree	4	2	0
Less than bachelor's degree	0	0	0
No certificate issued	1	1	1
TOTALS	52	52	52

Source: T. M. Stinnett, *op. cit.*, Table 2, p. 19.

General Requirements for Certificates

There are certain general requirements of the states for teachers' certificates. General requirements are those that all applicants for certificates must meet, as contrasted with the requirements that an applicant must meet to be authorized to teach a specific subject or on a specific school level. What are some of the general requirements? Thirty-two states require that an applicant for a teacher's certificate must be a citizen of the United States or have filed a declaration of intent. Twenty-five states require that the applicant take an oath of allegiance of loyalty. Eleven states require evidence of employment within the state, and forty-three states require that the applicant be recommended by his preparing college or, in the case of an experienced teacher, by his school employing official. Twenty-eight states require that the applicant must have attained the minimum age of eighteen; two states require a minimum age of seventeen; three states require a minimum age of nineteen; one requires a minimum age of twenty; and eighteen states do not specify a minimum age. Twenty-one states require a general health certificate. Six states require a special course, usually in the history and constitution of the particular state, a course that can only be secured, as a general rule, in institutions in that state.

Types of Certificates Issued

The several types of teachers' certificates issued by the states can be categorized in three ways: the term of the certificate, the level of college preparation of the holder, and the authorized teaching assignment of the holder. In the first category (term) are life, permanent, limited, continuing, and provisional or probationary certificates. In the second category are regular, standard, professional, and emergency or substandard. In the third category are blanket or general (with no teaching fields endorsed, only the school level of authorized teaching), endorsed (on which the authorized school level or subject and field of teaching are recorded), and special field (issued for each special field, such as art or music).

Twenty-seven states issue life or permanent certificates. The permanent certificate is not usually a life certificate, remaining valid only if the holder remains in teaching continuously or is not out of teaching beyond a specified number of years. Twelve states issue blanket or general high school certificates, on which the teaching fields and subjects that the holder is qualified to teach according to the requirements of the state are not endorsed. The enforcement of teaching assignments is left to local school administration and accrediting agencies. Forty-four states issue endorsed certificates for which the authorized teaching fields and subjects are stated as guides to employing school officers. In forty-one states special as well as academic fields are endorsed, while twelve states issue a separate certificate for each special field.

The Emergency-Certificate Practice

One of the persisting practices in all states, a practice vigorously resisted by practitioners in other professions and, in consequence, almost never resorted to in those professions, is the issuance of substandard or emergency certificates when qualified candidates for teaching positions are not available.

During World War II a chaotic situation developed in the teaching profession. Because teachers' salaries did not offer the compensation to be found in war industries and other higher-paying jobs, instructors left the profession by the thousands. High school graduates did not enter teacher-education courses in as large numbers as formerly. The result of these two factors was a severe, nation-wide shortage of teachers.

To keep the schools open, emergency certification was adopted. In many cases the teachers with these substandard certificates who came in to fill the ranks were married women who had left the profession but were able to return because their children were old enough to be in school. Some of those who were given emergency certificates had retired years before at advanced ages. Some had had but a few weeks' preparation beyond high school. Some of the so-called emergency teachers did good work, some mediocre, and some poor.

So much harm was done by some of the poorer of these emergency teachers, though, that there is a real question whether emergency certification should have been allowed. There were no emergency doctors, dentists, or nurses. Unfortunately, this practice of making up the shortage of qualified teachers by employing emergency teachers continues to be followed.

The number of substandard certificates issued reached fantastic proportions. At the peak of the teacher shortage during the war, some estimates placed the probable total as high as 140,000 emergency-certificate teachers employed in the schools of the United States. (The number of emergency teachers' certificates issued each year since 1945, as estimated by the NEA Research Division, is shown in the chart on page 435.)

The extent of the practice of issuing emergency certificates is indicated by the following: The number of persons employed who held substandard certificates was about 1 in 340 of the public school teachers in 1940–41; the proportion jumped to 1 in 7 by 1945–46; then the proportion declined until it reached 1 in 15 in 1960–61, and 1 in 20 in 1966–67.

Gains Being Made

In spite of the discouraging picture painted in the previous paragraphs, marked gains in certification standards and practices are being made. It has been previously pointed out that two states (Arizona and California) and the District of Columbia, in 1967, required five years of collegiate preparation for high school teachers of academic subjects, and forty-nine states and territories specified a minimum of four college years of preparation. For elementary school teachers forty-seven states and territories now require at least a bachelor's degree for certification.

As late as 1936 only five states required a degree for beginning elementary school teachers. By 1940 the number had grown to eleven; in 1946, to eighteen; and in 1967 to forty-seven.

Year	Number of Substandard Certificates *	Ratio of Emergency Teachers to Total Teaching Positions
1945–46	115,000–120,000	1 in 7
1946–47	110,000–115,000	1 in 8
1947–48	112,401	1 in 8
1948–49	105,267	1 in 9
1949–50	95,146	1 in 9
1950–51	75,079	1 in 12
1951–52	69,848	1 in 14
1952–53	69,626	1 in 14
1953–54	78,850	1 in 13
1954–55	80,674	1 in 13
1955–56	79,403	1 in 14
1956–57	86,616	1 in 14
1957–58	94,732	1 in 13
1958–59	94,010	1 in 14
1959–60	93,543	1 in 14
1960–61	93,917	1 in 15
1966–67	90,500	1 in 20

* For the years 1945–46 through 1949–50, see National Education Association, Research Division, "Teacher Forecast for the Public Schools," *Journal of Teacher Education*, March, 1953, 4:55. For the years 1950–51 through 1960–61, see National Education Association, Research Division, *Estimates of School Statistics, 1960–61*, Research Report 1960–R15. Washington, D.C.: The Association, 1954, p. 12, 1966–67 figures are estimates of the NEA Research Division.

ROLE OF THE PROFESSION IN CERTIFICATION

The rapid upgrading in minimum preparation requirements after 1946 can be attributed in large measure to the influence of the organized teaching profession. Disturbed by the prevailing low standards and public indifference to standards, the NEA in 1946 established the National Commission on Teacher Education and Professional Standards, and charged it with the task of stimulating the raising of standards for admission to the profession. NCTEPS immediately adopted a policy statement advocating the bachelor's degree as the minimum for which any teacher at any school level should be admitted to practice. The parallel state TEPS commissions gradually sought implementation of this policy. The results are shown in the upgrading in successive years.

What is the proper role of a profession in fixing and enforcing requirements for admission of its members to practice? What is the proper role of teachers regarding these functions? These questions can be answered by pointing out that a prime function of any professional group is to guarantee to the public the competence of its members to practice that profession. They can be answered, too, by pointing out that the American people have come to expect this basic service of the professions, that they have acted upon this expectation by vesting legal authority in virtually all the professions except teaching to perform these functions.

These powers are responsibilities that have slowly developed for teaching, too. Although, presently, the responsibilities or powers are largely extralegal for the teaching profession, nevertheless they are being exercised to some degree. In all but three states there now exists machinery by which the teaching profession exercises broad recommendatory powers regarding certification and preparation requirements. The machinery exists in the form of advisory councils on teacher education and certification, standing committees, state examining boards, or TEPS commissions. In twelve of these states the body is established by law; in the remainder they are extralegal, having been established by the chief state education legal agency.

Thus, the teaching profession is gradually moving toward a position to exercise, with the restrictions already described, similar powers and responsibilities over requirements for admission to practice as are the other professions. Two developments are yet needed: the sanction of law, and the achievement by the profession of the ability and willingness to assume these functions. These factors will be treated later in this chapter.

EFFORTS TO ACHIEVE RECIPROCITY IN CERTIFICATION

The great mobility of the American people is matched by that of teachers moving across state lines, seeking employment in other than their home states or states in which they went to college. This mobility of teachers has led to many efforts to devise a plan by which a qualified teacher could move freely from one state to another and be able to secure a certificate. Many plans have been tried, but still well-prepared, experienced teachers find state lines as serious barriers to certification and employment. Every state has its own set of requirements, which tend to penalize the teacher prepared in another state. Particularly since World War II has the problem become acute.

As early as 1890 New York State inaugurated an exchange-of-certificate plan. This plan was adopted by other states, and by 1921 some thirty-eight states were exchanging certificates. But the vast differences in standards for approving teacher-education institutions, the differences in state certification requirements, and the protests of in-state teachers that incoming teachers did not have to meet the same standards applied to them, caused growing dissatisfaction with the plan.

Consequently, the certificate-exchange idea declined after 1921, and presently no state will validate a teacher's certificate issued in another state. They must, instead, apply for a new certificate in the state to which they are transferring.

The state certification directors have, since about 1940, pursued concurrently two other means of bringing about reciprocity. The first was an effort to seek, through consultation in regional and national meetings, to bring the requirements of the respective states closer together. These efforts have been extremely fruitful. Many of the petty, irritating differences have been eliminated. The flow of teachers across state lines is much freer than is generally supposed. But many obstacles still remain, enough to defeat *free* migration of teachers. For example, at least six states have by law a special course requirement (such as state history) that the immigrating teacher must complete to achieve full certification. Some of these will accept the passing of an examination in the subject in lieu of the course. Prescribed course titles and hours are so diverse as to put unwarranted and irritating extra burdens upon migrating teachers.

The second of the parallel movements to bring about reciprocity in teacher certification has been the effort to establish regional reciprocity compacts. This plan is based upon the fact that, generally, the greatest exchange of teachers occurs among contiguous or nearby states. Thus, the state directors of certification in several geographical areas have worked out compacts or agreements by which each state in the compact would certificate teachers from the other states without penalty. The regional compacts worked out and the dates are as follows: the Ohio Valley Conference, 1938, involving eight states; the Southern States Compact, 1941, involving eleven states; the Eight-State Compact, 1949, involving the original six New England States, New York, and New Jersey, and later extended to include Delaware, Maryland, and Pennsylvania; and the Central States Conference, 1953, which involves six states.

The reciprocity-compact idea, like the effort to reconcile differences in certification requirements among the states, doubtless has been very fruitful in easing the obstacles to teacher migration across state lines. But the decline of the idea is evident. By 1967, all except the Northeast Compact have been abandoned.

The most recent and promising plan to bring about national reciprocity in teacher certification is to accept without penalty the credentials of a graduate of an institution accredited by the NCATE. This plan was proposed by the NASDTEC at its annual meeting at Bowling Green, Ohio, in 1958, and is based upon the assumption that the key to identification of a competent teacher is to be found in the type and quality of the program completed and the caliber of the institution offering it, rather than in detailed certification prescriptions.

In 1967 a total of 37 states use this plan to some degree, providing rather automatic acceptance of credentials of graduates of NCATE-approved institutions and the issuance of regular certificates to them without penalty.

ISSUES IN TEACHER CERTIFICATION

As the process by which legal sanction is given to the admission to practice of a member of the teaching profession, certification is of great importance to teachers and to the public. The importance of the process is reflected in the continuing issues that surround it. The following is a partial list of issues. There are many more, but the following are crucial:

1. *Who Shall Determine Certification Requirements?* If, as has been set forth many times in this book, a key mark of a profession is control over admission and expulsion of its members, then the answer to this question is clear: the profession should determine certification requirements. This is virtually universally true of other professions: state licensing bodies provided by law are made up of members of the profession involved, and the members are named or nominated by the state professional association. If one rejects the notion of professional autonomy for teaching, then, of course, the answer is indicated: the state board-of-education authority, generally composed of lay members, should set the requirements.

Presently, teaching is in a half-way position. It has, in most states, extralegal rights to participate in fixing certification requirements, with recommendations subject to veto by a lay board. That full legal rights will, in time, be vested in the profession seems obvious. In the meantime, how can the profession best exercise the recommendatory powers it now has? This question involves two aspects: What is the best machinery? Who should be involved?

As to the machinery, the predominant pattern, in 47 states, is that of an advisory council (or standing committee) on teacher education and certification, empowered to recommend what the requirements for certification should be. These councils vary in composition but, in general, they tend to provide representation to teacher-education institutions, to the practicing profession (classroom teachers, administrators, and special school service personnel), and to the state departments of education. But recent agitation is changing this composition to include representatives of liberal-arts fields.

While the present plan provides broad recommendatory powers to the profession regarding the fixing of certification requirements, lay state boards of education still retain veto powers. In the long look, then, teaching, to gain the same degree of control over admission and expulsion of its members, the kind of autonomy exercised by most other professions, must seek the creation of legal boards of professional members. By 1967 six states had established professional practices acts.

2. *The Issuance of Emergency Certificates.* This safety valve or escape hatch continues to be widely used by state departments of education. The reason is predicated upon the inability to find enough qualified teachers to fill all jobs. This is based upon a certain degree of logic. But it is a logic of expediency, often grossly abused, and so long as the teaching profession condones this undercutting of standards, just so long will status as a true profession be denied it. The probability is that the use of the emergency certificate has contributed materially to the chronic nature of the teacher shortage. This expedient device doubtless has repelled many potential teachers from preparing for entering or remaining in the profession.

The nature of this problem is reflected by the figures given on page 435. Emergency certificates can be abolished if the profession demands their discontinuance and the public is impelled to support professional salary schedules.

3. *Amount of Preparation to Be Required.* What is the minimum amount of preparation that should be required for initial certification of teachers? for continuing or permanent certification? We have traced, in the historical development of certification practices, the evolution of teaching from a poorly paid occupation for which no specific preparation was required, to one approaching professional status for which specific professional preparation is required. Will this trend toward more and more preparation, approaching that of other professions, be continued?

It is obvious that the teacher in the modern school, who must guide and assist the growth and development of the whole child, with an ever-mounting accumulation of new knowledge, must have an extended preparation. Four years of college preparation would seem to be little enough for the beginning teacher. States are beginning to mandate completion of a year of graduate work after three to five years of experience, and the prescription of five years of preservice preparation is on the horizon.

From analyses of evolving state certification requirements and of the annual production of teachers by colleges and universities, there is a fairly clear emerging trend as to the amount of preparation deemed necessary for qualified teachers. It has been pointed out previously that in 1967 a total of 47 states and territories required four college years of preparation for beginning elementary school teachers, and that all of the states required this minimum for high school teachers.

Again referring to the evolving state certification requirements, the trends or goals of preparation appear to be as follows: for beginning teachers, both elementary and secondary, completion of the bachelor's degree of teacher preparation for initial service and probationary certification, and completion of the fifth year of professional preparation after initial teaching service for permanent or continuing certification; for administrative, supervisory, and some special school service personnel, completion of a fifth year of preparation for initial service (with teaching experience as a prerequisite for initial certification and service), and the completion of the sixth year of preparation for full professional qualification and permanent or continuing certification. The task force of the NCTEPS special project on "New Horizons in Teacher Education and Professional Standards" has recommended that the goal for the future is five college years of preparation for beginning teachers. From this it can be assumed that the requirement for special school service personnel will be fixed first at six years, and finally at the doctor's degree. For school superintendents, already 19 states are requiring six years, and one, the doctor's degree.

4. *Types, Number, and Nomenclature of Certificates.* It is possible to observe two trends in regard to the number of certificates to be issued. On the one hand, there has been a movement to concentrate on a few types, rather than to continue with many. On the other hand, pressures are being exerted to issue an ever-increasing number of certificates as new service areas are added to the school program.

In a study made in 1949, it was found that the states issued about 1,000 separate-name certificates. Only five states issued a certificate with the same name, and in these five states the requirements for this certificate varied from two to five college years of preparation. This multiplicity of certificates has proved confusing and has resulted in a trend toward reducing the number of certificates issued by the states. In 1967 the number of separate-name certificates issued by the fifty-two states and territories had decreased to 550. The number ranged from one to 57; the median, 7. Connecticut, Hawaii, North Dakota, and Tennessee issue two certificates. These new regulations usually provide for two general teaching certificates, each one of which connotes the college years of preparation completed by the holder. The first, commonly called limited, probationary, or provisional, is issued to applicants who have completed the bachelor's degree of prescribed preparation, and is usually for a term of three to five years. The other certificate, issued upon completion of the fifth year of preparation and after three to five years of successful experience, is usually called permanent, continuing, standard, or professional, for terms ranging up to ten years in length. On these two certificates is endorsed each field or subject, or the school level, that the holder is qualified to teach.

5. *Life or Term Certificates.* Until a few years ago most states issued life certificates to teachers meeting the prescribed requirements. The practice has declined to the extent that presently twenty-seven states issue such certificates. These were supposed to indicate that the teacher was qualified to teach for as long as he lived. Whether the issuance of life or permanent certificates is a sound practice continues, however, to be a debatable issue among teachers.

Arguments against the practice cluster around the dynamic concept of the teacher's work. Teaching procedures change just as everything else in life, for nothing can stand still. Preparation for teaching must be a continuous process. Life or permanent certificates apparently are issued on the assumption that the finished preparation of teachers is reached at a given point. Experience has shown that many teachers, after receiving life certificates, did nothing to keep up to date. Holding life certificates impelled them to believe that their preparation was finished. The controversy regarding the wisdom of issuing such certificates received new emphasis as the result of unsatisfactory experiences with the practice during World War II.

Despite the admittedly undesirable experience of the past, there still remains considerable support among teachers for the policy of awarding permanent certificates upon completion of four or five college years of preparation. Those favoring this provision point out that other professions issue permanent certificates to practitioners. When a medical student, for example, has been awarded his M.D. degree, completed the required internship, and passed the required examination for state licensure, he is issued a permanent license to practice medicine. He is not compelled by the medical profession or state legal authority to return to medical college periodically for refresher work or to learn of new techniques. The proponents of the life-certificate policy for teachers contend that the teaching profession ought to follow this practice, that to hold a legal club over the heads of competent teachers who have completed the state's prescribed preparation is an undignified and unwarranted practice.

Those who argue that the issuance of life certificates for teachers is an unsound and undesirable policy emphasize that the teaching profession is different from the other professions. They assert that teaching is a public profession and is, to a great extent, noncompetitive, that the private professions, such as medicine, are highly competitive, and therefore the doctor is compelled to keep his preparation abreast of the latest developments if he is to retain a clientele. On the other hand, it is claimed, teachers have a compulsory clientele. Children are compelled by law to receive their services, and parents have little or no choice in selecting teachers for them, as they do when they employ a doctor to treat their children or themselves. Because of the noncompetitive nature of the teacher's work, the fact that tenure is provided most teachers after a few years of successful service and that parents and children do not, except in the most superficial manner, have any chance to pass judgment upon the efficiency of teachers, the state has an obligation to enforce professional-growth provisions for teachers.

Doubtless there is merit on both sides of this controversy. The evidence seems clear, however, that the practice of issuing life certificates to teachers has been a declining one. In 1967 there occurred the first increase in the number of states issuing life certification in two decades. The answer seems to lie in the shift from the issuance of life certificates to permanent certificates. The latter are long-term, usually ten years, and are renewable if the holder has taught for at least half of the life of the certificate. Additional renewal requirements, generally, are not based on completion of additional college work but on other evidence of professional growth. Where additional college work is mandated, this is usually done by local boards—not certification—for which special grants of funds are provided.

6. *Certification Renewal Requirements.*   Another issue in certification practices is closely related to the discussion about life certificates. The various aspects of this issue may be stated as follows: What are sound and desirable requirements for the renewal of teachers' certificates? Should renewal be based upon successful teaching experience plus evidence of professional growth required? If evidence of professional growth is required, what evidence: additional college credit or noncredit experiences, such as travel, committee work, research and writing, work in professional organizations? With respect to these issues, well-defined trends are evident in state certification policies and, particularly, in new requirements of states that have revised certification policies in recent years. With few exceptions, state certification regulations require teachers holding certificates based on preparation below the bachelor's degree to complete prescribed amounts of college work and teaching experience during the terms of the certificates. The prescriptions of additional college work to be completed vary widely. The typical practice seems to be the requirement of completion of six semester hours of college work each year, or six semester hours to be completed during the term of the certificate. The philosophy behind these provisions is that completion of the bachelor's degree of preparation should be the minimum standard for qualified teachers. Thus, all teachers certificated below this minimum are actually substandard in their preparation, and should be required to reach standard preparation.

While a few states renew certificates, based on the bachelor's degree, on successful teaching experience without requiring completion of additional work, the general practice is to require at least six hours of college work to be completed during the term of the certificate. When one year of graduate work has been completed, then a higher type of certificate is issued, and the requirement of additional college work is sometimes dropped.

Renewal requirements for certificates based upon completion of five college years of preparation usually specify that the holders must have taught for a prescribed number of years of the term, have completed additional college work, or must present other evidence of professional growth. This provision means that, at the five-year level of preparation, states do not consider it necessary or desirable to enforce completion of more college work, and that the noncredit experiences enumerated above are acceptable. And, within the framework of the discussion under life certificates, this seems sound. There ought to be a point of preparation beyond which professional growth is left to the qualified teacher and his employing school district to determine.

7. *Centralization of Authority.* The trend toward centralizing the issuing of teachers' certificates in state departments of education has been previously described in this chapter. It is apparent that the diffusion of certification authority among several agencies or officials within states is approaching complete abandonment. Apparently the passing of these controls from city and county administrative officials and state colleges has been accepted as the natural and desirable result of changing conditions. With transportation what it is today, and with the emphasis on more efficient school administrative units, there seems to be little reason to keep certification on a local basis. Nevertheless, there is a pronounced trend toward decentralizing the certification machinery by conferring more autonomy upon the profession in the formulation and enforcement of requirements, while retaining the legal authority in the state education agency. And there is a pronounced trend toward granting more autonomy to the accredited teacher-education institution in determining its own program of preparation.

8. *Certification by Examination.* The rise and decline of the practice of certification by examinations has already been described. Recently new trends in the use of the examination have been emerging.

This trend has been noticeable in large cities, many of which rely on the examination system for the selection of candidates for teaching positions. In many cases both a written and an oral examination are used. The trend seems to be to include a psychological or intelligence test, a personality test, and an aptitude test. The written portion usually also includes a subject-matter test upon the areas in which the teacher must instruct, questions on general and special methods, and sections on child growth and development. The oral examination is usually used to appraise the candidate's personality and general fitness to serve as a guide and counselor for young children.

The trend is also manifested in the use of the National Teacher Examinations to serve as a guide to employing officials. Some cities try to avoid employing teachers unless their credentials contain a record of the results attained on these examinations. A few states, (Georgia, North Carolina, and South Carolina) are also employing the National Teacher Examinations as a basis for the issuance of certificates or for determining the class of certificate to be issued. About a dozen states now use proficiency examinations for endorsement of certain special subjects.

An argument for such a plan is the example set by such professions as accounting, architecture, law, medicine, and dentistry. Examinations also serve to screen out applicants who are obviously unfit. Perhaps only the very poorest candidates are thus eliminated, but at least some undesirable prospects are kept out.

Through an examination system, institutions offering preparation to prospective teachers are kept on their toes. They cannot have too many of their graduates fail if they expect to stay in business.

A serious disadvantage of the examination system is that the curricula of teacher-education institutions would become more or less uniform. Instruction would emphasize materials designed to enable education students to pass the examination. The net effect of such uniformity would be to retard progress and make innovations difficult.

On the negative side, the principal argument against examinations is that they are not a fair test of teaching ability. One may be proficient in subject matter, but totally unable to serve as a guide and counselor of boys and girls. Even on the subject-matter side, one can know a great deal but not be able to teach it. Teaching is a profession in which one works with people rather than with things. It is difficult to judge, by means of written tests, how well one works with either children or adults.

West Virginia instituted in 1958 a proficiency examination for liberal-arts graduates applying for certification. There have been great pressures in recent years for some such provision, by which college graduates who had not completed prescribed education programs could enter teaching, or by which experienced teachers could qualify for additional teaching fields. The arguments advanced to justify such procedures are that many general college graduates can become good teachers by virtue of their broad educational backgrounds, interests, and related experiences. The fact that some 100,000 emergency certificates are issued annually to applicants who have not completed acceptable college curricula for teaching would seem to add some weight to these arguments. The issuance of these large numbers of substandard certificates doubtless is based upon the assumption of some degree of competence of the holders; otherwise their issuance could not be defended. There is, however, in the profession great resistance to the proficiency examination as a means of certification.

The basic argument is that the accepted route in all professions is completion of prescribed college or university curricula. To permit some to avoid this route would tend to destroy the concept of professional preparation and would, in time, return teaching to its earlier status of a profession without distinct preparation and admission requirements, that is, to a nonprofessional status. The experience in West Virginia does not seem to bear out this contention. In a four-year period 640 college graduates took the National Teacher Examinations in that state. Only 190 of these actually passed and secured certificates.

By far a more sweeping and significant issue is the employment of the qualifying examination for certification. This would require that graduates of accredited teacher-education programs pass a broad examination to qualify for certificates. The examinations would be open only to such graduates. Most of the other professions require such qualifying examinations. The arguments for their use are: (1) they would supplement and strengthen existing accrediting procedures; (2) they would reveal existing strengths and weaknesses in the preparing institutions; (3) they would weed out the incompetent or inferior candidates who manage somehow to get through almost every college or university; (4) they would demonstrate to the public that the teaching profession sets for itself discriminating standards for admission; and (5) they would tend to still the public clamor for differentiated scales of pay for teachers.

Arguments against the qualifying examinations are more vehemently advanced by colleges preparing teachers than by teachers themselves. The college teachers contend that their use would quickly force college faculties to teach to pass the exams rather than to concentrate upon the real needs of preparing teachers. They argue that such examinations would have little validity as measures of teacher competence.

Doubtless there are many valid arguments against the use of the qualifying examination. There seem, however, to be ample grounds for assuming that eventually its use will be adopted for admission to the teaching profession, as has been done in other professions.[9]

9. *Balance in the Requirements.* Recent and severe criticism of imbalance in state certification requirements has resulted in widespread review of current specifications. Especially have criticisms of excessive requirements in education courses been given evaluation. Many of these criticisms have been of an extreme nature—have exaggerated the facts. But some excesses have existed in education requirements, and often the teaching-field requirements have been too low. The criticisms have re-

[9] For further discussion of examinations for admission to teaching, see National Education Association, National Commission on Teacher Education and Professional Standards, *The Education of Teachers: Certification,* Report of the San Diego Conference. Washington, D.C.: The Association, 1961, pp. 232–52; or *Journal of Teacher Education,* June, 1960, *11*:223–43.

sulted in a healthy re-examination of existing practices. There are two ways to gauge the validity of requirements: by examining state certification specifications, and by examining those required for graduation by teacher-education institutions.

For elementary school teachers the requirements in professional education for certification among the states range from 15 to 36 semester hours; the median requirement is 24; the mode is 24. For high school teachers, the range is from 12 to 29 semester hours; the median is 18; the mode is 18. Thus, state requirements typically specify about 20 per cent of curriculum for elementary school teachers, and 15 per cent for high school teachers, to be in education courses. An examination of certification requirements in the teaching fields reveals more valid grounds for criticism, being far too low in many instances. For example, in the academic fields the requirements among the states range from 15 to 54 semester hours, with the median ranging from 15–27. The range and median of other fields are: modern languages, 15–48, 22; mathematics, 12–40, 18; chemistry, 12–40, 18; physics, 12–40, 18; biology, 8–30, 18; general science, 12–40, 18; social science, 15–54, 24.

From these figures it is apparent that in some states the minimum requirement for preparation in a teaching field or subject is lower than that specified in education. This has doubtless come about in an effort to meet the needs of small high schools where teachers, generally, have to teach several subjects or fields. Emerging trends indicate that state certification requirements in education will tend to cluster around 24 and 18 semester hours for the elementary and secondary school fields respectively, while institutional requirements will cluster around 30 and 24 hours respectively.

In specialization areas, state requirements seem to be moving toward concentration in a teaching major and minor of approximately 36 and 24 semester hours respectively, which will leave nearly one-half of the degree program for general education.

FUTURE ROLES OF CERTIFICATION

The foregoing provides a picture of existing certification practices and the issues that surround the process. What probable changes will be made to meet future needs and serve the profession of teaching better? Several considerations are suggested below.

What Functions Should Certification Serve?

That certification is trying to serve too many functions is obvious. In some states as many as a dozen or more functions are ascribed to certification, such as enforcing requirements regarding health, citizenship, good moral character, loyalty oaths, age, professional growth, teaching assignments, and ethical conduct, to name a few. Legal licensure cannot serve so many functions well. It ought not to be expected to do so. The profession itself should assume many of the tasks now performed by certification. The development of a self-directing profession of teaching will automatically remove many of these functions from licensure and vest responsibility for them in agencies of the profession.

In a sentence, the basic function that certification eventually ought to serve is to certify that the holder has been selected, prepared, and graduated from an accredited teacher-education program and recommended by the preparing institution as a competent practitioner in specified school levels, fields, or subjects. And, in time, the last specification may be dropped, leaving teaching assignment to other enforcement areas.

Evils of Proliferation of Certificates

It has been pointed out that some states issue as many as fifty to sixty separate-name certificates. This extraordinary proliferation is a result of the pressures from the teaching profession. Each specialized group has felt that a separate certificate enhanced its status, but this practice has some great disadvantages.

In recent years certification has more and more tended to serve the interests of specialized professional groups through detailed prescriptions for endorsement. Of course, the basic intent of these prescriptions was to guarantee competence. But whether these prescriptions, adopted almost always at the request of the specialized groups, always serve this broad function is a moot question. Another basic function of legal licensure is to protect the qualified against the unfair competition of the unqualified. Whether certification is the sole, or even the most effective, means of doing this needs critical examination. The specific certificate is a direct means of legal protection. Thus, the demand for such certificates has proliferated, until the profession is threatened with disintegration by fragmentation. We are tending to become many professions rather than one, with each specialized field constituting a small lake with only tenuous connection with the central stream. Alongside these demands must be laid the yardstick of what is best for education and best for society.

Certification Functions of Professional Organizations

If the functions to be served by legal licensure are to be reduced, these functions must be served by other agencies. What agencies will assume them? We can draw a parallel with other professions and surmise that eventually the appropriate professional associations will assume many of them.

One suggestion is that the state legal authorities should have the legal responsibility for issuing the general practitioner's credentials. Beyond that, the profession would issue the specialized credentials. State legal licensure would be restricted to certification that the holder has completed a program designed to turn out the competent general practitioner. Beyond that, the profession would assume responsibility and issue certificates of membership based on demonstrated competence in the respective subject-matter associations. These "certificates of membership" (or specialized certificates) would have no legal validity; they would serve only as authoritative guides to the employing school officer in making teaching assignments. For example, the medical profession expects legal licensure only of the general practitioner. The fields of specialization (internal medicine, surgery, eye-ear-nose and throat, etc.) are certified through additional specialized preparation and examination by the American Medical Association. These special certificates in medicine have no legal validity. But they have extraordinary powers in the assignment of doctors by other doctors seeking competent consultant services for a patient, and for hospitals selecting experts for service in the specialized fields.

In like manner, as a guide to local school administrators in making teaching assignments, membership in the usual academic teaching-field or subject associations, such as the National Science Teachers Association, the National Council of English Teachers, the National Council of Teachers of Mathematics, or the National Council for the Social Studies, and others, would be based upon and certify evidence of competence.

Kinney has made an eloquent plea for the issuance of a certificate as evidence of membership in the profession, leaving state licensure to satisfy legal requirements, the prerequisite to which would be the certificate of membership in the profession.[11]

This procedure would provide every practitioner with a basic legal credential, and it would tend to relieve state legal authorities of the difficult task of examining candidates and certifying competences in the subject or special school service fields. It would eliminate a mountain of specific course prescriptions, which tend to become so specialized and detailed that a competent practitioner in one state is a maverick in another.

The task force of the "New Horizons in Teacher Education and Professional Standards" project, in its report to the National Commission on Teacher Education and Professional Standards, recommended that the states issue one teachers' certificate, with the fields or subjects for which the holder is qualified to teach endorsed on the certificate. The argument

[11] Lucien B. Kinney, *Certification in Education.* Englewood Cliffs, New Jersey: Prentice-Hall, 1964, 178 pp.

for this procedure is that the proliferation of certificates tends to divide the teaching profession into many professions. It is pointed out that for all other professions only one legal certificate is issued, and all practitioners are required to hold that certificate. Competence in a given field of specialization is attested not by an additional legal certificate or by endorsements, but by professional associations themselves, either through membership requirements or by issuing a certificate of competence based upon additional preparation and examination.

REFERENCES

ANDERSON, EARL W., and RUSHER, ELFREDA M., "Staff—Certification," in HARRIS, CHESTER (ed.) *Encyclopedia of Educational Research*, 3rd ed. New York: Macmillan Company, 1960, pp. 1354–57.

ARMSTRONG, W. EARL, and STINNETT, T. M., *A Manual on Certification Requirements for School Personnel in the United States* (Biennial editions, 1951–1961 and 1964). National Commission on Teacher Education and Professional Standards, National Education Association, Washington, D.C.: The Association.

BEGGS, WALTER K., *The Education of Teachers*. New York: Center for Applied Research in Education, Inc., 1965, Chap. 3, "The Current Situation—Certification," pp. 44–61.

BOOZER, H. R., "External Examinations as Predictors of Competence," *Journal of Teacher Education*, June, 1965, 16:210–14.

BROUDY, H. S., "Conant on *The Education of Teachers*," *Education Forum*, January, 1964, 28:199–210.

CONANT, JAMES B., *The Education of American Teachers*. New York: McGraw-Hill Book Co., 1963, Chap. 3, "Patterns of Certification," pp. 42–55.

COREY, A. F., "CTA Speaks Out for Higher Standards in Licensure of Teachers," *California Education*, March, 1966, 3:3–6+.

CRESSMAN, GEORGE R., and BENDA, HAROLD W., *Public Education in America*, 3rd ed. New York: Appleton-Century-Crofts, 1966, "Legal Requirements for Teaching," pp. 149–156.

EDWARDS, NEWTON, and RICHEY, HERMAN G., *The School in the American Social Order*. Boston: Houghton Mifflin Company, 1963.

KINNEY, LUCIEN B., *Certification in Education*. Englewood Cliffs, N.J.: Prentice-Hall, Inc., 1964.

LIEBERMAN, MYRON, *Education as a Profession*. Englewood Cliffs, New Jersey: Prentice-Hall, 1956, Chap 5, "Certification as a Professional Problem," pp. 124–56.

————, *The Future of Public Education*. Chicago: University of Chicago Press, 1960, pp. 90–95, 102–108.

LINDNER, FRANCES LOUISE (SISTER MARY JOHN, D.C.). *State Certification of Teachers in Catholic Elementary and Secondary Schools.* Unpublished doctoral thesis. New York: St. John's University, February, 1966.

LINDSEY, MARGARET (ed.) *New Horizons for the Teaching Profession.* Washington, D.C.: National Commission on Teacher Education and Professional Standards, National Education Association, 1961, Chap. 6, "A License to Teach," pp. 141–59.

MELARO, C. L., "Comments on Teacher Certification," *NEA Journal*, September, 1966, 55:18–19.

"Migrating Educator? What About Your Teaching Credentials?" *Phi Delta Kappan*, March, 1966, 47:372–4.

MOSIER, EARL E., "Proficiency Examinations—A Wise or Unwise Policy?" *Journal of Teacher Education*, June, 1960, 11:223–30.

NATIONAL EDUCATION ASSOCIATION, National Commission on Teacher Education and Professional Standards, *Changes in Teacher Education: An Appraisal*, Report of the Columbus Conference. Washington, D.C.: The Association, 1964: KURLAND, NORMAN D., "Proficiency Examinations: A New Approach," pp. 89–102.

————, *The Education of Teachers: Certification*, Report of the San Diego Conference. Washington, D.C.: The Association, 1961. Includes Conference Working Papers from *Journal of Teacher Education*, June, 1960, 11:136–309.

————, *Professional Imperatives: Expertness and Self-Determination*, Report of the Fort Collins Conference. Washington, D.C.: The Association, 1962: WENDELL C. ALLEN, "Determining and Enforcing Standards of Accreditation, Certification, and Assignment," pp. 143–162.

PETTIT, M. L., "What College Graduates Say About Education Courses," *Journal of Teacher Education*, December, 1964, 15:378–81.

RICHEY, ROBERT W., *Planning for Teaching*, 3rd ed. New York: McGraw-Hill Book Company, 1963, Chap 4, "Certification and Future Professional Growth," pp. 90–117.

SIMANDLE, S., "Certification Across State Lines," *NEA Journal*, December, 1965, 54:46–7.

STINNETT, T. M., *A Manual on Certification Requirements for School Personnel in the United States*, 1967 ed. National Commission on Teacher Education and Professional Standards, National Education Association, Washington, D.C.: The Association, 1967.

————, "New Horizons in Teacher Certification," *The Future Challenges Teacher Education*, Eleventh Yearbook. Washington, D.C.: American Association of Colleges for Teacher Education, National Education Association, 1958, pp. 132–44.

STONE, J. C., "Teacher Education by Legislation: The California Story Continued," *Phi Delta Kappan*, February, 1966, 47:287–91.

WOELLNER, ROBERT C., and WOOD, M. AURILLA, *Requirements for Certification of Teachers, Counselors, Librarians, Administrators for Elementary Schools, Secondary Schools, Junior Colleges, 1966–67*, Thirty-first edition. Chicago: University of Chicago Press, 1967.

WOODRING, P., "Basic Principles for Development of State Certification Programmes: U.S.A.," *Yearbook of Education 1963*, pp. 521–9.

20: Professional
Accreditation of Teacher
Education

A ccreditation and its processes are unique to the United States. Accreditation is the process by which a voluntary agency, usually an association of schools, puts its stamp of approval upon the quality of the instructional program of institutions admitted to membership. The process is unique because, elsewhere, most countries maintain central legal ministries of education that dictate standards to be met by education institutions.[1] Here this process is extralegal and voluntary. In the United States, in part because our first schools were private and in part because education has been throughout our history a state responsibility, we have developed a historical reliance upon voluntary, rather than legal, enforcement of standards. Although states do maintain accrediting procedures for public elementary and secondary schools (and some states do for colleges), they have generally left to voluntary bodies the application of standards to colleges and universities, that is, left it to agencies or associations of educators to which colleges and universities may or may not, as they choose, subject themselves to examination in order to secure a stamp of approval. Such associations publish annual lists of accredited institutions.

In virtually all states, colleges and universities must secure the approval of the state department of education to engage in teacher education, if they wish their graduates to qualify for certificates to teach in the public schools. This process of approval is often referred to as accreditation, but in the pure meaning of the word it is not. "Approved for teacher

---

[1] John Dale Russell, "The Accrediting of Institutions of Higher Education," *Journal of Teacher Education,* June, 1950, 1:83.

education," rather than "accredited for teacher education" is the more definitive term as applied to the state legal process.

Significance for the Teaching Profession

Accrediting, for teacher education as well as for all professions, is of great importance. It is the means by which the teaching profession attempts to enforce a quality floor for the preparation of its members. And in the final analysis, it is the basic means by which a profession seeks to assure the public of competent practitioners. It is of great importance, therefore, that teachers understand the accrediting procedures for their profession and be prepared to participate in and give support to these procedures.

Actually there are three inseparable aspects of any profession's efforts to provide an adequate supply of qualified practitioners for service to the public. These three aspects are preparation for the profession, accreditation of the program of preparation, and certification (or licensure) of those who complete the prescribed program. For teaching, the three are teacher education, accreditation of teacher-education institutions, and teacher certification. These terms are often used as separate and unrelated ones. In reality they are integral parts of the process of getting qualified teachers into the classrooms. They cannot be separated; each undergirds and supports the other two.

Quite often, too, the three are erroneously grouped as accreditation. Particularly are accreditation and licensure mistakenly used as interchangeable terms. They are not, for each has its own clear function. Accreditation, as we have said, is the process by which an organization, association, or agency recognizes a program of study of a higher-education institution as meeting certain prescribed standards, and publishes annual lists of such institutions so recognized. Certification or licensure, on the other hand, is the process of giving legal approval to an individual to practice a profession. One is voluntary; the other is legal. The intent of accreditation is to protect the student from inferior programs of study; the intent of licensure is to protect the public from the unqualified or incompetent practitioners. The licensing authorities in the respective states rely heavily upon the extralegal accrediting bodies, especially those of the professions, in admitting applicants to examination for licensure or in issuing certificates.

THREE TYPES OF ACCREDITATION

As applied to teacher education, there are three types of accreditation that a college or university may seek: state, regional, and national. All three are voluntary in the sense that no institution is compelled by law to seek accreditation for teacher education, except, perhaps, state supported teacher education institutions; any institution may choose not to offer such a program.

State accreditation (which we have called approval) is basic, because a given institution cannot assure its graduates that they may secure a certificate to teach in the public schools in its state unless its program of teacher education is recognized by the chief state education authority (usually the state board of education, state department of education, or state department of public instruction). In 1967 there were a total of 1,200 colleges and universities approved by the fifty states, the District of Columbia, and Puerto Rico to offer teacher-education programs of some kind.

Six Regional Accrediting Associations

The second process, that of regional accrediting, was the first of the extralegal, voluntary procedures to be developed in the United States. There are six regional accrediting associations, all voluntary, made up of college and university teachers and officials and personnel from the secondary schools. State department-of-education personnel also have been very active in these associations, and maintain close working relationships in the accrediting processes, both state and regional, for high schools, colleges, and universities. The six regional accrediting associations have had profound influence in elevating the quality of education both in the high schools and in higher-education institutions. The regional associations accredit the total college or university program, and their recognition attests to the general excellence of the institution. The six regional associations are as follows: the New England Association of Colleges and Secondary Schools (1885), serving Connecticut, Maine, Massachusetts, New Hampshire, Rhode Island, and Vermont; the Middle States Association of Colleges and Secondary Schools (1892), serving Delaware, the District of Columbia, Maryland, New Jersey, New York, Pennsylvania, Puerto Rico, and the Canal Zone; the North Central Association of Colleges and Secondary Schools (1895), serving Arizona, Arkansas, Colorado, Illinois, Indiana, Iowa, Kansas, Michigan, Minnesota, Missouri, Nebraska, New Mexico, North Dakota, Ohio, Oklahoma, South Dakota, West Virginia, Wisconsin, and Wyoming; the Northwest Association of Secondary and Higher Schools (1918), serving Alaska, Idaho, Montana, Nevada, Oregon, Washington, and Utah; the Southern Association of Colleges and Secondary Schools (1895), serving Alabama, Florida, Georgia, Kentucky, Louisiana, Mississippi, North Carolina, South Carolina, Tennessee, Texas, and Virginia; and the Western College Association (1948), serving California, Hawaii, and Guam.

Evolution of Voluntary Accrediting

In the period from 1870 to 1912 there appeared to be emerging a legal national accrediting agency for colleges and universities. With the rapid multiplication of colleges and universities following the Civil War, the problems of admission standards, transfer of credit from one college to another, and the admission of college graduates to graduate schools became pressing ones. These problems were aggravated by the laxity of state laws regulating the chartering of institutions and by the paucity of state supervision of college practices.

The United States Bureau of Education (now the Office of Education, U.S. Department of Health, Education, and Welfare) was created in 1867 and charged with the responsibility of summarizing the educational activities taking place in the United States. To discharge this function, it was necessary for the bureau to list the number of colleges, college students, and college teachers. To do this, the bureau had to define a college. The list of institutions derived from its definition became, in a sense, an accredited list, because some colleges were excluded for failure to meet the definition. This list was continued until 1912, when violent reactions from the excluded institutions forced the abandonment of the annual listing.[2] Thus ended the trend toward a national list of accredited institutions by a legal agency. Between 1905 and 1948 the Association of American Universities did compile a national list for purposes of admission of students to graduate schools. The abandonment of this listing in 1948 ended another effort to establish voluntary accrediting for general college programs on a national basis.

Evolution of Professional Accrediting

As professions began to emerge in the United States, they gradually turned to the prescribed college and university courses of study and away from apprenticeship and learning-on-the-job preparation. Now, among the twenty-three recognized professions, completion of a prescribed curriculum, plus an examination in many professions, is the established route into licensure and practice in virtually all of them.

This development impelled the respective professional associations to seek some means of guaranteeing that the programs of preparation would be of acceptable quality. Without exception, the professions have been unwilling to rely exclusively upon state and regional accrediting, because state accrediting is too diverse, and regional associations accredit the whole institution rather than one part of it. Thus, each profession developed its own accrediting process and, unlike the regional associations, developed these as national bodies. This was done to assure simi-

[2] George E. Zook and M. E. Haggerty, *Principles of Accrediting Higher Institutions.* Chicago: The University of Chicago Press, 1936.

larity in preparation programs wherever the institutions are located, and thus to establish a national standard of competence for the practitioners wherever they may practice. Also, in establishing their accrediting agencies, the professions, unlike the regional associations, which put the process almost entirely in the hands of representatives of colleges and universities, turned to their own practicing members or to a combination of practitioners and representatives of the preparing schools. Often, licensing agencies also were included.

The first of the national professional accrediting bodies was established for medicine in 1907 by the American Medical Association, although its first standards were not published until 1912. Great impetus was given to this movement by the famous report by Abraham Flexner, issued in 1910 under the title, *Medical Education in the United States and Canada*.[3]

Flexner reported that many of the medical schools were nothing more than diploma mills and did not even require high school graduation for admission. They took a class in October and graduated them as full-fledged doctors the following April. He also reported that in many of these schools student fees were split among the faculty, and that chairs were so lucrative that often they went to the highest bidders. Flexner recommended that fully half of the then 158 schools should be closed. This the American Medical Association proceeded to bring about through rigorous accrediting requirements.

PROFESSIONAL ACCREDITING FOR TEACHER EDUCATION

Eventually the teaching profession had to face up to the same problem of accrediting as had all other professions in the United States. State accrediting was found to be too diverse. In many instances, state accrediting agencies were unable, because of political and other pressures, to impose discriminating standards upon colleges and universities wishing to engage in teacher education. Thus, the quality of teacher-education programs ranged from the superb to the ludicrous. Reciprocity in teacher certification among the states, because of the diversity of requirements, led to regional reciprocity compacts, but these were relatively ineffective; and teachers, highly qualified and broadly experienced, as they transferred to another state, ran into heavy assessments of deficiencies to be made up by further college work.

The teaching profession found, as did the other professions, that accreditation by the regional associations was not enough. Thus, in 1952

[3] Abraham Flexner, *Medical Education in the United States and Canada*, Bulletin No. 4. New York: The Carnegie Foundation for the Advancement of Teaching, 1910.

it established the National Council for Accreditation of Teacher Education, being the last of the then recognized professions to do so.

Before describing that organization, we should review the long, often bitter struggle of teaching to be recognized as a profession and to receive recognition of the right to a national professional accrediting process.

Emergence of Teacher Education

It will be remembered that teacher education as a professional process began with the founding of the normal schools in 1839. Throughout their history, almost to the beginning of this century, these were subcollegiate institutions, offering curricula first at the elementary school level, later reaching high school status, and finally offering two years of college work. It is not surprising that standard colleges took a dim view of these institutions. Teacher education, with these lowly beginnings, has a long history of alleged inferiority among the respected disciplines in higher education. When the normal schools began to be transformed into degree-granting teachers colleges, beginning about 1900 and continuing during the first three decades of this century, the latter inherited the low state imputed to the normal schools. With the converting of teachers colleges into state colleges and universities, which has transpired largely in the last two decades, the attitude of scorn has been ameliorated somewhat. The low respect for teacher education is reflected by the attitude of the regional accrediting associations and the struggle of the profession for decent accrediting procedures. The North Central Association of Colleges and Secondary Schools, for example, was founded in 1895, and issued its first list of accredited colleges in 1913, but not until 1918 did standards for teachers colleges develop. The Middle States Association debated the admission of teachers colleges at its first meeting in 1887, but not until 1934 did this association begin accrediting teachers colleges.[4] The New England Association, although until 1952 it was not actually an accrediting body, has only in the last few years admitted teachers colleges to membership.

History of Efforts to Establish Accrediting for Teacher Education

Prior to establishment of the NCATE in 1952, several efforts had been made to achieve an effective national body to improve teacher education. The first national association of teacher-education institutions was the National Education Association's Department of Normal Schools, founded in 1870. In 1902, the Council of Normal School Presidents was formed. This evolved in successive stages to merge in 1923 with the American Association of Teachers Colleges, founded in 1917. The American As-

---

[4] William K. Selden, "Why Accredit Teacher Education?" *Journal of Teacher Education,* June, 1960, *11*:185–190.

sociation of Colleges for Teacher Education was founded in 1948 by a merger of the American Association of Teachers Colleges with the National Association of Teacher Education Institutions in Metropolitan Areas and the National Association of Colleges and Departments of Education.

The AATC (American Association of Teachers Colleges) adopted accrediting standards in 1923, and began accrediting in 1927. The AACTE (American Association of Colleges for Teacher Education) carried on the function of national accrediting of teacher education until 1954, when the NCATE began formal accrediting operations. The AACTE was able to attain a membership of 284 institutions, including some liberal-arts colleges and universities. But the bulk of the some 1,150 approved teacher-education institutions continued to ignore its accrediting procedures.

The Founding of NCATE

In 1948 the first thrust of the organized teaching profession for a more effective accrediting process had its first beginning. One group in the Bowling Green National TEPS Conference recommended "that the National Commission on Teacher Education and Professional Standards call a national conference on accreditation." [5]

In 1950 the National Commission on Teacher Education and Professional Standards devoted its national conference (the Indiana Conference) to "Evaluative Criteria for Teacher Education Institutions." John Dale Russell, then director of the Division of Higher Education, United States Office of Education, in his keynote address advocated the establishment of a joint council for the accreditation of teacher education, broadly representative of the interested groups, including the teacher-education institutions, the organized teaching profession, the state education legal authorities, and local school administrative officials, professional and lay.[6]

This recommendation sparked the beginning of formal negotiations to establish such a council. A "Temporary Committee" with sixteen members, including representatives from the AACTE, NCTEPS, the Council of Chief State School Officers, and the National School Boards Association, was established to study the question and recommend a proposed organization. The Temporary Committee reported its findings in 1951, as follows:

That a national professional accrediting body for teacher education be established; that it be a joint council consisting of 21 members designated as follows: Six representatives to be appointed by the American Association of Colleges for

[5] H. B. Allman (recorder), "Accreditation and Development of Teacher Education Institutions," *The Education of Teachers—As Viewed By the Profession*, Report of the Bowling Green Conference. Washington, D.C.: National Commission on Teacher Education and Professional Standards, National Education Association, 1948, pp. 39–46.

[6] Ruth A. Stout, "The Indiana Conference Charts A Course," *Journal of Teacher Education*, September, 1950, 3:175–83. See also T. M. Stinnett, "Accreditation and the Professionalization of Teaching," *Journal of Teacher Education*, March, 1952, 3:30–39.

Teacher Education; six representatives to be appointed by the Executive Committee of the National Education Association, upon nomination by its National Commission on Teacher Education and Professional Standards; six representatives of the state education legal authorities, three to be appointed by the Council of Chief State School Officers, and three by the National Association of State Directors of Teacher Education and Certification; three representatives of local education legal agencies (school boards) to be appointed by the National School Boards Association.

These recommendations were approved by the five constituent agencies at annual meetings during 1951–52, and the joint council—the National Council for Accreditation of Teacher Education—was established, effective September 1, 1952.

The council, however, did not begin functioning as an active accrediting body until July 1, 1954, when W. Earl Armstrong became its executive director. On this date the council formally assumed the accrediting function that had been exercised from 1948 to 1954 by the AACTE. The council assumed the list of 284 institutions then on the accredited list of AACTE, but provided that these institutions would be re-evaluated as quickly as possible.

At the outset the NCATE faced major problems. Chief among these were inadequate financial support and the resistance of several college associations to the idea of a professional accrediting body for teacher education.

PROPOSAL FOR THE ESTABLISHMENT OF A NATIONAL COUNCIL FOR ACCREDITATION OF TEACHER EDUCATION

(Adopted April 27–29, 1951, by the Temporary Committee; amended at the meetings on September 22, 1951, and March 22, 1952)

I. Goals to Be Achieved by National Council

A. Recognition of teaching as a major profession *

B. Provision by all institutions preparing personnel for this profession of programs, facilities, and other resources adequate to insure professional competence.

Ability to achieve these goals within a reasonable time depends upon:

1. Clear designation of agencies responsible for legal accreditation and certification in the states and also of a representative voluntary agency to develop professional standards for all programs of teacher education.

2. Organization to insure full participation in the profession and laymen in the formulation of policies for accreditation and improvement of programs of teacher education.

3. Development of general public opinion in support of professional status for education.

II. Functions to Be Served by National Council

A. To formulate standards for teacher preparation through continuous research and through consideration of the recommendations of all organizations concerned with the improvement of the preparation of teachers.

* "Teaching" is to be interpreted broadly as the professional group.

B. To devise ways and means of evaluating institutional programs of teacher education by the application of these standards on the request of an institution, or state authority responsible for the accreditation desired by the institution.

C. To publish lists of institutions accredited by this Council.

III. Membership of National Council

The Council shall be composed of 21 * members to serve for three-year terms, no individual serving for more than two consecutive terms. Members of the Council shall be appointed as follows, each organization to arrange for the expiration of the terms of an equal number of its appointees each year.

A. Legal state education agencies. The National Council of Chief State School Officers shall name three members; the National Association of State Directors of Teacher Education and Certification shall name three members.

B. Practitioners. The National Commission on Teacher Education and Professional Standards shall name six members, broadly representative of the profession in the field.

C. Teacher-education institutions. The American Association of Colleges for Teacher Education shall name six members, broadly representative of institutions engaged in teacher education.

D. Boards of education. The National School Boards Association shall name three members.

* Reduced to nineteen in 1956 and expanded to 22 in 1966.

Source: "NEA to Act on Proposed Council," *Journal of Teacher Education*, June, 1952, 3:84.

In 1967 the NCATE had a budget of about $175,000. The NCATE is financed as follows: support from the NEA, through appropriating $42,000 a year to the budget of the National Commission on Teacher Education and Professional Standards; allotment by the AACTE of 18.5 per cent of its income from institutional membership, which yields about $40,000 a year; miscellaneous income from other sources equaling about $20,000 a year. In 1960 the NCATE for the first time inaugurated a fee for institutions seeking accreditation. This fee amounts to about $300 per institution on the average, and will add an estimated $50,000 a year to its budget. The council, however, is still underfinanced and understaffed. Under the fee plan, each institution is to be re-evaluated every ten years.

Resistances to Establishment of NCATE

The merger of the three organizations to form the AACTE in 1948 aroused apprehensions among presidents of higher-education institutions that the merger threatened the emergence of another national accrediting body, and had a part in bringing about the formation of the National Commission on Accrediting. By this time, administrative officials of higher-education institutions had become alarmed at the proliferation of accrediting agencies and their demands. The matter of the accrediting fees was beginning to be burdensome. But most of all was the threat of interference with institutional autonomy.

The NCATE, from the outset, faced vigorous criticism and apprehension from many colleges. These institutions were alarmed at the growing number of professional accrediting agencies which, from their viewpoint, tended to usurp the autonomy of the institutions by enforcing special demands. Second, there was great reluctance to recognize teaching as a profession and, therefore, to concede its right to a professional accrediting process similar to that accorded other professions. Third, these institutions were apprehensive that the NCATE would be dominated by the profession through the NEA, and by the legal agencies. Despite the fact that the NCATE was established as an autonomous, self-determining body, these fears continued, and from the start led to demands upon the National Commission on Accrediting to deny recognition to the NCATE as a professional accrediting agency. In the period between 1954 and 1956 the NCA studied both sides of the situation, and on October 10, 1956, recognized the NCATE as the official professional accrediting body for teacher education, subject to certain conditions.

The chief condition was that the structure of the council be changed to provide a majority of its membership from higher-education institutions. Accordingly, in 1957 the composition of NCATE was changed from twenty-one to nineteen members, distributed as follows: six representatives of the NEA, appointed by the NEA Executive Committee from nominations made by the National Commission on Teacher Education and Professional Standards; seven representatives of teacher-education institutions, appointed by the AACTE; three additional representatives of colleges, appointed by an *ad hoc* committee of the National Commission on Accrediting; two representatives from the state education legal agencies, one appointed by the Council of Chief State School Officers and one appointed by the National Association of State Directors of Teacher Education and Certification; and one representative appointed by the National School Boards Association.

This step mollified much of the criticism and fear of the NCATE, but not all of it. William Selden, executive secretary of the National Commission on Accrediting, the body that had to face the difficult problem of resolving the controversy, has summarized the arguments against recognizing the right of teaching to have its own professional accrediting process as follows:

In the first place, the liberal arts people, at least up until a few years ago, frequently objected to the argument that teaching is a profession like medicine or law. For one group of teachers to claim that teaching is not a profession is to proclaim a denial of their own birthright. Teaching shares an ancient heritage of professional status with law and medicine. Even though teaching in this country does not presently enjoy the preferred economic or social status of law or medicine, the facts of contemporary political life are clear that without an organized presentation of professional goals, improved economic and social status will not likely be attained . . . a second contention shared by many liberal arts people was that the extension of professional accrediting into this area of teacher education was completely unnecessary since it could be adequately served by the regional associations. This argument fails to take into account the fact that all professions, as early as medieval times, have sought to control the preparation for and admission into their ranks. In our country, as medicine so successfully proved, accreditation has been one of the most important mechanisms employed in this procedure.[7]

The National Commission on Accrediting

The NCA is not an accrediting body in the usual sense of the term. It is, in fact, an accrediting agency of accrediting agencies—that is, it recognizes and puts the stamp of approval on accrediting agencies that are acceptable to its constituent associations of higher education. It is empowered to act in this capacity by seven national associations of colleges and universities, as follows: American Association of Junior Colleges, American Association of Land-Grant Colleges and State Universities, Association of American Colleges, Association of American Universities, Association of Teacher Education Institutions (which was superseded by the newly formed—in 1961—Association of State Colleges and Universities), Association of Urban Universities, and National Association of State Universities. The NCA also has an institutional membership of some 1,200 colleges and universities.[8]

The NCA was formed in 1949 as successor to the Joint Committee on Accrediting, the latter having been formed in 1938 by the Association of Land-Grant Colleges and Universities and the National Association of State Universities. The emergence of the Joint Committee on Accrediting really represented a revolt against the proliferation of accrediting agencies. The major protests against accrediting bodies were the excessive number of them, the expense involved for colleges and universities, the threat to institutional autonomy, pressures for favoritism for certain departments or schools of a given college or university, and unwarranted interference with the administration of an institution. From the late 1930's on, the protests grew in volume and vehemence, resulting in the establishment of NCA in the hope of bringing some order out of a situation that had grown somewhat chaotic. The NCA consists of 42 members, each of the seven constituent associations selecting six members for three-year terms. The

---

[7] William K. Selden, op. cit., p. 188.

[8] For a fuller treatment of the history, purposes, and work of the NCA, see William K. Selden, "The National Commission on Accrediting," Accreditation in Higher Education (Lloyd E. Blauch, ed.), a publication of the U.S. Department of Health, Education, and Welfare, Office of Education. Washington, D.C.: U.S. Government Printing Office, 1959, Chap. 4, pp. 22–28.

NCA has declared as policy that it will recognize only one accrediting agency for a geographical area (regional association) and one agency for any one professional field. Thus, when the National Council for Accreditation of Teacher Education began to function in 1954, the problem of recognition by NCA precipitated somewhat of a hassle. The problem was resolved, as previously described, by NCA extending recognition to NCATE.

Criticisms have been directed both at NCA and NCATE over the agreement by which recognition was extended. The NCA was under great pressures from some of its constituent associations and from many of its institutional members to deny teaching a national professional accrediting agency. These pressures resulted largely from resistance to the notion that teaching is a profession and entitled to the rights accorded other recognized professions, such as medicine and law, and the contention that the regional accrediting association could adequately handle accrediting of institutions for teacher education. Despite these pressures, NCA maintained an attitude of fairness and recognized NCATE.

The NCATE, on the other hand, was bitterly criticized by some for what appeared to be knuckling under to the conditions laid down by NCA. The NEA and its National Commission on Teacher Education and Professional Standards were severely censured in some quarters for yielding to demands that a majority of NCATE members be representatives of colleges. Since the NEA represents fully three-fourths of the practicing members of the teaching profession, some felt that it should have demanded a majority of the membership. These viewpoints are all debatable, of course. Joint councils maintained by other professions (and the NCATE is a joint council) vary in size and composition. There is no set pattern. Most, however, contain representation from three groups or agencies: the practitioners, the preparing colleges and universities, and the legal licensing agencies. This structure obtains on NCATE, with one additional group represented: lay boards of education. It is true, however, that several professions (notably medicine and dentistry) do have control over their professional accrediting bodies, but they also include representatives from the three groups or agencies. In the long view, both NCA and NCATE will be commended for exercising statesmanship in the settlement of this difficult and delicate controversy.

In 1963 the National Commission on Accrediting began a review of the structure of the National Council for Accreditation of Teacher Education, and new requirements were to be proposed.

Criticisms of Structure of NCATE

It has been pointed out that the original structure of NCATE was changed from twenty-one to nineteen members in 1957, and provision was made to assure a majority (ten of nineteen) of college people on the council. The review of NCA beginning in 1963 resulted in a new structuring of NCATE. The number of members was changed to twenty-two— including 6 appointed by NEA, 10 appointed by AACTE, 3 representing the academic disciplines appointed by NCA, 2 representing state education departments, and one appointed by the National School Board Association. Thus, the proportion of practitioners was decreased, and that of college personnel increased.[9] But the restructurings of NCATE did not end criticism of its make-up. There is the criticism that there are too few from the liberal-arts fields, or academic disciplines, on the council. The fact that there are four representatives from liberal-arts colleges does not satisfy the critics. Their contention is that these are largely administrators, and there should be more scholars representing the academic fields. Others attack the council structure on the grounds that it contains too few classroom teachers from the public schools. Lieberman, especially, has criticized the council structure for this reason.[10]

The appropriate make-up of a professional accrediting agency is a matter about which there are varied opinions and viewpoints. Of twenty-one major professions (see Table 54), nine maintain associations of practi-

TABLE 54 Types of Accrediting Agencies Maintained by Twenty-Three Professions, and Dates of Establishment

An Association of Practitioners	An Association of Preparing Schools	Joint Council
Chemistry (1937)	Bible (1948)	Architecture (1914)
Chiropody (1951)	Business Administration (1916)	Dentistry (1909)
Forestry (1935)	Education (1927)	Engineering (1934)
Law * (1921)	Law *	Journalism (1945)
Library Science (1924)	Music (1924)	Pharmacy (1932)
Medicine (1907)	Nursing (1933)	Education (1952)
Optometry (1941)	Social Work (1927)	
Public Health (1946)	Theology (1936)	
Veterinary Medicine (1941)		

Source: T. M. Stinnett, "Accreditation and the Professionalization of Teaching," *Journal of Teacher Education*, March, 1952, 3:30–31.

* Law maintains accrediting by both a council and an association of law schools. Education now maintains only one, the joint Council.

[9] For a description of the controversy surrounding this restructuring see John Mayor, *Accreditation in Teacher Education. Its Influence on Higher Education.* Washington, D.C.: National Commission on Accrediting, 1963, 311 pp.

[10] See Myron Lieberman, *Education as a Profession.* Englewood Cliffs, New Jersey: Prentice-Hall, Inc., 1956, Chap. 6, "Accreditation and Professionalization," pp. 157–84.

tioners, eight have associations of preparing schools, and six maintain joint councils with representatives of the practitioners, the preparing schools, and the legal licensing agencies. The NCATE is in the last category. One of the criticisms of NCATE is that there are too few practitioners included in the membership. It depends upon what definition of practitioners is accepted. On this point, teaching cannot be compared with other professions, such as medicine, for example, where the practitioner is clearly separated from the personnel in preparing institutions. The members of NCATE, except the school board member, could all be considered practitioners, if one accepts the concept of the teaching profession as one profession. The critics, generally, do not accept this concept and regard only the classroom teachers from the public schools as practitioners.

Other critics contend that the NCATE should be controlled by the profession in the elementary and secondary schools, and that its membership should, therefore, consist entirely of practitioners from these schools. Persuasive arguments can be advanced for this viewpoint. And many observers believe that eventually this will be the case, that the present arrangement is an evolutionary step toward this end.

Current Status of NCATE

In 1967 there were 1,200 colleges and universities authorized to engage in teacher education—that is, this number of institutions were approved for teacher education by their respective state departments of education. Of these, a total of 1,062 were accredited by their regional associations, and 449 had received NCATE accreditation. Thus, about 136 of the institutions preparing teachers could not meet the standards of general excellence of the regional accrediting associations, and 749 at that time were not accredited by NCATE.

By 1967, the 449 NCATE-accredited colleges and universities produced about 75 per cent of the new teacher supply, new graduates prepared for teaching.

TEACHERS' ROLE IN ACCREDITATION

The importance of NCATE in the professionalization of teaching is many-fold. First, it will serve to establish a quality floor for teacher-education programs. Teaching has been without such a floor, so much so that the profession has frequently been mercilessly exploited by many colleges that used teacher education to entice enrollment into inferior programs. This quality floor, which will be constantly upgraded, will more and more tend to guarantee highly qualified entrants into the teaching profession. Moreover, it will tend to assure that new teachers, wherever they obtain their preparation, will have completed programs of greater similarity as to content and scholarly attainments. As Lieberman pointed out,[11] teachers have perhaps a stronger stake in the accreditation of teacher education than have other professional people. In the other professions state licensing requirements generally include a rigorous examination as an additional hurdle, whereas in teaching this is not the case. Such examinations tend to validate, to some degree, the equality of preparation. National accrediting of teacher education offers real hope for the elimination of cheap, shoddy shortcuts to entrance into the profession.

Also, as has been pointed out, NCATE accreditation offers real hope for achieving national reciprocity in teacher certification. By 1967 thirty-seven states, by the action of their state boards of education, had made reciprocity in certification rather automatic for graduates of NCATE accredited institutions. This does not mean that graduates of other institutions will be denied certification. And one professional association—the American Association of School Administrators—requires new members (since 1964) to be graduates of NCATE-accredited institutions.

As to the roles of teachers in the accrediting process, there are several:

1. The NCATE is structured to provide participation of practitioners in accrediting procedures. The practitioners (through the NEA) have six representatives on the council. In any profession the program of preparation for its members tends to take on the image of the profession. The impact of the individual teacher can be great, small, or none at all, depending upon his interest and willingness to become knowledgeable about the problems, issues, goals, and procedures involved. The respective state TEPS commissions, through study programs and conferences, seek to involve all teachers in participation in policy making and application. NCATE policies provide for a representative of the appropriate state education association (and its TEPS commission) to serve on each team selected to visit institutions seeking accreditation. Such responsibility involves the duty to know intimately the problems involved. A number of state education associations have conducted training schools or seminars for members designated to serve on future NCATE accrediting teams. If teachers want a part, and are to have a part, in the accrediting function, they must acquire the knowledge and skills to do so.

2. Teachers must provide intelligent support for the accrediting process in teacher education. If they are indifferent to the problem, then their profession will continue to be exploited and denied its proper status. Such support really denotes a "climate of public opinion" within the profession. Unawareness of what are accredited programs, and indifference to the certification of new teachers from such programs, are perhaps the most effective means, if adopted by a substantial portion of teachers, to prevent teaching from achieving a solid professional status.

[11] *Ibid.,* pp. 157–58.

3. The counseling of students seeking a college in which to enroll and to prepare for teaching is still another important role of teachers in the accrediting process. High school students, as a rule, do not know the intricacies of accrediting. Unless properly advised, they can choose colleges that have only state approval for teacher education. They should be advised of the advantages in choosing fully accredited institutions. In the choice of a college, prospective teachers should be advised that state approval for teacher education is basic, since without such approval there is no assurance of certification. Regional accrediting is essential for the transfer of credits and acceptance by other states for certification. NCATE accreditation (which requires that the institution be accredited by its regional association) will eventually tend to assure certification in any state.

PROFESSIONAL ACCREDITING BODIES RECOGNIZED BY NCA

Mayor [12] lists 28 professions maintaining national professional accrediting agencies as follows: architecture, art, business administration, chemistry, dental hygiene, dentistry, engineering, forestry, journalism, landscape architecture, law (American Bar Association), law education (Association of American Law Schools), librarianship, medical record librarianship, medical technology, medicine, music, nursing, occupational therapy, optometry, pharmacy, physical therapy, psychology, public health, social work, speech pathology and audiology, teacher education, theology, and veterinary medicine.

The Office of Education, U.S. Department of Health, Education, and Welfare, lists twenty-four professions with active, nationally recognized professional accrediting organizations as follows: anesthesia, architecture, Bible, business, chemistry, dentistry, engineering, forestry, journalism, law, library science, medicine, music, nursing, optometry, osteopathy, pharmacy, podiatry, public health, religious education, social work, teacher education, theology, and veterinary medicine.[13]

REFERENCES

AMERICAN ASSOCIATION OF COLLEGES FOR TEACHER EDUCATION, *Evaluative Criteria for Accrediting Teacher Education.* Washington, D.C.: The Association, 1967.

[12] John Mayor, *Accreditation in Teacher Education, op. cit.,* pp. 241–271.
[13] Theresa Birch Wilkins, *Accredited Higher Institutions,* U.S. Department of Health, Education, and Welfare, U.S. Office of Education, Bulletin 1960, No. 24. Washington, D.C.: U.S. Government Printing Office, 1960, p. 3.

BEGGS, WALTER K., *The Education of Teachers*. New York: Center for Applied Research in Education, Inc., 1965, Chap. 4, "The Current Situation—Accreditation of Programs in Teacher Education," pp. 62–83.

———, "Structure and Finance of the National Council for Accreditation of Teacher Education," *Journal of Teacher Education*, June, 1964, *15*: 136–47.

CONANT, JAMES B., *The Education of American Teachers*. New York: McGraw-Hill Book Co., 1963, Chaps. 3, 4, and 10.

COTTRELL, D. P., "NCATE Criteria and Procedures: An Analysis of Some Issues and Problems," *Journal of Teacher Education*, June, 1964, *15*:148–64.

EVERS, NATHANIEL, "Let's Be About Our Business," *Journal of Teacher Education*, June, 1961, *12*:132–38.

FLEXNER, ABRAHAM, *Medical Education in the United States and Canada*, Bulletin No. 4. New York: The Carnegie Foundation for the Advancement of Teaching, 1910.

LINDSEY, MARGARET (ed.) *New Horizons for the Teaching Profession*. Washington, D.C.: National Commission on Teacher Education and Professional Standards, National Education Association, 1961, Chap. 5, "Accreditation of Professional Preparatory Programs," pp. 109–40.

LIEBERMAN, MYRON, *Education as a Profession*. Englewood Cliffs, New Jersey: Prentice-Hall, 1956, Chap. 6, "Accreditation and Professionalization," pp. 157–84.

MAYOR, JOHN R., *Accreditation in Teacher Education, Its Influence on Higher Education*. Washington, D.C.: National Commission on Accrediting, 1965.

———, "Influence on Higher Education of Accreditation in Teacher Education," *Liberal Education*, March, 1965, *51*:44–53.

NATIONAL EDUCATION ASSOCIATION, National Commission on Teacher Education and Professional Standards, *Professional Imperatives: Expertness and Self-Determination*, Report of the Fort Collins Conference. Washington, D.C.: The Association, 1962: Wendell C. Allen, "Determining and Enforcing Standards of Accreditation, Certification, and Assignment," pp. 143–162.

RUSSELL, JOHN DALE, "The Accrediting of Institutions of Higher Education," *Journal of Teacher Education*, June, 1950, *1*:83–93.

———, "An Analysis of the Proposed National Council for Accreditation of Teacher Education," *Journal of Teacher Education*, June, 1952, *3*:87–93.

SELDEN, WILLIAM K., *Accreditation: The Struggle Over Standards in Higher Education*. New York: Harper & Brothers, 1960.

———, "Nationwide Standards and Accreditation," *AAUP Bulletin*, December, 1964, *50*:311–16.

STILES, L. J., "Reorganizing Accreditation for Teacher Education," *Phi Delta Kappan*, October, 1963, 45:31–7.

STINNETT, T. M., *A Manual on Certification Requirements for School Personnel in the United States*, 1967 ed. National Commission on Teacher Education and Professional Standards, National Education Association, Washington, D.C.: The Association, 1967.

THOMAS, M. B., "Purposes and Policies of the National Council on Accreditation of Teacher Education," *Journal of Teacher Education*, June, 1964, 15:130–5.

WILKINS, THERESA BIRCH, *Accredited Higher Institutions*. U.S. Department of Health, Education, and Welfare, Office of Education, Bulletin 1965, No. 1. Washington, D.C.: U.S. Government Printing Office, 1965.

Part Six
THE CHANGING SCENE IN TEACHING

21: The Competitive Struggle Among Teachers' Organizations

*I*ncluded in Chapter 17 was an extensive discussion of a wide variety of associations and organizations that seek to serve the general and specialized interests of teachers, at all levels of teaching. The discussions in that chapter referred largely to noncompeting organizations, although there generally is an overlapping of membership among them.

In recent years (since about 1960) there has developed an intense, competitive struggle for the membership of teachers, particularly those in the public schools. Fundamentally, the competition is between the two general national organizations and their affiliates—the National Education Association and the American Federation of Teachers. The affiliates of NEA are the respective state education associations, about 55 in number, including a few states that in 1967 still had two associations, the Overseas Education Association, and Puerto Rico, and some 9,000 local associations. The American Federation of Teachers has about 25 state federations and 700 local federations affiliated with it.

This competition between the two national organizations has great import for the future of teachers at all levels, but especially for public school teachers. Therefore, teachers should know the histories, philosophies, objectives, structures, and services of the NEA and AFT and their affiliates. Because of this necessity, Chapters 21 and 22 have been added to this edition.

HISTORY OF THE COMPETITION

The modern history of the struggle between these two great national rivals for the organizational loyalties of teachers, as already indicated, began about 1960. The real beginnings of the struggle date to the early years of this century. Although the American Federation of Teachers did not come into being until 1916, the actual beginnings of teachers' affiliation with organized labor began much earlier.

The inception of the movement of teachers to affiliate with labor was with the Chicago Federation of Teachers, organized in 1897, as a federation unaffiliated with labor. In 1902, the Chicago Federation of Teachers formally affiliated with the local labor organization, and in the same year it was admitted to membership in the American Federation of Labor (AFL). The San Antonio Teachers Association preceded the Chicago group in such affiliation by a few months. The AFL at that time declared that the time was ripe for organization of teachers in all parts of the United States.[1]

Although this pronouncement by AFL proved to be somewhat premature, other local teachers' groups, struggling to remedy the same economic, political, and educational conditions in their school districts as the Chicago Federation, did seek affiliation. Between 1902 and 1916 (when AFT was formed) some 20 local teachers' groups in 10 states affiliated with labor organizations. But in many instances these affiliated locals after short lives disappeared, perhaps for lack of a cohesive national force.

In 1915, the Chicago teachers, in a letter signed by officers and members of the Chicago Federation of Men Teachers, the Chicago Teachers Federation, and the Federation of Women High School Teachers, proposed the formation of a national federation of teachers to be affiliated with the American Federation of Labor. The three Chicago Federations and the Gary, Indiana, federation met on April 15, 1916, resulting in the formation of the American Federation of Teachers, providing for the first time a national focus for the efforts to align teachers with organized labor. Shortly thereafter, the original four locals were joined by the Teachers Union of the City of New York, the Oklahoma Teachers Federation, the Scranton, Pennsylvania, Teachers Association, and the High School Teachers Union of Washington, D.C.[2]

The basic cause for this break with tradition regarding the organizational affiliation of teachers was two-fold: (1) the desire to improve the economic lot of teachers; and (2) the apparent ineptness at that time of traditional teachers organizations in rectifying the existing conditions under which public school teachers were working.

At this point, it is interesting to note several parallels with the history of NEA. NEA came into being in 1857, somewhat like the AFT, as a result of the effort of 10 already existing state education associations, which

---

[1] For a comprehensive history of the movement toward teacher affiliation with organized labor, see *Organizing the Teaching Profession.* The Commission on Educational Reconstruction, AFT. Glencoe, Illinois: The Free Press, 1955, 320 pp.

[2] *Organizing the Teaching Profession, op. cit.,* Chap. 1, pp. 19–51.

were motivated by the need for a national focus to improve education and the status of teachers. Secondly, the period that saw the origin of affiliations of teachers with labor and the founding of AFT (1902–1916) was the period in which the NEA had come to be dominated largely by the presidents of prestigious universities, most of which were private. The ruling power structure of NEA during this period seemed to be oblivious to the desperate need of public school teachers for better salaries and better working conditions. Moreover, this power structure appeared unconcerned about the plight of the public school teachers in general. Not until about 1920—in significant measure due to the impact of the efforts of Ella Flagg Young, the first woman president of NEA, elected in 1910, and members of the teachers unions in Chicago—did a full-scale revolution in NEA structure occur, resulting in the unseating of the university presidents, the establishment of a representative assembly, the Research Division, the *NEA Journal,* and a Commission to wage a campaign for federal aid to the public schools.[3]

The situation that the teachers had to fight in Chicago was such that teachers were compelled to seek an alliance with a sympathetic power structure. The only one of significant influence at hand was organized labor.

There were involved in the Chicago situation at the turn of the century many of the factors that influenced the resurgence of teacher unionism in the 1950's and 1960's. In the first place, Chicago had skyrocketed in population between 1860 and 1890, from 100,000 to about 1,000,000. Chicago, at the beginning of the twentieth century, was a rapidly growing big city, experiencing impacts somewhat comparable to those resulting from the precipitate urbanization of the United States after World War II.

In this rapid expansion in Chicago, as was true of most large cities in the urbanization period referred to, the demand for public services outstripped the existing tax resources. This was true of school services. The city fell behind in construction of school buildings, and its schools became enmeshed in city politics, through appointment and domination of the Board of Education by the Mayor and City Council. The removal by the Mayor of noncompliant board members was common. At one time there were two boards of education in Chicago, each claiming to be the legal board. Political manipulations of the board and schools became increasingly apparent, culminating in the indictment and conviction of some members of the Board of Education. As late as 1945, certain personnel practices of the Chicago superintendent of schools came under fire from

[3] For a more comprehensive description see T. M. Stinnett, *Turmoil in Teaching.* New York: The Macmillan Company, 1968, Chap. 2, "Evolution of the Organizational Struggle," pp 17–39. Also see Edgar B. Wesley, *NEA: The First Hundred Years.* New York: Harper Brothers, 1957, Chap. 27, pp. 322–333.

citizens. The NEA investigated and found it necessary to expel the superintendent from NEA membership (See Chapter 15).

Prior to 1897, the salaries of Chicago teachers had been virtually un-
changed for two decades. The Chicago Teachers Federation was instrumental in securing raises in teachers' salaries in that year, but the gain
was short-lived, being cut back by the board in a retrenchment program.
As is often the case in any school retrenchment program, teachers' salaries
were the first to suffer most heavily. Incensed, the teachers under the
leadership of Margaret Haley and Catherine Goggin began to investigate
tax evasion and the low tax assessments of big corporations. A suit against
the evaders resulted in about $1,000,000 new revenue, which the Board
sought to divert to other needs than teachers' salaries. The Teachers Federation had to seek a court injunction to prevent the threatened diversion.
In both the tax evasion and tax assessment controversies, the federation
was supported by the Chicago Trades Federation, although the teachers
federation was not then formally affiliated with organized labor.

Backed now by a power structure of its own, the Chicago federation
continued and intensified its struggles for adequate school support and
teachers salaries against the low-tax interests in the city. Naturally, these
efforts led to retaliation. The Board struck back in 1915 with the Loeb
Rule, prohibiting membership of teachers in labor unions, thus seeking to
divorce the teachers from the chief source of their strength. This edict affected 3,000 teachers. With the aid of the Chicago Federation of Labor,
the teachers union was able to secure a temporary court injunction against
the enforcement of the rule, and later a permanent injunction was issued.
In apparent further efforts at retaliation, the Board of Education dismissed
68 union teachers, causing wide repercussions and resulting in state legislation in 1917 abolishing the Board of Education and establishing a new
board under a new code of law.

The Formative Years of AFT

Following the founding of AFT in 1916, the growth of the union movement among teachers was slow, but, except for an interlude or two,
gradual.

It must be remembered that in its beginning—up to about 1960—teachers
themselves, here and there, took the initiative in seeking affiliation with
labor. This happened in places, largely in cities, where conditions were allowed to deteriorate beyond the point of tolerance. Partisan political domination of the schools, disgracefully low teachers salaries, inadequate
supplies and instructional materials, often obsolete and unsafe school
buildings, were some of the motivating factors. In addition, there was the

domination of power groups over the operation of the schools, with low-tax advocates leading the domination, and the callous disregard of teachers' rights as American citizens and as competent professionals.

For recourse, teachers in several places turned to what appeared to them to be the only sympathetic power group available—organized labor. President Kennedy in his inaugural address in 1961 warned against the blocking of the legitimate aspirations of a free people for economic justice with the remark: "Those who make peaceful evolution impossible make violent revolution inevitable."

The teacher groups that constituted the leaders in the early movement to affiliate with labor, becoming locals of AFT, were the eight locals already mentioned, plus Atlanta (1919); Minneapolis (1919); Chattanooga (1919 and 1932); Cleveland (1934); West Suburban area of Chicago (1938); Toledo (1933); Springfield, Ohio (1934); Detroit (1920 and 1931); Gary (1937—second affiliation).

According to AFT's own history,[4] all these local affiliates came into existence because of intolerable conditions resulting from neglect of the schools during and after World War I and during the Great Depression years.

Too, all were born under adverse circumstances, generally fought by the newspapers, chambers of commerce, business groups, tax haters, school boards, and administrators. A wave of anti-unionism following the Great War inundated several of the newly formed locals. In Chicago, for example, the AFT's number 1 local, the Chicago Federation of Teachers, officially withdrew from AFT shortly after its affiliation, to assist in the reinstatement of 68 members discharged by the school board. By the end of 1920, AFT had lost more than half of its members.

Table 54 reflects how the membership of both AFT and NEA grew from the establishment of AFT.

It will be noted that the growth in members of AFT in the early years was spotty, and that it accelerated greatly during the turmoil of the depression decade, 1930–1940. Then the gains were steady and substantial thereafter. The really significant gains occurred after 1958, doubling between 1958 and 1965. NEA membership gained substantially every year cited since 1918. By 1967, NEA had in its membership about 52 per cent of all public school professional personnel and AFT about 7 per cent. In addition, the state education associations affiliated with NEA had in their membership over 90 per cent of all public school personnel in 1967.

It will be noted, too, that the real upsurge in AFT membership occurred from 1960 on. This date marked the beginning of all-out warfare between the teachers' unions and the professional associations.

[4] *Organizing the Teaching Profession, op. cit.* See Chap. I, pp. 19–51.

TABLE 55 *Membership in the National Education Association and the American Federation of Teachers in Selected Years, 1918 to 1967*

Years	NUMBER OF MEMBERS (NEAREST THOUSAND)	
	NEA	AFT
1918	10,000	1,500
1920	53,000	10,000
1930	172,000	7,000
1940	203,000	30,000
1950	454,000	41,000
1958	617,000	53,000
1959	667,000	55,000
1960	714,000	59,000
1961	766,000	61,000
1962	812,000	71,000
1963	860,000	82,000
1964	903,000	100,000
1965	943,000	110,000
1966	988,000	125,000
1967	1,028,456	140,000 (est.)
Aggregate Growth 1918 to 1967	1,018,456	138,500
Average Annual Growth 1918 to 1967	20,785	2,827

Source: *NEA Handbooks for Local, State, and National Associations* (published annually); and annual reports of the AFT national conventions.

WARFARE BETWEEN TEACHERS GENERAL ORGANIZATIONS

It has been previously stated that the mild competition between the professional associations of teachers and the teachers' unions exploded into open warfare in 1960. From 1916, when the AFT was founded, until 1960, the competition had proceeded quietly, with little sniping from either side. AFT had shown a respectable growth in membership, but was far outdistanced by the NEA, the state education associations, and their local affiliates.

The occasion for the explosion in 1960 was the collective bargaining election in the New York City schools, forced by a strike by members of the United Federation of Teachers, a local of the AFT.

During this contest for representation of New York City teachers, it became evident that organized labor, as represented by AFL-CIO, was giving aggressive backing to the AFT, in terms of money and organizing personnel. This fact revealed that AFL-CIO had decided upon an all-out organizing drive among white collar workers, and that teachers were the first major target. Prior to 1960, AFL-CIO had made sporadic efforts to gain a foothold in the white collar field, with few results. But with 1960 (the date is approximate) a vigorous national campaign was launched. The reasons appear to be obvious. (1) Organized labor had been losing membership during the industrial boom years of the late 1950's, despite the rapid increase in numbers of people in the labor force. (2) With the multiplication of jobs and the growth in automation and technology, the nature of the work force was changing drastically. The number of blue collar jobs was diminishing and the number of white collar jobs was increasing significantly. These factors dictated that organized labor had to shift gears and seek to organize the white collar worker to survive.

Of course, there are additional reasons. Labor felt that there must be a kinship among all workers to sustain the power of collective action, not only for the individual worker but also to propel forward social, political, and economic gains for the masses of Americans. Labor felt that it could improve the lot of the working individual more effectively than any other organization.

It is quite possible that President Kennedy's Executive Order 10,988, in early 1962, conferring the right of negotiation (not collective bargaining) upon federal employees, opened the vista of a fertile field for union organization among all public employees, including teachers.

Union Membership Drops

The membership of all labor unions in the United States reached a plateau in 1956 (at least before 1963 or 1964) with a total of 17,500,000 members. Then a decline set in, averaging about 100,000 members a year, until 1962 when the aggregate decrease amounted to more than 500,000. The following figures indicate the nature of the shift in the work force of the nation and the impacts of this shift on organized labor.

	1960	1962	Increase or Decrease
Total Civilian Labor Force	70,156,000	71,315,000	1,159,000+
Total Blue Collar Workers	26,309,000	26,244,000	65,000−
Total White Collar Workers	29,466,000	30,808,000	1,342,000+
Total Union Membership	17,100,000	16,586,000	514,000−
Total Union Membership of White Collar Workers	2,200,000	2,285,000	85,000+

Source: U.S. Department of Labor, Bureau of Labor Statistics, April, 1964.

In 1960, of the total union membership, 87 per cent were blue collar workers, and only 13 per cent were white collar workers. Labor in 1960 had organized only 24 per cent of the nation's civilian work force; by 1962 this had dropped to 22 per cent. With a steadily declining proportion of the total work force among its members, and a steadily declining proportion of the total work force being blue collar workers, labor was compelled to initiate a drive for white collar membership.

In the early 1960's the Industrial Union Department (IUD) of AFL-CIO appropriated $4,000,000 to finance an aggressive campaign to organize white collar workers, including professional people.

There is some evidence that the initial focus of this campaign was to be directed at teachers. There were good psychological reasons for this decision. Teachers had doggedly stuck to their professional organizations; they were a prestige group, with high idealism and dedication; they were a key group in influencing others; theirs was a seller's market with shortages almost everywhere; and finally, a breakthrough in the ranks of teachers would, it appeared, be a major selling point for the unions among other white collar and professional groups.

THE TEACHERS' UNION CAMPAIGN IN CITIES

For many reasons, the drive to organize teachers by labor centered upon the large industrial cities. Here labor was strongest politically. Here unionism among the masses was accepted as a way of life. Here school conditions (in the inner large cities) were deteriorating at an alarming rate. Here teachers were generally disgruntled—impatient with administrative bureaucracy, inadequate salaries, and low status.

The steadily worsening school situation in many cities was made to order for labor's capitalizing upon the growing unrest among teachers.

New York City Election Campaign

Among all the great cities, the largest presented the best target. New York City was chosen as the prime target for an organizing drive, and it became the showcase example of what collective action by teachers could accomplish.

Many have interpreted the drive to organize the teachers in New York City as the upsurge of a movement which will eventually bind teachers to organized labor. During the school year 1960–61 the United Federation of Teachers (an affiliate of the American Federation of Teachers), with a membership of about 5,000, sponsored a one-day strike of New York City teachers, in which a minority of the teachers participated. This was an effort to force the New York City Board of Education to adopt collective bargaining and to permit the teachers to designate a bargaining agent. Obviously, the UFT was driving to be recognized as the agent of the teachers, with a checkoff system of dues and other concessions. There were over 40,000 teachers in New York City who belonged to a multitude of organizations. No organization could at that time claim more than a small fraction of the total, and many, perhaps most, of the teachers were not affiliated with any organization.

While the Board of Education was awaiting the opinion of corporation counsel regarding the legality of collective bargaining (and, therefore, of the validity of holding an election among teachers regarding collective bargaining), the UFT called a strike to begin on November 7, 1960. Other teacher organizations in the city opposed the strike on the grounds that its purposes could be achieved without a strike and because of the illegality of teacher strikes under New York State law. There were conflicting claims regarding the effectiveness of the strike. There were predictions that 15,000 to 20,000 teachers would go out on strike, that the majority of schools would be closed, that organized labor would give full support to the strike, and that only a signed agreement with the Board of Education, granting all demands, would end the strike.

The Board of Education reported 5,900 teachers absent (out of 40,000); no schools were closed, although in some schools some classes had to be consolidated. Other results of the strike were that no other unions went out on strike, that actually labor leaders insisted the strike be called off, and that no signed agreement was obtained from the Board of Education. Striking teachers were permitted to return to their jobs, but were docked one day's pay.

The election on collective bargaining, which the New York City superintendent of schools and Board of Education had committed themselves, before the strike, to hold if such an election were found to be legal, was conducted during the summer of 1961. The New York City teachers voted overwhelmingly (27,000 to 9,000) for the designation of a bargaining agent for the city's 40,000 teachers.

Following this election, the NEA, which rarely ever had more than 1,000 members in New York City, entered the situation by sponsoring a coalition of teacher groups in the Teachers Bargaining Organization.

In November 1961 an election was authorized by the New York City Board of Education to select a bargaining agent for the teachers. The results of the election gave the United Federation of Teachers a clear majority of votes cast (about 20,000); the NEA-sponsored Teachers Bargaining Organization (TBO) polled about 10,000 votes; 2,500 voted for another or no organization; and about 10,000 teachers did not vote. The UFT presented its demands for adjustment of teachers' salaries to the school board, in January of 1962. Sustained negotiations failed to produce a commitment from the Board for an additional $53,000,000 for teachers' salaries. As a result, the UFT voted to strike, and on April 11 about 20,000 teachers walked out, about half of the teaching force. However, the number actually striking and the number refusing to cross picket lines are not known.

The strike lasted one day and was ended by an injunction issued by the New York State Supreme Court, directed at the UFT officials to refrain from picketing the schools and declared the strike illegal. The demands of the UFT were not met as a condition of returning to work. What the ultimate outcome of the overt action of the New York City teachers will be remains to be seen. The situation is a complicated and explosive one. Teacher strikes in New York are illegal (as they are in most other states) under the Condon-Wadlin Act, which states that striking teachers lose their jobs and tenure rights. They may be reinstated by the Board of Education, but pay raises are forfeited for a three-year period, and reinstated teachers are on probation for a period of five years.

The president of the New York City Board of Education, in commenting on the strike, said: "We are unanimous in the view that strike by teachers is illegal. . . . Under the circumstances that prevail the strike is particularly immoral, for this Board has done all that could be done within reason to meet the legitimate demands of our teachers. Those teachers who have abandoned their posts have betrayed their duty. They have been guilty of irresponsible behavior. The leadership of the union which encouraged and incited this strike is guilty of recklessness and irresponsible leadership; we believe it is also a betrayal of responsible unionism. In November 1960, when there was a one-day strike by teachers, responsible union leaders in the City gave public assurance there would never be a recurrence. The leadership of this union which has ordered this strike has betrayed this pledge." [5]

Moreover, after the April 11, 1962, teachers' strike, the New York City Board of Education voted to suspend further bargaining with UFT until its leaders would sign a no-strike pledge as part of the settlement of the salary question.

Involved in the New York City strike were other factors than teachers' salaries. Years of neglect of the needs of the schools, overcrowding, slum schools, obsolete buildings, and city and state politics. One columnist emphasized this factor as follows:

Less than 20 per cent of the elementary school teachers struck. More than 60 per cent of the high school teachers struck. But 75 per cent of the junior high school teachers struck. All these proportions surprised the Board of Edu-

[5] Statement by Max J. Rubin, *New York Times*, April 12, 1962, p. 36M.

cation, and the union, too. But there is a lesson for us all somewhere in them. Let us for just one moment forget money. Most of the elementary school teachers refused to strike; in the elementary schools there is hope for the pupils. Hope begins to die in junior high school where the students mark time and there is almost nothing for them to learn. It comes back a little in high school where the beaten students have dropped out, and a teacher can cling to the hope presented by the brightest of the survivors. It was in the junior high schools, where hope for the student goes to its lowest level, that the highest proportion of the teachers went out. Could the desperation which brought the teachers out yesterday be about not money but about the state of the New York school system? [6]

This raises the question of the appropriate use of teacher strikes as a means of shocking a community into correcting long-existing and intolerable conditions that threaten the welfare and the safety of children. There tends to be a public attitude of condemnation of teacher strikes over salaries (as reflected in state statutes forbidding them, and the law of no state authorizes them), but sympathy for use of the strike to improve conditions for children.

The Future of Collective Bargaining for Teachers

To what extent the experiences in New York City will affect methods of determining teachers' salaries cannot be predicted. But it does seem probable that, although the New York City situation is probably not unique, the occurrences there symbolize an unrest among teachers that has not been visible to the public. Almost within a decade, the United States has become predominantly an urban country. Presently about 70 per cent of the country's population is clustered in urban and surburban areas, and it is estimated that 85 per cent of future population growth will be in these areas. It is now evident that teachers, at least in large urban centers (of which there are in 1967 about 250) will become more aggressive in salary and other matters.

Partially as a result of the impacts of the New York City developments, the NEA instituted a special project to deal with the problems of urban education associations. Several factors influenced this action. First, it was made clear that the victory of the UFT, an affiliate of the American Federation of Teachers, in New York City was to be used by organized labor (the AFL-CIO) to secure a breakthrough in organizing the several million white collar workers in the United States. Automation and other factors have cut heavily into the membership of labor organizations. Blue collar jobs are declining percentagewise but white collar jobs are increasing. Organized labor, therefore, sees its own salvation in organizing the latter group. Thus, backed by AFL-CIO, the ATF announced that it would sponsor a vigorous drive to organize teachers in the urban areas.

[6] Murray Kempton, "The Day of Pride," *New York Post*, April 12, 1962, *Magazine*, p. 45.

A second factor was the rapidly increasing trend of urban education associations to employ full-time staffs (in 1967 more than 80 such associations had done so). These urban associations are demanding the development of aggressive programs, and they are calling upon the NEA for assistance. A third factor was the growing realization that the urban associations present a new cluster of complex problems that require specialized assistance.

The impact of these various factors probably was to compel state education associations and the NEA to sponsor state legislation mandating the right of teachers, through their associations, to negotiate with school boards in salary matters. In such legislation, the strike is banned, but mediation provisions would be included in cases of impasse. The seeking of such legislation was forced by the pressures of organized labor for legislation that mandates collective bargaining for teachers, regulated by state labor departments. By 1967, AFL-CIO had sponsored laws passed in six states; and the professional associations had secured passage of similar legislation in eight states. That such legislation will increase among the states seems obvious.

In fact, in amending its 1961 resolution (see pp. 164–65), the 1962 NEA Representative Assembly spelled out the demand for the legal right of teachers to negotiate as follows:

The National Education Association calls upon its members and upon boards of education to seek state legislation and local board action which clearly and firmly establishes these rights for the teaching profession.

The professional associations (NEA and state education associations), in seeking such legislation, would simply be proposing to formalize what is rapidly becoming informal practice in teacher-board salary agreements.

The National School Boards Association, however, has expressed opposition to such legislation in the following resolution:

The NSBA believes that, subject to the requirements of applicable law, ultimate decisions on all matters affecting local public schools, including the welfare of professional and non-professional personnel, should rest solely on school boards as representatives of the people; that it would be an abdication of their decision-making responsibility for school boards to enter into compromise agreements based on collective bargaining or negotiation, or to resort to mediation or arbitration, or to yield to threats of reprisal; and that concern for the public welfare requires that school boards resist by all lawful means the enactment of laws which would compel them to surrender any part of this responsibility.[7]

The resolution is specific and vigorous. But whether it, or indeed that of the NEA, is realistic in the face of new conditions and an apparently new climate of public opinion only time will tell.

[7] Resolution adopted at the NSBA Annual Convention, Philadelphia, April, 1961.

Enforcement of Salary Negotiation Principles. The position of the NEA favoring the principle of negotiation raises the question of enforcement of salary and other demands of teachers. The 1962 NEA Representative Assembly made its position regarding collective bargaining in the industrial sense clear in the following language:

Under no circumstances should the resolution of differences between professional associations and boards of education be sought through channels set up for handling industrial disputes. The teacher's situation is completely unlike that of an industrial employee. A board of education is not a private employer, and a teacher is not a private employee. Both are committed to serve the common, indivisible interest of all persons and groups in the community in the best possible education of their children. Teachers and boards of education can perform their indispensable functions only if they act in terms of their identity of purpose in carrying out this commitment. Industrial-disputes conciliation machinery, which assumes a conflict of interest and a diversity of purpose between persons and groups, is not appropriate to professional negotiations.

Moreover, the 1962 NEA Representative Assembly initiated, as an alternative to the strike as a means of enforcing salary agreements and professional working conditions, the use of professional sanctions as follows:

The National Education Association believes that, as a means for preventing unethical or arbitrary policies or practices that have a deleterious effect on the welfare of the schools, professional sanctions should be invoked. These sanctions would provide for appropriate disciplinary action by the organized profession.

What does the term "sanctions" mean? And how are they applied? These are yet to be spelled out fully. Briefly, a sanction is an action designed to enforce a law, a custom, or a moral mandate. It is used by legal bodies, by a concert of nations, and by professional and vocational groups.

There are many kinds of professional sanctions designed to enforce the policy of a professional group. And virtually every profession makes use of these: for example, preparation standards as a prerequisite to licensure and admission to practice, standards for employment of new persons to practice, standards for admission to membership in professional organizations, and many others. The sanctions regarding the enforcement of salary agreements and working conditions, for which there are precedents, are: censure of the school district, withdrawal of teacher placement services from a school, or, in extreme cases, the withdrawal of services to school districts of members of professional organizations. Public censure of unsatisfactory or intolerable conditions in a given school district has proved to be a powerful weapon. The NEA Defense Commission has used such censure effectively in many cases (see Chapter 15). A fair, impartial report of such conditions in a school district usually arouses public opinion to demand remedial action by the school board.

Withdrawal of teacher placement services is also an effective weapon against a school district that persists in violating standards of working conditions and personnel policies advocated by the profession. Such withdrawal tends to some degree to shut off the source of supply of qualified teachers of the district, forcing it to take substandard teachers or rectify the existing, unacceptable conditions.

Withdrawal of services to a school district simply refers to a professional association advising its members not to accept employment in the offending school district in the following school year, unless the indicated conditions are rectified. This is not a strike. Existing contracts are honored. Service to children is not interrupted during the term of teacher contracts. New contracts are not entered into. The net effect, if fully carried out, would be to declare the offending school district out of bounds as a source of employment for members of the professional association taking the action, until satisfactory adjustment of conditions is made by the school district. The effectiveness of the application of such a sanction (which has been invoked in several instances) depends upon a number of factors: (1) the gravity of the district's violation of reasonable standards; (2) the degree to which members of the professional association will comply with the invoked sanction; (3) the wisdom and fairness with which it is applied. Obviously, such a drastic action can only be invoked in extreme situations, when all other avenues of possible settlement have been exhausted. To many, this type of sanction appears to be nothing more than a strike, in a deferred sense. Proponents, however, contend that it is vastly different; that the offending district is given plenty of time to correct intolerable conditions; that if it deliberately chooses to impose inferior conditions of work, it is making the choice of providing inferior services for its children.

The use of sanctions by professional groups, as has been pointed out, has many precedents. But the types described above have been used infrequently.

The Aftermaths of New York

It became apparent immediately that the election victory of UFT in New York City was to become a showcase for both AFT and AFL-CIO. A vigorous national campaign was mapped by ATF to organize the nation's teachers. Walter Reuther, head of IUD, called the UFT victory in New York City one of the most important events in labor history in the last twenty years.

The first strike in New York City was prelude to further aggressiveness by UFT. A new impasse developed between the school board and UFT in April 1962, resulting in a strike vote of 2,544 for and 2,231 against, with overtones of a power struggle in the union over the election of officers in May.

As has been mentioned, the strike was held on April 11, 1962. About 20,500 of the city's 40,000 teachers remained away from work. By one estimate, as many as 25 of the city's 840 schools were forced to close during the day. The New York Supreme Court issued an injunction against the strike, under the Condon-Wadlin Act, upon request of the Board of Education. Under the threat of contempt of court, the UFT Executive Board called off the strike after one day. The UFT president denounced the court's action as a "slave labor injunction." The school board, as it did in the 1960 strike, declared an amnesty for the strikers. The president of the Board of Education denounced the strike as "reckless, irresponsible, and immoral," charging that it violated a pledge by responsible union leaders given after the 1960 strike.

UFT, having found a magic weapon—at least in New York City and later to be used widely by AFT: the illegal strike—threatened another strike in September 1963. This time the threat did not bring the desired results. But in its 1965–66 bargaining with the Board, UFT achieved a clear-cut, solid victory, including the creation of a teacher welfare fund of about $150 per teacher per year.

The New York City victory of the teachers union clearly was the kickoff of a national campaign to organize teachers under the banner of labor unions. The campaign was destined to become the cause of rancorous fighting between AFL and NEA. In other words, the New York City victory of UFT was the forerunner of a new climate in teachers organizations, a new attitude of aggressiveness and militancy among teachers, which were to alter drastically the administrative structure of the public schools.

The NEA, inept in the New York City fight, quickly girded itself for a sustained, long-time battle for survival. In 1961, the NEA Representative Assembly authorized a study of the needs of urban associations. This study revealed weaknesses of NEA services geared specifically to the needs of large city teachers. In March, 1962, it established the Urban Services Project, later changing this—in 1964—to the Urban Services Division. The onslaught of the teachers union in New York City exposed a long-standing weakness of NEA structure and services—the neglect of service to urban teachers. Throughout most of NEA's history, its strength had been predominantly in the rural areas and in small cities. While it had significant membership in many large cities, its membership in the industrial centers began to diminish somewhat after 1950.

With the development of the Urban Services Division, NEA began expanding its services to large city associations. By 1967, there were about eighty urban education associations with full-time staff members, in many instances with financial help from NEA. Moreover, it brought into being, through resolutions of the Representative Assembly in 1962, the instruments of professional negotiation and professional sanctions. (For comprehensive descriptions of these, see Chapter 22.)

So the battle began to shape up. After New York City, AFT won two easy victories in elections in Plainview, New York, in January, 1963, and in the Milwaukee Vocational Schools in June of the same year.

Large city elections or stipulations were won by NEA in Milwaukee (in February, 1964); Newark (December, 1964, and a second election in June, 1966); Buffalo (1966 and in 1967); New Rochelle (March, 1964); Madison, Wisconsin (June, 1964); Rochester, New York (December, 1964); Denver (by designation in 1964 and by election in April, 1967); Tulsa (January, 1965); New Haven (May, 1965); Seattle (1965); Flint, Michigan (1966); Dade County, Miami, Florida (1965); Fort Worth (1966); Buffalo (1967); and in Los Angeles and San Francisco, majorities on the negotiating council under the Winton Act.

AFT won in Detroit (May, 1964); Cleveland (June, 1964); Philadelphia (February, 1965); Boston (1966); Chicago (1966); Rochester (won in second election, 1966); Washington, D.C. (April, 1967); and Baltimore (June, 1967); and in some thirty other smaller districts.

The figures on 37 elections, following AFT's victory in New York, from January 1, 1963, to June 1, 1965, are as follows:

Total elections	37	(Teachers involved: 52,232)
Won by AFT	13	(30,749)
Won by NEA	23	(21,483)

It is evident from the number of teachers' affiliation won in these elections that the teachers' union tends to win in the larger cities, NEA in the smaller.

Figures on elections during the school year 1965–66 are as follows:

Number of elections	225	Per cent of elections won	
Won by AFT	26	by AFT	11%
Won by NEA	196	Per cent of elections won	
No choice of affiliation	3	by NEA	87%+

In addition, NEA won representation rights by stipulation in 588 school districts and AFT won 1, with no choice of affiliation in three cases. The term *by stipulation* means that the school board under existing law can recognize the organization with verified majority membership. Thus of the two methods (elections and stipulations), NEA won 784 or 96 per cent and AFT won 27 or 3 per cent, of the combined elections and stipulations cases.

By the end of the school year 1966–67, the NEA Research Division reported about 1,353 school districts, employing 574,621 teachers (more than one fourth of the instructional staff of all public schools), with professional negotiation agreements. Among these 1,353 school systems, NEA held representation rights in 1,179. AFT held representation rights in 35 districts. Thus NEA held negotiation rights in 93.4 per cent of the districts, representing nearly 400,000 teachers, or about 80 per cent of all personnel under agreements. AFT represented 103,095 (not counting Chicago) or about 20 per cent of personnel under agreements.

TABLE 56   *Gains in Membership of AFT and NEA (1960–1967)*
(Figures Rounded)

Year	AFT Membership	Gain Over Previous Year	No. of Affiliated Locals	NEA Membership	Gain Over Previous Year
1960	59,000	4,000	426	714,000	47,000
1961	61,000	2,000	433	766,000	52,000
1962	71,000	10,000	454	812,000	46,000
1963	82,000	11,000	476	860,000	48,000
1964	100,000	13,000	502	903,000	43,000
1965	110,000	10,000	560	943,000	40,000
1966	125,000	15,000	606	988,000	45,000
1967	142,000	15,000	686	1,028,000	40,000
Total Gains, 1960–67		81,000			314,000
Average Annual Gain		11,600			44,900

Source: *NEA Handbooks for Local, State, and National Associations* (Published annually) and *Reports of Annual Meetings of AFT.*

Philosophies and Procedures of the National Teachers Organizations

Historically, there has been a clear-cut dichotomy in both philosophies and procedures, between the American Federation of Teachers and the National Education Association. But in the years since 1962 (with the passage of the professional negotiation and sanctions resolutions by NEA) many observers have felt that the two organizations have grown more closely together in their procedures.

AFT has been, and is, tied to organized labor, with rather strict adherence to collective bargaining and the strike as defined in the National Labor Relations Act (1935), for workers in private industry. It should be pointed out that AFT did not fully embrace these processes until after the successes of UFT with strikes in New York City in 1960 and 1962.

Prior to that time, AFT had pressed for collective bargaining rights but had not advocated use of the strike by teachers; in fact, AFT had a clear no-strike policy. AFT had called for repeal of the no-strike ban for public employees in state laws. Until August, 1966, when the AFT annual convention adopted a restrictive membership policy, excluding in the future membership of professional school employees "from the principal up," AFT locals had been free to accept membership of all but the superintendent.

After the successful strikes in New York City, AFT officials declared their full alignment with AFL-CIO; they proudly asserted the status of the teachers' union as a trade union, with the obligation of full use of trade union tactics, and openly advocated strikes by teachers—even though strikes were illegal in every state—and the obligation of the national and local teachers unions to bring themselves within the orbit of AFL-CIO policies.

NEA, on the other hand, had historically adhered to the role of an independent, inclusive professional organization, unattached to any other segment of society, and operating through educational channels and state legislation to obtain its objectives.

In other words, NEA had historically operated on the basis of all-inclusive membership of professional school personnel, in which each member had "one voice and one vote." This philosophy rejected the notion that there is an inevitable adversary, conflict relationship between school boards-administrators and classroom teachers. NEA has put great emphasis upon its independent status. Its executive secretary has stated:

This is an independent organization. The difference between an independent professional organization and a branch of organized labor is not a superficial one. It goes to the heart of the unique function of public education in American democracy. The public school serves all the children of all the people, office workers, craftsmen, professional people, public officials, managers, and businessmen. Its personnel should not be affiliated to any one segment of the population.[8]

To these NEA claims, AFT maintains that:

1. It (AFT) is the only *bona fide* classroom teachers organization.
2. NEA is dominated by school administrators and classroom teachers can never secure economic justice and professional recognition in such an organization.
3. Affiliation with organized labor is essential because labor's political and economic power can gain for teachers the concessions requisite to professional status.

[8] William G. Carr, "The Turning Point," *Addresses and Proceedings of the 100th Annual Convention of the National Education Association*, Denver, July, 1962. Washington, D.C.: The Association, 1962, p. 22.

4. Teachers have the same problems as all workers; all workers must band together for their own welfare and the welfare of society as a whole.

In support of its claim of being the only organization exclusively devoted to the welfare of classroom teachers, AFT influenced the passage of an AFL-CIO resolution in 1957 branding NEA as a "company union." In labor law, this means a union organized by a given company and dominated by company management, to make certain that workers are prevented from making "unreasonable" demands upon the company for increased salaries and welfare benefits. The executive secretary of NEA, in a news release responded:

It is misleading to apply the term "company union" to the National Education Association. Our public schools are not a company; they are government services; they are not operated for profit. . . .

Reduced to its essentials, the controversy between the teachers union and the professional associations focuses at two points: (1) the charge of administrator domination of NEA on the one hand, and (2) AFT's affiliation with labor on the other. There are other related issues, to be sure, but these are fundamental.

With respect to the first, the point hinges on the proposition that an inclusive association, which accepts membership of all segments of the teaching profession, cannot adequately represent the interest of teachers. There can be no question that in the past NEA policies at many points have been influenced by administrative personnel out of all proportion to their membership numbers. And this has been true of many state and local education associations. This situation is now rapidly changing, with little question that AFT criticisms and charges have influenced greatly this development. This is quite another proposition, however, from that of asserting that inclusive associations cannot restrict themselves in such a manner as to serve fully the interest of classroom teachers. There are in existence many inclusive unions that seem to function equitably and effectively for all members. Also, as has been previously stated, until the summer of 1966, other than superintendents, administrative supervisory personnel could be and had been admitted to membership in AFT locals. And the 1966 action did not debar such personnel who were already members.

To state the matter another way, there is an "outness" and an "inness" of superintendents in participation in the operation of professional associations. In professional negotiation, superintendents are out as voting members, as executive officers of the school board. In all other professional matters, they are in as leaders of the professional staff.

The professional negotiation law passed in Connecticut in 1966, seems to provide a reasonable approach to this problem. That law permits a local school staff to determine by majority vote what personnel shall participate in representation of the staff.

Of course, in an inclusive association, whether it be local, state or national, provision must be made for an independent autonomous organization of classroom teachers, in which problems can be discussed in an uninhibited, untrammeled atmosphere.

The figures in Table 57 indicate that classroom teachers made up more than two thirds of the voting delegates in the 1966 NEA Representative Assembly. Administrators and supervisors constituted less than one fourth of the delegates. This is the policy making body of NEA.

TABLE 57   Composition of the 1966 NEA Representative Assembly (Miami Beach) By Teaching Positions

Position	Number of Delegates	Per Cent of Total Registration
Classroom Teachers	4,629	67.8
Superintendents, Principals, and other Supervisors	1,611	23.6
Retired Teachers	24	.4
Staff Members of State Education Association	239	3.5
Other Delegates	322	4.7
TOTALS	6,825	100.0

Source: NEA Department of Classroom Teachers *Bulletin,* November, 1966, p. 9.

A better case for the charge of administrator domination of NEA can be found in the constituency of the official bodies (Board of Trustees, Executive Committee, and Board of Directors) and commissions and committees of the Association. Among the 83 members of the NEA Board of Directors in 1966–67, 37 were classroom teachers (about 45 per cent); on the Executive Committee, 7 of 11 members were classroom teachers; and three of five members of the Board of Trustees were classroom teachers.

The Department of Classroom Teachers sponsored and secured passage of a resolution at the 1965 Representative Assembly providing that at least 50 per cent of the constituency of all NEA committees and commissions be classroom teachers. This resolution was aimed at correcting existing imbalances in the make-up of these bodies.

Rarely discussed is the drive of AFT to enroll all school personnel, professional and nonprofessional, including custodial workers, bus drivers, engineers, cafeteria workers, and so on, which raises questions to its claim as being an organization exclusively for classroom teachers.

Of the labor affiliation of teachers, the professional associations' position is that such an affiliation is neither to the advantage of the teachers' unions nor to organized labor, that teachers will be used to further the aims of labor, that educational policy will be determined largely by AFL-CIO instead of the teachers' union, that labor discipline will be applied to teachers, and that teachers will be expected to support strikes of other trade unions. Finally, union members will themselves resent, in the long run, the controls exercised by labor over the public schools.

On the issue of labor affiliation, the professional associations hold the view that teachers should seek the support of all segments of society of the public schools, but should not be maneuvered into an alliance with any segment that might jeopardize the independence, the academic freedom, and the authority of teachers. They point out that wherever teachers have been tied to a vested interest, their policies dictated or heavily influenced by outside groups, virtually without exception teachers have been demeaned, their profession has been debased, and the public good has suffered. These associations contend that teachers must be independent of any affiliation with outsiders, that it is easy to fall into the philosophical trap that a given segment's political and economic powers are indispensable to the welfare of teachers. The cost of such help is more than the profession should be willing to pay and more than the public interest can tolerate. These are the assertions of the professional associations.

Examples in defense of these assertions are cited by the professional associations as follows:

The AFT Executive Council in 1964, unauthorized by its delegate body, announced the support of the organization for the Elementary and Secondary Education Act, then pending in Congress, in order "to bring its policies more in line with AFL-CIO policy." This resulted in vigorous protests from the UFT, its largest local, because of provisions in the proposed law to provide some aid to private and parochial schools. AFT then decided to take a poll of its membership. This poll was not concluded until the bill had been passed and signed into law.

The associations also point to many cases in which locals or state affiliates of AFT had to oppose or remain silent about proposed sales and other excise taxes to provide needed funds for the public schools because AFL-CIO has consistently opposed such taxes. Some case examples cited by the associations occurred in Philadelphia, New Orleans, St. Louis, and the states of Indiana and Oklahoma.

On the matter of interference with teachers' academic freedoms, the associations point to the secondary boycott of the Kingsport Press (in

Tennessee) by AFL-CIO in support of the striking unions there, and called upon AFT and its locals to pressure their school boards to ban the school texts printed by this firm. The quality of the books did not enter into this action, only the charge of labor that the books were being printed by "scabs." The boards of New York City and a few other places actually voted in 1966 to ban the books. But the Supreme Court of New York State held this action by the New York City Board of Education to be illegal. A New York City teacher protested to the UFT on the action of banning the books and was told by the president of that organization, "It seems strange that we (teachers) would expect financial and other help from organized labor and not expect to help labor when it needed help." The National Labor Relations Board twice ruled, on complaints of the union of unfair labor practice, that the company was not guilty. By 1967, all five unions involved in the Kingsport Press case had been rejected by vote of their members as "bargaining agents." [9]

Teachers have been asked to go out on strike in sympathy with other unions—in Granite City, Illinois, in support of the cafeteria workers, for example. Teacher union members have been disciplined for failure to support a strike of the teachers union.

In a strike called by the Cook County College Teachers Union, about 20 members crossed picket lines and met their classes. They were immediately notified by the union that a vote would be taken to amend the bylaws to provide fines against members failing to observe union discipline during a strike. The proposed fines would include $45 a day for dishonoring picket lines; $30 a day for calling in sick or otherwise trying to collect pay and disassociate themselves from the strike; and $15 a day for refusing to picket, participate in the telephone chain, or otherwise support the union during a strike. The line-crossers were given a chance to demonstrate remorse by donating a day's pay to the union treasury.

One of the offending members of the teachers union responded as follows:

The house's (delegate body of the local) sudden decision to impose fines and its cynical, brutal, and insulting call for public confession of remorse are actions that no administration or college board would dare take. They show plainly that the most immediate danger to academic freedom is not from the radical right but rather from the spreading practice of granting exclusive bargaining rights to organizations such as this—organizations that bring in from outside the college their own political philosophy and their own traditions of conformity and control . . .

The college teacher resigned from the union, with the comment

[9] For a detailed account of this strike see Sylvester Petro, *The Kingsport Strike.* New Rochelle, New York: 1967, 238 pp.

that the "only remorse he felt was for joining the union in the first place." [10]

The professional associations also have discipline procedures for teachers who fail to support sanctions against a school district. In the Oklahoma case, NEA warned teachers not then employed in Oklahoma that acceptance of a teaching position in the state *might* be judged as unethical conduct. No teachers were disciplined in this case, but the threat of discipline was there, and such discipline doubtless will be used in time. The penalty could be censure, reprimand, suspension, or expulsion from membership. In fact, presumably growing out of the Oklahoma case in which some superintendents recruited teachers from out of the state, a resolution was adopted by the NEA Representative Assembly in 1965, which provided that the "offering of or acceptance of a teaching position in the sanctioned school district may be judged as a violation of the code of ethics."

Although this assertion was not made a part of the Code of Ethics, and the statement was not readopted by subsequent annual conventions, apprehension regarding application of the Code to superintendents who sought to fill positions in a sanctioned district prompted AASA to seek an interpretation from the NEA Ethics Committee. The ruling of the Committee was as follows (under date of July 27, 1967):

1. When the administrator has a legal responsibility to provide a teaching staff he would be in violation of this section if he willfully refused to do so. An effort to punish him for adhering to a legal order of the school board would be judged improper.
2. The superintendent has an affirmative obligation to inform prospective candidates for position openings as to the existence of a professional sanction as it related to the candidate's prospective conduct.
3. Principle IV, Section 3, states: "We fill no vacancy except where the terms, conditions, policies, and practices permit the exercise of our professional judgment and skill, and where a climate conducive to professional service exists." The NEA Committee states that the word "fill" does not refer to the superintendent's attempts to recruit and hire personnel. Rather, it refers only to persons who anticipate accepting a position in a district under sanction.

A high official of AFT has written:

The question of why AFT insists on affiliation with the AFL-CIO does deserve an answer, however. The first and most obvious reason, of course, is that of practicality. In any dispute with city and school officials, or with state officials, teachers rarely have the force to go it alone against the power structure. In every major city and in many state legislatures, the labor movement is a potent power bloc, and it is virtually the only friendly force available to teachers. You

[10] See editorials in the *Chicago Tribune*, Wednesday, February 15, 1967; and *Chicago Sun Times*, Tuesday, February 14, 1967.

may not like everything that these "labor blocs" do, but they are there and must be dealt with.[11]

The Use of Strikes

AFT now openly and vigorously advocates the use of the strike by teachers to enforce their demands. NEA has historically had a tacit no-strike policy, favoring instead other and legal means of securing gains for teachers. Both organizations have in significant measure changed their positions in recent years.

With respect to the strike, the AFT Executive Council adopted this statement in 1958: "The use of the strike is rejected as an instrument of policy of the American Federation of Teachers. The Executive Council and its national officers will not call a strike either nationally or in any local area of jurisdiction, nor in any way advise a local to strike."

After the UFT success in New York City, resolutions were adopted by the annual convention of AFT, in August 1963, the pertinent parts of which read: "That the American Federation of Teachers strongly supports the strike action of Local 2 (UFT)." A second resolution contained this wording: "That the AFT recognizes the right of locals to strike under certain circumstances." These resolutions urged AFL-CIO to support such strikes when they occur.

NEA, on the other hand, has not adopted a categorical policy for or against the strike. The several successive codes of ethics, dating back to the 1920's, which its members are obligated to observe have contained statements that clearly imply a no-strike policy. All of these statements have dealt with the obligation of members to observe faithfully the terms of a contract. The Code of Ethics of the Education Profession, adopted in 1963, and which has now been adopted by all state education associations, states:

> We regard the employment agreement as a solemn pledge to be executed in spirit and in fact in a manner consistent with the highest ideal of professional service. . . . In fulfilling our obligations to professional employment practices we . . . adhere to the conditions of a contract or the terms of an appointment until either has been terminated legally or by mutual consent. . . .

This declaration is a clear statement of a no-strike policy (without mentioning the strike), as applied to the conduct of an individual member. No mention is made of a concerted group action, and on this point the statement is vague or ambiguous. Several strikes or work stoppages of affiliates of NEA have occurred in recent years, with no reprimand or punitive action by NEA. What the future holds with respect to the position of the two national organizations cannot be predicted from their past history. It appears probable that NEA will not endorse strike action or

[11] David Selden, "Why the AFT Maintains its AFL-CIO Affiliation," *Phi Delta Kappan*, February, 1966, 67:6, pp. 298–300.

adopt a strike policy, so long as such acts are illegal, but will make vigorous use of sanctions. Plagued by its ambivalence on the strike issue, NEA at its 1967 convention in Minneapolis adopted a resolution that did not advocate teachers strikes but asserted that in case strikes occurred among its affiliates, NEA would extend aid to these affiliates.

RESOLUTION ON IMPASSE IN NEGOTIATION SITUATIONS PASSED BY NEA BOARD OF DIRECTORS JULY 1, 1967

The NEA recommends that the following procedures be used in the resolution of impasse between teachers associations and their employers:

Mediation. Mediation is the effort of a neutral third party to assist the parties to reach a voluntary agreement. Either party may initiate mediation.

Fact-finding. Fact-finding is the investigation by a neutral third party to discover the issues and to make recommendations for settlement to the parties. The recommendations are not binding, but may be made public. Either party may initiate fact-finding.

Arbitration. (When agreed upon by the parties.) Arbitration by a neutral third party results in a recommendation for settlement which is binding upon the parties. The parties must agree in advance that the matter at issue is to be submitted to binding arbitration.

Political action. Political action is comprised of a variety of activities which are pursued by the organized teaching profession to resolve impasses with, or influence decisions of, governmental bodies. It includes persuasion, recall elections, lobbying, and campaigns to convince citizens to support the public schools.

Sanctions. Sanctions are deterrents imposed against a public agency controlling the welfare of schools, or are one or more steps in the withholding of services. They include public censure, notification to educational and placement agencies and members of the profession of unsatisfactory conditions for professional service, refraining from extracurricular activities, and withholding of contracts.

The NEA believes that the above procedures should make the strike unnecessary. The NEA recommends that every effort be made to avoid the strike as a procedure for the resolution of impasse. The NEA recognizes that under conditions of severe stress, causing deterioration of the educational program, and when good faith attempts at resolution have been rejected, strikes have occurred and may occur in the future. In such instances, the NEA will offer all of the services at its command to help resolve the impasse.

One affiliated state education association (Massachusetts) has called for repeal of legislation banning strikes by teachers. And there have been several cases of teacher strikes in which state education associations affiliated with NEA have strongly supported the teachers in their strike actions, although the state associations did not advocate or encourage the strikes.

Following is a discussion of the paradox of the use of collective bargaining by public employees and the illegality of strikes by such employees:

Collective bargaining is "a practical impossibility" in public employment, and the sooner this fact is recognized, the sooner public employers and labor groups will find "an equitable solution to their differences," according to John N. Seaman, a Lansing attorney who retired last month after serving nine years on the Michigan Civil Service Commission. . . .

Michigan's Public Employee Relations Act, he said, "is the best example of an extraordinary paradox in public thinking today in public employee relations, which attempts to separate the use of collective bargaining from the right to strike, when, in fact, they are inseparable."

As Seaman sees it, there can be no meaningful collective bargaining without strikes, and he does not believe the public long will tolerate the interruption of government services. "As the unionization of public employees accelerates and attendant problems escalate, a substitute for true collective bargaining, requiring some sort of third party arbitration as the ultimate step, will be forced by law and public demand, in view of the work stoppages which are the inevitable by-product of attempts at true collective bargaining," he said.

"When a public employee attempts to bargain collectively through a union, the bargaining is not with a single employer-owner, as in private industry, but with every citizen within the governmental unit where he is employed. The citizens are his real employers, yet they do not sit at the bargaining table. . . .

"In private employment and the free collective bargaining process, the organized worker can strike, if necessary, and ordinarily the effect on the public as a whole is minimal, because the employer's competitors move in on his customers, supplying the public needed products or services. The pressure to settle on the employers is economic, and the economic concessions he can make are limited by competition and his profit margins.

"When the public employee groups strike, there is no competitor to step in and furnish the needed service to the public, and the public must do without. Doing without guards in our prisons, atendants at our mental hospitals, or police or fire protection, or many other government services is anarchy." [12]

SUMMARY

Since 1960, organized labor, through the American Federation of Teachers, has engaged in a vigorous drive to organize public school teachers of the nation. The campaign up to the present has been largely concentrated in the big industrial cities, but that this will eventually be a nation-wide drive is obvious. The weapons of the teacher union drive are (1) the claim of exclusive representation of classroom teachers, (2) the use of collective bargaining by law conferring upon public employees the rights already possessed by workers in private industry, (3) the use of teacher strikes, and (4) the reliance upon the political and economic power of organized labor.

The professional associations adhere to the viewpoint that a profession must be independent of alliance with any other segment of society, that a profession solves its own problems and does not rely upon outside forces. The professional associations espouse the inclusive membership concept,

[12] *Government Employee Relations Report,* February 6, 1967.

with proportional representation to assure one voice and one vote for each member in policy making.

The weapons of the professional associations are (1) professional negotiation mandate by law as the right of teachers, with all processes being kept within professional channels; (2) professional sanctions invoked against school districts as the ultimate step to force fair consideration of teachers rights, economic and professional; (3) the seeking of state legislation to improve the economic and professional status of teachers; and (4) a complete cluster of professional services to enable teachers to solve their own problems, including the improvement of the quality of education.

REFERENCES

BLANKE, VIRGIL E., "Teachers in Search of Power," *Education Forum,* January, 1966, *30*:231–238.

BOUTWELL, W. D., "What's Happening in Education? Is it Right for Teachers to Strike?" *PRA Magazine,* January, 1967, *61*:17–18.

CARR, WILLIAM G., "The Assault on Professional Independence," *Phi Delta Kappan,* September, 1964, *46*:17–18.

DASHIELL, DICK, "Teachers Choose the NEA," *NEA Journal,* September, 1966, *55*:43.

DOHERTY, ROBERT E., "The Law and Collective Bargaining for Teachers," *Teachers College Record,* October, 1966, Vol. 68.

EDUCATIONAL POLICIES COMMISSION, *The Public Interest in How Teachers Organize,* A Report prepared by the Commission. Washington: National Education Association, 1964.

ELAM, STANLEY, "Who's Ahead and Why: The NEA-AFT Rivalry," *Phi Delta Kappan,* September, 1964, *46*:12–15.

GROSS, CALVIN, "Ways to Deal with the New Teacher Militancy," *Phi Delta Kappan,* December, 1964, *46*:147–152.

LIEBERMAN, MYRON, "Teachers' Strikes: Acceptable Strategy?", *Phi Delta Kappan,* January, 1965, *46*:237–241.

MOSKOW, MICHAEL H., "Teacher Organizations: An Analysis of the Issues," *The Teachers College Record,* February, 1965, *66*:453–463.

"New Militants," *Time,* August 16, 1963, 2:45.

NOLTE, M. CHESTER, "Teachers Seek Greater Independence Through Legislative Channels," *American School Board Journal,* March, 1966, *152*:7–9.

SCANLON, JOHN, "Strikes, Sanctions and the Schools," *Saturday Review,* October 19, 1963, *46*:51–55, 70–74.

STARIE, JOHN H. and SPATAFORA, JACK, "Union or Professional Membership: A Matter of Philosophy and Program," *NEA Journal*, March, 1962, *51*:80–81.

STINNETT, T. M. *Turmoil in Teaching*. New York: Macmillan, 1968.

WEST, ALLAN M. "Professional Negotiations or Collective Bargaining?" *National Elementary Principal*, February, 1963, *42*:20–25.

WILDMAN, WESLEY A., "What Prompts Greater Teacher Militancy?" *The American School Board Journal*, March, 1967, *154*:27–32.

WILDMAN, WESLEY A. and PERRY, CHARLES R., "Group Conflict and School Organization," *Phi Delta Kappan*, December, 1966, *48*:156–9.

WOLLETT, DONALD H., "The Public Employee at the Bargaining Table: Promise or Illusion," *Labor Law Journal*, 1964, *15*:8.

22: Collective Action by Teachers

Involved in the organizational competition described in Chapter 21 is the drive of teachers for the right to collective action in matters relating to their welfare and status. The drive signified that the deeper aspirations of teachers could no longer be attained by the lone teacher competing with a well-entrenched power structure. The time had come for them to combine their individual efforts into collective action.

The processes of collective action were to be collective bargaining and strikes as used by the teachers' unions; professional negotiations and sanctions by the professional associations.

This most significant thrust of the public school teachers for new working conditions and status began to be evident about 1960. Although there had been several prior incidents (particularly in the period 1945–50) in which teachers by their aggressive action had indicated dissatisfaction with things as they were, these were largely unorganized isolated cases. These isolated incidents were, however, harbingers of a growing discontent and of the imminence of a teacher militancy unprecedented in the history of the public schools.

A new breed of teachers had arrived in the classrooms, and they were becoming vocal and insistent that they be accorded a real part in shaping the personnel and other policies of school districts. This mounting unrest was to grow in fervor and action, finally reaching the proportions of a revolution in the governance of the school by the mid-1960's. Also, this upsurge portended no less than a revolution in the status position of the teachers.

The scared, hired-hand, civil-servant posture of teachers was ending; a new concept of the nature and roles of the profession was beginning to emerge. The impact of this was that the governance of schools was in the process of changing from a vertical hierarchy, consisting of the board and administration, to a horizontal, coequal, collegial status among the professional staff. The day of paternalism, even of the benevolent type, was on its way out. The day of the participating creative teacher, with a real, not token, part in planning and executing school programs was on its way in. Collective action by teachers was on the way in—and to stay.

FACTORS AFFECTING TEACHER MILITANCY

It is difficult, if not impossible, to pinpoint precisely the events, actions, and factors that were the origin and motivation of the new development.

The new thrust of the teachers union is widely believed to be the predominant cause. Certainly, any informative study of the ferment from the mid-1950's to the mid-1960's would ascribe great influence to the American Federation of Teachers and its affiliates in accelerating the movement. Especially was great impetus given to the incipient movement by the successful forcing upon the school board of collective bargaining in New York City (and later elsewhere) by the use of the illegal teacher strike.

But the National Education Association began in the late 1950's to become aware of the growing restiveness of teachers and to adjust its own policies, actions, procedures, and services to meet the rapidly emerging new conditions.

The most probable explanation for the changed posture of both AFT and NEA was the flowing tide of discontent among teachers, motivated by a series of new factors that both organizations continued to be complacent about, until the tide threatened to inundate both.

Following the New York City teacher strikes in 1960 and 1962, it is quite clear that AFT sensed the full import of what was happening in the attitudes of teachers, perhaps more so than NEA, and moved more quickly and dramatically to capitalize upon the new aspirations of teachers. But this was a temporary phenomenon. NEA, beginning cautiously, gathered momentum; and by 1967 was matching the teachers union militancy with aggressive action, but with other processes than collective bargaining and the strike. It appears that the new tactics of both organizations were the result of, not the cause of, teacher militancy.

THE CAUSES OF THE TEACHER UPSURGE

What were the chief causes of the development throughout the 1950's of a new attitude of aggressiveness among teachers?

The first and perhaps most pronounced factor in the emergence of what came to be called the "new breed of teachers" was the rapidly increasing levels of preparation of teachers and thus of higher levels of competence. Almost within the scope of a little more than a decade the public school teachers had lifted themselves from the mass of under-prepared, substandard elements among the professions. As late as 1946, only 15 states were requiring the bachelor's degree for beginning elementary teachers; about 40 were enforcing the degree requirement for high school teachers. It has been estimated that in 1946 perhaps about half of all public school teachers had completed the bachelor's degree. By 1967, only 7 per cent were without at least the bachelor's degree and about 25 per cent had completed the master's degree; for men teachers about 35 per cent had completed five years or more of college preparation.

Out of the long tradition of the public schools, traditions of scanty preparation, poor pay, and routine roles as teachers, there had grown up another, and perhaps a natural, tradition. That tradition was one of the docile, subservient teacher who, by his very incompetence, had to be ordered about.

But by the late 1950's all this had largely changed. Moreover, the nature of education had changed, requiring constantly growing levels of competence and specialization. The same things had happened among public employees in general. A generation ago, government employees were viewed as holding political patronage jobs, jobs that any reasonably intelligent person could perform, and many of these jobs were held to be inconsequential or unnecessary. The status of such employees was low, and their treatment by the public and elected office holders matched this low esteem. But with the end of World War II, the rapid urbanization of the country, and the growth of technology, governments began demanding more and more professional, scientific, and technological experts, requiring a high level of university preparation. To compete with industry for such personnel, governments were compelled to match the status, the rewards, the fringe benefits, the job security, and the right to negotiate conditions of work.

This has happened to teachers, too. Two other significant factors in the teachers' upsurge were the increased proportion of men teachers and the rapidly dropping average age of the teaching staff.

A third factor was the growing size of the school districts, largely caused by the impacts of urbanization. Communication between the administration and the professional staff became extremely difficult, and in some instances impossible. Numerous bulletins, directives, and announcements in the local press gave the impression that teachers were faceless and mere cogs in a giant machine. This situation was bound, sooner or later to explode, by its very impersonality.

Of course, the galling position of the teacher also contributed. Typically, this involved intolerable overloading, with a galaxy of piddling routines that kept him from actual teaching, and a lack of recognition, so that he was always in the posture of a receiver and executor of orders from above. In short, he was the low man on the totem pole in the educational hierarchy, marked as being in a position that demeaned professionals and demeaned the importance of education.

But perhaps the dominant factor, quite often overlooked in the search for the causes of the new breed of teachers, was teacher idealism. This might seem a paradox: to juxtapose what appeared to be rebellion on the one hand and idealism on the other. Especially in the great cities, teachers, in their zeal to perform the crucial professional services for children for which they had spent years of their lives preparing, observed obsolete buildings, a dearth of teaching materials, shortages of textbooks, intolerable sanitary conditions, low salaries, deteriorating educational programs, and children short-changed in every way. The claim always was that the city could not afford to provide quality. Teachers knew this was not so and determined to do something about these conditions. Thus, the upsurge, the explosions resulting in charges of militancy and rebellion. Nothing short of this would have shocked the public into remedial action.

There are at least two other significant factors involved here. First, there were the intimations already evident in some places and among some groups, but largely obscured from the general population, of a coming revolution in education, a revolution arising from neglect and indifference to the educational needs of society, a coming revolution of vast proportions. Second, there was the flow of the times, a drastic change in the mores of people, which subsequently found expression in widespread dissent, rebellion, and activism among large groups of the American people. These were protests against the *status quo*, against the low status of these groups under existing conditions in society.

The Evolution of Collective Bargaining

The teachers unions had the processes that they were to use already at hand, tried and refined over a generation, by trial and error, by experience, by precedents of court decisions and decisions of regulatory bodies. The teachers' unions, borrowing from organized labor, had all these precedents but the strike of public employees. These precedents were collective bargaining and the strike, procedures made legal for workers in private industry by the Wagner Act (commonly called the National Labor Relations Act) passed by Congress in 1935. This law was subsequently amended by the Taft-Hartley Act (1947) and the Landrum-Griffith Act (1950), to add some restrictions to the power of unions and union leaders, and to seek a better balance of power between labor and management.

The passage of the Wagner Act was the successful culmination of a long and bitter struggle by organized labor to secure for workers in private industry the right, recognized in specific law, to bargain collectively with employers regarding wages and hours and working conditions and rules, and to spell these out in written contracts for a given period of time. The law also spelled out the legal right of workers in private industry to strike in case of impasses—where agreement on the terms of a contract could not be reached between the employees and management. Without such rights set forth in law, workers were at a great disadvantage, having to bargain individually with an employer of thousands who would suffer little, if at all, in the loss of one man's labor. The laborer on the other hand was powerless alone, because he had to have the job to sustain himself and family. This legislation constituted one of the greatest steps forward toward enlightened social legislation in our history. With the enactment of the Wagner Act, labor organizations boomed in size of membership and collective power.

The point at which the teachers unions have found it extremely difficult to make progress is that this legislation was specifically restricted to workers in private industry and was not applicable to public employees. This fact impelled the AFT to seek to force upon school boards the principle of collective bargaining for teachers to operate "beyond the horizon of the law" as enunciated by one of their leaders. This was also true of the use of the strike by teachers. In 1967, the laws of not a single state authorized strikes by public employees, including teachers. The laws of 13 states specifically prohibited such strikes. The laws of most states were silent on the matter of strikes by public employees. Many argue that silence of the law, in effect, gives assent. But this position is not sustained by existing court decisions. So the teachers unions have sought to transplant the Wagner Act processes to apply to teachers as public employees. Paralleling this effort has been a concerted drive in recent years by organized labor to secure legislation which would confer the same rights upon public employees, except the strike.

By 1967, legislation authorizing collective action by public employees, but not the right to strike, existed in 14 states. In Alaska, New Hampshire, Michigan, Wisconsin, Massachusetts, and Rhode Island, laws have been enacted sponsored by AFL-CIO; the professional associations have sponsored and passed professional negotiation laws in California, Connecticut, Florida, Oregon, and Washington. In addition, New York passed new legislation in 1967 to supplant the Condon-Wadlin Act, and Texas and Nebraska adopted permissive acts in that year.

A total of 110 teacher strikes occurred between 1940 and 1962, about two thirds of them between 1945–62. Of the 110 strikes, 91 involved public school teachers; 19 strikes involved teachers in private schools. In 58 of these 110 strikes, teachers were represented by unions; in 22 of the strikes, teachers were represented by professional associations; and in 30 of the strikes, teachers were represented by no organization. In other words, about 53 per cent of the 110 strikes occurred among teacher union affiliates; 20 per cent among professional association affiliates; and 27 per cent by independent teacher groups. Seventeen of the 110 strikes were classified by the Labor Bureau as major work stoppages, 14 of which were called by AFT affiliates; two were staged by independent organizations; and one apparently a joint effort of AFT and NEA affiliates.

Between 1962 and 1965, a total of 16 work stoppages were reported, making a total of 126 teacher strikes or work stoppages between 1940 and 1965. Eleven of these strikes were by AFT affiliates and four by NEA affiliates.

Between 1965 and 1967, there were at least 25 additional teacher strikes, and, in addition, at the beginning of the 1967–68 school term, there were strikes or withdrawal of teacher services in about 40 school districts.

Table 58 lists 36 major work stoppages of all types (strikes, walkouts, and professional holidays) in the school year 1960–61 through 1965–66 with the names of the school districts involved. "Professional holidays," declared by teachers in Utah, Oklahoma, and Kentucky, were called to protest the inadequacy of financing of the schools in these states and to dramatize the deleterious conditions existing in the schools, with the teachers offering to make up the missed days in school. But, of course, these were popularly characterized as teacher strikes.

THE ORIGIN OF PROFESSIONAL NEGOTIATION

In Chapter 7, the matters of professional negotiations and sanctions are discussed briefly. It is now essential that teachers understand fully the history and development of these two processes. Every indication is that both will be increasingly used in the future.

It is generally believed that the success of the teachers' unions, in the strikes forcing upon the New York City Board of Education the right of the teachers to use the collective bargaining, spurred NEA to seek counterprocesses—that is, to originate the processes called professional negotiation and professional sanctions. That viewpoint is only valid in part. It would be more accurate to say that the teachers' unions' success accelerated the adoption and use by NEA of the new processes.[1]

It is true that both procedures were not officially adopted by the NEA

[1] For a fuller description see T. M. Stinnett, Jack H. Kleinmann, and Martha L. Ware, *Professional Negotiations in Public Education.* New York: The Macmillan Company, 1966, Chap. 1, pp. 1–19.

TABLE 58   *Teachers Withdrawal of Services, by School Districts,*
School Years 1960–61 through 1965–66

Year	Month	School District	National Affiliate of Teachers	Days Duration
1960	August	MacCoupia County, Ill.	AFT	1
1960	November	New York City	AFT	1
1961	May	Portola Valley, Calif.	Prof. Assn.	1
1962	April	New York City	AFT	1
1963	May	Anderson, Ind.	AFT	5
1963	May	Gary, Ind.	AFT	1
1964	March	Jersey City, N.J.	Prof. Assn.	1
1964	May	East St. Louis, Ill.	AFT	5
1964	May	Utah (state-wide)	Prof. Assn.	2
1964	June	Hoboken, N.J.	Prof. Assn.	1
1964	June	New York City	AFT	1
1964	September	East St. Louis, Ill.	AFT	5
1964	October	Pautuckett, R.I.	AFT	9
1964	November	Lakeview, Ga.	Prof. Assn.	7
1964	November	Louisville, Ky.	AFT	6
1965	March	Belleville, N.J.	Prof. Assn.	1
1965	March	Pautuckett, R.I.	AFT	13
1965	April	Hamtramck, Mich.	AFT	4
1965	May	South Bend, Ind.	AFT	6
1965	November	Perth Amboy, N.J.	AFT	12
1965	December	Newark, N.J.	AFT	4
1966	February	Newark, N.J.	Prof. Assn.	2
1966	March	Plainview, N.Y.	AFT	4
1966	March	New Orleans, La.	AFT	3
1966	March	Thornon H.S., Ill.	AFT	2
1966	April	Tallmadre, Ohio	Prof. Assn.	1
1966	April	Wallace Village, Brownfield, Colo.	AFT	2
1966	April	Highland Park, Mich.	AFT	2
1966	June	Crestwood, Mich.	Prof. Assn.	7
1966	June	Flint, Mich.	Prof. Assn.	2
1966	June	Melvindale, Mich.	AFT	2
1966	June	N. Dearborn Heights, Mich.	AFT	5
1966	June	Taylor Township, Mich.	AFT	2
1966	June	Ecorse, Mich.	AFT	11
1966	June	Wayne, Mich.	Prof. Assn.	4
1966	June	Northville, Mich.	Prof. Assn.	2

Source: Reports of the National Education Association. This list is partial and does not include strikes during 1966–67, or at the opening of schools for the 1967–68 school year.

Representative Assembly until the summer of 1962 (after two teacher strikes in New York City). But both had been used in some form earlier.

NEA began the use of sanctions against school districts as early as 1948. The major elements of professional negotiations had been used in Connecticut since the courts' ruling in 1951 (on the Norwalk case in 1948 in which teachers engaged in a strike and won an agreement or contract with the school board) that boards of education could negotiate by these means; at the same time the courts ruled the strike illegal.

Following this decision, under the leadership of the state department of education, a procedure was developed containing the essential features of collective negotiation. This was formally approved by the State Board of Education in 1957. By 1965, some 68 school districts had adopted agreements under this plan.

As early as 1947, the NEA Executive Committee had called for the principle of professional negotiation in a resolution. This resolution was inspired by a dangerous state of unrest among teachers in many sections of the country, arising out of the failure to adjust teachers salaries to rapidly increasing consumer prices. The extent of the teacher unrest is evident in a series of teacher strikes from 1946 to 1948. The resolution stated:

> Group action is essential today. The former practice where teachers individually bargained with the superintendent of schools or the board of education for their salaries is largely past. For years there has been a steady movement in the direction of salary schedules applying to all teachers.
>
> In the present crises, it is especially important that there be professional negotiation on salary proposals. A salary committee composed of capable and trusted members of the group is necessary. This committee should be chosen by the entire teaching group and should have the authority to represent and act for the local educational association. This committee should be selected as early as possible each year.[2]

The principles of professional negotiation were considered by the executive secretaries of the state education associations in 1957. The NEA Representative Assembly in 1960 defeated a resolution to adopt the principles of professional negotiation. Although this proposed resolution was an intimation of the growing demand for the right to participate in policy formation, the delegates were not ready to embrace so radical a departure from the existing mores. The resolution was referred to the NEA Board of Directors for further study. This study continued for two years. Not until the NEA Denver Convention, in July, 1962, had opinions among teachers finally developed to the point that opposition of the traditionalists was swept aside, and the resolution (much stronger than the ones proposed in preceding years) was adopted. In addition, as a companion piece, the resolution on professional sanctions was adopted. Thus, both

[2] NEA Executive Committee, "The Professional Way to Meet the Crises," *NEA Journal*, February, 1947, 9:47.

processes were for the first time made official NEA policy, although, as has been stated, both had already been used by NEA and/or its affiliates. It is quite probable that the impact upon the delegates of the fiery speech before the 1962 NEA convention by James A. Carey, President of the International Union of Electrical Workers, attacking the alleged impotence of professional organizations, resulted in influencing passage of the two resolutions. Carey's speech was interpreted as a declaration of all-out war on professional organizations, especially of teachers, by organized labor.[3]

The professional negotiation resolution adopted by the Denver Convention in 1962 reads as follows:

RESOLUTION No. 18

The teaching profession has the ultimate aim of providing the best possible education for all the people. It is a professional calling and a public trust. Boards of education have the same aim and share this trust.

The National Education Association calls upon boards of education in all school districts to recognize their identity of interest with the teaching profession.

The National Education Association insists on the right of professional associations, through democratically selected representatives using professional channels, to participate with boards of education in the determination of policies of common concern, including salary and other conditions of professional service.

Recognizing both the legal authority of boards of education and the educational competencies of the teaching profession, the two groups should view the consideration of matters of mutual concern as a joint responsibility.

The seeking of consensus and mutual agreement on a professional basis should preclude the arbitrary exercise of unilateral authority by boards of education and the use of the strike by teachers.

The Association believes that procedures should be established which provide an orderly method for professional education associations and boards of education to reach mutually satisfactory agreements. *These procedures should include provisions for appeal through designated educational channels when agreement cannot be reached.*

Under no circumstances should the resolution of differences between professional associations and boards of education be sought through channels set up for handling industrial disputes. The teacher's situation is completely unlike that of an industrial employee. A board of education is not a private employer, and a teacher is not a private employee. Both are public servants. Both are committed to serve the common, indivisible interest of all persons and groups in the community in the best possible education for their children. Teachers and boards of education can perform their indispensable functions only if they act in terms of their identity of purpose in carrying out this commitment. Industrial disputes conciliation machinery, which assumes a conflict of interest and a diversity of purpose between persons and groups, is not appropriate to professional negotiations in public education.

[3] James A. Carey, "The Future of Public Education," *Addresses and Proceedings* (100th Annual Meeting of the National Education Association, Denver). Washington, D.C.: The Association: Vol. 100, 1962, pp. 48–49.

The National Education Association calls upon its members and upon boards of education to seek state legislation and local board action which clearly and firmly establishes these rights for the teaching profession.

This resolution was amended in subsequent conventions, at Seattle in 1964 and at New York City in 1965. But the essential elements remained.

As was to be expected, both the American Association of School Administrators (AASA) and the National School Boards Association (NSBA) reacted angrily to these actions by NEA.

The NSBA resolution said: "The National School Boards Association is opposed to sanctions, boycotts, strikes, or mandated mediation against school districts and does not consider them to be proper remedies for use in problem situations. The authority of the board of education is established by law and this authority may not be delegated to others." [4]

The AASA resolution, although much milder, expressed apprehension about the new trends.

By 1967, the NSBA had modified its position only in minor ways, but the number of states enacting legislation mandating that school boards engage in collective negotiation (either through collective bargaining or professional negotiation) was increasing. The enactment in the states of such laws negated the school board's assertion of exclusive legal authority which "may not be delegated to others."

Since 1962 the American Association of School Administrators has consistently modified its position, in resolutions, toward recognition of the steadily increasing practice of collective action for teachers. AASA's 1967 resolution constituted an endorsement of the processes of the professional associations of teachers. It reads as follows:

The AASA urges that the teaching profession commit itself to the establishment of truly professional negotiation procedures and, in communities where intolerable educational conditions cannot otherwise be remedied, to the intelligent application of sanctions as the means of demonstrating its determination to obtain suitable salaries, working conditions, and personnel policies. We deplore the use of strikes and affiliations which align educators exclusively with one segment of the American economic system. We recommend that organizations of educators include all professional personnel, and we deplore the current tendency to create, by membership restrictions, artificial barriers among those whose basic interests in education are the same.

Also, the AASA Convention in 1967 endorsed the statement of its Executive Committee approving the use of professional negotiations and sanctions, and spelling out the role of administrators in the processes. [5]

[4] *Resolutions Adopted by the 1963 Delegate Assembly.* Information Service Bulletin, Vol. 1, No. 8, Chicago: National School Boards Association, 1963. (Mimeographed).
[5] *School Administrators View Professional Negotiations.* Washington, D.C.: The American Association of School Administrators, 1966, 58 pp.

The Meaning of Professional Negotiation

Officials of AFT have repeatedly characterized professional negotiation as "collective begging," presumably because the assumption is that without the use of the strike there is no power structure to support professional negotiation. This has, in a measure at least, been disproved by the effectiveness of sanctions, described later. In simple language, professional negotiation is a set of written, officially adopted procedures by the recognized local staff organization and the school board, providing an orderly method for negotiation on matters of mutual concern, to reach agreement on these matters, and to provide mediation and appeal procedures, through educational channels, in cases of disagreements or impasses.

The recognized local staff organization may be determined by (1) an election in which teachers choose the organization to represent them; (2) by stipulation, through signed cards identifying the organization teachers prefer to represent them; or (3) by designation of the school board of the majority organization through verified membership count. Some laws specify only the election as the means of choosing the organization with exclusive negotiation rights.

Generally, school boards resisted the formalizing of professional negotiation procedures, as spelled out in the NEA resolution, on the grounds that (1) they already were carrying on consultation with teachers on matters of concern to them; therefore, there is no need for legislation; (2) the authority for final decision-making on school policies is vested by law in the school board and that anthority cannot be delegated to others; and (3) an appeals procedure would take from school boards the legal authority to make the final decision. The viewpoints of teachers regarding these assertions were as follows: Talking with the professional staff is not enough. Consulting with the staff may often be simply a paternalistic gesture, signifying only pleasant conversations, and too often having little or no bearing upon the decisions the board makes. Secondly, teachers want their right to negotiation spelled out in law, where the right is clear, and the roles of the negotiating parties are delineated. Third, teachers want an appeals or mediation procedure spelled out in law.

The NEA Research Division, in May, 1967, summarized the results to that date of the competition for teachers affiliation between NEA and its affiliated associations and AFT and its locals. Of 7,157 school systems surveyed, with enrollments of 1,000 or more, 5,549 districts responded. A total of 1,353 of these districts reported a written agreement with teachers in effect; 4,196 school systems (or nearly 76 per cent) reported no agreements. There were no agreements in seven states. In seven states there were agreements in only one school district each. But there were 256 agreements in California and 215 in Michigan. In 1,262 districts exclusive representation rights were held by NEA or AFT affiliates. NEA affiliates were the chosen organizations in 1,179 of the 1,262 districts; AFT affiliates were the choice in 32 districts. Thus by June 1, 1967, NEA affiliation had won representation rights in 93.4 per cent of districts with agreements; AFT affiliates had won 2.8 per cent of the districts. (These data did not include Chicago where the AFT had won representation rights because at the time of the survey a written contract had not been signed.)

PROFESSIONAL SANCTIONS

Professional sanctions, the use of which was officially endorsed by the NEA Representative Assembly at the Denver Convention in July of 1962, are generally viewed as the counterpart of the strike employed by AFT. The analogy is not precise, as will be explained.

Sanctions have a long history of use by professions. As used by professions, sanctions constitute a vital factor or element in the exercise of professional autonomy—the right of a given profession to manage the affairs of the profession. Professional sanctions are more of a persuasion instrument than a weapon. They have no inherent power, as does the strike, to force immediate action. Their power depends upon the impact of censure, reprimand, withdrawing of recognition, and in the final step the withdrawal of services of members of the profession. Actually, in the last case the impact of public opinion tends to clothe the process with power.

A dictionary definition of sanctions would read something like the following: a means or a declaration inducing observance of a standard or a custom, through imposing a deterrent or withholding a reward. For example, when NEA felt compelled to invoke sanctions state-wide against the schools of Utah (1963) and Oklahoma (1964), the declaration against these two school systems was that they were substandard and would be under a ban from the teaching profession until the deteriorating conditions were corrected. The quality of the school programs in these two states were advertised before the nation as below par, which was a powerful instrument in securing remedial action. The American Medical Association had taken a similar action against a hospital in Salt Lake City in 1948, declaring conditions and facilities of the institution substandard and that members of the Association would be enjoined from serving there until conditions were brought up to acceptable standards. This was a profession's way, and obligation, of alerting the public to conditions that might endanger the health and prevent proper treatment of patients. Similarly, a ban by the teaching profession alerts the public to inadequate educational programs for children. If this alert is supported by the facts the public will demand remedial action.

To state the use of sanctions in another way: they can express the teaching profession's disapproval of substandard conditions; they can alert the public to poor quality educational programs (something the public may not be aware of); they can protect children from being educationally short-changed; they can withhold professional services where these services could be used to continue poor conditions; they can protect members of the profession from having to enter into contracts where conditions of service are demeaning or compromising.

Several Types of Sanctions

Because in the public mind professional sanctions are often viewed as strikes under another name, the various types of sanctions available for use by the teaching profession should be understood. The equating of strikes and sanctions results from the belief that there is only one type of sanction and that is the ultimate one of withdrawing the services of teachers from the school district.

Discussed not necessarily in any order of importance, types of sanctions may involve:

1. *Disciplining members of the profession.* The teaching profession in 1963, at long last, achieved one Code of Ethics (the Code of Ethics for the Education Profession). A violation of this code could result in a charge against a teacher, a hearing and a declaration of censure, reprimand, suspension, or expulsion from membership if the member in question is found guilty of unethical conduct (see Chapter 15).

2. *Accreditation.* One of the oldest sanctions used by the teaching profession is that of accreditation, the placing of the stamp of approval of a voluntary association of educators upon the quality of the program of a given university, college, or secondary school. These institutions rely upon such approval for their very existence. Accreditation, in effect, says to the public that it can have confidence in the integrity of the institution and the quality of its education program. It says to other schools and colleges that they may properly accept credits for admission from other institutions so approved.

3. *Disaccreditation.* A converse sanction to (2) is that of disaccreditation, the withdrawing of the stamp of approval from a school or college whose program, for one reason or another, has been allowed to erode to the extent that it has fallen below acceptable standards. This is a very serious step to take, inasmuch as these institutions cannot long exist without accreditation. Students will not attend, because credits earned in the disaccredited institutions are not acceptable, and they cannot gain admission to other colleges or schools or to graduate and professional schools. There have been several cases in recent years in which a regional accrediting association has, because of persisting political interference, disaccredited colleges and universities, or even a whole state university system, until evidence was shown that such interference has ceased. These disaccreditations quickly brought about correction of the adverse conditions.

When, under the leadership of several NEA units and departments, notably NCTEPS, AACTE, and AASA, the National Council for Accreditation of Teacher Education was established in 1952, one of the prime objectives was to apply the positive sanction of accreditation to expedite interstate reciprocity in teacher certification.

4. *The withdrawal of service by teachers* is a fourth type of professional sanction. This is the type, as previously mentioned, that often is called a strike.

There are several steps or phases in the application of this type of sanction. The first would simply be a declaration, or a public announcement from NEA or one of its state or local affiliates that unsatisfactory conditions (specified) exist in a given school district; and unless remedies are provided with reasonable dispatch, the profession will be compelled to take further and more serious steps. This simply is an alert to all concerned parties that all is not well in the school district. This is a mild form of sanctions; but it is often quite effective and the only step the profession is required to take to set in motion remedial efforts. This step was used by NEA in 1963 and 1964 with reference to the conditions in the Overseas Dependents Schools. It was called an Urgent Advisory. The statement was sent to all state and local association affiliates, to placement services of colleges and universities, and to state departments of education, making it difficult to recruit an adequate supply of teachers.

The next step in the withdrawal of services is for the professional associations to request their members employed in other school districts not to seek or accept employment in the school districts under sanction. A third step is to request both the teachers employed in the school district and elsewhere not to accept service in the banned district until conditions are remedied. The most extreme step is to declare it unethical for any member of the profession to accept employment in the district, under threat of being judged guilty of unethical conduct and subject to reprimand, censure, suspension, or expulsion from membership. This ultimate step has not yet been employed, although it was voted by a state association in one case that was settled before this drastic measure had to be resorted to; and NEA stated in the Oklahoma case that outsiders taking jobs while the state was under sanction *might* be judged in ethical violation.

THE PROCEDURES FOR INVOKING SANCTIONS

Because the invoking of professional sanctions against a school district (or even a state) is a serious step, precautions had to be taken to make certain that the facts in a given case justify the action. Therefore, in the resolution officially endorsing the use of sanctions, the NEA Representative Assembly directed that the NEA staff, in collaboration with the state education associations affiliated with NEA, develop proposed guidelines clearly spelling out the procedures and steps by which sanctions would be invoked by the teaching profession.

Although the guidelines which were developed as a result of this directive recognized that there will be occasions in which a local association alone, or in collaboration with its state education association, will find it necessary to apply sanctions, they advocated the desirability of local, state, and NEA joint action, because such joint action reflects professional unity and constitutes a much more powerful effort than a local or local-state action. For example, the Overseas Education Association (teachers in the Overseas Dependent Schools affiliated with NEA) unilaterally invoked sanctions against the U.S. Department of Defense in the fall of 1962. This proved to be somewhat ineffective because the unilateral action represented the position of only about 2,500 teachers. In other words, the Overseas Dependent Schools were, thus, not under a ban of the total teaching profession. Subsequently, the NEA decided not to invoke sanctions, choosing other means of supporting the OEA.

At the heart of the procedural steps spelled out in the guidelines developed by the NEA staff and approved by the NEA Board of Directors, was the assertion that the invoking of sanctions by the NEA Executive Committee would occur after a comprehensive and objective investigation by a designated agency, usually the National Commission on Professional Rights and Responsibilities (the PR&R Commission). Although national sanctions could be invoked on *prima facie* evidence, this step has not as yet been used, and the guidelines stress the necessity of acting only upon clear and unbiased factual evidence. This is essential because, as has been pointed out, the real power in professional sanctions rests upon two basic factors: (1) united support of the teaching profession, and (2) public opinion. The two complement each other. Public opinion in a given school district will almost invariably support sanctions and demand remedial action if the facts reported show that children are being denied good educational conditions.

In order, then, to get the facts in an unbiased form the PR&R Commission always includes on its investigating committees (and a special committee is appointed in each case) outstanding lay citizens and others not affiliated with NEA. The lay members are usually members of local school boards not in any way connected with the school district involved. One or more well-known university professors are usually included on the investigating committees. As a general rule, such an investigation requires several months to search out the facts, publish the report, and to make a recommendation to the NEA Executive Committee for Action.[6]

[6] *Guidelines for Professional Sanctions,* by the National Commission on Professional Rights and Responsibilities, National Education Association. Washington, D.C.: the Association, 1963, 10 pp.

The wisdom of adhering closely to the comprehensive, objective investigation of conditions in a school district, for which a request has been received from its affiliated association(s), is illustrated in the Utah and Oklahoma cases. In each instance, a fact finding committee appointed by the governor—a committee consisting of distinguished citizens of the respective states—substantially confirmed the report of the NEA investigating committee. Thus, the integrity of both NEA's reporting the facts and of its position that educational conditions for children were subminimal were borne out. When the investigating committee has made its study, and if it has found conditions for good education to be unfavorable, the report is submitted to the NEA Executive Committee, which decides whether the adverse conditions are such as to warrant the imposition of sanctions. If sanctions are voted by the Executive Committee, the following steps may be taken: (1) Notice of the action to impose sanctions on a given school district is sent to the school board, the superintendent of schools, the mayor of the city, and the local and state education associations. The notice of sanctions will also specify the conditions for lifting or removing the sanctions. Sanctions may be lifted by the NEA Executive Committee upon recommendation of the PR&R Commission, or the investigating committee in the case when the evidence reflects that the unsatisfactory conditions have been corrected. (2) Release of the report to the press, to national and state journals, and the mass media, containing a censure of existing conditions. (3) Notification of the imposition of sanctions are sent to the state departments of education, college and university placement services, and to appropriate accrediting agencies. (4) Notification to NEA membership not currently employed in the school district involved, warning against acceptance of positions in the banned school district.

Are Sanctions the Same as a Strike?

Many observers find it difficult to distinguish between professional sanctions and strikes by teachers. The professional associations maintain that there are significant differences, that the withdrawing of the services of teachers where conditions are substandard is not a strike in the generally accepted connotation of the term.

To support this position, these associations point out:
1. There is no interruption of services to students.
2. Teachers fulfill their existing contracts for the current school year. There have been several cases of a local association using the sanction of withdrawing extracurricular services during the current school year, but these services, generally, did not involve contractual obligations or extra pay.
3. The imposition of sanctions is generally made effective with the en-

suing school year, allowing the school district several months in which to correct unsatisfactory conditions.

4. If the people of the school district involved elect to continue sub-minimal conditions, they can doubtless employ substandard or emergency teachers. There will be no picketing or other interference with the operation of the schools.

Whether the courts will equate sanctions with the strike is yet to be determined. As yet there has been no court test of this question. In the Little Lake, California, case a suit was brought in court to enjoin the California Teachers Association from withdrawing placement services to the school district. The suit was withdrawn without a decision, presumably because informal statements by the presiding judge to the effect that criticism of a public agency is an inherent right in American law seemed to point to an unfavorable decision, if the case were pursued. The governor of Oklahoma did threaten to file a court suit for damages allegedly accruing to the state as a result of NEA's blacklisting of its schools. The suit was never filed, which may or may not indicate that legal grounds existed for the threatened suit. Also in 1967 authorities of Parsons College sought an injunction in the Federal Courts to bar the North Central Association of Colleges and Secondary Schools from withdrawing accreditation of that college. The courts refused to interfere.

The Department of Defense, for a time refused to grant recognition to the Overseas Education Association under provisions of President Kennedy's Executive Order 10,988 granting the right of negotiation to Federal employees, which prohibited recognition to any organization that advovated a strike against the government. The withholding of recognition to the OEA ended when that organization rescinded its sanctions action. It appears clear that the Department of Defense interpreted the sanction action as a strike action or strike threat. Whether this interpretation would have been sustained by the courts still remains a question.

The National Labor Relations Board (NLRB) issued a decision in a labor–private industry controversy which seems to have some bearing on the withdrawal of services. A section of this decision reads:

> The broadest definition of a strike includes "quitting work" or "stoppage of work." Men cannot quit work before they are hired; they cannot stop work before they start. We reject, therefore, the contention that the alleged refusal to refer employees should be construed as a strike.[7]

Until there is a definitive court decision concerning the sanction of withdrawal of teachers services or the refusal of referral of teachers for employment by the professional association for a school district under ban, it cannot be determined whether sanctions are legal or are to be classified

---

[7] *Glazer's Union* (Joliet Contractor's Association) 30LRRM 1174 (1952).

as a strike. But the fact that various professions have widely invoked sanctions without interference from the Courts would seem to sustain the legality of sanctions.

SANCTIONS CASES

NEA has been invoking sanctions against school districts since 1947, when, with the Ohio Education Association, it applied sanctions against the North College Hill school board. This action was against the refusal of the board to renew the contract of the superintendent. The superintendent had refused to abdicate the right of nominating personnel for employment, a right which he had under existing law. The sanction invoked called for the resignation of the board majority. This case was won within a day after sanctions were applied. Other sanctions cases prior to the official adoption of the process by NEA in 1962 were Kelso, Washington (1950); and Polson, Montana (1950). In addition, there were several cases of sanctions being applied by state education associations in Connecticut, Colorado, and California.

An interesting and significant facet of the use of sanctions has been the action of Student National Education Association in a few states. SNEA is the professional orientation organization of college students preparing for teaching, a joint organization of NEA and the respective state education associations. The Connecticut Student Education Association voted to sanction two school districts in 1962, requesting its members not to seek or accept positions in these districts until conditions acceptable to the local education associations in the districts were provided. This action was taken in support of the teachers in these two districts who were in a sustained dispute with their school boards. The members of the CSEA, in effect, put the school boards of these districts on notice that they could not expect to fill any vacancies from the new supply of college graduates in the state. The Michigan Student Education Association took an equally significant step in 1965 with the adoption of a resolution requesting its members to refuse to seek or accept positions in school districts with starting salaries below $5,000 and maximum salaries of less than $8,000. For a list of sanctions applied, see Table 59 (page 520).

Sanctions Against States

Perhaps the sanctions cases that have attracted the widest attention were those against Utah and Oklahoma. In both cases NEA, after requests from the state education association and after sustained study of the conditions, voted sanctions against the state legislatures and the governors of the two states, thus putting a ban on all school districts in the two states, in 1964 and 1965, respectively. These were the first cases in which sanctions have been state-wide in application. In both cases the state authorities were indicted for allowing the quality of the education program to deteriorate to subminimal conditions. Action against state authorities were necessary because (1) the deteriorating conditions were general throughout the states, although there were exceptions in both states, and (2) the states were the only avenues for significant remedial action to correct the eroding school conditions. Both reasons serve to point up a situation that year-by-year tends to be true in all states. There is a rapid shift of the burden of financing public schools from local to state governments. In 1967, the NEA and the Florida Education Association invoked sanctions against the state of Florida for subminimal school support. In the Florida case, about half the state's teachers submitted resignations in the spring of 1968. This tactic was widely viewed as a strike, as was the New York City work stoppage in Sepember of 1967.

In Utah, the teachers had been fighting a losing battle since about 1950 to stop the deterioration in educational services and to provide adequate facilities, curriculum offerings, special school services, instructional materials, and teacher salaries. The teachers were consistently stymied by conservative elements in government and out, although a few minor victories were won. Finally in 1963, the teachers could no longer tolerate the failure of the governor and the legislature to recognize the steady deterioration of the school situation. (The state had dropped between 1948 and 1963 from first place among the states to thirty-sixth in per capita expenditures for the public schools.)

In the spring of 1963 when the legislature had adjourned without appreciable amelioration of the situation, the Utah Education Association requested NEA to sanction the state. Since NEA procedures (as spelled out in the guidelines) require an investigation of the facts, a special committee began the study late in the spring. This study could not be completed by the time of the NEA annual meeting in July. The PR&R Commission was, therefore, not in a position to recommend that conditions warranted the voting of immediate sanctions by the NEA Executive Committee. This caused a bitter fight on the floor of the NEA Representative Assembly, meeting in Detroit in July. Delegates from Utah knew the adverse facts were there and they felt that NEA was too legalistic and should act at once to support them in their fight against the state authorities. However, the Representative Assembly voted to uphold the procedures that it had adopted to guide itself in such cases, but also voted to extend financial aid to the Utah Education Association in pursuing the fight.

During the 1963–64 school year the investigating committee completed its study and found conditions to be about what the teachers had claimed.

TABLE 59 Professional Sanctions Imposed by Professional Association
(Against School Districts—State, County, and Local) 1962–66 *

Place	Date	Invoking Association
URGENT ADVISORY against Overseas Dependents Schools	November 1962	NEA
Waterbury, Conn. (Extra-curricular duties)	September 1963 Removed February 6, 1964	Waterbury Education Association
Waterbury (CTA) Postponed	November 1963 December 1963 Removed February 6, 1964	Connecticut Education Association
Little Lake, California	April 1962 Removed January 28, 1964	California Teachers Association
Springer, New Mexico	Fall 1965 Lifted May 1964	New Mexico Education Association
SECOND URGENT ADVISORY against Overseas Dependents Schools	February 1963 Removed October 14, 1966	NEA
Pleasantville, Iowa	February 1964	Iowa State Education Association
Utah	May 19, 1964 Lifted March 15, 1965	Utah Education Association & NEA
Recess in Utah (2 days)	May 18–19, 1964	Utah Education Association
Cauley, Wyoming	December 4, 1965 Lifted April 27, 1965	Wyoming Education Association
Oklahoma	March 6, 1965 Lifted September 18, 1965	Oklahoma Education Association
Oklahoma	May 11, 1965 Lifted September 24, 1965	NEA
Dade County, Florida	May 5, 1965 Lifted May 20, 1965	Dade County Teachers Association
Washington School District, Ohio	July 29, 1965	Ohio Education Association
Box Elder County, Utah	September 7, 1965 Lifted October 29, 1965	Utah Education Association
Duval County, Florida	October 1965 Lifted November 1965	Duval County Teachers Association
Nantucket, Massachusetts	Lifted April 22, 1966	Massachusetts Teacher Association
Springfield, Massachusetts	Lifted June 1966	Massachusetts Teacher Association
Newark, New Jersey	January 1966 Settled by strike February 1966	New Jersey Education Association and Newark Teachers Association
Finely, North Dakota	March 22, 1966 Lifted April 16, 1966	North Dakota Education Association
Portland, Maine	April 1966 Lifted June 1966	Maine Teachers Association
Herman, Maine	April 1966 Lifted June 1966	Maine Teachers Association
Baltimore, Maryland	June 1966	Baltimore Public School Teachers Association and Maryland State Teachers Association

TABLE 59 (*Continued*)

Place	Date	Invoking Association
Hillsborough County, Florida	June 1965 January 1966	Local Association
Duval County, Florida	October 1965 November 1965	Local Association
Volusia County, Florida	June 1965 September 1965	Local Association
Haysville (S.D. 261), Kansas	February 1966	Kansas State Teachers Association
Knoxville, Tennessee	March 1966	Knoxville Teachers League
Warren, Michigan	July 11, 1966 Lifted September 19, 1966	Michigan Education Association
Jersey City, New Jersey	Spring 1966	New Jersey Education Association
Asbury Park, New Jersey	1964	Asbury Park Teachers Association
Ecorse, Michigan	June 28, 1966	Michigan Education Association
Flint, Michigan	May 27, 1966 Lifted June 1966	Michigan Education Association
Southgate, Michigan	May 9, 1966 Lifted July 26, 1966	Michigan Education Association
Crestwood, Michigan	June 10, 1966 Lifted June 15, 1966	Michigan Education Association
West Brookfield, Massachusetts	August 18, 1966 Lifted September 26, 1966	Massachusetts Teachers Association
Farwell, Michigan	August 23, 1966 Lifted September 1, 1966	Michigan Education Association
Marian County, Florida	December 14, 1966	Florida Education Association
Fort Wayne, Indiana	February 9, 1967	Indiana State Teachers Association

Source: Reports of the National Education Association.

* This list necessarily must be considered as a partial one, since doubtless there have been cases of local or state association imposed sanctions not reported to NEA. Additional sanctions were invoked by NEA during the 1966–67 school year as follows: State of Florida, Baltimore City Schools.

In the meantime, the governor had appointed a fact-finding committee. The governor's committee issued its report a few weeks after that of the NEA, a report that verified the existence of inadequate conditions and recommended a special session of the legislature to vote the needed funds. The governor rejected both reports and refused to take action. NEA voted sanctions against the state in May, 1964. The sanction requested teachers employed outside Utah not to seek or accept positions there. But the Utah Education Association decided to strengthen the chances of success by organizing a political action program. More than 30 members of the legislature, the new governor, and the chairman of the State Board of

Education were elected with the help of the UEA. Thus, the 1965 legislature, upon recommendation of the newly elected governor, provided adequate appropriation and on March 15, 1965 (after the lapse of 300 days in which the nation-wide sanctions were in effect) the case in Utah was won.

Although the details differ widely, the same factors were involved in the voting of sanctions on Oklahoma by the NEA Executive Committee in April, 1965. These sanctions produced quick action by the legislature (a $28,000,000 appropriation for the schools, providing average teacher salary raises of about $550.) But much of the money needed to bring the schools up to acceptable quality depended upon action of the voters on a constitutional amendment, to be voted upon in September, 1965. Both OEA and NEA refused to lift sanctions pending this vote. The people by an overwhelming vote adopted the amendment permitting local elections to vote an additional 10 mill tax for the schools. This new provision could provide an estimated additional sum of $30,000,000 annually for the schools. In invoking sanctions against Oklahoma, out-of-state teachers were warned that acceptance of a position in the state *might* be interpreted as unethical conduct. Also, NEA set up services to assist Oklahoma teachers to secure positions in other states if they chose to do so. Although only about 600 Oklahoma teachers accepted jobs in other states, NEA received requests for about 10,000 teachers to fill vacancies.

In both the Utah and Oklahoma cases clear-cut victories were won, by the use of sanctions and other measures. But in both cases, sanctions proved effective over a much longer time period than many teachers, in highly emotional situations, are willing to wait for solutions. Clearly, the professional associations must find ways to speed up the process and develop quicker acting supplementary plans to compete with the instant urge to use the strike as a speedier weapon. However, it should be pointed out that subsequent sanctions will not require so much time. With these first two cases of state-wide sanctions there were widespread doubts both within the profession and without that sanctions would prove to be effective. With the winning of these two cases, the probability that state-wide sanctions will have to be applied diminishes. The reason is that states will want to avoid such extremely unfavorable publicity. There may, of course, be other such cases, but they will be rare.

GROWING TURMOIL

In the school year 1965–66, there were about 35 teacher strikes, about as many strikes as had occurred in the decade 1955–1965. And at the beginning of the 1967–68 school year, the turmoil reached a crescendo.

Teacher strikes in six states delayed the opening of the 1967–68 school year. There were teacher strikes in 36 school districts (affecting a total of 580 schools) in Michigan, involving about 500,000 children (300,000 in Detroit). There was a withdrawal of services through mass resignations of about 50,000 of the nearly 60,000 teachers in New York City, preventing the opening of three schools and involving over one million children. There was a teacher strike in Paducah, Kentucky (McCracken County). There was a teacher strike in Fort Lauderdale, Florida (Broward County), as well as threatened mass resignation among the state's 60,000 teachers— which did happen later in the year. Teachers in East St. Louis, Illinois, refused to open schools. Strikes in Newport, Rhode Island, and Youngstown, Ohio, were averted by last minute agreements. Other strikes during 1967–68 occurred in Pittsburgh, Cincinnati, Albuquerque and elsewhere.

Thus in six states upwards of 100,000 teachers were involved in walkouts or mass resignations in over 40 school districts, delaying the opening of schools, from a few days in some places to two weeks in New York City.

The mass resignation ploy was used in New York City and Broward County, Florida. This technique was used in New York City in an ostensible effort to avoid the penalties of the new Taylor Law (which became effective September 1, 1967) in New York state, prohibiting strikes by teachers with penalties directed chiefly at the teachers organization and officials holding representation rights. Using the mass resignation procedure, the United Federation of Teachers hoped to avoid the legal penalties of a teacher strike. Penalties, however, were assessed by the courts. A 15-day jail sentence was imposed on the president of UFT; and UFT was fined in the amount of $150,000. But the strike yielded great gains for teachers.

Obviously, the Broward County, Florida, teachers were using the mass resignation technique in lieu of a strike, which is illegal in that state. Some 35,000 of Florida's 60,000 teachers attended a rally in the Tangerine Bowl in Orlando on August 24 to protest the failure of the State Legislature and Governor Claude R. Kirk to seek a solution to the teacher salary situation. At this meeting thousands of Florida teachers signed resignation forms, to be used if the impasse continued.

NEA, through its DuShane Fund for Teacher Rights, provided $50,000 each for the Florida and Paducah, Kentucky, teachers, for interest free loans to tide them over the period of unemployment. Also, NEA announced free placement services for teachers in these areas who elect to secure positions in other states or school districts.

The full result of the Florida sanctions is not yet known. However, the Governor agreed to call a special session of the Legislature (in early 1968) if the FEA agreed to hold in abeyance the mass resignations. The new legislation did not satisfy the teachers and about half of the state's teachers did submit resignations. Apparently only a partial victory was won in Florida in the three-week walkout, with many of the teachers not being reinstated in their jobs.

SUMMARY

Teachers in the public schools of the United States are now widely involved in collective action to secure economic justice. But a larger goal appears to be the hunger to participate in policy making and the derivation of the educational program of their school systems. The latter is fundamentally a drive for professional status, to be recognized as competent professionals, and not mere functionaries in a routinized, mechanized system in which they had little voice in the planning. This is a search for academic freedom and authority. This is a wave of the future in the governance of the public schools which has great promise for better education and greater status for teachers.

Teachers will make their own judgments regarding their affiliations—whether with the professional associations or with the teachers' unions. Teachers, like other Americans, have the legal right to join or not to join the organization of their choice. Although NEA, the state education associations, and the local affiliates of both presently predominate in the organizational struggles for their affiliation, there is no way to predict what the future will bring.

Whether the growing militancy of teachers will tend to get out of the bounds of reasonableness and fairness remains to be seen. The strikes, or withdrawal of services, in 40 school districts at the beginning of the 1967–68 school year reflect the growing discontent of teachers with their economic status, their working conditions, and conditions generally in the public schools. Because state law has not in any state declared teacher strikes legal, sooner or later the public will demand one of two actions: (1) that strikes by teachers be made legal, or (2) that the penalties for teacher strikes as specified by law be enforced. No society can invite open insurrection by acquiescing to constant and widespread violation of its laws.

In recent years, collective action by public school teachers has proved to be highly effective. Doubtless collective action by teachers will continue, but many questions remain concerning the forms and processes to be used in such action.

REFERENCES

COHODES, AARON, "Teachers May Lose More than They Bargain For," *Nation's Schools,* January, 1967, 79:37.

DALY, RONALD O., "New Directions for Professional Negotiation," *NEA Journal,* October, 1966, 55:27–29.

EPSTEIN, BENJAMIN, "Why Principals Want to Negotiate for Themselves," *Nation's Schools,* October, 1966, 78:66–67.

EXTON, ELAIN. "NSBA at the Crossroads," *The American School Board Journal,* December, 1963, *147*:31–33.

GARBER, LEE O. and EDWARDS, NEWTON, *The Law Governing School Board Members and School Board Meetings.* Danville, Illinois: Interstate Printers and Publishers, 1963.

GROSS, CALVIN, "Ways to Deal with the New Teacher Militancy," *Phi Delta Kappan,* December, 1964, 46:147–152.

LIEBERMAN, MYRON, "Teachers' Strikes: An Analysis of the Issues," *Harvard Educational Review,* Winter, 1956, 26:39–70.

————, "Teachers' Strikes: Acceptable Strategy?" *Phi Delta Kappan,* January, 1965, *46*:237–241.

———— and MOSKOW, MICHAEL H., *Collective Negotiations for Teachers.* Chicago: Rand McNally and Company, 1966, 745 pp.

NATIONAL EDUCATION ASSOCIATION, Department of Classroom Teachers, *Classroom Teachers Speak on Professional Negotiations.* Washington, D.C.: The Department, 1963.

————, Field Operations and Urban Services, *Introduction to Professional Negotiations.* Washington, D.C.: The Association, 1966.

————, Research Division. *Professional Negotiation with School Boards: A Legal Analysis and Review,* Research Report 1965-R3, Washington, D.C.: The Association, March, 1965.

————, Salary Consultant Service and Department of Classroom Teachers, *Securing a Professional Negotiation Agreement,* Guidelines for Effective Work to Improve Teacher Salary Programs, No. 10. Washington, D.C.: The Association, 1965.

————, Office of Professional Development and Welfare, *Guidelines for Professional Negotiation,* Revised edition. Washington, D.C.: The Association, 1965.

————, Commission on Professional Rights and Responsibilities, *Guidelines for Professional Sanctions.* Washington, D.C.: The Association, 1966.

————, Research Division. *Negotiation Research Digest,* Washington, D.C.: The Association (published ten times per year, September through June).

SCANLON, JOHN, "Strikes, Sanctions and the Schools," *Saturday Review*, October 19, 1963, *45*:51–55, 70–74.

STINNETT, T. M. *Turmoil in Teaching*. New York: The Macmillan Co., 1968.

STINNETT, T. M., KLEINMANN, JACK H., and WARE, MARTHA L. *Professional Negotiation in Public Education*. New York: The Macmillan Company, 1966.

WOLLETT, DONALD H. "The Public Employee at the Bargaining Table: Promise or Illusion," *Labor Law Journal*, 1964, *15*:8.

Name Index

Subject Index